Organizational Learning

Organization Science

Series Editor: Arie Y. Lewin

Books from Sage Publications,
Organization Science, and the
Institute for Operations Research and the Management Sciences

The Sage Publications **Organization Science** book series reprints expanded Special Issues of *Organization Science*. Each individual volume is based on the original Special Issue that appeared in *Organization Science*. It includes all-new introductions by the editors as well as several chapters that did not appear in the original Special Issue. These new chapters may include reprints of papers that appeared in other issues of *Organization Science*, relevant papers that appeared in other journals, and also new original articles.

The book series is published by Sage Publications in partnership with INFORMS (the Institute for Operations Research and Management Sciences) the publisher of *Organization Science*. The Series Editor is Arie Y. Lewin, the Editor in Chief of *Organization Science*.

Organization Science was founded in 1989 as an international journal with the aim of advancing the field of organization studies by attracting, then publishing innovative research from across the social sciences. The term "Science" in the journal's title is interpreted in the broadest possible sense to include diverse methods and theoretical approaches. The editors of *Organization Science* believe that creative insight often occurs outside traditional approaches and topic areas, and that the role of *Organization Science* is to be broadly inclusive of the field by helping to integrate the diverse stands of organizational research. Authors are expected to describe theoretical concepts that give meaning to data, and to show how these concepts are relevant to organizations. Manuscripts that speculate beyond current thinking are more desirable than papers that use tried and true methods to study routine problems.

Initial books in this series:

**Longitudinal Field Research Methods: Studying Processes
of Organizational Change**
> *Edited by George P. Huber and Andrew H. Van de Ven*

Organizational Learning
> *Edited by Michael D. Cohen and Lee S. Sproull*

Cognition Within and Between Organizations
> *Edited by James R. Meindl, Charles Stubbart, and Joseph F. Porac*

For information on subscriptions to *Organization Science*, please contact INFORMS at 940-A Elkridge Landing Road, Linthicum, MD 21090-2909, 800-446-3676. For submission guidelines, contact INFORMS at 290 Westminster Street, Providence, RI 02903, 800-343-0062.

Organizational Learning

Michael D. Cohen
Lee S. Sproull
Editors

Organization Science

SAGE Publications
International Educational and Professional Publisher
Thousand Oaks   London   New Delhi

For information address:

SAGE Publications, Inc.
2455 Teller Road
Thousand Oaks, California 91320
E-mail: order@sagepub.com

SAGE Publications Ltd.
6 Bonhill Street
London EC2A 4PU
United Kingdom

SAGE Publications India Pvt. Ltd.
M-32 Market
Greater Kailash I
New Delhi 110 048 India

Printed in the United States of America

Library of Congress Cataloging-in-Publication Data

Main entry under title:

Organizational learning / edited by Michael D. Cohen, Lee S. Sproull.
    p. cm. — (Organization science)
  Includes bibliographical references and index.
  ISBN 0-8039-7088-9 (cloth: alk. paper). — ISBN 0-8039-7089-7
(pbk.: alk. paper)
    1. Organizational learning. I. Cohen, Michael D. II. Sproull,
Lee. III. Series.
HD58.82.O74 1995
302.3′5—dc20   95-35478

This book is printed on acid-free paper.

96 97 98 99 10 9 8 7 6 5 4 3 2

Sage Production Editor: Gillian Dickens
Sage Typesetter: Janelle LeMaster

Contents

Introduction   ix
Michael D. Cohen and *Lee S. Sproull*

1. Learning From Samples of One or Fewer   1
   James G. March, Lee S. Sproull, and *Michal Tamuz*

2. Organizing Work by Adaptation   20
   Edwin Hutchins

3. Organizational Learning and Communities-of-Practice:
   Toward a Unified View of Working, Learning, and Innovation   58
   John Seely Brown and *Paul Duguid*

4. Organizational Learning Curves: A Method for Investigating
   Intra-Plant Transfer of Knowledge Acquired Through
   Learning by Doing   83
   Dennis Epple, Linda Argote, and *Rukmini Devadas*

5. Exploration and Exploitation in Organizational Learning   101
   James G. March

6. Organizational Learning: The Contributing Processes
   and the Literatures   124
   George P. Huber

7. The Nontraditional Quality of Organizational Learning   163
   Karl E. Weick

8. Bounded Rationality and Organizational Learning   175
   Herbert A. Simon

9. Individual Learning and Organizational Routine:
   Emerging Connections   188
   Michael D. Cohen

10. Organizational Adaptation and Environmental Selection:
    Interrelated Processes of Change   195
    Daniel A. Levinthal

11. Technology Diffusion and Organizational Learning:
    The Case of Business Computing   203
    Paul Attewell

12. Organizational Learning and Personnel Turnover   230
    Kathleen Carley

13. An Organizational Learning Model of Convergence and
    Reorientation   267
    Theresa K. Lant and *Stephen J. Mezias*

14. Executive Succession and Organization Outcomes in
    Turbulent Environments: An Organization Learning Approach   302
    Beverly Virany, Michael L. Tushman,
    and *Elaine Romanelli*

15. Collective Mind in Organizations: Heedful Interrelating
    on Flight Decks   330
    Karl E. Weick and *Karlene H. Roberts*

16. Technological Change and the Management of
    Architectural Knowledge   359
    Rebecca M. Henderson

17. Organizational Evolution and the Social Ecology of Jobs   376
    Anne S. Miner

18. Organizational Routines Are Stored as Procedural Memory:
Evidence From a Laboratory Study   403
    Michael D. Cohen and *Paul Bacdayan*

19. Culture and Organizational Learning   430
    Scott D. N. Cook and *Dvora Yanow*

20. Organizing for Continuous Improvement: Evolutionary Theory
Meets the Quality Revolution   460
    Sidney G. Winter

21. Learning by Knowledge-Intensive Firms   484
    William H. Starbuck

22. Organizational Learning   516
    Barbara Levitt and *James G. March*

23. Learning Through Failure: The Strategy of Small Losses   541
    Sim B Sitkin

Index   579

About the Editors   603

About the Contributors   605

Introduction

MICHAEL D. COHEN
LEE S. SPROULL

This volume originated in a conference held at Carnegie Mellon University in May 1989 with the support of the National Science Foundation, the Xerox Corporation, and the university. Its goals were to advance the state of research on organizational learning and celebrate one of the field's leading scholars, James G. March.

Many of the conference papers were subsequently submitted to *Organization Science,* which had issued an open call for papers to be published in a special issue on organizational learning. All submissions were assessed via the journal's standard process of anonymous peer review, under our editorship. The result was the special issue of February 1991, *Organizational Learning: Papers in Honor of (and by) James G. March.*

Since the idea for the conference was first sketched in 1987, interest in organizational learning has continued to grow dramatically.[1] Thus we were delighted when Sage Publications offered to produce a collection based on the papers in the special issue—along with several that appeared in later numbers of *Organization Science*—because there were more high-quality submissions than the single issue could contain. The present volume has given us the opportunity not only to reprint the original selections, but also to include nine other papers on the topic that add to the variety and quality of the collection. We hope the volume will provide organizational researchers, practitioners, and students with a stimulating sample of the wide variety of approaches to organizational learning now being pursued.

In introducing the 1991 special issue, we argued that it was not yet time to draw lines around the field of organizational learning. Although we worried that confusion might be fostered if everything could claim to be organizational learning, we also felt that the area was too new, vital, and innovative to risk prematurely closing its borders.

We still hold this view and therefore still do not delineate what is, and what is not, "organizational learning." We have our own inclinations, of course, which are evident in those pieces of the collection we helped write. But for this introduction it seems more important to pursue two lines of clarification: (a) to suggest the dimensions that differentiate among studies of organizational learning and (b) to suggest trends that are emerging in many pieces of the recent literature. Although it is too soon to propose boundaries, we now have enough results to draw a rough map of the territory and offer some conjectures about where we may be headed. See Figure I.1.

DIMENSIONS OF DIFFERENCE

1. Is the knowledge that organizational learning builds in individual members procedural or declarative?

Chapter 18, "Organizational Routines Are Stored as Procedural Memory: Evidence From a Laboratory Study," introduces the distinction from contemporary psychology between procedural and declarative knowledge. Procedural knowledge has been found to characterize individual knowledge of well-practiced skills, both motor and cognitive. Declarative knowledge characterizes knowledge of facts and propositions. The two kinds of knowledge have markedly different properties, the former being more tacit and less rapidly forgotten. When translated to the organizational context, the distinction illuminates an important dimension among studies of organizational learning. What kind of knowledge is being built in member individuals? At the procedural end of the spectrum lie all the skills built through legitimate peripheral participation as discussed in Chapter 3, "Organizational Learning and Communities-of-Practice: Toward a Unified View of Working, Learning, and Innovation." At the declarative end are the many studies of how organizations acquire and distribute knowledge of significant facts and theories. This is the literature on which Chapter 6, "Organization Learning: The Contributing Processes and the Literatures," concentrates. The knowledge acquired by theoretical analysis of the experience of others, the central concern of Chapter 1, "Learning From Samples of One or Fewer," is also on this declarative side of the map.

2. Are the results of organizational learning stored in the minds of individual organizational members or in the relations among the individuals?

Many researchers have stressed the need to differentiate organizational learning from simple individual learning. But it is important to refine the distinction still further. Organizational learning may occur by changing the memories (whether procedural or declarative) of many individual members. Or it may be produced by modifying the relations among members—their roles, authority, communication channels, information technologies, explicit standard operating procedures, or even their shared vocabulary.[2]

On the individual side of the map, Chapter 6 reviews much literature of this type. For Huber, organizational learning is the acquisition of information that becomes available at widely distributed points in an organization. On the other side, Chapter 2, "Organizing Work by Adaptation," demonstrates the development of an inter-individual computational procedure. Chapter 15, "Collective Mind in Organizations: Heedful Interrelating on Flight Decks," and Chapter 16, "Technological Change and the Management of Architectural Knowledge," provide further examples of the relational form of organizational learning. Chapter 12, "Organizational Learning and Personnel Turnover," exhibits both these effects, with changes occurring in individuals and being induced in those with whom they work.

3. Does organizational learning reinforce existing action patterns or cause them to change?

A number of classic studies of the learning of routines, such as Allison (1971) and Nelson and Winter (1982), are centrally concerned with the stability of the resulting action patterns. More recently, Winter (1994) interprets the procedures of the modern quality movement as a design for learning that will produce change in routines. Chapter 16 provides a striking account of structural learning that at first fuels change, then accumulates to make further change impossible. Work in the learning curve tradition, such as in Chapter 4, "Organizational Learning Curves: A Method for Investigating Intra-Plant Transfer of Knowledge Acquired Through Learning by Doing," demonstrates processes that dramatically alter action patterns over time.

Taken together, these observations suggest a three-dimensional map of recent work in the field. Although these dimensions may have some correlation, they are distinctive enough that, for example, papers such as Chapters 1 and 3 can be close on one dimension and far apart on another. In the not-too-distant future the dimensions of a map such as this may help subdivide the field of organizational learning, so that we can more easily discern what kinds of learning a particular study (mainly) addresses and which other studies are most likely to be relevant. In Chapter 8, "Bounded Rationality and Organizational Learning," Simon argues eloquently that such a gain in precision is badly needed.

The papers presented here, and dozens of others that could not be included for limitations of space, challenge conventional organization theory in three fundamental ways.

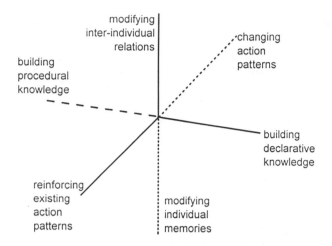

Figure I.1. Three Dimensions of Organizational Learning Research

1. They focus on action, rather than on choice.

Many studies attend to broader categories of action within organizations, deemphasizing the attention usually given to explicit choices. This is evident in the focus on routines in many organizational learning studies (Chapters 2 and 18), in the work that views an organizational culture as learning a characteristic way of doing things (Chapter 19), and in work that finds learning in changing role relations, job occupants, and job definitions (Chapter 11, "Technology Diffusion and Organizational Learning: The Case of Business Computing"; Chapter 12, "Organizational Learning and Personnel Turnover"; and Chapter 17, "Organizational Evolution and the Social Ecology of Jobs"), thus framing change in choices as a consequence rather than a cause.

An interest in organizational learning need not entail a deemphasis of choice. One can view learning as the result of a sequence of choices, and this has often occurred in formal modeling approaches (e.g., Levinthal & March, 1981). But it appears that the organizational learning literature is developing not just into an alternative to approaches assuming rational choice, but into an alternative to focusing on choice per se—rational or boundedly rational. (Chapter 8 forcefully argues against this trend.) The implication of the shift is that choice appears as one of many significant (learned) forms of organizational action, and rational choice as one (learned) form of choice. A learning view is helping us see that vast bulk of the iceberg of organizational action that lies beneath highly visible choices.

2. They emphasize dynamics, with stability interpreted in that context.

Learning, in virtually any definition, is a process that alters the character of action. Learning often replaces old actions with new ones, as Chapter 7, "The Nontraditional Quality of Organizational Learning," emphasizes. Sometimes, the dynamic rigidifies existing action patterns, to the frustration of would-be reengineers. (Chapter 5, "Exploration and Exploitation in Organizational Learning," contributes here to the theory of how this can happen.) In either case, attention to learning implies a central concern with how action patterns take shape within and are shaped by the stream of experience. This primacy of dynamics frames organizational stability in a new light. In contrast to the deep rationalist presumption that equilibrium is a natural, generally beneficial, state of affairs that is sometimes temporarily disturbed, a learning point of view suggests that stability may be an uncommon, hard won, and not always beneficial condition. Our eyes are opened, for example, to ecologies of learning systems and to organizations with learning occurring at multiple levels. In such settings, each element of a system may change in a way that can destabilize those of its neighbors that are learning to deal with it.

3. They explain organizational coherence, rather than assuming it.

There is ample documentation of organizations that fail to create or maintain coherence. And, of course, many studies assume—and some find—that organizations can be extremely coherent in their actions. Neither of these traditions aspires to show how the coherence of multiple actors forming a single organization could be possible and thereby provide a systematic account of how it might fail to be achieved. Yet the emergence of a (partially) coherent organizational entity from the activities of its component individuals probably deserves to be a fundamental explanandum of organization theory.

Again, in the recent literature one can discern a trend toward tackling this challenge. It is addressed in the Chapter 3 account of the generation of communities of practice. It is explored for very small organizations in Chapters 2 and 18. Chapter 15 attacks the question directly in the case of aircraft carrier deck crews. In this aspect, the literature on organizational learning displays some kinship with developments in the literature on "complex adaptive systems" and its focus on "emergent phenomena" (Holland, 1995).

Taken together, these trends in recent work show that organizational learning research is beginning to address more squarely some of the most fundamental, outstanding issues in the study of organization. Its future seems bright.

ONE ELEMENT OF STABILITY
IN A CHANGING LITERATURE

Listing trends in organizational learning research obscures one of its most constant factors: the influence of James G. March. Barnett's (1994) study of the literature isolated 17 key publications that were cited 3,876 times between 1956 and 1993. Two works by March and his colleagues accounted for 57% of the citations between 1981 and 1985. From 1991 through 1993, March's work with three colleagues accounts for 64%! We are proud to conclude this new introduction by reprinting the concluding portion of the introduction to the 1991 special issue. This volume, like that special issue, celebrates March's continuing contributions in its subtitle, *Organizational Learning: Papers in Honor of (and by) James G. March.*

> In the present volume there is no paper that is not in his intellectual debt, even though the papers stem from very diverse traditions. And, of course, there are [three] papers authored or co-authored by Jim as well. Thus the volume, like the conference, evidence his continuing leadership of the quest for a solid understanding of organizations, one that cheerfully seeks to account for both the triumphs and failures of people confronting a world complex beyond rational mastery.
>
> At the conference, there was an evening set aside to appreciate Jim, at which he was given a first English edition of Cervantes' *Don Quixote.* It is a story he loves, and it is fitting that he should admire a book in which the often absurd encounter between the world and human distortions of the world exalts striving and yields both illumination and laughter. Many of us found that our feelings for Jim March share much with Sancho Panza's admiration for Don Quixote: he may seem "crazy," but "he says things that, to my mind, and indeed everybody's that listens to him, are so wise and run in such a straight furrow that the devil himself couldn't have said them better" (Part II, ch. xxxiii). A whole discipline can be proud to follow him.

NOTES

1. An informal indicator is the wide popularity of Senge's *Fifth Discipline* (1990); a more formal one is Barnett's (1994) finding that a set of central articles offering definitions of organizational learning were cited 744 times in the period 1991-1993, with 20% increases each year.

2. These relations may also reduce ultimately to changes in individuals, of course, but an additional step is involved, and these changes have a more marked inter-individual character, so that they might persist, even in the event of personnel turnover.

REFERENCES

Allison, G. (1971). *Essence of decision: Explaining the Cuban missile crisis.* Boston: Little, Brown.

Barnett, C. K. (1994). Organizational learning theories: A review and synthesis of the literature. *Academy of Management Review.* Manuscript submitted for publication.

Holland, J. H. (1995). *Hidden order: How adaptation builds complexity.* Redding, MA: Addison-Wesley.

Levinthal, D. A., & March, J. G. (1981). A model of adaptive organizational search. *Journal of Economic Behavior and Organization, 2,* 307-333.

Nelson, R., & Winter, S. (1982). *An evolutionary theory of economic change.* Cambridge, MA: Belknap.

Senge, P. M. (1990). *The fifth discipline.* New York: Doubleday/Currency.

Winter, S. G. (1994). Organizing for continuous improvement. In J. A. C. Baum & J. Singh (Eds.), *The evolutionary dynamics of organizations.* New York: Oxford University Press.

1

Learning From Samples of One or Fewer

JAMES G. MARCH
LEE S. SPROULL
MICHAL TAMUZ

Organizations learn from experience. Sometimes, however, history is not generous with experience. We explore how organizations convert infrequent events into
interpretations of history, and how they balance the need to achieve agreement on
interpretations with the need to interpret history correctly. We ask what methods
are used, what problems are involved, and what improvements might be made.
Although the methods we observe are not guaranteed to lead to consistent
agreement on interpretations, valid knowledge, improved organizational performance, or organizational survival, they provide possible insights into the possibilities for and problems of learning from fragments of history.

(ORGANIZATIONAL LEARNING; LEARNING
FROM EXPERIENCE; SMALL SAMPLES)

Organizations learn from experience, but learning seems problematic when
history offers only meager samples of experience. Historical events are
observed, and inferences about historical processes are formed, but the
paucity of historical events conspires against effective learning. We consider
situations in which organizations seek to learn from history on the basis of
very small samples of experience. For example:

This chapter appeared originally in *Organization Science,* Vol. 2, No. 1, February 1991.

Case 1. A military organization has rarely fought in a battle. Yet it wants to learn from its history how to improve its ability to engage in warfare.

Case 2. A business firm has little experience with foreign acquisitions. Yet it wants to learn from its history whether and how to make such investments.

Case 3. An airline rarely has fatal accidents. Yet it wants to learn from its history how to reduce the chances of such disasters.

Case 4. A business firm rarely makes major marketable discoveries. Yet it wants to learn from its history how to increase the chances of such innovations.

Case 5. A power company rarely has nuclear accidents. Yet it wants to learn from its history how to minimize the chances of such catastrophes.

In the next section, we examine how organizations convert meager experience into interpretations of history by experiencing infrequent events richly. In Section 2, we examine processes for simulating hypothetical histories. In Section 3, we examine some justifications for these two learning strategies and some of the problems involved.

1. EXPERIENCING HISTORY RICHLY

Historical events are unique enough to make accumulating knowledge difficult. Each event is a single, unrepeated data point, and accumulation seems to require pooling across diverse contexts. Organizations attempt such pooling, but they also seek to increase the information extracted from their own limited historical experience by treating unique historical incidents as detailed stories rather than single data points. They elaborate experience by discovering more aspects of experience, more interpretations of experience, and more preferences by which to evaluate experience.

Experiencing More Aspects of Experience. Characterizing history as small samples of unique occurrences overlooks the wealth of experience that is represented in each historical event. The apparent stinginess of history is moderated by attending to more aspects of experience (Campbell, 1979). For example, learning about a decision involves monitoring its outcomes. But long before an organization experiences many of the outcomes of a typical decision, it experiences a variety of collateral consequences associated with the making of the decision and its implementation. Learning and evaluation occur through these experiences prior to outcome-based learning. For example, participants appreciate collateral experiences such as "a bold move" or "a good meeting."

When early collateral experiences are positive, organizations, like individuals, are prone to exhibit self-reinforcing decision behavior. Especially when outcome feedback is slow or unclear, an organization is likely to repeat decisions simply because it has made them before. Thus, in a study of decisions about foreign direct investments by Finnish firms, Björkman (1989) found that, prior to receiving information on the results of their first investments and simply as a result of their experience in making the first decisions, firms increased their propensity to make more investments. This did not appear to be a consequence of any explicit intention to spread risk. Apparently, the organizations extracted lessons from the choice process itself, lessons about the competence and character of relevant actors and the pleasure of deciding to invest. Learning was embedded richly in the taking of action, rather than simply in considering its ultimate consequences.

Making a decision also induces anticipations of its future costs and benefits (Merton, 1968). The anticipations are experienced prior to the consequences and are an independent basis for learning. Since expectations for chosen alternatives will generally be positive, they ordinarily reinforce a repetition of the action. On the other hand, negative expectations might be experienced in situations involving coercion or peril, or when learning takes place in an alienated part of the organization, or among opposition groups. In such cases, the effect of making a decision reduces the propensity to repeat it. In general, decision processes in organizations lead to overly optimistic expectations and thus are vulnerable to subsequent disappointment with results (Harrison & March, 1984). These optimistic errors in anticipations are likely to make the short-run lessons of experience more reinforcing of action than the long-run lessons. The inconsistency in learning is reduced by the tendency for actual experience to be both delayed and more ambiguous than anticipations, thus allowing optimistic expectations about experience to be confirmed by retrospective sense-making of it (Aronson, 1968; Salancik, 1977).

Organizations also enhance the richness of history by focusing intensively on critical incidents. For example, when a large section of the metal skin of an Aloha Airlines aircraft peeled away in mid-air, the event attracted considerable attention and triggered a major modification in FAA-mandated maintenance programs. Close examination of what happened revealed significant features of aircraft engineering and maintenance that had not been noted earlier. By identifying those features and their implications, the organizations learned. Similarly, when a computer science graduate student propagated a "virus" among many computer networks, producing breakdowns in hundreds of systems, and considerable publicity, the incident stimulated analyses that identified weaknesses in the underlying computer code and in how people and systems were organized to respond to such events.

Three aspects of an event seem to make it critical. The first is its place in the course of history. Events that change the world are critical incidents. They are branching points of historical development. From such an incident, one learns about changed implications for the future rather than about how to predict or control similar occurrences in the future. A classic example is the invention of the printing press.

The second aspect of an event that makes it critical is its place in the development of belief. Events that change what is believed about the world are critical incidents. In a way consistent with conventional ideas about the relation between surprise and information value (Raiffa, 1968), criticality is associated with the surprise an event evokes for current belief. A single incident is typically unsurprising because it can be interpreted as consistent with sampling variation within existing theories (Fischhoff, 1975; Fischhoff & Beyth, 1975). But sometimes a solitary event provides an unexpected contradiction to our beliefs, as for example in the Aloha Airlines and computer virus cases.

A third aspect that makes an event critical is its metaphorical power. Events that evoke meaning, interest, and attention for organizational participants are critical incidents. Anecdotes and stories are standard features of pedagogical practice. Skill at story telling is a major factor in endowing experience with metaphorical force. But the raw material of experience also affects the development of stories. Critical incidents have a quality of simplicity and representativeness that is not entirely imposed on them. Some historical events are better vehicles for meaning than others.

Experiencing More Interpretations. Organizations often augment history by attending to multiple observers or interpretations. The consequences of an action are experienced differently throughout the organization. Conflicts of interest or differences in culture, in particular, stimulate multiple interpretations. Because different individuals and groups experience historical events differently, they learn different lessons from the same experience (Dearborn & Simon, 1958; Sproull & Hofmeister, 1986). As a result, organizational experience leads to a variety of interpretations, and an organization's repertoire may come to include several different, possibly contradictory, story lines. Differences in perspectives lead to differences in interpretations and create a mosaic of conflicting lessons.

To be sure, efforts to make multiple interpretations consistent are also routine in organizations. Formal proceedings, findings, informal conversations, and the diffusion of stories tend to create a shared, interpretive history. Interpretations of individual or group responsibility for mistakes or failures (or brilliant moves or successes) come to be shared. However, such efforts are not always successful (Brunsson, 1989). The structure of internal competition and conflict divides many organizations into advocates and opponents for organizational policies and actions. The contending groups interpret history differently and draw different lessons from it.

Experiencing More Preferences. Organizations discover values, aspirations, and identities in the process of experiencing the consequences of their actions. They learn how to distinguish success from failure, and thus affect considerably the other lessons they take from their experience. While the interpretation of a particular outcome as a success or failure is not arbitrary, neither is it always self-evident. The preferences and values in terms of which organizations distinguish successes from failures are themselves transformed in the process of learning. By acting, reflecting, and interpreting, organizations learn what they are. By observing their own actions, they learn what they want (Weick, 1979). Whether these changes are seen as learning new implications of alternative actions for stable preferences, or as transforming preferences, is partly a matter of intellectual taste (Becker & Stigler, 1977).

For any given dimension of organizational preferences, aspiration levels change in response to an organization's own experience and to the experience of other organizations to which it compares itself (Cyert & March, 1963; Lant & Montgomery, 1987), thereby loosening the link between performance and outcomes, on the one hand, and evaluations of success and failure (and thus learning), on the other. Because experiencing an outcome as a success or failure depends on the relation between the outcome and adaptive aspirations for it, what is learned from any particular kind of experience can vary substantially across time and across organizations. Consider, for example, the efforts of a business firm to learn from its marketing experience. Whether a particular marketing strategy is viewed as a success (to be reinforced) or a failure (to be extinguished) will depend as much on the organization's aspirations as on the marketing outcomes. In a similar way, election results are experienced by political parties and movements in terms of a comparison between outcomes and aspirations rather than simply in terms of the former.

The dimensions of preferences also change. As we have noted above, a rich examination of an individual case uncovers a variety of features and consequences of action. These experiences become bases for organizational interpretations not only of the world and its rewards but also of the organization, particularly its preferences, values, and character (Zald & Denton, 1963). For example, when the Coca-Cola Company reinstated old coke as Coca-Cola Classic (after having first withdrawn it from the market in favor of a replacement), it learned from its behavior that it was a "flexible company that listened to its customers" (Oliver, 1986). Anything that predisposes parts of an organization to find pleasure in consequences, for example, an upbeat mood (Isen, Schalker, Clark, & Karp, 1978) or a sense of responsibility for action (March & Olsen, 1975), tends to increase the likelihood of identifying positive aspects of unanticipated consequences, thus of transforming preferences.

2. SIMULATING EXPERIENCE

In trying to understand unique experiences, organizations make implicit choices between two alternative perspectives on history. In the first perspective, realized events are seen as necessary consequences of antecedent historical conditions. In the second perspective, realized events are seen as *draws* from a distribution of possible events. If historical events are (possibly unlikely) draws from a wealth of possibilities, an understanding of history requires attention to the whole distribution of possible events, including those that did not occur (Fischhoff, 1980; Hogarth, 1983). The organizational problem is to infer an underlying distribution of possible events from a series of realized events having varying, but possibly quite low, probabilities. The merging of empirical and theoretical knowledge required to understand these underlying distributions raises some complicated problems of inference and method.

We consider two closely related techniques for organizational simulation of hypothetical events: the first technique is to define and elaborate a class of historical non-events that can be called near-histories—events that almost happened. The second technique is to define and elaborate a class of historical non-events that can be called hypothetical histories—events that might have happened under certain unrealized but plausible conditions.

Near-Histories. If a basketball game is decided by one point, one team wins and the other team loses, with consequences that may be vital for a championship. But the outcome will normally be interpreted by experts as a draw from some probability distribution over possible outcomes rather than simply as a "win" by one team and a "loss" by the other. In general, if a relatively small change in some conditions would have transformed one outcome into another, the former will be experienced to some degree as having been the latter. In such a spirit, the National Research Council (1980) has defined a safety "incident" as an event that, under slightly different circumstances, could have been an accident.

Air traffic systems illustrate how organizations learn from near-histories or "incidents" (Tamuz, 1987). By collecting information about near-accidents from pilots and air traffic controllers, air safety reporting systems considerably enlarge the sample of events that can be treated as relevant to understanding aviation safety. Information on near-accidents augments the relatively sparse history of real accidents and has been used to redesign aircraft, air traffic control systems, airports, cockpit routines, and pilot training procedures.

Near-histories are useful antidotes to a tendency to over generalize from the drama of great disasters or victories (Fischhoff, 1982). For example, students of the Battle of Midway have suggested a number of quite likely alternative scenarios for that battle that would have led to notably different outcomes (Prange, 1982). Future admirals learn not only from the battle but also from its near-histories. Standard folkloric observations that great failures often are the consequence of bad luck or timing and great successes the consequence of good luck or timing suggest an implicit distribution of possible outcomes around the observed outliers. They emphasize that the near-histories of genius and foolishness are more similar than their realized histories.

Hypothetical histories. Near-histories are a special case of a more general approach—the construction of hypothetical histories. Hypothetical histories play a role in organizational learning similar to that of mental models or simulations in studies of individual learning (Johnson-Laird, 1983; Kahneman & Tversky, 1982a). Organizations use small samples of specific historical events to construct theories about events, and then simulate hypothetical histories that can be treated as having interpretive significance comparable to, or even greater than, the history actually experienced. In this process, the analysis of unique historical outcomes emphasizes identifying the underlying distribution from which that realization was drawn rather than explaining the particular draw (Stinchcombe, 1978).

A pervasive contemporary version of hypothetical histories is found in the use of spread sheets to explore the implications of alternative assumptions or shifts in variables in a system of equations that portrays organizational relations. More generally, many modern techniques of planning in organizations involve the simulation of hypothetical future scenarios, which in the present terms are indistinguishable from hypothetical histories (Hax & Majluf, 1984). The logic is simple: small pieces of experience are used to construct a theory of history from which a variety of unrealized, but possible, additional scenarios are generated. In this way, ideas about historical processes drawn from detailed case studies are used to develop distributions of possible futures.

Organizations expand their comprehension of history by making experience richer, by considering multiple interpretations of experience, by using experience to discover and modify their preferences, and by simulating near-events and hypothetical histories. They try to learn from samples of one or fewer. Many of the techniques organizations use to learn from small samples of history, however, are clearly suspect. They can lead to learning false lessons, to superstitious learning, to exaggerated confidence in historical understandings. As a result, discussions of organizational learning from small samples tend to be framed by a mood of despair over the futility of the effort. In Section 3, we turn to an examination of how such learning might be understood, evaluated, and improved.

3. ASSESSING AND IMPROVING
LEARNING FROM SMALL HISTORIES

In Sections 1 and 2, we have described some of the ways organizations learn from fragments of history. In this section, we assess their effectiveness in terms of two common criteria: reliability and validity. A reliable learning process is one by which an organization develops common understandings of its experience and makes its interpretations public, stable, and shared. A valid learning process is one by which an organization is able to understand, predict, and control its environment. Neither reliability nor validity is assured. Because different people and groups in an organization approach historical experience with different expectations and beliefs, shared understandings cannot be assumed. And because historical events are produced by particular (and often complicated) combinations of factors occurring in non-repetitive contexts, learning validly from small samples of historical experience is difficult (Brehmer, 1980; Kiesler & Sproull, 1982).

If individual beliefs converge to an accurate understanding of reality, then they become simultaneously shared and valid. Such a convergence might be expected in worlds of stable knowledge and cumulative discovery. Alternatively, if socially constructed beliefs are enacted into reality (Weick, 1979), the enactment brings high levels of both reliability and validity. For example, organizational beliefs about power, legitimacy, competence, and responsibility are based upon interpretations of shared experiences that are themselves considerably affected by the beliefs.

The more general situation, however, is one of partial conflict between the dual requirements of reliability and validity. Stable, shared knowledge interferes with the discovery of contrary experience from which valid learning arises, and the exploration of novel ideas interferes with the reliable maintenance and sharing of interpretations (March, 1990). As a result, organizational learning involves balancing the two. The trade-offs between reliability and validity made by the learning procedures we observe are less a result of conscious choice than a collection of evolving practices, imperfectly justified and incompletely comprehended. For example, the extent and character of subgroup differentiation in organizations and the mechanisms by which they are sustained or changed are important means by which the trade-off between reliability and validity is made.

The Reliability of Learning: The Construction and Sharing of Belief. Stability in shared understandings is important for organizational effectiveness and survival (Beyer, 1981; March & Olsen, 1989), as it is for social systems (Durkheim, 1973) and knowledge in general (Rorty, 1985). However, the ambiguities of history make common understandings of organizational experience difficult to sustain. Meaning is not self-evident but must be constructed and shared. Many different interpretations are both supportable and refutable.

Some standard mechanisms of individual sense-making contribute to reliability. The retrieval of history from memory exaggerates the consistency of experience with prior conceptions (Fischhoff, 1975; Pearson, Ross, & Dawes, 1990). Incorrect predictions are not noticed or are interpreted as irrelevant anomalies or measurement errors (Einhorn & Hogarth, 1978; Lord, Lepper, & Ross, 1979). Missing data are experienced as consistent with the model and are remembered as real (Cohen & Ebbesen, 1979; Loftus, 1979).

The apparatus of organizational information processing and decision making supplements these individual and social cognitive processes. Information is gathered and distributed more to interpret decisions than to inform them (Feldman & March, 1981; March & Sevón, 1984). Meetings are organized more to share stories and explanations than to take action (Brunsson, 1985, 1989). Organizations develop robust understandings that are resilient to contradictory information (Sproull, Weiner, & Wolf, 1978; Starbuck, 1983). Conceptions of identity in organizations tend also to be conserved by interpretations of experience. Decision makers in organizations discover what they are and how they should behave by taking actions (Weick, 1979). Making a decision leads to defining a personal and organizational identity consistent with that decision. Similarly, the social construction of aspirations tends to be conservative, to reinforce shared behavioral preferences.

Pressures toward reliability are easily orchestrated within an emphasis on critical incidents. Defining an event as critical focuses attention on interpreting and responding to the event. Because of the ambiguities associated with any single incident, responses and interpretations tend to be adopted more as a result of their temporal proximity, cognitive availability, or political convenience than by virtue of their obvious validity (Cohen, March, & Olsen, 1972; Cyert, Dill, & March, 1958).

The learning process is generally conservative, sustaining existing structures of belief, including existing differences, while coping with surprises in the unfolding of history. Organizations create the same kinds of coherent systems of belief that in science are called knowledge, in religion are called morality, and in other people's societies are called myths. Experience is used to strengthen and elaborate previously believed theories of life.

Such a description is, however, incomplete. There are limits to the conservation of belief (Higgins & Bargh, 1987; Martin & Siehl, 1983). Both success and failure contain the seeds of change. A persistent subjective sense of success leads to a sense of competence and a willingness to experiment (March & Shapira, 1987). A persistent subjective sense of failure produces instability in beliefs and disagreement among organizational participants with respect to both preferences and action (Sproull, Weiner, & Wolf, 1978). In addition, pressures toward subgroup homogeneity lead to internal differentiation and limit organizational homogeneity (Cangelosi & Dill, 1965; Lawrence & Lorsch, 1967).

The Validity of Learning: The Construction of Causal Belief. The confusions of history often obscure what happened, why it happened, and how we should learn from it. The general problem is not simply one of eliminating known biases in historical interpretation by organizations. The experimental design and sample sizes of history are inadequate for making inferences about it (Levitt & March, 1988; Lounamaa & March, 1987). Estimation from historical events is subject to two major kinds of variability. The first stems from the fact that some of the processes by which history is produced may be genuinely stochastic. Understanding those processes requires approximating the underlying distributions from which a realized event is drawn. The expected error in estimation can be decreased by aggregating over several events, but history limits the number of comparable events. Lacking multiple events, organizations use whatever information they can extract from single cases to discern the historical processes that determine those underlying distributions.

The second kind of variability in estimation stems from the measurement and interpretation of historical events by observers. Measurement error, model misspecification, and system complexity introduce substantial noise into observations and interpretations. With large samples of events, organizations can tolerate a relatively large amount of noise, aggregating over events to extract a signal. With small samples, however, aggregation is a less powerful procedure. Two organizational responses are common. First, since variability in interpretation with respect to any information is partly a function of the effort expended in examining it, the expected error can be decreased through a more intense examination of the individual case. Second, since the processes of measurement and interpretation yield a distribution of possible observations, the expected error can be decreased by aggregating over multiple observers.

Most of the ways organizations increase the validity of learning from historical experience can be seen as reflecting such considerations. Organizations attempt to overcome the limitations in the experimental design and sample sizes of history by enhancing the knowledge they have. They attempt to experience history more richly to formulate more interpretations of that experience, and to supplement history by experiencing more of the events that did not occur but could have.

Consider, first, efforts to experience history more richly. Every unique historical event is a collection of micro events, each of which can be experienced. In this sense, the learning potential of any historical event is indeterminate. Because both the scope of an event and the depth of its decomposition into elements are arbitrary, so also is the richness of experience. By considering additional aspects of experience and new dimensions of preferences, an organization expands the information gained from a particular case. The pursuit of rich experience, however, requires a method for absorbing detail without molding it. Great organizational histories, like great novels, are written, not by first constructing interpretations of events and then filling in the details, but by first identifying the details and allowing the interpretations to emerge from them. As a result, openness to a variety of (possibly irrelevant) dimensions of experience and preference is often more valuable than a clear prior model and unambiguous objectives (Maier, 1963; March, 1978, 1987).

Moving from rich experiences of history to valid inferences about history involves a logic that is not very well-defined but is different from the logic of classical statistical inference. It assumes that the various micro events associated with an event are in some way interconnected. They are clearly not independent samples of some universe in the standard statistical sense. But they provide scraps of information about an underlying reality that cumulate, much the way various elements of a portrait cumulate to provide information about its subject.

Consider, second, efforts to interpret experience in more ways. Imagination in generating alternatives of interpretation reduces the standard confirmatory bias of experience, at the cost of also reducing the speed at which a correct interpretation is recognized and confirmed. Janis and Mann (1977) and George (1980) have each pointed out the advantages of pooling perceptions and judgments across individuals who interpret history differently. A similar argument is made into a methodological point by Allison (1971) and Neustadt and May (1986). Such observations suggest an important trade-off in attempts to improve the precision of estimates: an organization can opt to increase the number of events to be observed and interpreted or, alternatively, to increase the number and diversity of observers for a single event. Whether it is better to invest in additional events or in additional observers depends both on the relative cost of the two and on the relative magnitudes of the two sources of variability. But in pursuing an understanding of organizational history, greater reduction in uncertainty can often be achieved by pooling observers than by pooling events, particularly if the observers are relatively independent.

Consider, third, efforts to experience more of the events that did not happen. The presumption is that the processes of history are both more stable than their realized outcomes and more susceptible to understanding through rich descriptions. Near-histories and hypothetical histories produce distributions of unrealized, possible events. By treating events that did not occur as having significance similar to those that did occur, hypothetical histories exploit the information contained in rich descriptions of historical processes to provide a more judicious assessment of the probability distribution of future events.

In addition to providing a wider range of experience from which to draw, near-histories may be more easily interpreted than realized history. Tamuz (1988) suggests that understanding actual aviation accidents is heavily compromised by the legal and financial contexts which provide individual and organizational incentives for discovering particular self-interested interpretations. She argues that although the reporting of near-accidents is affected by publicity, politics, and perceived reporting incentives, the analysis of these near-accidents often introduces fewer biases than those of accidents, thus producing understandings that are more consistent with broader social constructions and theories of evidence.

Although near-histories make useful contributions to learning, supplementing realized events with hypothetical ones introduces certain complications. First, constructing hypothetical histories can be expensive. Sometimes the substantial costs of such activities are shared by professional associations and governmental agencies, as they are in the air transportation industry. But often the ordinary branchings of history make it difficult to gather and interpret information on consequences of hypothetical histories that are not immediate. Imagine an organization that wanted to compare the ultimate careers and productivity of its employees with those job applicants it almost hired, or of applicants to whom it offered employment but who chose to work elsewhere. Assembling information on such a collection of historical branches involving outsiders, and interpreting the information, are substantial tasks.

Second, the impact of hypothetical histories ordinarily cannot compare with the dramatic power of realized history (Fischhoff & Beyth, 1975; Kiesler & Sproull, 1982). It is difficult to match the powerful effect of actual events (for example, the 1987 Challenger explosion) on beliefs. As a result, a vital part of the telling of history is the evocation of imagination (Tolstoy,

1869). The probable dependence of imagination on vividness (Shedler & Manis, 1986) and rich detail (Krieger, 1983) provides at least a partial reason for emphasizing such stories in organizations (Clark, 1972; Martin, 1982). In the stories of Three-Mile Island, the Aloha Airlines flight, and the Cornell computer virus, vivid historical events were used to dramatize a hypothetical story of even greater potential disaster. The drama mobilized attention and learning across a wide spectrum of groups.

Third, hypothetical histories may be ambiguous and thus unpersuasive. Where organizations face possible events of great consequence but small likelihood, the use of near-histories to augment simple experience is sometimes controversial. If the probability of disaster is very low, near-histories will tend to picture greater risk than will be experienced directly by most organizations or individuals in a reasonable length of time. In such case, near-histories are likely to be treated as generating too pessimistic a picture. For example, long before the fatal Challenger flight, the spacecraft flew a series of successful missions despite its faulty O-rings. Some engineers interpreted the indications of O-ring problems during these early flights as symptoms that past successes had been relatively lucky draws from a distribution in which the probability of disaster was relatively high (Bell & Esch, 1987; Boisjoly, 1987). Others, including some key personnel in NASA, considered these estimates of danger as exaggerated because, in the realized history, the system had been robust enough to tolerate such problems (Starbuck & Milliken, 1988).

Conversely, if the probability of success is very low, most short sequences of realized experience will contain no successes. The direct experience of most organizations and individuals with projects offering very low probability of very high return will be less favorable than will an analysis of near-successes. In such cases, near-histories are likely to be treated as providing too optimistic a picture. One such case involves organizations searching unsuccessfully for major innovations and treating assertions of "near-discoveries" as an unduly optimistic basis for sustaining investment in research.

As these examples suggest, the most obvious learning problem with near-histories is the necessary ambiguity of their interpretation. If an organization is concerned with product quality and uses an inspection system to reject items that do not meet standards, every rejected item provides information on two things—the likelihood of substandard production and the likelihood of discovering the inadequacy. Each event, therefore, is both a failure and a success. Similarly, every time a pilot avoids a collision, the event provides evidence both for the threat and for its irrelevance. It is not clear whether the learning should emphasize how close the organization came to a disaster, thus the reality of danger in the guise of safety, or the fact that disaster was avoided, thus the reality of safety in the guise of danger.

4. FOUR QUESTIONS

Organizational efforts to learn reliably and validly from small histories are marked by two conspicuous things: first, we try to learn from them, often believing that we do so (Allison, 1971; George & McKeown, 1985), or can do so (Fischhoff, 1982; Kahneman & Tversky, 1982b), and often believing that we do not and cannot (Fischhoff, 1980; Dawes, Faust, & Meehl, 1989). Second, we do not have a shared conception of how we learn from small histories or what distinguishes single cases that are informative from those that are not (Herbst, 1970; Mohr, 1985).

We have not invented a general logic for learning from history that can fully rationalize what we have described, nor do we imagine that such a total rationalization is possible. Many of the ways in which organizations treat small histories are difficult to justify as either leading to shared beliefs, exhibiting intelligence, or producing competitive advantage. Learning processes sometimes result in confusion and mistakes.

Nevertheless, we are disposed to see elements of intelligence in organizational efforts to organize, construct, and interpret experience, so as to move toward a shared understanding of it. We think organizations learn from their histories in ways that are, at times, remarkably subtle adaptations to the inferential inadequacies of historical experience. We recognize some advantages in having stable, shared beliefs about experience even if misinterpretations are embedded in those beliefs. We see possibilities for expanding and enhancing unique, ambiguous events, so as to learn more richly and validly from them. We believe that usable knowledge can be extracted from fragments of history and that intensive examinations of individual cases can be used imaginatively to construct meaningful hypothetical histories.

Such beliefs depend ultimately on confidence in being able to resolve some fundamental issues in historical inference. These include four critical questions:

1. What is the evidential standing of imagination? Organizations use near-histories and hypothetical histories to learn from samples of one or fewer. The procedures seem to have elements of intelligence in them, but they mix theoretical and empirical knowledge in ways that are not considered comprehensively in our theories of inference.

2. What is a proper process for combining prior expectations and interrelated, cumulated aspects of a rich description into an interpretation of history? Organizations develop and modify stories about history on the basis of detailed examinations of individual cases. It is clear that radically different stories may be told about the same history. But it also seems clear that the evaluation of stories is not arbitrary, that there are criteria for differentiating between good and bad stories.

3. What is the proper trade-off between reliability and validity in historical interpretation? As organizations develop theories of their experiences, they balance gains and losses in validity against gains and losses in reliability. The metric and the procedures for the trade-off are ill-defined, but there seems little doubt that an intelligent organization will sometimes sacrifice conventional notions of validity in order to achieve or sustain reliability in interpretation.

4. What are the relative values of multiple observations of events and multiple interpretations of them? Improving precision in estimates involves pooling over observations and over observers. Theories of historical inference tend to emphasize pooling over observations. Pooling over observers appears to have advantages in some common situations, but in the absence of a clearer formulation of the gains and losses involved, it is hard to specify the precise conditions favoring one strategy or the other.

These questions invite heroic philosophical and methodological efforts to clarify and extend the uses of historical experience in the construction and sharing of meaning. The problems involved are not trivial. Nevertheless, we think modest progress can be made without waiting for a revolution in epistemology and within reasonably conventional modes of thinking about historical inference and learning from experience. The present paper is in that spirit. By examining the ways organizations actually seek to learn from small histories, and by trying to make sense of some of the things they do, we have tried to suggest some possible directions for understanding how meaning is extracted from sample sizes of one or fewer.

Acknowledgments

The research has been supported by the National Science Foundation, the Spencer Foundation, the Stanford Graduate School of Business, the System Development Foundation, and the Xerox Corporation. We are grateful for the comments of Michael Cohen, Robyn Dawes, Kristian Kreiner, Arie Lewin, Allyn Romanow, Sim Sitkin, and Suzanne Stout.

REFERENCES

Allison, G. T. (1971). *Essence of decision.* Boston: Little, Brown.

Aronson, E. (1968). Disconfirmed expectancies and bad decisions—Discussion: Expectancy vs. other motive. In R. P. Abelson, E. Aronson, W. McGuire, T. Newcombe, M. Rosenberg, & P. H. Tannenbaum (Eds.), *Theories of cognitive consistency* (pp. 491-493). Chicago: Rand McNally.

Becker, G. S., & Stigler, G. J. (1977). De gustibus non est disputandum. *American Economic Review, 67,* 76-90.

Bell, T. E., & Esch, K. (1987). The fatal flow in flight 51-L. *IEEE Spectator, 24*(2), 36-51.

Beyer, J. M. (1981). Ideologies, values and decision-making in organizations. In P. C. Nystrom & W. H. Starbuck (Eds.), *Handbook of organizational design* (Vol. 2, pp. 166-202). Oxford, UK: Oxford University Press.

Björkman, I. (1989). *Foreign direct investments: An empirical analysis of decision making in seven Finnish firms.* Helsinki: Svenska Handelhögskolan.

Boisjoly, R. (1987). Ethical decisions—Morton Thiokol and the space shuttle Challenger disaster. *American Society of Mechanical Engineering,* 87-WA/TS-4, 1-13.

Brehmer, B. (1980). In one word: Not from experience. *Acta Psychologica, 45,* 223-241.

Brunsson, N. (1985). *The irrational organization: Irrationality as a basis for organizational action and change.* Chichester, UK: Wiley.

Brunsson, N. (1989). *The organization of hypocrisy.* Chichester, UK: Wiley.

Campbell, D. (1979). Degrees of freedom and the case study. In T. D. Cook & C. S. Reichardt (Eds.), *Qualitative and quantitative methods in evaluations research* (pp. 49-67). Beverly Hills, CA: Sage.

Cangelosi, V., & Dill, W. R. (1965). Organizational learning: Observations toward a theory. *Administrative Science Quarterly, 10,* 175-203.

Clark, B. R. (1972). The organizational saga in higher education. *Administrative Science Quarterly, 17,* 178-184.

Cohen, C. E., & Ebbesen, E. B. (1979). Observational goals and schema activation: A theoretical framework for behavior perception. *Journal of Experimental Social Psychology, 15,* 305-329.

Cohen, M. D., March, J. G., & Olsen, J. P. (1972). A garbage can model of organizational choice. *Administrative Science Quarterly, 17,* 25.

Cyert, R. M., Dill, W., & March, J. G. (1958). The role of expectations in business decision making. *Administrative Science Quarterly, 3,* 307-340.

Cyert, R. M., & March, J. G. (1963). *A behavioral theory of the firm.* Englewood Cliffs, NJ: Prentice Hall.

Dawes, R. M., Faust, D., & Meehl, P. E. (1989). Clinical versus actuarial judgment. *SCI, 243,* 1668-1674.

Dearborn, D. C., & Simon, H. A. (1958). Selective perception: A note on the departmental identification of executives. *Sociometry, 21,* 140-144.

Durkheim, E. (1973). *On morality and society* (R. N. Bellah, Trans.). Chicago: University of Chicago Press.

Einhorn, H., & Hogarth, R. (1978). Confidence in judgment: Persistence in the illusion of validity. *Psychological Review, 85,* 395-416.

Feldman, M. S., & March, J. G. (1981). Information as signal and symbol. *Administrative Science Quarterly, 26,* 171-186.

Fischhoff, B. (1975). Hindsight ≠ Foresight: The effect of outcome knowledge on judgment under uncertainty. *Journal of Experimental Psychology: Human Perception and Performance, 1,* 288-299.

Fischhoff, B. (1980). For those condemned to study the past: Reflections on historical judgment. In R. A. Shweder & D. W. Fiske (Eds.), *New directions for methodology of behavioral science* (pp. 79-93). San Francisco: Jossey-Bass.

Fischhoff, B. (1982). Debiasing. In D. Kahneman, P. Slovic, & A. Tversky (Eds.), *Judgment under uncertainty: Heuristics and biases* (pp. 422-444). Cambridge, UK: Cambridge University Press.

Fischhoff, B., & Beyth, R. (1975). "I knew it would happen"—Remembered probabilities of once-future things. *Organizational Behavior and Human Performance, 13,* 1-16.

George, A. L. (1980). *Presidential decision making in foreign policy: The effective use of information and advice.* Boulder, CO: Westview.

George, A. L., & McKeown, T. (1985). Case studies and theories of organizational decision making. In R. F. Coulam & R. A. Smith (Eds.), *Advances in information processing in organizations* (Vol. 2, pp. 21-58). Greenwich, CT: JAI.

Harrison, J. R., & March, J. G. (1984). Decision-making and postdecision surprises. *Administrative Science Quarterly, 29,* 26-42.

Hax, A. C., & Majluf, N. S. (1984). *Strategic management: An integrated perspective.* Englewood Cliffs, NJ: Prentice Hall.

Herbst, P. G. (1970). *Behavioral worlds: The study of single cases.* London: Tavistock.

Higgins, E. T., & Bargh, J. A. (1987). Social cognition and social perception. *Annual Review of Psychology, 38,* 369-425.

Hogarth, R. (1983). *Small probabilities: Imagination as experience* (Working paper). Chicago: University of Chicago Center for Decision Research.

Isen, A. M., Schalker, T. E., Clark, M., & Karp, L. (1978). Affect, accessibility of material in memory, and behavior: A cognitive loop? *Journal of Personality and Social Psychology, 36,* 1-12.

Janis, I. L., & Mann, L. (1977). *Decision-making: A psychological analysis of conflict, choice and commitment.* New York: Free Press.

Johnson-Laird, P. N. (1983). *Mental models: Towards a cognitive science of language, inference, and consciousness.* Cambridge, MA: Harvard University Press.

Kahneman, D., & Tversky, A. (1982a). The simulation heuristic. In D. Kahneman, P. Slovic, & A. Tversky (Eds.), *Judgment under uncertainty: Heuristics and biases* (pp. 201-208). Cambridge, UK: Cambridge University Press.

Kahneman, D., & Tversky, A. (1982b). Intuitive prediction: Biases and corrective procedures. In D. Kahneman, P. Slovic, & A. Tversky (Eds.), *Judgment under uncertainty: Heuristics and biases* (pp. 414-421). Cambridge, UK: Cambridge University Press,

Kiesler, S., & Sproull, L. S. (1982). Managerial response to changing environments: Perspectives on problem sensing from social cognition. *Administrative Science Quarterly, 27,* 548-570.

Krieger, S. (1983). Fiction and social science. In S. Krieger (Ed.), *The mirror dance: Identity in a women's community* (pp. 173-199). Philadelphia: Temple University Press.

Lant, T. K., & Montgomery, D. B. (1987). Learning from strategic success and failure. *Journal of Business Research, 15,* 503-518.

Lawrence, P., & Lorsch, J. (1967). *Organization and environment: Managing differentiation and integration.* Boston: Harvard Graduate School of Business Administration.

Levitt, B., & March, J. G. (1988). Organizational learning. *Annual Review of Sociology, 14,* 319-340.

Loftus, E. (1979). *Eyewitness testimony.* Cambridge, MA: Harvard University Press.

Lord, C., Lepper, M. R., & Ross, L. (1979). Biased assimilation and attitude polarization: The effects of prior theories on subsequently considered evidence. *Journal of Personality and Social Psychology, 37,* 2098-2110.

Lounamaa, P. H., & March, J. G. (1987). Adaptive coordination of a learning team. *Management Science, 33,* 107-123.

Maier, N. R. F. (1963). *Problem-solving discussions and conferences: Leadership methods and skills.* New York: McGraw-Hill.

March, J. G. (1978). Bounded rationality, ambiguity, and the engineering of choice. *Bell Journal of Economics, 9,* 587-608.

March, J. G. (1987). Ambiguity and accounting: The elusive link between information and decision making. *Accounting, Organization, and Society, 12,* 153-168.

March, J. G. (1990). Exploration and exploitation in organizational learning. *Organization Science, 2*(1), 71-87.

March, J. G., & Olsen, J. P. (1975). The uncertainty of the past: Organizational learning under ambiguity. *European Journal of Political Research, 3,* 147-171.

March, J. G., & Olsen, J. P. (1989). *Rediscovering institutions: The organizational basis of politics.* New York: Free Press.

March. J. G., & Sevón, G. (1984). Gossip, information, and decision making. In L. S. Sproull & J. P. Crecine (Eds.), *Advances in information processing in organizations* (Vol. 1, pp. 95-107). Greenwich, CT: JAI.

March, J. G., & Shapira, Z. (1987). Managerial perspectives on risk and risk taking. *Management Science, 33,* 1404-1418.

Martin, J. (1982). Stories and scripts in organizational settings. In A. H. Hasdorf & A. M. Isen (Eds.), *Cognitive social psychology* (pp. 255-305). New York: Elsevier-North Holland.

Martin, J., & Siehl, C. (1983, Autumn). Organizational culture and counter culture: An uneasy symbiosis. *Organizational Dynamics,* pp. 52-64.

Merton, R. (1968). *Social theory and social structure.* New York: Free Press.

Mohr, L. B. (1985). The reliability of the case study as a source of information. In R. F. Coulam & R. A. Smith (Eds.), *Advances in information processing in organizations* (Vol. 2, pp. 65-94). Greenwich, CT: JAI.

National Research Council (Assembly of Engineering Committee on FAA Airworthiness Certification Procedures). (1980). *Improving aircraft safety: FAA certification of commercial passenger aircraft.* Washington, DC: National Academy of Sciences.

Neustadt, R. E., & May, E. R. (1986). *Thinking in time: The uses of history for decision-makers.* New York: Free Press.

Oliver, T. (1986). *The real coke, the real story.* New York: Penguin.

Pearson, R. W., Ross, M., & Dawes, R. M. (1990). Personal recall and the limits of retrospective questions in surveys. In J. Tanur (Ed.), *Questions about survey questions.* Beverly Hills, CA: Sage.

Prange, G. W. (1982). *Miracle at midway.* New York: McGraw-Hill.

Raiffa, H. (1968). *Decision analysis.* Reading, MA: Addison-Wesley.

Rorty, R. (1985). Solidarity and objectivity. In J. Rajchman & C. West (Eds.), *Post-analytic philosophy* (pp. 3-19). New York: Columbia University Press.

Salancik, G. R. (1977). Commitment and control of organizational behavior and belief. In B. M. Staw & G. R. Salancik (Eds.), *New directions in organizational behavior* (pp. 1-54). Chicago: St. Clair.

Shedler, J., & Manis, M. (1986). Can the availability heuristic explain vividness effects? *Journal of Personality and Social Psychology, 51,* 26-36.

Sproull, L. S., & Hofmeister, K. R. (1986). Thinking about implementation. *Journal of Management, 12,* 43-60.

Sproull, L. S., Weiner, S., & Wolf, D. (1978). *Organizing an anarchy: Belief, bureaucracy, and politics in the National Institute of Education.* Chicago: University of Chicago Press.

Starbuck, W. H. (1983). Organizations as action generators. *American Sociological Review, 48,* 91-102.

Starbuck, W. H., & Milliken, F. K. (1988). Challenger: Fine-tuning the odds until something breaks. *Journal of Management Studies, 25*(4), 319-340.

Stinchcombe, A. (1978). *Theoretical methods in social history.* New York: Academic Press.

Tamuz, M. (1987). The impact of computer surveillance on air safety reporting. *Columbia Journal of World Business, 22,* 69-77.

Tamuz, M. (1988). *Monitoring dangers in the air: Studies in ambiguity and information.* Doctoral dissertation, Stanford University.

Tolstoy, L. N. (1869). *War and peace* (R. Edmonds, Trans.). Harmondsworth, UK: Penguin.

Weick, K. (1979). *The social psychology of organizing* (2nd ed.). Reading, MA: Addison-Wesley.

Zald, M. N., & Denton, P. (1963). From evangelism to general service: The transformation of the YMCA. *Administrative Science Quarterly, 8,* 214-234.

2

Organizing Work by Adaptation

EDWIN HUTCHINS

Common sense suggests that work is organized in accordance with plans that are created by designers who reflect on the work setting and manipulate representations of the work process in order to determine new and efficient organizational structures. Or, even if "outside" designers are not involved, the reorganization of work is normally attributed to the conscious reflection by members of the work group itself. A detailed examination of the response of a real-world group to a sudden and unexpected change in its informational environment shows that these common sense assumptions may be quite misleading.

While entering a harbor, a large ship suffered an engineering breakdown that disabled an important piece of navigational equipment. This paper considers the response of the ship's navigation team to the changed task demands imposed by the loss of this equipment. Following a rather chaotic search of the space of computational and social organizational alternatives, the team arrived at a new stable work configuration.

In retrospect, this solution appears to be just the sort of solution we would hope designers could produce. However, while some aspects of the response appear to be the products of conscious reflection, others, particularly those concerning the division of cognitive labor, are shown to arise without reflection from adaptations by individuals to what appear to them as local task demands. It is argued that while the participants may have represented and thus learned the solution after it came into being, the solution was clearly discovered by the organization itself before it was discovered by any of the participants.

(NAVIGATION; ORGANIZATIONAL DESIGN;
SOCIAL INTERACTION; MENTAL ARITHMETIC)

This chapter appeared originally in *Organization Science,* Vol. 2, No. 1, February 1991. Copyright © 1991, The Institute of Management Sciences.

INTRODUCTION

This paper attempts to raise some questions about the processes by which the organization of work arises. Common sense suggests that work is organized in accordance with plans that are created by designers who reflect on the work setting and manipulate representations of the work process in order to determine new and efficient organizational structures. Or, even if "outside" designers are not involved, the reorganization of work is attributed to the conscious reflection by members of the work group itself. Here I examine the response of a work group to a change in its informational environment. I will argue that several important aspects of a new organization are achieved not by conscious reflection but by local adaptations. The solution reached is one that we recognize in retrospect as being just the sort of solution we would hope designers could produce, yet it is a product of adaptation rather than of design.

The setting is the pilothouse or navigation of a large navy ship. The bridge is the "brain" of the ship. It is where the captain sits, where the helmsman stands and steers, and where the navigation team works to ensure that the ship knows where it is located and where it is going at all times. Several years ago, while I was recording both video and audio data of the performance of an actual navigation team bringing a real ship into a narrow harbor, the ship's propulsion system failed unexpectedly. This was a bit of bad luck for the ship, simultaneously robbing it of its ability to maneuver and interrupting all electrical production. The loss of electrical power caused a cascade of failures of electrical devices including one that is literally and figuratively instrumental to navigation. This incident provided an opportunity to witness and record the response of a complex organizational system to a very real crisis situation. In this paper I will describe the way a navigation team adapted to the loss of an important piece of navigational equipment while the ship was entering a harbor. Before doing so, it is necessary to provide some background on the nature of navigation work and the navigation team.

NAVIGATING LARGE SHIPS

Guiding a large ship into or out of a harbor is a difficult task. Ships are massive objects: their inertia makes them slow to respond to changes in propeller speed or rudder position. Because of this response lag, changes in direction or speed must be anticipated and planned well in advance. Depending on the characteristics of the ship and its velocity, the actions that will bring it to a stop or turn it around, for example, may need to be taken tens of seconds, or even minutes, before the ship arrives at the desired turning or stopping point. Aboard naval vessels, a continuous plot of the position of the ship is maintained to support decisions concerning its motion.[1] The *conning officer* is nominally responsible for the decisions about the motion of the ship, but usually, such decisions are actually made by the navigation team and passed to the conning officer as recommendations, such as, "Recommend coming right to zero one seven at this time." The conning officer considers the recommendation in the light of the ship's overall situation, and if the recommendation is appropriate, he acts upon it by giving orders to the *helmsman,* who steers the ship, or to the *leehelmsman,* who controls the ship's engines.

The navigation activity is event-driven in the sense that the navigation team must keep pace with the movements of the ship. Unlike many decision-making settings, when something goes wrong aboard ship, quitting the task or starting over from scratch are not available options. The work must go on. In fact, the conditions under which the task is most difficult are usually the conditions under which its correct and timely performance is most important.

Position Fixing by Visual Bearings

In order to plan the motions of the ship, the navigation team must establish the position of the ship and compute its future positions. The most important piece of technology in this task is the navigation chart, a specially constructed model of a real geographical space. The ship is somewhere in space, and to determine or "fix" the position of the ship is to find the location on the appropriate chart that corresponds to the position of the ship in the world.

The simplest form of position fixing, and the one that concerns us here, is position fixing by visual bearings. For this, one needs a chart of the region around the ship, and a way to measure the direction, conventionally with respect to north, of the line of sight connecting the ship and some landmark on the shore. The direction of a landmark from the ship is called the landmark's *bearing.* A line drawn on the chart starting at the location of the symbol for the landmark and extending past the assumed location of the ship is called a *line of position.* The ship must have been somewhere on that line when the bearing was observed. If we have another line of position, constructed on the basis of the direction of the line of sight to another known landmark, then we know that the ship is also on that line. If the ship was on both of these lines at the same time, the only place it can have been is where the lines intersect. In practice, a third line of position with respect to another landmark is constructed. The three lines of position form a triangle, and the size of the triangle formed is an indication of the quality of the position fix.

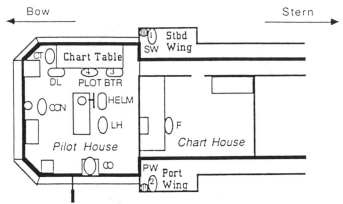

Watchstander Positions for Sea and Anchor Detail

Figure 2.1. Plan View of the Navigation Bridge Showing the Location of the Chart
Table and the Main Navigation Duty Stations

NOTE: Position 1, starboard wing bearing taker; Position 2, port wing bearing taker; Position 3, bearing timer; Position 4, plotter.

It is sometimes said that the anxiety of the navigator is proportional to the size of the fix triangle.

The Fix

The necessity for continuously plotting the ship's position, projecting the future track, and preparing to plot the next position is satisfied by a cycle of activity called the fix cycle. When the ship is operating near land, the work of the fix cycle is distributed across a team of six people.[2] The duty stations of the members of the team in the configuration called Sea and Anchor Detail are shown in Figure 2.1 as elliptical shapes. We can follow the fix cycle by following the trajectory of information through the system.

New information about the location of the ship comes from the bearing takers on the wings of the ship (Position 1 and 2 in Figure 2.1). They find landmarks on the shore in the vicinity of the ship and measure the bearings of the landmarks (direction with respect to north) with a special telescopic sighting device called an *alidade*. The true north directional reference is provided by a gyrocompass repeater that is mounted under the alidade. A prism in the alidade permits the image of the gyrocompass scale to be superimposed on the view of the landmark. (An illustration depicting the view through such a sight is shown in Figure 2.2.) The bearing takers read

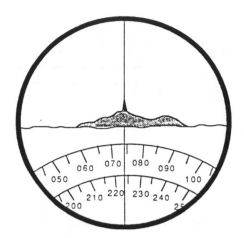

Figure 2.2. The View Through the Alidade

NOTE: The upper scale shows bearings relative to the ship's head, the lower scale swings with the gyrocompass and shows true bearings.

the measured bearings and then report them over a telephone circuit to the bearing timer.

The bearing timer (Position 3 in Figure 2.1) stands at the chart table inside the pilothouse. He talks to the bearing takers out on the wings and writes the reported bearings in a book called the bearing log which he keeps on the chart table in front of him.

The plotter (Position 4 in Figure 2.1) plots the reported bearings. He normally has no direct communication with the bearing takers, but either is told the bearings by the bearing timer, or reads them out of the bearing log. From the perspective of the plotter, the bearing timer is an information buffer. In order to make a high-quality fix, the bearings should be observed as quickly and as nearly simultaneously as possible. Since it takes much longer to plot a line of position than it does to make the observation of the bearing, the activities of the plotter and the bearing takers have different distributions in time. The activities of the bearing timer not only provide a permanent record of the observations made, but also permit the bearing takers and the plotter to work, each at his most productive rate, without having to coordinate their activities in time.

Once he has plotted the ship's position, the plotter also projects where the ship will be at the time of the next few fix observations. To do this he needs to know the heading and speed of the ship. The plotter normally reads these from the deck log, which lies on the chart table near his left hand.

When the projected position of the ship has been plotted, the bearing timer consults with the plotter to decide which landmarks will be appropriately situated for the next position fix, and assigns the chosen landmarks to the bearing takers by talking to them on the phone circuit. The bearing timer times the fix intervals, and about 10 seconds before the next fix time, he says "Stand by to mark." This alerts the bearing takers that they should find their landmarks and aim their telescopic sights at them.

At the time chosen for the fix observations, the bearing timer says "Mark," and the bearing takers observe and report the bearings of the landmarks they have been assigned. Thus the cycle begins again.

THE CASUALTY

Crisis

After several days at sea, the USS Palau[3] was returning to port, making approximately 10 knots in the narrow channel between Ballast Point and North Island at the entrance to San Diego harbor. A junior officer had the con under the supervision of the navigator and the captain was on the bridge. Morale in the pilothouse had sagged during two frustrating hours of engineering drills conducted just outside the mouth of the harbor, but was on the rise now that the ship was headed toward the pier. Some of the crew talked about where they should go for dinner ashore and joked about going all the way to the pier at 15 knots, so they could get off the ship before nightfall.

The bearing timer had just given the command, "Standby to mark time three eight"[4] and the fathometer operator was reporting the depth of water under the ship, when the intercom erupted with the voice of the engineer of the watch, "Bridge, Main Control. I am losing steam drum pressure. No apparent cause. I'm shutting my throttles." Moving quickly to the intercom, the conning officer acknowledged, "Shutting throttles, aye." The navigator moved to the captain's chair repeating, "Captain, the engineer is losing ah steam on the boiler for no apparent cause." Possibly because he realized that the loss of steam might affect the steering of the ship, the conning officer ordered the rudder amidships. As the helmsman spun the wheel to bring the rudder angle indicator to the centerline, he answered the conning officer, "Rudder amidships, aye sir." The captain began to speak, saying, "Notify . . . ," but the engineer was back on the intercom, alarm in his voice this time, speaking rapidly, almost shouting, "Bridge, Main Control, I'm going to secure number two boiler at this time. Recommend you drop the anchor!" The captain had been stopped in mid-sentence by the blaring intercom, but before the engineer could finish speaking, the captain restarted in a loud, but cool, voice, "Notify the bosun." It is standard procedure on large ships to have an anchor prepared to drop in case the ship loses its ability to maneuver while in restricted waters. With the propulsion plant out, the bosun, who was standing by with a crew forward, ready to drop the anchor, was notified that he might be called into action. The failing intonation of the Captain's command gave it a cast of resignation, or perhaps boredom, and made it sound entirely routine.

In fact, the situation was anything but routine. The occasional cracking voice, a muttered curse, the removal of a jacket that revealed a perspiration soaked shirt on this cool spring afternoon, told the real story: the Palau was not fully under control, and careers, and possibly lives, were in jeopardy.

The heart of the propulsion plant had stopped. The immediate consequences of this event were potentially grave. Despite the crew's correct responses, the loss of main steam put the ship in danger. Without steam, it could not reverse its propeller, which is the only way to slow a large ship efficiently. The friction of the water on the ship's hull will eventually reduce its speed, but the Palau would coast for several miles before coming to a stop. The engineering officer's recommendation that the anchor be dropped was not appropriate. Since the ship was still traveling at a high rate of speed, the only viable option was to attempt to keep the ship in the deep water of the channel and coast until it had lost enough speed to safely drop an anchor.

Within 40 seconds of the report of loss of steam pressure, the steam drum was exhausted and all steam turbine operated machinery came to a halt. This machinery includes the turbine generators which generate the ship's electrical power. All electrical power was lost throughout the ship and all electrical devices without emergency power backup ceased to operate. In the pilothouse a high pitched alarm sounded for a few seconds, signaling an undervoltage condition for one of the pieces of equipment. Then the pilothouse fell eerily silent as the electric motors in the radars and other devices spun down and stopped. The port wing bearing taker called in to the bearing timer, "John, this gyro just went nuts."

"Yah, I know, I know, we're havin' a casualty."

Because the main steering gear is operated with electric motors, the ship now not only had no way to arrest its still considerable forward motion, it also had no way to quickly change the angle of its rudder. The helm does have a manual backup system located in a compartment called *after-steering* in the stern of the ship, a worm gear mechanism powered by two men. However, even strong men working hard with this mechanism can change the angle of the massive rudder only very slowly.

Shortly after the loss of power, the captain said to the navigator, who is the most experienced conning officer on board, "O.K., ah, Gator, I'd like you to take the con." The navigator answered "Aye, sir," and turning away from the captain announced to the pilothouse, "Attention in the pilothouse. This is the navigator. I have the con." As required, the quartermaster of the watch acknowledged, "Quartermaster, aye," and the helmsman reported, "Sir, my rudder is amidships." The navigator had been looking over the bow of the ship trying to detect any turning motion. He answered the helmsman, "Very well. Right five degrees rudder." Before the helmsman could reply, the navigator increased the ordered angle, "Increase your rudder right ten degrees." The rudder angle indicator on the helm station has two parts, one shows the rudder angle that is ordered, and the other the actual angle of the rudder. The helmsman spun the wheel causing the desired rudder angle indicator to move to right ten degrees, but the actual rudder angle indicator seemed not to move at all. "Sir, I have no helm sir!" he reported.

Meanwhile, the men on the worm gear were straining to move the rudder to the desired angle. Without direct helm control, the conning officer acknowledged the helmsman's report and sought to make contact with after-steering by way of one of the bridge phone talkers. "Very well. After-steering, Bridge." The navigator then turned to the helmsman, "Let me know if you get it back." And before he could finish his sentence, the helmsman responded, "I have it back, sir." When the navigator acknowledged the report, the ship was on the right side of the channel, but heading far to the left of track. "Very well, increase your rudder to right fifteen." "Aye, sir. My rudder is right fifteen degrees. No new course given." The navigator acknowledged, "Very well," and then looking out over the bow of the ship itself whispered, "Come on, damn it, swing!" Just then, the starboard wing bearing taker spoke on the phone circuit, "John, it looks like we're gonna hit this buoy over here." The bearing timer had been concentrating on the chart and hadn't heard. "Say again," he said. The starboard wing bearing taker leaned over the railing of his platform to watch the buoy pass beneath him. It moved quickly down the side of the ship staying just a few feet from the hull. When it appeared that it would not hit the ship, he said, "Nuthin," and that ended the conversation. Inside, they never knew how close they had come. Several subsequent helm commands were answered, "Sir, I have no helm." When asked by the captain how he was doing, the navigator, referring to their common background as helicopter pilots, quipped, "First time I ever dead-sticked[5] a ship, captain." Steering a ship requires fine judgments about the angular velocity of the ship. Even if helm response were instantaneous, there would still be a considerable lag between the time a helm command was given and the time the ship's response to the changed rudder angle was first detectable as the movement of the bow with respect to objects in the distance. Operating with this manual system, the conning officer did not always know what the actual rudder angle was, and could not know how long to expect to wait to see if the ordered command was having the desired effect. Because of the slowed response time of the rudder, the conning officer ordered more extreme rudder angles than usual, causing the Palau to weave erratically from one side of the channel to the other.

Within three minutes, the emergency diesel electric generators were brought on the line and electrical power was restored to vital systems throughout the ship. Control of the rudder was partially restored, but remained intermittent for an additional four minutes. Although the ship still could not control its speed, it could at least now keep itself in the dredged portion of the narrow channel. Based on the slowing down over the first fifteen minutes following the casualty, it became possible to estimate when and where the ship would be moving slowly enough to drop the anchor. The navigator conned the ship toward the chosen spot.

About five hundred yards short of the intended anchorage, a sailboat took a course that would lead it to cross in front of the Palau. The Palau's enormous horn is steam driven and could not sound. The keeper of the deck log was ordered outside with a small manually pumped horn. Men on the flight deck ran to the bow to watch the impending collision. Five feeble blasts were sounded from the middle of the flight deck, two stories below. There is no way to know whether or not the signal was heard by the sailboat—by then it was directly ahead of the ship, and so close that only the tip of its mast was visible from the pilothouse. A few seconds later, the sailboat emerged, still sailing, from under the starboard bow and the keeper of the deck log continued to the bow to take up a position there in case other horn blasts were required.

The Consequences for the Navigation Team

The immediate response of the navigation team to the loss of steam and electrical power was simply to continue with the fix they were in the midst of taking. However, one of the pieces of electrical equipment that was subjected to loss of power was the Mark-19 gyrocompass. There are two layers of redundant protection for the gyrocompass function—independent emergency electrical power and a backup gyrocompass. Unfortunately, the emergency power supply for the gyrocompass failed, and the backup gyrocompass had been taken out of service earlier, due to a maintenance problem. So when the power failed, the Mark-19 lost power. The gyrocompass did not fail completely when the lights went out, but it did appear to be mortally wounded. Sixteen minutes after the loss of power, the Palau's speed had dropped to less than 4 knots and the ship was less than half a mile from its intended temporary anchorage, when word was passed to the bridge from the forward IC room that the gyrocompass had ceased operation. This was an especially critical period for the navigation team. The chosen anchorage location was out of the navigation channel, and near an area where the water shoaled rapidly. Dropping the anchor too soon would leave the ship obstructing traffic in the channel, while dropping too late would risk the ship swinging over and grounding upon a shoal. Simply restoring the power to a gyrocompass is not sufficient to bring it to a usable state; several hours are usually required for the gyro to "settle-in" and provide reliable readings.

As we saw in the description of the normal activities of the navigation team provided earlier, the gyrocompass provides input to the determination of true bearings of landmarks for position fixing. For the navigation team, then, the primary consequence of the power outage was the loss of the only remaining functioning gyrocompass on the ship.

Computational Structure of the Task

Figure 2.3 shows the relationships among the various terms of the computation. With the gyrocompass working, the alidade (telescopic sight) mounted on the pelorus permits the direct measurement of the direction of the bearing of the landmark with respect to true north (TB in Figure 2.3). When the gyrocompass failed, all that could be measured by the bearing takers with the pelorus was the direction of the landmark with respect to the ship's head (RB in Figure 2.3). In order to compute the true bearing of the landmark, once the relative bearing has been determined, it is necessary to determine the direction of the ship's head with respect to true north. The compass measures the direction of the ship's head with respect to magnetic north (C in Figure 2.3). But the compass reading must first be corrected for errors, called deviation, that are specific to the compass and dependent upon heading (D in Figure 2.3). Cartographers measure the difference between true north and magnetic north for all mapped regions of the world. This is called the variation (V in Figure 2.3). The sum of these terms is the true bearing of the landmark, that which was directly measured when the gyrocompass was working.

There is a mnemonic in the culture of navigation that summarizes the relations among the terms that make up the ship's true head. It is "Can Dead Men Vote Twice?" and it stands for the expression "C + D = M, M + V = T" or "compass heading plus deviation equals magnetic heading, magnetic heading plus variation equals true heading." This specifies a meaningful order for the addition of the terms in which every sum is a culturally meaningful object in the world of navigation. Every competent navigation practitioner can recite this mnemonic, and most can give an accurate account of what it means. The knowledge that is embodied in this formula will be an important component of the solution discovered by the navigation team. Notice, however, that this mnemonic says nothing about relative bearings.

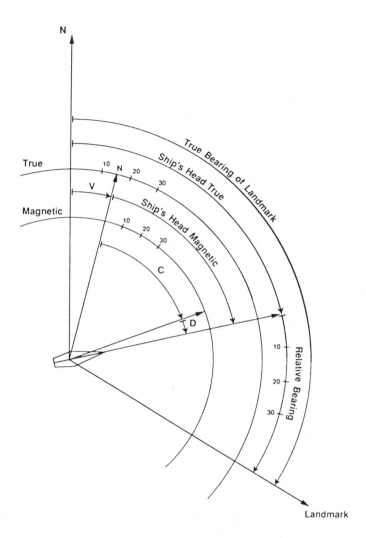

Figure 2.3. The Relationships Among the Terms of the Bearing Correction Computation
NOTE: True bearing of landmark from ship equals compass heading (C), plus deviation (D), plus magnetic variation (V), plus relative bearing (RB).

The computational structure of the task is well known. As described above, computing true bearings for landmarks from relative bearings involves adding together the ship's compass heading, the compass deviation for that heading, the magnetic variation appropriate for the geographic location, and the bearing of the landmark relative to the ship's head. The procedure for a single line of position, therefore, requires three addition operations. If one used this procedure for each line of position, the set of three lines of position that makes up a position fix would require nine addition operations. There is a substantial savings of computational effort to be had, however, by modularizing the computation in a particular way. Since all three lines of position in any given fix are observed as nearly simultaneously as is possible, the ship's head for all of them must be the same. Thus, one can compute the ship's true heading (sum of compass heading, deviation and variation) just once, and then add each of the three relative bearings to that intermediate sum. This procedure requires only five addition operations for the entire fix, two for the ship's true head and one for each of the relative bearings, while nine addition operations are required by the nonmodularized procedure. As we shall see when we consider the details of the actual performance of the team, even a small savings of computational effort can be very helpful in this high workload environment.

THE PROBLEM OF ORGANIZATION

A search of ship's operations and training materials revealed many documents that describe in detail the nominal division of labor among the members of the navigation team in the normal crew configurations, and many that describe the computational requirements for deriving a single line of position from compass heading, deviation, variation, and relative bearing. There was, however, no evidence of a procedure that describes how the computational work involved in doing position fixing by visual observations of relative bearings should be distributed among the members of the navigation team when the gyrocompass has failed. The absence of such a procedure is not surprising. After all, if the ship had a procedure for this situation, it should have one for hundreds of other situations that are more likely to occur, and it is simply impossible to train a large number of procedures in an organization characterized by high rates of personnel turnover.

Even though no such procedure exists, since this event did occur, we may ask what a procedure for dealing with it should be like. Clearly, the design of a procedure for this situation should take advantage of the benefits of modularizing the computation. Perhaps one would design a procedure that calls for the initial computation of ship's true head followed by the computation of each of the true bearings in turn. That much seems straightforward, but how should one organize the activities of the separate team members so that they can each do what is necessary and also get the new job done in an efficient way? This is a non-trivial problem because there are so many possibilities for permutations and combinations of distributions of human effort across the many components of the computational task. The design should spread the workload across the members of the team to avoid over-loading any individual. It should incorporate sequence control measures of some kind to avoid dis-coordinations, in which crew members undo each other's work; collisions, in which two or more team members attempt to use a single resource at the same time; and conflicts in which members of the team are working at cross purposes. It should exploit the potential of temporally parallel activity among the members of the team and, where possible, avoid bottlenecks in the computation.

As specified, it is quite a complicated design problem, and it looks even more difficult when we examine the relationships between the members of the navigation team and their computational environment. Given the nature of the task they were performing, the navigation team did not have the luxury of engaging in such design activities. They had to keep doing their jobs, and in the minutes between the loss of the gyrocompass and the arrival of the ship at anchor, the requirements of the job itself far exceeded the available resources.

THE ADAPTIVE RESPONSE

Viewing the navigation team as the cognitive system leads us to ask where in the navigation team this additional computational load was taken up and how the new tasks were accomplished. To summarize before examining the performance of the team in detail, the additional computation originally fell to the quartermaster chief who was acting as plotter. To correct the relative bearings passed to him, he attempted to do the added computations using mental arithmetic, but it was more than he could do within the severe time constraints imposed by the need for fixes on one-minute intervals. By trading some accuracy for computational speed, he was able to determine when the ship had arrived at its intended anchorage. After the Palau came to anchor, the plotter introduced a hand-held calculator to relieve the burden of mental arithmetic under stress, and recruited the assistance of the bearing timer in the performance of the computation. There was no explicit plan for the division of the labor involved in this added task between the plotter and bearing timer. Each had other duties that were related to this problem that had to be attended to as well.

Since this correction computation has well defined subparts, we may ask how the subparts of the task were distributed among the participants. But here we find that at the outset there was no consistent pattern. The order in which the various correction terms were added, and who did the adding, varied from one line of position to the next, and even the number of correction terms applied changed over the course of the 66 LOPs that were shot, corrected, and plotted between the loss of the gyrocompasses and the arrival of the Palau at its berth. Gradually, an organized structure emerged out of the initial chaos. The sequence of computational and social organizational configurations through which the team passed is shown in Figure 2.4. After correcting and plotting about 30 LOPs, a consistent pattern of action appeared in which the order of application of the correction terms and the division of labor between plotter and bearing timer stabilized. While the computational structure of this stable configuration seems to have been, at least in part, intended by the plotter, the social structure (division of labor) seems to have emerged from the interactions among the participants without any explicit planning.

Analysis

The bearing takers out on the wings of the ship were only slightly affected by the loss of the gyrocompass. For them, it meant only that they had to remember to shoot the bearings relative to ship's head, the outer rather than the inner of the two azimuth circles in the alluded view-finder (see Figure 2.2). The analysis will therefore focus on the activities of the plotter, a quartermaster chief (designated "P" in the analysis), and the bearing timer, a quartermaster second class (designated "S" in the analysis).

We can consider the behavior of the plotter and the bearing timer to be a search in a very complex space for a computational structure and a social structure that fit each other and that get the job done. As Figure 2.4 shows, on their way to a stable configuration, these two explored 13 different computational structures and many social configurations.

How can we account for this seemingly bizarre search of computational and social space? I will claim that there are four main principles of the organization of computation involved. They are:

1. computational structure driven by the availability of data,
2. the use of a normative description to organize computation,
3. the computational advantages of modularizing the addition task,
4. the fit between computational and social organization.

The events between the failure of the gyrocompass and the end of the task can be partitioned into four regions based on these principles. In the first region, Lines of Position (LOPs) 1-15, P does all the computation himself and the computational structure is driven primarily by the availability of data. The end of this region is marked by the introduction of an electronic calculator. In the second region, LOPs 16-24, P begins to push some of the computational load onto the bearing timer, S, and while providing the bearing timer instruction on how to do the computation, begins to use a normative description to organize the computation. In the third region, LOPs 25-33, the modularity of the computation becomes a shared resource for the two workers through their joint performance of the modular procedure. In the forth and final region, LOPs 34-66, they discover a division of labor that fits the computation, and they coin a lexical term for the modular sum, thus crystallizing the conceptual discovery in a shared artifact. Let's look now at the details of the work at the chart table, considering the lines of position plotted from the time the gyrocompass failed until the system had settled into its new stable configuration (refer to Figure 2.4).

Region 1: Computational Structure
Driven by Data Availability

The first 12 lines of position are computed by P, using what would normally be called mental arithmetic. In some cases, this arithmetic is aided by artifacts in the environment. In the very first LOP, for example, he uses the scale of the hoey (chart plotting tool) as a medium for addition, lining up the scale index with 29 (the compass course), sliding it 52 gradations upward (the relative bearing), etc., and in LOP 2 he uses the bearing log itself as a memory during the computation, tracing out the addition columns with his fingers. LOPs 8 and 9 were computed using paper and pencil in the margins of the chart. P had a good deal of trouble keeping up with the demands of the task, as shown by the fact that the first fix has only two LOPs in it, the second fix has but one LOP and the third fix has two LOPs. The anchor was dropped at 17:06 in the afternoon just before the fifth line of position was plotted. Once the anchor was down, the team went from one-minute-fix intervals to six-minute-fix intervals, but P was still having trouble keeping up while doing mental arithmetic.

P's behavior in this region can be described as opportunistic. He used three different computational orderings and several different media in computing the first twelve lines of position. While at first glance this behavior looks unsystematic, there is a simple but powerful regularity in it. The order in which P took the terms for addition depends upon where the terms were in his environment, and on when and with how much effort he could get access to them. For example, in LOP 8, P returned to the chart table verbally rehearsing the ship's magnetic heading. He began his computation with that term. In LOP 9, where P had to consult S in order to establish the identity of

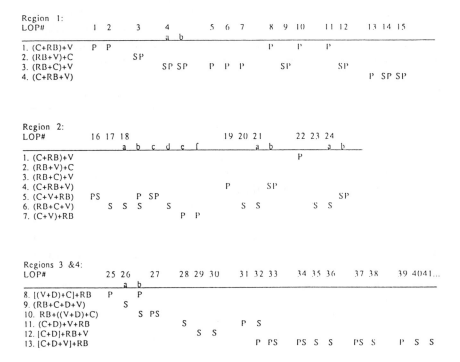

Figure 2.4. Line of Position Computations

NOTE: The structure of the computation performed is given in the left hand column. Lines of position are numbered across the top of each section of the table. "P" indicates an LOP computation performed entirely by the plotter. "S" indicates an LOP computation performed entirely by S. "SP" indicates an LOP computation begun by or structured by S and completed by P. "PS" indicates a computation begun by or structured by P and completed by S.

the next relative bearing to add, he began his computation with relative bearing. In LOP 10, P was again doing the calculation on his own and again he began with ship's magnetic head. These patterns are hints to a more general organizing principle that we will see throughout this event. An examination of Figure 2.4 shows that in the first two regions, twelve out of fifteen LOPs for which the computation is initiated by P begin with the ship's magnetic head, and thirteen out of eighteen computations initiated by S begin with the relative bearing of the landmark.

This regularity appears to be a consequence of local strategies for individual cognitive economy. From the perspective of a person trying to do the addition, if one of the terms is already in working memory when it is time to begin the computation, then it is most efficient to start with that term.

Consider the situation of the bearing timer. When the computations are done on-line, the bearing timer is in interaction with the bearing takers. He has listened to, written down and verbally acknowledged relative bearings. These activities, although not part of the addition procedure itself, influence the course of the addition procedure because they put the RB term into the working memory of the bearing taker. With RB already in working memory, in order to do the computation in the order that supports modularization, (C + V + RB), S must either somehow keep RB active in working memory, or he must overwrite RB in working memory and read it again later when it is needed. If he chooses to maintain RB in working memory, then it must remain unaltered (and must not alter the other number representations present) during the reading of C, the recall of V and the addition of C and V. This may require him to maintain up to 11 digits in working memory (eight for the addition of V + C, plus up to three for RB). If the memory load of that task is too great, S may choose to let RB be overwritten in working memory and read it in again later. Of course, doing that involves wasted effort overwriting and rereading RB.

In contrast to the costs of this "preferred" order, taking the terms in the order (RB + C + V) or (RB + V + C) involves lighter loads on working memory and no wasted effort. Thus, from the bearing taker's local perspective, it was simply easier and more efficient to begin each computation with the relative bearing.

P was in a different position. In most cases, he went to the helm station to get the ship's compass head while the relative bearings were being reported. This puts the C term into P's working memory at the beginning of the fix. Notice in Figure 2.4 that except for LOPs 5-7, every LOP initiated by P himself begins with C as the first term. But interaction with S or with other representational systems can change P's position in the computation. In each case where P began by asking S for a term to add, that term was the relative bearing and the relative bearing was taken as the first item in the addition. On closer inspection, the apparent exceptions to the rule in LOPs 5-7 are not exceptions at all. These computations were not done while the data were coming in. The observations of the three relative bearings were made while P worked to determine the location of the anchor. Then he set out to compute the LOPs with all of the data in the book in front of him— relative bearings in the left hand columns of the bearing book page and the ship's magnetic head in the rightmost column. This interaction with the bearing book changed the temporal pattern of availability of data, which in turn changed the organization of the most efficient ordering of terms for the performance of mental arithmetic.

It is unlikely that either man was ever aware of having made a decision concerning the order in which to add the terms. Rather, each was simply trying to do the additions as correctly and as efficiently as possible. Since the two participants at the chart table experienced different patterns of availability of data, this principle produced characteristically different results for each of them.

The principle at work so far can be summarized as follows: individual actors can locally minimize their workload by allowing the sequence of terms in the sum to be driven by the availability of data in the environment. But, since data become available primarily via social interactions, the computational structure is largely an unplanned side effect of this interactional structure. The interactional structure itself is chaotic because it is shaped by interference from other tasks and social interactions with other members of the navigation team and members of other work teams on the bridge.

After LOP 12, S initiated a round of bearings on a two-minute interval. P instructed him to take the fix on six-minute intervals, and complained about trying to keep up doing mental arithmetic. When asked if he had been able to keep up with the work he said,

> **P:** No, I was running it through my head and it wouldn't add. It wouldn't make numbers, so I was making making right right angles in my head to see where the hell it was at.
>
> **S:** You take the variation out of it.
>
> **P:** Yes, you add the, you add the magnetic head, then you add the variation.

This conversation is the first evidence of reflection on the structure of the computation. P explicitly names the variables, saying, ". . . you add the magnetic head, then you add the variation." After this, P remarked that the only way to keep up with the work would be to use a calculator. Shortly after this conversation, P went to the chart house and returned with a navigation calculator.[6]

The use of the calculator eliminated the need for the intermediate sums that P computed when doing mental arithmetic. In LOPs 13-15, P keyed in the data. He started each LOP computation by keying in C +, then he looked for RB in the bearing book, keyed RB +, then keyed V = . Here the calculator was not only a computational device; P also used it as a temporary external memory for the C term while he looked for the RB term. The immediate consequences of the introduction of the calculator were that it eliminated that production of intermediate sums (this will be important in the development of the modular solution below), and it changed the memory requirements for P by serving as an external memory. It did not change the fact that the order in which the terms were added was dependent on the pattern of availability of data in the task environment.

The dependence of the computational sequence on the availability of data is the main characteristic of events in the first region. It will survive into later regions in the behavior of the bearing timer, but the introduction of the calculator marks the beginning of the end of this sort of data-driven task organization for P. Up until and including the first calculator round, S has sometimes fed values of RB to P, but has done no arithmetic, mental or otherwise. That is about to change.

Region 2: The Emergence of Mediating Structure

The most important consequence of the introduction of the calculator was that it created a new context of interaction between P and S, in which P gave S instruction in the procedure. For example, in LOP 16, P returned from the helm station where he had read the compass heading and keyed in the value of C.

> **LOP 16:** $(C + V + RB)$
> *P returns from helm.*
> **P:** 2 3 1. What have we got? {231 + }
> *(Then slides the calculator to S.)*
> **P:** Here, add these things.
> **P:** You want . . . You want the head. You want the head
>
> | which is
>
> 2 3 1.
> **S:** | and add
> variation.
> **P:** Plus variation.
> **S:** Oh, 231 is the head?
> **P:** 2 3 1. Here {Clear 2 3 1}
> **S:** I got it. *(puts his hands on the keys.)* {clear, 2 3 1}
> **P:** Plus 14.
> **S:** {+ 14} Okay.
> **P:** Okay. *(intermediate sum not computed)*
> **S:** { + **0 0 7** = } is 252 on Silvergate.
> **P:** 2 5 2 Silvergate.

P controlled the order of the arguments in this LOP. S seemed surprised that he started with the ship's head.

In LOPs 17 and 18a, P was busy plotting a previous bearing. S initiated the computation himself by reading the RB from the book and beginning with it. In LOP 18a, the result was in error because the bearing that was reported was misread by the bearing taker. But the context of the error provided an opportunity to restructure the work. S slid the calculator over in front of P and began to dictate values starting with what was, for him, the most salient term, RB. P, however, ignored S and began keying in the data in the sequence C + V. P made an error and cleared the calculator. S, having seen the sequence in which P wanted to add the terms, dictated the terms in the order C + V + RB as seen in LOP 18c.

LOP 18c: (C + V + RB)
    S: 2 3 1, Chief, plus 14, plus |
    P: (2 3 1 + 1 4 +) | Okay, what was ah,
    S: The bearing was 1 5 7. (3 sec) | Okay
    P: {1 5 7 = } | 4 0 2
    S: Minus 3 60 | is
    P: {– | 3 60 = } is 0 4 2. No it ain't. It isn't no 0 4 2. It's just not working. Look where 0 4 2 goes. (*P points to the chart.*) If it's 0 4 2, we're sitting over on Shelter Island!

There were three more attempts to compute this LOP. In LOP 18d, S made a data entry error and passed the calculator to P in frustration. In LOP 18e, P made a data entry error, cleared the calculator and began again.

We might have thought that the importance of the introduction of the calculator would be its power as a computational device. In fact we see that using the calculator, the team was neither faster nor more accurate than they were without it! The important contribution of the calculator was that it changed the relation of the workers to the task. When P pushed the calculator over to S and told him to add the terms, he engaged in a new task, that of instructing S in the computation, and he organized his instructional efforts in terms of the normative computational structure, "C + D = M + V = T." This was evident in LOP 16 where P named the variables, "You want the head, which is 2 3 1 . . . plus variation." Note that S did not seem to learn from the explicit statements of P. He returned to taking the RB first in LOPs 17, 18a and b. However, once P had articulated this structure, it became a resource he could use to organize his own performance of the task. In LOP 18b, in spite of S having dictated the RB to him first, he keyed in C + V. There, S verbally shadowed P's keystrokes. This joint performance was the first time S had taken ship's head as the first term. Once P began behaving this way, S was able to internalize that which appeared in interpersonal work and, under certain social conditions, could use it to organize his own behavior. Thus, in LOP 18c where S took the role of dictating the values to P who was keying them in, S said, "2 3 1, Chief, plus 14, plus . . . " But the structure was not yet well established for S. In the next attempt, LOP 18d, a new RB was observed and, driven by the data, S began the computation with it.

The introduction of the calculator and the errors that were committed with it provided a context for instruction in which the sequence of terms could be explicitly discussed. The errors they were responding to were not sequence errors, but simple key pressing errors, yet they still served as contexts for sequence specification. P appeared to learn from his own instructional statements (intended for S) and changed his own behavior. Until he tried to instruct S on what to do, he took the terms in the order in which they were presented by the environment. S appeared to change his own behavior to fit with what P *did,* not what he *said.* This newly emergent normative structure dominated P's instructional efforts and came to dominate the organization of his task performance as well.

In LOP 21a, S made a key pressing error while adding the terms in the order (RB + C + V). The error drew P's attention and he turned to watch S.

LOP 21b: (C + RB + V) & ((C + V) + RB) = ((C + V) + RB + V)
  S: {clear **2 2 1 | + 14**}
  P: | plus 14 is 2 3 5. (C + V. *P does it in his head.*)
  S: 2 3 5?
  P: Yah, its 2 3 5 plus 1 1 8.   ((C + V) + RB)

  S: Oh. {clear} (*S doesn't realize that hitting* = *would have produced* 235.)
  P: 2 3 5 is | 3 3 5, 3 4 5, how about 3 5 3. Right?
  S: {235 | + **1 1 8** + 14 =}   How about 0 0 7.

                              (C + V) + RB + V)

  P: 0 0 7.
  S: Chief, the computer just beat you. (*Chief glares at S*)
          Just kidding. (*all laugh 4 sec*) The modern technology.
  P: I'll modern technology you.

Here, in LOP 21b, two important things happened. First, S demonstrated that he could produce the normative sequence when trying to show P he could do the addition correctly. Second, this was the first time P had organized a properly modular computation. Unfortunately, it is also clear that S did not yet understand the meaning of the intermediate sum (C + V), which is the key to the modularization. He mistook it for C alone, and added in RB and V, generating an error. P seemed intimidated by the calculator and did not challenge the result. It lead to a poor fix, but he had been getting really poor fixes all along. Fortunately, the anchor was holding and they were in no danger, but at this point if they had had to rely on the quality of the fixes, they would have been in trouble.

P performed LOP 23 with the non-standard sequence (C + RB + V). However, this is not a violation of the principles described above. P did not get C from the helm at the beginning of the fix as he usually did. Instead, he was busy asking whether the anchor was being hoisted at this time. S announced C when P returned to the table. P looked in the bearing book for C. He read it aloud, and while still leaning over the book he added in the RB nearest him in the book, pointing to the place digits in it with the butt of his pencil as he added the numbers. Once again, the availability of data in the environment drove the organization of the computation.

LOP 24a: (RB + C + V)
   S: 1 1 2 plus 2 2 6 plus 14, 3 5 2 on ship's head. (*means Hamm's light*)
   P: Which tower is he shooting for North Island Tower? (*P leaves table for wing*)
   P: Hey, which tower are you shooting for North Island Tower? (*PW points to tower*) You are? Okay.
   PW: Is that the right one?
   P: Yep.
        (*P returns to table*)

LOP 24b: (C + V + RB)
   S: Which tower   I wa—
   P: I And ah, what was Hamm's?
   S: And Hamm's was {2 2 6 + 1 4 + 1 1 2 =} 3 5 2. (5 sec) Time 56 Chief.

In LOP 24a S, working on his own, took the terms in the order (RB + C + V). A few moments later when P asked S what the bearing was to Hamm's, instead of remembering it, S re-computed it. This time, LOP 24b, he did it in the prescribed order, (C + V + RB). This is evidence that he knew the sequence preferred by P, but he seemed to produce it only in interactions with P.

This is the end of the second region. In this region we have seen that a mediating structure is being remembered by P, but S's organization of the computation is still driven largely by the pattern of availability of data. The clear boundary between this region and the first one is not marked by the introduction of the calculator, but by P's order "Here, add these things." The change in computational structure follows from a social innovation that was made possible by a technological change rather than from the technological innovation itself.

Region 3: Partial Modularization

In the description of the computational structure of the task given above, we noted that the true bearing is the sum of four terms: ship's magnetic head, C; deviation, D; variation, V; and relative bearing, RB. By now the team had computed and plotted 24 lines of position and the deviation term was not included in any of them. This seems surprising, since we have ample evidence that both of them knew well what deviation is and how to use it. One can only surmise that they were so busy trying to do the job that they forgot this term. The absence of the deviation term had no effect on the quality of the fixes plotted until LOP 22, because until then the ship was on a heading for which the deviation was near zero. Just before LOP 22, however, the ship's head swung southwest, and on that heading there was a three-degree deviation. The fix triangles started opening up, and it became clear to P that something was wrong. He lay the hoey on the chart from various landmarks and moved it slightly, seeing what sort of different bearings would make the triangle smaller. LOPs 25-27 are a re-working of LOPs 22-24, this time taking deviation into account.

1. **P:** I keep getting these monstrous goddamn, these monstrous frigging goddamn triangles. I'm trying to figure out which one is fucking off.
2. **S:** You need another round?
3. **P:** No, no no, uhuh. 1 2 0 I know what he's doing. Let me try, let me try *(turns and moves to helm station)* let me try, with my new ones, say three *(reads deviation card posted on compass stand)*. Say three, add three to everything.
4. **S:** Add three?
5. **P:** Yah.
6. **S:** 'Cause he's using magnetic? *(S does not get it yet.)*

LOP 25: ([(V + D) + C] + RB)

7. **P:** On a southwest heading add three. So its (14 + 3 =)17 plus 2 2, 17 plus 2 2 6 is ah, 2 3 ah
8. **S:** Plus 2 2 6 is 3 4 is 2 4 3 *(S working on paper with pencil)*

$$((V + D) + C)$$

9. **P:** Okay, 2 4 3 and 0 1 3 is 2 5 6. 2 | 5 6

$$([(V + D) + C] + RB)$$

10. **S:** | 2 5 9 *(this is an error)*
11. **P:** 2 5 nuhuh?
12. **S:** 2 5 9, plus 0 1 3? It's 2 5 9.
13. **P:** 2 5 9 that's right. Okay. And plus 1 1 2 was what?

LOP 26a

14. **S:** 1 1 2 plus 2 2 6. (*Here is clear evidence that S doesn't understand the attempt to modularize.* (**RB + C**))

LOP 26b: ([(V + D) + C] + RB) & (RB + [(V + D) + C])

15. **P:** Plus 2 4 3, 2 4 3 plus 1 1 2.
    [(V + D) + C] + RB)

16. **S:** 1 1 2 plus 2 4 3 is 5 5, 3 5 5 (*still working on paper*), (**RB + [(V + D) + C]**)

In P's moment of discovery, line 3, where he said "I know what he's doing," he noticed that the geometry of the triangle was such that a small clockwise rotation of each of the lines of the previous fix would make the triangle smaller. Any small error that belongs to all the LOPs suggests deviation. He went to the helm station and consulted the deviation card to determine the deviation for this heading. Although he describes the results as "much better," with deviation included, the two errors introduced by S still result in a poor fix.

The computation of 243 as the ship's true head, and its use in LOP 26b is the very first full modularization of the computation. P has control of the computations in all three LOPs, although in LOP 26b he has to fight S's strong propensity to put the RB first. S clearly does not yet understand either the benefits of modularization or the necessity to add the RB last in the modular form. The structure of LOP 27 was modular too, but the value of ship's true head, while properly computed, was not correctly remembered.

P seems to have taken the discovery of deviation and the recomputation of the bearings as an opportunity to think about the structure of the computation itself. The reflection that came in the wake of the introduction of the calculator led him to organize the computation in accordance with the normative form. The reflection that came with the addition of the deviation term led him to the modular structure. He never explicitly mentioned the advantages of modularization, but if he was not aware of the advantages when he organized the computation, he must certainly have been aware of them once the computation had been performed.

S computed LOP 28 while P explained to the keeper of the deck log why the gyrocompass could not be restarted in time to help, and why they will therefore make the remainder of the trip using magnetic bearings. P's conversation was interrupted by S who checked on the procedure for using the deviation table.

LOP 28: ([(C + D] + V + RB)
    S: Charles? (2 sec) Head?
    H: 2 2 6.

S: 2 2 6.

S: So it's 2 2 6. You wanna add 3, right? On a southerly course? (3 sec) Chief?

P: Say again.

S: You wanna add 3 to that /?/ southerly course? (*pointing at the entry on the deviation table*) (2 sec). It's 2 2 6. The magnetic head is 2 2 6.

P: Yah.

S: 2 2 6 plus | 3, okay, so that makes 2 2 9. {**2 2 9 + 14**}

P: | right.

S: {+1 1 5 =} (3 sec) 3 5 8 on Hamm's light.

      ([C + D] + V + RB)

Thus, S took the arguments in the right order in LOP 28, but did only a partial modularization. He computed (C + D) = 229 as a modular sum. Then he added V and added RB without producing ship's true head as an intermediate sum. In LOPs 29 and 30, S started with the partially modular sum, and added the terms in the order [C + D] + RB + V. Even this partial modularization is an important step forward for S. It appears to be due to two factors. First, including deviation in the computation may have made the C term more salient. Second, S's location in the computation had changed. He recorded the relative bearings as usual, but he had to go to the helm station himself to get the compass heading because P was otherwise occupied. At that point he had the C term in working memory and it was time to begin the computation. This change in position meant that what was best for the computation was also easiest for S. This is not the best division of labor, but it is one for which there is a momentary local fit between social and computational structure. The pattern of availability of data was not running counter to the computational structure. Paradoxically, then, the extra work that took P away from the chart table (a burden on the system) may have been a factor that permitted the system to improve.

Weighed Anchor

LOPs 32-33 are a turning point in the procedure. In LOP 32 there is a clear conflict of understanding between P and S. In LOP 33 they perform what will be the stable configuration for the first time.

LOP 32: ([(C + D) + V] + RB)

    1. **S:** You want the aero beacon?

    2. **P:** Yah, I want the aero beacon now, yah. It's just . . . 1 8 7, 8 8, 8 7, 8 8.

    3. **S:** 0 2 0, what's the ship's head?

4. **P:** Huh? 0 8 7. 8 7. It's | 1 west
5. **S:** | 0 87 it's 1 west, 7
6. **P:** its 8 6 (**C + D**)
7. **S:** {8 6.}
8. **P:** And 14| is 1 0 0 (**(C + D) + V**)
9. **S:** |{ **+ 14**}
10. **S:** {**+ 1 0 0**}, hold it
11. **P:** No, it's 1 0 0 plus whatever. (**[(C + D) + V] + RB**)
12. **S:** 1 0, where are you getting? . . .
13. **P:** 1 0 0 is the heading, the whole thing, | plus relative.
14. **S:** |Oh, the whole thing, plus
                             relative, { **+ 20** = }.
                             1 20.
15. **P:** Okay
16. **S:** 1 20 |is for North Island Tower.

LOP 33: (**[(C + D) + V] + RB**)

17. **P:** |and Hamm's? (2 sec) 1 0|0 plus whatever for Hamm's.
18. **S:** |Hamm's
19. Okay, {100 + **2 2 4** =}. 3 2 4 on|Hamm's
20. **P:** |3 2 4. That's all three of 'em. I got 'em all.
21. **S:** Okay
22. **P:** Looks good. Right on. Perfect. Pinpoint fix.
23. **S:** Alright!

In LOP 32, P works with S to recompute the ship's true heading. This joint work in lines 4-16 provides the opportunity for S to understand that the "whole thing" is the modular sum to which the RB can be added. The order in which S added the terms still followed the pattern of data availability, but P actively constructed the pattern of data availability such that the sequence produced by S was the desired one. That is, P acted as a mediator between the pattern of data availability in the task environment and the addition activities of S.

The most salient features of this region were the emergence of the partial modularization of the computation and the conflicts between P's newly solidified conceptual schema, and S's practices. In this region, P began to provide mediating structure that changed the pattern of data availability experienced by S. In LOP 33, S showed signs of using this mediating structure himself. For S, the addition activity was no longer on the surface being applied opportunistically. It now lay behind a conceptual and social organization that fed it the terms of the expression in a particular order.

Region 4: The New, Stable Solution

In the previous section, we saw how the behavior of one individual can act as a mediating device that controls the pattern of availability of data for the other. In this, the last region, the team discovered a division of labor in which each of them could use a computational sequence that followed the availability of data in the task environment (thus minimizing memory load and wasted effort) while each simultaneously produced for the other patterns of data availability that supported the modular form of the computation. In this region the computational structure was still driven primarily by the pattern of availability of data, but the availability of data itself was determined by the social organization of the actions of the members of the team. Thus, the issue here is the fit between the constraints of cognitive processing (memory limitations, e.g.) and the social organization of work (distribution of cognitive labor), as mediated by the structure of the computational task (modularity of addition).

In LOPs 34-36 they tuned their division of labor, jointly computing the modular sum in LOP 34, and S remembering it in LOPs 35 and 36.

LOP 34: **([(C + D) + V] + RB)**

    P: Okay, what's he on? (to helm) What are ya on right

          now? 8, 8 5. 8 5, 0 8 5, 0 8l4 plus 14 0 9 8.   **((C + D) + V)**

    S: l0 8 5 is/ 0 8 4 plus 14, (8 4 + 14 =} that's

    P: Okay

    S: 98

    P: 9 8 and 2 6

    S: 9 8 (+ 2 6 = } 1 2 4. **([(C + D) + V] + RB)**

    P: l1 2 4

    S: l1 2 4 North Island Tower

    P: Okay

LOP 35:

    S: (9 6 + 2 1 2 =) 3 0 8 on Hamm's light. **([(C + D) + V] + RB)**

    (S has mis-remembered the true head. Should be 98, not 96)

    P: Okay

LOP 36:

    S: {98 + 3 5 7}

    P: Damn near reciprocals.

    S: {−3 6 0 =}

    P: 3 60 isl0 9 5

    S: ahl0 9 5   **([(C + D) + V] + RB)**

This is essentially the pattern of work they would maintain all the way to the dock. By LOP 38 the final pattern was achieved. In this, P computed the modular sum alone, finding C and D at the helm station and recalling V from long term memory. Meanwhile, S recorded the relative bearings. P then added the first relative bearing to the modular sum, usually while S was recording the last of the relative bearings. P announced the modular sum to S, and S then added each of the other relative bearings to the modular sum. The only important event not included in these first 38 LOPs was the advent of a linguistic label for the ship's true head. They called it "total" in LOP 42 at 18:42. Once they had a name for it, they could pass it around among themselves more easily. The "publication" of the modular sum is essential to the final solution, since it acts as the bridge between the portion of the computation done by P and that done by S.

DISCUSSION

It appears that four forces control the navigation team's bizarre search of the space of computational and social structures. They are (1) the advantages of operating first on the contents of working memory which leads computational sequence to be entrained by the pattern of availability of data, (2) the use of normative computational structure, which permitted the discovery of (3) the advantages of modularization of computation, and (4) the fit of social to computational structure. Each region of the adaptation process is dominated by one of these forces. In fact, all of them, except the advantages of modularization, are present to some extent in all regions of the adaptation history.

Memory Limitations and the Availability of Data

In the beginning, the structure of the computation seems to be driven exclusively by an interaction of limitations of the human cognitive system, specifically memory limitations, and the availability of data in the environment (Anderson, 1983; Newell & Simon, 1972). Memory limitations make it advantageous to add the terms of the correction in the order they become available. The availability of data depends on the pattern of social interactions. This seems to characterize P's behavior until he assumes a different relation to the computation at LOP 16. It describes S's behavior at least until LOP 32, and possibly to the end of the task.

At LOP 16, the introduction of the calculator gave rise to a new social arrangement (S punching keys while P told him which keys to press) that gave P a new relation to the computational task, that led, in turn, to the introduction of the normative computational structure. What P remembered was acted out in interaction with S. When S took dictation from P while keying in values, P was mediating the task for him. P was changing S's relation to the task such that what was convenient for S was also what was effective for the computation.

The Normative Computational Sequence, $C + D = M, M + V = T, T + RB = TB$

There is no doubt that P's computations were shaped by variants of the normative structure from LOP 16 on. There was only one exception to this (LOP 19), and in that case the RB had a value that was particularly easy to handle: 0 0 7. P maintained this structure even when it ran counter to the pattern of availability of data as in LOP 18b.

S appeared to be capable of producing the normative sequence when in interaction with P (LOPs 24b, 27); but when on his own, he seemed clearly driven by the availability of data. Thus, when computing the true bearings on-line as he recorded the values of relative bearings, he always took the RB as the first term. Before the discovery of the deviation term he used the sequence (RB + C + V) and after the inclusion of deviation (RB + C + D + V). In one instance, however, P was removed from the table by another task, and S computed the true bearings alone. After having recorded the relative bearings and having obtained the ship's magnetic head from the helmsman (C term in working memory), he began with the C term.

The computational importance of the normative sequence is that it makes the modularization possible. Since addition is a commutative operation, there is no difference in the sum achieved by adding the terms in any of the 24 possible sequences. But if the addition is to take advantage of the modularity of ship's true head, the terms C, D, and V will have to be added together before any of them is added to a relative bearing. The normative structure provides a rationale for doing this, and it provides culturally meaningful interpretations of the intermediate sums that are lacking from such non-normative additions as (RB + V) or (V + D) (see Figure 2.3).

The Modular Computation

The modular organization of the computation emerges haltingly from P's attempts to apply the normative form, but it seems unlikely that P took up the normative form for its links to modularized form of the computation. It is more likely that it gave him a better understanding of what was going on by providing intermediate sums that have meaningful interpretations in the world of the ship. For an experienced navigator, a bearing is not simply a number, it is a body-centered feeling about a direction in space. Taking the terms in non-normative sequence results in intermediate sums that are just numbers. Taking them in normative sequence results in intermediate sums that are meaningful directions in the world of the navigator. In this form they become directions that make sense (or don't), and this gives the navigator another opportunity to detect error or to sense that the computation is going well or badly even before it is completed.

There was a hint of modularity in LOPs 18e and f where P computed $C + V$ and then asked for the RB. Similarly in LOP 21b he said, ". . . it's 2 3 5 $(C + V)$ plus 1 1 8 (RB)." In each of these cases, there was only one LOP involved, so it was not possible to exploit the advantages of modularization. The first unambiguous case of modular computation was in the LOPs 25-27, that introduced the deviation term. These were performed in the non-standard sequence $([(V + D) + C] + RB)$. It is probably significant that P chose to perform these calculations with paper and pencil rather than with the calculator. The paper and pencil computation produced, as a natural side effect, a written record of the sum $[(V + D) + C]$ which was then easily at hand for addition to each of the relative bearings. The written record of the modular sum in this instance was functionally similar to the verbal "publishing" of the labeled modular sum in the later fixes.

The Fit of Social and Computational

The modular form of the computation only became stable when a new division of cognitive labor was established in LOPs 32 and 33. The pattern of availability of data produced by the division of labor in this stable configuration fit the computational structure of the problem. P obtained C from the helmsman and D from the deviation table, added them and then added the variation (easily available in memory). At the same time, S recorded the relative bearings of the landmarks. P told S the modular sum, which S recorded, and S provided P with the first relative bearing. P added this relative bearing to the remembered modular sum. While P plotted the first LOP, S then added each of the other recorded relative bearings to the modular sum. Thus, the team arrived at a division of cognitive labor in which the behavior of each of the participants provided the necessary elements of the information environment of the other, just when they were needed. Each could behave as though driven by the availability of data in the world; and at the same time, as a team, they performed the additions in the sequence that provided the benefits of modularization.

Adaptation by Design?

Since the work of Cyert and March (1963), organization theory has viewed routines as fundamental building blocks. Thus the processes that change routines are very important to study. The description of the behavior of the four factors shows how a variety of solutions may be explored, but it does not in itself answer the question of how better solutions may become the routine operations of the system.

A classical view of organizational change (a folk view?) is that an analyst looks at the behavior of the system, represents it explicitly and plans a better solution (e.g., Chandler's [1966] well-known account of the reorganization of Dupont). The better solution is expressed as an explicit description of system operation that is subsequently implemented in the real system by somehow altering the behavior of the participants to bring it into line with the designed solution. We often think of the organization of a system as a consequence of this sort of planning or design. We imagine an "outside" observer who observes the system's performance, represents it, operates on the representation to determine how to change the system, and then uses a channel of communication from outside the system to effect the changes (see Figure 2.5).

In her work on energy policy analysts, Feldman (1989, p. 136) adds some complexity. She describes organizational routines as "complex sets of inter-locking behaviors held in place through common agreement on the relevant roles and expectations." She says, "Any particular set of agreements about rules and roles is a sort of equilibrium satisfying the demands of many different parties" (p. 136). A similar view is expressed by Nelson and Winter (1982) when they characterize routines as memory, truce, and target. This is a more subtle and interactive sense of the nature of the solutions to the problem of organization. An organization has many parts, and the operation of the whole emerges from the interactions of those parts. Each part may simultaneously provide constraints on the behavior of other parts and be constrained by the behavior of other parts. Elsewhere (Hutchins, in press), I have referred to this sort of system of mutually adaptive computational sub-parts as a "cognitive ecology." This describes the sort of solution discovered by the navigation team. The parties to the computation are the plotter and the bearing recorder, and the demands on them are constructed in the interactions among their cognitive processing capabilities, the structure of the computation, the availability of data, and the fit between computational and social organization. They settled into a solution that simultaneously satisfied all these constraints. Feldman (1989) continues in the same vein:

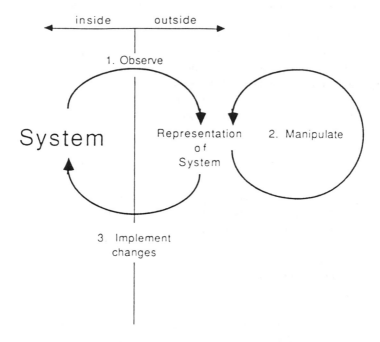

Figure 2.5. The Basic Design Process

NOTE: A representation that is "about" the entire system is created from observations of the system. This representation is manipulated in order to plan an intervention in the system.

> Many organizations or parts of organizations must coordinate their behavior in such a way that each can cope adequately with the pressures and constraints it has to satisfy. While there may be many possible solutions to such a problem, they are not necessarily easy to find. (p. 136)

The question is now posed. Given that organizations are the kinds of systems that consist of many interlocking, interacting, and mutually dependent parts, how can solutions to the organization problem be discovered? Feldman (1989) provides one answer as follows:

> Even if one of the participants finds a new solution that will satisfy the constraints of all parties, the problems of persuading everyone else that this would be a beneficial change may still be considerable. (pp. 136-137)

Clearly the process described in this passage must happen frequently. Parts of the behavior of the navigation team fit this description nicely. P's use of the normative computation scheme and his attempts to make that scheme explicit for S are examples. But this answer is a retreat to the classical view. It posits a designer, albeit "one of the participants" who "finds a new solution," and then must "persuade everyone else" that it is a good solution. And there remain aspects of the adaptive responses of the members of the navigation team, particularly those involving the changing division of labor, that are simply not captured by *any* description which relies on explicit representation of the shape of the solution.

ADAPTATION AND LOCAL DESIGN

In the analysis presented above, there are no instances of anyone reflecting on the whole process. P seems occasionally to represent the entire computation, but there is no evidence he ever imagined the structure of the division of labor. The adaptation process seemed to take place by way of local interactions, mostly of two types. First, team members put constraints on each other by presenting each other with partial computational products. When there is no previously worked out division of labor and assignments of responsibility for various parts of the computation, team members negotiate the division of labor by doing some (what they can, or what is convenient) and hoping that others can do whatever else is required. These are changes that result from the interactions among the behaviors of the subparts of the system as they adapt to the information environment and to each other's behaviors. There is no need to invoke any representation of the behavior of any part of the system to account for these adaptations. The way the computation was driven by the availability of data is an example of this kind of unreflective adaptation process. Even though they are not planned, these changes are not necessarily chaotic. If one part of the system behaves in a systematic way, another part may come to behave in a systematic way by adapting to the behavior of the first. In the interaction between P and S we saw that the behavior of one subsystem can be entrained by that of another.

A second adaptive process involves local design. When implicit negotiations of the division of labor fail, an actor may become aware of his own inability to keep up with the computation and attempt to recruit others to take on parts of it. Thus, the most striking thing P said during the search for a new configuration was something he said to S while falling behind in his attempts to compute bearing corrections with a pocket calculator. He pushed the calculator at the timer and said, "Here, add these things." There is no need to attribute a global awareness of the process to P to account for this. He doesn't have enough time to do his own work, much less reflect on the overall

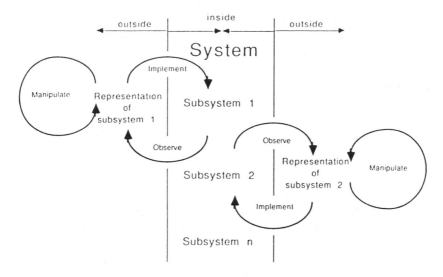

Figure 2.6. Local Design Activity

NOTE: Subsystems interact with each other and adapt to each other's behaviors. Representations of local subsystem behavior are created and manipulated in order to plan changes to subsystem operation. These changes may trigger adaptive responses in other subsystems.

division of labor. He is just acutely aware that he is falling behind and that he needs help to catch up. This is a case of local design. As shown in Figure 2.6, design processes may be local to subsystems. Figure 2.6 depicts an overall system that can change in three modes:

1. Without any design activity at all, through the adaptive interactions among the subsystems.

2. Through local design activities in which manipulations are performed on representations of local subsystems in order to discover more adaptive relationships with the subsystem's environment. These changes may, in turn, lead to adaptive changes, either designed or not, by the other subsystems.

3. Through classical global activities in which the representation is of the entire system of interest.

The response of the system to the change in its environment was eventually successful, but it was the consequence of a large number of local interactions and adjustments, some of which led the system away from the eventual solution. Many of these adjustments appear to have been local design decisions by the participants. Prior to its discovery by the system as a whole, however, the final configuration appears not to have been represented or understood by any of the participants. To the extent that the acquisition of a useful adaptation to a changing environment counts as learning, we must say that this is a case of organizational learning.

Evolution and Design

It seems to me that there is an important difference between the process of change by supervisory reflection and intervention imagined in the classical view, and the process of change by local adjustment described above. It strongly resembles the difference between design and evolution (Alexander, 1964).

Both evolution and design can be characterized as searches. The evolutionary search is conducted by the system itself in terms of itself, while the design search is conducted by an "outsider" on representations of the system. The evolutionary search is the process of adaptation (cf. Weick's view of enactment, 1979), while the design search precedes and guides an implementation of the, hopefully adaptive, design. Pure evolution is, in fact, a process without design (Dawkins, 1986). What we see in the case of the adaptation by the navigation team is an organizational change that is produced in part by an evolutionary process (adaptive search without representation of the search space), and in part by a process that is something that lies between evolution and classical global-perspective design.

From this perspective, human institutions can be quite complex because they are composed of subsystems (people) that are "aware" in the sense of having representations of themselves and their relationships with their surroundings. Whether we consider a particular change at the upper system level to be the result of evolution or the result of design depends on what we believe about the scope of the awareness of the subsystems. If we think that some of the subsystems have global awareness, and can represent and anticipate the consequences of possible changes, then we may view an organizational change as a result of design. If we believe that the subsystems do not form and manipulate representations of system operation, then we must view organizational change as evolutionary. What do we say when the individual subsystems only engage in local design activity—say, crying out for help when one is overworked? In that case, design is clearly involved, and the change in the local environment of the individual that adapts this way is a *designed* change. Now, that local designed change may have undesigned and unanticipated consequences for other parts of the system. It may thus provoke local adaptations by other parts of the system as all of the parts seek (either by design or not) to satisfy the new environment of constraints produced by the changes in the behaviors of other parts. Ultimately, this process may produce a change in the behavior of the system as a whole. Even when many local design decisions are involved, such an adaptation that occurs at the system level appears to be evolutionary in the sense that the system level change that resulted was never represented. I believe most of the phenomena labeled as social or organizational "evolution" are instances of this kind of change.

Is the navigation task setting primarily the product of evolution or of design? When we consider human systems, we have to acknowledge that every participant in the system can be both inside and outside some systems in this sense. The changes in the organization of the navigation team were brought about by changes in the thinking of the participants of the system, that is, the agreements about rules and roles that constitute the organizational routine. To this extent, the structure of the setting is a product of design. But, since the observed reorganization was never fully represented by any of the participants in the system, the actors' designs alone cannot account for the solution that was achieved. Thus, the organization of the navigation task is also a product of evolution. Finally, while the participants may have represented and thus learned the solution after it came into being, the solution was clearly discovered by the organization itself before it was discovered by any of the participants.

Acknowledgments

A preliminary version of this manuscript was prepared for the conference on Organizational Learning, May 18-20, 1989, at Carnegie Mellon University. June 1990 editorial revisions made by Michael Cohen and Lee Sproull.

Appendix
Transcription Conventions

Speakers

    P: Quartermaster Chief, acting as plotter. The Chief is the ranking enlisted man in the navigation department. Also has the title Assistant to the Navigator.

    S: Quartermaster Second Class, acting as bearing timer-recorder. Sometimes referred to by his first name, John.

    H: The helmsman who is steering the ship. First name, Charles.

  PW: Port Wing bearing taker.

Conventions for Transcription

( )   Words enclosed in parentheses are comments or annotations of the actions observed in the video record. Never verbatim transcription.

| Vertical bars are used in adjacent lines of transcription to indicate simultaneity of occurrence.

/?/   Unintelligible portion of utterance.

{ }   Numbers and actions enclosed in curb brackets denote key presses on the calculator.

{3 +}   Numbers and actions in bold font enclosed in curly brackets are key presses on the calculator that are verbally shadowed. This would mean a person pressed the 3 and the + key while saying "Three plus." In addition to numbers, the most frequent key presses are +, −, = and clear.

1 20   Spoken numbers have been transcribed mostly as numerals for convenience. If they are separated by spaces, each numeral was pronounced separately. If they are not separated by space, then they are read as conventional numbers. This example could also have been transcribed, "One twenty."

Formulas for the Computation

C   The compass heading of the ship with no corrections.

D   Compass deviation. A function of heading.

V   Magnetic variation. Approximately 14 degrees East in San Diego Harbor.

RB   The relative bearing of a landmark. This is the bearing of the landmark with respect to ship's head.

TB   True bearing $(T + RB)$.

M   Ship's magnetic heading $(C + V)$.

T   Ship's true head $(M + V)$.

( )   Terms enclosed in parenthesis were entered into the calculator with only plus or minus operators among them. The = operator closes the parenthesis. Thus $(C + V + RB)$ means the three terms were added together as a group, whereas $((C + V) + RB)$ means that the = operator was applied to $(C + V)$ which was then added to RB.

[ ]   Sums in square brackets were spoken as intermediate sums. Thus, +RB) denotes the following actions: key V, key +, key D, key =, key +, key C, key =, read the displayed value aloud, key +, key RB, key =

NOTES

1. Such complete records are not always kept aboard merchant vessels and are not absolutely essential to the task of navigating the ship in restricted waters. It is possible for an experienced pilot to "eyeball" the passage and make judgments concerning control of the ship without the support of the computations that are carried out on the chart. Aboard naval vessels, however, such records are always kept for reasons of safety primarily, but also for purposes of accountability so that, should there be a problem, the ship will be able to show exactly what it was doing and where it was at the time of the mishap.

2. On other ships, and on this ship in different circumstances, the team may be somewhat larger or smaller depending on the availability of qualified personnel.

3. All of the names appearing in this document are pseudonyms, including that of the ship itself.

4. All of the discourse reported in this passage is direct transcription from the audio record of actual events. Rather than presenting the transcript itself with annotation, I have combined the transcript and annotation into a single narrative structure. The purpose of this passage is to convey a sense of the drama of the situation and to set the scene for subsequent events that will be analyzed in detail.

5. To "dead stick" an aircraft is to fly it after the engine has died.

6. The calculator was capable of computing a number of specialized navigation functions, but only addition and subtraction were used in what follows.

REFERENCES

Alexander, C. (1964). *Notes on the synthesis of form.* Cambridge, MA: Harvard University Press.

Anderson, J. (1983). *Architecture of cognition.* Cambridge, MA: Harvard University Press.

Chandler, A. (1966). *Strategy and structure.* Cambridge, MA: Harvard University Press.

Cyert, R. M., & March, J. G. (1963). *A behavioral theory of the firm.* Englewood Cliffs, NJ: Prentice Hall.

Dawkins, R. (1986). *The blind watchmaker.* New York: Norton.

Feldman, M. S. (1989). *Order without design.* Berkeley: University of California Press.

Hutchins, E. (in press). The social organization of distributed cognition. In L. Resnick & J. Levine (Eds.), *Perspectives on socially shared cognition.* Washington, DC: American Psychological Association.

Nelson, R., & Winter, S. (1982). *An evolutionary theory of economic change.* Cambridge, MA: Harvard University Press.

Newell, A., & Simon, H. (1972). *Human problem solving.* Englewood Cliffs, NJ: Prentice Hall.

Weick, K. E. (1979). *Social psychology of organizing.* Reading, MA: Addison-Wesley.

3

Organizational Learning and Communities-of-Practice

Toward a Unified View of Working, Learning, and Innovation

JOHN SEELY BROWN
PAUL DUGUID

Recent ethnographic studies of workplace practices indicate that the ways people actually work usually differ fundamentally from the ways organizations describe that work in manuals, training programs, organizational charts, and job descriptions. Nevertheless, organizations tend to rely on the latter in their attempts to understand and improve work practice. We examine one such study. We then relate its conclusions to compatible investigations of learning and of innovation to argue that conventional descriptions of jobs mask not only the ways people work, but also significant learning and innovation generated in the informal communities-of-practice in which they work. By reassessing work, learning, and innovation in the context of actual communities and actual practices, we suggest that the connections between these three become apparent. With a unified view of working, learning, and innovating, it should be possible to reconceive of and redesign organizations to improve all three.

(LEARNING; INNOVATION; GROUPS; DOWNSKILLING; ORGANIZATIONAL CULTURES; NONCANONICAL PRACTICE)

INTRODUCTION

Working, learning, and innovating are closely related forms of human activity that are conventionally thought to conflict with each other. Work practice is generally viewed as conservative and resistant to change; learning

This chapter appeared originally in *Organization Science*, Vol. 2, No. 1, February 1991. Copyright © 1991, The Institute of Management Sciences.

is generally viewed as distinct from working and problematic in the face of change; and innovation is generally viewed as the disruptive but necessary imposition of change on the other two. To see that working, learning, and innovating are interrelated and compatible and thus potentially complementary, not conflicting forces requires a distinct conceptual shift. By bringing together recent research into working, learning, and innovating, we attempt to indicate the nature and explore the significance of such a shift.

The source of the oppositions perceived between working, learning, and innovating lies primarily in the gulf between precepts and practice. Formal descriptions of work (e.g., "office procedures") and of learning (e.g., "subject matter") are abstracted from actual practice. They inevitably and intentionally omit the details. In a society that attaches particular value to "abstract knowledge," the details of practice have come to be seen as nonessential, unimportant, and easily developed once the relevant abstractions have been grasped. Thus education, training, and technology design generally focus on abstract representations to the detriment, if not exclusion, of actual practice. We, by contrast, suggest that practice is central to understanding work. Abstractions *detached from practice* distort or obscure intricacies of that practice. Without a clear understanding of those intricacies and the role they play, the practice itself cannot be well understood, engendered (through training), or enhanced (through innovation).

We begin by looking at the variance between a major organization's formal descriptions of work both in its training programs and manuals and the actual work practices performed by its members. Orr's (1987a, 1987b, 1990a, 1990b) detailed ethnographic studies of service technicians illustrate how an organization's view of work can overlook and even oppose what and who it takes to get a job done. Based on Orr's specific insights, we make the more general claim that reliance on espoused practice (which we refer to as *canonical practice*) can blind an organization's core to the actual, and usually valuable practices of its members (including *noncanonical practices,* such as "work arounds"). It is the actual practices, however, that determine the success or failure of organizations.

Next, we turn to learning and, in particular, to Lave and Wenger's (1990) practice-based theory of learning as "legitimate peripheral participation" in "communities-of-practice." Much conventional learning theory, including that implicit in most training courses, tends to endorse the valuation of abstract knowledge over actual practice and as a result to separate learning from working and, more significantly, learners from workers. Together Lave and Wenger's analysis and Orr's empirical investigation indicate that this knowledge-practice separation is unsound, both in theory and in practice. We argue that the composite concept of "learning-in-working" best represents the fluid evolution of learning through practice.

From this practice-based standpoint, we view learning as the bridge between working and innovating. We use Daft and Weick's (1984) interpretive account of "enacting" organizations to place innovation in the context of changes in a community's "way of seeing" or interpretive view. Both Orr's (1987a, 1987b, 1990a, 1990b) and Lave and Wenger's (1990) research emphasize that to understand working and learning, it is necessary to focus on the formation and change of the communities in which work takes place. Taking all three theories together, we argue that, through their constant adapting to changing membership and changing circumstances, evolving communities-of-practice are significant sites of innovating.

1. WORKING

a. Canonical Practice

Orr's (1987a, 1987b, 1990a, 1990b) ethnography of service technicians (reps) in training and at work in a large corporation paints a clear picture of the divergence between espoused practice and actual practice, of the ways this divergence develops, and of the trouble it can cause. His work provides a "thick" (see Geertz, 1973), detailed description of the way work actually progresses. Orr contrasts his findings with the way the same work is thinly described in the corporation's manuals, training courses, and job descriptions.[1]

The importance of such an approach to work in progress is emphasized by Bourdieu (1977), who distinguishes the *modus operandi* from the *opus operatum*—that is, the way a task, as it unfolds over time, looks to someone at work on it, while many of the options and dilemmas remain unresolved, as opposed to the way it looks with hindsight as a finished task. Ryle (1954) makes a similar point. The *opus operatum,* the finished view, tends to see the action in terms of the task alone and cannot see the way in which the process of doing the task is actually structured by the constantly changing conditions of work and the world. Bourdieu makes a useful analogy with reference to a journey as actually carried out on the ground and as seen on a map ("an abstract space, devoid of any landmarks or any privileged centre" [p. 2]). The latter, like the *opus operatum,* inevitably smooths over the myriad decisions made with regard to changing conditions: road works, diversions, Memorial Day parades, earthquakes, personal fatigue, conflicting opinions, wrong-headed instructions, relations of authority, inaccuracies on the map, and the like. The map, though potentially useful, by *itself* provides little insight into how *ad hoc* decisions presented by changing conditions can be resolved (and, of course, each resolved decision changes the conditions once more). As a journey becomes more complex, the map increasingly conceals what is actually needed to make the journey. Thick description, by contrast, ascends from the abstraction to the concrete circumstances of actual practice, reconnecting the map and the mapped.

Orr's (1987a, 1987b, 1990a, 1990b) study shows how an organization's maps can dramatically distort its view of the routes its members take. This "misrecognition," as Bourdieu (1977) calls it, can be traced to many places, including pedagogic theory and practice. Often it has its more immediate cause in the strategy to downskill positions. Many organizations are willing to assume that complex tasks can be successfully mapped onto a set of simple, Tayloristic, canonical steps that can be followed without need of significant understanding or insight (and thus without need of significant investment in training or skilled technicians). But as Bourdieu, Suchman (1987a), and Orr show, actual practice inevitably involves tricky interpolations between abstract accounts and situated demands. Orr's reps' skills, for instance, are most evident in the improvised strategies they deploy to cope with the clash between prescriptive documentation and the sophisticated, yet unpredictable, machines they work with. Nonetheless, in the corporation's eyes practices that deviate from the canonical are, by definition, deviant practices. Through a reliance on canonical descriptions (to the extent of overlooking even their own noncanonical improvisations), managers develop a conceptual outlook that cannot comprehend the importance of noncanonical practices. People are typically viewed as performing their jobs according to formal job descriptions, despite the fact that daily evidence points to the contrary (Suchman, 1987b). They are held accountable to the map, not to road conditions.[2]

In Orr's (1987a, 1987b, 1990a, 1990b) case, the canonical map comes in the form of "directive" documentation aimed at "single point failures" of machines. Indeed, the documentation is less like a map than a single predetermined route with no alternatives: it provides a decision tree for diagnosis and repair that assumes both predictable machines and an unproblematic process of making diagnoses and repairs through blindly following diagnostic instructions. Both assumptions are mistaken. Abstractions of repair work fall short of the complexity of the actual practices from which they were abstracted. The account of actual practice we describe below is anything but the blind following of instructions.

The inadequacies of this corporation's directive approach actually make a rep's work more difficult to accomplish and thus perversely demands more, not fewer, improvisational skills. An ostensible downskilling and actual upskilling therefore proceed simultaneously. Although the documentation becomes more prescriptive and ostensibly more simple, in actuality the task becomes more improvisational and more complex. The reps develop sophisticated noncanonical practices to bridge the gulf between their corporation's canonical approach and successful work practices, laden with the dilemmas, inconsistencies, and unpredictability of everyday life. The directive documentation does not "deprive the workers of the skills they have"; rather, "it merely reduces the amount of information given them" (Orr, 1990a, p. 26). The burden of making up the difference between what is provided and what is needed then rests with the reps, who in bridging the gap actually protect the organization from its own shortsightedness. If the reps adhered to the canonical approach, their corporation's services would be in chaos.

Because this corporation's training programs follow a similar downskilling approach, the reps regard them as generally unhelpful. As a result, a wedge is driven between the corporation and its reps: the corporation assumes the reps are untrainable, uncooperative, and unskilled; whereas the reps view the overly simplistic training programs as a reflection of the corporation's low estimation of their worth and skills. In fact, their valuation is a testament to the depth of the rep's insight. They recognize the superficiality of the training because they are conscious of the full complexity of the technology and what it takes to keep it running. The corporation, on the other hand, blinkered by its implicit faith in formal training and canonical practice and its misinterpretation of the rep's behavior, is unable to appreciate either aspect of their insight.

In essence, Orr (1987a, 1987b, 1990a, 1990b) shows that in order to do their job the reps must—and do—learn to make better sense of the machines they work with than their employer either expects or allows. Thus they develop their understanding of the machine not in the training programs, but in the very conditions from which the programs separate them—the authentic activity of their daily work. For the reps (and for the corporation, though it is unaware of it), learning-in-working is an occupational necessity.

b. Noncanonical Practice

Orr's analyses of actual practice provide various examples of how the reps diverge from canonical descriptions. For example, on one service call (Orr, 1987b, 1990b) a rep confronted a machine that produced copious raw information in the form of error codes and obligingly crashed when tested. But the error codes and the nature of the crashes did not tally. Such a case immediately fell outside the directive training and documentation provided by the organization, which tie errors to error codes. Unfortunately, the problem also fell outside the rep's accumulated, improvised experience. He summoned his technical specialist, whose job combines "trouble-shooting consultant, supervisor, and occasional instructor." The specialist was equally baffled. Yet, though the canonical approach to repair was exhausted, with their combined range of noncanonical practices, the rep and technical specialist still had options to pursue.

One option—indeed the only option left by canonical practice now that its strategies for repair had been quickly exhausted—was to abandon repair altogether and to replace the malfunctioning machine. But both the rep and the specialist realized that the resulting loss of face for the company, loss of the customer's faith in the reps, loss of their own credit within their organization, and loss of money to the corporation made this their last resort. Loss of face or faith has considerable ramifications beyond mere embarrassment. A rep's ability to enlist the future support of customers and colleagues is jeopardized. There is evidently strong social pressure from a variety of sources to solve problems without exchanging machines. The reps' work is not simply about maintaining machines; it is also and equally importantly, about maintaining social relations: "A large part of service work might better be described as repair and maintenance of the social setting" (Orr, 1990b, p. 169). The training and documentation, of course, are about maintaining machines.

Solving the problem *in situ* required constructing a coherent account of the malfunction out of the incoherence of the data and documentation. To do this, the rep and the specialist embarked on a long story-telling procedure. The machine, with its erratic behavior, mixed with information from the user and memories from the technicians, provided essential ingredients that the two aimed to account for in a composite story. The process of forming a story was, centrally, one of diagnosis. This process, it should be noted, *begins* as well as ends in a communal understanding of the machine that is wholly unavailable from the canonical documents.

While they explored the machine or waited for it to crash, the rep and specialist (with contributions from the ethnographer) recalled and discussed other occasions on which they had encountered some of the present symptoms. Each story presented an exchangeable account that could be examined and reflected upon to provoke old memories and new insights. Yet more tests and more stories were thereby generated:

> The key element of diagnosis is the situated production of understanding through narration, in that the integration of the various facts of the situation is accomplished through a verbal consideration of those facts with a primary criterion of coherence. The process is situated, in Suchman's terms, in that both the damaged machine and the social context of the user site are essential resources for both the definition of the problem and its resolution. . . . They are faced with a failing machine displaying diagnostic information which has previously proved worthless

and in which no one has any particular confidence this time. They do not know where they are going to find the information they need to understand and solve this problem. In their search for inspiration, they tell stories. (Orr, 1990b, pp. 178-179)

The story-telling process continued throughout the morning, over lunch, and back in front of the machine, throughout the afternoon, forming a long but purposeful progression from incoherence to coherence: "The final trouble-shooting session was a five hour effort. . . . This session yielded a dozen anecdotes told during the trouble shooting, taking a variety of forms and serving a variety of purposes" (Orr, 1990b, p. 10). Ultimately, these stories generated sufficient interplay among memories, tests, the machine's responses, and the ensuing insights to lead to diagnosis and repair. The final diagnosis developed from what Orr calls an "antiphonal recitation" in which the two told different versions of the same story: "They are talking about personal encounters with the same problem, but the two versions are significantly different" (Orr, 1987b, p. 177). Through story telling, these separate experiences converged, leading to a shared diagnosis of certain previously encountered but unresolved symptoms. The two (and the ethnographer) had constructed a communal interpretation of hitherto uninterpretable data and individual experience. Rep and specialist were now in a position to modify previous stories and build a more insightful one. They both increased their own understanding and added to their community's collective knowledge. Such stories are passed around, becoming part of the repertoire available to all reps. Orr reports hearing a concise, assimilated version of this particular false error code passed among reps over a game of cribbage in the lunch room three months later (Orr, 1990b, p. 181ff). A story, once in the possession of the community, can then be used—and further modified—in similar diagnostic sessions.

c. Central Features of Work Practice

In this section, we analyze Orr's thick description of the rep's practice through the overlapping categories, "narration," "collaboration," and "social construction"—categories that get to the heart of what the reps do and yet which, significantly, have no place in the organization's abstracted, canonical accounts of their work.

Narration. The first aspect of the reps' practice worth highlighting is the extensive narration used. This way of working is quite distinct from following the branches of decision tree. Stories and their telling can reflect the complex social web within which work takes place and the relationship of the narrative, narrator, and audience to the specific events of practice. The stories have a flexible generality that makes them both adaptable and particular. They function, rather like the common law, as a usefully underconstrained means to interpret each new situation in the light of accumulated wisdom and constantly changing circumstances.

The practice of creating and exchanging of stories has two important aspects. First of all, telling stories helps to diagnose the state of a troublesome machine. Reps begin by extracting a history from the users of the machine, the users' story, and with this and the machine as their starting point, they construct their own account. If they cannot tell an adequate story on their own, then they seek help—either by summoning a specialist, as in the case above, or by discussing the problem with colleagues over coffee or lunch. If necessary, they work together at the machine, articulating hunches, insights, misconceptions, and the like, to dissect and augment their developing understanding. Story telling allows them to keep track of the sequences of behavior and of their theories, and thereby to work towards a coherent account of the current state of the machine. The reps try to impose coherence on an apparently random sequence of events in order that they can decide what to do next. Unlike the documentation, which tells reps *what* to do but not *why*, the reps' stories help them develop causal accounts of machines, which are essential when documentation breaks down. (As we have suggested, documentation, like machines, will always break down, however well it is designed.) What the reps do in their story telling is develop a causal map out of their experience to replace the impoverished directive route that they have been furnished by the corporation. In the absence of such support, the reps Orr studied cater to their own needs as well as they can. Their narratives yield a story of the machine fundamentally different from the prescriptive account provided by the documentation, a story that is built in response to the particulars of breakdown.

Despite the assumptions behind the downskilling process, to do their job in any significant sense, reps need these complex causal stories and they produce and circulate them as part of their regular noncanonical work practice. An important part of the reps' skill, though not recognized by the corporation, comprises the ability to create, to trade, and to understand highly elliptical, highly referential, and to the initiated, highly informative war stories. Zuboff (1988) in her analysis of the skills people develop working on complex systems describes similar cases of story telling and argues that it is a necessary practice for dealing with "smart" but unpredictable machines. The irony, as Orr points out, is that for purposes of diagnosis the reps have no smart machines, just inadequate documentation and "their own very traditional skills."

It is worth stressing at this point that we are not arguing that communities simply can and thus should work without assistance from trainers and the corporation in general. Indeed, we suggest in our conclusion that situations inevitably occur when group improvisation simply cannot bridge the gap between what the corporation supplies and what a particular community actually needs. What we are claiming is that corporations must provide support that corresponds to the real needs of the community rather than just to the abstract expectations of the corporation. And what those needs are can only be understood by understanding the details and sophistications of actual practice. In Orr's account, what the reps needed was the means to understand the machine causally and to relate this causal map to the inevitable intricacies of practice. To discern such needs, however, will require that corporations develop a less formal and more practice-based approach to communities and their work.

The second characteristic of story telling is that the stories also act as repositories of accumulated wisdom. In particular, community narratives protect the reps' ability to work from the ravages of modern idealizations of work and related downskilling practices. In Orr's example, the canonical decision trees, privileging the decontextualized over the situated, effectively sweep away the clutter of practice. But it is in the face of just this clutter that the reps' skills are needed. Improvisational skills that allow the reps to circumvent the inadequacies of both the machines and the documentation are not only developed but also preserved in community story telling.

Jordan's (1989) work similarly draws attention to the central, dual role of informal stories. She studied the clash between midwifery as it is prescribed by officials from Mexico City and as it is practiced in rural Yucatan. The officials ignore important details and realities of practice. For instance, the officials instruct the midwives in practices that demand sterile instruments though the midwives work in villages that lack adequate means for sterilization. The midwives' noncanonical practices, however, circumvent the possibility of surgical operations being carried out with unsterile instruments. These effective practices survive, despite the government's worryingly decontextualized attempts to replace them with canonical practices, through story telling. Jordan notes that the two aspects of story telling, diagnosis and preservation, are inseparable. Orr also suggests that "The use of story telling both to preserve knowledge and to consider it in subsequent diagnoses coincides with the narrative character of diagnosis" (Orr, 1990b, p. 178). We have pulled them apart for the purpose of analysis only.

Collaboration. Based as it is on shared narratives, a second important aspect of the reps' work is that it is obviously communal and thereby *collaborative.* In Orr's example, the rep and specialist went through a collective, not individual process. Not only is the learning in this case inseparable from working, but also individual learning is inseparable from collective learning. The insight accumulated is not a private substance, but socially constructed and distributed. Thus, faced with a difficult problem reps like to work together and to discuss problems in groups. In the case of this particular problem, the individual rep tried what he knew, failed, and there met his limits. With the specialist he was able to trade stories, develop insights, and construct new options. Each had a story about the condition of the machine, but it was in telling it antiphonally that the significance emerged.

While it might seem trivial, it is important to emphasize the collaborative work within the reps' community, for in the corporation's eyes their work is viewed individually. Their documentation and training implicitly maintain that the work is individual and the central relationship of the rep is that between an individual and the corporation:

> The activities defined by management are those which one worker will do, and work as the relationship of employment is discussed in terms of a single worker's relationship to the corporation. I suspect the incidence of workers alone in relations of employment is quite low, and the existence of coworkers must contribute to those activities done in the name of work. . . . The fact that work is commonly done by a group of workers together is only sometimes acknowledged in the literature, and the usual presence of such a community has not entered into the definition of work. (Orr, 1990a, p. 15)

In fact, as Orr's studies show, not only do reps work with specialists, as in the example given here, but throughout the day they meet for coffee or for meals and trade stories back and forth.

Social Construction. A third important aspect of Orr's account of practice, and one which is interfused with the previous two and separated here only to help in clarification, involves *social construction.* This has two parts. First and most evident in Orr's example, the reps constructed a shared understanding out of bountiful conflicting and confusing data. This constructed understanding reflects the reps' view of the world. They developed a *rep's* model of the machine, not a trainer's, which had already proved unsatisfactory, nor even an engineer's, which was not available to them (and might well have been unhelpful, though Orr interestingly points out that reps cultivate connections throughout the corporation to help them circumvent the barriers to understanding built by their documentation and training). The reps' view, evident in their stories, interweaves generalities about "this model" with particularities about "this site" and "this machine."

Such an approach is highly situated and highly improvisational. Reps respond to whatever the situation itself—both social and physical—throws at them, a process very similar to Levi-Strauss's (1966) concept of *bricolage:* the ability to "make do with 'whatever is to hand' " (p. 17). What reps need for *bricolage* are not the partial, rigid models of the sort directive documentation provides, but help to build, *ad hoc* and collaboratively, robust models that do justice to the particular difficulties in which they find themselves. Hutchins (1991, in press), in his analysis of navigation teams in the U.S. Navy, similarly notes the way in which understanding is constructed within and distributed throughout teams.

The second feature of social construction, as important but less evident than the first, is that in telling these stories an individual rep contributes to the construction and development of his or her own identity as a rep and reciprocally to the construction and development of the community of reps in which he or she works. Individually, in telling stories the rep is becoming a member. Orr (1990b) notes, "this construction of their identity as technicians occurs both in doing the work and in their stories, and their stories of themselves fixing machines show their world in what they consider the appropriate perspective" (p. 187). Simultaneously and interdependently, the reps are contributing to the construction and evolution of the community that they are joining—what we might call a "community of interpretation," for it is through the continual development of these communities that the shared means for interpreting complex activity get formed, transformed, and transmitted.

The significance of both these points should become apparent in the following sections, first, as we turn to a theory of learning (Lave & Wenger, 1990) that, like Orr's analysis of work, takes formation of identity and community membership as central units of analysis; and second as we argue that innovation can be seen as at base a function of changes in community values and views.

2. LEARNING

The theories of learning implicated in the documentation and training view learning from the abstract stance of pedagogy. Training is thought of as the *transmission* of explicit, abstract knowledge from the head of someone who knows to the head of someone who does not in surroundings that specifically exclude the complexities of practice and the communities of practitioners. The setting for learning is simply assumed not to matter.

Concepts of knowledge or information transfer, however, have been under increasing attack in recent years from a variety of sources (e.g., Reddy,

1979). In particular, learning theorists (e.g., Lave, 1988; Lave & Wenger, 1990) have rejected transfer models, which isolate knowledge from practice, and developed a view of learning as social construction, putting knowledge back into the contexts in which it has meaning (see also Brown, Collins, & Duguid, 1989; Brown & Duguid, in press; Pea, 1990). From this perspective, learners can in one way or another be seen to construct their understanding out of a wide range of materials that include ambient social and physical circumstances and the histories and social relations of the people involved. Like a magpie with a nest, learning is built out of the materials to hand and in relation to the structuring resources of local conditions. (For the importance of including the structuring resources in any account of learning, see Lave, 1988.) What is learned is profoundly connected to the conditions in which it is learned.

Lave and Wenger (1990), with their concept of *legitimate peripheral participation* (LPP), provide one of the most versatile accounts of this constructive view of learning. LPP, it must quickly be asserted, is *not* a method of education. It is an analytical category or tool for understanding learning across different methods, different historical periods, and different social and physical environments. It attempts to account for learning, not teaching or instruction. Thus this approach escapes problems that arise through examinations of learning from pedagogy's viewpoint. It makes the conditions of learning, rather than just abstract subject matter, central to understanding what is learned.

Learning, from the viewpoint of LPP, essentially involves becoming an "insider." Learners do not receive or even construct abstract, "objective," individual knowledge; rather, they learn to function in a community—be it a community of nuclear physicists, cabinet makers, high school classmates, street-corner society, or, as in the case under study, service technicians. They acquire that particular community's subjective viewpoint and learn to speak its language. In short, they are enculturated (Brown et al., 1989). Learners are acquiring not explicit, formal "expert knowledge," but the embodied ability to behave as community members. For example, learners learn to tell and appreciate community-appropriate stories, discovering in doing so, all the narrative-based resources we outlined above. As Jordan (1989) argues in her analysis of midwifery, "To acquire a store of appropriate stories and, even more importantly, to know what are appropriate occasions for telling them, is then part of what it means to become a midwife" (p. 935).

Workplace learning is best understood, then, in terms of the communities being formed or joined and personal identities being changed. The central issue in learning is *becoming* a practitioner not learning *about* practice. This approach draws attention away from abstract knowledge and cranial processes and situates it in the practices and communities in which knowledge takes on significance. Learning about new devices, such as the machines Orr's technicians worked with, is best understood (and best achieved) in the context of the community in which the devices are used and that community's particular interpretive conventions. Lave and Wenger (1990) argue that learning, understanding, and interpretation involve a great deal that is not explicit or explicable, developed and framed in a crucially *communal* context.

Orr's (1990a) study reveals this sort of learning going on in the process of and inseparable from work. The rep was not just an observer of the technical specialist. He was also an important participant in this process of diagnosis and story telling, whose participation could legitimately grow in from the periphery as a function of his developing understanding not of some extrinsically structured training. His legitimacy here is an important function of the social relations between the different levels of service technician, which are surprisingly egalitarian, perhaps as a result of the inherent incoherence of the problems this sort of technology presents: a specialist cannot hope to exert hierarchical control over knowledge that he or she must first construct cooperatively. "Occupational communities . . . have little hierarchy; the only real status is that of member" (p. 33).

a. Groups and Communities

Having characterized both working and learning in terms of communities, it is worth pausing to establish relations between our own account and recent work on groups in the workplace. Much important work has been done in this area (see, for example, the collections by Hackman [1990] and Goodman and Associates [1988]) and many of the findings support our own view of work activity. There is, however, a significant distinction between our views and this work. Group theory in general focuses on groups as canonical, bounded entities that lie within an organization and that are organized or at least sanctioned by that organization and its view of tasks (see Hackman, 1990, pp. 4-5). The communities that we discern are, by contrast, often non-canonical and not recognized by the organization. They are more fluid and interpenetrative than bounded, often crossing the restrictive boundaries of the organization to incorporate people from outside. (Orr's reps can in an important sense be said to work in a community that includes both suppliers and customers.) Indeed, the canonical organization becomes a questionable unit of analysis from this perspective. And significantly, communities are emergent. That is to say their shape and membership emerges in the process of activity, as opposed to being created to carry out a task. (Note, by contrast, how much of the literature refers to the *design* or *creation* of new groups [e.g., Goodman & Associates, 1988]. From our viewpoint, the central questions more involve the *detection* and *support* of emergent or existing communities.)

If this distinction is correct then it has two particularly important corollaries. First, work practice and learning need to be understood not in terms of the groups that are ordained (e.g., "task forces" or "trainees"), but in terms of the communities that emerge. The latter are likely to be noncanonical (though not necessarily so) while the former are likely to be canonical. Looking only at canonical groups, whose configuration often conceals extremely influential interstitial communities, will not provide a clear picture of how work or learning is actually organized and accomplished. It will only reflect the dominant assumptions of the organizational core.

Second, attempts to introduce "teams" and "work groups" into the workplace to enhance learning or work practice are often based on an assumption that without impetus from above, an organization's members configure themselves as individuals. In fact, as we suggest, people work and learn collaboratively and vital interstitial communities are continually being formed and reformed. The reorganization of the workplace into canonical groups can wittingly or unwittingly disrupt these highly functional noncanonical—and therefore often invisible—communities. Orr (1990a) argues:

> The process of working and learning together creates a work situation which
> the workers value, and they resist having it disrupted by their employers
> through events such as a reorganization of the work. This resistance can surprise
> employers who think of labor as a commodity to arrange to suit their ends. The
> problem for the workers is that this community which they have created was not
> part of the series of discrete employment agreements by which the employer
> populated the work place, nor is the role of the community in doing the work
> acknowledged. *The work can only continue free of disruption if the employer*
> *can be persuaded to see the community as necessary to accomplishing work.*
> (p. 48, emphasis added)

b. Fostering Learning

Given a community-based analysis of learning so congruent with Orr's analysis of working, the question arises, how is it possible to foster learning-in-working? The answer is inevitably complex, not least because all the intricacies of context, which the pedagogic approach has always assumed could be stripped away, now have to be taken back into consideration. On the other hand, the ability of people to learn *in situ* suggests that as a fundamental principle for supporting learning, attempts to strip away context should be examined with caution. If learners need access to practitioners at work, it is essential to question didactic approaches, with their tendency to separate learners from the target community and the authentic work practices. Learning is fostered by fostering access to and membership of the target community-of-practice, not by explicating abstractions of individual practice. Thus central to the process are the recognition and legitimation of community practices.

Reliance on formal descriptions of work, explicit syllabuses for learning about it, and canonical groups to carry it out immediately set organizations at a disadvantage. This approach, as we have noted, can simply blind management to the practices and communities that actually make things happen. In particular, it can lead to the isolation of learners, who will then be unable to acquire the implicit practices required for work. Marshall (in Lave & Wenger, 1990) describes a case of apprenticeship for butchers in which learning was extremely restricted because, among other things, "apprentices . . . could not watch journeymen cut and saw meat" (p. 19). Formal training in cutting and sawing is quite different from the understanding of practice gleaned through informal observation that copresence makes possible and absence obviously excludes. These trainees were simply denied the chance to become legitimate peripheral participants. If training is designed so that learners cannot observe the activity of practitioners, learning is inevitably impoverished.

Legitimacy and peripherality are intertwined in a complex way. Occasionally, learners (like the apprentice butchers) are granted legitimacy but are denied peripherality. Conversely, they can be granted peripherality but denied legitimacy. Martin (1982) gives examples of organizations in which legitimacy is explicitly denied in instances of "open door" management, where members come to realize that, though the door is open, it is wiser not to cross the threshold. If either legitimacy or peripherality is denied, learning will be significantly more difficult.

For learners, then, a position on the periphery of practice is important. It is also easily overlooked and increasingly risks being "designed out," leaving people physically or socially isolated and justifiably uncertain whether, for instance, their errors are inevitable or the result of personal inadequacies. It is a significant challenge for design to ensure that new collaborative technologies, designed as they so often are around formal descriptions of work, do not exclude this sort of implicit, extendable, informal periphery. Learners need legitimate access to the periphery of communication—to computer mail, to formal and informal meetings, to telephone conversations, etc., and, of course, to war stories. They pick up invaluable "know how"—not just information but also manner and technique—from being on the periphery of competent practitioners going about their business. Furthermore, it is important to consider the periphery not only because it is an important site of learning, but also because, as the next section proposes, it can be an important site for innovation.

3. INNOVATING

One of the central benefits of these small, self-constituting communities we have been describing is that they evade the ossifying tendencies of large organizations. Canonical accounts of work are not only hard to apply and hard to learn, they are also hard to change. Yet the actual behaviors of communities-of-practice are constantly changing both as newcomers replace old timers and as the demands of practice force the community to revise its relationship to its environment. Communities-of-practice like the reps' continue to develop a rich, fluid, noncanonical world view to bridge the gap between their organization's static canonical view and the challenge of changing practice. This process of development is inherently innovative. "Maverick" communities of this sort offer the core of a large organization a means and a model to examine the potential of alternative views of organizational activity through spontaneously occurring experiments that are simultaneously informed and checked by experience. These, it has been argued (Hedberg, Nystrom, & Starbuck, 1976; Schein, 1990), drive innovation by allowing the parts of an organization to step outside the organization's inevitably limited core worldview and simply try something new. Unfortunately, people in the core of large organizations too often regard these noncanonical practices (if they see them at all) as counterproductive.

For a theoretical account of this sort of innovation, we turn to Daft and Weick's (1984) discussion of interpretive innovation. They propose a matrix of four different kinds of organization, each characterized by its relationship to its environment. They name these relationships "undirected viewing," "conditioned viewing," "discovering," and "enacting." Only the last two concern us here. It is important to note that Daft and Weick too see the community and not the individual "inventor" as the central unit of analysis in understanding innovating practice.

The *discovering organization* is the archetype of the conventional innovative organization, one which responds—often with great efficiency—to changes it detects in its environment. The organization presupposes an essentially prestructured environment and implicitly assumes that there is a correct response to any condition it discovers there. By contrast, the *enacting organization* is proactive and highly interpretive. Not only does it respond to its environment, but also, in a fundamental way, it creates many of the conditions to which it must respond. Daft and Weick (1984) describe enacting organizations as follows:

> These organizations construct their own environments. They gather information by trying new behaviors and seeing what happens. They experiment, test, and stimulate, and they ignore precedent, rules, and traditional expectations. (p. 288)

Innovation, in this view, is not simply a response to empirical observations of the environment. The source of innovation lies on the interface between an organization and its environment. And the process of innovating involves actively constructing a conceptual framework, imposing it on the environment, and reflecting on their interaction. With few changes, this could be a description of the activity of inventive, noncanonical groups, such as Orr's reps, who similarly "ignore precedent, rules, and traditional expectations" and break conventional boundaries. Like story telling, enacting is a process of interpretive sense making and controlled change.

A brief example of enacting can be seen in the introduction of the IBM Mag-I memory typewriter "as a new way of organizing office work" (Pava, cited in Barley, 1988). In order to make sense and full use of the power of this typewriter, the conditions in which it was to be used had to be reconceived. In the old conception of office work, the potential of the machine could not be realized. In a newly conceived understanding of office practice, however, the machine could prove highly innovative. Though this new conception could not be achieved without the new machine, the new machine could not be fully realized without the conception. The two changes went along together. Neither is wholly either cause or effect. Enacting organizations differ from discovering ones in that in this reciprocal way, instead of waiting for changed practices to emerge and responding, they enable them to emerge and anticipate their effects.

Reregistering the environment is widely recognized as a powerful source of innovation that moves organizations beyond the paradigms in which they begin their analysis and within which, without such a reformation, they must inevitably end it. This is the problem which Deetz and Kersten (1983) describe as closure: "Many organizations fail because . . . closure prohibits adaptation to current social conditions" (p. 166). Putnam (1983) argues that closure-generating structures appear to be "fixtures that exist independent of the processes that create and transform them" (p. 36). Interpretive or enacting organizations, aware as they are that their environment is not a given, can potentially adopt new viewpoints that allow them to see beyond the closure-imposing boundary of a single worldview.

The question remains, however, how is this reregistering brought about by organizations that seem inescapably trapped within their own worldview? We are claiming that the actual noncanonical practices of interstitial communities are continually developing new interpretations of the world because they have a practical rather than formal connection to that world. (For a theoretical account of the way practice drives change in worldview, see Bloch, 1977.) To pursue our connection with the work of the reps, closure is the likely result of rigid adherence to the reps' training and documentation and the formal account of work that they encompass. In order to get on with their work, reps overcome closure by reregistering their interpretation of the machine and its ever changing milieu. Rejection of a canonical, predetermined view and the construction through narration of an alternative view, such as Orr describes, involve, at heart, the complex intuitive process of bringing the communicative, community schema into harmony with the environment by reformulating both. The potential of such innovation is, however, lost to an organization that remains blind to noncanonical practice.

An enacting organization must also be capable of reconceiving not only its environment but also its own identity, for in a significant sense the two are mutually constitutive. Again, this reconceptualization is something that people who develop noncanonical practices are continuously doing, forging their own and their community's identity in their own terms so that they can break out of the restrictive hold of the formal descriptions of practice. Enacting organizations similarly regard both their environment and themselves as in some sense unanalyzed and therefore malleable. They do not assume that there is an ineluctable structure, a "right" answer, or a universal view to be discovered; rather, they continually look for innovative ways to impose new structure, ask new questions, develop a new view, become a new organization. By asking different questions, by seeking different *sorts* of explanations, and by looking from different points of view, different answers emerge—indeed different environments and different organizations mutually reconstitute each other dialectically or reciprocally. Daft and Weick (1984) argue, the interpretation can "shape the environment more than the environment shapes the interpretation" (p. 287).

Carlson's attempts to interest people in the idea of dry photocopying—xerography—provide an example of organizational tendencies to resist enacting innovation. Carlson and the Batelle Institute, which backed his research, approached most of the major innovative corporations of the time—RCA, IBM, A. B. Dick, Kodak. All turned down the idea of a dry copier. They did not reject a flawed machine. Indeed, they all agreed that it worked. But they rejected the *concept* of an office copier. They could see no use for it. Even when Haloid bought the patent, the marketing firms they hired consistently reported that the new device had no role in office practice (Dessauer, 1971). In some sense it was necessary both for Haloid to reconceive itself (as Xerox) and for Xerox's machine to help bring about a reconceptualization of an area of office practice for the new machine to be put into manufacture and use.

What the evaluations saw was that an expensive machine was not needed to make a record copy of original documents. For the most part, carbon paper already did that admirably and cheaply. What they failed to see was that a copier allowed the proliferation of copies and of copies of copies. The quantitative leap in copies and their importance independent of the original then produced a qualitative leap in the way they were used. They no longer served merely as records of an original. Instead, they participated in the productive interactions of organizations' members in a unprecedented way. (See Latour's, 1986, description of the organizational role of "immutable mobiles.") Only in use in the office, enabling and enhancing new forms of work, did the copier forge the conceptual lenses under which its value became inescapable.

It is this process of seeing the world anew that allows organizations reciprocally to see themselves anew and to overcome discontinuities in their environment and their structure. As von Hippel (1988), Barley (1988), and others point out, innovating is not always radical. Incremental improvements occur throughout an innovative organization. Enacting and innovating can be conceived of as at root sense-making, congruence-seeking, identity-building activities of the sort engaged in by the reps. Innovating and learning in daily activity lie at one end of a continuum of innovating practices that stretches to radical innovation cultivated in research laboratories at the far end.

Alternative worldviews, then, do not lie in the laboratory or strategic planning office alone, condemning everyone else in the organization to submit to a unitary culture. Alternatives are inevitably distributed throughout all the different communities that make up the organization. For it is the organization's communities, at all levels, who are in contact with the environment and involved in interpretive sense making, congruence finding, and adapting. It is from any site of such interactions that new insights can be coproduced. If an organizational core overlooks or curtails the enacting in its midst by ignoring or disrupting its communities-of-practice, it threatens its own survival in two ways. It will not only threaten to destroy the very working and learning practices by which it, knowingly or unknowingly, survives. It will also cut itself off from a major source of potential innovation that inevitably arises in the course of that working and learning.

4. CONCLUSION: ORGANIZATIONS AS COMMUNITIES-OF-COMMUNITIES

The complex of contradictory forces that put an organization's assumptions and core beliefs in direct conflict with members' working, learning, and innovating arises from a thorough misunderstanding of what working, learning, and innovating are. As a result of such misunderstandings, many modern processes and technologies, particularly those designed to downskill, threaten the robust working, learning, and innovating communities and practice of the workplace. Between Braverman's (1974) pessimistic view and Adler's (1987) optimistic one, lies Barley's (1988) complex argument, pointing out that the intent to downskill does not *necessarily* lead to downskilling (as Orr's reps show). But the intent to downskill may first drive noncanonical practice and communities yet further underground so that the insights gained through work are more completely hidden from the organization as a whole. Then later changes or reorganizations, whether or not intended to downskill, may disrupt what they do not notice. The gap between espoused and actual practice may become too large for noncanonical practices to bridge.

To foster working, learning, and innovating, an organization must close that gap. To do so, it needs to reconceive of itself as a community-of-communities, acknowledging in the process the many noncanonical communities in its midst. It must see beyond its canonical abstractions of practice to the rich, full-blooded activities themselves. And it must legitimize and support the myriad enacting activities perpetrated by its different members. This support cannot be intrusive, or it risks merely bringing potential innovators under the restrictive influence of the existing canonical view. Rather, as others have argued (Hedberg, 1981; Nystrom & Starbuck, 1984; Schein, 1990) communities-of-practice must be allowed some latitude to shake themselves free of received wisdom.

A major entailment of this argument may be quite surprising. Conventional wisdom tends to hold that large organizations are particularly poor at innovating and adapting. Tushman and Anderson (1988), for example, argue justifiably that the *typical,* large organization is unlikely to produce discontinuous innovation. But size may not be the single determining feature here. Large, *atypical,* enacting organizations have the potential to be highly innovative and adaptive. Within an organization perceived as a collective of communities, not simply of individuals, in which enacting experiments are legitimate, separate community perspectives can be amplified by interchanges among communities. Out of this friction of competing ideas can come the sort of improvisational sparks necessary for igniting organizational innovation. Thus large organizations, *reflectively structured,* are perhaps particularly well positioned to be highly innovative and to deal with discontinuities. If their internal communities have a reasonable degree of autonomy and independence from the dominant worldview, large organizations might actually accelerate innovation. Such organizations are uniquely positioned to generate innovative discontinuities incrementally, thereby diminishing the disruptiveness of the periodic radical reorganization that Nadler (1988) calls "frame breaking." This occurs when conventional organizations swing wholesale from one paradigm to another (see also Bartunek, 1984). An organization whose core is aware that it is the synergistic aggregate of agile, semiautonomous, self-constituting communities and not a brittle monolith is likely to be capable of extensible "frame bending" well beyond conventional breaking point.

The important interplay of separate communities with independent (though interrelated) worldviews may in part account for von Hippel's (1988) account of the sources of innovation and other descriptions of the innovative nature of business alliances. Von Hippel argues that sources of innovation can lie outside an organization among its customers and suppliers. Emergent communities of the sort we have outlined that span the boundaries of an organization would then seem a likely conduit of external and innovative views into an organization. Similarly, the alliances Powell (1990) describes bring together different organizations with different interpretive schemes so that the composite group they make up has several enacting options to choose from. Because the separate communities enter as independent members of an alliance rather than as members of a rigid hierarchy, the alternative conceptual viewpoints are presumably legitimate and do not get hidden from the core. There is no concealed noncanonical practice where there is no concealing canonical practice.

The means to harness innovative energy in any enacting organization or alliance must ultimately be considered in the design of organizational architecture and the ways communities are linked to each other. This architecture should preserve and enhance the healthy autonomy of communities, while simultaneously building an interconnectedness through which to disseminate the results of separate communities' experiments. In some form or another the stories that support learning-in-working and innovation should be allowed to circulate. The technological potential to support this distribution— e-mail, bulletin boards, and other devices that are capable of supporting narrative exchanges—is available. But narratives, as we have argued, are embedded in the social system in which they arise and are used. They cannot simply be uprooted and repackaged for circulation without becoming prey to exactly those problems that beset the old abstracted canonical accounts.

Moreover, information cannot be assumed to circulate freely just because technology to support circulation is available (Feldman & March, 1981). Eckert (1989), for instance, argues that information travels differently within different socio-economic groups. Organizational assumptions that given the "right" medium people will exchange information freely overlook the way in which certain socio-economic groups, organizations, and in particular, corporations, implicitly treat information as a commodity to be hoarded and exchanged. Working-class groups, Eckert contends, do pass information freely and Orr (1990a) notes that the reps are remarkably open with each other about what they know. *Within* these communities, news travels fast; community knowledge is readily available to community members. But these communities must function within corporations that treat information as a commodity and that have superior bargaining power in negotiating the terms of exchange. In such unequal conditions, internal communities cannot reasonably be expected to surrender their knowledge freely.

As we have been arguing throughout, to understand the way information is constructed and travels within an organization, it is first necessary to understand the different communities that are formed within it and the distribution of power among them. Conceptual reorganization to accommodate learning-in-working and innovation, then, must stretch from the level of individual communities-of-practice and the technology and practices used there to the level of the overarching organizational architecture, the community-of-communities.

It has been our unstated assumption that a unified understanding of working, learning, and innovating is potentially highly beneficial, allowing, it seems likely, a synergistic collaboration rather than a conflicting separation among workers, learners, and innovators. But similarly, we have left unstated the companion assumption that attempts to foster such synergy through a conceptual reorganization will produce enormous difficulties from the perspective of the conventional workplace. Work and learning are set out in formal descriptions so that people (and organizations) can be held accountable; groups are organized to define responsibility; organizations are bounded to enhance concepts of competition; peripheries are closed off to maintain secrecy and privacy. Changing the way these things are arranged will produce problems as well as benefits. An examination of both problems and benefits has been left out of this paper, whose single purpose has been to show where constraints and resources lie, rather than the rewards and costs of deploying them. Our argument is simply that for working, learning, and innovating to thrive collectively depends on linking these three, in theory and in practice, more closely, more realistically, and more reflectively than is generally the case at present.

Acknowledgments

This paper was written at the Institute for Research on Learning with the invaluable help of many of our colleagues, in particular Jean Lave, Julian Orr, and Etienne Wenger, whose work, with that of Daft and Weick, provides the canonical texts on which we based our commentary.

NOTES

1. For a historical overview of anthropology of the workplace, see Burawoy (1979).

2. Not all the blame should be laid on the managers' desk. As several anthropologists, including Suchman (1987a) and Bourdieu (1977) point out, "informants" often describe their jobs in canonical terms though they carry them out in noncanonical ways. Lave (1988) argues that informants, like most people in our society, tend to privilege abstract knowledge. Thus they describe their actions in its terms.

REFERENCES

Adler, P. S. (1987). Automation and skill: New directions. *International Journal of Technology Management, 2*(5/6), 761-771.

Barley, S. R. (1988). Technology, power, and the social organization of work: Towards a pragmatic theory of skilling and deskilling. *Research in the Sociology of Organizations, 6,* 33-80.

Bartunek, J. M. (1984). Changing interpretive schemes and organizational restructuring: The example of a religious order. *Administrative Science Quarterly, 29,* 355-372.

Bourdieu, P. (1977). *Outline of a theory of practice* (R. Nice, Trans.). Cambridge, MA: Cambridge University Press.

Bloch, M. (1977). The past and the present in the present. *Man [NS], 12,* 278-292.

Braverman, H. (1974). *Labor and monopoly capitalism: The degradation of work in the twentieth century.* New York: Monthly Review Press.

Brown, J. S., & Duguid, P. (in press). Enacting design. In P. Adler (Ed.), *Designing automation for usability.* New York: Oxford University Press.

Brown, J. S., Collins, A., & Duguid, P. (1989). Situated cognition and the culture of learning. *Education Researcher, 18*(1), 32-42.

Burawoy, M. (1979). The anthropology of industrial work. *Annual Review of Anthropology, 8,* 231-266.

Daft, R. L., & Weick, K. E. (1984). Toward a model of organizations as interpretation systems. *Academy of Management Review, 9*(2), 284-295.

Deetz, S. A., & Kersten, A. (1983). Critical models of interpretive research. In L. L. Putnam & M. E. Pacanowsky (Eds.), *Communication and organizations: An interpretive approach.* Beverly Hills, CA: Sage.

Dessauer, J. H. (1971). *My years with Xerox: The billions nobody wanted.* Garden City, NY: Doubleday.

Eckert, P. (1989). *Jocks and burnouts.* New York: Teachers College Press.

Feldman, M. S., & March, J. G. (1981). Information in organizations as signal and symbol. *Administrative Science Quarterly, 26,* 171-186.

Geertz, C. (1973). *Interpretation of cultures: Selected essays.* New York: Basic Books.

Goodman, P., & Associates. (1988). *Designing effective work groups.* San Francisco: Jossey-Bass.

Hackman, J. R. (Ed.). (1990). *Groups that work (and those that don't).* San Francisco: Jossey-Bass.

Hedberg, B. (1981). How organizations learn and unlearn. In P. C. Nystrom & W. H. Starbuck (Eds.), *Handbook of organizational design* (Vol. 1, pp. 3-27). New York: Oxford University Press.

Hedberg, B., Nystrom, P. C., & Starbuck, W. H. (1976). Designing organizations to match tomorrow. In P. C. Nystrom & W. H. Starbuck (Eds.), *Prescriptive models of organizations* (pp. 41-65). Amsterdam: North-Holland.

Hutchins, E. (1991). Organizing work by adaptation. *Organization Science, 2*(1), 14-39.

Hutchins, E. (in press). Learning to navigate. In S. Chalkin & J. Lave (Eds.), *Situated learning.* Cambridge, UK: Cambridge University Press.

Jordan, B. (1989). Cosmopolitical obstetrics: Some insights from the training of traditional midwives. *Social Science and Medicine, 28*(9), 925-944.

Latour, B. (1986). Visualization and cognition: Thinking with eyes and hands. *Knowledge and Society, 6,* 1-40.

Lave, J. (1988). *Cognition in practice: Mind, mathematics, and culture in everyday life.* New York: Cambridge University Press.

Lave, J., & Wenger, E. (1990). *Situated learning: Legitimate peripheral participation* (IRL report 90-0013). Palo Alto, CA: Institute for Research on Learning.

Levi-Strauss, C. (1966). *The savage mind.* Chicago: University of Chicago Press.

Martin, J. (1982). Stories and scripts in organizational settings. In A. H. Hastorf & A. M. Isen (Eds.), *Cognitive and social psychology* (pp. 255-305). Amsterdam: Elsevier.

Nadler, D. (1988). Organizational frame bending: Types of change in the complex organization. In R. H. Kilman, T. J. Covin, & Associates (Eds.), *Corporate transformation: Revitalizing organizations for a competitive world.* San Francisco: Jossey-Bass.

Nystrom, P. C., & Starbuck, W. H. (1984, Spring). To avoid organizational crises, unlearn. *Organizational Dynamics,* pp. 53-65.

Orr, J. (1987a, June). Narratives at work: Story telling as cooperative diagnostic activity. *Field Service Manager,* pp. 47-60.

Orr, J. (1987b). *Talking about machines: Social aspects of expertise.* Report for the Intelligent Systems Laboratory, Xerox Palo Alto Research Center, Palo Alto, CA.

Orr, J. (1990a). *Talking about machines: An ethnography of a modern job.* Doctoral dissertation, Cornell University.

Orr, J. (1990b). Sharing knowledge, celebrating identity: War stories and community memory in a service culture. In D. S. Middleton & D. Edwards (Eds.), *Collective remembering: Memory in society* (pp. 169-189). Beverly Hills, CA: Sage.

Pea, R. D. (1990). *Distributed cognition* (IRL Report 90-0015). Palo Alto, CA: Institute for Research on Learning.

Powell, W. W. (1990). Neither market nor hierarchy: Network forms of organization. In B. M. Staw & L. L. Cummings (Eds.), *Research in organizational behavior* (pp. 295-336). Greenwich, CT: JAI.

Putnam, L. L. (1983). The interpretive perspective: An alternative to functionalism. In L. L. Putnam & M. E. Pacanowsky (Eds.), *Communication and organizations: An interpretive approach.* Beverly Hills, CA: Sage.

Reddy, M. J. (1979). The conduit metaphor. In A. Ortony (Ed.), *Metaphor and thought* (pp. 284-324). Cambridge, UK: Cambridge University Press.

Ryle, G. (1954). *Dilemmas: The tarner lectures.* Cambridge, UK: Cambridge University Press.

Schein, E. H. (1990). Organizational culture. *American Psychologist, 45*(2), 109-119.

Scribner, S. (1984). Studying working intelligence. In B. Rogoff & J. Lave (Eds.), *Everyday cognition: Its development in social context.* Cambridge, MA: Harvard University Press.

Suchman, L. (1987a). *Plans and situated actions: The problem of human-machine communication.* New York: Cambridge University Press.

Suchman, L. (1987b). Common sense in interface design. *Techné, 1*(1), 38-40.

Tushman, M. L., & Anderson, P. (1988). Technological discontinuities and organization environments. In A. M. Pettigrew (Ed.), *The management of strategic change.* Oxford: Basil Blackwell.

von Hippel, E. (1988). *The sources of innovation.* New York: Oxford University Press.

Zuboff, S. (1988). *In the age of the smart machine: The future of work and power.* New York: Basic Books.

4

Organizational Learning Curves

A Method for Investigating Intra-Plant Transfer of Knowledge Acquired Through Learning by Doing

DENNIS EPPLE
LINDA ARGOTE
RUKMINI DEVADAS

This paper illustrates how a learning-curve model can be generalized to investigate potential explanations of organizational learning. The paper examines the hypothesis that knowledge acquired through learning by doing is embodied in an organization's technology by analyzing the amount of transfer that occurs across shifts within a plant. If knowledge becomes completely embodied in technology, transfer across shifts should be complete since both shifts use the same technology. Methods that can be used for studying intra-plant transfer of knowledge are presented. The methods are illustrated by analyzing data from a plant that began production with one shift and then added a second shift several months into the production program. Three aspects of transfer are analyzed: (1) carry forward of knowledge when the plant makes the transition from one to two shifts, (2) transfer across shifts after both shifts are operating, and (3) transfer across time. Results indicate that substantial, but less than complete, transfer of knowledge occurred when the second shift was introduced. Once both shifts were operating, partial transfer across them occurred. Implications of the results for a theory of organizational learning and practical applications are discussed.

(LEARNING CURVES; PRODUCTIVITY;
TECHNOLOGY TRANSFER)

This chapter appeared originally in *Organization Science,* Vol. 2, No. 1, February 1991. Copyright © 1991, The Institute of Management Sciences.

OVERVIEW

As organizations produce more of a product, the unit cost of production typically decreases at a decreasing rate. This pattern, or close variants of it, has been named the "learning curve" or "experience curve" or "progress curve," and the realization of improvements in productivity through experience with production has been termed "learning by doing."

The presence of a learning curve has been documented in the manufacture of a wide variety of products (Yelle, 1979). There is considerable variation, however, in the rate at which organizations learn (Argote & Epple, 1990; Dutton & Thomas, 1984; Hayes & Clark, 1986; Yelle, 1979). This paper illustrates how the conventional learning-curve model can be generalized to investigate potential explanations of this variation.

RESEARCH ON
ORGANIZATIONAL LEARNING CURVES

Since Wright's (1936) early piece on organizational learning curves, much of the work on organizational learning curves has focused on investigating the functional form of the relationship between unit cost and cumulative output, and on analyzing the relationship in different industries (Yelle, 1979). Reviews can be found in Yelle (1979) and Dutton and Thomas (1984).

Promising starts have been made in developing a theory of organizational learning (Muth, 1986), but the research has not progressed to the point of explaining the variation of learning rates observed across organizations. Further, despite much speculation about what accounts for the phenomenon of organizational learning curves, little empirical evidence about these factors has emerged (Dutton & Thomas, 1984; Lieberman, 1984; Yelle, 1979). Factors suggested as being responsible for organizational learning include: increased proficiency of individuals, including direct labor, management, and engineering staff; greater standardization of procedures; improvements in scheduling; improvements in the flow of materials; improvements in product design; improvements in tooling, layout, materials, and equipment; better coordination; division of labor and specialization; incentives; leadership; and learning by firms outside the focal firm, including suppliers and other firms in the industry (e.g., see Hayes & Wheelwright, 1984; Hirsch, 1952; Joskow & Rose, 1985; Wright, 1936).

Yelle (1979) organized these potential explanations for organizational learning into two general categories, labor learning and organizational learning, including technological learning. The distinction between individual and organizational learning is a useful heuristic. At one extreme, if productivity is invariant to worker experience, learning is embodied entirely in the organization. At the other, if the organization is unchanging and learning increases, learning is embodied entirely in workers. Intermediate cases, however, are possible. If improvements in organization provide the potential for higher productivity, but experienced workers are required to exploit the potential, then knowledge is embodied in both individuals and the organization. To the categories of individual and organizational learning, we would add a third category: learning from the experience of others since organizations may benefit from knowledge acquired by others (Dutton & Thomas, 1984; Levitt & March, 1988; Levy, 1965).

Alternative explanations for organizational learning yield differing implications as to where knowledge acquired by learning by doing resides and for the extent to which knowledge transfers within and across firms. For example, suppose learning is embodied in improvements in technology (plant layout, equipment, computer software and other physical aspects of the production process). Since both shifts at a plant use the same technology, knowledge embodied in physical facilities and equipment should be fully transferred both from the period of one-shift-a-day operation to the period of two-shift-a-day operation and from one shift to another during the operation of two shifts.

As a second example, if industrial learning is embodied primarily in individual production workers, then transfer across shifts may be limited. Carry forward from the period of one-shift-a-day operation to the period of two-shift-a-day operation will depend on the training that new workers receive, their previous experience, and on the relative proportions of experienced workers assigned to the new crews formed when the second shift is introduced. These examples illustrate ways in which empirical regularities regarding the accumulation and transfer of knowledge can potentially illuminate the learning process.

Transfer of learning has been examined by psychologists for many years. Psychologists typically examine how performing one task affects the performance of another task by the same individual. More recently, researchers have begun to examine the transfer of knowledge across different organizations (Argote, Beckman, & Epple, 1990; Joskow & Rose, 1985; Zimmerman, 1982). These researchers examine whether productivity gains associated with experience can be transferred across firms. Zimmerman found evidence of transfer of learning in the construction of nuclear power plants: industry experience was a significant predictor of the unit cost of construction. Firm experience, however, was more significant than industry experience in the study. Joskow and Rose found that architect-engineer experience and utility experience were significant predictors of the costs of constructing coal-burning generating units while industry experience was not significant.

Argote et al. found that organizations beginning operation at a later date were more productive than those with early start dates. Once organizations began production, however, they did not appear to benefit from knowledge acquired through production at other organizations.

Day and Montgomery (1983) emphasized the importance of estimating the amount of transfer from shared experience. They indicated that sharing of experience is usually assessed by applying expert judgment to each cost element. They suggested that the paucity of published research on the topic of shared experience is due to the formidable amount of work entailed in such an element-by-element assessment. Our approach for studying shared experience does not require such disaggregated analysis.

Researchers have also examined transfer across time within organizations. Baloff (1970) and Hirsch (1952) presented suggestive empirical evidence that forgetting occurred when the production process was interrupted in organizations. Argote et al. (1990) found evidence of depreciation of knowledge in shipbuilding after controlling for factor inputs. Recent output was a more important predictor of current production than cumulative output.

In addition to furthering understanding of the learning process, methods for studying the transfer of learning can provide important information for managerial decision making regarding the trade-off between number of plants to operate and number of shifts per plant. Information about the extent to which knowledge carries forward from a period of operating with one shift to a period of operating with multiple shifts and the extent of transfer across shifts when multiple shifts are operating can be useful in deciding when to make the transition from one-shift-a-day to multiple-shift-a-day operation.

Thus, a goal of this paper is to demonstrate how a conventional learning curve can be generalized to investigate factors responsible for organizational learning. We focus on the transfer of knowledge across shifts at a plant. Three aspects of transfer are investigated: (1) carry forward of knowledge when the plant makes the transition from one-shift-a-day operation to two shifts per day, (2) transfer across shifts after two-shift-a-day operation is underway, and (3) transfer across time or the persistence of knowledge.

THE CONVENTIONAL
INDUSTRIAL LEARNING CURVE

To illustrate our approach and its relationship to the conventional learning curve, we present and estimate a sequence of increasingly general models, beginning with the conventional learning curve model.

The learning curve is commonly written in the form:

$$l/q = CQ^{-\gamma} \qquad (1)$$

where, at each date, q denotes output, l denotes hours worked, Q is cumulative output, and C and γ are constants.[1] The larger the coefficient γ, the more rapidly productivity increases due to learning.

The rate of learning is often expressed in terms of the progress ratio which is related to γ in equation (1) by

$$p = 2^{-\gamma}. \qquad (2)$$

This ratio indicates the percentage by which average labor hours per unit fall with a doubling of cumulative output. For example, if $\gamma = 0.3$, then $p = 0.8$, indicating that unit labor costs fall to 80% of their previous level when cumulative output doubles.

For purposes of comparison with more general models developed below, we invert both sides of equation (1) and let $A = 1/C$ to obtain the equivalent form

$$q/l = AQ^{-\gamma}. \qquad (3)$$

To express equation (3) in a form estimable with data measured for discrete time intervals, we introduce time subscripts and an error term

$$q_t/l_t = AQ^{\gamma}_{t-1}e^{\varepsilon_t}. \qquad (4)$$

In our analysis, the unit of time is a week. Thus, q_t and l_t are respectively output and hours worked during week t. The term ε_t in equation (4) represents random factors affecting the production process.

The time subscript on Q_{t-1} indicates that cumulative output at the end of the previous week appears on the right-hand side of equation (4). Cumulative output is a proxy for knowledge acquired through past production. Thus, in the learning curve for a given week, it is natural to include cumulative output through the end of the previous week. Further, cumulative output through the end of week t is equal to cumulative output at the end of the previous week, plus production in week t: $Q_t = Q_{t-1} + q_t$. Thus, if Q_t rather than Q_{t-1} were included on the right-hand side of equation (4), current output q_t would appear not only on the left side of (4) but indirectly on the right-hand side as well. This would render least-squares estimation inappropriate and considerably complicate the estimation problem. Thus, on both logical and statistical grounds, inclusion of Q_{t-1} rather than Q_t on the right-hand side of (4) is the preferred specification.

Taking logarithms of equation (4) and letting $a = \text{Ln}(A)$, we express the relationship in a form that is more convenient for estimation:

$$\text{Ln}(q_t / l_t) = a + \gamma \text{Ln } Q_{t-1} + \varepsilon_t . \tag{5}$$

DATA

Our data are from a North American truck plant producing a single vehicle. The plant, which is unionized, began production in the 1980s with one shift and added a second shift several months into the production program. Employees were trained initially on the first shift and then moved to the second shift. While some experienced employees moved to the second shift, proportionately fewer experienced employees worked on the second shift than on the first. We have weekly data beginning at the start of production for a period of 19 weeks of operation with one shift and 80 weeks of operation with two shifts.[2]

A learning curve plotted from our data is shown in Figure 4.1. This figure shows the characteristic learning curve pattern: the direct labor hours required per truck decreased at a decreasing rate as the cumulative number of trucks produced increased. The figure also shows the effect of adding the second shift. Direct labor hours per unit decreased until the second shift was introduced. Unit labor hours increased when the second shift was added (marked on horizontal axis of Figure 4.1). Unit costs then fell as the organization gained experience operating with both shifts.

ESTIMATION OF THE
CONVENTIONAL LEARNING-CURVE MODEL

The results from estimating equation (5) are reported in column (1) of Table 4.1.[3] This equation provides strong evidence of learning—output per person hour increases significantly with cumulative output as indicated by the highly significant estimate of γ.

We estimated equation (5) allowing for first-order autocorrelation of the residuals. Parameter η in Table 4.1 is the first-order autocorrelation coefficient, and it is highly significant.[4]

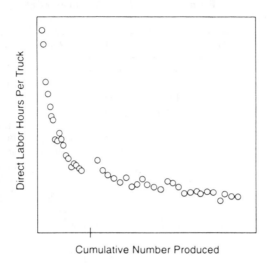

Figure 4.1. Relation Between Direct Labor Hours per Truck and Cumulative Number
       Produced
NOTE: Units are not shown to protect confidentiality of data.

RETURNS TO INCREASING LABOR HOURS

The conventional learning curve specification implies that, for a given
level of cumulative output, output per week increases proportionately with
hours worked per week. Diminishing returns to labor may eventually be
reached if larger and larger numbers of labor hours were added per week in
a fixed physical facility. To allow for this possibility, we write the production
function in the following more general form:[5]

$$\text{Ln } q_t = a + \alpha \text{ Ln } l_t + \gamma \text{ Ln } Q_{t-1} + \varepsilon_t . \tag{6}$$

A value of $\alpha < 1$ implies diminishing returns to labor, $\alpha = 1$ implies constant
returns to labor, and $\alpha > 1$ implies increasing returns. Equation (5) is the
special case of equation (6) in which $\alpha = 1$.

Column (2) of Table 4.1 is the result obtained from estimating equation
(6), again allowing for first-order autocorrelation.[6] The estimate of the
coefficient of labor hours is very close to one, suggesting that diminishing
returns to labor does not occur in these data.

TABLE 4.1 Coefficient Estimates for Several Formulations of the Learning Model

Coefficient	(1)	(2)	(3)	(4)	(5)	(6)
Learning	0.15	0.14	0.14	0.28	1.15	1.50
Parameter, γ	(0.02)	(0.02)	(0.02)	(0.04)	(0.37)	(0.30)
Labor hours		1.03	1.02	1.02	1.02	0.94
Coefficient, α		(0.02)	(0.06)	(0.06)	(0.06)	(0.06)
Days per week			1.04	1.04	1.01	1.05
Coefficient, β			(0.02)	(0.02)	(0.02)	(0.02)
Depreciation				0.92	1.0	0.99
Parameter, γ				(0.04)	(0.08)	(0.04)
Learning Decline					−0.04	−0.06
Parameter, δ					(0.02)	(0.01)
Carry Forward						0.69
Parameter, ρ						(0.10)
Transfer						0.56
Parameter, θ						(0.31)
Autocorrelation	0.79	0.79	0.78	0.67	0.39	0.20
Coefficient, η	(0.05)	(0.05)	(0.05)	(0.06)	(0.09)	(0.10)
R^2	0.9756	0.9946	0.9946	0.9951	0.9958	0.9962
Log Likelihood	187.66	189.27	189.35	193.99	201.49	207.36

NOTE: Standard errors are reported in parentheses beneath the coefficients. Coefficients γ, α, β, λ, and ρ are significantly different from 0 at $p < 0.001$. Coefficient δ has significance level $p = 0.05$ in column (5) and $p < 0.001$ in column (6). Coefficient θ has a significance level of approximately 0.07.

Diminishing returns to labor could be more pronounced with an increase in hours per shift than with an increase in shifts per week. This possibility is permitted by

$$\text{Ln } q_t = a + \alpha \text{ Ln } h_t + \beta \text{ Ln } n_t + \gamma \text{Ln } Q_{t-1} + \varepsilon_t. \qquad (7)$$

Here, h_t is hours per shift and n_t is shifts per week. By definition, $l_t = h_t n_t$. Thus when $\alpha = \beta$, equation (7) reduces to equation (6).

Column (3) of Table 4.1 is the result obtained from estimating equation (7), allowing for first-order autocorrelation. A likelihood ratio test contrasting the result in column (3) to that in column (2) reveals that α and β are not significantly different from each other (i.e., there is no evidence to reject the null hypothesis that $\alpha = \beta$). Thus, there is no evidence that the returns to increasing labor hours per shift are different from increasing shifts per week. These generalizations of the model do not alter the conclusion that significant learning occurs; productivity increases significantly with cumulative output.

DEPRECIATION OF KNOWLEDGE

Implicit in the conventional learning curve model and the generalizations discussed thus far is the assumption that knowledge acquired through learning by doing does not depreciate. The next generalization allows for the possibility that depreciation of knowledge occurs:

$$\text{Ln } q_t = a + \alpha \text{ Ln } h_t + \beta \text{ Ln } n_t + \gamma \text{ Ln } K_{t-1} + \varepsilon_t, \tag{8a}$$

where

$$K_t = \lambda K_{t-1} + q_t. \tag{8b}$$

This specification differs from (7) by allowing for the possibility that not all past knowledge is carried forward from one week to the next. In particular, if $\lambda < 1$ in equation (8b), then less than complete carry forward of knowledge from one period to the next occurs. If $\lambda = 1$, then $K_t = Q_t$, and this model reduces to equation (7).

To estimate equations (8a) and (8b), we first rewrite equation (8b) in the following equivalent form:

$$K_t = \sum_{s=1}^{t} \lambda^{t-s} q_s. \tag{8b'}$$

This expresses the stock of knowledge in terms of the history of production and the depreciation parameter λ, which is to be estimated. Substituting this result into (8a), we obtain

$$\text{Ln } q_t = a + \alpha \text{ Ln } h_t + \beta \text{ Ln } n_t + \gamma \text{ Ln} \left(\sum_{s=1}^{t-1} \gamma^{t-s-1} q_s \right) + \varepsilon_t. \tag{9}$$

This equation is clearly a highly nonlinear function of parameter λ. Hence, we estimate the model using maximum likelihood.[7]

Results from estimation of equation (9) are presented in column (4) of Table 4.1. The estimate of λ is significantly less than 1 ($p = 0.05$), suggesting that knowledge acquired through learning depreciates relatively rapidly over time. The estimated learning coefficient γ changes substantially when we allow for depreciation of knowledge. Changes in the coefficient γ are not surprising since the variable that γ multiplies changes substantially when depreciation of knowledge occurs.

CHANGING RATE OF LEARNING AS
THE STOCK OF KNOWLEDGE GROWS

The rate of learning may decline as the organization gains experience in production. Hence, we generalize the model as follows:

$$\text{Ln } q_t = a + \alpha \text{ Ln } h_t + \beta \text{ Ln } n_t + \gamma \text{ Ln } K_{t-1} + \delta(\text{Ln } K_{t-1})^2 + \varepsilon_t, \quad (10)$$

where K_t is defined as in (8b). In this equation, $\delta < 0$ implies that the rate of acquisition of knowledge declines as the stock of knowledge grows, and $\delta > 0$ implies an accelerating rate of acquisition of knowledge. If $\delta = 0$, then equation (10) reduces to equation (8a).[8]

Results from estimating this model are presented in column (5) of Table 4.1. These results suggest that the rate of acquisition of knowledge does indeed decline as the stock of knowledge increases, since δ is significantly less than zero. Moreover, with this specification, the estimated depreciation parameter is now 1.0, implying that little depreciation occurs. The value of γ changes markedly between columns (4) and (5) of Table 4.1. When the quadratic in $\text{Ln}K_{t-1}$ is introduced, learning is captured by the term $\gamma \text{ Ln}K_{t-1} + \delta(\text{Ln}K_{t-1})^2$. With this more general specification learning effects must take account of the values of both γ and δ. Hence, a change in γ is expected if δ is significantly different from zero—as it is in our estimates in column (5), Table 4.1.

A MODEL OF INTRA-PLANT
TRANSFER OF KNOWLEDGE

Our findings thus far on the rate of learning and depreciation of learning might also be due to incomplete carry forward of knowledge from the period of one-shift-a-day operation to the period of two-shift-a-day operation or to incomplete transfer of knowledge across shifts during the operation of both shifts. Our final generalizations of the model allow for incomplete carry forward of knowledge and incomplete transfer across shifts.

The equation relating production to inputs and knowledge is written on a per-shift basis as follows:

$$\text{Ln } q_{it} = a + \alpha \text{ Ln } h_{it} + \beta\text{Ln } n_{it} + \gamma \text{ Ln } K_{it-1} + \delta(\text{Ln } K_{it-1})^2 + \varepsilon_{it}. \quad (11a)$$

Subscript i may take on one of the three values: $i = 0$ denotes observations during the period of one-shift operation, $i = 1$ denotes shift one during the period of two-shift operation, and $i = 2$ denotes shift two during the period of two-shift operation.

Let S denote the last week of one-shift operation. The model of knowledge acquisition, retention, and transfer is

$$K_{0t} = \lambda K_{0t-1} + q_{0t}, \qquad\qquad t \leq S, \qquad\qquad (11b)$$

$$K_{iS} = \rho_i K_{0S}, \qquad\qquad i = 1, 2, \qquad\qquad (11c)$$

$$K_{it} = \lambda K_{it-1} + q_{it} + \theta_i q_{jt}, \qquad i, j = 1, 2, \qquad i \neq j; t \geq S + 1. \qquad (11d)$$

Equation (11b) applies during the period of one-shift operation exactly as before. Equations (11c) allow for partial carry forward of knowledge from the period of one-shift to the period of two-shift operation. If $\rho_i < 1$, less than complete carry forward to shift i occurs; if $\rho_i = 1$, full carry forward occurs. Equations (11d) apply during the period of two-shift operation. Parameter θ_i denotes the amount of transfer to shift i from shift j. If $\theta_i < 1$, less than complete transfer occurs; if $\theta_i = 1$, full transfer occurs.

With shift-level data, one can proceed with direct estimation of the model in equations (11). We do not have data disaggregated by shift for the plant we are studying. The model is estimable, however, for the special case in which the two shifts are treated symmetrically. Results for this case serve to illustrate our approach and prove to be quite suggestive.

Symmetric treatment of the two shifts involves two sets of assumptions. One set involves assumptions about values of the variables, namely, that hours per shift, days worked per week per shift, and random components are the same for the two shifts. That is,

$$h_t = h_{1t} = h_{2t,} \ n_{1t} = n_{2t} = n_t / 2, \text{ and } \varepsilon_{1t} = \varepsilon_{2t} = \varepsilon_t.$$

The assumptions about hours per shift and days per week are, we believe, close approximations. The assumption about the random shocks may be a good one where the shock is associated with labor relations, is caused by external events such as problems with parts and materials delivered by external suppliers, or is due to extended technical problems with equipment. Other shocks such as temporary equipment breakdowns will typically be shift-specific, and the quality of our assumption about these depends on the extent to which they average out across shifts during the course of a week.

The other set of symmetry assumptions involves the parameters that characterize carry forward and transfer of knowledge. We assume that the carry forward of knowledge from the period of one-shift-a-day production to the period of two-shift-a-day production is the same for the day as for the night shift, $\rho_1 = \rho_2 = \rho$, and that the transfer of knowledge across shifts after the start of two-shift-a-day production is symmetric, $\theta_1 = \theta_2 = \theta$.

It is useful to note that these symmetry assumptions are implicit in the conventional learning-curve model. In particular the model in (11) specialized to the case with full carry forward ($\rho_i = \rho_j = 1$) and complete transfer ($\theta_i = \theta_j = 1$) reduces to that in (10). Hence, the symmetric case is of particular interest to test.

With the above symmetry assumptions, the production function for $t > S$ becomes

$$\text{Ln}(q_t/2) = a + \alpha \, \text{Ln} \, h_t + \beta \, \text{Ln}(n_t/2) + \gamma \, \text{Ln} \, K_{t-1} + \delta (\text{Ln}K_{t-1})^2 + \varepsilon_t, \quad \text{12a}$$

and the accumulated stock of knowledge at date $t > S$ can be written as

$$K_t = \lambda \, K_{t-1} + (1 + \theta)\frac{q_t}{2}. \quad \text{12b}$$

The production function for $t \le S$ is equation (11a) with subscript $i = 0$, and the accumulated stock of knowledge for $t \le S$ is given in equation (11b).[9]

Results from estimation of the above model are presented in column (6) of Table 4.1. The results in Table 4.1 fit the data quite well,[10] the algebraic signs of the coefficients are all as anticipated, and the magnitudes of the coefficients are all quite reasonable. The estimated exponent of labor hours per shift, $\hat{\alpha} = 0.94$, is less than one, suggesting that the marginal product of labor decreases as labor hours per shift increases, as one would expect. However, this estimate is not significantly different from one so the hypothesis that output increases proportionately with labor hours per shift would not be rejected. The estimated exponent of days per week, $\hat{\beta} = 1.05$, is significantly greater than one, suggesting a modest increase in returns to increasing days worked per week.

The estimated exponents of the knowledge variable and the squared knowledge variable are $\hat{\gamma} = 1.5$ and $\hat{\delta} = -0.06$, and both are large and highly significant. These estimates indicate that learning by doing yields large productivity gains as production progresses and knowledge is accumulated, but that the rate of accumulation of knowledge declines as the stock of knowledge grows. Using the results in Table 4.1 we calculated that, for a given level of labor inputs, a 2.9 fold increase in output per week would have occurred between the first week in our sample and the same week one year later—a remarkable 190% growth in productivity in one year.

The remaining parameters are of particular interest in characterizing the transfer and depreciation of learning. The estimated carry forward from one to two-shift-per-day operation is given by $\hat{\rho} = 0.69$. This parameter estimate is significantly greater than zero and significantly less than one ($p < 0.001$). It indicates that 69% of knowledge acquired during the period of one-shift-a-day operation is carried forward to the period of two-shift-per-day operation.

The estimated transfer between day and night shifts during the period after two-shift-a-day operation begins is given by $\hat{\theta} = 0.56$. This parameter indicates that 56% of the knowledge acquired on one shift is transferred to the other. The estimate of $\hat{\theta}$ is significantly different from zero at $p \approx 0.07$ and significantly less than one at $p \approx 0.08$. Thus, this result suggests that roughly half of the knowledge acquired on one shift is transferred to the other shift once both shifts are in operation.

The estimated persistence parameter is $\hat{\gamma} = 0.99$. A weekly depreciation parameter of this magnitude translates into substantial depreciation of knowledge over the course of a year. Taken literally, this result implies that 60% ($= 0.99^{52}$) of the stock of knowledge at the beginning of a year would remain at the end of the year if the stock were not replenished by continuing production. However, it is important to note that the estimate of this parameter is not very precise. The estimate is not significantly different from the case of no depreciation, $\lambda = 1$. Moreover, the null hypothesis that $\lambda = 0.95$—a very rapid weekly rate of depreciation—would not be rejected at the 0.10 level. Thus, there is not sufficient information in the data to obtain a precise estimate of the depreciation parameter.

Two further generalizations of the model were investigated. A time trend was included as a proxy for technical progress to investigate the possibility that part of the productivity increase might be due to increasing technical knowledge acquired from the larger environment. The coefficient of time is both small (0.002) and statistically insignificant ($p \geq 0.15$). While this proxy is imperfect, it provides no evidence to suggest that the productivity increases realized at this plant are due to importation of knowledge from outside the plant.

The other generalization was to investigate the possibility of higher-order autocorrelation of the residuals. The second-order autocorrelation coefficient is small (0.03) and statistically insignificant ($p \geq 0.7$). There is no evidence of higher-order autocorrelation.

It is standard industrial practice to assume a learning curve of the form in equation (1). This implicitly assumes that $\alpha = \beta = \lambda = \rho = \theta = 1$ and $\delta = 0$. Performing a likelihood ratio test of the model in column (6) of Table 4.1 against that in column (1), we find that these constraints are very strongly rejected ($\chi^2_6 = 39.4$, $p \leq 0.0001$). Thus, the more general formulation suggested here yields a very substantial improvement in the fit to the data.[11]

DISCUSSION

The results tell an interesting story regarding intra-plant transfer of knowledge. Substantial but less than complete transfer of knowledge occurred at the time the second shift was introduced. The hypothesis of complete transfer ($\rho = 1$) is strongly rejected ($p < 0.01$). Once production with two shifts is underway, the evidence suggests that partial transfer occurred. The hypothesis of complete transfer ($\theta = 1$) is rejected ($p \approx 0.08$), and the hypothesis of no transfer ($\theta = 0$) is rejected at $p \approx 0.07$. The hypothesis of complete transfer both at the time of startup and thereafter ($\rho = 1$ and $\theta = 1$) is very strongly rejected ($p \leq 0.005$).

These results provide evidence against the hypothesis that knowledge becomes completely embodied in the technology (tooling, programming, assembly line layout and balancing, and so on). If it did become so embodied, then transfer of knowledge over time and across shifts would be complete since both shifts use the same production facilities. Our results suggest that part, but not all, of the accumulated knowledge becomes embodied in the organization's technology.

Our results indicate that a substantial proportion of knowledge carried forward from the period of one-shift to the period of two-shift operation. A large investment in training was made before the second shift was introduced. The substantial amount of knowledge carried forward to two-shift-a-day operation may reflect this investment in training.[12] If this is correct, it leaves open the question of whether the benefits of training are in the development of individual skills, development of managerial skills, and/or development of a network of coordination and communication among members of the workforce. Development of strategies for assessing the relative importance of these factors is an important issue for future research.

It is of interest to contrast our results on intra-plant transfer of knowledge in automotive production to results on inter-plant transfer of knowledge in shipbuilding (Argote et al., 1990). The investigation of shipbuilding indicated that plants starting production later had higher initial productivity levels than plants starting earlier. This is analogous to our finding of partial carry forward of knowledge in the change from one to two shifts. Once shipyards began production, they did not benefit from knowledge acquired at other yards. Thus, our results suggest that greater transfer across shifts within a plant occurs than across production facilities that are geographically separated.

Our findings on persistence in automotive production also provide an interesting supplement to those found in shipbuilding. In shipbuilding, estimated monthly persistence parameters were in the range from 0.65 to 0.88. By contrast, our estimate for automotive production suggests little evidence of depreciation. However, the estimate in the case of automotive production is not sufficiently precise to permit us to reject weekly depreciation parameters on the order of 0.95—which imply monthly depreciation rates on the order of 0.81 (= 0.95^4). These are within the range of values of monthly parameters estimated for shipbuilding.

CONCLUSIONS

Within the confines of the assumptions we have made, our model fits the data quite well. Our estimates yield interesting implications regarding intra-plant transfer of learning. The results suggest that our approach to investigating intra-plant transfer has promise for further application. Such applications have the potential both to illuminate the nature of the learning process and to provide valuable information for managers about the extent to which knowledge can be shared within production facilities.

For managers, the extent of transfer provides important information for decisions about trade-offs between multiple-plant operation and multiple-shift operation within individual plants. In addition, methods for quantifying the extent to which knowledge is carried forward from one-shift to two-shift operations can provide the basis for managers to assess the effectiveness of alternative strategies to enhance the amount of knowledge that is carried forward. Similarly, the ability to quantify the extent of transfer across shifts may prove valuable in investigating the effectiveness of measures to increase transfer across shifts.

Field research on learning almost inevitably involves investigating non-experimental data. A challenge for such research is to find quasi-experiments in the field that make it possible to control for some factors while varying others. Since both shifts within a plant use the same equipment and physical facilities, the effects of equipment and facilities are held constant when intra-plant transfer is investigated. In addition, in most manufacturing environments, including the one we study, the same product is produced by both shifts. Hence, the effects of product characteristics are held constant as well. Studying intra-plant transfer in such settings provides an opportunity to disentangle the extent to which learning becomes embodied in the technology from learning that does not. This is what makes the study of intra-plant transfer valuable from the standpoint of researching the learning process.

Acknowledgments

We gratefully acknowledge the support of the National Science Foundation's Decision, Risk, and Management Science Program (Grant Numbers SES-8808711 and SES-9009930) and of the Center for the Management of Technology and Information in Organizations at Carnegie Mellon University. We wish to thank Paul Goodman, Tim McGuire, Tom Morton, and the reviewers for their very helpful comments. An earlier draft of this paper was presented at the ORSA/INFORMS meeting, New York, October 1989.

NOTES

1. In industrial applications, the learning curve is often written

$$L/Q = BQ^{-\gamma} \tag{1'}$$

where, at each date throughout the production program, Q is cumulative output, L is cumulative hours worked, and B and γ are constants. Equation (1) of the text derives from (1') upon multiplying by Q, differentiating with respect to time, dividing by $Q = q$, and substituting $L = l$. When random factors affect production, the form of the learning curve in equation (1) of the text is generally more appropriate as a foundation for empirical analysis than equation (1'). As a production program evolves over time, Q and L become increasingly large. As a consequence, even quite large weekly fluctuations in output per labor hour are masked by adding current values of hours and output to their entire past histories when computing the numerator and denominator on the left-hand side of equation (1'). Production histories plotted or estimated using equation (1') give a misleading impression of decreasing variance in output per labor hour even if the weekly variance in output per labor hour is constant or increasing. The form in equation (1) of the text does not suffer from this problem.

2. In choosing the sample for estimation, we deleted five observations that were not representative of normal operating conditions. One of these observations was deleted because there was a materials shortage from an external supplier that week and only one day was worked. The remaining four observations are for the period of transition from one-shift-a-day to two-shift-a-day operation. During part of the transition, the crews for the two shifts worked partially overlapping hours. Thus, production during this period was not typical of either one-shift-a-day operation or two-shift-a-day operation. Modeling the transition process may be of interest in its own right, but is beyond the scope of this paper.

3. The estimate of the constant term is not of particular interest for purposes of this paper. To help preserve confidentially of our data, we do not report the constant terms from our regressions.

4. Maddala (1988, Section 6.4) discusses estimation of regression models with first-order autocorrelation of the residuals. Higher-order correlation of the errors may also be present. To simplify exposition, we present several extensions of the basic model. We then report results of testing for higher-order autocorrelation after these extensions are developed.

5. The equations that we estimate may be thought of as increasingly general forms for the production function. The quantity of physical capital (e.g., plant and equipment) changed little over the time period of production that we study. The effects of this fixed capital stock are impounded in the constant term in the equations we estimate. This does not rule out the possi-

bility that learning by doing occurred via modifications in the existing capital stock. To the extent that such changes are the source of learning they may be captured by the knowledge variable in our equations.

6. The potential for simultaneous equation bias here is minimal because labor contracts give managers little discretion to change labor hours within a given week.

7. Thus far, well-known methods for estimating models with autoregressive errors have been used (Maddala, 1988, Section 6.4). The presence of λ in equation (9) complicates estimation. We do estimation using a grid search in increments of 0.01 over values of λ in the interval $[0,1]$. For each value of λ, we calculate the implied K_t series recursively using equation (8b) and $K_0 = 0$. Equivalently, K_t may be calculated using: $K_t = \Sigma_{s=1}^{t} \gamma^{t-s} q_s$. With a series for K_t, the remaining parameters can be estimated using standard methods for estimating models with autocorrelated errors (Maddala, 1988, Section 6.4). Our estimates are then the value of λ and the associated values of the other parameters that maximize the likelihood function.

To compute estimated standard errors of the parameters, we use the procedure described in Judge, Griffiths, Hill, and Lee (1980, Chap. 17). Further details are available upon request.

8. We use the quadratic function of $\text{Ln } K_{t-1}$ to approximate the true but unknown functional form. With $\gamma > 0$ and $\delta < 0$, the function in (10) reaches a maximum where $\text{Ln } K_{t-1} = \gamma / 2\delta$. For all observations in our sample, $\text{Ln } K_{t-1} < \hat{\gamma}/2\hat{\delta}$.

9. This model is estimated as follows. For a given value of λ, a series for K_{0t} for $t \leq S$ can be computed recursively as before. Alternatively, as before, this may be calculated using $K_{0t} = \Sigma_{t=1}^{t} \gamma^{t-s} q_s$ for $t \leq S$. For $t > S$, knowledge may be written as follows. Accumulated knowledge at date S is K_{0S}. Let $R_t = \Sigma_{s=s+1}^{t} \gamma^{t-s} q_s$. Then equations (11) and the symmetry assumptions imply that $K_t = pK_{0S} + ((1 + \theta)/2)R_t$ for $t > S$.

Let I, be an indicator variable defined as follows: $I_t = 1$ for $t \leq S$ and $I_t = 0$ for $t > S$. Then the series for knowledge can be written as

$$K_t = I_t K_{0t} + (1 - I_t) [pK_{0S} + ((1 + \theta)/2)R_t] \text{ for all } t.$$

Estimation proceeds by substituting this expression for K_t into equation (11a). A generalization of the search procedure described in footnote 7 is used. Details are available upon request.

10. We have included the likelihood function values to illustrate that each model in columns (4)-(6) results in very significant improvement in fit relative to the immediately preceding column.

11. It is also of interest to note the decrease in the first-order autoregressive parameter η across the columns in Table 4.1 as the model is generalized. This suggests that what appears in column (1) to be a relatively high degree of persistence in the process generating shocks to the production process may in fact be a result of using an unduly restrictive model. When variables increase across observations, as $\text{Ln } q_t$ and $\text{Ln } K_t$ do in our data, an autoregressive error process may appear to be present if a linear relationship is assumed when a nonlinear relationship is present. The drop in η between columns (4) and (5) of Table 4.1 suggests that the relatively high value of η in column (4) is due to imposing a linear relationship between $\text{Ln } q_t$ and $\text{Ln } K_{t-1}$ when a nonlinear relationship is present. The further drop in η between columns (5) and (6) suggests that part of the apparent autocorrelation of errors in column (5) is in fact due to the assumption in the model column (5) of full carry forward and complete transfer when two-shift operation is introduced.

12. In addition to being an investment that enhances future productivity, labor hours devoted to training might affect current productivity if workers in training assist (or impede) production. We investigated the possibility that training hours might affect current production by including the logarithm of training hours as an additional variable in the model in column (6) of Table 4.1. The coefficient of this variable was both negligible (–0.004) in magnitude and statistically

insignificant. This evidence suggests that the effect of training hours, if any, is on future production. With data for only a single plant, we cannot test the hypothesis that training enhances the carry forward of knowledge from one to two-shift-a-day operations. Such a test would require comparing different plants that engaged in different levels of training prior to adding a second shift.

REFERENCES

Argote, L., Beckman, S. L., & Epple, D. (1990). The persistence and transfer of learning in industrial settings. *Management Science, 36,* 140-154.

Argote, L., & Epple, D. (1990). Learning curves in manufacturing. *Science, 247,* 920-924.

Baloff, N. (1970). Startup management. *IEEE Transactions, EM-17,* 132-141.

Day, G. S., & Montgomery, D. B. (1983). Diagnosing the experience curve. *Journal of Marketing, 47,* 44-58.

Dutton, J. M., & Thomas, A. (1984). Treating progress functions as a managerial opportunity. *Academy of Management Review, 9,* 235-247.

Hayes, R. H., & Clark, K. B. (1986). Why some factories are more productive than others. *Harvard Business Review, 64,* 66-73.

Hayes, R. H., & Wheelwright, S. C. (1984). *Restoring our competitive edge: Competing through manufacturing.* New York: John Wiley.

Hirsch, W. Z. (1952). Manufacturing progress functions. *Review of Economics and Statistics, 34,* 143-155.

Joskow, P. L., & Rose, N. L. (1985). The effects of technological change, experience, and environmental regulation on the construction cost of coal-burning generating units. *Rand Journal of Economics, 16,* 1-27.

Judge, G. J., Griffiths, W. E., Hill, R. C., & Lee, T. C. (1980). *The theory and practice of econometrics.* New York: John Wiley.

Levitt, B., & March, J. G. (1988). Organizational learning. *Annual Review of Sociology, 14,* 319-340.

Levy, F. K. (1965). Adaptation in the production process. *Management Science, 11,* B136-B154.

Lieberman, M. B. (1984). The learning curve and pricing in the chemical processing industries. *Rand Journal of Economics, 15,* 213-228.

Maddala, G. S. (1988). *Introduction to econometrics.* New York: Macmillan.

Muth, J. F. (1986). Search theory and the manufacturing progress function. *Management Science, 32,* 948-962.

Wright, T. P. (1936). Factors affecting the cost of airplanes. *Journal of the Aeronautical Sciences, 3,* 122-128.

Yelle, L. E. (1979). The learning curve: Historical review and comprehensive survey. *Decision Sciences, 10,* 302-328.

Zimmerman, M. B. (1982). Learning effects and the commercialization of the new energy technologies. *Bell Journal of Economics, 13,* 297-310.

5

Exploration and Exploitation in Organizational Learning

JAMES G. MARCH

This paper considers the relation between the exploration of new possibilities and the exploitation of old certainties in organizational learning. It examines some complications in allocating resources between the two, particularly those introduced by the distribution of costs and benefits across time and space, and the effects of ecological interaction. Two general situations involving the development and use of knowledge in organizations are modeled. The first is the case of mutual learning between members of an organization and an organizational code. The second is the case of learning and competitive advantage in competition for primacy. The paper develops an argument that adaptive processes, by refining exploitation more rapidly than exploration, are likely to become effective in the short run but self-destructive in the long run. The possibility that certain common organizational practices ameliorate that tendency is assessed.

(ORGANIZATIONAL LEARNING; RISK TAKING; KNOWLEDGE AND COMPETITIVE ADVANTAGE)

A central concern of studies of adaptive processes is the relation between the exploration of new possibilities and the exploitation of old certainties (Holland, 1975; Kuran, 1988; Schumpeter, 1934). Exploration includes things captured by terms such as search, variation, risk taking, experimenta-

This chapter appeared originally in *Organization Science*, Vol. 2, No. 1, February 1991. Copyright © 1991, The Institute of Management Sciences.

tion, play, flexibility, discovery, innovation. Exploitation includes such things as refinement, choice, production, efficiency, selection, implementation, execution. Adaptive systems that engage in exploration to the exclusion of exploitation are likely to find that they suffer the costs of experimentation without gaining many of its benefits. They exhibit too many undeveloped new ideas and too little distinctive competence. Conversely, systems that engage in exploitation to the exclusion of exploration are likely to find themselves trapped in suboptimal stable equilibria. As a result, maintaining an appropriate balance between exploration and exploitation is a primary factor in system survival and prosperity.

This paper considers some aspects of such problems in the context of organizations. Both exploration and exploitation are essential for organizations, but they compete for scarce resources. As a result, organizations make explicit and implicit choices between the two. The explicit choices are found in calculated decisions about alternative investments and competitive strategies. The implicit choices are buried in many features of organizational forms and customs, for example, in organizational procedures for accumulating and reducing slack, in search rules and practices, in the ways in which targets are set and changed, and in incentive systems. Understanding the choices and improving the balance between exploration and exploitation are complicated by the fact that returns from the two options vary not only with respect to their expected values, but also with respect to their variability, their timing, and their distribution within and beyond the organization. Processes for allocating resources between them, therefore, embody intertemporal, interinstitutional, and interpersonal comparisons, as well as risk preferences. The difficulties involved in making such comparisons lead to complications in specifying appropriate trade-offs, and in achieving them.

1. THE EXPLORATION/EXPLOITATION TRADE-OFF

Exploration and Exploitation in Theories of Organizational Action

In rational models of choice, the balance between exploration and exploitation is discussed classically in terms of a theory of rational search (Hey, 1982; Radner & Rothschild, 1975). It is assumed that there are several alternative investment opportunities, each characterized by a probability distribution over returns that is initially unknown. Information about the distribution is accumulated over time, but choices must be made between gaining new information about alternatives and thus improving future returns (which suggests allocating part of the investment to searching among uncertain alternatives), and using the information currently available to improve present returns (which suggests concentrating the investment on the apparently best alternative). The problem is complicated by the possibilities that new investment alternatives may appear, that probability distributions may not be stable, or that they may depend on the choices made by others.

In theories of limited rationality, discussions of the choice between exploration and exploitation emphasize the role of targets or aspiration levels in regulating allocations to search (Cyert & March, 1963). The usual assumption is that search is inhibited if the most preferred alternative is above (but in the neighborhood of) the target. On the other hand, search is stimulated if the most preferred known alternative is below the target. Such ideas are found both in theories of satisficing (Simon, 1955) and in prospect theory (Kahneman & Tversky, 1979). They have led to attempts to specify conditions under which target-oriented search rules are optimal (Day, 1967). Because of the role of targets, discussions of search in the limited rationality tradition emphasize the significance of the adaptive character of aspirations themselves (March, 1988).

In studies of organizational learning, the problem of balancing exploration and exploitation is exhibited in distinctions made between refinement of an existing technology and invention of a new one (Levinthal & March, 1981; Winter, 1971). It is clear that exploration of new alternatives reduces the speed with which skills at existing ones are improved. It is also clear that improvements in competence at existing procedures make experimentation with others less attractive (Levitt & March, 1988). Finding an appropriate balance is made particularly difficult by the fact that the same issues occur at levels of a nested system—at the individual level, the organizational level, and the social system level.

In evolutionary models of organizational forms and technologies, discussions of the choice between exploration and exploitation are framed in terms of balancing the twin processes of variation and selection (Ashby, 1960; Hannan & Freeman, 1987). Effective selection among forms, routines, or practices is essential to survival, but so also is the generation of new alternative practices, particularly in a changing environment. Because of the links among environmental turbulence, organizational diversity, and competitive advantage, the evolutionary dominance of an organizational practice is sensitive to the relation between the rate of exploratory variation reflected by the practice and the rate of change in the environment. In this spirit, for example, it has been argued that the persistence of garbage-can decision processes in organizations is related to the diversity advantage they provide in a world of relatively unstable environments, when paired with the selective efficiency of conventional rationality (Cohen, 1986).

The Vulnerability of Exploration

Compared to returns from exploitation, returns from exploration are systematically less certain, more remote in time, and organizationally more distant from the locus of action and adaption. What is good in the long run is not always good in the short run. What is good at a particular historical moment is not always good at another time. What is good for one part of an organization is not always good for another part. What is good for an organization is not always good for a larger social system of which it is a part. As organizations learn from experience how to divide resources between exploitation and exploration, this distribution of consequences across time and space affects the lessons learned. The certainty, speed, proximity, and clarity of feedback ties exploitation to its consequences more quickly and more precisely than is the case with exploration. The story is told in many forms. Basic research has less certain outcomes, longer time horizons, and more diffuse effects than does product development. The search for new ideas, markets, or relations has less certain outcomes, longer time horizons, and more diffuse effects than does further development of existing ones.

Because of these differences, adaptive processes characteristically improve exploitation more rapidly than exploration. These advantages for exploitation cumulate. Each increase in competence at an activity increases the likelihood of rewards for engaging in that activity, thereby further increasing the competence and the likelihood (Argyris & Schön, 1978; David, 1985). The effects extend, through network externalities, to others with whom the learning organization interacts (David & Bunn, 1988; Katz & Shapiro, 1986). Reason inhibits foolishness; learning and imitation inhibit experimentation. This is not an accident but is a consequence of the temporal and spatial proximity of the effects of exploitation, as well as their precision and interconnectedness.

Since performance is a joint function of potential return from an activity and present competence of an organization at it, organizations exhibit increasing returns to experience (Arthur, 1984). Positive local feedback produces strong path dependence (David, 1990) and can lead to suboptimal equilibria. It is quite possible for competence in an inferior activity to become great enough to exclude superior activities with which an organization has little experience (Herriott, Levinthal, & March, 1985). Since long-run intelligence depends on sustaining a reasonable level of exploration, these tendencies to increase exploitation and reduce exploration make adaptive processes potentially self-destructive.

The Social Context of Organizational Learning

The trade-off between exploration and exploitation exhibits some special features in the social context of organizations. The next two sections of the present paper describe two simple models of adaptation, use them to elaborate the relation between exploitation and exploration, and explore some implications of the relation for the accumulation and utilization of knowledge in organizations. The models identify some reasons why organizations may want to control learning and suggest some procedures by which they do so.

Two distinctive features of the social context are considered. The first is the mutual learning of an organization and the individuals in it. Organizations store knowledge in their procedures, norms, rules, and forms. They accumulate such knowledge over time, learning from their members. At the same time, individuals in an organization are socialized to organizational beliefs. Such mutual learning has implications for understanding and managing the trade-off between exploration and exploitation in organizations. The second feature of organizational learning considered here is the context of competition for primacy. Organizations often compete with each other under conditions in which relative position matters. The mixed contribution of knowledge to competitive advantage in cases involving competition for primacy creates difficulties for defining and arranging an appropriate balance between exploration and exploitation in an organizational setting.

2. MUTUAL LEARNING IN THE DEVELOPMENT OF KNOWLEDGE

Organizational knowledge and faiths are diffused to individuals through various forms of instruction, indoctrination, and exemplification. An organization socializes recruits to the languages, beliefs, and practices that comprise the organizational code (Van Maanen, 1973; Whyte, 1957). Simultaneously, the organizational code is adapting to individual beliefs. This form of mutual learning has consequences both for the individuals involved and for an organization as a whole. In particular, the trade-off between exploration and exploitation in mutual learning involves conflicts between short-run and long-run concerns and between gains to individual knowledge and gains to collective knowledge.

A Model of Mutual Learning

Consider a simple model of the development and diffusion of organizational knowledge. There are four key features to the model:

1. There is an external reality that is independent of beliefs about it. Reality is described as having m dimensions, each of which has a value of 1 or –1. The (independent) probability that any one dimension will have a value of 1 is 0.5.
2. At each time period, beliefs about reality are held by each of n individuals in an organization and by an organizational code of received truth. For each of the m dimensions of reality, each belief has a value of 1, 0, or –1. This value may change over time.
3. Individuals modify their beliefs continuously as a consequence of socialization into the organization and education into its code of beliefs. Specifically, if the code is 0 on a particular dimension, individual belief is not affected. In each period in which the code differs on any particular dimension from the belief of an individual, individual belief changes to that of the code with probability, p_1. Thus, p_1 is a parameter reflecting the effectiveness of socialization, i.e., learning *from* the code. Changes on the several dimensions are assumed to be independent of each other.
4. At the same time, the organizational code adapts to the beliefs of those individuals whose beliefs correspond with reality on more dimensions than does the code. The probability that the beliefs of the code will be adjusted to conform to the dominant belief within the superior group on any particular dimension depends on the level of agreement among individuals in the superior group and on p_2.[1] Thus, p_2 is a parameter reflecting the effectiveness of learning *by* the code. Changes on the several dimensions are assumed to be independent of each other.

Within this system, initial conditions include: a reality m-tuple (m dimensions, each of which has a value of 1 or –1, with independent equal probability); an organizational code m-tuple (m dimensions, each of which is initially 0); and n individual m-tuples (m dimensions, with values equal 1, 0, or –1, with equal probabilities).

Thus, the process begins with an organizational code characterized by neutral beliefs on all dimensions and a set of individuals with varying beliefs that exhibit, on average, no knowledge. Over time, the organizational code affects the beliefs of individuals, even while it is being affected by those beliefs. The beliefs of individuals do not affect the beliefs of other individuals directly but only through affecting the code. The effects of reality are also indirect. Neither the individuals nor the organizations experience reality.

Improvement in knowledge comes by the code mimicking the beliefs (including the false beliefs) of superior individuals and by individuals mimicking the code (including its false beliefs).

Basic Properties of the Model in a Closed System

Consider such a model of mutual learning first within a closed system having fixed organizational membership and a stable reality. Since realizations of the process are subject to stochastic variability, repeated simulations using the same initial conditions and parameters are used to estimate the distribution of outcomes. In all of the results reported here, the number of dimensions of reality (m) is set at 30, the number of individuals (n) is set at 50, and the number of repeated simulations is 80. The quantitative levels of the results and the magnitude of the stochastic fluctuations reported depend on these specifications, but the qualitative results are insensitive to values of m and n.

Since reality is specified, the state of knowledge at any particular time period can be assessed in two ways. First, the proportion of reality that is correctly represented in the organizational code can be calculated for any period. This is the knowledge level of the code for that period. Second, the proportion of reality that is correctly represented in individual beliefs (on average) can be calculated for any period. This is the average knowledge level of the individuals for that period.

Within this closed system, the model yields time paths of organizational and individual beliefs, thus knowledge levels, that depend stochastically on the initial conditions and the parameters affecting learning. The basic features of these histories can be summarized simply: Each of the adjustments in beliefs serves to eliminate differences between the individuals and the code. Consequently, the beliefs of individuals and the code converge over time. As individuals in the organization become more knowledgeable, they also become more homogeneous with respect to knowledge. An equilibrium is reached at which all individuals and the code share the same (not necessarily accurate) belief with respect to each dimension. The equilibrium is stable.

Effects of Learning Rates. Higher rates of learning lead, on average, to achieving equilibrium earlier. The equilibrium level of knowledge attained by an organization also depends interactively on the two learning parameters. Figure 5.1 shows the results when we assume that p_1 is the same for all individuals. Slower socialization (lower p_1) leads to greater knowledge at equilibrium than does faster socialization, particularly when the code learns

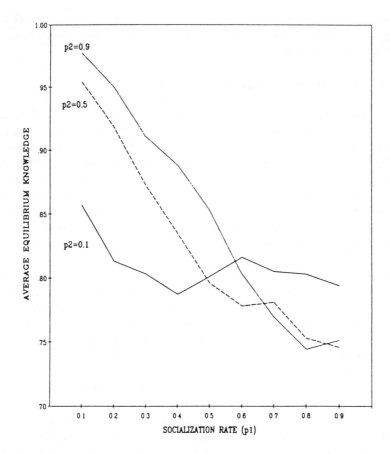

Figure 5.1. Effect of Learning Rates (p_1, p_2) on Equilibrium Knowledge
NOTE: M = 30; N = 50; 80 Iterations.

rapidly (high p_2). When socialization is slow, more rapid learning by the code leads to greater knowledge at equilibrium; but when socialization is rapid, greater equilibrium knowledge is achieved through slower learning by the code. By far the highest equilibrium knowledge occurs when the code learns rapidly from individuals whose socialization to the code is slow.

The results pictured in Figure 5.1 confirm the observation that rapid learning is not always desirable (Herriott et al., 1985; Lounamaa & March, 1987). In previous work, it was shown that slower learning allows for greater exploration of possible alternatives and greater balance in the development of specialized competences. In the present model, a different version of the same general phenomenon is observed. The gains to individuals from adapting rapidly to the code (which is consistently closer to reality than the average individual) are offset by second-order losses stemming from the fact that the code can learn only from individuals who deviate from it. Slow learning on the part of individuals maintains diversity longer, thereby providing the exploration that allows the knowledge found in the organizational code to improve.

Effects of Learning Rate Heterogeneity. The fact that fast individual learning from the code tends to have a favorable first-order effect on individual knowledge but an adverse effect on improvement in organizational knowledge and thereby on long-term individual improvement suggests that there might be some advantage to having a mix of fast and slow learners in an organization. Suppose the population of individuals in an organization is divided into two groups, one consisting of individuals who learn rapidly from the code ($p_1 = 0.9$) and the other consisting of individuals who learn slowly ($p_1 = 0.1$).

If an organization is partitioned into two groups in this way, the mutual learning process achieves an equilibrium in which all individuals and the code share the same beliefs. As would be expected from the results above with respect to homogeneous socialization rates, larger fractions of fast learners result in the process reaching equilibrium faster and in lower levels of knowledge at equilibrium than do smaller fractions of fast learners. However, as Figure 5.2 shows, for any average rate of learning from the code, it is better from the point of view of equilibrium knowledge to have that average reflect a mix of fast and slow learners rather than a homogeneous population. For equivalent average values of the socialization learning parameter (p_1), the heterogeneous population consistently produces higher equilibrium knowledge.

On the way to equilibrium, the knowledge gains from variability are disproportionately due to contributions by slow learners, but they are disproportionately realized (in their own knowledge) by fast learners. Figure 5.3 shows the effects on period-20 knowledge of varying the fraction of the population of individuals who are fast learners ($p_1 = 0.9$) rather than slow learners ($p_1 = 0.1$). Prior to reaching equilibrium, individuals with a high value for p_1 gain from being in an organization in which there are individuals having a low value for p_1, but the converse is not true.

These results indicate that the fraction of slow learners in an organization is a significant factor in organizational learning. In the model, that fraction is treated as a parameter. Disparities in the returns to the two groups and their interdependence make optimizing with respect to the fraction of slow learners problematic if the rates of individual learning are subject to individual control. Since there are no obvious individual incentives for learning slowly

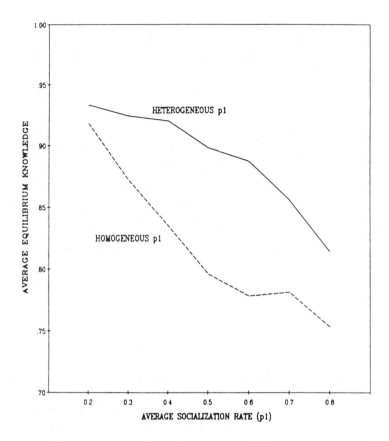

Figure 5.2. Effect of Heterogeneous Socialization Rates ($p_1 = 0.1, 0.9$) on Equilib-
           rium Knowledge

NOTE: $M = 30$; $N = 50$; $p_2 = 0.5$; 80 Iterations.

in a population in which others are learning rapidly, it may be difficult to
arrive at a fraction of slow learners that is optimal from the point of view of
the code if learning rates are voluntarily chosen by individuals.

Basic Properties of the Model
in a More Open System

These results can be extended by examining some alternative routes to
selective slow learning in a somewhat more open system. Specifically, the
role of turnover in the organization and turbulence in the environment are

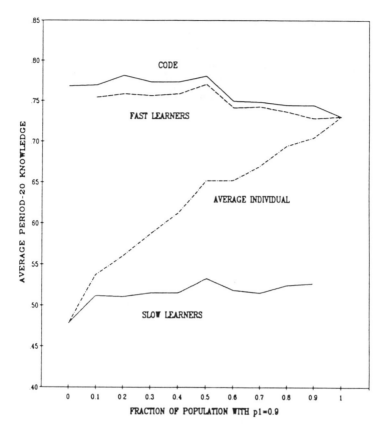

Figure 5.3. Effect of Heterogeneous Socialization Rates ($p_1 = 0.1, 0.9$) on Period-20 Knowledge

NOTE: $M = 30$; $N = 50$; $p_1 = 0.1, 0.9$; $p_2 = 0.5$; 80 Iterations.

considered. In the case of turnover, organizational membership is treated as changing. In the case of turbulence, environmental reality is treated as changing.

Effects of Personnel Turnover. In the previous section, it was shown that variability is sustained by low values of p_1. Slow learners stay deviant long enough for the code to learn from them. An alternative way of producing variability in an organization is to introduce personnel turnover. Suppose that each time period each individual has a probability, p_3, of leaving the organization and being replaced by a new individual with a set of naive beliefs

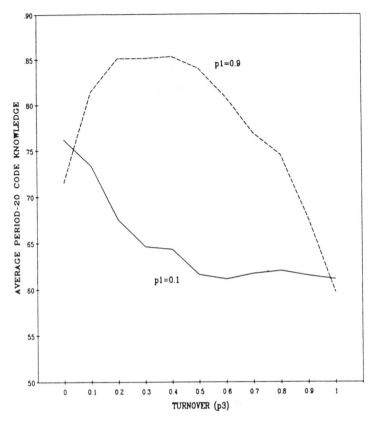

Figure 5.4. Effect of Turnover (p_3) and Socialization Rate ($p_1 = 0.1, 0.9$) on Period-20
          Knowledge

NOTE: $M = 30$; $N = 50$; $p_1 = 0.1, 0.9$; $p_2 = 0.5$; 80 Iterations.

described by an m-tuple, having values equal to 1, 0, or -1, with equal
probabilities. As might be expected, there is a consistent negative first-order
effect of turnover on average individual knowledge. Since there is a positive
relation between length of service in the organization and individual knowledge, the greater the turnover, the shorter the average length of service and
the lower the average individual knowledge at any point. This effect is
strong.

The effect of turnover on the organizational code is more complicated and
reflects a trade-off between learning rate and turnover rate. Figure 5.4 shows
the period-20 results for two different values of the socialization rate (p_1). If

p_1 is relatively low, period-20 code knowledge declines with increasing turnover. The combination of slow learning and rapid turnover leads to inadequate exploitation. However, if p_1 is relatively high, moderate amounts of turnover improve the organizational code. Rapid socialization of individuals into the procedures and beliefs of an organization tends to reduce exploration. A modest level of turnover, by introducing less socialized people, increases exploration, and thereby improves aggregate knowledge. The level of knowledge reflected by the organizational code is increased, as is the average individual knowledge of those individuals who have been in the organization for some time. Note that this effect does not come from the superior knowledge of the average new recruit. Recruits are, on average, less knowledgeable than the individuals they replace. The gains come from their diversity.

Turnover, like heterogeneity in learning rates, produces a distribution problem. Contributions to improving the code (and subsequently individual knowledge) come from the occasional newcomers who deviate from the code in a favorable way. Old-timers, on average, know more, but what they know is redundant with knowledge already reflected in the code. They are less likely to contribute new knowledge on the margin. Novices know less on average, but what they know is less redundant with the code and occasionally better, thus more likely to contribute to improving the code.

Effects of Environmental Turbulence. Since learning processes involve lags in adjustment to changes, the contribution of learning to knowledge depends on the amount of turbulence in the environment. Suppose that the value of any given dimension of reality shifts (from 1 to −1 or −1 to 1) in a given time period with probability p_4. This captures in an elementary way the idea that understanding the world may be complicated by turbulence in the world. Exogenous environmental change makes adaptation essential, but it also makes learning from experience difficult (Weick, 1979). In the model, the level of knowledge achieved in a particular (relatively early) time period decreases with increasing turbulence.

In addition, mutual learning has a dramatic long-run degenerate property under conditions of exogenous turbulence. As the beliefs of individuals and the code converge, the possibilities for improvement in either decline. Once a knowledge equilibrium is achieved, it is sustained indefinitely. The beliefs reflected in the code and those held by all individuals remain identical and unchanging, regardless of changes in reality. Even before equilibrium is achieved, the capabilities for change fall below the rate of change in the environment. As a result, after an initial period of increasing accuracy, the knowledge of the code and individuals is systematically degraded through

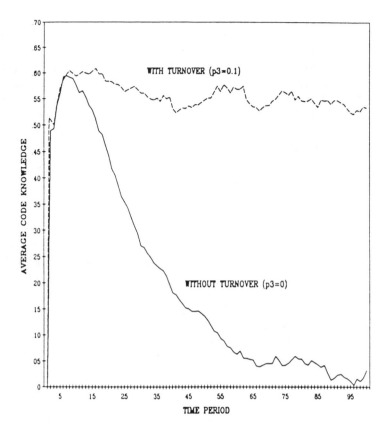

Figure 5.5. Effect of Turbulence (p_4) on Code Knowledge Over Time With and Without
              Turnover (p_3)
NOTE: $M = 30$; $N = 50$; $p_1 = 0.1$; $p_2 = 0.5$; $p_4 = 0.02$; 80 Iterations.

changes in reality. Ultimately, the accuracy of belief reaches chance (i.e.,
where a random change in reality is as likely to increase accuracy of beliefs
as it is to decrease it). The process becomes a random walk.

The degeneracy is avoided if there is turnover. Figure 5.5 plots the average
level of code knowledge over time under conditions of turbulence ($p_4 = 0.02$).
Two cases of learning are plotted, one without turnover ($p_3 = 0$), the other
with moderate turnover ($p_3 = 0.1$). Where there is turbulence without turnover, code knowledge first rises to a moderate level, and then declines to 0,
from which it subsequently wanders randomly. With turnover, the degeneracy is avoided and a moderate level of code knowledge is sustained in the
face of environmental change. The positive effects of moderate turnover

depend, of course, on the rules for selecting new recruits. In the present case, recruitment is not affected by the code. Replacing departing individuals with recruits closer to the current organizational code would significantly reduce the efficiency of turnover as a source of exploration.

Turnover is useful in the face of turbulence, but it produces a disparity between code knowledge and the average knowledge of individuals in the organization. As a result, the match between turnover rate and level of turbulence that is desirable from the point of view of the organization's knowledge is not necessarily desirable from the point of view of the knowledge of every individual in it, or individuals on average. In particular, where there is turbulence, there is considerable individual advantage to having tenure in an organization that has turnover. This seems likely to produce pressures by individuals to secure tenure for themselves while restricting it for others.

3. KNOWLEDGE AND ECOLOGIES OF COMPETITION

The model in the previous section examines one aspect of the social context of adaptation in organizations, the ways in which individual beliefs and an organizational code draw from each other over time. A second major feature of the social context of organizational learning is the competitive ecology within which learning occurs and knowledge is used. External competitive processes pit organizations against each other in pursuit of scarce environmental resources and opportunities. Examples are competition among business firms for customers and governmental subsidies. Internal competitive processes pit individuals in the organization against each other in competition for scarce organizational resources and opportunities. Examples are competition among managers for internal resources and hierarchical promotion. In these ecologies of competition, the competitive consequences of learning by one organization depend on learning by other organizations. In this section, these links among learning, performance, and position in an ecology of competition are discussed by considering some ways in which competitive advantage is affected by the accumulation of knowledge.

Competition and the Importance of Relative Performance

Suppose that an organization's realized performance on a particular occasion is a draw from a probability distribution that can be characterized in terms of some measure of average value (x) and some measure of variability (*v*). Knowledge, and the learning process that produces it, can be described in terms of their effects on these two measures. A change in an organization's performance distribution that increases average performance (i.e., makes $x' > x$) will often be beneficial to an organization, but such a result is not assured when relative position within a group of competing organizations is important. Where returns to one competitor are not strictly determined by that competitor's own performance but depend on the relative standings of the competitors, returns to changes in knowledge depend not only on the magnitude of the changes in the expected value but also on changes in variability and on the number of competitors.

To illustrate the phenomenon, consider the case of competition for primacy between a reference organization and N other organizations, each having normal performance distributions with mean $= x$ and variance $= v$. The chance of the reference organization having the best performance within a group of identical competitors is $1/(N + 1)$. We compare this situation to one in which the reference organization has a normal performance distribution with mean $= x'$ and variance $= v'$. We evaluate the probability, $P*$, that the (x', v') organization will outperform all of the N (x, v) organizations. A performance distribution with a mean of x' and a variance of v' provides a competitive advantage in a competition for primacy if $P*$ is greater than $1/(N + 1)$. It results in a competitive disadvantage if $P*$ is less than $1/(N + 1)$.

If an organization faces only one competitor $(N = 1)$, it is easy to see that any advantage in mean performance on the part of the reference organization makes $P*$ greater than $1/(N + 1) = 0.5$, regardless of the variance. Thus, in bilateral competition involving normal performance distributions, learning that increases the mean always pays off, and changes in the variance— whether positive or negative—have no effect.

The situation changes as N increases. Figure 5.6 shows the competitive success (failure) of an organization having a normal performance distribution with a mean $= x'$ and a variance $= v'$, when that organization is faced with N identical and independent competitors whose performance-distributions are normal with mean $= 0$ and variance $= 1$. Each point in the space in Figure 5.6 represents a different possible normal performance distribution (x', v'). Each line in the figure is associated with a particular N and connects the (x', v') pairs for which $p* = 1/(N + 1)$.[2] The area to the right and above a line includes (x', v') combinations for which $P*$ is greater than $1/(N + 1)$, thus that yield a competitive advantage relative to $(0,1)$. The area to the left and below a line includes (x', v') combinations for which $P*$ is less than $1/(N + 1)$, thus that yield a competitive disadvantage relative to $(0,1)$.

The pattern is clear. If N is greater than 1 (but finite), increases in either the mean or the variance have a positive effect on competitive advantage, and sufficiently large increases in either can offset decreases in the other. The

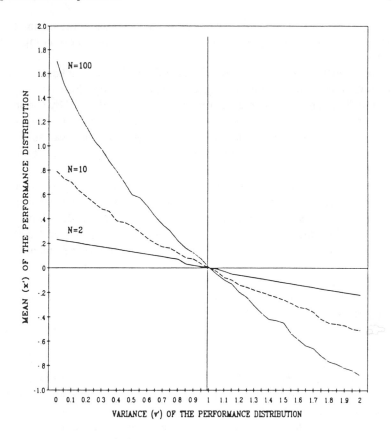

Figure 5.6. Competitive Equality Lines ($P^* = 1/(N + 1)$) for One ($x'\ v'$) Organization
Competing With N (0, 1) Organizations (Normal Performance Distributions)

trade-off between increases in the mean and increases in the variance is strongly affected by N. As the number of competitors increases, the contribution of the variance to competitive advantage increases until at the limit, as N goes to infinity, the mean becomes irrelevant.

Learning, Knowledge, and Competitive Advantage

The effects of learning are realized in changes in the performance distribution. The analysis indicates that if learning increases both the mean and the variance of a normal performance distribution, it will improve competitive advantage in a competition for primacy. The model also suggests that increases in the variance may compensate for decreases in the mean; decreases in the variance may nullify gains from increases in the mean. These variance effects are particularly significant when the number of competitors is large.

The underlying argument does not depend on competition being only for primacy. Such competition is a special case of competition for relative position. The general principle that relative position is affected by variability, and increasingly so as the number of competitors increases, is true for any position. In competition to achieve relatively high positions, variability has a positive effect. In competition to avoid relatively low positions, variability has a negative effect.

Nor does the underlying argument depend on the assumption of normality or other symmetry in the performance distributions. Normal performance distributions are special cases in which the tails of the distribution are specified when the mean and variance are specified. For general distributions, as the number of competitors increases, the likelihood of finishing first depends increasingly on the right-hand tail of the performance distribution, and the likelihood of finishing last depends increasingly on the left-hand tail (David, 1981). If learning has different effects on the two tails of the distribution, the right-hand tail effect will be much more important in competition for primacy among many competitors. The left-hand tail will be much more important in competition to avoid finishing last.

Some learning processes increase both average performance and variability. A standard example would be the short-run consequences from adoption of a new technology. If a new technology is so clearly superior as to overcome the disadvantages of unfamiliarity with it, it will offer a higher expected value than the old technology. At the same time, the limited experience with the new technology (relative to experience with the old) will lead to an increased variance. A similar result might be expected with the introduction of a new body of knowledge or new elements of cultural diversity to an organization, for example, through the introduction of individuals with untypical skills, attitudes, ethnicity, or gender.

Learning processes do not necessarily lead to increases in both average performance and variation, however. Increased knowledge seems often to reduce the variability of performance rather than to increase it. Knowledge makes performance more reliable. As work is standardized, as techniques are learned, variability, both in the time required to accomplish tasks and in the quality of task performance, is reduced. Insofar as that increase in reliability comes from a reduction in the left-hand tail, the likelihood of finishing last in a competition among many is reduced without changing the likelihood of finishing first. However, if knowledge has the effect of reducing the right-hand tail of the distribution, it may easily decrease the chance of being best among several competitors even though it also increases average performance. The question is whether you can do exceptionally well, as opposed to better than average, without leaving the confines of conventional action. The answer is complicated, for it depends on a more careful specification of the kind of knowledge involved and its precise effects on the right-hand tail of the distribution. But knowledge that simultaneously increases average performance and its reliability is not a guarantee of competitive advantage.

Consider, for example, the case of modern information and decision technology based on computers. In cases where time is particularly important, information technology has a major effect on the mean, less on the variance. Some problems in environmental scanning for surprises, changes, or opportunities probably fall into such a category. Under such conditions, appropriate use of information technology seems likely to improve competitive position. On the other hand, in many situations the main effect of information technology is to make outcomes more reliable. For example, additional data, or more detailed analyses, seem likely to increase reliability in decisions more rapidly than they will increase their average returns. In such cases, the effects on the tails are likely to dominate the effects on the mean. The net effect of the improved technology on the chance of avoiding being the worst competitor will be positive, but the effect on the chance of finishing at the head of the pack may well be negative.

Similarly, multiple, independent projects may have an advantage over a single, coordinated effort. The average result from independent projects is likely to be lower than that realized from a coordinated one, but their right-hand side variability can compensate for the reduced mean in a competition for primacy. The argument can be extended more generally to the effects of close collaboration or cooperative information exchange. Organizations that develop effective instruments of coordination and communication probably can be expected to do better (on average) than those that are more loosely coupled, and they also probably can be expected to become more reliable, less likely to deviate significantly from the mean of their performance distributions. The price of reliability, however, is a smaller chance of primacy among competitors.

Competition for Relative Position and Strategic Action

The arguments above assume that the several individual performances of competitors are independent draws from a distribution of possible performances, and that the distribution cannot be arbitrarily chosen by the competitors. Such a perspective is incomplete. It is possible to see both the mean and the reliability of a performance distribution (at least partially) as choices made strategically. In the long run, they represent the result of organizational choices between investments in learning and in consumption of the fruits of current capabilities, thus the central focus of this paper. In the short run, the choice of mean can be seen as a choice of effort or attention. By varying effort, an organization selects a performance mean between an entitlement (zero-effort) and a capability (maximum-effort) level. Similarly, in the short run, variations in the reliability of performance can be seen as choices of knowledge or risk that can be set willfully within the range of available alternatives.

These choices, insofar as they are made rationally, will not, in general, be independent of competition. If relative position matters, as the number of competitors increases, strategies for increasing the mean through increased effort or greater knowledge become less attractive relative to strategies for increasing variability. In the more general situation, suppose organizations face competition from numerous competitors who vary in their average capabilities but who can choose their variances. If payoffs and preferences are such that finishing near the top matters a great deal, those organizations with performance distributions characterized by comparatively low means will (if they can) be willing to sacrifice average performance in order to augment the right-hand tails of their performance distributions. In this way, they improve their chances of winning, thus force their more talented competitors to do likewise, and thereby convert the competition into a right-hand tail "race" in which average performance (due to ability and effort) becomes irrelevant. These dynamics comprise powerful countervailing forces to the tendency for experience to eliminate exploration and are a reminder that the learning dominance of exploitation is, under some circumstances, constrained not only by slow learning and turnover but also by reason.

4. LITTLE MODELS AND OLD WISDOM

Learning, analysis, imitation, regeneration, and technological change are major components of any effort to improve organizational performance and strengthen competitive advantage. Each involves adaptation and a delicate trade-off between exploration and exploitation. The present argument has been that these trade-offs are affected by their contexts of distributed costs and benefits and ecological interaction. The essence of exploitation is the refinement and extension of existing competences, technologies, and paradigms. Its returns are positive, proximate, and predictable. The essence of exploration is experimentation with new alternatives. Its returns are uncertain, distant, and often negative. Thus, the distance in time and space between the locus of learning and the locus for the realization of returns is generally greater in the case of exploration than in the case of exploitation, as is the uncertainty.

Such features of the context of adaptation lead to a tendency to substitute exploitation of known alternatives for the exploration of unknown ones, to increase the reliability of performance rather more than its mean. This property of adaptive processes is potentially self-destructive. As we have seen, it degrades organizational learning in a mutual learning situation. Mutual learning leads to convergence between organizational and individual beliefs. The convergence is generally useful both for individuals and for an organization. However, a major threat to the effectiveness of such learning is the possibility that individuals will adjust to an organizational code before the code can learn from them. Relatively slow socialization of new organizational members and moderate turnover sustain variability in individual beliefs, thereby improving organizational and average individual knowledge in the long run.

An emphasis on exploitation also compromises competitive position where finishing near the top is important. Knowledge-based increases in average performance can be insufficient to overcome the adverse effects produced by reductions in variability. The ambiguous usefulness of learning in a competitive race is not simply an artifact of representing knowledge in terms of the mean and variance of a normal distribution. The key factor is the effect of knowledge on the right-hand tail of the performance distribution. Thus, in the end, the effects stem from the relation between knowledge and discovery. Polanyi (1963), commenting on one of his contributions to physics, observed that "I would never have conceived my theory, let alone have made a great effort to verify it, if I had been more familiar with major developments in physics that were taking place. Moreover, my initial ignorance of the powerful, false objections that were raised against my ideas protected those ideas from being nipped in the bud" (p. 1013).

These observations do not overturn the renaissance. Knowledge, learning, and education remain as profoundly important instruments of human well-being. At best, the models presented here suggest some of the considerations involved in thinking about choices between exploration and exploitation and in sustaining exploration in the face of adaptive processes that tend to inhibit it. The complexity of the distribution of costs and returns across time and groups makes an explicit determination of optimality a nontrivial exercise. But it may be instructive to reconfirm some elements of folk wisdom asserting that the returns to fast learning are not all positive, that rapid socialization may hurt the socializers even as it helps the socialized, that the development of knowledge may depend on maintaining an influx of the naive and ignorant, and that competitive victory does not reliably go to the properly educated.

Acknowledgments

This research has been supported by the Spencer Foundation and the Graduate School of Business, Stanford University. The author is grateful for the assistance of Michael Pich and Suzanne Stout and for the comments of Michael Cohen, Julie Elworth, Thomas Finholt, J. Michael Harrison, J. Richard Harrison, David Matheson, Martin Schulz, Sim Sitkin and Lee Sproull.

NOTES

1. More precisely, if the code is the same as the majority view among those individuals whose overall knowledge score is superior to that of the code, the code remains unchanged. If the code differs from the majority view on a particular dimension at the start of a time period, the probability that it will be unchanged at the end of period is $(1 - p_2)k$, where k $(k > 0)$ is the number of individuals (within the superior group) who differ from the code on this dimension minus the number who do not. This formulation makes the effective rate of code learning dependent on k, which probably depends on n. In the present simulations, n is not varied.

2. The lines are constructed by estimating, for each value of v' from 0 to 2 in steps of 0.05, the value of x' for which $p^* = 1/(N + 1)$. Each estimate is based on 5000 simulations. Since if $x' = 0$ and $v' = 1$, $P^* = 1/(N + 1)$ for any N, each of the lines is constrained to pass through the $(0,1)$ point.

REFERENCES

Argyris, C., & Schön, D. (1978). *Organizational learning*. Reading, MA: Addison-Wesley.

Arthur, W. B. (1984). Competing technologies and economic prediction. *ILASA Options, 2,* 10-13.

Ashby, W. R. (1960). *Design for a brain* (2nd ed.). New York: John Wiley.

Cohen, M. D. (1986). Artificial intelligence and the dynamic performance of organizational designs. In J. G. March & R. Weissinger-Baylon (Eds.), *Ambiguity and command: Organizational perspectives on military decision making* (pp. 53-71). Boston, MA: Ballinger.

Cyert, R. M., & March, J. G. (1963). *A behavioral theory of the firm*. Englewood Cliffs, NJ: Prentice Hall.

David, H. A. (1981). *Order statistics* (2nd ed.). New York: John Wiley.

David, P. A. (1985). Clio and the economics of QWERTY. *American Economic Review, 75,* 332-337.

David, P. A. (1990). The hero and the herd in technological history: Reflections on Thomas Edison and "the battle of the systems." In P. Higgonet & H. Rosovsky (Eds.), *Economic development past and present: Opportunities and constraints* (pp. 72-119). Cambridge, MA: Harvard University Press.

David, P. A., & Bunn, J. A. (1988). The economics of gateway technologies and network evolution. *Information Economics and Policy, 3,* 165-202.

Day, R. H. (1967). Profits, learning, and the convergence of satisficing to marginalism. *Quarterly Journal of Economics, 81,* 302-311.

Hannan, M. T., & Freeman, J. (1987). The ecology of organizational foundings: American labor unions, 1836-1985. *American Journal of Sociology, 92,* 910-943.

Herriott, S. R., Levinthal, D. A., & March, J. G. (1985). Learning from experience in organizations. *American Economic Review, 75,* 298-302.

Hey, J. D. (1982). Search for rules for search. *Journal of Economic Behavior and Organization, 3,* 65-81.

Holland, J. H. (1975). *Adaptation in natural and artificial systems.* Ann Arbor: University of Michigan Press.

Kahneman, D., & Tversky, A. (1979). Prospect theory: An analysis of decision under risk. *Econometrica, 47,* 263-291.

Katz, M. L., & Shapiro, C. (1986). Technology adoption in the presence of network externalities. *Journal of Political Economy, 94,* 822-841.

Kuran, T. (1988). The tenacious past: Theories of personal and collective conservatism. *Journal of Economic Behavior and Organization, 10,* 143-171.

Levinthal, D. A., & March, J. G. (1981). A model of adaptive organizational search. *Journal of Economic Behavior and Organization, 2,* 307-333.

Levitt, B., & March, J. G. (1988). Organizational learning. *Annual Review of Sociology, 14,* 319-340.

Lounamaa, P. H., & March, J. G. (1987). Adaptive coordination of a learning team. *Management Science, 33,* 107-123.

March, J. G. (1988). Variable risk preferences and adaptive aspirations. *Journal of Economic Behavior and Organization, 9,* 5-24.

Polanyi, M. (1963). The potential theory of adsorption: Authority in science has its uses and its dangers. *Science, 141,* 1010-1013.

Radner, R., & Rothschild, M. (1975). On the allocation of effort. *Journal of Economic Theory, 10,* 358-376.

Schumpeter, J. A. (1934). *The theory of economic development.* Cambridge, MA: Harvard University Press.

Simon, H. A. (1955). A behavioral model of rational choice. *Quarterly Journal of Economics, 69,* 99-118.

Van Maanen, J. (1973). Observations on the making of policemen. *Human Organization, 32,* 407-418.

Weick, K. E. (1979). *The social psychology of organizing* (2nd ed.). Reading, MA: Addison-Wesley.

Whyte, W. H., Jr. (1957). *The organization man.* Garden City, NY: Doubleday.

Winter, S. G. (1971). Satisficing, selection, and the innovating remnant. *Quarterly Journal of Economics, 85,* 237-261.

6

Organizational Learning

The Contributing Processes and the Literatures

GEORGE P. HUBER

This paper differs from previous examinations of organizational learning in that it is broader in scope and more evaluative of the literatures. Four constructs related to organizational learning (knowledge acquisition, information distribution, information interpretation, and organizational memory) are articulated, and the literatures related to each are described and critiqued.

The literature on *knowledge acquisition* is voluminous and multi-faceted, and so the knowledge acquisition construct is portrayed here as consisting of five subconstructs or subprocesses: (1) drawing on knowledge available at the organization's birth, (2) learning from experience, (3) learning by observing other organizations, (4) grafting on to itself components that possess knowledge needed but not possessed by the organization, and (5) noticing or searching for information about the organization's environment and performance. Examination of the related literatures indicates that much has been learned about learning from experience, but also that there is a lack of cumulative work and a lack of integration of work from different research groups. Similarly, much has been learned about organizational search, but there is a lack of conceptual work, and there is a lack of both cumulative work and syntheses with which to create a more mature literature. Congenital learning, vicarious learning, and grafting are information acquisition subprocesses about which relatively little has been learned.

The literature concerning *information distribution* is rich and mature, but an aspect of information distribution that is central to an organization's benefiting from its learning, namely how units that possess information and units that need this

This chapter appeared originally in *Organization Science,* Vol. 2, No. 1, February 1991. Copyright © 1991, The Institute of Management Sciences.

information can find each other quickly and with a high likelihood, is unexplored. *Information interpretation,* as an organizational process, rather than an individual process, requires empirical work for further advancement. *Organizational memory* is much in need of systematic investigation, particularly by those whose special concerns are improving organizational learning and decision making.

(ORGANIZATIONAL ADAPTATION;
ORGANIZATIONAL CHANGE;
ORGANIZATIONAL INFORMATION PROCESSING;
ORGANIZATIONAL LEARNING)

The purpose of this paper is to contribute to a more complete understanding of organizational learning. The paper elaborates four constructs integrally linked to organizational learning (knowledge acquisition, information distribution, information interpretation, and organizational memory) and describes needs and opportunities for further research and for integration of work already completed. It differs from previous examinations of organizational learning (Fiol & Lyles, 1985; Hedberg, 1981; Levitt & March, 1988; Shrivastava, 1983) in that it is broader in the scope of its subject matter and it evaluates the literatures more critically. In particular, the paper notes and attempts to explain the general lack of cumulative work and the lack of synthesis of work from different research groups. It also notes that thus far only a very small proportion of the work is presented in forms and forums that give it social or administrative value.

Intentional learning is the focal process in the lives of scientists and educators. Small wonder that when organizational scientists think about organizational learning, they often think of it as an intentional process directed at improving effectiveness. The prominence of this instrumental perspective in the managerial literature (Porter, 1980; Sammon, Kurland, & Spitalnic, 1984) undoubtedly contributes additionally to its pervasiveness in the organizational science literature. Some authors (Argyris & Schön, 1978, p. 323; Fiol & Lyles, 1985, p. 803) have gone so far as to imply that organizational effectiveness must be enhanced in order to claim that organizational learning has occurred.

It is important to challenge narrow concepts of organizational learning, or of any phenomenon early in the history of inquiry, as narrow conceptions decrease the chances of encountering useful findings or ideas. Consequently, it seems important to highlight that learning need not be conscious or intentional, as is apparent in discussions of operant conditioning in humans and other animals (Bower & Hilgard, 1981) and in case studies of organizational learning (March & Olsen, 1979).

Further, learning does not always increase the learner's effectiveness, or even potential effectiveness. Learning does not always lead to veridical knowledge. Sample data are not always representative and new findings sometimes overturn what was previously "known to be true." Entities can incorrectly learn, and they can correctly learn that which is incorrect.

Finally, learning need not result in observable changes in behavior.

> Change resulting from learning need not be visibly behavioral. Learning may result in new and significant insights and awareness that dictate no behavioral change. In this sense the crucial element in learning is that the organism be consciously aware of differences and alternatives and have consciously chosen one of these alternatives. The choice may be not to reconstruct behavior but, rather, to change one's cognitive maps or understandings. (Friedlander, 1983, p. 194)

In view of the above, here a more behavioral perspective is taken: *An entity learns if, through its processing of information, the range of its potential behaviors is changed.* This definition holds whether the entity is a human or other animal, a group, an organization, an industry, or a society. The information processing can involve acquiring, distributing, or interpreting information.[1] When the entity is an organization, these processes are frequently interpersonal or social, but they are occasionally more mechanical, and they can often be usefully viewed as logistical processes.

More meaning is given to organizational learning by characterizing it in terms of attributes. Four seem especially germane—existence, breadth, elaborateness, and thoroughness. With respect to the *existence* of organizational learning, let us assume that *an organization learns if any of its units acquires knowledge that it recognizes as potentially useful to the organization.*[2] A corollary assumption is that an organization learns something even if not every one of its components learns that something. These two assumptions are not universally held, but are widely held. For fuller discussions of the assumptions see Beer (1972), Douglas (1986), Morgan (1986), Sandelands and Stablein (1987), and Sims, Gioia, and Associates (1986).

It will be argued in Section 2 that *more organizational learning occurs when more of the organization's components obtain this knowledge and recognize it as potentially useful.* This assertion addresses the *breadth* of organizational learning. It will be contended in Section 3 that, with regard to an item of information, *more organizational learning occurs when more and more varied interpretations are developed,* because such development changes the range of potential behaviors. This assertion is concerned with

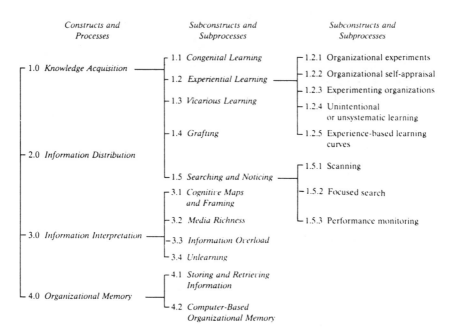

Constructs and Processes — *Subconstructs and Subprocesses* — *Subconstructs and Subprocesses*

1.0 *Knowledge Acquisition*
— 1.1 *Congenital Learning*
— 1.2 *Experiential Learning*
— 1.2.1 Organizational experiments
— 1.2.2 Organizational self-appraisal
— 1.2.3 Experimenting organizations
— 1.2.4 Unintentional or unsystematic learning
— 1.2.5 Experience-based learning curves
— 1.3 *Vicarious Learning*
— 1.4 *Grafting*
— 1.5 *Searching and Noticing*
— 1.5.1 Scanning
— 1.5.2 Focused search
— 1.5.3 Performance monitoring

2.0 *Information Distribution*

3.0 *Information Interpretation*
— 3.1 *Cognitive Maps and Framing*
— 3.2 *Media Richness*
— 3.3 *Information Overload*
— 3.4 *Unlearning*

4.0 *Organizational Memory*
— 4.1 *Storing and Retrieving Information*
— 4.2 *Computer-Based Organizational Memory*

Figure 6.1. Constructs and Processes Associated With Organizational Learning

the elaborateness of organizational learning. Finally, again in Section 3, it will be argued that *more organizational learning occurs when more organizational units develop uniform comprehensions of the various interpretations.* What is uniform here is not necessarily the perceived value or validity of the interpretation, as would be the case in "groupthink" (Janis, 1972). Rather, what is uniform are the understandings across units of the possibly different interpretations. *Thoroughness* of organizational learning is the attribute addressed with this assertion.

The paper deals with four learning-related constructs (see Figure 6.1). Each is treated in a subsequent section of the paper. *Knowledge acquisition* is the process by which knowledge is obtained. *Information distribution* is the process by which information from different sources is shared and thereby leads to new information or understanding. *Information interpretation* is the process by which distributed information is given one or more commonly understood interpretations. *Organizational memory* is the means by which knowledge is stored for future use. The last section of the paper contains some suggestions for researchers interested in learning more about organizational learning.

1. KNOWLEDGE ACQUISITION

Many formal organizational activities are intended to acquire information or knowledge. Examples are customer surveys, research and development activities, performance reviews, and analyses of competitor's products. Many informal behaviors also are directed toward obtaining information or knowledge, for example, reading the *Wall Street Journal* or listening to coffee break "news." The following discussion is organized around five processes through which organizations acquire information or knowledge: (1) congenital learning, (2) experiential learning, (3) vicarious learning, (4) grafting, and (5) searching (see Figure 6.1).

1.1. Congenital Learning

Organizations do not begin their lives with clean slates. The individuals or organizations that create new organizations have knowledge about the new organization's initial environment and about the processes the organization can use to carry out its creator's intentions, and they make this knowledge available to the new organization's members. More generally, "organizations are driven to incorporate the practices and procedures defined by prevailing rationalized concepts of organizational work and institutionalized in society" (Meyer & Rowan, 1977, p. 340). From a new organization's perspective, both the institutionalized knowledge referred to by Meyer and Rowan and the more context specific knowledge imparted by the organization's creators are *inherited knowledge.*

There invariably exists a time interval between when an organization is first conceived of and the rather arbitrarily defined birth event (when, for example, an organization is "incorporated" or is formally granted a mission and resources by its parent organization). During this interval the organization's founders employ vicarious learning, grafting, or searching to learn on behalf of the organization-to-be. Thus an organization's *congenital knowledge* is a combination of the knowledge inherited at its conception and the additional knowledge acquired prior to its birth.

The nature of an organization is greatly influenced by the nature of its founders and its founding (Boeker, 1988, 1989; Kimberly, 1979; Schein, 1984; Stinchcombe, 1965). What an organization knows at its birth will determine what it searches for, what it experiences, and how it interprets what it encounters. While there seems to be universal agreement that congenital knowledge strongly influences future learning, many of the rich details of the matter are yet to be investigated.

1.2. Experimental Learning

After their birth, organizations acquire some of their knowledge through direct experience. Sometimes this learning is a result of intentional, systematic efforts. Much more frequently it is acquired unintentionally or unsystematically. The literature related to experimental learning is quite varied, and is discussed here under the following subheadings: (1) organizational experiments, (2) organizational self-appraisal, (3) experimenting organizations, (4) unintentional or unsystematic learning, and (5) experience-based learning curves. This subsection closes with an evaluation of the literature on learning from experience.

1.2.1. Organizational Experiments. Experiential learning is enhanced by the availability and analysis of feedback. One approach to facilitating intentional organizational learning is to increase the accuracy of feedback about cause-effect relationships between organizational actions and outcomes. Another is to ensure the collection and analysis of such feedback. Both approaches are included in formal organizational experiments (cf. Lawler, 1977; Staw, 1977; Warner, 1984; Wildavsky, 1972), or in formal post hoc analyses of "natural" experiments (cf. Huber, Ullman, & Leifer, 1979; Landau, 1973; Sitkin, forthcoming). Except for the relatively well-understood processes involved in research and development and test marketing (Jelinek, 1979; Tushman & Moore, 1988), formal organizational experiments are not widely authorized by organizational administrators. One reason is that the need to project an image of decisiveness sometimes causes administrators and other leaders not to admit to the uncertainty that would motivate an experiment. In the case of either formal experiments or post hoc analyses of natural experiments, proprietary and political concerns tend to inhibit dissemination of any but positive findings (R. K. Carter, 1971; Weiss, 1973).

In spite of the importance of organizational experiments as learning mechanisms (e.g., experiments that test the market acceptability of new products or the effectiveness of new human services delivery programs), the literature contains very few studies of experimentation by organizations. What antecedent conditions favor or lead to organizational experiments? High trust? High needs for performance? A culture where tolerance for mistakes is central? (See Peters, 1987, for radical ideas on how to create such a culture.) An exception to the general lack of empirical study of organizational experiments (evidenced in the review by Warner, 1981) is the literature on program evaluation (Rossi & Freeman, 1989; Weiss, 1973), where in effect a program is an experiment even though that is not its purpose. Of course from this literature we do not find much insight into why or how organizational experiments are initiated.

The literature on organizational decision making describes two decision-making processes where successful use requires intentional learning from feedback. One, Lindblom's (1959) method of "successive limited comparisons" involves proposing (e.g., in the form of legislation) movement to some condition or position other than the present undesirable condition or position, and obtaining feedback from those affected by the proposed movement. If the proposal passes this "trial balloon" political adversity test, the proposal is authorized and implemented. If the observed outcome of the implementation is favorable, but the new situation is still not satisfactory, the process is repeated, with the proposed movement in the same general direction as the previous movement. When the outcome of a movement is negative, movement in a new direction is proposed. At each step of this process, learning occurs and affects action. The second process, related to Lindblom's method, is Quinn's (1980) somewhat more focused process of "logical incrementalism" in which the organization's

> executives artfully blend formal analysis, behavioral techniques, and power politics to bring [about] cohesive step-by-step movements toward ends which initially are broadly conceived, but which are then constantly refined and re-shaped as new information appears. (Hax & Majluf, 1988, p. 104)

1.2.2. Organizational self-appraisal is another form of experiential learning. Under this term I group a number of overlapping approaches that tend to focus on member interaction and participation as critical to learning, and on improving the organizational members' mental-health and relationships as important goals of learning. These foci contrast with a focus on monitoring more objective measures of performance, such as assessing adherence to prior plans, a subject discussed in Section 1.5.3. *Action research,* a relatively data intensive approach to organizational self-appraisal, includes gathering information about problems, concerns, and needed changes from organizational members, organizing this information, sharing it with the members, and involving the members in choosing, planning, and implementing actions to correct problems identified (Argyris, 1983; Lewin, 1949; MacNamara & Weeks, 1982; Peters & Robinson, 1984; Trist, 1983). Action research is one of several approaches employed in the field of *organizational development,* a field devoted to inducing change in organizations (Beer & Walton, 1987; Burke, 1982; French & Bell, 1990) in order to improve the quality of working life of the organization's members (Faucheux, Amado, & Laurent, 1982).

Some organizational self-appraisal literature stresses cognitive aspects of learning and focuses on learning new frames of reference (Dery, 1983;

Shrivastava & Schneider, 1984). Argyris and Schön (1974, 1978) and Argyris (1982) articulate this concept in the form of a dichotomy, "single-loop" versus "double-loop" learning, where the latter is related to an organization's frame of reference:

> One type (of organizational learning) involves the production of matches, or the detection and correction of mismatches, without change in the underlying governing policies or values. This is called *single-loop learning*. A second type, *double-loop learning,* does require re-examination and change of the governing values. Single-loop learning is usually related to the routine, immediate task. Double-loop learning is related to the nonroutine, the long-range outcome. (Argyris, 1983, p. 116)

This conceptual distinction between learning within a frame of reference and learning a new frame of reference seems critically important, but empirical study of fundamental changes in organizational frames of reference (e.g., changes in organizational culture) has been limited primarily to case studies (cf. Argyris, 1983; Tunstall, 1983). It may be that more systematic empirical studies will not find the two types of learning to be distinct in practice. It will be interesting to see if organizational scientists can verify the case study findings by drawing on data bases involving many major organizational changes (such as Miller & Friesen's studies of "Momentum and Revolution in Organizational Adaption," 1980a, and "Archetypes of Organizational Transition," 1980b).

1.2.3. Experimenting Organizations. "Adaption to a particular niche . . . while it leads to short-run survival, is never adequate for survival in the long run. . . . Adaptability is the capacity to expand niches or to find new niches" (Boulding, 1978, p. 111). Organizational experiments and self-appraisals are generally directed toward enhancing *adaptation,* while maintaining organizational experiments is generally directed toward enhancing *adaptability.*

How can organizations obtain and maintain adaptability? One group of researchers has suggested that organizations should operate themselves as "experimenting" or "self-designing" organizations, i.e., should maintain themselves in a state of frequent, nearly-continuous change in structures, processes, domains, goals, etc., even in the face of apparently optimal adaption (Hedberg, Nystrom, & Starbuck, 1976; Nystrom, Hedberg, & Starbuck, 1976; Starbuck, 1983). Hedberg, Nystrom, and Starbuck (1977) argue that operating in this mode is efficacious, perhaps even required, for survival in fast changing and unpredictable environments. They reason that probable and desirable consequences of an ongoing state of experimentation are that organizations learn about a variety of design features and remain flexible.

Experimenting organizations would thus be less resistant to adopting unfamiliar features or engaging unfamiliar environments, i.e., they would be adaptable. It is interesting to contrast this reasoning with the observation of Levitt and March (1988, p. 334):

> Since frequent changes accentuate the sample size problem by modifying a situation before it can be comprehended, such behavior is likely to lead to random drift rather than improvement (Lounamaa & March, 1987). Reducing the frequency or magnitude of change, therefore, is often an aid to comprehension, though the benefits of added information about one situation are purchased at a cost of reduction in information about others (Levinthal & Yao, 1988).

The proposal that organizations should operate themselves as experimenting organizations has had almost no effect on either practice or research. But the utility of many novel ideas is not immediately recognized—there may be instances or conditions in which experimenting organizations do or might thrive and survive (cf. Mintzberg & McHugh's, 1985; description of the National Film Board of Canada, especially p. 189; and also Nonaka's, 1988, discussion of certain learning-enhancing practices in Japanese firms). Do experimenting organizations or close approximations exist? What are the enabling conditions? Why has the idea of experimenting organizations received so little attention in the literature, except for attention from its originators? These questions beg to be answered by those seeking a full understanding of the domain of organizational learning.

1.2.4. Unintentional or unsystematic learning has been studied experimentally, analytically, and through interpretation of archival data. Experimental studies of learning by groups appeared during the late 1950s and early 1960s (Cangelosi & Dill, 1965; Chapman, Kennedy, Newell, & Biel, 1959; Dill & Doppelt, 1963). Judged by today's standards, these studies were not methodologically sophisticated, and they were minimally cumulative in that they tended not to draw upon or extend the results of previous studies. They did, however, often lead to observations that have not been contradicted, e.g., that group or organizational learning is often haphazard and multi-faceted. Experimental work on organizational learning has nearly ceased (but see Miles & Randolph, 1980, for an exception). Why this has occurred is unclear. Its demise seems unfortunate.

Analytic work was more common during the 1980s. Levinthal and March (1981) studied the nature and consequences of adaptive search in the context of a firm searching for new technologies. Cohen (1981) examined the effects of organizational structure on the effectiveness of search. Harrison and

March (1984) demonstrated that post-decisional feedback about decision outcomes is necessarily more likely than not to be disappointing, and that the degree of disappointment is a function of the number of alternatives considered and the accuracy of the estimates of the payoffs associated with choosing the alternatives. Herriott, Levinthal, and March (1985) examined the effects of several variables on experiential learning in the context of budgeting resources across return-producing activities. Lounamaa and March (1987) studied learning by modeling a two-person team whose members learn about each other in the process of coordinating their actions. These works provide interesting findings, but are decidedly noncumulative. The interesting finding that fast learning is sometimes disadvantageous (Herriott et al., 1985; Levinthal & March, 1981; Lounamaa & March, 1987) seems plausible as developed and discussed by Levitt and March (1988), but the frequency and nature of this phenomenon deserve investigation in field settings.

March and Olsen (1979) describe instances of unintentional or unsystematic organization learning in real organizations. Other than these retrospective interpretations, there appear to be few if any published observational or archival studies where unintentional or unsystematic organizational learning was the focal topic of interest. Systematic field studies of unintentional organizational learning would considerably enhance our understanding of the phenomenon and could serve as bases for critiquing and guiding laboratory and analytic work.

1.2.5. Experience-Based Learning Curves. What is the hard evidence that an organization's experience enhances its performance? Using years in the industry as a proxy for experience, and even after controlling for size and the development of resource-enhancing linkages, Brittain (1989) found experience to predict organizational survival. An extensive literature (Dutton, Thomas, & Butler, 1984; Mody, 1989; Muth, 1986; Yelle, 1979) documents the positive effect of experience on performance—as manufacturing organizations gain experience in producing a new product, their production cost and production time per unit decrease. The magnitudes of the reductions are often predictable from a mathematical model (sometimes called an "experience curve" or a "learning curve"), and the predictions are frequently used in planning. Recent work (Epple, Argote, & Devadas, this volume) demonstrates how nonsimple learning-curve models can be used to investigate possible explanations of organizational learning. This is an important use of such models, as empirical studies (cf. Joskow & Rose, 1985; Zimmerman, 1982) make clear that a number of contingency variables may be required for an accurate explanation to be achieved.

TABLE 6.1 A Sample of Obstacles to Organizational Learning From Experience

The organization's members, as sensors of experience, function imperfectly (Feldman, 1989). Some of these shortcomings are pervasive (Harrison & March, 1984; Hogarth, 1987; Schwenk, 1984) and others depend on the member's position, background, and style (Dearborn & Simon, 1958; Ireland et al., 1987; Nutt, 1986).

Feedback of the results of organizational action is often distorted or suppressed (Huber, 1982; Weiss, 1980) or arrives after the need for learning as a basis for changing the action has passed (Starbuck & Milliken, 1988).

Units capable of learning from the experience of other units may not have access to this experience, as a consequence of either routine rules for message routing (Huber, 1982) or organizational politics (Newman, 1985).

Apparent "consequences of organizational actions" may be unrelated to organizational actions; "superstitious learning" occurs (Levitt & March, 1988; Ouchi, 1984, pp. 3-4).

As a result of its having developed a high level of competence in one process when comparing this process to other processes, an organization may come to perceive this process as superior to other processes in which it has less competence. The latter processes may actually be superior, and would have been found to be so if the organization had developed competencies in them equal to its competence in the process that was observed to be more effective (Levitt & March, 1988).

1.2.6. Evaluation of the Literature on Learning From Experience. A desirable feature of the literature on learning from experience is that the studies employ multiple methods (e.g., laboratory experiments, mathematical analysis, computer simulations, and retrospective analysis of organizational events). Another desirable characteristic is that the literature is replete with fresh insights. Some observations about the difficulties encountered in organizational learning from experience, especially when the learning is unintentional or unsystematic, are shown in Table 6.1.

Examining the literature on experiential learning makes clear that a great deal has been learned, but also raises four concerns. The first relates to the nature of the literature. Holding aside the literature on experience-based learning curves, the literature on organizational learning from experience contains very few formal, systematic field studies. The second concern is that the number of independent investigators examining any particular issue is small. The third concern has to do with the relative absence of studies that build on the results of previous studies. For example, in contrast to the studies concerning the effects of experience in manufacturing, the analytic studies of unintentional or unsystematic organizational learning tend only to reference, rather than draw upon, the previous results of analytic studies.[3] The fourth concern is the lack of intellectual interaction among investigators from different groups. Work reported by any one group rarely builds on findings or ideas from other groups. If the issues investigated were so unique that attention to the work of outsiders would be dysfunctionally distracting, then this parochial behavior would be understandable, but the issues are not conceptually that different.

We have examined processes where the experience leading to learning was firsthand. The next two processes to be examined involve organizations acquiring knowledge through second-hand experience.

1.3. Vicarious Learning: Acquiring Second-Hand Experience

Organizations commonly attempt to learn about the strategies, administrative practices, and especially technologies (Czepiel, 1975; Sahal, 1982) of other organizations. For example,

> borrowing from other organizations is one form of organizational learning. Manufacturers such as automobile and computer companies have for years routinely examined in detail their competitors' products as they appear in the marketplace. (Eells & Nehemiks, 1984)

"Corporate intelligence" is the term associated with the idea of searching for information about what corporate competitors are doing and how they do it (Fuld, 1988; Gilad & Gilad, 1988; Porter, 1980; Sammon, Kurland, & Spitalnic, 1984). Channels for acquiring this information include consultants, professional meetings, trade shows, publications, vendors and suppliers and, in less competitive environments, networks of professionals.

"Institutional theory" (Meyer & Rowan, 1977; Zucker, 1987) holds that organizations pervasively imitate other organizations because doing so minimizes sanctions from a variety of stakeholders. House and Singh (1987), drawing considerably on March (1981), state that mimicry occurs particularly "when technologies are poorly understood and when goals are ambiguous" (p. 709). In contrast, it appears that mimicry is not efficacious when environments are both competitive and fast-changing. Based on their empirical study of organizations in just such an environment, Bourgeois and Eisenhardt (1988) concluded that "Imitation is often not viable . . . as it implies both waiting and jumping into an occupied niche" (p. 833). A rich discussion of the circumstances where acquiring second-hand experience through imitation is, and is not, to be preferred over learning through first-hand experience is provided by Dutton and Freedman (1985).

The literature on diffusion of technologies and administrative practices has been suggested by Dutton and Freedman (1985) and Levitt and March (1988) as a source of information for researchers interested in organizational learning through imitation. However, Mahajan, Sharma, and Bettis (1988) provide reasoning and data that do not support the diffusion model, and suggest that imitation may be a more limited form of organizational learning than has been suggested previously. Accurate models of learning through imitation may require some degree of complexity. For example, in their study of cross-organizational learning in shipyards, Argote, Beckman, and Epple (1990) found that imitation played a much larger role at the time that shipyards initiated production than after production was ongoing. Whether organizations imitate high status organizations (e.g., Toyota, IBM) as a result of the same forces that cause people to imitate the actions of celebrities or other high status individuals is a matter in need of theoretical and empirical investigation.

1.4. Grafting

Organizations frequently increase their store of knowledge by acquiring and grafting on new members who possess knowledge not previously available within the organization. Sometimes grafting-on of carriers of new knowledge is done on a large-scale basis, as in the case of an acquisition of a whole organization by another. A well-known example is General Motors' acquisition of Ross Perot's corporation, EDS, in order to obtain the information systems expertise possessed by EDS. For acquiring complex forms of information or knowledge, grafting is often faster than acquisition through experience and more complete than acquisition through imitation.

Empirical studies of knowledge acquisition through grafting are scarce, but see Lyles's (1988) examination of knowledge acquisition through joint ventures. The work of Jemison and Sitkin (1986) on the necessity of attending to the process dimension of mergers is relevant and perhaps indicative of the type of work that will be useful in the future. We can expect that, as the rate at which organizations must assimilate new knowledge continues to increase (Drucker, 1988; Huber, 1984), grafting will become a more frequently used approach for organizations to acquire quickly knowledge that is new to them.

The last of the five information acquisition processes to be discussed is learning by searching or noticing. The literature seems to indicate that searching is the process most consciously pursued by managers on a day-to-day basis.

1.5. Searching and Noticing

Organizational information acquisition through search can be viewed as occurring in three forms: (1) scanning, (2) focused search, and (3) performance monitoring. *Scanning* refers to the relatively wide-ranging sensing of the organization's external environment. *Focused search* occurs when organizational members or units actively search in a narrow segment of the organization's internal or external environment, often in response to actual or suspected problems or opportunities. *Performance monitoring* is used to mean both focused and wide-ranging sensing of the organization's effectiveness in fulfilling its own pre-established goals or the requirements of stakeholders. *Noticing* is the unintended acquisition of information about the organization's external environment, internal conditions, or performance. Space constraints preclude further discussion of noticing, but see Starbuck and Milliken (1988).

1.5.1. Scanning. Organizational environments change. If the lack of fit between an organization and its environment becomes too great, the organization either fails to survive or undergoes a costly transformation (Miller & Friesen, 1980a, 1980b; Tushman & Romanelli, 1985). In recognition of this, organizations scan their environments for information about changes (Fahey, King, & Narayanan, 1981; Wilensky, 1967). Scanning varies in intensity from high vigilance, active scanning, to the routine scanning or mere maintenance of a state of alertness for nonroutine (but relevant) information, as in the "passive search" noted by Mintzberg, Raisinghani, and Theoret (1976, p. 255).

Two literatures relate to scanning, one in which the organization or department is the unit of analysis (the "macro" literature) and one in which the individual is the unit of analysis (the "micro" literature). The macro literature (cf. Aguilar, 1967; Dutton & Freedman, 1985; Hambrick, 1982; Jemison, 1984) is dominated by research related to environmental scanning for enhancing strategic management effectiveness. Fundamental to this literature is the assumption that scanning contributes to performance, an assumption that has been validated in a variety of studies (Daft, Sormunen, & Parks, 1988; Dollinger, 1984; Tushman & Katz, 1980).

The micro literature on scanning focuses on boundary-spanning personnel as sensors of the organization's environment. Two streams of research are apparent. One, on gatekeepers in the research and development industry, is relatively mature—empirical studies build on earlier conceptualizations and empirical studies (Gerstenfeld & Berger, 1980; Tushman, 1977). A modest theory linking gatekeeper characteristics and behavior to organizational performance has been developed by Tushman and his associates (Tushman, 1977; Tushman & Katz, 1980; Tushman & Scanlan, 1981). A second and still developing stream of research deals with the environmental monitoring behavior of upper-level managers. It is less mature, consisting largely of field studies of managerial activities (Dollinger, 1984; Keegan, 1974; Kurke &

Aldrich, 1983; Mintzberg, 1975). Theory-testing studies of boundary span-
ners as sensors of the environment are not common (but see Blandin &
Brown, 1977; Hambrick, 1982; Leifer & Huber, 1977; Schwab, Ungson, &
Brown, 1985).

1.5.2. Focused Search. The organizational science literature related to focused search has dealt primarily with two matters: the antecedents to focused
search and the nature of focused search. With respect to antecedents, early
authorities noted that the initiation of focused search is not a casual behavioral change. For example, Reitzel (1958) emphasizes that there seems to be
a general reluctance to initiate focused search unless it is clearly necessary.

> Not until the element of novelty in a problem situation has become clearly
> explicit will a significant disruption of the relationship between the environ-
> ment and the organism be sharply felt and a search begin for alternatives to
> the habitual response. Then and only then does a more or less conscious and
> deliberate decision-making process get initiated. (p. 4)

Downs (1966, p. 190) and Ansoff (1975) also suggested that for search-
prompting signals to have an effect they must be very "loud" and received
from multiple sources, and Feldman and Kanter (1965) stated that "the
organization will search for additional alternatives when the consequences
of the present alternatives do not satisfy its goals" (p. 622). In addition, it is
apparently not only that the need for focused search be clear, but also that
effort directed toward resolving the problem (or capitalizing on the opportunity) be viewed as having a satisfactory probability of success (Glueck,
1976, p. 70; Schwab et al., 1985).

   Cyert and March (1963, pp. 44-82, 120-122) observe that search tends to
be focused in the vicinity of the problem symptoms or the current alternative,
i.e., on options that are readily available or that have been directed at similar
problems in the past, and O'Reilly (1982) and Culnan (1983) find that the
choice of information sources is greatly affected by source accessibility.
Together these ideas suggest that some sort of threshold must be exceeded
before search will take place, where the threshold is defined both in terms of
the costs and benefits associated with searching versus not searching and in
terms of the probabilities that these costs and benefits will be incurred.
Mintzberg et al.'s (1976) discussion of a search initiation threshold is in
terms of these variables. Thus the thrust of much of the literature is that
organizations will initiate focused search when (1) a problem is recognized
and (2) some heuristic assessment of the costs, benefits, and probabilities
involved suggests that a search-justifying threshold value has been reached

or exceeded. Cyert and March argued that these two conditions are both necessary and sufficient for focused search to occur—such search will not be initiated unless such conditions occur and will be initiated if they occur. In contrast to this emphasis on recognition of a problem as the impetus for search, in his extension of Cyert and March's *A Behavioral Theory of the Firm,* Carter (1971) observes internally initiated search in the form of search for opportunities in the environment:

> The procedure was for the president to initiate probes by mentioning, either in casual conversation or by explicit memorandum, that Comcor was interested in purchasing certain types of companies. Staff members could then seek companies that fit the requirements. (p. 420)

Whether focused search is largely reactive or proactive is related to the issue of determinism versus voluntarism in organizational change (Astley & Van de Ven, 1983; Hambrick & Finkelstein, 1987). My speculation is that in organizational subunits and at lower organizational levels search is largely reactive to problems, but that in autonomous organizations and at higher organizational levels a significant proportion of search is a consequence of proactive managerial initiatives. Underlying these possible relationships is the likelihood that organizational slack and managerial discretion (Allen, 1979; Hambrick & Finkelstein, 1987) are more frequent at higher organizational levels, and that slack and discretion are key determinants of whether search behavior will be proactively initiated.

1.5.3. Performance Monitoring. One of the clearest and most pervasive forms of organizational search is performance monitoring. Organizations formally and routinely assess how well they are meeting both their own standards, such as inventory levels, and the expectations of external constituencies and stakeholders. In addition, as Mintzberg (1975) makes clear, managers informally monitor conditions in their organization. While performance monitoring has as its ultimate purpose improving performance, Crozier (1965) takes a very pessimistic view and argues that bureaucratic organizations simply "cannot correct their behavior by learning from their errors" (p. 186). Wildavsky (1972), Landau (1973), and Staw and Ross (1987) present somewhat more broadly based analyses of when and how it is that organizations do not use feedback to improve their performance.

1.5.4. Evaluation of the literature on learning by searching indicates that much has been learned, but identifies two problems. One of these is the *lack of conceptual work.* For example, no distinction has been made between focused search for solutions and focused search for information about already identified solutions (the former being more a matter of discovery or identification and the latter being more one of investigation). The distinction might be useful, as the various forms of search might have different antecedents or might be carried out by different types of organizational units or with different types of search processes. Some support for this idea is Fredrickson's (1985) finding that preferred search processes varied according to whether the stimulus was a problem or an opportunity, and also Dutton and Jackson's (1987) thoughts about how the labeling of a situation as a threat or opportunity might affect organizational actions.

Another example of conceptual work that might be useful concerns the *information environment,* the set of symbols, data, and other indicators of the environment that is subject to being sensed by the organization and that stands conceptually between the actual environment and the perceived environment (Huber & Daft, 1987). Once conceptualized, the information environment can be thought of as having characteristics, such as completeness, unbiasedness, and clarity, that may be important predictors of organizational learning and that seem subject to enhancement through managerial action.

The second problem identified when evaluating the organizational search literature is that, while early field studies (Cyert & March, 1963) were used to build and to test theory (E. E. Carter, 1971; Gerwin, 1969; Weber, 1965), in recent years there has been a *lack of theory-testing field work.*

Before closing this section on search, it seems worthwhile to note that not all organizational search is carried out for the purpose of learning. For example, organizational decision makers must frequently legitimate their decisions to others. Sabatier (1978) discusses this point at some length and notes a number of field studies where information was sought for the explicit purpose of legitimating decisions reached on other grounds. Similarly, their extensive interview study of mid-to-high level public officials led Weiss (1980) to state that:

> If research (information) is used, it usually . . . is expected to convince other people of the credibility and legitimacy of one's position. Several people spoke about . . . the use of research (information) as ammunition in the political wars. (p. 388)

The needs to reduce their post-decisional dissonance, to legitimate decisions to others, and to project an image of thoroughness and objectivity frequently cause organizations and their members to search for more information than is necessary to solve the focal problem. This may be a partial explanation for the oft-repeated observation that decision makers acquire "too much" information. (See Connolly, 1988, for a review and critique of the literature that supports this point of view. Also see Feldman & March, 1981, for a discussion of the conspicuous display of information search behavior as a mechanism for managing perceptions, and March & Sevón, 1984, for a discussion of still other uses of information and information-related behaviors in and by organizations.)

To some extent the five information-acquisition processes just discussed can be substitutes for each other. On the other hand, some have characteristics that favor their use in certain situations. For example, vicarious learning and grafting seem like they would be faster than experiential learning for obtaining technical "know how." As another example, given the difficulties inherent in changing an individual's or an organization's frame of reference, it seems that under some circumstances experience would be a very poor teacher and that vicarious learning, grafting, or searching would therefore be necessary for learning to occur. Under other circumstances only experience would convince a recalcitrant learner/adapter that the externally observed frame of reference was locally valid.

Many organizational members and units that serve as knowledge acquirers also have, as part of their role, sharing what they have acquired with other organizational components. This brings us to the subject of information distribution.

2. INFORMATION DISTRIBUTION

Information distribution is a determinant of both the occurrence and breadth of organizational learning. With regard to occurrence of organizational learning, consider that organizational components commonly develop "new" information by piecing together items of information that they obtain from other organizational units, as when a shipping department learns that a shortage problem exists by comparing information from the warehouse with information from the sales department.

With respect to the idea that information distribution leads to more broadly based organizational learning, consider the fact that organizations often do not know what they know. Except for their systems that routinely index and store "hard" information, organizations tend to have only weak systems for finding where a certain item of information is known to the organization. But when information is widely distributed in an organization, so that more and more varied sources for it exist, retrieval efforts are more likely to succeed and individuals and units are more likely to be able to learn. Thus, information distribution leads to *more broadly based* organizational

TABLE 6.2 Propositions Concerning Information Distribution in Organizations

The probability that organizational member or unit A will rout information to member or unit B is:
1. positively related to A's view of the information's relevance to B,
2. positively related to B's power and status,
3. negatively related to A's view of A's costs of routing the information to B
4. negatively related to A's workload,
5. positively related to the rewards and negatively related to the penalties that A expects to result from the routing, and
6. positively related to the frequency with which A has previously routed information to B in the recent past.

The probability or extent of delay in the routing of information by A to B is:
1. positively related to the workload of A,
2. positively related to the number of sequential links in the communication chain connecting A to B, and
3. negatively related to A's view of the timeliness of the information for B

The probability or extent of information distortion by A when communicating to B is:
1. positively related to A's view of the consequent increase in A's goal attainment that will result from the distortion,
2. negatively related to the penalty that A expects to incur as a result of introducing the distortion,
3. positively related to the amount of discretion allowed in the presentation format,
4. positively related to the difference between the actual information and the desired or expected information,
5. positively related to A's work overload, and
6. positively related to the number of sequential links in the communication chain connecting A with B.

SOURCE: From Huber (1982) and Huber and Daft (1987).

learning. This is in contrast to the previous idea that information distribution leads to *new* organizational learning.

Researchers in organizational behavior and organizational communications have learned a great deal about information distribution in organizations, and reviews are numerous (Farace & McDonald, 1974; Guetzkow, 1965; Huber, 1982; Krone, Jablin, & Putnam, 1987; O'Reilly & Pondy, 1980; Porter & Roberts, 1976; Thayer, 1967). Drawing on these reviews allows us to summarize much of what is relevant for our immediate purpose in the form of a modest number of propositions (see Table 6.2).

Organizational units with potentially synergistic information are often not aware of where such information could serve, and so do not route it to these destinations. Also, units which might be able to use information synergistically often do not know of its existence or whereabouts. How those who possess nonroutine information and those who need this information find each other is relatively unstudied, but deserves the attention of researchers interested in organizational learning. One organizational process that facilitates the coupling of those who need nonroutine information and those who have it is internal employee transfer, both employee-initiated and employer-initiated. The role of this process in intra-organizational information distribution is a prime candidate for empirical study.

Combining information from different subunits leads not only to new information but also to new understanding. This fact highlights the role of information distribution as a precursor to aspects of organizational learning that involve information interpretation:

> . . . it is assumed that the organizational interpretation process is something more than what occurs by individuals [who] come and go. . . . Organizations preserve knowledge, behaviors, mental maps, norms, and values over time. The distinctive feature of organization level information activity is sharing. (Daft & Weick, 1984, p. 285)

3. INFORMATION INTERPRETATION

Daft and Weick (1984) define interpretation as "the process through which information is given meaning" (p. 294), and also as "the process of translating events and developing shared understandings and conceptual schemes" (p. 286). Do these definitions imply that, if all organizational units develop a common interpretation about an item of information, then more organization learning has occurred? Or has more organizational learning occurred if all units interpret the information differently? In other words, should organizational learning be defined in terms of the commonality of interpretation, or should it be defined in terms of the variety of interpretations held by the organization's various units? It seems reasonable to conclude that more learning has occurred when more and more varied interpretations have been developed, because such development changes the range of the organization's potential behaviors, and this is congruent with the definition of learning. It also seems reasonable to conclude that more learning has occurred when more of the organization's units understand the nature of the various interpretations held by other units. For example, more complete understanding can either enhance cooperation and thus increase the range of potential behaviors, or can inhibit cooperation and thus decrease the range of potential behaviors. In either case, more complete understanding leads to a change in the range of potential behaviors, i.e., to organizational learning.

There seems to have been little systematic study of the development of shared understanding among organizational units about particular events or items of information, but there has been some, and there are related literatures. For reviews of related literatures, see Isabella's (1990) review of the cognitive aspects of interpretation in organizations and her study of the temporal nature of interpretation, Jablin's (1984, 1987) reviews of socialization of new members, and Sproull's (1981) review of the role of face-to-face communication in constructing and maintaining interpretations of situations. Dutton, Fahey, and Narayanan (1983) provide a rich conceptual description of interpretation in the context of development of corporate strategy. How organizations develop interpretations of history from scattered and unique experiences is explained by March, Sproull, and Tamuz (this volume).

It seems likely that the extent of shared interpretation of new information is affected by (1) the uniformity of prior *cognitive maps* possessed by the organizational units, (2) the uniformity of the *framing* of the information as it is communicated, (3) the *richness of the media* used to convey the information, (4) the *information load* on the interpreting units, and (5) the amount of *unlearning* that might be necessary before a new interpretation could be generated. Other variables may also be determinants of shared interpretations (Bartunek, 1984; Milliken, 1990), but these five either follow from our earlier discussions or have been singled out in the literature as especially relevant. Each is discussed below.

3.1. Cognitive Maps and Framing

The facts that a person's prior cognitive map (or belief structure or mental representation or frame of reference) will shape his or her interpretation of information, and that these cognitive maps vary across organizational units having different responsibilities, are well established (Dearborn & Simon, 1958; Ireland, Hitt, Bettis, & DePorras, 1987; Kennedy, 1983; Walker, 1985; Zajonc & Wolfe, 1966). Similarly, it is well established that how information is framed or labeled affects its interpretation (Dutton & Jackson, 1987; Tversky & Kahneman, 1985). If information is not uniformly framed when distributed to different units, uniform interpretations are less likely to be achieved. Of course, differences in language or cognitive maps across units may require that idiosyncratic messages be used to create uniform framings. An important feature of interpretations in organizations is that they are socially constructed (Sims, Gioia, & Associates, 1986). This fact introduces the role of communication media in the construction of common meaning.

3.2. Media Richness

Media richness is a determinant of the extent to which information is given common meaning by the sender and receiver of a message. It is defined as the communication "medium's capacity to change mental representations within a specific time interval" (Daft & Huber, 1987, p. 14; Daft & Lengel, 1984). It has two underlying dimensions—the variety of cues that the medium can convey and the rapidity of feedback that the medium can provide. Research supports the notion that managers who consider media richness when choosing a communication medium are more effective (Daft, Lengel, & Trevino, 1987), and thus provides some support for the idea that media richness affects the development of common understanding.

Media can convey too great a range of symbols for some aspects of the interpretation task. For example, when assessing the effectiveness of various media, Short, Williams, and Christie (1976)

> found more opinion change via audio-only media. Kiesler et al. (1984) found significantly higher choice shift in computer-conferencing groups, although Hiltz and Turoff (1978) present contradictory evidence. Short et al. (1976) conclude that, whatever the benefits of face-to-face communication, it also distracts communicators from the task and from vocal cues that might indicate lying. By directing too much attention toward the communicators, face-to-face interactions may lead to ineffective task outcomes. (Culnan & Markus, 1987, pp. 428-429)

Before leaving this discussion of information interpretation, it is appropriate to note that shared interpretation of information is not necessary for organizational units to agree on action. For example, Donnellon, Gray, and Bougon (1986) interpret Weick (1979) as arguing that

> only minimal shared understanding is required, because organization is based primarily on exchange (e.g., of work for pay). That is, in order to produce organized action, group members need only share the knowledge that the exchange will continue. It is not necessary that members subscribe to the same goals or share the same interpretations of their joint action. (p. 43)

The empirical study by Donnellon et al. (1986) supports Weick's argument. Eisenberg (1984) and Eisenberg and Witten (1987) go further and argue that ambiguity facilitates agreement on actions in that it allows each unit to believe whatever is necessary to achieve consensus. See Weick and Bougon (1986) for further development of the idea of shared understanding. With regard to the relationships among clarity of communication, information interpretation, and organizational effectiveness, it seems important to move from speculation to empirical research.

3.3. Information Overload

Interpretation within or across organizational units is less effective if the information to be interpreted exceeds the units' capacity to process the information adequately (see the study by Meier, 1963, and the reviews by Driver & Streufert, 1969; Miller, 1978, chap. 5). This fact was vividly portrayed by Schlesinger (1970) in his testimony to the Senate Subcommittee on National Security and International Operations:

> What happened in Viet Nam is that we were simply drowned in statistics; we were drowned in information. A very small proportion of this information was adequately analyzed. We would have been much better off to have a much smaller take of information and to have done a better job of interpreting what that information meant. (p. 482)

Clearly, overload detracts from effective interpretation. Further, as a result of variability in cognitive maps across units, even uniform overload, by creating ambiguity in the perceived input, will lead to nonuniform interpretation. This is because

> presented with a complex stimulus, the subject perceives in it what it is ready to perceive; the more complex or ambiguous the stimulus, the more perception will be determined by what is already "in" the subject and the less by what is in the stimulus. (Bruner, 1957, pp. 132-133)

Overload that is not uniform across units leads, of course, to even greater disparities in the uniformity of interpretation and learning.

In his discussion of information overload, Simon (1973) concludes that organization designs that minimize the need for information distribution among the organization's units reduce the information load on the units, and should be adopted by organizations in excessively rich information environments. But this "design for informational autonomy" would reduce information sharing across units and would consequently curtail some types of organizational learning. For arguments supporting this latter point, in the research and development context, see Sitkin (forthcoming). Clearly the informational interconnectedness of units affects organizational learning in complex ways, and is one of the variables that should be investigated in future research.

3.4. Unlearning and Its Effects on Learning

"Unlearning" is an attention-catching term that appears in the organization and management literature (Hedberg, 1981; Klein, 1989; Nystrom &
Starbuck, 1984) and that begs to be addressed in a paper dealing with
organizational learning. Hedberg is an early and frequently cited reference
on unlearning. He defines unlearning as "a process through which learners
discard knowledge" (p. 18). By emphasizing unlearning as the discarding of
"obsolete and misleading knowledge" (p. 3), he implies that unlearning is
functional, and perhaps intentional: "to forget" means not only "to lose the
remembrance of" (*Webster's New Collegiate Dictionary,* 1987, p. 484), but
also means "to disregard intentionally" (*Webster's New Collegiate Dictionary,* 1987, p. 484).

In attempting to define unlearning, it is important to note that an entity
can unlearn behaviors, and it can unlearn constraints on behaviors. Thus
unlearning can lead to either a decrease, or an increase, in the range of
potential behaviors. It follows then, from the earlier definition of learning,
that unlearning is conceptually subsumable under learning. Use of the word
"unlearning" serves primarily to emphasize a decrease in the range of
potential behaviors, rather than to indicate a qualitatively different process.

There are several effects of unlearning. One is that, because the organization is without a fact, belief, or script that it previously used, it becomes at
least temporarily inactive in the context where this knowledge had been used.
A second effect, if there is impetus for action, is that focused search is
initiated to obtain a substitute fact, belief, or script that plays a parallel role
in the organization's functioning: Whether search would be focused in the
vicinity of that which was just unlearned, as might be suggested by either
the thinking of Lindblom (1959) or Cyert and March (1963, p. 121), or would
be focused far from this vicinity, as might be imagined if that which is being
unlearned is quite aversive, is a question that merits empirical study. A third
possible effect of unlearning is that unlearning opens the way for new
learning to take place; the reasoning is analogous to Lewin's (1951) idea that
organizational change can best be implemented if a felt need for change is
first created, if an "unfreezing" occurs. An extreme form of intentional
unlearning by organizations is the discharge of employees, especially managers who are unable to move from outdated ways of doing things (Tunstall,
1983).

An unusual effect of unlearning results from socialization of new organizational members. Socialization sometimes causes new members to unlearn. A consequence can be that the knowledge that the new members
possessed upon entry becomes unavailable to the organization. Whether,
when, and how socialization of those new members who have been brought

in for the purpose of increasing the organization's knowledge (see Section 1.4 on grafting) should take place is a research opportunity with considerable significance for administrative practice.

4. ORGANIZATIONAL MEMORY

Everyday experience and some research make clear that the human components of organizational memories are often less than satisfactory. Considering the many factors that contribute to inaccurate learning and incomplete recall (Kahneman, Slovic, & Tversky, 1982; Nisbett & Ross, 1980; Starbuck & Milliken, 1988), this is not surprising. The problem of poor organizational memory is, however, much more complex than simple considerations of the deficiencies of humans as repositories of organizational information and knowledge might suggest. Everyday observations make clear (1) that personnel turnover creates great loss for the human components of an organization's memory, (2) that nonanticipation of future needs for certain information causes great amounts of information not to be stored (e.g., blackboards get erased, task completion times are not recorded) or not to be stored such that it can be easily retrieved (e.g., solutions to problems, even if stored, are often only crudely indexed), and (3) that organizational members with information needs frequently do not know of the existence or whereabouts of information possessed or stored by other members. It follows that variables likely to influence the ongoing effectiveness of organizational memory include (1) membership attrition, (2) information distribution and organizational interpretation of information, (3) the norms and methods for storing information, and (4) the methods for locating and retrieving stored information. We need not discuss membership attrition, as its deleterious effects on organizational memory are obvious, especially with respect to retention of tacit knowledge. In addition, we need not examine information distribution and interpretation, as the main idea—that the location of information and common interpretation in multiple memory nodes is associated with "more" learning—was discussed earlier.

4.1. Storing and Retrieving Information

Organizations store a great deal of "hard" information on a routine basis, sometimes for operating reasons and sometimes to satisfy the reporting requirements of other units or organizations. A great deal of organizational knowledge about how to do things is stored in the form of standard operating procedures, routines, and scripts (Feldman, 1989; Gioia & Poole, 1984; Nelson & Winter, 1982, pp. 99-107), and, as Mintzberg's (1975) work indicates, managers and others routinely acquire and mentally store "soft" information as well.

What is not well understood, and would be an interesting subject for empirical research, is the extent to which nonroutine information is deliberately stored to be used as a basis for future decision making. This behavior could involve anticipating future needs for the information. What variables determine such behavior? Several possibilities come to mind: the degree to which the future needs are predictable; the scope of future needs that the member can envision; the commitment to the well-being of the organization (or to other subunits if storage is not for oneself); and the accessibility and utility of the channels and mechanisms available for storage.

As a result of specialization, differentiation, and departmentalization, organizations frequently do not know what they know. The potential for reducing this problem by including computers as part of the organization's memory is considerable, and deserves investigation by organizational scientists as well as by computer scientists and information systems designers.

4.2. Computer-Based Organizational Memory

Information concerning the times necessary to complete fabrication of certain products, to receive shipments of ordered materials, to recruit or train various types of employees, or to deliver certain types of services are more and more frequently resident in computers as transactions artifacts, either those created and transmitted internally using the organization's electronic mail, electronic bulletin board, or electronic blackboard systems, or those exchanged electronically across the organization's boundaries (e.g., letters, billings, and contracts). Case-by-case foresight, smart indexing or, in the future, artificial intelligence (Johansen, 1988, pp. 34-36) can facilitate retrieval of information from these artifacts. Automatic capturing and sophisticated retrieval of such information result in computer-resident organizational memories with certain properties, such as completeness and precision, that are superior to the human components of organizational memories. On-going increases in the "friendliness" and capability of computer-based information retrieval systems are lowering some obstacles to the implementation of the above ideas and practices.

What about "soft" information? Much of what an organization learns is stored in the minds of its members. In many cases organizations grow their own experts. These people are expert not in a whole discipline or broad category of problems, but rather have had organizational experiences that made them expert with respect to specific intellectual tasks such as (1) diagnosing quality problems or equipment malfunctions; (2) learning the identities of extra-organizational experts, influence peddlers, resource providers, or other nonmembers who may be useful to the organization; and (3) locating information or other resources not locatable using official, standard sources. Using the knowledge of these home-grown experts, organizations are creating computer-based expert systems (Rao & Lingaraj, 1988; Rauch-Hindin, 1988; Waterman, 1986). Such expert systems have some properties, such as accessibility, reliability, and "own-ability," that are superior to those of human experts and that, in some situations, are useful components of organizational memories. Thus, even though expert systems have other properties that are inferior to those of human experts, as the friendliness and capability of expert systems increase, the proportion of an organization's "soft" and local information that is computer-resident increases. Research questions pertaining to the organizational issues involved in obtaining soft information and storing it in computers are noted in Huber (1990).

In closing this section, it seems appropriate to emphasize again the critical role of organizational memory in organizational learning. Two points seem worth noting. The first is that to demonstrate or use learning, that which has been learned must be stored in memory and then brought forth from memory; both the demonstrability and usability of learning depend on the effectiveness of the organization's memory. The second point is multifaceted: (1) *information acquisition* depends in many instances on attention, which is directed by previous learning retained in memory; (2) *information distribution* is affected by organizational decisions made using criteria implied in Table 6.2, which are applied using information contained in memory; (3) *information interpretation* is greatly affected by cognitive maps or frames of reference, which are undefinable except in terms of a memory. Thus the basic processes that contribute to the occurrence, breadth, and depth of organizational learning depend on organizational memory. The construct of organizational memory is clearly important to the idea of organizational learning, but has received relatively little empirical study. For a historical study demonstrating the perceived importance of organizational memory to managers, see Yates (1990). For a critique of the organizational science literature on organizational memory, see Walsh and Ungson (1991).

5. SUMMARY

In this paper, four constructs related to organizational learning (knowledge acquisition, information distribution, information interpretation, and organizational memory) were examined, and the literature related to each was described and critiqued. Because the literature on *knowledge acquisition* is voluminous and multi-faceted, the process was portrayed as consisting of five subconstructs or subprocesses: (1) congenital learning, (2) experiential learning, (3) vicarious learning, (4) grafting, and (5) searching or noticing. Examination of the related literatures indicated that, while much has been learned about experiential learning, there is a lack of cumulative work and a lack of synthesis of work from different research groups. Similarly, it was found that much has been learned about organizational search, but that there is a lack of conceptual work and a lack both of continuing empirical work and of integration with which to create a more mature literature. Congenital learning, vicarious learning, and grafting were found to be information acquisition subprocesses about which relatively little has been learned beyond the fact that they occur.

The literature concerning *information distribution* was found to be rich and mature. However, a key aspect of information distribution, namely how organizational units possessing information and units needing this information can find each other quickly and with a high likelihood, was found to be unexplored. *Information interpretation,* as an organizational process rather than as an individual process, was found to require empirical work for further advancement. Finally, *organizational memory,* as a determinant of organizational learning and decision making, was found to be much in need of systematic investigation.

A number of conclusions follow from this examination of organizational learning. One is that the organizational processes and subprocesses that contribute to changes in the range of an organization's potential behaviors are more numerous and varied than a small sampling of the organizational science literature might suggest. While any one research group can ignore this fact with little peril to itself, the field as a whole cannot. A second conclusion is that, with few exceptions (e.g., experience-based learning curves and information distribution), there is little in the way of substantiated theory concerning organizational learning and there is considerable need and opportunity to fill in the many gaps.

The third conclusion flies in the face of the normal science paradigm and contributes to the just-noted lack of substantiated theory—the researchers who have studied organizational learning apparently have, to a surprising degree, not used the results from previous research to design or interpret their own research. Another conclusion, also contrary to the advice that scientists frequently give to each other, is that there is little cross-fertilization or synthesis of work done by different research groups or on different but related aspects of organizational learning. (An exception to this conclusion is that March has made important contributions in a number of areas and has provided a number of integrative works.)

No clear indication exists as to why research on organizational learning has not conformed to recommended practice. Why is there so little cumulative work? Why has so little integration taken place? There are no answers in the literature, but there are clues. One clue is that, in general, the landscape of research on organizational learning is sparsely populated. Consequently, it may be difficult for researchers to find one another in the disparate literatures where their works appear. Further, because there is little agreement on what organizational learning is or how it should be assessed, the encounters that do occur tend not to be fruitful.

A second clue concerning the paucity of cumulative work is found in the review by Levitt and March (1988). Speaking about inter-organizational learning, they observe that:

> Ecologies of learning include various types of interactions among learners (e.g., groups of researchers), but the classical type is a collection of competitors. . . . There is a tendency for organizations (e.g., groups of researchers) to specialize and for faster learners to specialize in inferior technologies. (pp. 331-332; parenthetical phrases added)

Science-making is a competitive industry, as well as a cooperative one. Scientists tend not to follow in the trails of others if blazing their own trail leads to ownership of part of the landscape. Further, this tendency not to follow the trail of others is exacerbated when lack of agreement on definitions and measures makes the identity of the right trail problematic. Finally, initial success tends to lead to specialization and, while specialization leads to competence and therefore more success, specialization also leads to niches and regions uninhabited by competitors, and so ignorance of the work of others persists. Scientists, like organizations, tend to learn well what they do, and tend to do what they have learned to do well.

What will change this state of affairs? What will lead to work in organizational learning that is cumulative and integrative? One possible answer is exposure to facts and findings from other research groups and streams that can be used to extend the boundaries of one's own work. This paper is an attempt to create such exposure. Another answer, perhaps more compelling, was noted earlier—as the landscape of research on organizational learning becomes more densely populated, much of what an investigator might do might have been done, and so the investigator is compelled to do work closely adjacent to and interfacing with the work of others. Finally, again as the research landscape becomes densely populated, ownership rights become of concern, and researchers are forced by professional norms and journal editors to acknowledge the work of others, and in so doing they will sometimes see ways to capitalize on it. Because the topic of organizational learning is intellectually attractive and of practical importance, it seems quite likely that a denser landscape of studies and researchers will develop, and that this in turn will lead to cumulation and synthesis, and eventually to a rich and elaborate understanding of the phenomenon.

The last conclusion that follows from this examination of organizational learning is of singular importance. With very few exceptions (e.g., the work on organizational self-appraisal and on media richness), work on organizational learning has not led to research-based guidelines for increasing the effectiveness of organizational learning. Nor has it been presented in forums or media typically monitored by those who guide organizational processes. These two conditions certainly seem deserving of attention and remedial action, as organizational adaption and innovation, both critical in a rapidly changing world, could undoubtedly be improved if organizational designers and administrators knew more about how organizations learn and about how organizations might be guided to learn more effectively.

Acknowledgments

This research was supported in part by the Army Research Institute for the Behavioral and Social Sciences. I am indebted to Janice Beyer, Fred Jablin, David Jemison, Arie Lewin, Reuben McDaniel, Chet Miller, Karl Weick, and Claire Weinstein and the reviewers and editors of this special issue for their many useful suggestions and constructive comments on earlier drafts of this paper.

NOTES

1. The words information and knowledge will be used interchangeably in this paper. I have, however, tried to use *information* when referring to data that give meaning by reducing ambiguity, equivocality, or uncertainty, or when referring to data which indicate that conditions are not as presupposed, and have tried to use *knowledge* when referring to more complex products of learning, such as interpretations of information, beliefs about cause-effect relationships, or, more generally, "know-how." While I believe that most readers will be comfortable with this usage, I note that cognitive psychologists (cf. Paris, Lipson, & Wixson, 1983) have developed their own terminology and divide knowledge into "declarative" (i.e., facts), "procedural" (e.g., know-how, scripts), and "conditional" (as in "under what circumstances does this apply").

2. Living systems sense and otherwise process enormous amounts of data. For some purposes even a fleeting, unintended storage in the entity's short-term memory should be viewed as learning. Given the length and purposes of this paper, however, employing the phrase "that it recognizes as potentially useful" is helpful in that it avoids having to deal with the murky construct of "latent information," data acquired but unrecognized by any organizational unit as having any potential use.

3. It may be that the difference between the extent of cumulation in these two example clusters is a consequence of the size or density of the clusters. In dense clusters of studies, such as the experience-curve cluster, there may not be niches for additional free-standing studies—much of what an investigator might do may have been done, and so the investigator adds (marginally) to previous work. In contrast, in sparse clusters, such as the analytic studies of organizational learning, the benefits from relatively divergent, unconnected studies may outweigh the benefits from superimposed, cumulative studies.

REFERENCES

Aguilar, F. J. (1967). *Scanning the business environment.* New York: Macmillan.

Allen, S. A. (1979). Understanding reorganizations of divisionalized companies. *Academy of Management Journal, 22,* 641-671.

Ansoff, H. I. (1975). Managing strategic surprise by response to weak signals. *California Management Review, 18,* 21-33.

Argote, L., Beckman, S. L., & Epple, D. (1990). The persistence and transfer of learning in industrial settings. *Management Science, 36*(2), 140-154.

Argyris, C. (1982). *Reasoning, learning, and action: Individual and organizational.* San Francisco: Jossey-Bass.

Argyris, C. (1983). Action science and intervention. *Journal of Applied Behavioral Science, 19,* 115-140.

Argyris, C., & Schön, D. A. (1974). *Theory in practice: Increasing professional effectiveness.* San Francisco: Jossey-Bass.

Argyris, C., & Schön, D. A. (1978). *Organizational learning: A theory of action perspective.* Reading, MA: Addison-Wesley.

Astley, W. G., & Van de Ven, A. (1983). Central perspectives and debates in organization theory. *Administrative Science Quarterly, 28,* 245-273.

Bartunek, J. M. (1984). Changing interpretive schemes and organizational restructuring: The example of a religious order. *Administrative Science Quarterly, 29,* 355-372.

Beer, M., & Walton, A. E. (1987). Organization change and development. *Annual Review of Psychology, 38,* 339-367.

Beer, S. (1972). *Brain of the firm.* Harmondsworth, UK: Allen Lane, Penguin.

Blandin, J. S., & Brown, W. B. (1977). Uncertainty and management's search for information. *IEEE Transactions on Management, EM-24,* 114-119.

Boeker, W. (1988). Organizational origins: Entrepreneurial and environmental imprinting at founding. In G. Carroll (Ed.), *Ecological models of organization.* New York: Ballinger.

Boeker, W. (1989). Strategic change: The effects of founding and history. *Academy of Management Journal, 32,* 489-515.

Boulding, K. E. (1978). *Ecodynamics: A new theory of social evolution.* Beverly Hills, CA: Sage.

Bourgeois, L. J., III, & Eisenhardt, K. M. (1988). Strategic decision processes in high velocity environments: Four cases in the microcomputer industry. *Management Science, 34*(7), 816-835.

Bower, G. H., & Hilgard, E. R. (1981). *Theories of learning.* Englewood Cliffs, NJ: Prentice Hall.

Brittain, J. (1989). Strategy and time-dependent failure probabilities: Experience, obsolescence, and strategic change. *Academy of Management Proceedings,* 173-177.

Bruner, J. S. (1957). On perceptual readiness. *Psychological Review, 64,* 132-133.

Burke, W. W. (1982). *Organization development: Principles and practices.* Boston: Little, Brown.

Cangelosi, V. E., & Dill, W. R. (1965). Organizational learning: Observations toward a theory. *Administrative Science Quarterly, 10,* 175-203.

Carter, E. E. (1971). The behavioral theory of the firm and top-level corporate decisions. *Administrative Science Quarterly, 16,* 413-428.

Carter, R. K. (1971). Client's resistance to negative findings and the latent conservative function of evaluation studies. *American Sociologist, 6,* 118-124.

Chapman, R. L., Kennedy, J. L., Newell, A., & Biel, C. (1959). The systems research laboratory's air defense experiments. *Management Science, 5,* 250-269.

Cohen, M. D. (1981). The power of parallel thinking. *Journal of Economic Behavior and Organization, 2,* 285-306.

Connolly, T. (1988). Studies of information purchase processes. In B. Brehmer & C. R. B. Joyce (Eds.), *Human judgement: A social judgement theory.* Amsterdam: North-Holland.

Crozier, M. (1965). *The bureaucratic phenomenon.* New York: Oxford University Press.

Culnan, M. J. (1983). Environmental scanning: The effects of task complexity and source accessibility on information gathering behavior. *Decision Sciences, 14,* 194-206.

Culnan, M. J., & Markus, M. L. (1987). Information technologies. In F. M. Jablin, L. L. Putnam, K. H. Roberts, & L. W. Porter (Eds.), *Handbook of organizational communication* (pp. 420-443). Newbury Park, CA: Sage.

Cyert, R. M., & March, J. G. (1963). *A behavioral theory of the firm.* Englewood Cliffs, NJ: Prentice Hall.

Czepiel, J. A. (1975). Patterns of interorganizational communications and the diffusion of a major technological innovation in a competitive industrial community. *Academy of Management Journal, 18,* 6-24.

Daft, R. L., & Huber, G. P. (1987). How organizations learn: A communication framework. *Research in the Sociology of Organizations, 5,* 1-36.

Daft, R. L., & Lengel, R. H. (1984). Information richness: A new approach to managerial behavior and organization design. *Research in Organizational Behavior, 6,* 191-233.

Daft, R. L., Sormunen, J., & Parks, D. (1988). Chief executive scanning, environmental characteristics, and company performance: An empirical study. *Strategic Management Journal, 9,* 123-139.

Daft, R. L., Lengel, R. H., & Trevino, L. K. (1987). Message equivocality, media selection, and manager performance: Implications for information systems. *MIS Quarterly, 11,* 355-368.

Daft, R. L., & Weick, K. E. (1984). Toward a model of organizations as interpretation systems. *Academy of Management Review, 9,* 284-295.

Dearborn, D. C., & Simon, H. A. (1958). Selective perception: A note on the departmental identification of executives. *Sociometry, 21,* 140-144.

Dery, D. (1983). Decision-making, problem-solving, and organizational learning. *Omega, 11,* 321-328.

Dill, W. R., & Doppelt, N. (1963). The acquisition of experience in a complex management game. *Management Science, 10,* 30-46.

Dollinger, M. J. (1984). Environmental boundary spanning and information processing effects on organizational performance. *Academy of Management Journal, 27,* 351-368.

Donnellon, A., Gray, B., & Bougon, M. G. (1986). Communication, meaning, and organized action. *Administrative Science Quarterly, 31,* 43-55.

Douglas, M. (1986). *How institutions think.* Syracuse, NY: Syracuse University Press.

Downs, A. (1966). *Inside bureaucracy.* Boston: Little, Brown.

Driver, M. J., & Steufert, S. (1969). Integrative complexity: An approach to individuals and groups as information processing systems. *Administrative Science Quarterly, 14,* 272-285.

Drucker, P. F. (1988). The coming of the new organization. *Harvard Business Review,* 45-53.

Dutton, J. E., Fahey, L., & Narayanan, V. K. (1983). Toward understanding strategic issue diagnosis. *Strategic Management Journal, 4,* 307-323.

Dutton, J. E., & Jackson, S. E. (1987). Categorizing strategic issues: Links to organizational action. *Academy of Management Review, 12,* 76-90.

Dutton, J. M., & Freedman, R. D. (1985). External environment and internal strategies: Calculating, experimenting, and imitating in organizations. In R. Lamb & P. Shrivastava (Eds.), *Advances in strategic management* (Vol. 3, pp. 39-67). Greenwich, CT: JAI.

Dutton, J. M., Thomas, A., & Butler, J. E. (1984). The history of progress functions as a managerial technology. *Business History Review, 58,* 204-233.

Eells, R., & Nehemiks, P. (1984). *Corporate intelligence and espionage.* New York: Macmillan.

Eisenberg, E. M. (1984). Ambiguity as strategy in organizational communication. *Communication Monographs, 51,* 227-242.

Eisenberg, E. M., & Witten, M. G. (1987). Reconsidering openness in organizational communication. *Academy of Management Review, 12,* 418-426.

Fahey, L., King, W. R., & Narayanan, V. K. (1981). Environmental scanning and forecasting in strategic planning—The state of the art. *Long Range Planning, 14,* 32-39.

Farace, R. V., & MacDonald, D. (1974). New directions in the study of organizational communication. *Personnel Psychology, 27,* 1-19.

Faucheux, C., Amado, G., & Laurent, A. (1982). Organizational development and change. *Annual Review of Psychology, 33,* 343-370.

Feldman, J., & Kanter, H. E. (1965). Organizational decision making. In J. G. March (Ed.), *Handbook of organizations* (pp. 614-649). Chicago: Rand McNally.

Feldman, M. (1989). *Order without design: Information production and policy making.* Stanford, CA: Stanford University Press.

Feldman, M., & March, J. (1981). Information in organizations as signal and symbol. *Administrative Science Quarterly, 26,* 171-186.

Fiol, C. M., & Lyles, M. A. (1985). Organizational learning. *Academy of Management Review, 10,* 803-813.

Fredrickson, J. W. (1985). Effects of decision motive and organizational performance level on strategy decision processes. *Academy of Management Journal, 28*(4), 821-843.

French, W. L., & Bell, C. H. (1990). *Organization development.* Englewood Cliffs, NJ: Prentice Hall.

Friedlander, F. (1983). Patterns of individual and organizational learning. In S. Srivastva & Associates (Eds.), *The executive mind: New insights on managerial thought and action.* San Francisco: Jossey-Bass.

Fuld, L. M. (1988). *Monitoring the competition: Find out what's really going on over there.* New York: John Wiley.

Gerstenfeld, A., & Berger, P. (1980). An analysis of utilization differences for scientific and technical information. *Management Science, 26,* 165-179.

Gerwin, D. (1969). Towards a theory of public budgetary decision making. *Administrative Science Quarterly, 14,* 33-46.

Gilad, B., & Gilad, T. (1988). *The business intelligence system.* New York: American Management Association.

Gioia, D. A., & Poole, P. P. (1984). Scripts in organizational behavior. *Academy of Management Review, 9,* 449-459.

Glueck, W. (1976). *Business policy: Strategy formation and management action* (2nd ed.). New York: McGraw-Hill.

Guetzkow, H. (1965). Communications in organizations. In J. G. March (Ed.), *Handbook of organizations.* Chicago: Rand McNally.

Hambrick, D. C. (1982). Environmental scanning and organizational strategy. *Strategic Management Journal, 3,* 159-174.

Hambrick, D. C., & Finkelstein, S. (1987). Managerial discretion: A bridge between polar views of organizational outcomes. In L. L. Cummings & B. M. Staw (Eds.), *Research in organizational behavior* (pp. 369-406). Greenwich, CT: JAI.

Harrison, J. R., & March, J. G. (1984). Decision making and postdecision surprises. *Administrative Science Quarterly, 29,* 26-42.

Hax, A. C., & Majluf, N. S. (1988). The concept of strategy and the strategy formation process. *Interfaces, 19,* 99-109.

Hedberg, B. L. T. (1981). How organizations learn and unlearn. In P. C. Nystrom & W. H. Starbuck (Eds.), *Handbook of organizational design* (Vol. 1, pp. 3-27). New York: Oxford University Press.

Hedberg, B. L. T., Nystrom, P. C., & Starbuck, W. H. (1976). Camping on seesaws: Prescriptions for a self-designing organization. *Administration Science Quarterly, 2,* 39-52.

Hedberg, B. L. T., Nystrom, P. C., & Starbuck, W. H. (1977). Designing organization to match tomorrow. In P. C. Nystrom & W. H. Starbuck (Eds.), *Prescriptive models of organizations* (pp. 41-65). Amsterdam: North-Holland.

Herriott, S. R., Levinthal, D., & March, J. G. (1985). Learning from experience in organizations. *American Economic Review, 75,* 298-302.

Hiltz, S. R., & Turoff, M. (1978). *The network nation: Human communication via computer.* Reading, MA: Addison-Wesley.

Hogarth, R. M. (1987). *Judgement and choice.* Chichester, UK: Wiley.

House, R. J., & Singh, J. V. (1987). Organizational behavior: Some new directions for I/O psychology. *Annual Review of Psychology, 38,* 669-718.

Huber, G. P. (1982). Organizational information systems: Determinants of their performance and behavior. *Management Science, 28,* 135-155.

Huber, G. P. (1984). The nature and design of post-industrial organizations. *Management Science, 30,* 928-951.

Huber, G. P. (1990). A theory of the effects of advanced information technologies on organizational design, intelligence, and decision making. *Academy of Management Review, 15,* 47-71.

Huber, G. P., & Daft, R. L. (1987). The information environments of organizations. In F. M. Jablin, L. L. Putnam, K. H. Roberts, & L. W. Porter (Eds.), *Handbook of organizational communication* (pp. 130-164). Newbury Park, CA: Sage.

Huber, G. P., Ullman, J., & Leifer, R. (1979). Optimum organization design: An analytic-adoptive approach. *Academy of Management Review, 4,* 567-578.

Ireland, R. D., Hitt, M. A., Bettis, R. A., & DePorras, D. A. (1987). Strategy formulation processes: Differences in perceptions of strength and weaknesses indicators and environmental uncertainty by managerial level. *Strategic Management Journal, 8,* 469-485.

Isabella, L. A. (1990). Evolving interpretations as a change unfolds: How managers construe key organizational events. *Academy of Management Journal, 33,* 7-41.

Jablin, F. M. (1984). Assimilating new members into organizations. *Communication Yearbook, 8.* Beverly Hills, CA: Sage.

Jablin, F. M. (1987). Organizational entry, assimilation, and exit. In F. M. Jablin, L. L. Putnam, K. H. Roberts, & L. W. Porter (Eds.), *Handbook of organization communication.* Newbury Park, CA: Sage.

Janis, I. L. (1972). *Victims of groupthink.* Boston: Houghton Mifflin.

Jelinek, M. (1979). *Institutionalizing innovation: A study of organizational learning systems.* New York: Praeger.

Jemison, D. B. (1984). The importance of boundary-spanning roles in strategic decision making. *Journal of Management Studies, 21,* 131-152.

Jemison, D. B., & Sitkin, S. B. (1986). Corporate acquisitions: A process perspective. *Academy of Management Review, 11,* 145-163.

Johansen, R. (1988). *Groupware: Computer support for business teams.* New York: Free Press.

Joskow, P. L., & Rose, N. L. (1985). The effects of technological change, experience, and environmental regulation on the construction cost of coal-burning generating units. *Rand Journal of Economics, 16,* 1-27.

Kahneman, D., Slovic, P., & Tversky, A. (1982). *Judgement under uncertainty: Heuristics and biases.* Cambridge, UK: Cambridge University Press.

Keegan, W. J. (1974). Multinational scanning: A study of information sources utilized by headquarters executives in multinational companies. *Administrative Science Quarterly, 19,* 411-421.

Kennedy, M. M. (1983). Working knowledge. *Knowledge: Creation, Diffusion, Utilization, 5,* 193-211.

Kiesler, S., Siegel, J., & McGuire, J. W. (1984). Social psychological aspects of computer-mediated communication. *American Psychologist, 39,* 1123-1134.

Kimberly, J. R. (1979). Issues in the creation of organizations: Initiation, innovation, and institutionalization. *Academy of Management Journal, 22,* 437-457.

Klein, J. I. (1989). Parenthetic learning in organizations: Toward the unlearning of the unlearning model. *Journal of Management Studies, 26,* 291-308.

Krone, K. J., Jablin, F. M., & Putnam, L. L. (1987). Communication theory and organizational communication: Multiple perspectives. In F. M. Jablin, L. L. Putnam, K. H. Roberts, & L. W. Porter (Eds.), *Handbook of organizational communication.* Newbury Park, CA: Sage.

Kurke, L. B., & Aldrich, H. B. (1983). Mintzberg was right! A replication and extension of the nature of managerial work. *Management Science, 29,* 975-984.

Landau, M. (1973). On the concept of a self-correcting organization. *Public Administration Review, 33,* 533-542.

Lawler, E. E., III. (1977). Adaptive experiments: An approach to organizational behavior research. *Academy of Management Review, 2,* 567-585.

Leifer, R., & Huber, G. P. (1977). Relations among perceived environmental uncertainty, organization structure, and boundary-spanning behavior. *Administrative Science Quarterly, 22,* 235-247.

Levinthal, D., & March, J. G. (1981). A model of adaptive organizational search. *Journal of Economic Behavior and Organization, 2,* 307-333.

Levinthal, D., & Yao, D. A. (1988). *The search for excellence: Organizational inertia and adaption.* Unpublished manuscript.

Levitt, B., & March, J. G. (1988). Organizational learning. *Annual Review of Sociology, 14,* 319-340.

Lewin, K. (1949). *Field theory in social science.* New York: Harper & Row.

Lindblom, C. E. (1959). The science of muddling through. *Public Administration Review, 19,* 78-88.

Lounamaa, P. H., & March, J. G. (1987). Adaptive coordination of a learning team. *Management Science, 33,* 107-123.

Lyles, M. A. (1988). Learning among joint-venture sophisticated firms. *Management International Review, 28,* 85-98.

MacNamara, M., & Weeks, W. H. (1982). The action learning model of experiential learning for developing managers. *Human Relations, 35,* 879-902.

Mahajan, V., Sharma, S., & Bettis, R. A. (1988). The adoption of the *M*-Form organizational structure: A test of imitation hypothesis. *Management Science, 34,* 1188-1201.

March, J. G. (1981). Decision in organizations and theories of choice. In A. H. Van de Ven & W. Joyce (Eds.), *Perspectives on organization design and behavior* (pp. 563-577). New York: John Wiley.

March, J. G., & Olsen, J. P. (1979). *Ambiguity and choice in organizations* (2nd ed.). Bergen, Norway: Universitetsforlaget.

March, J. G., & Sevón, G. (1984). Gossip, information, and decision making. In L. S. Sproull & P. D. Larkey (Eds.), *Advances in information processing in organizations* (Vol. 1). Greenwich, CT: JAI.

Meier, R. L. (1963). Communications overload: Proposals from the study of a university library. *Administrative Science Quarterly, 4,* 521-544.

Meyer, J. W., & Rowan, B. (1977). Institutionalized organizations: Formal structure as myth and ceremony. *American Journal of Sociology, 83,* 440-463.

Miles, R. H., & Randolph, W. A. (1980). Influence of organizational learning styles on early development. In J. R. Kimberly & R. H. Miles (Eds.), *The organizational life cycle.* San Francisco: Jossey-Bass.

Miller, D., & Friesen, P. H. (1980a). Archetypes of organizational transition. *Administrative Science Quarterly, 25,* 268-299.

Miller, D., & Friesen, P. H. (1980b). Momentum and revolution in organizational adaption. *Academy of Management Journal, 25,* 591-614.

Miller, J. G. (1978). *Living systems.* New York: McGraw-Hill.

Milliken, F. J. (1990). Perceiving and interpreting environmental change: An examination of college administrators' interpretation of changing demographics. *Academy of Management Journal, 33,* 42-63.

Mintzberg, H. (1975). The manager's job: Folklore and fact. *Harvard Business Review, 53,* 49-61.

Mintzberg, H., & McHugh, A. (1985). Strategy formation in an adhocracy. *Administrative Science Quarterly, 30,* 160-197.

Mintzberg, H., Raisinghani, D., & Theoret, A. (1976). The structure of unstructured decision processes. *Administrative Science Quarterly, 21,* 246-275.

Mody, A. (1989). Firm strategies for costly engineering learning. *Management Science, 35,* 496-512.

Morgan, G. (1986). *Images of organizations.* Newbury Park, CA: Sage.

Muth, J. F. (1986). Search theory and the manufacturing progress function. *Management Science, 32,* 948-962.

Nelson, R., & Winter, S. (1982). *An evolutionary theory of economic change.* Cambridge, MA: Belknap Press of Harvard University Press.

Newman, M. (1985). Managerial access to information: Strategies for prevention and promotion. *Journal of Management Studies, 22,* 193-212.

Nisbett, R., & Ross, L. (1980). *Human inference: Strategies and shortcomings of social judgement.* Englewood Cliffs, NJ: Prentice Hall.

Nonaka, I. (1988). Creating organizational order out of chaos: Self-renewal in Japanese firms. *California Management Review, 30,* 57-73.

Nutt, P. C. (1986). Decision style and strategic decisions of top executives. *Technological Forecasting and Social Change, 30,* 39-62.

Nystrom, P. C., Hedberg, B. L. T., & Starbuck, W. H. (1976). Interacting processes as organizational designs. In R. H. Kilman, L. R. Pondy, & D. P. Slevin (Eds.), *The management of organization designs* (pp. 41-65). Amsterdam: North-Holland.

Nystrom, P. C., & Starbuck, W. (1984). To avoid organizational crises, unlearn. *Organizational Dynamics, 13,* 53-65.

O'Reilly, C. (1982). Variations in use of decision makers' use of information sources: The impact of quality versus accessibility of information. *Academy of Management Journal, 25,* 756-771.

O'Reilly, C., & Pondy, L. (1980). Organizational communication. In S. Kerr (Ed.), *Organizational behavior.* Columbus, OH: Grid.

Ouchi, W. G. (1984). *The M-Form society.* New York: Avon.

Paris, S. G., Lipson, M. Y., & Wixson, K. K. (1983). Becoming a strategic reader. *Contemporary Educational Psychology, 8,* 293-316.

Peters, M., & Robinson, V. (1984). The origins and status of action research. *Journal of Applied Behavioral Science, 20,* 113-124.

Peters, T. (1987). *Thriving on chaos.* New York: Harper & Row.

Porter, L. W., & Roberts, K. H. (1976). Communications in organizations. In M. D. Dunnette (Ed.), *Handbook of industrial and organizational psychology.* Chicago: Rand McNally.

Porter, M. E. (1980). *Competitive strategy: Techniques for analyzing industries and competitors.* New York: Free Press.

Quinn, J. B. (1980). *Strategies for change: Logical incrementalism.* Homewood, IL: Irwin.

Rao, H. R., & Lingaraj, B. P. (1988). Expert systems in production and operations management. *Interfaces, 18,* 80-91.

Rauch-Hindin, W. B. (1988). *A guide to commercial artificial intelligence.* Englewood Cliffs, NJ: Prentice Hall.

Reitzel, W. A. (1958). *Background to decision making.* Newport, RI: U.S. Naval War College.

Rossi, P. H., & Freeman, H. E. (1989). *Evaluation: A systematic approach* (4th ed.). Newbury Park, CA: Sage.

Sabatier, P. (1978). The acquisition and utilization of technical information by administrative agencies. *Administrative Science Quarterly, 23,* 396-417.

Sahal, D. (1982). *The transfer and utilization of technical knowledge.* Lexington, MA: Lexington Books.

Sammon, W. L., Kurland, M. A., & Spitalnic, R. (1984). *Business competitor intelligence: Methods for collecting, organizing, and using information.* New York: John Wiley.

Sandelands, L. E., & Stablein, R. E. (1987). The concept of organization mind. *Research in the Sociology of Organizations, 5,* 135-162.

Schein, E. H. (1984). Coming to a new awareness of organizational culture. *Sloan Management Review, 12*(1), 3-16.

Schlesinger, J. R. (1970). *Planning, programming, budgeting, inquiry of the Subcommittee on National Security and International Operations for the Senate Committee on Government Operations.* 91 Cong. 1 Sess., p. 482.

Schwab, R. C., Ungson, G. R., & Brown, W. B. (1985). Redefining the boundary spanning-environment relationship. *Journal of Management, 11,* 75-86.

Schwenk, C. R. (1984). Cognitive simplification processes in strategic decision making. *Strategic Management Journal, 5,* 111-128.

Short, J., Williams, E., & Christie, B. (1976). *The social psychology of telecommunications.* New York: John Wiley.

Shrivastava, P. (1983). A typology of organizational learning systems. *Journal of Management Studies, 20,* 1-28.

Shrivastava, P., & Schneider, S. (1984). Organizational frames of reference. *Human Relations, 37,* 795-809.

Simon, H. A. (1973). Applying information technology to organization design. *Public Administration Review, 33,* 268-278.

Sims, H. P., Jr., Gioia, D. A., & Associates. (1986). *The thinking organization.* San Francisco: Jossey-Bass.

Sitkin, S. B. (forthcoming). Learning through failure: The strategy of small losses. In B. M. Staw & L. L. Cummings (Eds.), *Research in organizational behavior.* Greenwich, CT: JAI.

Sproull, L. S. (1981). Beliefs in organizations. In P. C. Nystrom & W. H. Starbuck (Eds.), *Handbook of organizational design* (Vol. 2, pp. 203-244). New York: Oxford University Press.

Starbuck, W. H. (1983). Organizations as action generators. *American Sociological Review, 48,* 91-102.

Starbuck, W. H., & Milliken, F. J. (1988). Executives' perceptual filters: What they notice and how they make sense. In D. Hambrick (Ed.), *The executive effect: Concepts and methods for studying top managers* (pp. 35-66). Greenwich, CT: JAI.

Staw, B. M. (1977). The experimenting organization: Problems and prospects. In *Psychological foundations of organization behavior.* Pacific Palisades, CA: Goodyear.

Staw, B. M., & Ross, J. (1987). Behavior in escalation situations: Antecedents, prototypes, and solutions. In L. L. Cummings & B. M. Staw (Eds.), *Research in organizational behavior* (Vol. 9, pp. 39-78). Greenwich, CT: JAI.

Stinchcombe, A. L. (1965). Social structure and organizations. In J. G. March (Ed.), *Handbook of organizations* (pp. 142-193). Chicago: Rand McNally.

Thayer, L. (1967). Communication and organization theory. In F. E. X. Dance (Ed.), *Human communication theory: Original essays.* New York: Holt, Rinehart & Winston.

Trist, E. (1983). Referent-organizations and the development of inter-organizational domains. *Human Relations, 36,* 269-284.

Tunstall, W. B. (1983). Cultural transition at AT&T. *Sloan Management Review, 25,* 18.

Tushman, M. L. (1977). Communications across organizational boundaries: Special boundary roles in the innovation process. *Administrative Science Quarterly, 22,* 587-605.

Tushman, M. L., & Katz, R. (1980). External communication and project performance: An investigation into the role of gatekeepers. *Management Science, 26,* 1071-1085.

Tushman, M. L., & Moore, W. L. (Eds.). (1988). *Readings in the management of innovation.* Cambridge, MA: Ballinger.

Tushman, M. L., & Romanelli, E. (1985). Organizational evolution: A metamorphosis model of convergence and reorientation. In L. L. Cummings & B. M. Staw (Eds.), *Research in organizational behavior* (Vol. 7, pp. 171-222). Greenwich, CT: JAI.

Tushman, M. L., & Scanlan, T. J. (1981). Boundary-spanning individuals: Their role in information transfer and their antecedents. *Academy of Management Journal, 24,* 289-305.

Tversky, A., & Kahneman, D. (1985). The framing of decisions and the psychology of choice. In G. Wright (Ed.), *Behavioral decision making.* New York: Plenum.

Walker, G. (1985). Network position and cognition in a computer software firm. *Administrative Science Quarterly, 30,* 103-130.

Walsh, J. P., & Ungson, G. R. (1991). Organizational memory. *Academy of Management Review.*

Warner, M. (1981). Organizational experiments and social innovations. In P. C. Nystrom & W. H. Starbuck (Eds.), *Handbook of organizational design* (Vol. 1). New York: Oxford University Press.

Warner, M. (1984). *Organizations and experiments.* New York: John Wiley.

Waterman, D. A. (1986). *A guide to expert systems.* Reading, MA: Addison-Wesley.

Weber, C. E. (1965). Intraorganizational decision processes influencing the EDP staff budget. *Management Science, 13,* 69-93.

Webster's new collegiate dictionary. (1977). Springfield, MA: G. & C. Merriam.

Weick, K. E. (1979). Cognitive processes in organizations. *Research in Organizational Behavior, 1,* 41-74.

Weick, K. E., & Bougon, M. G. (1986). Organizations as cognitive maps: Charting ways to success and failure. In H. P. Sims, Jr., D. A. Gioia, & Associates (Eds.), *The thinking organization*. San Francisco: Jossey-Bass.

Weiss, C. H. (1973). *Evaluating action programs: Readings in social action and education.* Boston: Allyn & Bacon.

Weiss, C. H. (1980). Knowledge creep and decision accretion. *Knowledge: Creation, Diffusion, Utilization, 1,* 381-404.

Wildavsky, A. (1972). The self-evaluating organization. *Public Administration Review, 32,* 509-520.

Wilensky, H. (1967). *Organizational intelligence.* Berkeley: University of California Press.

Yates, J. (1990). *For the record: The embodiment of organizational memory, 1850-1920.* Paper presented at the Business History Conference.

Yelle, L. E. (1979). The learning curve: Historical review and comprehensive survey. *Decision Sciences, 10,* 302-308.

Zajonc, R., & Wolfe, D. (1966). Cognitive consequences of a person's position in a formal organization. *Human Relations, 19,* 139-150.

Zimmerman, M. B. (1982). Learning effects and the commercialization of new energy technologies: The case of nuclear power. *Bell Journal of Economics, 13,* 297-310.

Zucker, L. G. (1987). Institutional theories of organization. *Annual Review of Sociology, 13,* 443-464.

7

The Nontraditional Quality
of Organizational Learning

KARL E. WEICK

The traditional definition of learning as a shift in performance when the stimulus situation remains essentially the same implies a set of conditions that occur rarely in organizations. Thus, either organizational learning is an infrequent event, or it occurs frequently but takes a nontraditional form. Both possibilities are reviewed and implications for research strategy are suggested.

(ORGANIZATIONAL LEARNING)

It has always bothered me that people in organizational theory began to talk about learning (e.g., Cangolesi & Dill, 1965) just about the time psychologists began to desert the concept. I worry that scholars of organizations may have made their inquiries even more difficult by adopting a concept that didn't work for others, and will not work for them. This essay is an attempt to come to grips with this concern.

Koch (1985) described the movement of psychologists away from learning in this way:

There has been a marked realignment in the relative "glamour" of major areas of fundamental psychology. . . . Though "radical behaviorism" and a number of "mediation" theories seeking to integrate S-R and cognitive concepts (e.g., "cognitive

This chapter appeared originally in *Organization Science,* Vol. 2, No. 1, February 1991. Copyright © 1991, The Institute of Management Sciences.

learning theory," "social learning theory") are still on the scene, interest in learning in most of the senses pursued by the learning theorists of the Age of Theory
is approaching the vestigial. And it is of interest to note that the strongholds of
influence of both "radical" and "liberalized" behaviorism are *now* to be found in
applied (especially clinical) rather than fundamental psychology. . . . *(N)o* field
or family of concepts within fundamental psychology commands anything like
the breadth of allegiance that did S-R learning theory during the Age of Theory.
If "cognitive science" is now, in some sense, the "basic" field, this is so mainly
in the eyes of cognitive scientists. (p. 933)

To better understand why students of organizations might intentionally
treat as central what others treat as vestigial, we need to look more closely
at traditional definitions of learning and at unique properties of organizations
which complicate the application of these definitions. These complications
create difficult issues of intellectual strategy for students of organizational
learning. Resolution of these difficulties will affect whether investigators are
able to produce important new knowledge and create a viable alternative to
the rational choice model.

The following analysis will be grounded in a traditional definition of
learning that is representative:

> to become able to respond to task-demand or an environmental pressure in a
> different way as a result of earlier response to the same task (practice) or as a
> result of other intervening relevant experience. . . . The sign of learning is not
> a shift of response or performance as a consequence of change in stimulus-
> situation or in motivation, but rather a shift in performance when the stimulus-
> situation and the motivation are essentially the same. Such change in perfor-
> mance is said to require hypothesizing a change in the responding organism.
> (English & English, 1958, p. 289; see Bower & Hilgard, 1981, p. 11 for a
> similar definition)

The defining property of learning is the combination of same stimulus and
different response. If this combination is difficult to observe or difficult to
create, then an inference of learning is difficult to sustain. The point I want
to argue is that the combination of same stimulus, different response is rare
in organizations meaning either that organizations don't learn or that organizations learn but in nontraditional ways. Choice between these two possibilities has important consequences for understanding.

The combination of same stimulus different response is rare in organizations for three basic reasons. First, each of the two elements *separately* do
not occur often and it is more common to observe their opposites (different

stimulus, same response). Second, the *sequence* of same-different occurs less often than do the other three combinations (same-same, different-different, different-same). And third, when the sequence same-different does occur in organizations, it occurs for reasons other than learning.

DIFFERENT STIMULI, SAME RESPONSES

Stimulus situations in organizations tend to be unstable and changing. This instability makes it hard to establish sufficient stimulus similarity so that it becomes possible to make a different response. Most process theories of organization, such as organized anarchy (Cohen, March, & Olson, 1972), structuration (Riley, 1983), or interpretation systems (Daft & Weick, 1984), portray both organizations and their environments as changing flows from which a variety of stimuli can be carved. When there is flux, there is both no stimulus and a changing stimulus, but there is seldom the same stimulus.

Furthermore, most organizations have a response system which is designed to emit the same response. Organizational response systems which emphasize relatively constant responding are called routines (e.g., Feldman, 1989; Levitt & March, 1988). These basic building blocks represent efficient tools designed to transform variable inputs into less variable outputs through a standardized sequence of operations. The routines themselves encode and perpetuate what has been learned in the past, but individual routines are slow to change. When they do change, this typically occurs through the addition of new subroutines. Thus, there is more variety across routines, which suggests that the portfolio of routines may be the site of organizational learning.

The point, however, is that organizations are more notable for the sameness of their responses than for the difference in their responding. Sameness results from practices such as division of labor (which produces higher adherence to the routines of a specialty), formalization (which creates constant responding), and socialization (which is designed to reduce variation in responding), as well as from establishment of routines.

NONLEARNING SEQUENCES
OF STIMULUS-RESPONSE PATTERNS

All three nonlearning sequences, same-same, different-different, different-same, are at least as common in organizations as is the learning sequence, same-different.

The pattern, same stimulus-same response, is explicit in the repeated observation that organizations are inertial structures (e.g., Grandoori, 1987, p. 85) and implicit in the observation that organizations "satisfice" (March & Simon, 1958, pp. 140-141). A sufficient response to a stimulus tends to be the same response that was made to a related stimulus in the past. When search for causes of a problem is circumspect and local, the responses turned up tend to resemble closely those responses that have been used in the past.

The pattern of same-same is also common when people adopt a logic of appropriateness and match behavior routines to situations (Levitt & March, 1988, p. 320). Canonical organizational practices such as those discussed by Brown and Duguid (this volume) are the antithesis of response change, as is the tendency for members of organizations to change the justifications for their performance rather than their performance (Cangolesi & Dill, 1965, p. 193).

The pattern, different stimulus-different response, is visible when, in response to a changed situation, people become mindful and improvise a response, execute a generate and test routine (Dennett, 1978, pp. 71-89), or do what they saw someone else do in a related situation. Although each of these responses could be traced back to some earlier incident of learning, none of them represents a changed response to the same task demands. Instead, they represent a novel response to a novel stimulus.

The pattern, different stimulus-same response, is probably the most common sequence found in organizations. Since this sequence appears to be the opposite of traditional learning, it raises the most interesting set of issues about organizational learning.

I say "appears to be opposite" because some different-same sequences may imply a same-different sequence. Suppose, for example, that stimulus X leads to response Y, but through a process of stimulus generalization, stimulus Z now leads to response Y. The question now becomes, with what was stimulus Z associated before it was attached to Y? If Z was attached previously to response W, then the change from ZW to ZY represents same-different, or traditional, learning. However, Z may not have been attached to anything, which means learning is not the issue. While stimulus generalization (different-same) may imply response generalization (same-different), that is not always the case.

Although the pattern different-same may index learning under some conditions, it also reflects other dynamics that operate in organizations. For example, the pattern different-same is common when a change in stimuli is judged to be transient or unimportant. If the different stimulus will soon revert to a stimulus which is more familiar, there is little incentive to change the response.

But the pattern different-same may also reflect a much more active organization. The same response may intensify in the face of changing stimulation, in an effort to undo or manipulate (Hedberg, Nystrom, & Starbuck, 1976) the change, and enact a stimulus-situation that is closer to one which the organization can deal with. Discussions of negotiated environments (Pfeffer & Salancik, 1978, chap. 7) focus on processes by which concerted, forceful responding is exerted to transform a different stimulus situation back into one which is more consistent with an existing repertoire of responses. New learning is not involved in this sequence. Instead, organizations act so that their old learning proves adequate.

NONLEARNING EXPLANATIONS
OF "LEARNING" SEQUENCES

The final sequence, same-different, which is the traditional sequence associated with individual learning, does occur in organizations. The problem is, when it does occur there is often a nonlearning explanation for what has happened. For example, responses to the same stimulus may change because responding occurs in social situations. There is considerable evidence that the mere presence of people can be drive-arousing, which alters response hierarchies and responses that are emitted (Schmitt, Gilovich, Goore, & Joseph, 1986). The same stimulus may evoke different responses, but change has little to do with learning. It has more to do with the fact that arousal favors the emission of simpler more overlearned responses and discourages the emission of more complex, more recently learned response.

The pattern of same-different should be common when people forget how they responded to the same stimulus in the past, when they respond to the same stimulus differently in an attempt to relieve boredom or overload (Klapp, 1986), when turnover is high, participation is fluid, socialization is informal, and mergers and acquisitions are common. In each of these cases, action is less history-dependent because there is less organizational history salient for each actor. Instead, guidance comes from more idiosyncratic, more diverse personal experience, which results in different responses to the same stimulus.

Technically, in each of these cases there is no evidence of learning simply because we failed to exclude competing explanations. The point, however, is that the ecology of organizational action often creates nonlearning dynamics in sequences that would ordinarily be associated with learning. Thus, such normal accompaniments of organized life as audiences, arousal, boredom, and overload can prevent intentional efforts to construct a different response to the same situation.

INTELLECTUAL STRATEGIES TO
PURSUE ORGANIZATIONAL LEARNING

The preceding section raises the intriguing possibility that traditional learning may not be the form that change takes in organizations. When stimulus situations change continuously, a history-dependent process such as learning is of little help since the basic precondition, same stimulus, can be achieved only by generalization. The price of such an achievement is a loss in perceptual accuracy. This is a constraint on the stimulus side. But there is also a constraint on the response side. Routines restrict the differential responding that is essential if one is to respond in a new way to an old stimulus.

Perhaps organizations are not built to learn. Instead, they are patterns of means-ends relations deliberately designed to make the same routine response to different stimuli, a pattern which is antithetical to learning in the traditional sense. Organizations are fixed tools in search of new problems, and learning is a relatively minor part of this search. Or perhaps organizations are built to learn, but they do so in novel ways.

Given these puzzles, what intellectual strategies are available to improve our understanding of organizational learning? Two options will be reviewed.

Strategy 1: Retain Traditional Definition

The first option is to retain the traditional definition of learning, conclude that organizational learning is rare when viewed in light of this definition, and search for those types of organizations and those contexts where conditions for traditional learning *are* met.

Thus, we might argue that, for an organization to learn, it must stabilize the stimulus situation (it can do this either cognitively or by action), determine its modal response to this stabilized stimulus situation, change this modal response, and then apply this changed response to a situation which presumably has remained stable. With this recipe in mind, it would appear that the only organizations capable of learning are those with either strong cultures (they lump different stimuli into a handful of stable categories and create stimulus similarity) or persistent enactment (they change heterogeneous stimuli into stimuli that are more homogeneous), who also have weak routines that permit discretionary responding or strong routines whose substance encourages experimentation.

This intellectual strategy has both advantages and disadvantages.

A considerable advantage is that it focuses attention on behavior. To equate learning with same-different is to emphasize its resemblance to response generalization (a particular stimulus becomes effective in eliciting other responses) rather than to stimulus generalization. This emphasis is consistent with the salience of action in organizational theory (Weick, 1987). Organizations are action generators (Starbuck, 1983). When people leave organizations, action routines persist (Weick & Gilfillan, 1971) and provide a structure which supplies continuity. Learning is triggered by performance gaps (Cangolesi & Dill, 1965) and departures from aspiration level (Cyert & March, 1963). People act their way into meaning (Bem, 1972; Weick, 1979) which means that a focus on behavior need not rule out attention to cognition. All four stages in the organizational cycle of choice (March & Olsen, 1975, p. 149), a cycle which is cited in many learning formulations, involve acts, choices, and behaviors. And finally, a significant form of organizational learning identified by Fiol and Lyles (1985, p. 806) is "behavioral development," and this form is the basis of the definition that guides Strategy 1.

A further advantage of this strategy is that it treats learning as problematic rather than automatic, and it suggests a process explanation for inertia. Organizations persist in old behaviors because they are unable or unwilling to create the conditions of same-different that are necessary for learning.

There are, however, also several disadvantages to Strategy 1.

First, the SR notation, which can seem arbitrary (e.g., Tolman, 1959, p. 95), tends to obscure process and transition. If we say that learning has occurred when a person makes a different response to the same stimulus, that is a static assertion because it describes neither what preceded the learning (e.g., different-different) nor what follows once learning occurs (e.g., situation becomes same-same as habituation develops for the newly acquired response). Thus, the conclusion that learning is rare in organizations may be an artifact of observing too small a portion of the change process, an oversight which is encouraged by this analytic unit.

A related problem is that many of the illustrations of nonlearning, such as routines, would themselves appear to be the result of earlier learning. Thus, the evidence we cite for nonlearning may mask earlier learning. While masking is a distinct possibility, our analysis presumes that many processes and events in organizations arise through nonlearning mechanisms such as deviation amplifying loops (Maruyama, 1963) and increasing return mechanisms (Arthur, 1990). These mechanisms transform small accidental variations into large, stable structures. These mechanisms are common in organizations and may be the source of many structures which others attribute to intention and learning.

Finally, specification of who is learning what can shift in the same setting, depending on whose actions are the focus of attention. For example, efforts of *INC Magazine* (Hyatt, 1990) to understand why the book *Swimming with Sharks* became a business bestseller revealed that the author, envelope manufacturer Harvey MacKay, engaged in a number of data collection and self-promotional activities that had heretofore been unknown in publishing. These activities were simply the same ones MacKay had used all along to sell envelopes. That the product was now a book made no difference, so, to MacKay, selling sharks is a different stimulus (books not envelopes) to which he makes the same response (e.g., use Rolodex to call people and drum up interest in product). However, to the publishers, with their established routines of ways to sign, produce, and market books (e.g., small initial print run with unknown author), MacKay's actions forced them into a different response than they were used to. Thus the selling of sharks, in the eyes of the publishers, was the same stimulus (one more book to sell) to which they made a different response (initial print run 6 times larger than normal for a new author).

If we adhere to the argument that same-different is learning, then the publishers learned but MacKay didn't. But if we say that in MacKay's eyes selling a book had previously evoked some other response than that of treating it as an envelope, then he too learned when the same stimulus of a book to sell now evoked a different response than he ordinarily would have made.

Strategy 2: Replace Traditional Definition

A second strategy is to discard the traditional definition of learning, replace it with a definition that is tied more closely to properties of organizations (disruptions of the learning cycle, aggregation), and pursue the idea that organizational change does involve learning albeit a different kind of learning than has been described in the past.

An example of an alternative definition is Duncan and Weiss's (1979) description of knowledge as the outcome of learning. Learning is "the process within the organization by which knowledge about action-outcome relationships and the effect of the environment on these relationships is developed" (p. 84). This definition is not interchangeable with a definition involving changed responses, because it is often the case that changed knowledge makes behavior change unnecessary.

A more radical approach to redefinition would be to take the position that individual learning occurs when people give a different response to the same stimulus, but organizational learning occurs when groups of people give the same response to different stimuli. If organizations learn when they develop routines, then this should be visible as different responses become resolved down to a singular response, and an increasingly wide variety of stimuli now trigger this singular response. Consider the example of learning curves that develop as people gain more experience with production tasks (Epple,

Argote, & Devadas, this volume; Shrivastava, 1983, pp. 14-16). Suppose that one month after an auto plant opens, a completed car rolls off the assembly line every 10 minutes. Ten months later a completed car rolls off every 6.5 minutes. At first glance it looks like the response remains the same (a car is produced) and the stimulus of material inputs remains the same. Thus, there seems to be no learning behind the learning curve.

More detailed inspection suggests the possibility of a different story. At the macro level, materials and technology change over the 10 months as suppliers and technicians make adjustments (different stimuli), but cars continue to be produced (same response). A basic routine is broadened to include a wider variety of stimuli. At the individual level, however, we observe numerous small changes in response (e.g., Chambliss, 1989) to relatively the same material and technology each individual started with. The different responses arise from a mixture of practice, experimentation, and discussion. Thus, learning occurs at both levels of analysis, but it takes opposite forms.

There are at least three advantages to the second strategy of replacing the traditional definition.

First, it favors adoption of the influential information processing view of learning (e.g., Huber & Daft, 1987). An information processing perspective portrays the stimulus terms not as physical terms, but as events that are perceived and interpreted by the learner. "The product of a learning experience resides in memory for relationships between encoded stimulus information and behavioral dispositions. In the information-processing approach, one probes more deeply into what the individual is doing while learning is taking place. The goal is to construct a theoretical representation of the sequence of events that occur while stimulus information is transformed by perceptual and cognitive operations into the encoded forms that are preserved in organized memory" (Estes, 1988, p. 352).

Two other advantages involve interpretation systems. First, the view that knowledge development constitutes learning is compatible with the idea that organizations consist in part of "shared agreements." Second, the idea that learning involves the development of knowledge fits better with the proposal of people like Brown and Duguid (this volume) and Duncan and Weiss (1979, p. 90) that learning resembles sensemaking.

There are, however, at least three disadvantages to this second strategy. First, the preoccupation with memory, encoding, and representations may lead people to ignore the important link from cognition to action or to assume that this link is automatic. Second, by making the learning process more private, investigation is made more difficult, access is less direct, and the temptation to create increasingly exotic mediating processes is stronger.

Third, this strategy tends to discourage borrowing and whatever cumulation might be possible with more established but dated positions in learning theory (e.g., Mandler, 1985, pp. 108-118). Investigators tend to emphasize differences rather than similarities and to miss fundamental building blocks (e.g., discussion of attention rules in Mead, 1934, p. 94) that might be shared among positions.

CONCLUSION

This review of two strategies to deal with the "problems" created by a definition that no one seems to believe anyway may lead some readers to wonder if, perhaps, I missed the point of Werner's remark that, "My teacher, Stern, used to say that psychologists were in the habit of putting obstacles in their path, and then as they removed them one by one, calling attention to the progress they were making" (cited in Crovitz, 1970, p. 1). This essay may represent nothing more than a victory over narcissistic handicapping, but I think there is more involved than that.

Previous efforts to grasp the phenomenon of organizational learning have mixed together change, learning, and adaption, with only casual attention to levels of analysis and to referents for the activity itself. One way to untangle this mixture is to designate an explicit anchor, which I have done by constructing this review around a traditional psychological definition of learning, and then ask, when do conditions necessary for traditional learning occur in organizations? Having asked that question, I then began to see potential nonlearning sources of change in organizations as well as novel forms which learning itself might take. And these discoveries, in turn, intensified the need to examine the phenomenon of organizational learning itself more closely.

Thus, intense initial pursuit of Strategy 1 encourages eventual movement to Strategy 2, followed by empirical grounding such as we find represented in work by Feldman (1989), Orr (1990), Paconowsky (1988), Hutchins (1988), and Hackman (1990). "Bad" definitions can be instrumental to good outcomes, which is why I am personally in no hurry to abandon insights about learning embedded in traditional psychological definitions. Systematic extension of these definitions makes clear the potential uniqueness of organizational learning in ways which link that uniqueness to what we already know about individual learning. That linkage, in turn, is a step toward specifying ways in which emergent organizational learning is foreshadowed by indigenous individual learning.

Acknowledgments

This essay is a revised version of a talk given at the Conference on Organizational Learning held at Carnegie-Mellon University in May 1989. I am grateful to Michael Cohen for helping me to think through the argument presented here.

REFERENCES

Arthur, W. B. (1990, February). Positive feedbacks in the economy. *Scientific American,* pp. 92-99.

Bem, D. J. (1972). Self-perception theory. In L. Berkowitz (Ed.), *Advances in experimental social psychology* (Vol. 6). New York: Academic.

Bower, G. H., & Hilgard, E. R. (1981). *Theories of learning* (5th ed.). Englewood Cliffs, NJ: Prentice Hall.

Cangelosi, V. E., & Dill, W. R. (1965). Organizational learning: Observations toward a theory. *Administrative Science Quarterly, 10,* 175-203.

Chambliss, D. F. (1989). The mundanity of excellence; An ethnographic report on stratification and Olympic swimmers. *Sociological Theory, 7*(1), 70-86.

Cohen, M. D., March, J. G., & Olsen, J. P. (1972). A garbage can model of organizational choice. *Administrative Science Quarterly, 17,* 1-25.

Crovitz, H. F. (1970). *Galton's walk.* New York: Harper & Row.

Cyert, R. M., & March, J. G. (1963). *A behavioral theory of the firm.* Englewood Cliffs, NJ: Prentice Hall.

Daft, R., & Weick, K. E. (1984). Toward a model of organizations as interpretations systems. *Academy of Management Review, 9,* 284-295.

Dennett, D. C. (1978). *Brainstorms.* Montgomery, VT: Bradford.

Duncan, R., & Weiss, A. (1979). Organizational learning: Implications for organizational design. In B. Staw & L. L. Cummings (Eds.), *Research in organizational behavior* (Vol. 1, pp. 75-132). Greenwich, CT: JAI.

English, H. B., & English, A. C. (1958). *A comprehensive dictionary of psychological and psychoanalytical terms.* New York: Longmans, Green.

Estes, W. K. (1988). Human learning and memory. In R. C. Atkinson, R. J. Herrnstein, G. Lindzey, & R. D. Luce (Eds.), *Stevens handbook of experimental psychology* (Vol. 2, pp. 351-415). New York: John Wiley.

Feldman, M. S. (1989). *Order without design.* Stanford, CA: Stanford University Press.

Fiol, C. M., & Lyles, M. A. (1985). Organizational learning. *Academy of Management Review, 10,* 803-813.

Grandoori, A. (1987). *Perspectives on organization theory.* Boston: Ballinger.

Hackman, J. R. (Ed.). (1990). *Groups that work.* San Francisco: Jossey-Bass.

Hedberg, B. L. T., Nystrom, P. C., & Starbuck, W. H. (1976). Camping on seesaws: Prescriptions for a self-designing organization. *Administrative Science Quarterly, 21,* 41-65.

Huber, G. P., & Daft, R. L. (1987). The information environments of organizations. In F. M. Jablin, L. L. Putnam, K. H. Roberts, & L. W. Porter (Eds.), *Handbook of organizational communication* (pp. 130-164). Newbury Park, CA: Sage.

Hutchins, E. (1988). *Organizing work by evolution and by design.* Unpublished manuscript.

Hyatt, J. (1990, March). How to write a business best-seller. *INC,* pp. 64-75.

Klapp, O. E. (1986). *Overload and boredom.* New York: Greenwood.

Koch, S. (1985). Afterword. In S. Koch & D. E. Leary (Eds.), *A century of psychology as science* (pp. 928-950). New York: McGraw-Hill.

Levitt, B., & March, J. G. (1988). Organizational learning. *Annual Review of Sociology, 14,* 319-340.

Mandler, G. (1985). *Cognitive psychology.* Hillsdale, NJ: Lawrence Erlbaum.

March, J. G., & Olsen, J. P. (1975). The uncertainty of the past: Organizational learning under ambiguity. *European Journal of Political Research, 3,* 141-171.

March, J. G., & Simon, H. A. (1958). *Organizations.* New York: John Wiley.

Maruyama, M. (1963). The second cybernetics: Deviation-amplifying mutual causal processes. *American Scientist, 51,* 164-179, 250-256.

Mead, G. H. (1934). *Mind, self, and society.* Chicago: University of Chicago Press.

Orr, J. E. (1990). Sharing knowledge, celebrating identity: Community memory in a service culture. In D. Middleton & D. Edwards (Eds.), *Collective remembering* (pp. 169-189). Newbury Park, CA: Sage.

Paconowsky, M. (1988). Communicating in the empowering organization. In J. A. Anderson (Ed.), *Communication yearbook, 11* (pp. 310-334). Newbury Park, CA: Sage.

Pfeffer, J., & Salancik, G. R. (1978). *The external control of organizations: A resource dependence perspective.* New York: Harper & Row.

Riley, P. (1983). A structurationist account of political culture. *Administrative Science Quarterly, 28,* 414-437.

Schmitt, B. H., Gilovich, T., Goore, N., & Joseph, L. (1986). Mere presence and social facilitation: One more time. *Journal of Experimental Social Psychology, 22,* 242-248.

Shrivastava, P. (1983). A typology of organizational learning systems. *Journal of Management Studies, 20,* 7-28.

Starbuck, W. H. (1983). Organizations as action generators. *American Sociological Review, 48,* 91-102.

Tolman, E. C. (1959). Principles of purposive behavior. In S. Koch (Ed.), *Psychology: A study of a science* (Vol. 2, pp. 92-157). New York: McGraw-Hill.

Weick, K. E. (1979). *The social psychology of organizing* (2nd ed.). Reading, MA: Addison-Wesley.

Weick, K. E. (1987). Perspectives on action in organizations. In J. Lorsch (Ed.), *Handbook of organizational behavior* (pp. 10-28). Englewood Cliffs, NJ: Prentice Hall.

Weick, K. E., & Gilfillan, D. P. (1971). Fate of arbitrary traditions in a laboratory microculture. *Journal of Personality and Social Psychology, 17,* 179-191.

8

Bounded Rationality
and Organizational Learning

HERBERT A. SIMON

As I understand it, the manifest function of this gathering is to discuss the topic of organizational learning, whereas the latent function is to honor James March. Or is it the other way around? In either case, it is a valuable and pleasurable undertaking. Shakespeare subdivided human life into five major stages. We can refine the latter portion of his scale by taking note, at any given time in our lives, of whom we are just then honoring. Not long after we received our Ph.D.s, it was time to honor our teachers, as they began to reach the appropriate level of dignity for such accolades. A couple of decades later, we found ourselves honoring our contemporaries and colleagues. Still later, those of us who are lucky enough to survive have the opportunity of honoring our students.

Of course, Jim March was never my student. (In my memory of him, back to our earliest acquaintance, he never exhibited that quality of docility that befits students.) Nevertheless, I did offer him his first job, and he did accept. Offering was easy. I met him in New Haven, and had dinner with him, and reached an immediate decision. I probably had to clear the decision with the Dean, Lee Bach, but in those happy days we didn't worry about faculty committees, so it didn't take long. I recount all this as evidence of my sound judgment and ability to learn very rapidly. But it wasn't very hard, at that dinner, to learn that I was dealing with a young political scientist of unusual promise. And how right I was!

This chapter appeared originally in *Organization Science,* Vol. 2, No. 1, February 1991. Copyright © 1991, The Institute of Management Sciences.

THE ORGANIZATIONAL LEVEL

One can question whether this anecdote serves as an example of organizational learning—my assigned topic. It was learning by an individual that had consequences for an organizational decision—it provided new factual decision premises that led to an offer. But we must be careful not to adopt too strict a definition of organizational learning, or we will define our topic out of existence, thereby denying the legitimacy of this conference. All learning takes place inside individual human heads; an organization learns in only two ways: (a) by the learning of its members, or (b) by ingesting new members who have knowledge the organization didn't previously have.

But what is stored in any one head in an organization may not be unrelated to what is stored in other heads; and the relation between those two (and other) stores may have a great bearing on how the organization operates. What an individual learns in an organization is very much dependent on what is already known to (or believed by) other members of the organization and what kinds of information are present in the organizational environment. As we shall see, an important component of organizational learning is internal learning—that is, transmission of information from one organizational member or group of members to another. Individual learning in organizations is very much a social, not a solitary, phenomenon.

However, we must be careful about reifying the organization and talking about it as "knowing" something or "learning" something. It is usually important to specify *where* in the organization particular knowledge is stored, or *who* has learned it. Depending on its actual locus, knowledge may or may not be available at the decision points where it would be relevant. Since what has been learned is stored in individual heads (or in files or data banks), its transience or permanence depends on what people leave behind them when they depart from an organization or move from one position to another. Has what they have learned been transmitted to others or stored in ways that will permit it to be recovered when relevant?

The justification of a conference on organizational learning, exemplified in the papers already presented, is that human learning in the context of an organization is very much influenced by the organization, has consequences for the organization, and produces phenomena at the organizational level that go beyond anything we could infer simply by observing learning processes in isolated individuals. It is those consequences and those phenomena that we are trying to understand here. And my task is to show how some of those consequences and phenomena arise from the fact that human rationality is very approximate in the face of the complexities of everyday organizational life. Along the way, I will have some comments on ways in which we can do research and thereby gain new knowledge about these phenomena—learn about organizational learning.

Let me perseverate for a moment on that term "organizational level." Readers of the book, *Organizations* (1958), that Jim March and I wrote more than 30 years ago have sometimes complained that it was not a book on organizations at all but on the social psychology of people living in an organizational environment. The complaint was usually registered by sociologists, and was not without merit.

We need an organization theory because some phenomena are more conveniently described in terms of organizations and parts of organizations than in terms of the individual human beings who inhabit those parts. There is nothing more surprising in the existence of those phenomena than in the existence of phenomena that make it convenient for chemists to speak about molecules rather than quarks. Employing a more aggregate level of discourse is not a declaration of philosophical anti-reductionism, but simply a recognition that most natural systems do have hierarchical structure, and that it is sometimes possible to say a great deal about aggregate components without specifying the details of the phenomena going on within these components.

Hence, in what follows, I will have little or nothing to say about the mechanisms that enable an individual human being to learn, but will focus on the ways in which information is acquired by organizations, is stored in them, and is transmitted from one part of an organization to another. I will be concerned with what are usually called emergent phenomena at the organizational level, and hope that sociologists will find this essay more "organizational" than was our book.

THE STRUCTURE OF ROLES

For purposes of discussing organization learning, organizations are best viewed as systems of interrelated roles, and that is the way I have been viewing them here. How can we conceptualize roles so as to make this concept useful for organization theory?

The point has perhaps not been emphasized in the sociological literature as often as it should be that a role is not a system of prescribed behaviors but a system of prescribed decision premises. Roles tell organization members how to reason about the problems and decisions that face them: where to look for appropriate and legitimate informational premises and goal (evaluative) premises, and what techniques to use in processing these premises. The fact that behavior is structured in roles says nothing, one way or the other, about how flexible or inflexible it is.

Each of the roles in an organization presumes the appropriate enactment of the other roles that surround it and interact with it. Thus, the organization is a role *system.*

ORGANIZATIONAL LEARNING AND INNOVATION

Since the organizations I know best are universities, and since I have not engaged in recent years in any systematic organizational research, I will have to draw upon my university experiences for most of my examples of organizational learning phenomena. Let us take the case of a university that wants to innovate along some dimension of educational practice—perhaps by building its instruction around the Great Books, or by focusing on something it calls liberal-professional education. I'll use the latter example, which is closer to home.

The graduate schools from which a university draws its new teachers are organized in disciplines, some of which are saturated with the values of liberal education (and transmit them to their students), others of which are devoted to professional education. There are no disciplines, to the best of my knowledge, that fly the banner of "liberal-professional" education. Clearly, a university that wishes to implement this kind of instruction is faced with a major learning problem for its new (and probably its old) faculty members. It has no chance of accomplishing its goal without substantial education, and reeducation, of its inductees. Moreover, the reeducation is not a one-time task but a continuing one, unless the educational climate of the environing society changes so that it begins to produce graduates already indoctrinated with the desired goals.

Effects of Turnover

Turnover in organizations is sometimes considered a process that facilitates organizational innovation—getting out of the current rut. But in the case before us, where the organization is trying to distance itself from general social norms, turnover becomes a barrier to innovation, because it increases training (socialization) costs. To preserve its distinct culture, an organization of this kind may try to train its own personnel from the ground up, instead of relying on outside institutions to provide that training. Such inbreeding will have other organizational consequences. (I state these conclusions very confidently, but they should really be stated as researchable hypotheses.)

Contrast this with the organization that finds in its environment training organizations that share a common culture with it. The Forest Service, in Kaufman's (1960) classical account of it, is such an organization, counting on schools of forestry to provide it with new employees who are already indoctrinated with its values and even its standard operating procedures. The same thing occurs, less precisely but on a larger scale in such professions as engineering, where there are close links between the engineering colleges and the industries, with a feedback of influence from industry to the engineering curricula.

An Experiment on Stability

If turnover is sufficiently low, organizational values and practices can be stabilized by the fact that each new inductee finds himself or herself confronted with a social system that is already well established and prepared to mold newcomers to its procedures. This phenomenon can be produced in the laboratory (and I believe actually *has* been produced, but I cannot put my hands on the appropriate reference).

In a certain experimental paradigm in social psychology (often called the Bavelas communication network) different patterns of communication are induced in five-person groups. In one pattern (the wheel) one member of the group serves as leader or coordinator and all the other members communicate with him or her, and not directly with each other. In another pattern (the circle) the members are arranged in a symmetric circular network, each member communicating only with the two who are immediately adjacent. The groups are performing a task that requires them to share information that is given to the members individually (Bavelas, 1950).

Now consider two groups whose members are $A1$, $A2$, $A3$, $A4$, $A5$, and $B1$, $B2$, $B3$, $B4$, $B5$, respectively, where the As are in the wheel pattern and the Bs in the circle pattern. After they are thoroughly trained in the task, we open all the communication channels so that each member can communicate directly with all the others in that group. If they are under sufficient pressure to perform rapidly, the first group will likely continue to use the wheel pattern of communication and the second group the circle pattern.

After a number of additional trials, interchange $A1$ and $B1$. One would predict that the groups would continue to use their respective patterns. After a few more trials, interchange $A2$ with $B2$, then $A3$ with $B3$, and so on until the original wheel group is populated by $B1$ through $B5$, and the original circle group by $A1$ through $A5$. We would predict that the As would now be communicating in a circle pattern and the Bs in a wheel pattern. As I said, I believe the experiment has been run, but I do not know where the results were published. If it works as predicted, it demonstrates an emergent property of an organization—a persistence of pattern that survives a complete replacement of the individuals who enact the pattern.

Let us return to the topic of organizations that deviate from their surrounding cultures. The example of the deviant university can be extended to virtually all organizational innovation. Among the costs of being first— whether in products, in methods of marketing, in organizational procedures, or what not—are the costs of instilling in members of the organization the knowledge, beliefs, and values that are necessary for implementing the new goals. And these costs can be exceedingly large (as they are in the case I used as my example). The tasks of management are quite different in organizations that can recruit employees who are prefashioned, so to speak, than they are in organizations that wish to create and maintain, along some dimensions, idiosyncratic subcultures.

A major topic, therefore, in organizational learning is an understanding of the mechanisms that can be used to enable an organization to deviate from the culture in which it is embedded. As my university example suggests, this topic can be examined in the field, and particularly in a historical vein, by following the course of events in organizations that are identified as distancing themselves along one or more dimensions from the surrounding culture. If we are concerned about the imprecision of case studies as research data, we can console ourselves by noting that a man named Darwin was able to write a very persuasive (perhaps even correct) book on the origin of species on the basis of a study of the Galapagos Islands and a few other cases. To the best of my recollection, there are no statistics in Darwin's book.

Organizational Memory

The process of retaining unique traits within an organization is a part of the more general phenomena of organizational memory. Since much of the memory of organizations is stored in human heads, and only a little of it in procedures put down on paper (or held in computer memories), turnover of personnel is a great enemy of long-term organizational memory. This natural erosion of memory with time has, of course, both its advantages and disadvantages. In the previous section I emphasized one of its disadvantages. Its advantage is that it automatically removes outdated irrelevancies (but without discriminating between the relevant and the irrelevant). Leaving aside the erosion problem, how are we to characterize an organization's memories?

Research in cognitive psychology in recent years has made great progress in understanding human expertise (Simon, 1981, chap. 4). What has been learned can be summed up in a few generalizations. First, expertise is based on extensive knowledge—no knowledge, no expertise. A world-class expert in any field (several domains have been studied in some detail) holds in memory some 50,000 chunks (familiar units) of relevant information. (The

50,000 should not be taken too literally, but it is correct within an order of magnitude.)

This body of knowledge is stored in the form of an indexed encyclopedia, which is technically referred to as a *production system*. Associated with each chunk is a set of cues which, whenever evoked by a stimulus, will provide access to that chunk in semantic memory. The memory content may be of many kinds: the name associated with the cue, information about the cued phenomenon, things to do about it, and so on. The physician who sees the symptom (the cue) is reminded of the name of a disease often associated with it, information about the likely course of the disease, possible medical action to cure it, additional tests that would increase the reliability of the diagnosis, and so on.

Armed with knowledge stored in his or her production system, the expert is prepared (but only in the domain of expertise) to respond to many situations "intuitively"—that is, by recognizing the situation and evoking an appropriate response—and also to draw on the stored productions for more protracted and systematic analysis of difficult problems.

We know also that no one—literally no one—becomes a world class expert in any professional domain with less than ten years of full-time dedication to learning, to acquiring the 50,000 indexed chunks organized in the production system. The evidence for this time requirement is overwhelming, and child prodigies provide no exceptions (Bloom, 1985; Hayes, 1989, chap. 11).

Against the background of this picture of expertise, the memories of an organization can be represented as a vast collection of production systems. This representation becomes much more than a metaphor as we see more and more examples of human expertise captured in automated expert systems. One motive for such automation, but certainly not the only one, is that it makes organizational memory less vulnerable to personnel turnover.

INGESTING INNOVATIONS FROM WITHOUT

My previous example had to do with organizations trying to retain their identities in a world of alien ideas, fighting the threat of increasing entropy that comes with the ingestion of personnel. The other side of the coin is the problem of assimilating innovations that originate outside the organization, or that have to be transmitted from a point of origin in the organization to points of implementation. Here, let me take the research and design process as my example, but again in the context of universities. The translation to corporate situations will follow.

Research as a Learning Mechanism

So-called research universities usually proclaim that they have a dual mission: to create new knowledge and to transmit that knowledge to their students. Research accomplishes the former, and instruction the latter. Of course the real pattern is much more complicated than that. In the first place, the new knowledge produced by research is usually not initially transmitted to students at the same university, but to researchers throughout the world, mainly by publication. In the second place, most of the knowledge transmitted to students in a university is not produced at that university. Is there really any reason why the research (which is one process of learning) and the instruction (another learning process) should go on in the same institution?

When we examine the research process more closely, we see that it differs rather fundamentally from the usual description. In any given research laboratory, only a tiny fraction of the new knowledge acquired by the research staff is knowledge created by that laboratory; most of it is knowledge created by research elsewhere. We can think of a research scientist as a person who directs one eye at nature and the other at the literature of his or her field. And in most laboratories, probably all laboratories, much more information comes in through the eye that is scanning the journals than the eye that is looking through the laboratory microscope.

It is probably true, and certainly widely suspected, that in any field of research a large fraction of the less distinguished laboratories could vanish without seriously reducing the rate at which new knowledge is created. Does that mean that these dispensable laboratories (dispensable in terms of the creation of knowledge) do not pay their way? The conclusion does not follow if the main function of a laboratory is not the creation of knowledge but the acquisition of knowledge. In military parlance, we would label such laboratories intelligence units rather than research units. They are units of the organization that are specialized for the function of learning from the outside world (and perhaps, incidentally, sometimes creating new knowledge themselves).

As a matter of fact, in our more honest moments in universities, we sometimes recognize the intelligence function of "research." When we are asked why we require faculty members who are primarily teachers to publish in order to gain promotion or tenure, we answer that if they do not do research, they will not remain intellectually alive. Their teaching will not keep up with the progress of their disciplines. It is not their research products that we value, but their engagement in research which guarantees their attention to the literature—to the new knowledge being produced elsewhere.

It can be highly dysfunctional for a laboratory to live with the belief that its main product is the new knowledge produced by its in-house research. Such a belief produces the NIH (Not Invented Here) phenomenon, with a consequent reinvention of many wheels.

R&D and Manufacturing

The problems of organizational learning have just begun when an intelligence unit extracts some possibly relevant new knowledge from the environment (or invents it itself). The problem of developing new products from (local or imported) research ideas and of carrying them to the stage of successful manufacture and marketing is a classical organizational problem of this kind. A successful product must satisfy a whole range of constraints, the knowledge of which may originate in many parts of the organization. Among these are constraints on product characteristics determined by end use and markets, constraints determined by manufacturing considerations, and constraints determined by natural laws over and above those involved in the nuclear concept.

End Use and Market Constraints. An idea for a better mousetrap originating in a research laboratory has to satisfy the needs and demands of real-world markets. Research and development is usually conceived to begin with a key scientific idea which is elaborated through a development process. The development process annexes a succession of constraints to the initial research idea, continually modifying the idea until it satisfies them (or until it appears that they cannot be satisfied). Acquiring knowledge of the appropriate constraints is an important learning process, since that knowledge is generally widely distributed throughout the organization and elsewhere, and is seldom all available to the research and development staff at the beginning of the process (Simon, 1976, chap. 17).

In some industries, control gear would be an example, a considerable fraction of ideas for new products originates with a knowledge of customers' needs and problems—the nature and uses of the equipment to be controlled. In these cases, the sales engineers need to be incorporated in the intelligence process that initiates new product development. Here there is a reverse flow of instruction from the usual conception of the R&D process.

In whichever direction the ideas flow through the organization, it is clear that nothing will happen unless they do flow. Normally, the learning associated with a new product must be highly diffused through the organization— many people have to learn many things, and such lateral diffusion and transfer is far from automatic or easy. It must overcome motivation obstacles (I have already mentioned the NIH syndrome), and it must cross cognitive boundaries.

Manufacturing Constraints. A common complaint about contemporary American practice in new product design is that the design process is carried quite far before manufacturing expertise is brought to bear on it. But ease and cheapness of manufacture can be a key to the prospects of a product in competitive markets, and failure to consider manufacturability at an early stage usually causes extensive redesign with a corresponding increase in the time interval from initial idea to a manufactured product. These time delays are thought to be a major factor in the poor showing of many American industries in competing with the Japanese.

We know some, if not all, of the conditions for making communications between designers and manufacturing engineers effective. Each group must respect the expertise of the other, and must acknowledge the relevance of that expertise to their own problems. Moreover, each must have a sufficient knowledge and understanding of the others' problems to be able to communicate effectively about them. Experience shows that these conditions are unlikely to be satisfied unless members of each group (or a sufficient number of members of each group) have had actual experience with the activities and responsibilities of the other group. In typical Japanese manufacturing practice, this shared understanding and ability to communicate is brought about by extensive lateral transfer of engineers in the course of their careers.

These examples will illustrate some of the kinds of learning involved, some of the problems of bringing it about, and some of the mechanisms for solving those problems when an organization brings in innovations from outside or tries to transport them from one organizational unit to another.

ACQUIRING NEW PROBLEM REPRESENTATIONS

In my earlier discussion of a culturally deviant organization, I contrasted the way in which roles (decision premises) are acquired in such an organization from the way in which they are acquired in an organization that builds upon the culture of the society that provides it with new members.

In my discussion of research and development, I examined the ways in which new decision premises may be injected into organizations and diffused through them. In neither discussion did I distinguish sharply between learning that brings new knowledge to bear within an existing culture and knowledge that changes the culture itself in fundamental ways. I would like to turn now to that distinction (which clearly is a relative, and not an absolute one).

In the literature of problem solving, the topic I am now taking up is called "problem representation." In the past 30 years, a great deal has been learned about how people solve problems by searching selectively through a problem space defined by a particular problem representation. Much less has been learned about how people acquire a representation for dealing with a new problem—one they haven't previously encountered (but see March, Sproull, & Tamuz, this volume).

Two cases must be distinguished: (1) The learner is presented with an appropriate problem representation, and has to learn how to use it effectively. That is essentially what is involved when organizations, already formed, ingest new members from an alien culture. (2) The organization is faced with a totally new situation, and must create a problem representation to deal with it, then enable its members to acquire skill in using that representation. In the extreme case, a new organization is created to deal with a new task. A new problem representation, that is to say, a role system, is created.

Creating an Organization

Some years ago I was fortunate enough to have a grandstand seat at the creation of the Economic Cooperation Administration (ECA), the U.S. governmental organization that administered the Marshall Plan of aid to Western European countries. In that process, which extended through most of the year 1948, competing problem representations emerged from the very first days, each implying a quite different organization structure, set of organizational roles, from the others. These problem representations were not made out of whole cloth, but arose from analogies between the presumed task of the ECA and other tasks that were familiar to the inventors of the representations from their previous training and experience.

For example, some participants in the planning drew an analogy between the ECA and wartime organizations that had supplied essential goods to the allies. Others thought of it as an exercise in investment banking. Others were reminded of the theory of international trade balances. From each of these views, a set of organizational roles could be inferred, and each such structure of roles was quite different from the others. Which representations took root in which parts of the burgeoning organization depended heavily on the cultures from which these parts recruited their new members.

I have told elsewhere the story of how this competition was resolved (Simon, 1976, chap. 16). One technique used was to disseminate a document that presented one of the representations (the one based on the balance of trade analogy) persuasively, and which mapped out its organizational implications. Another technique was to starve out the units dedicated to other representations by denying them new personnel.

Why Representation Matters

In my remarks thus far I have said only a little about bounded rationality —about the limits upon the ability of human beings to adapt optimally, or even satisfactorily, to complex environments. Attention to the limits of human rationality helps us to understand why representation is important, and how policy statements imply representations. About a decade ago, the U.S. Steel Corporation began to contract its steel operations and to divert a major part of its capital to the acquisition of assets in the oil industry. The motivation of these moves was a particular representation of the corporation's purposes.

If, a few years ago, you had asked executives of U.S. Steel what the corporation's goals were, they might have answered: "To manufacture and market steel efficiently and profitably." If you had persisted further, they might even have agreed that profit was the "bottom line." But it would have been hard or impossible for them to describe the company without strong emphasis on its focus on steel. Their views might have been paraphrased: "We are out to make profits, but the way for us to make profits is to be an efficient steel manufacturer. That is a domain in which we have knowledge and expertise, and in which we can make good decisions."

For the conglomerate that U.S.X. has become, an entirely different representation is required. The corporation has product divisions that can still be described in ways that resemble the earlier corporation—the word "steel" applying to some divisions, and "oil" to others. But in the new representation, these divisions are only components operating within a larger framework in which the fundamental policy is to invest available funds in the directions that will yield the greatest returns. Within that framework, new expertise is required: essentially the expertise of an investment banker.

Change in representation implies change—here very fundamental change—in organizational knowledge and skills. It should not be surprising that under these conditions we often see massive turnover of personnel at all levels. It is often cheaper and quicker to import the new expertise and dismiss the old than to engage in massive reeducation.

CONCLUSION

In this paper, my intent has been to show how concepts that have arisen in contemporary cognitive psychology for describing human learning and problem solving processes, and human expertise, can be applied to the analysis of organizational learning. I have made no attempt to be complete or comprehensive in my account. Instead, I have been satisfied to present some examples of how specific organizational situations can be understood in terms of these concepts.

Along the way, I have made a few comments on research strategy. I have remarked on how experiments may be useful for studying mechanisms. But above all else, I have emphasized the role of careful case studies in research on organizational learning. By "careful," I mean studies that explore the contents of important organizational memories, the ways in which those contents are accessed (or ignored) in the decision-making process, and the ways in which they are acquired by organizations and transmitted from one part of an organization to another. Among the contents of organizational memories perhaps the most important are the representation of the organization itself and its goals, for it is this representation (or representations, if it is not uniform throughout the organization) that provides the basis for defining the roles of organization members.

If organization theory finds it useful to draw upon some of the ideas that have emerged in cognitive psychology, it will be advantageous to borrow also the terminology used in discussing these ideas. Without working toward a higher level of consistency in terminology than prevails in organization theory today, it will be difficult or impossible to cumulate and assemble into a coherent structure the knowledge we are gaining from individual case studies and experiments. We will be continually reinventing wheels. That is a luxury we cannot afford. The happy band of researchers on organization theory is sufficiently small to be kept fully occupied discovering and verifying the theory just once.

Acknowledgments

This research was supported by the Personnel and Training Programs, Psychological Sciences Division, Office of Naval Research, under Contract No. N00014-86-K-0768.

REFERENCES

Bavelas, A. (1950). Communication patterns in task-oriented groups. *Journal of Acoustical Society of America, 22,* 725-730.

Bloom, B. S. (Ed.). (1985). *Developing talent in young people.* New York: Ballantine.

Hayes, J. R. (1989). *The complete problem solver* (2nd ed.). Hillsdale, NJ: Lawrence Erlbaum.

Kaufman, H. (1960). *The forest ranger.* Baltimore: Johns Hopkins University Press.

March, J. G., & Simon, H. A. (1958). *Organizations.* New York: John Wiley.

Simon, H. A. (1976). *Administrative behavior* (3rd ed.). New York: Macmillan.

Simon, H. A. (1981). *The sciences of the artificial* (2nd ed.). Cambridge: MIT Press.

9

Individual Learning and Organizational Routine

Emerging Connections

MICHAEL D. COHEN

The intent of this review essay is to draw attention to a striking convergence of work on learning being done—separately until now—by students of organizational learning and by psychologists interested in memory and in skilled performance. Issues being raised in the study of organizational learning are nicely complemented by current developments in psychology. They provide both confirmation of what organization theorists have intuited about individuals and a more differentiated understanding of skill-learning and memory that should enrich organizational theorizing and observation. The plan of the essay is to sketch an interesting example of recent work on both the organizational and psychological sides, then to discuss their points of contact.

In *Information and Organizations,* Stinchcombe (1990) has made a large-scale effort to extract and reframe central organization theory assertions of major figures such as Schumpeter, Chandler, and Simon. He synthesizes them with insights derived from his own observations of manufacturing, oil extraction, construction, and university administration to obtain a distinctive new perspective on organizations.

The result is a very stimulating argument that the variety of organizational forms we see about us are the product of a fundamental organizational dynamic: the seeking and processing of information about the organization's key uncertainties. In effect, organizational structure is viewed as a design for

This chapter appeared originally in *Organization Science,* Vol. 2, No. 1, February 1991. Copyright © 1991, The Institute of Management Sciences.

organizational learning, for acquiring information about the state of the world, and for improving what the organization can do.

The foundation of organizational capabilities, in Stinchcombe's (1990) view, are the skills of its individual members. These he compares to small computer programs: "the parts of an individual's skill which are completely routinized are the parts that he or she does not have to think about—once a routine is switched on in the worker's mind, it goes on the end without further consultation of the higher faculties" (p. 63). The view is somewhat similar to that of Nelson and Winter (1982).

Information about uncertainties ("the news" as Stinchcombe, 1990, often calls it) serves two purposes with respect to the repertoire of skills: in building/modifying its contents, the routines themselves, and in switching activation among those routines potentially relevant to the current context.

Building and modifying the repertoire are fundamental activities because they embody learning in routines, thus constituting a major form of organizational memory. The steady refinement of that repertoire generates much of the performance improvement we see in learning curve research. The *rate* of such improvement can be dramatic, which causes Stinchcombe (1990) to remark that "at the beginning of a production run there is not much one can do that is as inefficient as buying the same activities today that one bought yesterday" (p. 372/133).

The *content* of the improvement can also vary greatly, depending on the organizationally determined flows of information that surround the learning. Hence the significance of the decision by DuPont, made famous by Chandler (1962), to place production of a new product under the control of those in contact with its buyers rather than under the control of those committed to efficient production of many different products.

In Stinchcombe's (1990) perspective, improving speed of routines and changing their detailed contents, along with accurate switching among existing routines, are major sources of competitive advantage or other forms of organizational success. Therefore organizational arrangements should be, and frequently will be, designed to acquire, as quickly and as reliably as possible, the information needed to drive these processes.

Stinchcombe (1990) exploits this view to produce illuminating discussions of many issues. For example: the tension captured in Schumpeter's distinction of invention from innovation (the best organization for the information requirements of invention may be systematically poor for its subsequent propagation); the organizational histories in Chandler (to Stinchcombe the account of DuPont seems largely correct, but that of Sears may not be); and Sabel's (1982) history of semiskilled factory production ("fordism" continued the long-term movement of the building of routines and of the switching among them from the level of the craftsman to the level of the factory management).

Given the centrality of building and exercising skills in the approach to organization developed by Stinchcombe (1990)—and by distinguished predecessors such as Nelson and Winter (1982) and Cyert and March (1963), it is salutary that cognitive psychology is exhibiting renewed interest in the learning and exercise of skills by individuals. An extremely interesting recent example is the work of Singley and Anderson (1989). They show that modern experimental and computer modeling technique can cast considerable new light on how skills are acquired, and enacted. Their results, and those of other psychologists working in the area, reinforce many aspects of Stinchcombe's observations, suggest some corrections of his views, and offer many possibilities for deepening the development of a conception of organizations as processing information to learn and apply skilled routines.

The problem of transfer of learning has a very distinguished history in psychology, in large part because of its fundamental significance for education (Thorndike & Woodworth, 1901). The early history of the subject was stimulated by questions such as, "Does learning Latin increase a student's ability to write clear English or to think logically about problems?" The answers to such questions must depend on the nature and extent of the overlap between the skills acquired in the initial learning (of, say, Latin) and those useful in the target task(s).

Singley and Anderson (1989) argue that this is a promising time to return to working on transfer of learning, after more than a decade in which psychology paid it relatively little heed, because modeling methods developed in cognitive science, in particular production system modeling, provide a natural framework for theory and observation. They feel that the production, the basic building block of such models, a small rule-like package with an activation condition and a action to be taken when that condition is met, provides an ideal formal analog for a component of a skill. Thus their central argument: the greater the overlap between the components (productions) acquired in learning one skill and those required for performance of a new target task, the greater the anticipated transfer of learning.

Singley and Anderson (1989) use data gathered through computerized tutorial programs to build production system models of performance in areas such as LISP programming, and problem solving in introductory calculus and geometry. They then show that the degree-of-overlap idea can be used to make predictions about transfer to new target tasks, and that the predictions generally agree rather well with the observed performance of human subjects.

A key idea in their results is the distinction between what they call declarative and procedural forms of memory, and their identification of corresponding forms of skill. Here they connect their work on skill to a growing body of memory research showing that established skilled performance—both cognitive and motor—can be stored in a form of memory ("procedural") that has distinctive properties quite different from the properties of memory for facts, events, or propositions ("declarative" memory).

Singley and Anderson (1989) illustrate the difference between these forms of memory for skill by means of an analogy to computer programs, which may exist as complied machine language (procedural), or as high level language source code (declarative). The former is rapidly executable, but difficult to repair and closely tied to a specific hardware environment. The latter can be repaired or generalized to other environments more easily, but can be executed, in a typical case, only by a very slow interpretation process. There are many similarities and some interesting differences with the view of individual skills offered by Stinchcombe (1990) and quoted above.

Many of the key studies behind the procedural/declarative distinction have been done with amnesia patients who may be unable to remember the daily visits of therapists or daily exposure to apparatus, instruction, and task, but still show task improvement. For example, such patients have been able to learn to solve the Tower of Hanoi Puzzle or to improve their play at checkers (Cohen, 1984). Such results are the basis of the inference that skills may be acquired and stored in a form different from the storage and access of memories for episodes of personal interaction or for abstract statements of rules. Another striking feature of such patients is that their responses in priming experiments are nearly normal even when their recall is severely impaired. Cues in context elicit established responses although the patients may not recall previous similar episodes.[1]

If research continues to develop the idea that individual skills have distinctive properties derived from their being stored in a particular kind of memory, there may be many important organizational implications. Four are sketched here, presented in the context of the perspective developed by Stinchcombe (1989). They are not conceived as resolving established research questions, but rather in the spirit of indicating the kind of fertile development that is now taking shape, defining an area of coming beneficial interaction between organization theory and psychology.

1. The results indicate that many of the properties of skills, for example their ability to operate with substantial independence of long-term memory of events or episodes, can be found in both motor and cognitive skills. Most familiar examples used by organization theorists are for motor operations, such as driving a car or touch typing. But now we can expect to find this independence in cognitive activity too. Consider this extreme observation reported by McCulloch (1965):

I have seen a man of over 80 years of age walk into a meeting of a Board of
Directors and for over 8 hours work out from scratch all the details necessary
for the sale of a complete railroad. He pushed the other men so as to get every
piece of evidence on the table. His judgment was remarkably solid. The amount
of detail involved in the transaction was enormous, and it actually took over 6
hours to get all the requisite details on the map. He summarized that detail at the
end of the meeting, in a period of half an hour, very brilliantly, and when he came
out he sat down, answered two letters that were on his desk, turned to his secretary, and said, "I have a feeling that I should have gone to a Board of Directors
Meeting." He was not then, or at any later time, able to recall one iota of that
meeting. (pp. 88-89)

Good observers of organization have often noticed a dissociation of
skilled action from verbal deliberation in organizations, but frequently
attribute it to a mind/body difference. Zuboff (1988) in her work on impacts
of computers on workplaces follows such a line and then must struggle to
interpret the similarities of insurance claim processors to factory workers. A
procedural/declarative distinction makes it much easier to see how workers
in the two settings can be like each other in their reactions to computing and
unlike their managers.

2. Stinchcombe (1990) closes his volume with the qualification that he has
not been able to provide "a theory of errors." That is, his reasoning often
rests on the assumption that forms of organization persist because, on
average, they work better than alternatives. But he cannot say as much as he
might like about when and how they may work badly. The more detailed
development of the psychology of skill offers the possibility of progress
against such limitations.

Much of the psychological work is centered on the ability to characterize
errors. VanLehn's (1989) models of learning to subtract are verified by
detailed predictions of errors made on tests. Singley and Anderson (1989)
identify a characteristic kind of error, which they argue is the main form of
negative transfer of learning, as identical to the Einstellung (or "set") effects
studied since the 1940s. In such experiments familiar features of a context
evoke well-established action patterns (activate procedural knowledge),
even though a more reasoned analysis (involving declarative representations) would indicate another, more suitable course of action. In the laboratory, subjects can often be induced to form routines for tasks so that they
will miss "obvious" opportunities for improved performance (i.e., they make
the equivalent of three right turns when they could have made one left).

At the organizational level, consider the famous story from the Cuban
missile crisis study by Allison (1971, p. 109): Russian soldiers told to main-

tain secrecy of their arrival and dressed in civilian clothes went onto the docks and nonetheless formed up into ranks and marched away, making themselves easy to identify and count.

3. Procedural memory in individuals also appears to be more specific to the mode of communication in which it is initiated (e.g., verbal vs. written) than is the case with declarative memory (Graf, Shimamura, & Squire, 1985). A skill learned in one mode may not be available if triggering information is presented in another mode. As a result there may be interesting implications for the recurring tension between "theory" and "practice" found in large organizations trying to systematize behavior learned in small work groups. (Brown & Duguid discuss such tensions in their contribution to this volume.) Observations by Powell (1989) on efforts to learn from joint ventures indicate that diffusion of new practices throughout a partner organization may be better achieved by means of personnel rotations than via publication of research studies documenting the joint venture practices.

4. Declarative memory appears to decay more rapidly than procedural. This is consistent with many observations, including the finding that people can speak correct sentences in a language they once knew, long after they have forgotten the formal grammatical rules they were taught (Bahrick, 1984). It is also consistent with observations often reported by systems analysts trying to define computer programs to duplicate current behavior: there are practices in organizations that are performed regularly long after the actors have ceased to be able to give a convincing account of their purposes (Sheil, 1981). With some additional work, we may become better able to characterize the domains in which actions can persist while reasons come and go (Allison, 1971; Zald, 1970).

This point, especially taken together with its predecessors, begins to suggest that organizations may have a counterpart of what has been called for individuals a "cognitive unconscious" (Rozin, 1976), a stock of memory and know-how that is not readily accessible to ordinary recollection and analysis.

It is, as has been noted, too early to be sure about the generality of examples such as those just discussed. But it is the right time to assert that students of organizational learning are going to benefit from working out the detailed implications and validity of a rich (re)new(ed) source of ideas.

NOTE

1. Excellent reviews are in Squire (1987) and Tulving and Schachter (1990).

REFERENCES

Allison, G. (1971). *Essence of decision: Explaining the Cuban missile crisis.* Boston: Little, Brown.

Anderson, J. R. (1983). *The architecture of cognition.* Cambridge, MA: Harvard University Press.

Bahrick, H. P. (1984). Semantic memory content in permastore: 50 years of memory for Spanish learned in school. *Journal of Experimental Psychology, General, 113,* 1-29.

Chandler, A. D. (1962). *Strategy and structure: Chapters in the history of the industrial enterprise.* Cambridge: MIT Press.

Cohen, N. J. (1984). Preserved learning capacity in amnesia: Evidence for multiple memory systems. In L. Squire & N. Butters (Eds.), *Neuropsychology of memory* (pp. 88-103). New York: Guilford.

Cyert, R. M., & March, J. G. (1963). *A behavioral theory of the firm.* Englewood Cliffs, NJ: Prentice Hall.

Graf, P., Shimamura, A. P., & Squire, L. R. (1985). Priming across modalities and across category levels: Extending the domain of preserved function in amnesia. *Journal of Experimental Psychology [Learning, Memory, Cognition], 11,* 386-396.

Luchins, A. S. (1942). Mechanization in problem solving. *Psychological Monographs, 54.*

McCulloch, W. S. (1965). Why the mind is in the head. In W. S. McCulloch (Ed.), *Embodiments of mind* (pp. 72-141). Cambridge: MIT Press.

Nelson, R., & Winter, S. (1982). *An evolutionary theory of economic change.* Cambridge, MA: Belknap Press.

Powell, W. W. (1989, May). *Learning in international business alliances.* Paper presented at the NSF Conference on Organizational Learning, Pittsburgh, PA.

Rozin, P. (1976). The evolution of intelligence and access to the cognitive unconscious. *Progress in Psychobiology and Physiological Psychology, 6,* 245-280.

Sabel, C. F. (1982). *Work and politics: The division of labor in industry.* Cambridge, UK: Cambridge University Press.

Sheil, B. (1981). *Coping with complexity* (Working paper). Palo Alto, CA: Xerox Palo Alto Research Center, Laboratory for Artificial Intelligence.

Singley, M. K., & Anderson, J. R. (1989). *The transfer of cognitive skill.* Cambridge, MA: Harvard University Press.

Squire, L. R. (1987). *Memory and brain.* New York: Oxford University Press.

Stinchcombe, A. L. (1990). *Information and organizations.* Berkeley: University of California Press.

Thorndike, E. L., & Woodworth, R. S. (1901). The influence of improvement in one mental function upon the efficiency of other functions. *Psychological Review, 8,* 247-261.

Tulving, E., & Schachter, D. L. (1990). Priming and human memory systems. *Science, 247,* 301-306.

VanLehn, K. (1989). *Mind bugs: The origins of procedural misconception.* Cambridge: MIT Press.

Zald, M. N. (1970). *Organizational change: The political economy of the YMCA.* Chicago: University of Chicago Press.

Zuboff, S. (1988). *In the age of the smart machine: The future of work and power.* New York: Basic Books.

10

Organizational Adaptation and Environmental Selection

Interrelated Processes of Change

DANIEL A. LEVINTHAL

Research on organizational change has been animated by two conflicting perspectives. One line of research has emphasized organizational adaptation (Child, 1972; Cyert & March, 1963; Lawrence & Lorsch, 1967), while Hannan and Freeman (1977) have posed an alternative paradigm in which variation in organizational forms within a population is explained by differential rates of birth and death. Astley and Van de Ven (1983) and Scott (1987) have offered a reconciliation of these divergent perspectives, suggesting that they are in fact complementary. In particular, Scott argued that a selection perspective is useful in explaining the core features of organizations, the survival rates of relatively small organizations, and in accounting for changes over long periods of time. In contrast, Scott proposed that adaptation perspectives are a useful complement in examining peripheral features of organizations, survival of larger and more powerful organizations, and change over shorter periods of time.

Much recent research has pursued an empirical agenda consistent with this idea that each approach has its own appropriate domain. Both variation in the frequency with which change occurs (Amburgey, Kelley, & Barnett, 1990; Baum, 1990; Haveman, 1990) and in the impact of change on the survival rates of organizations (Amburgey et al., 1990; Miner, Amburgey, &

This chapter appeared originally in *Organization Science*, Vol. 2, No. 1, February 1991. Copyright © 1991, The Institute of Management Sciences.

Stearns, 1990; Singh, House, & Tucker, 1986) have been examined. As Winter (1990) notes, "the emerging consensus is not on a particular sweeping generalization about the levels of adaptability/rationality or inertia/ irrationality that organizations display, but an emerging agreement that arguing about the generalizations is less interesting than sorting out the cases and testing the strength of competing interpretations" (pp. 292-293).

This essay proposes a different conception of the relationship of adaptation and selection processes. In reviewing some of the most recent advances in the literature, the essay uncovers a view of adaptation and selection not as mutually exclusive alternatives, each with its own domain of applicability, but rather as fundamentally interdependent processes. On the one hand, organizational learning contributes, in part, to organizational inertia, which, in turn, is the basis of selection processes. On the other hand, far from being incompatible with adaptive learning, inertial forces are a prerequisite for intelligent adaptation.

In complex decision problems the discovery of the optimum is an extremely difficult task, with an astronomical number of alternatives. This makes it imperative to use building blocks derived from previous "good" solutions (Holland, 1975) even though so doing contributes to inertia. Retaining elements of prior solutions enhances organizational reliability, as suggested by Hannan and Freeman (1984, 1989), and it also facilitates intelligent adaptation in that it allows for clearer inferences to be made regarding the efficacy of any experiment in organizational change. But the presence of such inertia implies that organizations cannot adapt perfectly to their environments, which, in turn, suggests that selection processes are a powerful source of change. This essay explores these connections between processes of selection and adaptation in two specific contexts: the relationship between organizational age and both organizational inertia and mortality, and the relationship between organizational change and mortality.

AGE DEPENDENCE

A robust result from empirical analysis of mortality patterns of organizations is that the rate of failure declines with organizational age (Carroll, 1983). Given this empirical regularity, the question remains as to what are the underlying processes. One possibility is that the result is simply a spurious effect of heterogeneity in the population studied. If organizational failure rates vary in the population but are themselves stable over time, one would still observe a declining hazard rate in the overall population. Those organizations with a high risk of failure are more likely to be selected out early on. As a result, the population of surviving organizations will tend to consist of those organizations with a low risk of failure.

However, the pattern of a declining hazard rate over time is still observed when researchers control for possible sources of heterogeneity, such as organizational size (Freeman, Carroll, & Hannan, 1983). More recent studies have incorporated unobserved sources of heterogeneity (Hannan & Freeman, 1989). Even in these more general analyses in which the nature of heterogeneity is not specified a priori, the familiar pattern of negative age dependency is still observed.

These results suggest that there is a relationship between the age of an individual organization and the likelihood of survival. This relationship, in turn, may stem from two basic properties of organizational learning. First, learning is typically reflected in an enhancement of an organization's competence at its current activities. This process is conventionally thought of in the context of a learning curve and a firm's production cost, but it also is consistent with richer and more general characterizations of the accumulation of skills and knowledge (Cohen & Levinthal, 1990; Nelson & Winter, 1982). Greater competence over time should lead to a lower risk of mortality.

Second, learning often reduces the variation in performance, as distinct from increasing its expectation.[1] It is this second implication of organizational learning that is the basis of Hannan and Freeman's (1984, 1989) argument for a relationship between organizational age and mortality. They argue that selection processes operate so as to eliminate those organizations within a population with low reliability or accountability. Reliability is, in turn, enhanced by processes of institutionalization and the creation of highly standardized routines, which form the basis of continuity in an organization's behavior over time (Nelson & Winter, 1982). Thus, Hannan and Freeman suggest that organizational mortality declines with age due to the increasing reliability of organizational behavior over time.

March (this volume) provides an explicit account of how a learning process may result in both a decline in variance and an increase in average performance. He models the development of organizational knowledge, both among individuals and within the organization as a whole. Learning tends to be self-limiting, in that as learning occurs, beliefs of individual members of the organizations converge, average knowledge level increases, and the diversity of beliefs that is necessary for further adaptation is eliminated.[2] Thus, older organizations would tend to exhibit higher mean performance, greater reliability in their performance and higher levels of inertia in their behaviors.

This model exhibits behavior that reflects the broader notion of competency traps (Levitt & March, 1988). As an organization gains experience and, thereby, proficiency with the current activities, procedures, or technologies, it becomes less likely that experimentation with alternatives will appear attractive or, if attempted, prove desirable. There is a general tendency for systems of learning to drive out experimentation, leading again to an association of higher performance, greater reliability, and increasing inertia with organizational age.

Models of adaptive learning could also be used to explore the presence of occasional, radical reorientations in an organization's strategy and structure (Tushman & Romanelli, 1985). Tushman and Romanelli argue that such reorientations tend to occur after periods of sustained poor performance and a change in top management. Adaptive learning perspectives (Cyert & March, 1963) would suggest that poor performance would lead to greater search for new "solutions" and, following the logic of March's model described above, this turnover in the top management team should lead to greater variation in the set of proposed solutions.

ORGANIZATIONAL MORTALITY AND ORGANIZATIONAL CHANGE

Organizational change engenders two types of gambles. The first reflects the uncertainty of the change process itself, while the second risk, more familiar in discussions of population ecology, is the uncertainty associated with the organization's fitness with the environment. This dichotomy is reflected in the business policy literature, which has historically centered on two distinct sets of questions: the study of process (e.g., organizational decision making, implementation of decisions) and the study of content (e.g., the impact of firm policies on firm and industry profitability).

Hannan and Freeman's (1989) recent discussion of structural inertia represents an important advance, as it incorporates this dual nature of change processes in analyses of organizational mortality. They characterize adaptation as a process involving competing risks. Not only is there the usual risk of failure associated with a possible reduction of an organization's fit with its environment, but efforts to realign an organization with a changing environment pose a second risk: that of reorganization. For instance, the introduction of a new product not only presents a risk associated with market acceptance, but it may also disrupt organizational processes, due to different production requirements or new demands on the sales and marketing personnel. If one accepts the view that organizations whose performance falls below their aspiration level are more likely to engage in organizational change (Cyert & March, 1963; March & Simon, 1958), then, given the risk of reorganization, for some organizations "efforts to survive will have speeded up the process of failure" (March, 1982, p. 567).

With the exception of Amburgey et al. (1990), efforts to empirically examine the adaptiveness of organizations have not reflected these competing risks. Whether a given change in organizational behavior is adaptive or not has typically been analyzed by examining the effect of that change on the organization's risk of failure. More precisely, researchers have examined the effect of such changes on the parameter of age-dependence. However, such analyses conflate what would appear to be two separate risks. A change process may be adaptive in that it lowers the asymptotic value of the hazard rate, yet it may lead to an increase in the likelihood of failure due to the short-run risk of reorganization. Thus, the net effect of even such "adaptive" changes on survival probabilities is ambiguous.

Amburgey et al. (1990) find that the immediate impact of change is to greatly heighten the risk of failure. Longer term, those organizations that survive the immediate threat of the change event tend to face a lower risk of failure. Thus, their findings suggest both that there is tremendous risk associated with the process of change, and that these changes themselves tend to be adaptive. Acknowledging the dual effect of organizational changes provides at least a partial rationale for the distinction between core and periphery changes made by Hannan and Freeman (1984). Core changes— changes in central goals, forms of authority, core technology, or marketing strategy—need not be any less adaptive than peripheral changes in terms of their effect on the long-run probability of survival (i.e., the asymptotic hazard rate). However, core changes are likely to pose a much greater risk of reorganization.

Hannan and Freeman (1989, pp. 88-89) suggest that the more decoupled is the subunit undergoing change and the less complex is the change, the lower is the risk of reorganization. This argument is readily justified if one examines a nested learning model as in Herriott, Levinthal, and March (1985) and Lounamaa and March (1987). While adaptive learning for isolated subunits can be quite effective (Cyert & March, 1963; Lave & March, 1975), simultaneous learning at multiple levels need not be (Lounamaa & March, 1987).

Lounamaa and March (1987) consider experimental learning in the context of a simple team problem, examining the interaction produced by simultaneous learning at two levels in an organization. In environments in which performance is a noisy reflection of organizational decisions, highly interactive learning and adaptation fail. Inferences from experience becomes problematic because the relationship between the actions of individuals in the organization and overall organizational performance is confounded by the simultaneous learning of other actors and by errors in perceiving performance. Lounamaa and March (1987) suggest that "relatively efficient rules for learning in multi-level organizations involve simplifying the 'experimental design' of natural experience by inhibiting learning in one part of the organization in order to facilitate learning in another, changing learning in different parts of the team from a parallel to a sequential process" (p. 118).

Lounamaa and March (1987) develop an analytic structure which illustrates the importance of inertial forces for organizational learning and, in turn, organizational performance. Thus, while Hannan and Freeman (1984) have pointed out that March (1982) has suggested that organizations change continuously and effortlessly, it is clear from March's own work that such changes need not enhance organizational survival. Furthermore, the Lounamaa and March model provides a basis for distinguishing between core and periphery changes. Core changes, by definition, will involve a more interactive learning process. As a result, not only is the intelligent adjustment of core decision rules problematic, but such adjustment confounds the learning processes.

Models of adaptive learning provide a sense of the complexity and risks associated with organizational changes, and offer a rationale for some of the central assumptions of Hannan and Freeman's characterization of the relationship between organizational change and organizational survival, a central issue in the study of selection processes. Far from being incompatible with adaptive learning, inertial forces are a prerequisite for intelligent adaptation (Holland, 1975). As illustrated in the context of the Lounamaa and March (1987) model, a high degree of inertia may be necessary for intelligent inferences to be made. Peripheral, rather than core, changes provide a more promising opportunity for intelligent learning.

CONCLUSION

This brief essay can only be suggestive, both in extent and scope. With respect to the former attribute, only a small number of possible exemplars of research linking models of organizational learning with ecological analysis of organizational survival have been discussed. An important limitation on the scope of this essay is that it neglects higher levels of analysis. Learning processes are present at the population and community levels, most prominently in the form of imitative behavior (Lant & Mezias, 1990; Levitt & March, 1988).

The narrow intention of this essay has been to suggest that models of organizational change may provide a useful basis for exploring selection processes. Processes of organizational evolution engender much of the persistent variation within organizational populations on which selection processes operate. It is in this sense that organizational adaptation and environment selection are not conflicting perspectives on change as suggested by early writings, nor simply complementary views as suggested by more recent literature, but are fundamentally interrelated processes of change.

Acknowledgments

I have benefited from comments on a prior draft by Arie Lewin, Jitendra Singh, and especially, Michael Cohen. The work, in large part, stems from my own learning experiences with Jim March.

NOTES

1. This dual effect of learning is consistent with Bowman's (1980, 1982) finding that firm profitability and the variability of profits are negatively correlated.

2. In contrast, Amburgey et al. (1990), building on Nelson and Winter (1982), suggest that learning processes enhance an organization's ability to change. They argue that the more standardized routines become, the more readily innovation may occur through the recombination of existing routines. As Nelson and Winter state, "Reliable routines of well-understood scope provide the best components of new combinations. In this sense, success at the innovative frontier may depend on the quality of the support from the civilized regions of established routine" (p. 131).

REFERENCES

Amburgey, T. L., Kelly, D., & Barnett, W. P. (1990). Resetting the clock: The dynamics of organizational change and failure. *Academy of Management Best Papers Proceedings*, pp. 160-164.

Astley, W. G., & Van de Ven, A. (1983). Central perspectives and debates in organizational theory. *Administrative Science Quarterly, 28*, 245-273.

Baum, J. A. C. (1990). Inertial and adaptive patterns in the dynamics of organizational change. *Academy of Management Best Papers Proceedings*, pp. 165-169.

Bowman, E. H. (1980). A risk-return paradox for strategic management. *Sloan Management Review, 21*, 17-31.

Baum, J. A. C. (1982). Risk seeking by troubled firms. *Sloan Management Review, 23*, 33-42.

Carroll, G. R. (1983). A stochastic model of organizational mortality: Review and reanalysis. *Social Science Research, 12*, 303-329.

Child, J. (1972). Organizational structure, environment and performance: The role of strategic choice. *Sociology, 6*, 1-22.

Cohen, W. M., & Levinthal, D. A. (1990). Absorptive capacity: A new perspective on learning and innovation. *Administrative Science Quarterly, 35,* 128-152.

Cyert, R. M., & March, J. G. (1963). *A behavioral theory of the firm.* Englewood Cliffs, NJ: Prentice Hall.

Freeman, J., Carroll, G. R., & Hannan, M. T. (1983). The liability of newness: Age dependence in organizational death rates. *American Sociological Review, 48,* 692-710.

Hannan, M. T., & Freeman, J. (1977). The population ecology of organizations. *American Journal of Sociology, 82,* 929-964.

Hannan, M. T., & Freeman, J. (1984). Structural inertia and organizational change. *American Sociological Review, 49,* 149-164.

Hannan, M. T., & Freeman, J. (1989). *Organizational ecology.* Cambridge, MA: Harvard University Press.

Haveman, H. A. (1990). *Structural inertia revisited: Diversification and performance in California savings and loans.* Unpublished Ph.D. dissertation, University of California at Berkeley.

Herriott, S. R., Levinthal, D., & March, J. G. (1984). Learning from experience in organizations. *American Economic Review, 75,* 298-302.

Holland, J. (1975). *Adaptation in natural and artificial systems.* Ann Arbor: University of Michigan Press.

Lant, T. K., & Mezias, S. J. (1990). An organizational learning model of convergence and reorientation. *Strategic Management Journal, 11,* 147-179.

Lave, C. A., & March, J. G. (1975). *An introduction to models in the social sciences.* New York: Harper & Row.

Lawrence, P. R., & Lorsch, J. W. (1967). *Organization and environment: Managing differentiation and integration.* Boston, MA: Graduate School of Business Administration.

Levitt, B., & March, J. G. (1988). Organizational learning. *Annual Review of Sociology, 14,* 319-340.

Lounamaa, P. H., & March, J. G. (1987). Adaptive coordination of a learning team. *Management Science, 33,* 107-123.

March, J. G. (1982). Footnotes to organizational change. *Administrative Science Quarterly, 26,* 563-577.

March, J. G., & Simon, H. A. (1958). *Organizations.* New York: John Wiley.

Miner, A. S., Amburgey, T., & Stearns, T. (1990). Interorganizational linkages and population dynamics: Buffering and transformational shields. *Administrative Science Quarterly, 35,* 689-713.

Nelson, R. R., & Winter, S. G. (1982). *An evolutionary theory of economic change.* Cambridge, MA: Harvard University Press.

Scott, W. R. (1987). *Organizations: Rational, natural, and open systems.* Englewood Cliffs, NJ: Prentice Hall.

Singh, J. V., House, R. J., & Tucker, D. J. (1986). Organizational change and organizational mortality. *Administrative Science Quarterly, 31,* 587-611.

Tushman, M. L., & Romanelli, E. (1985). Organizational evolution: A metamorphosis model of convergence and reorientation. *Research in Organizational Behavior, 7,* 171-222.

Winter, S. G. (1990). Survival, selection, and inheritance in evolutionary theories of organization. In J. Singh (Ed.), *Organizational evolution: New directions* (pp. 269-297). Newbury Park, CA: Sage.

11

Technology Diffusion and Organizational Learning

The Case of Business Computing

PAUL ATTEWELL

The dominant explanation for the spread of technological innovations emphasizes processes of influence and information flow. Firms which are closely connected to pre-existing users of an innovation learn about it and adopt it early on. Firms at the periphery of communication networks are slower to adopt.

This paper develops an alternative model which emphasizes the role of know-how and organizational learning as potential barriers to adoption of innovations. Firms delay in-house adoption of complex technology until they obtain sufficient technical know-how to implement and operate it successfully.

In response to knowledge barriers, new institutions come into existence which progressively lower those barriers, and make it easier for firms to adopt and use the technology without extensive in-house expertise. Service bureaus, consultants, and simplification of the technology are examples. As knowledge barriers are lowered, diffusion speeds up, and one observes a transition from an early pattern in which the new technology is typically obtained as a service to a later pattern of in-house provision of the technology.

Thus the diffusion of technology is reconceptualized in terms of organizational learning, skill development, and knowledge barriers. The utility of this approach is shown through an empirical study of the diffusion of business computing in the United States, reporting survey and ethnographic data on the spread of business computing, on the learning processes and skills required, and on the changing institutional practices that facilitated diffusion.

(ORGANIZATIONAL LEARNING; DIFFUSION OF TECHNOLOGY)

INTRODUCTION

The recent spread of computer and related technologies throughout the U.S. economy, coinciding with a period of intense competition from overseas, has convinced many policy makers that America's economic future depends on the rapid diffusion and successful utilization of new technologies in the workplace (President's Commission, 1985, p. 18). However, several scholars have questioned the usefulness of current theories of technology diffusion for understanding the spread of complex new production technologies. They have called for new perspectives better suited to understanding the dissemination of these technologies (Brown, 1981; Eveland & Tornatzky, 1990; Kelly & Kranzberg, 1978).

In this paper, I review established theories of innovation diffusion, and summarize recent criticisms made of them. I then construct a perspective on technology diffusion that places at its core the issue of organizational learning and know-how. Survey, interview, and archival data on the recent diffusion of business computing are then analyzed, in order to demonstrate the empirical validity of this new theoretical formulation, and its utility in explaining institutional patterns of diffusion.

THE THEORY OF INNOVATION DIFFUSION

At the most general level, two metaphors or images inform innovation diffusion research. Perhaps the dominant image is that diffusion is a process of communication and influence whereby potential users become informed about the availability of new technology and are persuaded to adopt, through communication with prior users (Rogers, 1983). This implies that patterns of adoption across populations of organizations reflect patterns of communication flow. Researchers examine the roles of persons within innovating firms who are especially well linked to outside networks and organizations, and also study patterns of communication and influence within the adopting firm.

The second metaphor is an economic one which views diffusion primarily in terms of cost and benefit: the higher the cost, the slower diffusion will occur. The higher the perceived profit from an innovation, the faster adoption will occur (Mansfield, 1968).

1. Adopter Studies

Both the communication/influence imagery and the economic imagery inform one style of diffusion research which focuses upon adoption by individuals or by single firms. Typically, early adopters are contrasted with late adopters to generate a list of factors related to early adoption. For example:

1. Firm size: large firms adopt innovations before smaller ones (Davies, 1979, p. 118).
2. Profitability: those firms for whom an innovation is most profitable become early adopters (Davies, 1979; von Hippel, 1988).
3. Innovation champions inside the adopting firm: Rothwell and Zegveld (1985) identify three roles—the product champion, the business innovator, and the technological gatekeeper.
4. Organization and environmental attributes: intensity of competition, firm size, mass versus batch production, degree of centralization, organizational slack, proportion of specialists, and functional differentiation have been linked to adoption by Abernathy and Utterback (1978), Aiken and Hage (1971), Kimberley and Evanisko (1981), Tornatzky and Fleischer (1990), and others.

2. Macro-Diffusion

Macroscopic studies of innovation examine the diffusion of new technologies across entire populations of organizations. One strand of research takes a spatial approach, representing the spread of innovations by a "gravity model" (Rogers, 1983). Speed of adoption is a function of the population size of an area, and secondarily of the distance of that area from other centers of population. (Population and proximity to population centers are indirect measures of density of communication, akin to Durkheim's notion of "moral density.") Applied to the U.S., an innovation is predicted to appear earliest in the two major coastal conurbations (Boston to Washington D.C.; Southern California), then in the next largest metropolitan areas (inland), and spread after a considerable lag to areas of low population density (Hunt & Chambers, 1976, p. 48). The gravity model successfully describes the diffusion of social innovations from TV stations to heroin addiction, but it appears less useful in explaining industrial innovations, perhaps because certain types of manufacturing concentrate in smaller towns (Mansfield, 1968; Pred, 1977).

A second theme in the macroscopic study of innovation focuses on the S-shaped curve which describes adoption over time: early on few firms adopt, then there is a sudden "take off," followed by a slowing in the rate of adoption (Mahajan & Peterson, 1985). Economists explain the S-shape of the curve in terms of the shifting balance of supply and demand, which is a function of the investment required to adopt a technology and the profitability of that technology (Freeman, 1982; Jowett, 1986; Mansfield, 1968, 1977;

von Hippel, 1988). The steep "take off" of the S-curve is often due to a substantial drop in the price of the new technology, causing a surge in demand.

Burt (1987), a sociologist, has analyzed the S-curve differently, arguing that distinctive mechanisms of diffusion (structural equivalence versus cohesion) imply different shapes of S-curve. Structural equivalence means that those who adopt at one point in time are similarly situated *vis à vis* other actors. Cohesion suggests that adoption results from direct communication between a potential user and prior users. Burt has tested the relative importance of these two mechanisms, arguing that structural equivalence plays a larger role in explaining diffusion of tetracycline than does cohesion. He suggests that interpersonal communication is less important for diffusion than traditional diffusion theory suggests, especially in contexts where marketers use multiple channels to get news of the innovation to potential users (p. 1328).

Markus (1987) has shown that modifications to the traditional S-curve are required to account for interactive communications media, from telephones to electronic mail, to facsimile machines. For such media, adoption becomes progressively more attractive, the more it has already been adopted by others. Conversely, in their early stages these media face start-up problems and discontinuance, because many people with whom one wishes to communicate are not yet using that medium. This is the reverse of traditional diffusion theory, which posits the highest gains to be associated with early adoption, and discontinuance to be associated with late adopters (Rogers, 1983, p. 188). Markus's diffusion curve for successful interactive technologies is exponential rather than S-shaped.

For both sociologists and economists, research at the macroscopic level typically proceeds by attempting to fit a mathematical model of the diffusion process to empirical data describing the diffusion of an innovation over time (Mahajan & Peterson, 1985). For example, Chow (1967) and Stoneman (1976, 1983, pp. 135-141) have examined the diffusion of mainframe computing in the U.S. from an economic perspective. Both used economy-wide time-series data on the number of mainframes sold (dependent variable), on the price of those computers, controlling for quality, and on overall economic growth (independent variables). Despite the evident sophistication of these econometric studies, their *empirical* ability to model the diffusion of computing proved disappointing. Neither price nor output growth (GNP) proved to be statistically-significant predictors of the numbers of computers diffused. (Other researchers, applying a similar approach to other technologies, have been more successful.)

CRITIQUES OF CURRENT DIFFUSION THEORY

In an influential review, Brown (1981) has criticized the view of adoption as "primarily the outcome of a learning or communications process." That perspective emphasizes *demand* for an innovation, and assumes that everyone has an equal opportunity to adopt, limited only by their "innovativeness." This places too much emphasis on the demand side and not enough on supply-side institutions of diffusion. Institutions that supply and actively market innovations affect the spread of innovations, and determine to some degree who adopts and when. Since supply-side institutions often focus their marketing and educational activities in certain areas or on certain types of firm, it is unlikely that each firm will have an equal opportunity to adopt. Thus, he argues, research should go beyond the individualistic perspective which stresses the innovativeness of potential adopters, and should examine instead the institutional and market structures that channel new technologies to users (cf. Robertson & Gatignon, 1987).

Economic studies of diffusion are not immune from Brown's (1981) criticism, despite the fact that they analyze both supply and demand variables. For the economic approach is theoretically indifferent to *institutional factors* on either the supply or demand side. By focusing solely on price and profitability, it ignores nonmonetary barriers and facilitators to diffusion that are the raison d'etre of other schools of diffusion theory.

A different set of criticisms of current diffusion theory is provided by Eveland and Tornatzky (1990), who suggest "Problems arise when the diffusion model is applied in situations where its basic assumptions are not met—that is to say, virtually every case involving complex, advanced technology" (p. 123). They point out that diffusion theory has tended to focus on adoption decisions by an individual, and upon a relatively rationalistic adoption decision. Yet for advanced production technologies, "Decisions are often many (and reversed), and technologies are often too big and complex to be grasped by a single person's cognitive power—or usually, to be acquired or deployed within the discretionary authority of any single organizational participant" (p. 124). When adoption is not a single event, and when complex organizational processes rather than individual decision-making come to the fore, the classical diffusion model (e.g., Coleman, Katz, & Menzel, 1966), based on an individual's decision being primarily influenced via communication with external agents, seems less applicable.

Eveland and Tornatzky (1990) recommend instead a perspective that views diffusion and adoption as occurring within contexts that constrain and mold choices. They enumerate five elements of context: nature of the technology itself, user characteristics, the characteristics of deployers, boundaries within and between deployers and users, and characteristics of communication and transaction mechanisms. Of particular relevance are their observations that diffusing or deploying a technology is more difficult if (1) its scientific base is abstract or complex, (2) the technology is fragile (in the sense that it does not work consistently), (3) it requires "hand-holding"—aid and advice to adopters after initial sale, (4) it is "lumpy" ("affects huge swaths of the user organization"), and (5) it is not easily "productized"— made into a standard commodity or a complete package. They note that many advanced workplace technologies fulfill several of these criteria, suggesting that their diffusion is problematic for both producer and user firms.

Communication Versus Knowledge
in Technology Diffusion

The limitations of previous diffusion theory become evident if one considers more closely the role of information and knowledge. The classical studies stressed the *flow* of information and ideas, and the importance of contact between originators of the technology and potential users (Coleman et al., 1966). A core idea was that nonadopters lag behind early adopters because the former have not yet learned of the existence of an innovation, or have not yet been influenced about its desirability by better-informed contacts. Diffusion is therefore limited by the timing and pattern of communication.

Unfortunately, the classical studies failed to distinguish between two different types of communication (or information) involved in the diffusion process: signaling versus know-how or technical knowledge. Differentiating between these two leads to very different perspectives on technology diffusion.

Signaling refers to communication about the existence and potential gains of a new innovation. Unless a potential adopter knows about an innovation, and is informed persuasively about the benefits of using it, the innovation is unlikely to be adopted. The classical diffusion studies assumed that signaling information took different lengths of time getting to different potential users (according to their centrality to communications networks and links to prior adopters), resulting in the S-curve of early, middle, and late adopters. Signaling was therefore viewed as central to explaining the diffusion process.

However, one may question whether signaling information remains a limiting factor in contexts where information about the existence of new production technologies and their benefits is widely broadcast by manufacturers' advertisements, by specialized business journals, and by trade associations (cf. Burt, 1987). Mansfield (1985) has documented that signaling about new production technology in the U.S. can be very fast and widespread, implying that it is not a limiting factor, one shaping the pattern or timing of diffusion.[1]

Learning and/or communicating the technical knowledge required to use a complex innovation successfully places far greater demands on potential users and on supply-side organizations than does signaling. The amount and detail of information is far greater in the former case. If obtaining technical knowledge is slower and more problematic, one may hypothesize that it plays a more important role in patterning the diffusion process of complex technologies than does signaling. It should therefore move to center stage in any theory of complex technology diffusion (as detailed below).

A substantial literature examines the technical knowledge base of innovation: research and development centers, the patent system, university-industry links, trade associations and industry consortia (Pavitt, 1985; Tornatzky, 1983; Tornatzky & Fleischer, 1990). One focus is on the *sources* of technological knowledge instantiated in an innovation—whether the knowledge originated in a public institution, a manufacturer, or a user organization (Freeman, 1963, 1968; Nasbeth & Ray, 1974; Pavitt, 1985; Ray, 1969, 1988; von Hippel, 1988).

The present paper shares with this literature its interest in supply-side institutions and technical knowledge, but departs from this school in one important respect. Most studies of supply-side institutions in innovation conceptualize the diffusion process in terms of knowledge *transfer.* They replicate the traditional diffusion model, insofar as an innovation and its accompanying technical knowledge are viewed as being transferred from the originating institution to user organizations. At the risk of overstatement, one might argue that such studies treat the movement of complex technical knowledge under a model of communication most appropriate for signaling.

There are, however, compelling empirical and theoretical reasons for avoiding the concept of knowledge transfer when applied to complex technologies. Studies have shown that, although one can readily buy the machinery that embodies an innovation, the knowledge needed to use modern production innovations is acquired much more slowly and with considerably more difficulty. Arrow (1962) argues that manufacturers using new process technologies are "learning by doing"—their productivity improves for several years after adopting a new technology, as they learn to use the technology to best effect (cf. Dutton & Thomas, 1985). Ray (1969), Pavitt (1985), von Hippel (1988), and others detail the way that production innovations, before they become useful, have to be substantially modified inside user firms. Tushman and Anderson (1986) suggest that innovative technologies can either be competence-destroying or competence-enhancing for firms, according to whether they render obsolete or build upon preexisting skills and knowledge.

Absorbing a new complex technology not only requires modification and mastery of the technology, viewed in a narrow mechanical sense, but it also often requires (frequently unanticipated) modifications in organizational practices and procedures: these too have to be learned the hard way (Johnson & Rice, 1987; Stasz, Bikson, & Shapiro, 1986).

Thus implementing a complex new technology requires both individual and organizational learning. Individual learning involves the distillation of an individual's experiences regarding a technology into understandings that may be viewed as personal skills and knowledge. Organizational learning is built out of this individual learning of members of an organization, but is distinctive. The organization learns only insofar as individual insights and skills become embodied in organizational routines, practices, and beliefs that outlast the presence of the originating individual. These routines may reflect an amalgam of individual learning or skills, and need not correspond to any one individual's understanding. Furthermore the link between learning and experience is often, but not always, lost to the organization, so that the particular learning experiences that led to any particular routine may be lost, even though the "lesson" remains instantiated in the organizational routine, practice or policy (Levitt & March, 1988).

Rosenberg (1982) has extended Arrow's (1962) notion of learning by doing, suggesting that it is not only new process technologies (e.g., in manufacturers), that are learned in this fashion. The ultimate or end users of complex products also face what Rosenberg calls "learning by using." He argues that, for complex technologies, the products are so multi-faceted, with interactions occurring between subsystems, that it is impossible for the designer to know in advance quite how they will perform when used. The result is "learning by using": the end user spends several years developing an understanding of the strengths and weaknesses of the technology. The knowledge gained by these users becomes very important to manufacturers for designing new generations of equipment (cf. Eveland & Tornatzky, 1990, p. 120).

Neither "learning by doing" nor "learning by using" is the result of knowledge transfer from the originator to the user of the technology. Indeed the point of the concepts is the opposite: to highlight the need for learning and skill formation *in situ*, far from the originator. Rice and Rogers (1980) have labeled this process "reinvention," to dramatize the importance of knowledge creation by the user (see also Clark, 1987).

The implication of these studies is that know-how, far from being readily or easily transferred from the originator to the user of a technology, faces barriers and is relatively immobile (Boyle, 1986; Eveland & Tornatzky, 1990, p. 139). Knowledge often has to be discovered *de novo* within the user organization. Using an imagery of information *transfer* for technical knowledge is therefore unwise: it obscures more than it enlightens.

Theoretical considerations also suggest an alternative conception than transfer. The Schumpeterian thesis argues that the incentive to develop a new technology derives from the inventor's desire to monopolize the use of the innovation. The faster it diffuses, the sooner one's advantage and ability to profit from it go away. A major part of the economics of innovation examines whether licensing arrangements, patents, joint ventures, and other special institutional arrangements intended to make it profitable for innovators to share their innovations, actually do so (Kamien & Schwartz, 1982). The existence of these special inducements to share knowledge underlines the fact that the initial inclination of businesses is to hoard and hide know-how, rather than transfer or diffuse it.

These critiques and studies imply that a different theory is needed to analyze the role of learning and technical knowledge in the diffusion of advanced production technologies, one that avoids the traditional notions built around signaling or transfer. The following section sketches such a perspective.

A KNOWLEDGE-BARRIER
INSTITUTIONAL-NETWORK APPROACH

1. Organizational Learning Is Partly a Consequence of Immobility of Technical Knowledge

Far from flowing easily from manufacturers and distributors of complex technology into user organizations, technical know-how is relatively immobile, and often has to be recreated by user organizations. Reinvention and learning by doing are, in part, responses to the difficulty or incompleteness of technical knowledge transfer between firms.

2. The Burden of Developing Technical Know-How (Organizational Learning) Becomes a Hurdle to Adoption

As Rosenberg (1982) put it: ". . . an intuitive familiarity with learning by using, and the time that must often elapse before performance uncertainties are resolved, may constitute an important reason for the decision of private firms to postpone the adoption of an innovation" (p. 140; see also Gerwin, 1988).

3. Given Such Hurdles, the Relationships Between Supply-Side and User Organizations in a Network Go Beyond Selling and Buying Equipment

They become structured around the task of reducing knowledge hurdles for potential adopters of an advanced technology. An appropriate image is of a network of supplier and user organizations with technical knowledge distributed quite unevenly across the network (Tornatzky & Fleischer, 1990, p. 121). The institutional network changes as new mechanisms are developed for lowering or circumventing knowledge barriers to adoption.

4. Mediating Institutions Come Into Existence Where Technical Knowledge Is Scarce and/or Organizational Learning Around a Technology Is Burdensome

These supply-side institutions specialize in creating and accumulating technical know-how regarding complex, uncertain, dynamic technologies. They "stand between" a user and a complex technology (hence "mediating").

5. Mediating Institutions Capture Economies of Scale in Learning

By the time a mediating firm has written its tenth compiler or installed its tenth inventory system, it has ironed out errors and learned from earlier attempts. This option of learning through repetition is restricted for demand-side institutions: few customers would have the occasion to develop a computerized inventory system ten times over. Economies of scale are greatest for "rare event learning"—distilling knowledge from events which occur infrequently. Rare event learning occurs when new products/systems are being developed, when unusual combinations of hardware and software are being installed, and in repair.

6. The S-Curve Reflects Changing Knowledge Barriers Over Time

The changing numbers of adopters over time need not be viewed solely or primarily in terms of shifting equilibria between costs of equipment and profitability (the economic model). Instead, the S-curve may be viewed more broadly, in terms of the changing height of hurdles (both know-how and machinery cost) to in-house adoption. Such hurdles include the difficulties of obtaining knowledge and skilled personnel and the effort of in-house organizational learning about technologies. This construct clearly exceeds the purchase price of machinery that is the typical operationalization of cost in economic diffusion studies.

7. Service Is an Alternative to Adoption or Nonadoption

A third alternative exists beyond "adopt" and "not adopt" a technology in-house—namely to purchase the fruits of that technology on a market, as a *service* from a mediating institution. Service institutions decouple the benefits of new technologies from the customer's need to acquire technical expertise about them. Consumers obtain the benefits of the new technology by getting someone else to provide it as a service, rather than by taking on the formidable task of organizing the technology in-house for themselves. To the extent that expertise and use can be decoupled in this way, knowledge barriers are lowered, and the process of technology diffusion is accelerated.

8. Technology Services Are an Alternative to Knowledge Transfer

Taking the burden of learning off the back of a potential user is *not* the same as transferring knowledge. Running users' data for them, writing software for a customer organization, installing a system for a firm, or advising what equipment to purchase, does not transfer a consultant's know-how or skills to the user organization. These services do not usually enable the customer to carry out the tasks unaided on subsequent occasions. But the provision of these services by mediating institutions does enable user organizations to adopt a complex technology without (initially) having to acquire a full range of technical knowledge in-house, and hence is functional for diffusion.

9. A Transition Occurs From Service to Self-Service

As expertise hurdles are reduced over time—both by manufacturers self-consciously seeking ways to reduce the knowledge burden on end users, and by the training and diffusion of knowledgeable persons (Ettlie, 1980)—the balance shifts from "buy" (a technology service) to "make" (deploy the technology in-house), from technological service to self-service. Firms that have already tasted the benefits of the technology, via a service provider, constitute a pool of already-primed potential adopters, likely to adopt in-house once knowledge and other barriers fall.

The same process occurs for diffusion within individual organizations. With high initial knowledge barriers, one finds at first a highly-centralized provision of the technology within a firm, with one department essentially offering the technology as a service to other parts of the firm. As knowledge and expertise barriers are lowered, the technology diffuses, and the norm becomes decentralized "self-service" in end-user departments.

METHODOLOGY

There is a dearth of government or publicly-available survey data on the diffusion of computing, a situation which has led to complaints that scholars are missing a golden opportunity to study a major technological revolution (Hunt & Hunt, 1986, p. 17). However, some market research firms have carried out large-scale surveys of the extent of computer use in representative samples of firms. I obtained market surveys for 1979, 1982, and 1985 from one firm. On-site interviews with managers of a representative sample of New York area firms were carried out by the author and colleagues as part of a study of computer impacts (Rule & Attewell, 1989). Qualitative materials from these interviews flesh out the survey data. Third, the policies and roles of manufacturers are accessible because lawsuits forced companies to document their competitive practices (Fisher, McKie, & Mancke, 1983).

INSTITUTIONAL FEATURES OF THE
DIFFUSION OF BUSINESS COMPUTING

Use of in-house computers by businesses began in the late 1950s, but the machines were so complex and expensive that they remained mainly the preserve of large companies until the end of the 1960s. Diffusion "took off" toward the end of the 1970s (Jowett, 1986). The 1980s have seen the spread of computing to even the smallest of businesses, and a parallel diffusion of personal and minicomputers into individual departments within firms. Table 11.1 documents diffusion by size from 1979 to 1985.

Diffusion and the Question of Expertise

The theory advanced earlier implies that business computing is not just a matter of purchasing objects (the computer and software) but requires considerable skills. Evidence that this can be a barrier can be found in the most extreme case, where firms buy computers but are unable to operate them. About 3% of the firms in the 1985 survey reported having purchased in-house computers but had no applications running on their computer(s). Similarly the site-visits revealed that a handful of firms had abandoned or never used their computers, due to technical problems or a lack of anyone able to operate them. (Similar knowledge-deficit abandonment effects have been documented for other advanced technologies, such as machine vision systems. See Eveland & Tornatzky, 1990, p. 123.)

Given the need for expertise, large firms hire professional experts in-house: by 1986 the numbers of computer operators, programmers, and

TABLE 11.1 Company Utilization Rates 1979-1985: % With Any In-House
Computing

Establishment Size	1979	1982	1985
1-19 employees	2.5	9.1	26.9
20-99 employees	22.7	34.7	47.8
100-249 employees	48.3	59.6	62.8
250-499 employees	50.8	71.9	73.0

SOURCE: Author's analyses of market research surveys by Focus Inc.

systems analysts had grown to 1,739,000 persons. However, it is striking that many computerized businesses don't employ computer professionals. In the 1982 survey, 70% of computerized firms with under 20 employees had no in-house computer specialist, and 42% of computerized businesses with 250-499 employees lacked a programming professional. This was not just a feature of very simple computer systems: the 42% of firms without programmers had an average of 9.5 terminals (*not* PCs) per firm—implying quite complex multi-user systems.

What is striking about the computer revolution was the emergence of institutional arrangements that removed a large part of the burden of knowledge acquisition from the backs of potential users, and enabled a relatively complex technology to diffuse rapidly into firms that initially lacked expert knowledge and did not employ in-house specialists.

The Importance of Computer Bureaus for Diffusion

A two-stage process in which firms initially purchased computer data-processing *services* from other organizations, and later purchased in-house computers was especially important in the early decades of diffusion. Computer or data processing service bureaus emerged in the 1960s as one of many strategies to increase the sales of mainframe computers. Manufacturers like IBM and Honeywell opened bureaus, along with nonmanufacturers like ADP and Digicon. Although it is today a multibillion dollar industry, the theoretical importance of the service bureau as an agent of technological diffusion has not been recognized by scholars.

A bureau typically owns mainframe computers and employs a staff of systems professionals. Client companies either send the bureau written data on business transactions (e.g., accounts receivable) or enter data from terminals in their own establishments linked to the bureau's computer by phonelines. The bureau processes this data and returns reports, payroll checks, or invoices that the client firm then uses in its daily business. Alternatively, the customer firm may have both terminals and printers at its own site and use the bureau's computer and software for remote processing ("time-sharing") (Negus, 1972).

There are several reasons for purchasing data processing services rather than obtaining computers for in-house use. Prior to the advent of personal computers, using a bureau required far less capital investment than buying a computer. Also bureaus could capture the economies of scale of processing huge numbers of payroll or receivables; most customer-firms would not have sufficient processing needs to reach such economies of scale. Bureaus could also amortize the costs of developing software across numerous clients, and fully utilize systems professionals where smaller firms could not.

But from a knowledge barrier perspective, using a computer bureau enables a customer firm to enjoy the benefits of computer technology without having to develop in-house technical knowledge about computing. It was and is a way of experiencing the new technology "at arm's length." The economies of scale in learning that bureaus enjoyed enabled them to offer technical services that it would have been hard for a customer to re-create in-house. Bureaus were pioneers in developing transaction processing software for specific kinds of businesses, and were early experts at integrating software written by one manufacturer with hardware from another (Fisher et al., 1983, p. 324).

Survey data reveal what an important role service bureaus have played in diffusion. In 1962, a government agency surveyed 17,414 establishments in New York State that together employed over half of the state's workforce. Only 3.4% of establishments had in-house computing at that time, while about eight times as many (27%) had access to computing either from an outside bureau or from a "pseudo-bureau" (a separate establishment providing processing services to other parts of a firm). See Table 11.2.

Obtaining computer services, as distinct from computing in-house, was important for both small and large establishments in 1962. Only in the very largest establishments (2,000 employees) did one find in-house computing predominating over bureau or pseudo-bureau services. In medium and small establishments, "outside" processing was far more common than in-house.

Twenty years later one finds a pattern similar to that in 1962: small firms are more likely to use a bureau than large firms. But by 1979 the employment-size "cut off" for bureau use has moved lower: more large and medium-sized firms have shifted to in-house processing. (See Table 11.3.)

Notwithstanding the proportional shift to in-house computing over time, the DP bureau industry continues to grow in absolute or dollar terms because the market for business computing is not yet saturated (U.S. Department of Commerce, 1989, p. 45-2).

TABLE 11.2 Establishments With Electronic Data Processing in New York State in 1962

Establishment Size	N	In-House Computer	Bureau	"Pseudo-Bureau"
< 50 workers	3067	3%	11%	87%
50-99	415	3	29	69
100-199	326	20	13	67
200-499	390	36	18	46
500-999	199	47	22	31
1000-1999	139	63	11	27
2000-4999	98	76	5	19
5000 or more	49	92	6	2

SOURCE: New York State (1968).
NOTE: "Pseudo-bureau" means using data processing services provided by a part of one's firm located elsewhere.

TABLE 11.3 1979 Survey on Primary Mode of Data Processing

Establishment Size	Manual*	In-House Computer	Bureau	"Pseudo-Bureau"
< 25 workers	74%	12%	10%	4%
25-100	48	32	15	5
100-200	25	54	14	7
200-500	12	67	7	9

SOURCE: Author's analyses of market research surveys by Focus Inc.
*Includes accounting machines.

The emergence of a computer bureau industry speeded the diffusion of a new technology by decoupling (user) expertise from the benefits of innovation, by acting as a mediating institution standing between the technology and the user. Other mechanisms for easing the knowledge demands of this new technology also proved important: the role of manufacturers, the recycling of software, the use of consultants, and the emergence of informal experts.

Manufacturers and Knowledge Barriers

Early manufacturers of hardware understood that a user's knowledge acquisition could be a potential barrier to adoption, and responded to this in several ways. They provided manuals and standard operating procedures, and provided hardware training for users. They also removed from the customer the knowledge-intensive burden for maintenance and repair of hardware. IBM initially made its reputation by promising to fix hardware problems, fast.

But by far the largest knowledge barrier in introducing computing into a firm involves software. Designing and writing programs for the particular applications of a business is a time-consuming task requiring a large set of technical skills. In this area also we see the emergence of a series of mechanisms whose joint effect was to remove a large part of the knowledge acquisition burden from the user.

In the 1950s and into the 1960s, organizations seeking to automate voluminous clerical transactional data turned to IBM and other hardware manufacturers for software as well as hardware: the manufacturers were the only ones with sufficient expertise to develop the software. A symbiotic relationship existed, especially between IBM and its largest customers like the Social Security Administration and the IRS. These customers paid for IBM to develop file management utilities, databases, and other then-novel software necessary for their activities.[2] IBM later sold the general-purpose parts of this software along with their hardware to subsequent customers.

Although this resulted in the accumulation of knowledge and experience (by the manufacturer) and the transfer of the product of that knowledge to multiple customers, it only removed a part of the software development burden from users. The applications programs—the software that processed checks, invoices, etc.—still had to be written. For their very largest customers, manufacturers did provide the programming know-how and staff for specific applications. Thus, IBM pioneered methodologies for analyzing the information requirements of large firms (Business Systems Planning) which it provided as a service, and IBM staff coded the software indicated by these requirements analyses.

The provision of maintenance, software, and training along with the hardware was known in the industry as "bundling." These ancillary services were included in the price of the hardware during the 1950s and 1960s. Indeed IBM mandated maintenance and repair being bundled with its hardware until it was forced to stop that practice, in a consent agreement to an anti-trust suit in 1956. Bundling continued as a central but now voluntary part of IBM's marketing strategy, and was copied by its competitors, until about 1969 (Fisher et al., 1983, pp. 34, 96, 172).

The Role of Consultants

Very large firms set up specialized staff departments (the Data Processing or MIS Department) whose staff wrote applications software for the firm. However many medium and small firms could afford neither to build an in-house programming staff nor to purchase IBM's "total solution" of hardware and customer-written software. Instead, these firms hired outside firms of consultants to advise them over purchases of equipment and to plan whole systems, to program and install software, and to integrate computers into networks. This temporary infusion of expertise has proved to be far from a transitional phenomenon. It has spawned an enormous industry: today, the computer professional services industry does about $32 billion p.a. in business, split with one-third going to consulting and training, one-third to systems integration and one-third to programming (U.S. Department of Commerce, 1989).

One important role of consultants today, and an even more dominant one a decade or more ago, was the development and programming of software. Several of the firms in our New York sample commissioned such custom-built software. However writing complex programs from scratch is a difficult task: errors (bugs) abound, deadlines are often exceeded, budgets are used up before the work is completed (Brooks, 1974). A substantial minority of interview sample firms told of disaster stories: of software that never worked right, of consultants unable to make software run on requisite hardware, leaving firms in the lurch. Others were more successful, but this era of custom programming seems to have been fraught with difficulty in many settings. Over time however, practices altered to make software acquisition less problematic.

Recycling Software

Private-sector businesses share many activities in common, even if their products or line of business differ dramatically. Accounts receivable, payroll, the general ledger are functions that recur across all manner of firms. It would seem practical to write "generic" software programs for basic business functions, and to customize them for the special needs of a particular customer. This approach became popular during the 1970s. Either taking code written for a previous client, or purchasing a package they then intended to modify, consultants developed applications programs for particular customers.

The logical extreme of this was the appearance of a software industry during the 1960s that offered "off the shelf" or "package" software packages that were supposedly ready to run, without programming by the user. The software industry experienced explosive growth, as IBM and other manufacturers found themselves unable to keep up with the burgeoning demand for applications software and "unbundled" applications software from 1969 on (Fisher et al., 1983, p. 174). Today programming services are a $9.7 billion industry (U.S. Department of Commerce, 1989, p. 45-2).

Although the rapid growth of the software industry suggests that "off the shelf" and recycled software are successful products, it is worth pointing out some limitations of this attempt to shortcut one stage in technology transfer. In Greek myth, Procrustes preyed upon unsuspecting travelers, offering them shelter and a bed in his home. The original Procrustean bed was fatal: a tall guest, whose head or limbs dangled off the end of the bed, had the overlap chopped off (by Procrustes); a short guest was racked and stretched until he fit. An analogous fate was reported by some of those firms in our sample which used off-the-shelf or lightly modified software. The particularities of the firm's business did not match the way the generic software had been written, resulting in great inconvenience. For example a clothing manufacturer bought well-regarded inventory software. But this industry has a lot of merchandise returned by its customers as a part of its normal way of doing business. The generic inventory software could only process these returns of merchandise in the most tortuous time-consuming way, wiping out all the productivity gains of using the program.

Until recently, the only recourse of firms suffering the Procrustean bed was either to scrap the software and buy another package or to employ someone to customize it further to their needs. Either course of action added expense and delay. Lately however, the problem seems less common, because highly industry-specific recycled software is usurping the role of generic software. Thus instead of purchasing a generic inventory package, a firm (say a stationery wholesaler) may choose among several competing packages, each of which is designed specifically for the wholesale stationery trade.

Today, specific inventory packages are available for meat wholesalers, liquor stores, and dozens of other industry segments. This kind of highly-specialized off-the-shelf software—"niche software"—has eased the prior problem of finding expert programmers to modify generic software and has lessened the knowledge-acquisition burden on adopters.

Analogous forms of "niche" customization have been reported for other technologies. Ray (1969, 1988) noted that the oxygen process in steel production was held back until different versions were developed to meet the distinctive needs of producers of various specialized types of steel: the generic process placed too much of a development and modification burden for most potential users.

Standards, Shells, and Interfaces

The factors mentioned thus far reduced the need for knowledge transfer by reducing the necessity for programming knowledge on the part of potential adopters. In addition, a series of developments have made software easier to operate for nonprogrammer end users. On mainframes, operating systems automated more and more activities; job control languages became simpler from the user's perspective. The development of shells—programs that link multiple applications and enable end users to move from one to another via simple menu choices rather than complex command sequences—also helped. And most recently, user-friendly graphics-based interfaces, modeled on the Macintosh's desktop, enable end users to direct computers without knowing procedural languages or complex commands.

Troubleshooting Expertise: Help Lines and Users Groups

Industrial sociologists have noted that highly-automated technologies may require relatively less skill to operate when they are working normally, but require correspondingly large amounts of skill when things go wrong. Operating skills recede in importance compared to troubleshooting and diagnostic skills. Developing in-house operating know-how is relatively straightforward: it accumulates almost continuously as the technology is used. But troubleshooting know-how depends on learning from (relatively) rare events.

From manufacturer-provided on-site repair, to writing software with "help screens" available at the touch of a button, to toll-free telephone numbers for technical assistance, to sponsoring user groups and electronically-accessible bulletin boards—one can trace a series of innovations intended to remove, or at least lighten, the burden of "rare event learning" for end users. When an unfamiliar problem occurs, there is someone to turn to. One of the most recent of these innovations is the development of "remote operating software." These programs allow an expert troubleshooter located far away from a customer to dial up the customer's microcomputer, and watch remotely as the user attempts some task on the computer which is proving problematic. While watching, the remote expert may identify a mistake that the user is making. Or the remote expert may "take control" over the user's machine and run diagnostic software to identify the problem, even though s/he is located far away.

Dynamics Within the User Firm: Centralized to Self-Service

The dynamics of diffusion within individual firms shared many of the characteristics of macro-diffusion. During the 1960s and 1970s, large firms provided computer services to their numerous operating departments in a centralized way. Data processing or MIS departments operated mainframes, wrote code, and essentially acted as computer bureaus for the rest of the firm (Table 11.2). Operating departments might have terminals connected to the corporate mainframe, but were very dependent for expertise and hardware upon centralized computer departments, which offered access and expertise as a service.

The monopoly of centralized processing unraveled in the 1970s and 1980s in many, but not all firms, encouraged by several developments (Leigh & Burgess, 1987). Programming bottlenecks were widespread, as central data processing staff were inundated with requests from operating departments for debugging and modification of existing software, as well as requests for new applications. Often central DP focused on one or two critical areas, leaving other potential users disenfranchised (Iacono & Kling, 1988). At the same time, the availability of first minicomputers and then microcomputers, meant that obtaining in-house processing power became financially feasible for operating units. The spread of off-the-shelf and niche software meant that operating departments could aspire to using new applications, without having to program them from scratch. Taken together, this led to a rapid diffusion of computing activity beyond central DP. What ensued was a period of strife, as some central DP departments tried to hold onto their monopoly, sometimes citing the need for standards, sometimes invoking the idea that distributed computing was wasteful, while centralized computing realized economies of scale (Kling & Iacono, 1984). In most firms, diffusion seems irreversible (Rockart & Flannery, 1983). Central DP have adapted by redefining their role to include provision of end-user advice centers, planning, and providing the communications/interconnectivity infrastructure of the firm (Sprague & McNurlin, 1986). Key high-volume financial and transactional software typically remain within the jurisdiction of central DP, and run on mainframe systems.

Mavens and Gurus: Informal Expertise

Given the discussion so far, one might infer that the knowledge-acquisition or skill burden on the end user of business computing is minimal, given the range of service provision and the simplification of software interfaces, etc. That would be quite incorrect. Even when the knowledge-burden of maintenance, programming, and activating programs has been removed from the end user, there remains the not-inconsequential task of learning how best to apply the technology in the business context. Fieldwork among computer users reveals that using applications programs and applying computer applications to business tasks requires a surprising depth of skill and knowledge. Part of this involves discovering "work arounds" or "kludges"—methods of circumventing awkwardnesses or bugs in programs. Another part consists of methods of making programs do things they weren't designed to do: clerks append memos in blank database fields to alert fellow workers to problems with a particular transaction, thus creating a crude electronic mail where none was provided. Managers twist spreadsheet programs to perform tasks never envisioned by their vendors. (The tip of this knowledge iceberg appears in the letter columns of computer magazines where word processor and spreadsheet users share their latest tricks.)

A final area of skill-acquisition occurs when users find ways in which the technology can change how their firm does business. From managers who use spreadsheets to pore over figures to find new ways of reducing costs to the low-level employee at American Hospital Supply who first suggested placing a terminal in a customer's office—end users have experimented with the technology to enhance their business activity.

My fieldwork experiences suggest that informal computer experts are a very important feature of staff and operations departments where computers are used extensively. There is a folk terminology for describing people who are especially skilled or knowledgeable: computer gurus, computer mavens, power users. Office workers and managers alike depend upon such people for advice, for training, for figuring solutions to new problems, for troubleshooting malfunctioning programs. These skills are developed by people whose main responsibilities are doing work, not building systems. Their abilities and role may even go unnoticed by higher management or by a firm's formal computer specialists. This is very different from acquiring computer expertise in the traditional sense, which required hiring a formally-trained staff of computer professionals.

In sum, the mechanisms described earlier that lowered the knowledge threshold for adopting computers have not, thereby, eliminated learning and knowledge on the part of computer users. They have simply shifted the locus of that learning.

DISCUSSION

This paper developed a theoretical framework for examining the diffusion of complex production technologies which are (in Eveland & Tornatzky's, 1990, terms) scientifically demanding, fragile, and lumpy—the antithesis of a reliable commodity. In such situations, knowledge and technical know-how become important barriers to diffusion, and supply-side institutions have to innovate, not only in their design of products, but especially in the development of novel institutional mechanisms for reducing this knowledge or learning burden upon end users.

The institutional history of business computing suggests a sequence of ways that an organizational network lowered knowledge barriers. Early on, supply-side organizations provided services rather than simply selling machinery. Initially these were comprehensive: operating services, installation services, programming, repair. These services reduced the burden of in-house learning for users, and speeded diffusion, but were costly. This phase was fraught with difficulties for many users.

The long-term solution to this demand for expertise was to automate and to standardize. From the development of assemblers and compilers, to the use of high level languages, to the development of shells and user-friendly interfaces—work that once required substantial skills has been given to the machine. This increased the complexity of software and the demands placed on hardware, but that complexity is inside the machine, largely hidden from the user. This has stimulated a shift away from service to a self-service mass market for computer technology.

Know-how based services remain an important component of the network, but their scope contracts and centers on the most complex knowledge areas, for example, new product development, installation, and repair. Most users are able to manage the day to day exigencies of operating the technology, with help from home-grown gurus, and occasional appeals to service firms.

Gershuny and Miles (1982) argue that the movement from service to self-service is a widespread socio-economic dynamic, applying to shifts from movie houses to VCRs and from laundries to washing machines as much as to production technologies. I would be more cautious. The trajectory can reverse for particular technologies. Technological advances can increase complexity and uncertainty, making end users dependent again on specialized experts, building new knowledge hurdles for potential adopters. One example is LANs, which have made many end-user departments dependent on central MIS again. Even more recently, Kodak Corporation has given up jurisdiction over operating its centralized mainframe computing centers, preferring to have IBM provide this as a service.

It is also clear that, in the case of complex production technologies like business computing, there is not a zero-sum choice between computing as a purchased service versus self-service or in-house computing. For while the historical trend has certainly been from service to in-house for *operating* computers, the role of computer services has not diminished. This suggests that service and in-house should be viewed as complements, rather than opposites. Even as the knowledge burdens are reduced in one area (e.g., computer operations) and that activity moves in-house, the complexity and knowledge burden in other facets of computing increase, leading to expansion of service in that area (e.g., consulting over connectivity and computer networks). One could argue that, *in order to* reduce the complexity and uncertainty in one area, complexity and uncertainty increase in another. Thus the price of making computer operations user-friendly (icon interfaces and menus, help screens, query-by-example, communications) has been extra complexity in hardware and software, that has raised the knowledge burdens of hardware and software design and manufacture. Within an organizational learning framework, this means that even as some activities are routinized, making in-house learning-by-doing an attractive option, others become more complex, so much a matter of rare event learning that user organizations prefer to let other organizations specialize in providing them.

Insofar as this model of technology diffusion highlights the interplay and choice between service versus in-house, it parallels Williamson's (1975, 1981) notions of markets (buy a good or service) versus hierarchy (make, bring in-house). One may therefore question whether this paper's "knowledge barrier institutional network" approach to diffusion is simply a special case of transaction-cost economics. However, in the most immediate reading, transaction-cost analysis would predict the *opposite* institutional trajectory from that found for the diffusion of business computing.

The transaction-cost approach assumes that purchasing on a market would normally be more efficient than producing within a hierarchy. This general advantage of markets is only reversed when certain costs of doing transactions on a market exceed the inefficiencies of producing within one's own firm. The most significant aspect of these transaction costs involve the *specificity* of assets. Asset specificity refers to the idea that in order to make a transaction with a particular seller, the buyer may have to commit certain investments, much of which would be lost if the buyer were to have to shift to a different supplier. In-house production becomes more attractive if asset specificity increases; it becomes less attractive if assets become less specific, more interchangeable.

For Malone, Banjamin, and Yates (1987) information technology has tended to reduce transaction costs, and make various information processes and products *less specific,* and is therefore leading to a broad shift away from hierarchy, towards markets. This leaves a riddle as to why computing technology itself has diffused with the opposite trajectory: from services purchased on a market to more in-house (hierarchy) deployment.

It would be hard to argue that assets involved with computing have become more specific with time (as Williamson's theory usually explains shifts towards hierarchy). Software that a decade ago could only be run on one machine is now usable on several platforms. Where once code was typically custom-written, today it is much more often obtainable off-the-shelf. Software development expertise that was a decade ago highly-specific to IBM is today more highly diffused across a highly-competitive market of suppliers. At the hardware level, more manufacturers have entered the fray, and the adoption of industry-wide standards makes more machines inter-changeable. In terms of skilled personnel, the various technical computer occupations have expanded rapidly, and rapid circulation of personnel allows for circulation of expertises (Ettlie, 1980).

In sum, the trajectory of business computing from service to in-house is the reverse of what would be expected from a simple transaction-cost approach. The direction is understandable if changes from market services to in-house deployment result mainly from a progressive lowering of know-how barriers and cheapening of equipment, rather than from changes in transaction costs. It therefore seems sensible to treat a knowledge barrier approach to technology diffusion as a distinct theory in its own right.

Acknowledgments

This research was supported in part by a grant from the National Science Foundation's Program on Information Technology and Organizations. I would like to thank my colleagues James Rule, Kevin Delaney, and Stephen Cohen for their assistance in the New York Area computing study.

NOTES

1. Some European economists, however, believe differently. Nasbeth and Ray (1974, pp. 299-301) report that late adopters received information of the existence of numerically-controlled machine tools *ten years* after early adopters. By contrast Mansfield (1985) reported signaling within one year. Coleman et al.'s (1966) study of the diffusion of tetracycline also documented very rapid signaling (cf. Burt, 1987).

2. I am grateful to Kenneth Laudon for this point.

REFERENCES

Abernathy, W. J., & Utterback, J. M. (1978). Patterns of industrial innovation. *Technology Review, 80,* 40-47.

Aiken, M., & Hage, J. (1971). The organic organization and innovation. *Sociology, 5,* 63-82.

Arrow, K. (1962). The economic implications of learning by doing. *Review of Economic Studies, 29,* 166-170.

Boyle, K. (1986). Technology transfer between universities and the UK offshore industry. *IEEE Transactions on Engineering Management, 33,* 33-42.

Brooks, F. (1974, December). The mythical man month. *Datamation,* pp. 45-52.

Brown, L. (1981). *Innovation diffusion.* London: Methuen.

Burt, R. (1987). Social contagion and innovation: Cohesion versus structural equivalence. *American Journal of Sociology, 92,* 1287-1335.

Chow, G. C. (1967). Technological change and the demand for computers. *American Economic Review, 57,* 1117-1130.

Clark, P. (1987). *Anglo-American innovation.* New York: Walter de Gruyter.

Coleman, J. S., Katz, E., & Menzel, H. (1966). *Medical innovation: A diffusion study.* New York: Bobbs-Merrill.

Davies, S. (1979). *The diffusion of process innovations.* Cambridge, UK: Cambridge University Press.

Dutton, J., & Thomas, A. (1985). Relating technological change and learning by doing. *Research on Technological Innovation, Management and Policy, 2,* 187-124.

Ettlie, J. E. (1980). Manpower flows and the innovation process. *Management Science, 26,* 1086-1095.

Eveland, J. D., & Tornatzky, L. (1990). The deployment of technology. In L. Tornatzky & M. Fleischer (Eds.), *The processes of technological innovation* (chap. 6). Lexington, MA: Lexington Books.

Fisher, F., McKie, J., & Mancke, R. (1983). *IBM and the U.S. data processing industry: An economic history.* New York: Praeger.

Freeman, C. (1963). The plastics industry: A comparative study of research and innovation. *National Institute Economic Review, 26,* 22-62.

Freeman, C. (1965). Research and development in electronic capital goods. *National Institute Economic Review, 34,* 40-91.

Freeman, C. (1968). Chemical process plant: Innovation and the world market. *National Institute Economic Review, 45,* 29-74.

Freeman, C. (1982). *The economics of industrial innovation.* Cambridge: MIT Press.

Gershuny, J., & Miles, I. (1982). *The new service economy.* New York: Praeger.

Gerwin, D. (1988). A theory of innovation processes for computer-aided manufacturing technology. *IEEE Transactions on Engineering Management, 35*(2), 90-100.

Hunt, H. A., & Hunt, T. C. (1986). *Clerical employment and technological change.* Kalamazoo, MI: W. E. Upjohn Institute for Employment Research.

Hunt, L. G., & Chambers, C. C. (1976). *The heroin epidemics.* New York: Halsted.

Iacono, S., & Kling, R. (1988). Computer systems as institutions: Social dimensions of computing in institutions. In J. DeGross & M. Olson (Eds.), *Proceedings of the ninth international conference on information systems* (pp. 101-110). Minneapolis, MN: ICIS.

Johnson, B., & Rice, R. (1987). *Managing organizational innovation.* New York: Columbia University Press.

Jowett, P. (1986). *The economics of information technology.* New York: St. Martin's.

Kamien, M., & Schwartz, N. (1982). *Market structure and innovation.* Cambridge, UK: Cambridge University Press.

Kelly, P., & Kranzberg, M. (1978). *Technological innovations: A critical review of current knowledge.* San Francisco: San Francisco University Press.

Kimberley, J., & Evanisko, M. (1981). Organizational innovation: The influence of individual, organizational, and contextual factors on hospital adoption of technological and administrative innovations. *Academy of Management Journal, 124*(4), 689-713.

Kling, R., & Iacono, S. (1984). The control of information systems developments after implementation. *Communications of the ACM, 27*(12), 1218-1226.

Leigh, W., & Burgess, C. (1987). *Distributed intelligence: Trade offs and decisions for computer information systems.* Cincinnati: South-Western Publishing.

Levitt, B., & March, J. G. (1988). Organizational learning. *Annual Review of Sociology, 14,* 319-340.

Mahajan, V., & Peterson, R. (1985). *Models for innovation diffusion.* Beverly Hills, CA: Sage.

Malone, T. W., Benjamin, R. I., & Yates, J. (1987). Electronic markets and electronic hierarchies: Effects of information technology on market structure and corporate strategies. *Communications of the ACM, 30*(6), 484-497.

Mansfield, E. (1968). *Industrial research and technological innovation: An econometric analysis.* New York: Norton.

Mansfield, E. (1977). The diffusion of eight major industrial innovations. In N. E. Terleckjy (Ed.), *The state of science and research: Some new indicators.* Boulder, CO: Westview.

Mansfield, E. (1985). How rapidly does new industrial technology leak out? *Journal of Industrial Economics, 34*(2), 217-223.

Markus, M. L. (1987). Toward a "critical mass" theory of interactive media. *Communications Research, 24*(5), 491-511.

Nasbeth, L., & Ray, G. F. (1974). *The diffusion of new industrial processes.* Cambridge, UK: Cambridge University Press.

Nasbeth, L., & Ray, G. F. (1984). *The diffusion of mature technologies.* Cambridge, UK: Cambridge University Press.

Negus, R. (1972). *A guide to computer bureau services.* New York: Pitman.

New York State. (1968). *Manpower impacts of electronic data processing.* New York: New York State Department of Labor, Division of Research and Statistics.

Pavitt, K. (1985). Sectoral patterns of technical change. *Research Policy, 13,* 343-373.

Pred, A. R. (1977). *City systems in advanced economies: Past growth, present processes, and future development options.* New York: Halsted.

President's Commission on Industrial Competitiveness. (1985). *Global competition: The new reality* (Vol. 1). Washington, DC: Government Printing Office.

Ray, G. F. (1969). The diffusion of new technology. *National Institute Economic Review, 48,* 40-83.

Ray, G. F. (1988). The diffusion of innovations: An update. *National Institute Economic Review, 126,* 51-56.

Rice, R., & Rogers, E. (1980). Reinvention in the innovation process. *Knowledge: Creation, Diffusion, Utilization, 1,*(4), 499-514.

Robertson, T., & Gatignon, H. (1987). The diffusion of high technology innovations: A marketing perspective. In J. Pennings & A. Buitendam (Eds.), *New technology as organizational innovation* (pp. 179-196). Cambridge, MA Ballinger.

Rockart, J., & Flannery, L. (1983). The management of end user computing. *Communications of the ACM, 26*(10), 776-784.

Rogers, E. (1983). *The diffusion of innovation* (3rd ed.). New York: Free Press.

Rosenberg, N. (1976). *Perspectives on technology.* Cambridge, UK: Cambridge University Press.

Rosenberg, N. (1982). *Inside the black box: Technology and economics.* Cambridge, UK: Cambridge University Press.

Rothwell, R., & Zegveld, W. (1985). *Reindustrialization and technology.* Armonk, NY: M. E. Sharpe Inc.

Rule, J., & Attewell, P. (1989). What do computers do? *Social Problems, 36*(3), 225-241.

Sprague, R., & McNurlin, B. (1986). *Information systems management in practice.* Englewood Cliffs, NJ: Prentice Hall.

Stasz, C., Bikson, T. K., & Shapiro, N. Z. (1986). *Assessing the forest service's implementation of an agency-wide information system.* Santa Monica, CA: RAND.

Stoneman, P. (1976). *Technological diffusion and the computer revolution.* Cambridge, UK: Cambridge University Press.

Stoneman, P. (1983). *An economic analysis of technological change.* Oxford, UK: Oxford University Press.

Tornatzky, L. (1983). *The process of technological innovation: Reviewing the literature.* Washington, DC: National Science Foundation.

Tornatzky, L., & Fleischer, M. (1990). *The processes of technological innovation.* Lexington, MA: Lexington Books.

Tushman, M., & Anderson, P. (1986). Technological discontinuities and organizational environments. *Administrative Science Quarterly, 31,* 439-465.

United States Department of Commerce. (1989). *U.S. industrial outlook.* Washington, DC: Government Printing Office.

Williamson, O. E. (1975). *Markets and hierarchies.* New York: Free Press.

Williamson, O. E. (1981). The economics of organization: The transaction cost approach. *American Journal of Sociology, 87*(3), 548-577.

von Hippel, E. (1988). *The sources of innovation.* New York: Oxford University Press.

12

Organizational Learning and Personnel Turnover

KATHLEEN CARLEY

The impact of personnel turnover on an organization's ability to learn, and hence on its ultimate performance, is explored for organizations with different structures and different tasks. A model of organizational decision making is presented where: (1) the organization is faced with a continuous sequence of similar but not identical problems; (2) each problem is so complex that no one person has access to all of the information nor the skill to comprehend all of the information necessary to make the decision; (3) individual decision makers base their decisions on their own previous experience; and (4) there is personnel turnover. Using simulation the impact of turnover on the rate and level of learning for hierarchies and teams is examined. This research suggests that while teams in general learn faster and better than hierarchies, hierarchies are less affected by high turnover rates particularly when the task is nondecomposable. Institutionalized memory, as embodied in the memories of distributed individuals and in the advisory relationships between individuals, determines the consequences of personnel turnover.

(SIMULATION; PERSONNEL TURNOVER; LEARNING; INSTITUTIONAL MEMORY)

For individuals, experience is expected to lead to improved performance and a higher percentage of "correct" decisions. Since organizational or group performance is dependent on the experience and capabilities of individual

This chapter appeared originally in *Organization Science,* Vol. 3, No. 1, February 1992. Copyright © 1992, The Institute of Management Sciences.

members (see Hastie, 1986; Shaw, 1981, for reviews), organizations should learn as their personnel learn. Since experience is a function of the individual's position in the organization and the relationships among individuals (Cohen, 1962; Cohen, Robinson, & Edwards, 1969; Shaw, 1954, 1981), organizations with different structures should exhibit different abilities to learn. Since turnover affects the balance and location of experience in the organization, turnover should also affect the organization's ability to learn and its performance.

However, the relationship among turnover, performance, and organizational structure is problematic. When people leave, without mechanisms for transferring personal experience among decision makers, the lessons of history are lost, knowledge disappears, the institution's memory is reduced (Carroll, 1984; Grusky, 1964; Neustadt & May, 1986), and the organization's effectiveness and productivity decrease (Price, 1977). Yet, when new skills are gained, turnover can benefit the organization (Dalton & Tudor, 1979; Price, 1977; Price & Mueller, 1981). Although turnover and experience are related, experience alone does not suffice to explain the impact of turnover for certain tasks (Argote, Beckman, & Epple, 1987). Moreover, at certain organizational levels, such as executives (Tushman, Virany, & Romanelli, 1989), the impact of turnover seems independent of experience. Since individuals at each level in the organization (executive, staff, analysts . . .) have to face different information-processing demands and garner different types of experience, turnover at different levels may affect the organization differently. For example, although Price and Mueller (1981) suggest it may take a 50% turnover rate among nurses before the net effect is negative, few would suggest that hospitals could withstand the same rate of turnover among doctors.

In this paper, the impact of personnel turnover on across-problem[1] organizational learning in hierarchies and teams is examined using a model of organizational decision making in which individuals base their decisions on their experience. Thus, this paper is in a long tradition of interest in organizational decision making in which the organization's behavior is seen as affected by the intendedly, but boundedly, rational behavior of individual decision makers (Carley, 1986a; Cyert & March, 1963; March & Olsen, 1975; March & Simon, 1958; Padgett, 1980a; Simon, 1947; Steinbruner, 1974). What matters is not the quality or correctness of a specific decision but the organization's ability to learn to make a greater proportion of correct decisions over time. This paper emphasizes organizational across-problem learning as a function of individual across-problem learning in a distributed decision-making task. In such a task it is not necessary (and often not possible) for individuals to reach consensus; information pooling occurs through institutional design rather than individual choice (Panning, 1986). Thus, this study differs from research that emphasizes the historical development of routines, standard operating procedures, and accounting procedures (Cyert & March, 1963; Johnson & Kaplan, 1987; Levitt & March, 1988; March, 1981; March & Olsen, 1975; Nelson & Winter, 1982), cumulative production skills (Argote et al., 1987; Dutton & Thomas, 1984; Preston & Keachie, 1964; Rosenberg, 1982), single-problem learning,[2] mutual influence, and the production of consensus (Bavelas, 1950; Cohen, 1962; Cohen et al., 1969; DeGroot, 1974; Hastie, 1986), decision making when information is redundant (Hastie, 1986),[3] determination of the optimal decision rule (DeGroot, 1970; Grofman & Owen, 1986; Marschak, 1955; McGuire & Radner, 1986), and the learning of (or emergence of) effective communication structures (Cohen, 1962; Guetzkow & Dill, 1957; Leavitt, 1951; Shaw, 1954; Shaw & Rothschild, 1956).[4]

Types of Structure

Hierarchies and teams as idealized structural types are of particular interest because they may be differentially affected by turnover. Hierarchies are characterized by a set of decision makers that are organized in a chain of command[5] (Cohen's, 1986, hierarchical authority structure) such that decision makers at different levels have access not only to different information but also to different types of information (Chandler & Dames, 1980; Downs, 1967; Weber, 1922) and such that the top manager makes the ultimate decision (Carley, 1986b; Padgett, 1980a). By contrast, teams are characterized by a set of decision makers that act autonomously (there is no chain of command), have access to different information, and have equal voice in the final decision.

Hierarchies have a variety of advantages and disadvantages. Hierarchies enable specialization (Duncan, 1973), emerge in response to distributed or specialized information (Cohen, 1962), potentially decrease competition and deception and admit better auditing (Williamson, 1975), reduce coordination costs (Malone, 1986, 1987), and are most effective when the task and technology are simple (Thompson, 1967). Experimental evidence also suggests that when the task is simple such centralized structures tend to solve problems more quickly and with fewer errors than decentralized structures (Cohen, 1962; Shaw, 1981, pp. 150-161).[6] However, when the task is more complex the opposite is the case (Shaw, 1981, pp. 150-161). In addition, hierarchies may exhibit lower performance than other organizational forms due to information distortion (Jablin, Putnam, Roberts, & Porter, 1986, pp. 610-613) which may result from condensing information as it goes up the chain of command (Downs, 1967, p. 269) or from uncertainty absorption (March & Simon, 1958). Further, information channeling within the hierarchy may inhibit innovation and discovery (Burns & Stalker, 1961).

Alternate structures have been proposed that, in contrast to hierarchies, provide more effective communication for single-problem learning (Galbraith, 1973; Simon, 1973; Wilensky, 1967), permit more rapid problem solving (Carley, Lehoczky, Rajkumar, Sha, Tokuda, & Wang, 1988), optimize the decision for a single problem (DeGroot, 1970; Grofman & Owen, 1986; Marschak, 1955; McGuire & Radner, 1986), admit flexibility (Davis & Lawrence, 1977), or are more egalitarian (O'Neill, 1984). While none of these structures is identical to the teams examined in this paper, they do bear certain resemblances.[7] They are decentralized and there is no chain of command (Anderson & Fischer, 1986; Cohen, March, & Olsen, 1972; Masuch & LaPotin, 1989). Masuch and LaPotin, contrasting such structures with hierarchies, found that randomness decreased productivity, and hierarchical authority relations improved performance only when decision makers were committed. Markets, like teams are decentralized, and Williamson (1975) argued that they are highly efficient on a variety of dimensions as long as specialization is not required.[8] Further teams without managers must be explicitly coordinated to perform effectively. Though such coordination may be done through negotiation (Bar-Shalom & Tse, 1973; Strand, 1971; Tsitsiklis & Athans, 1984), the equal allocation of resources and effort that can result may not be the optimal coordination strategy (Arrow & Radner, 1979; Carley, 1988).

In summary, hierarchies and teams (or extremely similar structures) have emerged as organizational structures of great interest. The relative ability of these structures to exhibit across-problem learning when decisions and not information are communicated and their resiliency in the face of turnover have not been systematically examined. However, the literature does make several predictions (at least by analogy with single-problem learning) which include but are not limited to the following. Teams will learn faster and better than hierarchies when the task is complex, but hierarchies will fare better when the task is simple. Due to the speed with which they learn, teams should be less affected than hierarchies by increasing task complexity and turnover.

LEARNING BEHAVIOR

To examine this problem a model of organizational behavior is developed and analyzed. This model's main assumptions are based on the following four observations. First, organizational behavior is historically based. Organizations rely on experience, incrementally adapting their response to similar problems as they receive feedback on their previous decisions (Levitt & March, 1988; Lindblom, 1959; Steinbruner, 1974). Second, organizational learning depends, at least in part, on the memories of individuals and their ability to learn (Hastie, Park, & Weber, 1984; Johnson & Hasher, 1987). Third, organizations are disorderly (Cohen et al., 1972; March & Romelaer, 1976; Padgett, 1980a). One source of disorderliness which may be particularly crippling is personnel turnover and the movement of decision makers between decision arenas (Carley, 1986b; Grusky, 1963; March & Romelaer, 1976; March & Shapira, 1982; Pfeffer & Salancik, 1978; Tushman, Virany, & Romanelli, 1985, 1989). Fourth, while organizations often are faced with highly similar problems, they are rarely faced with exactly the same problem. The problems faced are so complex that different types of expertise may be required; no one decision maker in the organization may be able to cope with, let alone have access to, all of the information needed to make a decision. I refer to sets of problems with these characteristics as quasi-repetitive integrated decision-making tasks.

A task is quasi-repetitive if the same type of problem is faced multiple times but some of the information, constraints, parameters, etc., are different each decision period, thus producing slightly different decisions. A task is integrated[9] if the final organizational decision is determined by combining into a single decision a plethora of previous smaller or component decisions made by various decision makers (DMs) within the organization. Such quasi-repetitive integrated decision-making tasks are quite common in the organizational arena. At a very general level such tasks include determining whether the positive implications of a possible policy outweigh the negative implications (e.g., determining for a new line of research or a new product whether the chances for success outweigh the chances for failure). At a more specific level, tasks with these characteristics include air traffic control (La Porte & Consolini, 1988; Steeb et al., 1980; Thorndyke, McArthur, & Cammarata, 1981), sensor data interpretation (Smith, 1980), and budgeting (Padgett, 1980b). Despite the prevalence of such tasks in organizations, the relative ability of organizations with different structures to learn, despite turnover, when faced with such a task has not been explored analytically.[10]

The proposed model is based on assumptions which reflect these observations. Individuals are treated as perfect historians whose decisions are based on their personal previous experience. Thus, individual decision makers are intendedly adaptive (March & Olsen, 1975). Further, in keeping with work in behavioral decision theory, individuals are modeled as imperfect statisticians insensitive to sample size (Tversky & Kahneman, 1971), but adjusting their expectations on the basis of additional information

(Tversky & Kahneman, 1974), and effectively overconfident of their ability to correctly predict outcomes (Lichtenstein & Fischhoff, 1977). In keeping with the work in distributed decision making, individual decision makers are modeled as engaged in cooperative behavior (for an overview, see Bond & Gasser, 1988). The organization is modeled as a set of decision makers who change over time and are engaged in a quasi-repetitive integrated decision making task for which there is unambiguous and rapid feedback. Illustrative organizations with many, if not all of these characteristics, are air traffic control and financial trading.

Simulation[11] of the proposed model is used to explore the impact of personnel turnover and organizational structure on the rate and level of learning achieved by the organization, while controlling for other factors that affect the experience of individuals (task complexity, task type, and personal experience). In theoretical analyses the researcher typically derives logically implied consequences from a minimal set of premises. As models increase in complexity our ability to locate analytic solutions decreases in which case simulation becomes an attractive alternate method for deriving theoretical consequences. Thus, the simulation results should be viewed as derived predictions which can be tested empirically. Further, the results should not be viewed as tests against nature but as tests of the ability of the model's assumptions to generate observable outcomes.

1. MODEL

The organization operates across a sequence of decision-making periods. Each period the organization faces a new problem that is similar, but not identical, to previous problems. During each period, information on the new problem is evaluated by analysts acting autonomously, a final organizational decision is made, and then each member of the organization receives feedback. This feedback is the "true" decision for that problem. How the final organizational decision is made is different for the team and the hierarchy. Further, even though the organization and its members know what type of decision is supposed to be made, the individual decision makers do not necessarily know when to make a specific decision. Rather, they have to learn the rules that associate specific inputs with specific decisions. For example, radar operators may know they are to determine whether the radar configuration signals that a missile is approaching; however, they do not know initially, and thus must learn, which particular configurations correspond to missiles. A brief outline of the model is provided in Appendix 1.[12]

1.1. Organizational Structure

Two organizational structures are examined: the centralized hierarchy and the team which differ only in the presence of upper-level management.

Centralized Hierarchy. The centralized hierarchy is modeled as a three-tier organization composed of a chief executive officer (CEO), a set of assistant executive officers (AEOs), and a set of analysts. In this paper, the specific centralized hierarchy examined has 13 DMs[13] with 3 under each "manager" or "executive." There are 9 analysts. Each analyst, each decision period, receives some information on the problem (a subproblem), integrates the information to make a decision (yes or no), and sends this decision to his or her AEO. The AEO uses the 3 analysts' decisions to make an integrated decision (yes or no), and sends this decision to the CEO. The CEO integrates the AEOs' decisions and makes the final, organizational, decision (yes or no). Then all DMs are given, as feedback, the "true" decision. The true decision is the decision for the entire problem that a perfect DM given the entire problem and having perfect knowledge of what pattern corresponds to which solution would give as the answer. The DM's experience thus includes what patterns of information the DM has seen, and the number of times in that DM's experience that when that pattern was observed the true decision was a yes (or no).

Team. The team is modeled as a single-tier organization composed of a set of 9 analysts.[14] Each decision period, each analyst receives information (a subproblem), and makes a decision (yes or no) independent of the other analysts. The final, organizational, decision is the majority vote of the analysts.[15] Next, the analysts find out the true decision.

1.2. Task

The task is a very general one involving elements of both pattern matching, and determining statistical relationships. The organization must determine which configuration of 1s and 0s in a binary word of length N goes with a yes or no answer. The decision makers do not know initially whether the correct pattern-response configuration is majority classification, even/odd classification, parity, etc. By altering which pieces of information or "bits" in the word a particular analyst sees or by altering the probability that the true decision is a "1" or "0" tasks with different characteristics can be examined.

Task complexity is defined as the number of bits or positions in that word that can be 1 or 0 (N). For a given level of task complexity (N) there are potentially 2^N problems. Thus, as task complexity increases the likelihood of seeing an identical problem two periods in a row decreases. Task complexity has several real world analogues such as the amount of information that needs to be processed for a task or the number of different variables that need to be examined. For example, adapting off-the-shelf inventory control software for small personal businesses is a less complex task than designing and building specialized inventory systems for large hospitals in part because it involves fewer design variables. Task complexity does not change over time. In this paper, four levels of task complexity are examined: very low ($N = 9$), low ($N = 27$), medium ($N = 45$), and high ($N = 63$).[16]

Each decision period the organization is faced with a particular problem. Problem solution requires integrating the decisions made by the analysts. For each problem there is a decision provided by the organization (the final decision) and a true decision. Such a problem is divisible into a set of subproblems, each of which is a portion of the word. Each analyst has a distinct subproblem; that is, each position or "bit" in the word is evaluated by only one analyst. Given a subproblem each analyst must decide—yes ("I think the answer is 1," represented by a 1) or no ("I think the answer is 0," represented by a 0). In addition, in the hierarchy, the AEOs and CEO take as their subproblem the decisions of their subordinates and then, like the analysts, decide—yes ("I think the answer is 1," represented by a 1) or no ("I think the answer is 0," represented by a 0). Thus, each decision maker is making a recommendation for what he or she thinks the final decision should be. The individual decision maker by passing on a 1/0 decision rather than the number of 1s has compressed information; hence, there is information loss. And the degree of information loss is higher the more complex the task.

Which of the potential problems the organization faces and how the problem is divided across analysts determines the "type of task." Two task types are considered in detail—nondecomposable and decomposable-consensual. A problem is decomposable given a particular organizational structure if the subproblems given to the analysts are independent and the set of solutions to these subproblems accurately reflects all incoming information. In general we can think of a problem as decomposable if a division of a problem into "x" subproblems does not yield a different answer than a division into "less than x" subproblems. When problems are not decomposable, pertinent information may be lost when decisions are made on subproblems thus resulting in potentially incorrect final decisions. An example of a nondecomposable task is design, e.g., aircraft or car design. A problem is consensual given a particular organizational structure if the correct solutions to the subproblems given to the analysts are identical. A problem where each analyst sees an identical subproblem is consensual. In theory, tasks such as proposal evaluation where each analyst evaluates the same set of proposals have this consensual property. These task types are examined as they represent idealized types that are interesting due to their prevalence in real organizations and on which hierarchies and teams may perform differently.

Nondecomposable Task. A problem is a word drawn from this set of 2^N words with replacement such that all problems are equally likely to be drawn. This guarantees that 1s and 0s are equally likely in every bit and that the bits are independent. Each analyst has a distinct subproblem that is a contiguous set of positions and each position in the word is evaluated by only one analyst. For example, we can imagine an organization with 3 analysts that is faced with the problem—101010001; in this case, the first analyst sees the first 3 positions (101), the second analyst sees the next three positions (010), and the third analyst sees the last three positions (001). In the nondecomposable task no one analyst, or set of analysts, has enough information to always make the true decision. Each analyst, however, as he or she gains experience by seeing a sequence of subproblems learns what patterns typically are associated with what response. For example, an analyst might learn that when the subproblem 110 is observed the true decision is typically 1.

Decomposable-Consensual Task. A problem is a word drawn from the set of 2^N words with replacement such that all subproblems are identical. As in the nondecomposable task, each analyst has a distinct subproblem that is a contiguous set of positions; each position in the word is evaluated by only one analyst. For example, we can imagine an organization with 3 analysts that is faced with the problem—101101101; in this case, the first analyst sees the first 3 positions (101), the second analyst sees the second three positions (101), and the third analyst sees the last three positions (101). In the decomposable-consensual task each analyst has enough information to always make the true decision. Each analyst always makes the correct decision after gaining enough experience to know what pattern is associated with what response. This happens after seeing the pattern once.

These two tasks can be thought of as extreme points in a continuum of tasks. For the nondecomposable task each analyst sees a somewhat different subproblem whose pattern is indicative of, but not completely diagnostic of, the final result. In contrast, for the decomposable-consensual task each analyst sees the identical subproblem whose pattern is diagnostic of the overall pattern. The decomposable-consensual task is an "easier" task; i.e., when consensuality is enforced, for the same level of task complexity, the number of possible problems is lower for the decomposable-consensual task than for the nondecomposable task. Consequently both teams and hierarchies should learn faster when they work on a decomposable-consensual task than when they work on a nondecomposable task.

1.3. Decision Procedure and Learning

All DMs, regardless of position (analyst, AEO, or CEO), learn from experience and employ the same learning algorithm. Each DM keeps a cumulative record of the subproblems it receives and the true decision. For each DM each subproblem falls into a particular class. A class is a particular pattern of 1s and 0s, such as 010. For the two types of tasks examined the classes of subproblems seen by the analysts are identical and all classes of subproblems are equally likely. As task complexity increases (9, 27, 45, 63), the number of bits of information seen by each analyst increases (1, 3, 5, 7) and the number of classes of subproblems or patterns that the analyst must choose between increases (2, 8, 32, 128).[17] Regardless of task complexity managers always see the same number of bits—3. As the DM encounters subproblems it builds up, for each class of subproblems, an expectation as to whether its decision when it sees a problem in that class is a 0 or a 1. Each DM basically keeps two counters for each class of subproblems—the number of times the true decision was a 0, and the number of times the true decision was a 1. Each decision cycle, each DM simply ups the appropriate counter. Since each DM sees the true decision, organizational structure does not affect what is learned. The DM's expectation that its answer is a 0 (1) is defined as the proportion of times in this DM's experience that, given this class of subproblems, the true decision was a 0 (1). When the DM is faced with a subproblem, the DM uses this experiential information to make a decision using the following procedure:

1. Determine what class the subproblem is in.
2. If the expectation of a 0 is greater than the expectation of a 1, return 0 as the decision.
3. If the expectation of a 0 is less than the expectation of a 1, return 1 as the decision.
4. If the expectation of a 0 is equal to the expectation of a 1, return either a 0 or a 1 as the decision with equal likelihood. In other words, in the absence of sufficient information—guess.

This learning procedure guarantees that each DM learns the conditional probabilities that the true decision is a 1 (or 0) given a particular pattern. The decision procedure guarantees that the DM will pass on as his or her decision the value whose conditional probability is higher. By using this decision/learning procedure the DMs learn to match incoming information to possible decisions in much the same way that parallel distributed processing systems learn to match particular patterns to particular outputs (McClelland et al.,

1986; Rumelhart et al., 1986). The proposed procedure in effect is weighting each input separately and equally. As such, this learning procedure guarantees that the decision maker will come to attend more to that incoming information that "will match" the correct response. Given the right sequence of problems this learning procedure will produce what might be interpreted as superstitious learning, i.e., doing what one did last time because it worked. Further, this same learning procedure in the short run, and in the face of turnover, creates the appearance that upper-level managers attend more to those analysts who have a history of producing correct decisions.[18]

1.4. Turnover

Organizational turnover occurs when members of the organization leave and are replaced by new personnel. Turnover is implemented by having a DM leave the organization, and another immediately enter the organization periodically over time as a Poisson process. Which DM leaves the organization is determined randomly; all DMs at the same organizational level are equally likely to be chosen to leave. I define the rate of turnover as 1 over the mean number of decision periods between these exits/entrances (mean interarrival time). Four turnover rates are examined: (1) no turnover; (2) low —0.01 arrivals per decision periods (ADPs) for analysts, 0.0033 ADPs for AEOs, and 0.0011 ADPs for CEOs; (3) medium—0.02 ADPs for analysts, 0.0067 ADPs for AEOs, and 0.0022 ADPs for CEOs; and (4) high—0.1 ADPs for analysts, 0.033 ADPs for AEOs, and 0.011 ADPs for CEOs. These are chosen so that, if the same turnover rate is used at all levels in the organization, the probability of a particular individual leaving during a particular time period is the same for all individuals regardless of level.

When turnover occurs the organization loses the expertise and experience of the DM who leaves and gains the experience of the DM who joins the organization. The level of DM experience is the number of subproblems it has observed. The type of DM experience is defined by the task it has faced. Incoming analysts can differ in level and type of experience. For analysts, three different forms of experience are examined: (1) novice—no experience, (2) good fit—moderate experience (500 subproblems) with exactly the same task, and (3) poor fit—moderate experience (500 subproblems) in an organization with a slightly different task (one in which likelihood of a 0 in each bit is 54% rather than 50%). In contrast all new managers are treated as novices. This reflects the assumption that new managers do not enter new jobs with preconceptions about which of their subordinates are most likely to produce correct decisions, but rather, adapt to their new job by "listening first."

2. ORGANIZATIONAL PERFORMANCE

The organization's performance at a particular time is a function of whether the final, organizational, decision is a correct decision. A correct decision occurs if the final decision matches the true decision. The organization's performance can be determined analytically when (1) the true decision is known, (2) the frequency of each pattern of subproblem is known, and (3) the conditional probability of a 1 (or 0) given a particular subproblem is known. For example, in this paper, unbeknownst to the individual decision makers, 1s and 0s are equally likely and the true decision is a "1" if there really are more 1s than 0s in the problem and "0" if there really are more 0s than 1s.[19] Initially, for all organizations examined, all DMs are novices and so randomly guess. In this case, the model can be solved analytically, with the result that initially the organization makes the correct decision only 50% of the time.

2.1. Ultimate Performance

Organizational performance is not dependent on the vagaries of individual experience once individuals are fully trained and know which pattern corresponds to which solution. Under such conditions structural and task factors should dominate. For complex tasks teams should outperform hierarchies (Shaw, 1981) as hierarchies have greater information distortion (Downs, 1967; Jablin et al., 1986), greater uncertainty absorption (March & Simon, 1958), and less flexibility (Davis & Lawrence, 1977); whereas, for simple tasks, hierarchies should be more efficient and exhibit better performance (Shaw, 1981; Thompson, 1967). Further, performance should decrease as tasks increase in complexity due to the increased likelihood of error (Perrow, 1984) and the increased information-processing and decision-making demands (Galbraith, 1973).

For the proposed model, ultimately all DMs, regardless of level,[20] will act as majority classifiers and so can be thought of as employing as a standard operating procedure "propose as their guess about the global majority whatever is in their local majority." The performance of an organization with such a standard operating procedure can be analytically determined[21] and the result is the theoretical optimum performance level (see Table 12.1).

In contrast to traditional expectations, the proposed model suggests that hierarchies do not outperform teams even when the task is simple and that task type in addition to task complexity and organizational structure determines organizational performance. We see in Table 12.1 that, ultimately, when there is no turnover: (1) when the task is decomposable-consensual all

TABLE 12.1 Theoretical Optimum Performance Levels

Task Complexity	Very Low	Low	Medium	High
Hierarchies				
nondecomposable task	89.415	80.450	79.071	78.443
decomposable task	100.000	100.000	100.000	100.000
Teams				
nondecomposable task	100.000	85.173	83.240	82.419
decomposable task	100.000	100.000	100.000	100.000

NOTE: Each cell contains the limiting probability times 100 for one type of organization faced with a particular type of task with a particular level of task complexity.

organizations learn to make all decisions correctly, (2) when the task is nondecomposable organizational performance decreases as complexity increases, and (3) when the task is nondecomposable teams learn more than hierarchies and so come to outperform them. In addition, the proposed model suggests that even in a stable environment in which the task does not change, experiential learning improves performance but does not guarantee perfect performance. Specifically, errors will still occur if the task is complex and nondecomposable. This is analogous to Perrow's observation (1984) that in tightly-coupled complex systems accidents are inevitable.

Two factors determine the organization's theoretical performance limit. First, information reduction occurs as analysts compress information into a decision. The greater the task complexity the greater the information reduction and consequently the lower the ultimate performance. Only when the task complexity is 9, and so each analyst sees only one bit of information, is no information lost when the analyst passes on his or her decision. The more diagnostic the task the lower the information reduction and consequently the higher the ultimate performance: since the decomposable-consensual task is completely diagnostic no pertinent information is lost as the analysts make their decisions and so the theoretical optimum level always is 100%. Second, information reduction occurs as DMs combine their decisions. Analysts, whether in teams or hierarchies, learn exactly the same thing when faced with the same problem. Thus performance differences across organizational structures have to do with the way the analysts' decisions are combined. In the hierarchy, information reduction occurs three times (when the analysts, AEOs, and CEO integrate information to make a decision) and information channeling occurs twice (when different information is distributed across analysts, and then AEOs). In teams, information reduction occurs twice (once by the analysts and once when the vote is taken) and information channeling occurs only once (when information is distributed across analysts). The more levels at which decisions are combined the greater the information reduction and the lower the ultimate performance. Thus, hierarchies are more severely affected than teams. Further, one would expect that the "flatter" the hierarchy (fewer levels) the less its performance would be affected. The more consensual a task the less information is lost as decisions are combined and the higher the ultimate performance. Since the decomposable-consensual task is completely consensual all analysts produce identical decisions and so no information is lost as their decisions are combined.

2.2. Simulation and Measuring Learning

Organizations, however, rarely operate in this optimal mode. Rather, personnel may be poorly trained or may leave the organization. Consequently it is important to consider whether the foregoing conclusions hold even when the organization is still learning or when there is turnover. The proposed model cannot be solved analytically under these conditions as the DMs' decision rules continually change and the proportion of DMs using each rule is not known. Thus, to examine organizational performance under less than optimal conditions it is necessary to turn to simulation.

In the foregoing discussion the following parameters were identified: organizational structure, task complexity, turnover rate, experience, and task type. To determine the impact of varying these parameters on organizational learning Monte Carlo analysis is used. Each organization is simulated 400 times (400 runs). Within each of these 400 runs each organization is simulated for 2500 decision periods (hence it is faced with a sequence of 2500 problems).[22] The random sequences for both turnover and problem are not repeated across runs nor across organizational types in order to prevent bias from a particular random sequence choice.[23]

Two measures of learning are used—final level of learning (or final performance level) and rate of learning. The final level of learning is defined as the percentage of correct decisions made between decision period 2300 and 2500 by the 400 organizations of that type. This final level is a measure of how much the organization can learn, and hence how well it can ultimately perform. Most organizations examined have stabilized their behavior by this point. Each value for final level of learning is based on 80,000 decisions. This averaging approach is taken to reduce the variance of the estimator. Since the percentage of correct decisions, denoted by p, is based on the sum of 80,000 binary decisions the standard deviation of this percentage can be determined as: $(p(1 - p)/80,000)^{0.5}$. If p is 0.5 then the standard deviation is 0.0018, if p is 0.8 then the standard deviation is 0.0014, and if p is 0.9 then the standard deviation is 0.0010. In general, for the organizations examined, the percentage of correct decisions ranges between 50% and 90% and the standard deviation thus ranges between 0.18% and 0.10%.

The rate of learning is defined as the average number of decision periods it takes until the organization has increased its performance by 10% (learned to make 60% rather than 50% of its decisions correctly) as measured in ten decision time period windows. By definition, if a 10% performance increase does not occur during the 2500 decision periods it will be defined as occurring at time 2495 (the middle of the last time window).[24] The standard deviations provided are the standard deviations of these means. In order to measure the resiliency of organizations in the face of turnover I use as a baseline their performance when there is no turnover.[25]

By varying these parameters many types of organizations can be identified. In this paper, 256 types of organizations are examined. Both hierarchies and teams, for both types of tasks, for the 3 turnover rates among analysts greater than none, for all 4 levels of task complexity, for the 3 types of experience are simulated (144 types), as are hierarchies and teams for both types of tasks for all complexity levels when there is no turnover (16 types). Thus, there are 80 matched pairs of organization types such that one member is a team and the other is a hierarchy. In addition, in order to examine the impact of executive turnover, hierarchies for both types of tasks for the 3 turnover rates among managers greater than none, for all 4 levels of analyst turnover, for all 4 levels of complexity are simulated (96 types).

3. SIMULATION RESULTS

As previously discussed, performance degrades with complexity and teams outperform hierarchies unless the task is decomposable-consensual (in which case all organizations perform perfectly). Such ultimate performance occurs once the organization, and all its members, have learned all that can be learned. Now, simulation will be used to examine (1) whether structure and task have the same impact on rate of learning that they do on ultimate performance and (2) whether the relation among structure, task, rate, and level of learning holds in the face of turnover. Complete data from these simulations are provided in Appendix 2. (See note 12.)

3.1. Structure, Task, and Rate of Learning

In the organizations examined, typically, teams learn more quickly than hierarchies, organizations facing low-complexity tasks learn more quickly than those facing high-complexity tasks,[26] and organizations facing decomposable-consensual tasks learn more quickly than those facing nondecomposable tasks.[27] For teams the average learning rate is 177.5 ($\sigma = 61.0$) whereas, for hierarchies (both with and without executive turnover), the average learning rate is 453.2 ($\sigma = 60.3$).[28] This difference is significant (one-tailed $t = 33.639$, $p < 0.0005$, df = 79). For organizations faced with a very low complexity task the average learning rate is 20.9 ($\sigma = 2.8$); whereas, for organizations faced with a high complexity task, the average learning rate is 799.4 ($\sigma = 125.5$). This difference is significant (one-tailed $t = 6.2$, $p < 0.0005$, df = 63). For organizations faced with a nondecomposable task the average learning rate is 710.5 ($\sigma = 82.1$); whereas for organizations faced with the decomposable-consensual task the average learning rate is 23.5 ($\sigma = 1.9$). This difference is significant (one-tailed $t = 8.4$, $p < 0.0005$, df = 127).

In the proposed model, analysts, whether in a team or hierarchy, learn at the same rate and ultimately achieve the same performance level for the same task. Since the tasks examined are quasi-repetitive and individuals have "perfect" memories, the rate at which individuals learn is a function of how frequently the same problem repeats. The simpler the task the more frequently problems repeat. Thus, learning is faster in low-complexity and decomposable-consensual tasks. But for teams and hierarchies organizational performance differences are attributable to structural factors. Teams learn faster than hierarchies as the organizational learning rate is controlled by the analysts' learning rate; whereas, in the hierarchy, it is also dependent on the managerial learning rate. Consequently, in hierarchies, managerial learning slows the rate of organizational learning. To demonstrate this point, I will contrast the 16 hierarchies in which there is no managerial turnover and all new personnel are novices (4 rates of turnover for each of the 4 levels of complexity) under conditions where managers do not learn but instead perform optimally by simply employing a majority classification rule and so always attend equally to each DM under them[29] with these same 16 hierarchies where managers learn (as previously specified). When managers learn the average final performance level is 71.99 and the average learning rate is 788.8; whereas, when managers always act optimally the average final performance level is 72.46 and the average learning rate is 365. Thus, managerial learning does not significantly alter how much the hierarchy learns (one-tailed $t = 0.111$, $p > 0.25$, df = 15) but it does significantly reduce how fast the hierarchy learns (one-tailed $t = 1.493$, $p = 0.077$, df = 15).

These results confirm traditional expectations with the exception that hierarchies do not learn faster than teams even when the task is simple. These results, however, are "on average" results. A closer examination of the data reveals that hierarchies learn faster than teams when the task is nondecomposable, complex, and the new personnel are a poor fit with the organization. Of the 80 pairs of organizational types, such that the only difference is

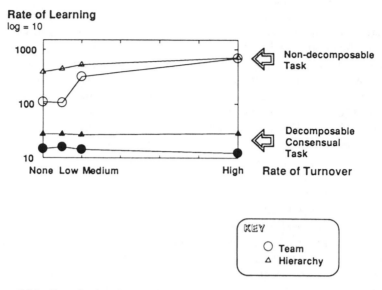

Figure 12.1. Organizations Learn Slower the Higher the Turnover

NOTE: The average rate of learning, plotted on a log 10 scale, for hierarchies (triangles) and teams (circles) for both decomposable-consensual (bottom) and nondecomposable (top) tasks as the turnover rate among analysts increases is shown. In the hierarchies there is no executive turnover. Each mark indicates the average number of time periods until all organizations with that structure, faced with that type of task, and level of turnover (regardless of personnel experience or task complexity) learn to make 60% of their decisions correctly. Thus, the higher the mark the lower the rate of learning. When there is no turnover each mark represents the average of 400 organizations of 4 types, thus $N = 1,600$. When there is turnover, the new personnel can be either novices, or have a good fit or poor fit with the organization and so each mark represents the average of 400 organizations of 12 types ($N = 4,800$).

organizational structure, in 62 of the pairs teams learn as much or more than the hierarchies and in 77 of the pairs teams learn as fast or faster than the hierarchies. Teams are slower and learn less when personnel who are a poor fit are hired. For the remaining 176 organizational types, which are hierarchies with executive turnover, the corresponding team always learns as fast or faster and more than the hierarchies.

3.2. Turnover and the Organization's Ability to Learn

In the organizations examined, typically, organizations learn slower (Figure 12.1) and less (Figure 12.2) the higher the turnover rate.[30] As expected, organizations facing simple tasks (decomposable-consensual or low complexity) are more resilient in the face of turnover and still outperform their counterparts facing complex tasks.[31] However, in contrast to the prediction, teams are more affected than hierarchies by turnover. For the same increase

Final Performance Level

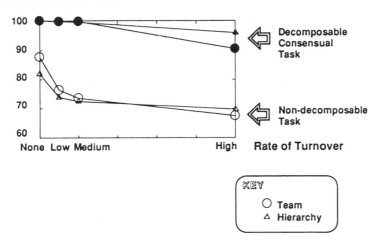

Figure 12.2. Organizations Learn Less the Higher the Turnover

NOTE: The average final performance level for hierarchies (triangles) and teams (circles) for both decomposable-consensual (top) and nondecomposable (bottom) tasks as the turnover rate among analysts increases is shown. In the hierarchies there is no executive turnover. When there is no turnover each mark represents the percentage of decisions made by 400 organizations of 4 types over 200 decision periods that are correct, thus $N = 320,000$. When there is turnover, the new personnel can be either novices, or have a good fit or poor fit with the organization and so each mark represents the percentage of decisions made by 400 organizations of 12 types over 200 decision periods that are correct ($N = 960,000$).

in turnover teams experience a greater decrease in how much is learned than hierarchies (hierarchies make 8.1% fewer correct decisions when analyst turnover is high and there is no executive turnover than when there is no turnover, whereas teams make 13.9% fewer correct decisions). Consequently when turnover is severe, hierarchies are more resilient and actually may come to outperform teams, but will do so exceedingly slowly.

Turnover reduces organizational performance because portions of the institution's memory leave as personnel leave. The higher the turnover the more likely it is that personnel leave before they are fully trained and consequently the lower the organization's final level of learning. Simpler tasks require less training; consequently, it takes a much higher turnover rate before organizations facing such tasks are even affected by turnover. Hierarchies are more resilient than teams as they are less vulnerable to the single random analyst. In the worst case, turnover converts analysts into random guessers. In a fully-trained organization one analyst randomly guessing will decrease organizational performance in just those cases where one analyst's

TABLE 12.2 Theoretical Final Performance When One Analyst Is Random

Task Complexity	Very Low	Low	Medium	High
Hierarchies				
nondecomposable task	89.415	80.450	79.071	78.443
one-random	81.660	75.821	74.817	74.466
Teams				
nondecomposable task	100.000	85.173	83.240	82.419
one-random	86.325	79.136	77.824	77.417

NOTE: Each cell contains the limiting probability times 100 for one type of organization faced with a nondecomposable task with a particular level of task complexity. In the fully-trained organization all analysts act like majority classifiers. In the one-random organization 8 analysts act like majority classifier and one analyst acts randomly.

decision makes a difference. This problem can be solved analytically. As can be seen in Table 12.2, when a single analyst acts randomly the team's ultimate performance is more affected than is the hierarchy's; for example, when task complexity is low teams make 14% more errors when a single analyst guesses whereas hierarchies make only 8% more errors. Teams are more vulnerable than hierarchies to a single random analyst as there are more cases when one analyst's decision makes a difference in the team (70 cases) than in the hierarchy (64 cases).[32] Further, since hierarchies composed of a single random analyst and otherwise fully-trained analysts exhibit high resiliency, it can be concluded that resiliency is due to structure not learning. These results suggest that, in hierarchies, upper management serves as a form of institutional memory buffering the organization from the "big mistakes" that employees might make while they come up to speed (learning and re-learning). Managers, by reducing the number of cases in which an analyst can affect the organization, act as a buffer zone in which institutional memory takes precedence over lower level decisions. Whereas, in the team, institutional memory is housed within each analyst and so becomes integrated into the lower level decisions. Thus, the team, whose performance is dependent on the unbuffered performance of its members, is more prone than the hierarchy to making the same "mistake" over and over again.

Vulnerability is modulated by a variety of factors. The fewer analysts who are fully-trained, the greater the number of cases where a single analyst's decision matters. For the decomposable-consensual task the only time a single analyst's decision matters is when other analysts are also guessing. Indeed, in the nondecomposable task increased executive turnover increases the hierarchy's resiliency in the face of analyst turnover (see Table 12.3).

TABLE 12.3 Regardless of Rate of Executive Turnover, Hierarchies Are More Resilient Than Teams in How Much They Learn if the Task Is Nondecomposable

	For a Task Complexity of:			
	Very Low	Low	Med	High
Nondecomposable Task				
Hierarchies				
Rate of Executive Turnover				
None	7.8	17.4	22.7	26.9
Low	8.0	17.4	18.2	14.7
Medium	7.1	16.4	16.6	12.6
High	4.2	9.6	9.1	5.8
Teams	12.3	20.5	24.5	28.5
Decomposable-Consensual Task				
Hierarchies				
Rate of Executive Turnover				
None	0.0	0.1	2.7	19.1
Low	0.0	0.3	3.2	19.0
Medium	0.0	0.4	3.4	18.9
High	0.2	1.3	4.1	19.1
Teams	0.0	0.0	2.3	17.7

NOTE: Each cell contains data on the resiliency of the one type of organization defined by the cell's position. Resiliency is defined as final performance with no turnover minus final performance when there is a high rate of analyst turnover. All new analysts are novices. The cell value is based on comparing the final performance level for 400 pairs of organizations. Since final performance level is based on averaging 200 time periods, $N = 80,000$.

3.2.1. Modulation of the Impact of Turnover Due to New Employee's Experience.

Contrary to previous literature and predictions, turnover always degrades the organization's final performance level even when experienced personnel are hired. However, hiring experienced personnel can increase the learning rate. In keeping with the predictions, organizations faced with simple tasks are less affected by hiring experienced personnel than are organizations faced with complex tasks. And, in contrast to the prediction, training alone is not sufficient as even a very small amount of inappropriate experience can actually be worse than no experience. Further, the relationship between structure and experience is complex. While hierarchies typically learn faster (Figure 12.3) and better (Figure 12.4) when they hire experienced personnel as opposed to novices, teams do worse by hiring novices than appropriately trained personnel and still worse by hiring personnel with inappropriate experience particularly if they work on a nondecomposable task.[33]

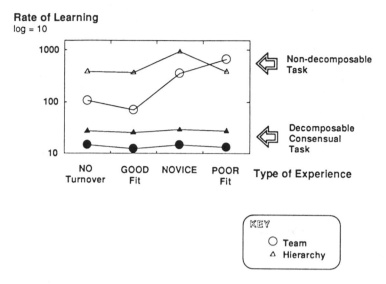

Figure 12.3. Hierarchies Learn Faster by Hiring Experienced Personnel

NOTE: The average rate of learning, plotted on a log 10 scale, for hierarchies (triangles) and teams (circles) for both decomposable-consensual (bottom) and nondecomposable (top) tasks for the different types of experience that the analysts might have is shown. In the hierarchies there is no executive turnover. Each mark indicates the average number of time periods until all organizations with that structure, faced with that type of task, and that type of new personnel (regardless of level of turnover or task complexity) learn to make 60% of their decisions correctly. Thus, the higher the mark the lower the rate of learning. When there is no turnover each mark represents the average of 400 organizations of 4 types, thus $N = 1,600$. When there is turnover, for each type of new personnel 3 rates of turnover and 4 levels of complexity are simulated and so each mark represents the average of 400 organizations of 12 types ($N = 4,800$).

Organizations learn more quickly when they hire appropriately trained personnel as the new analysts do not just guess but instead return the majority decision more often than chance. The more appropriate the previous experience the more likely it is that personnel will become majority classifiers prior to turnover and consequently the higher the organization's final level of learning. When inappropriately trained personnel are hired, organizational performance is affected by two competing mechanisms. First, some of the experience may be transferable. In this study, only 4% of the problems seen by the inappropriately trained personnel were "different." Thus, 96% of what they had previously learned should be transferable. Second, the inappropriate experience may make the analyst less likely than chance to make the correct decision. Teams, because they are more vulnerable to the erroneous analyst, will be more affected by inappropriately trained analysts than will hierar-

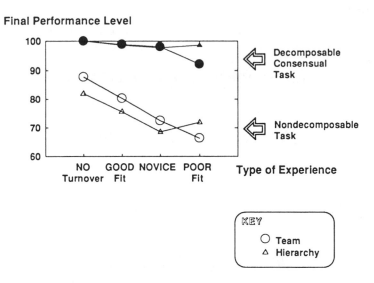

Figure 12.4. Teams Learn the Most When Hiring Personnel Who Are a Good Fit, but for Hierarchies Any Type of Experience Will Do

NOTE: The average final performance level for hierarchies (triangles) and teams (circles) for both decomposable-consensual (top) and nondecomposable (bottom) tasks for the different types of experience that the analysts might have is shown. In the hierarchies there is no executive turnover. When there is no turnover each mark represents the percentage of decisions made by 400 organizations of 4 types over 200 decision periods that are correct, thus $N = 320,000$. When there is turnover, for each type of new personnel 3 rates of turnover and 4 levels of complexity are simulated and so each mark represents the percentage of decisions made by 400 organizations of 12 types over 200 decision periods that are correct ($N = 960,000$).

chies. Thus, when incoming personnel have inappropriate experience, the team starts out learning, but as more people with inappropriate experience are hired the team's performance deteriorates and it "unlearns" (see Figure 12.5 for an example). Consequently by hiring the right personnel the team can outperform the hierarchy, but if the wrong personnel are hired the team is devastated. Since management buffers the hierarchy from the mistakes of lower-level personnel the hierarchy, unlike the team, can take advantage of any experience. Teams, however, are more vulnerable to analyst error, cannot take advantage of experienced transfers, and so are less resilient to turnover when they hire inappropriately trained personnel.

3.2.2. The Relative Effect of Executive and Analyst Turnover. Since managers "see the big picture," require more extensive training, make less struc-

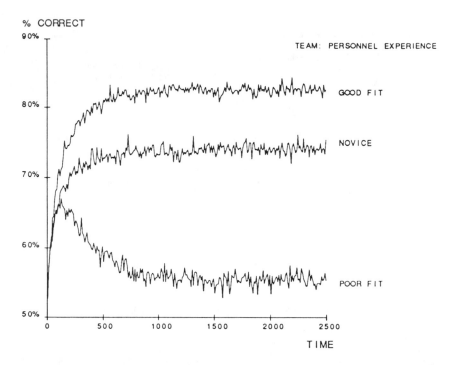

Figure 12.5. Teams Are Devastated by Inappropriate Employee Experience
NOTE: The percentage of correct decisions made by teams who hire personnel with different types of experience are plotted over time. The three types of experience, going from top to bottom, are: good fit—new personnel were trained on 500 problems drawn from a slightly different task, novices—new personnel have no experience, and poor fit—new personnel were trained on 500 problems drawn from a slightly different task (4% 0 bias). Each line represents the averaged behavior of 400 teams with a medium turnover rate.

tured decisions, and so on, managerial turnover generally is presumed to be more debilitating than turnover at lower levels. The proposed model, however, suggests that although executive turnover is more debilitating than analyst turnover when task complexity is low (i.e., the same turnover rate leads to lower final levels of learning), when task complexity is high the opposite is true (Figure 12.6). As task complexity increases a shift occurs in where the greatest information loss occurs in the hierarchy. At the managerial level, regardless of task complexity, information loss due to reduction and channeling is constant. However, as task complexity increases the information loss at the analyst level increases. Consequently as task complexity increases the proportion of information lost at the analyst level increases and so the value of the analyst relative to executive increases.

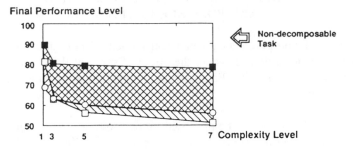

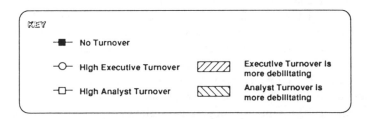

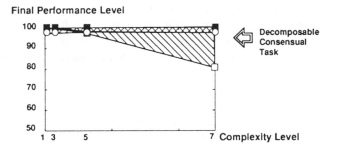

Figure 12.6. Executive Turnover Is More Debilitating When Task Complexity Is Low, but Analyst Turnover Is More Debilitating When Task Complexity Is High

NOTE: The average final performance level for hierarchies for both nondecomposable (top) tasks and decomposable-consensual tasks (bottom) as the level of task complexity increases is shown. The top line (marked with black squares) is the case where there is no turnover among analysts or executives. The line marked with circles is the case where there is high executive turnover and no analyst turnover. The line marked with white squares is the case where there is high analyst turnover and no executive turnover. The difference between the top line (no turnover) and the other shows the degradation in performance attributable to that type of turnover. Both new executives and new analysts are novices. Each mark represents the percentage of decisions made by 400 organizations of that type over 200 decision periods that are correct ($N = 80,000$).

4. DISCUSSION OF MODEL LIMITATIONS
AND POSSIBLE EXTENSIONS

The model proposed is an oversimplification of individual and organizational behavior. Let us consider the effect of some of these simplifications on the observed results. Future work should consider eliminating these simplifications.

Individual Behavior. In the proposed model, individuals do not exhibit all of the cognitive limitations known to affect humans. For example, there are no framing effects (all subproblems are correctly categorized) and there are no saliency effects (all previous experience is remembered and used) which have been demonstrated to affect individual (Nisbett & Ross, 1980; Tversky & Kahneman, 1973, 1981) and organizational (Argote et al., 1987; Levitt & March, 1988) decision making. As a result the predicted rate and level of learning and length of recovery from turnover may be higher than would be observed in human organizations.

Cooperation. In the proposed model decision makers are engaged in effectively cooperative behavior relative to the organizational goal, despite often having different personal goals. Although the model captures many of the nuances of goal related intendedly rational behavior, by focusing on cooperative behavior, the effect of such forces as differential goal setting, negotiation, bargaining, persuasion, and gaming are missing from this formulation. And, it is assuredly the case that within organizations such behaviors do occur (March & Shapira, 1982). Typically it is assumed that such noncooperative behavior decreases the organization's ability to learn as it increases the ambiguity inherent in the organization. If so, then modeling decision makers as essentially cooperative leads to organizations that learn faster and better than would uncooperative organizations.

Turnover. Turnover in the proposed model is treated as a Poisson process where all DMs at the same level are equally likely to leave. Yet, in real organizations, there often are systemic controls on who leaves such as tenure or performance. Typically, performance improves with tenure (Price & Mueller, 1981). Were leaving positively correlated with tenure, the organizations would have exhibited lower final levels of learning as the people who were making the most correct decisions would be leaving. Were leaving based on poor performance, on average the newest people would be leaving, and the organization's final level of learning would have been higher. A mixed firing strategy would probably have produced results similar to those observed.

Task. Performance limits cannot be overcome by changing the turnover rate or the experience of the personnel. Rather, overcoming performance limits requires organizations to change tasks (move to a different complexity), break the task up differently (change the organizational structure), or add redundancy to the system by giving different decision makers access to the same information. Such abilities represent other forms of organizational learning in which the organizations could engage.

Consider two hybrid tasks. In the first hybrid task, input is unequally weighted. For example, the information received by one analyst is much more important than that received by other analysts. In the second hybrid task one analyst, or subset of analysts, always receives information that is diagnostic of the result and information received by other analysts is indicative of the right answer. In the hybrid tasks, unlike those examined in this paper, different analysts (and hence different upper-level managers) have different probabilities for receiving the same information. Since the decision/learning procedure guarantees that DMs will learn to attend more to the incoming information that "will match" the correct response the analysts receiving the more important (heavily weighted) input or more diagnostic input will learn faster and better than his or her fellow analysts. An analyst can become a star simply by being in the right place, that is, by having access to better information.

The team cannot take advantage of such differentiation in information and learning as the final decision is made by equally weighting all analysts' decisions. The hierarchy, however, can take advantage of differentiation as the manager who manages the "stars" will learn to attend to them and weigh their inputs more heavily. This process will make the manager who manages "stars" a star, and cause his or her manager to attend more to him or her. For these hybrid tasks hierarchies actually may learn faster than teams. This may be more true for the diagnostic than the weighted hybrid task as the diagnostic task is at least partially decomposable and the weighted task (depending on the weights) still may be nondecomposable.

Stable Environment. In the proposed model the organization is faced with a quasi-stable environment; i.e., the specific problems change over time but the task does not. This quasi-stability guarantees that experience is useful and that personnel and organizations can learn. In contrast, were the environment unstable, perhaps because the task changed, different results might emerge. In particular, in a highly turbulent environment turnover even may be beneficial to the organization.

This point is particularly relevant to the issue of executive succession where researchers have found that turnover among executives improves (Pettigrew, 1985; Tushman et al., 1989), has no effect on (Grusky, 1963), and degrades (Grusky, 1964; Tushman et al., 1989) organizational performance depending on the conditions under which turnover occurs (see Tushman et al., 1989, for an overview). For example, Tushman et al. found that in stable environments where organizations performed well executive turnover degraded performance (turnover destroys competency); whereas, in a turbulent environment, executive turnover seemed necessary if the organization was to adapt to the changing environment (turnover enhances competency). The proposed model assumes a stable environment, in terms of task complexity and type of task, and predicts that executive turnover will reduce performance. Thus, as far as the model goes, it is in accord with the findings previously cited. Further, the proposed model is consistent with an argument that a changing environment (changing tasks) may necessitate executive turnover in order to maintain high performance levels as the old executives have no training on the new task and hence may slow the rate of adaptation over hiring new executives trained in that task. Moreover, the proposed model suggests that executive succession will have little effect on future performance when the organization is faced with extremely high turnover at other levels and is working on a highly complex task.

Organizational Learning. In this study, improved performance over time is attributable to improvements in the distributed memory, i.e., to improvements in the memories of the separate decision makers and, in the case of the hierarchy, to changes in the relationships between managers and their subordinates. Thus, turnover leads to information loss and a reduction in institutional memory as there is no repository for knowledge in the organization other than personnel. In contrast, other studies have shown or argued for improvements in performance due to increases in routinization (Cyert & March, 1963; Levitt & March, 1988; March & Olsen, 1975) or in socially shared cognitions or memories (Argyris & Schön, 1978; Daft & Weick, 1984; Hedberg, 1981). These alternate learning modes require external knowledge repositories, such as standard operating procedures, forms in file cabinets, and computerized data bases. Adding such repositories to the model would probably make the organization's performance less susceptible to turnover.

Model as General Framework. Despite limitations, the proposed model captures many of the features of organizational behavior that relate to organizational learning. Thus, this model can serve as a framework to look at many of the issues just discussed. This model can be thought of as a series of interlinking modules—(1) problem generation, (2) decision making, (3) decision feedback, and (4) turnover—which are embedded within a loop such that each step is repeated each time period. In this paper, several different problem generation and turnover modules have been employed. For example, problem generation modules with different levels of task complexity and types of tasks were examined. Alternatively, other modules could have been explored such as turnover modules with different ratios of executive to staff turnover or even different types of turnover such as performance based or tenure based. As another example, this model could be adapted to explore whether the amount of information shared by personnel alters the impact of turnover on organizational performance. As a final example, this framework could be used to look at the impact of the timeliness and accuracy of feedback on organizational learning and hence performance.

5. CONCLUSION

This study suggests that while teams learn faster and often come to outperform hierarchies, hierarchies can buffer the organization from the effects of turnover. More specifically, teams learn faster and better than hierarchies when new personnel are novices or fit well with the organization, whereas hierarchies act as information warehouses and are less affected than teams by turnover. And in hierarchies the upper management acts as a buffer zone protecting the organization from turnover and personnel who make mistakes. Three basic mechanisms are at work: information loss through information reduction, managerial learning, and structural buffering. The less information is reduced, the faster and more the organization learns. Teams reduce information less and so learn faster and better than hierarchies. Managerial learning, by definition, only occurs in hierarchies and reduces the rate at which hierarchies learn relative to teams. Structural buffering occurs in hierarchies where the channeling of information to managers actually limits the "damage" a single analyst can do, thereby making hierarchies more resilient than teams. Since institutional memory is embodied in the memory of distributed individuals and the relationships between them, these three mechanisms combine to make hierarchies more resilient than teams. The team, without such relationships, is more vulnerable to the whims of individuals.

These findings resulted from a theoretical exploration of the impact of personnel turnover and organizational structure on organizational learning when the organization is faced with a quasi-repetitive integrated decision-making task while controlling for various environmental conditions (task complexity, type of task, and personnel experience) conducted via simulation. These findings should not be treated as "facts" about organizations, but as model-based predictions. Despite the simplicity of the proposed model, it enables an analytic treatment of complex issues and makes interesting predictions which, in turn, have interesting policy implications. Let us consider a few of these.

This study suggests that which organizational structure is "the best" is contingent on a variety of factors, but such contingencies are highly systematic. Thus two organizations in the same industry (and hence facing similar tasks with comparable complexity) can have different structures yet similar performance if they use different turnover rates or employ different types of personnel. Similarly, organizations in different industries may evolve the same structure but exhibit vastly different performance due to task differences or personnel turnover differences. But, because of the systematic way in which such contingencies affect organizational performance, the behavior of the organization can be characterized and possibly predicted.

There is a trade-off between single-problem performance and across-problem performance. In the team, unlike the hierarchy, institutional memory is decentralized. Consequently, in the team, there is less information loss per problem and higher single-problem performance than in the hierarchy, but at the cost of greater organizational subjugation to personal memory and hence greater information loss across problems when personnel leave. There is also a trade-off between performance and vulnerability. Hierarchies, by channeling different information to different managers, reduce organizational vulnerability by buffering the organization from the mistakes of personnel, but at the cost of greater information loss per problem and hence generally lower final performance and a slower learning rate. Thus the hierarchy plods along slowly and relentlessly, continues to learn and to make use of the lessons of history, despite high turnover levels, high complexity tasks, and hiring inappropriate personnel. In contrast, teams can exhibit high performance but at the cost of increased vulnerability. Thus, teams can skyrocket to a high performance position, only to suffer institutional senility as personnel start leaving. These results imply that in new areas where there are no existing practitioners it would be more efficacious to set up teams than hierarchies. For ease of learning, startup companies might be formed of a loose group of more or less equivalent individuals but will (or should) move to a hierarchical structure as they are faced with personnel turnover. Since teams have less latitude in their hiring decisions than do hierarchies, teams might take longer to hire and more intensely screen new personnel than might hierarchies.

Organizations are subject to performance limits such that although individuals continue to learn the organization does not. In a stable environment experience-based learning leads to a certain coherence and consistency in individual behavior as new experiences serve to reinforce the lessons of history. Such performance limits might be overcome if now and then personnel played a hunch or took a risk. March (1981; March & Olsen, 1975) has argued that, within organizations, consistency limits learning and ambiguity in preferences is advantageous as learning often results from fortuitous accidents. In contrast, this paper suggests that even though consistency limits performance and occasional inconsistency improves performance on a single problem, learning may not accrue from such fortuitous accidents. The sheer rarity in which the hunch works, coupled with information loss due to nondecomposability, leads to such a dearth of information that learning is not possible. There are mechanisms which go beyond the personal memories of the decision participants and integrate information across individual decision makers that can be used to record the fortuitous accident and so reduce information loss in solving a particular problem. These include standard operating procedures, information sharing, institution-wide data bases, and lower levels of specialization. This research suggests that without such institution-wide mechanisms the lesson of the fortuitous accident will be lost. Thus, while institutional memory, as embodied in the memory of distributed individuals and the relationships between them, may be sufficient to buffer the hierarchy from the deleterious effects of turnover, institution-wide recording mechanisms may be necessary if the lessons of the fortuitous accident are not to be lost.

Acknowledgments

This research was supported by the NSF under grant No. SES-8707005. A previous version of this paper was presented at the NSF-sponsored Conference on Organizational Learning—Carnegie Mellon University, May 18-20, 1989. Thanks go to Linda Argote, Michael Cohen, Pat Larkey, and Lee Sproull for their comments on an earlier draft of this paper.

NOTES

1. This is also referred to as across-trial learning.
2. This also is referred to as within-trial learning.
3. As noted by Hastie (1986) ". . . research is needed to investigate the relationship between information pooling and accuracy. In the empirical literature the most glaring omission we found was the lack of research on group accuracy under conditions in which nonredundant sources of information are pooled. On the theoretical side there are no treatments of information-pooling processes and group accuracy" (p. 157). The symbol task used by Cohen (1962, 1969), however, does require individuals to pool information that is only partially redundant.
4. Cohen (1962, 1969) considers across-problem learning; however, unlike this study he focuses on the emergence of structure rather than performance improvements.

5. Although Mintzberg (1979, 1983) has demonstrated that there are communication structures other than the command and information access structures, in this study the only lines of communication are the authority relations.

6. These communication studies follow in the tradition of Bavelas (1950) and Leavitt (1951), and use an experimental setup in which decision makers typically communicate while solving the problem, do not turn over, and are given different initial information but information of the same type. Even the most centralized of the communication networks analyzed (the wheels) are not organizational hierarchies as all decision makers get the same type of information and the group's final decision is not made by a single individual. Moreover, the most decentralized structures (the completely connected networks) are not teams as the group members do not act autonomously but communicate in order to solve the problem.

7. Actually, the organizations of team theory (Marschak, 1955; McGuire & Radner, 1986; Radner, 1987), when there is no communication while solving a single problem, are similar to the teams studied herein. However, team theory is concerned with locating the optimal decision rule and not with learning.

8. Markets differ from teams in that members may not work cooperatively toward a single goal. Moreover, markets typically are modeled as completely connected or decentralized communication networks whose members may communicate while solving a problem.

9. Integrated tasks do not require individual decision makers to reach a consensus in order to make a group decision.

10. Experimental studies have employed such tasks (Cohen, 1962; Cohen et al., 1969; Leavitt, 1951, for example) but have focused on the emergence of structure (do humans learn who to communicate with) rather than changes in task performance.

11. The simulation program is written in C, will run on a UNIX workstation, and is available from the author upon request.

12. Appendix available upon request from *Organization Science's* Editorial Office at IN-FORMS, 290 Westminster Street, Providence, RI 02903.

13. A hierarchy of 13 DMs is the minimum nontrivial hierarchy that can be examined such that the hierarchy has 3 levels and an odd number of DMs under each "manager."

14. The team has 9 DMs in order to match the number of analysts in the hierarchy. The number of analysts, rather than total DMs, is matched so that the complexity of the subproblem seen by each analyst is identical for teams and hierarchies for the same size problem while maintaining no overlap in the subproblems seen by the different analysts.

15. The simple voting scheme is employed in order to focus the results on the impact of organizational structure (i.e., the fact that hierarchies have more levels of information integration and segregation than teams).

16. Given the constraints that (1) there is no overlap in the subproblems seen by different analysts, (2) the number of bits in the full problem must be odd in order to guarantee an unambiguous true decision, and (3) the number of analysts is 9, then the possible choices of task complexity are odd multiples of 9 (9, 27, 45, 63, . . .). Nine, although a trivial case (each analyst has access to only one piece of information), is considered for the sake of completeness. In addition, task complexities of 27, 45, and 63 are examined. These values were chosen as they represent the simplest cases that can be examined and yet have a difference in task complexity.

17. Since each analyst sees the same number of bits, each will be faced with $2^{N/9}$ classes of subproblems, where N is the level of task complexity.

18. Actually, this procedure results in upper-level managers attending more to those analysts who are either consistently correct or consistently wrong. However, since the learning procedure results in analysts trying to be right, in effect the upper-level managers end up attending just to those analysts who are consistently correct.

19. For the problems examined, the word size is odd (9, 27, 45, and 63) and there is a true decision.

20. The manager will attend to the analyst who has a history of being correct. In the limit, since the bits are independent and weighted equally, this is equivalent to being a majority classifier.

21. Computing these theoretical performance limits requires calculating the conditional probabilities for each individual decision maker. Consequently for the nondecomposable task generally it is not practical to compute these optimums as to do so involves solving 2^N problems. Thus, the numbers in Table 12.1 for nondecomposable tasks are estimates based on solving 1,000,000 problems.

22. The exception here is organizations with no turnover. These organizations were simulated for a sufficient period of time that they reached their ultimate performance level. For all other organizations, i.e., those with turnover, 2500 was chosen as this provided sufficient time that, in trial runs, the learning curve was no longer rising during the last 200 to 500 time periods.

23. Although the hierarchy and team each sees a different set of 100 sequences of 2500 problems, this does not affect the results as these sets are drawn from the same underlying distribution. Similarly, although which DM leaves is different for hierarchies and teams this does not affect the results as the DMs selected are drawn from the same underlying distribution. And, although when a DM leaves is different for hierarchies and teams, this does not affect the results as the exit times are drawn from the same underlying distribution.

24. This definition has little impact on the reported results. First, only 24 of the 256 organizations exhibit such slow learning and of these cases, 17 occur when there is executive turnover. In only one case do comparable teams—and hierarchies both exhibit such slow learning. Further, since the learning rate degrades monotonically with respect to turnover rate and task complexity the interpretation of the results is not affected by any numeric bias that limiting the learning rate to 2495 might impute.

25. This is equivalent to using the "majority rule SOP" as a baseline.

26. In this analysis the size of the organization is fixed. Since organization size and task complexity together determine the size of the analyst's subproblems and hence the rate at which analysts learn, the ratio of the two also determines the rate and level of organizational learning. For the same complexity of task, larger organizations will fair better, as analyst's subproblem will be smaller, and there will be less to learn. The results in this paper suggest that the effect is nonlinear, although this is a point for future research. A more important effect of size, however, may be that for a task of a given complexity the larger the organization the greater the level of information redundancy it can achieve while keeping the size of all analysts' subproblems the same. Whether such redundancy improves performance is a point for future research.

27. Identical "on average" results occur for the final level of learning.

28. In addition, as task complexity increases the drop in the learning rate is greater for hierarchies than for teams (hierarchies take 643 decision periods more, on average, to make 60% of their decisions correctly when task complexity is high than when it is low, whereas teams take only 486 more decision periods). Ultimately, however, hierarchies are more resilient than teams to task complexity (when task complexity is high hierarchies make 15.4% fewer correct decisions than when it is low, whereas teams make 21.6% fewer correct decisions). Increased task complexity increases information loss for the nondecomposable task and so increases the likelihood of making an incorrect decision. In the hierarchy, the additional information loss due to information reduction and channeling at the managerial level already was causing the hierarchy to make some of these same mistakes. Consequently the hierarchy is more resilient to complexity.

29. The 16 specified organizational types were simulated, using the same Monte Carlo procedure specified earlier. The only difference between the model simulated, and the model described in this paper, is that the managers do not learn. The results for the 16 simulated

organizations where managers do not learn are given in Table A3 in Appendix 2, which is available upon request from *Organization Science*'s Editorial Office at INFORMS, P.O. Box 64794, Baltimore, MD 21264-4794.

30. Since organization size and turnover rate jointly determine the amount of information lost when personnel leave they combine to determine the rate and level of organizational learning. For the same turnover rate, larger organizations will fair better as less information will be lost when personnel leave. Whether larger organizations are more able to withstand the same proportional loss in information due to turnover is a point for future research.

31. Similarly, in hierarchies, as the managerial turnover rate increases these organizations learn more slowly and less and still perform the best and are the most resilient when the task is simple.

32. In the team, a single analyst can change the final decision only when without that analyst there is a tie. Since there are 9 analysts in the organizations examined, ties can occur among 8 analysts in $\binom{8}{4}$ or 70 ways. In the hierarchy, a single analyst can change the final decision only when its AEO without knowing the random analyst's decision is faced with a tie and the two other AEOs disagree. There are two ways in which the random analyst's AEO can be faced with a tie. And the two other AEOs will disagree just in case there are 3 ones, or only one of the two AEOs has exactly two ones, or only one of the two AEOs has exactly two zeroes. Thus, there are $\binom{6}{3} + 2 \times \binom{3}{2}$ ways in which the two other AEOs can disagree. Consequently in the hierarchy there are only $2 \times (\binom{6}{3} + 2 \times \binom{3}{2})$ or 64 ways in which a single analyst can make a difference.

33. The foregoing results are fairly impervious to executive turnover in the hierarchy as long as the rate of turnover among executives is lower than it is among analysts.

REFERENCES

Anderson, P. A., & Fischer, G. W. (1986). A Monte Carlo model of a garbage can decision process. In J. March & R. Weissinger-Baylon (Eds.), *Ambiguity and command: Organizational perspectives on military decision making*. Boston, MA: Pitman.

Argote, L., Beckman, S., & Epple, D. (1987). *The persistence and transfer of learning in industrial settings*. Paper presented at the St. Louis meetings of The Institute of Management Sciences (TIMS) and the Operations Research Society of America (ORSA).

Argyris, C., & Schön, D. A. (1978). *Organizational learning: A theory of action perspective*. Reading, MA: Addison-Wesley.

Arrow, K. J., & Radner, R. (1979). Allocation of resources in large teams. *Econometrica, 47*, 361-385.

Bar-Shalom, Y., & Tse, E. (1973). Tracking in a cluttered environment with probabilistic data association. *Proceedings of the Fourth Symposium on Nonlinear Estimation*. San Diego: University of California, San Diego.

Bavelas, A. (1950). Communication pattern in task-oriented groups. *Journal of Acoustical Society of America, 22*, 730-735.

Bond, A., & Gasser, L. (1988). *Readings in distributed artificial intelligence*. San Mateo, CA: Kaufmann.

Burns, T., & Stalker, G. (1961). *The management of innovation*. London: Tavistock.

Carley, K. M. (1986a). Efficiency in a garbage can, implications for crisis management. In J. March & R. Weissinger-Baylon (Eds.), *Ambiguity and command: Organizational perspectives on military decision making*. Boston: Pitman.

Carley, K. M. (1986b). Measuring efficiency in a garbage can hierarchy. In J. March & R. Weissinger-Baylon (Eds.), *Ambiguity and command: Organizational perspectives on military decision making.* Boston: Pitman.

Carley, K. M., Lehoczky, J., Rajkumar, R., Sha, L., Tokuda , H., & Wang, L. (1988). *Comparing approaches for achieving near optimal solutions in a distributed decision making environment* (Working paper).

Carroll, G. R. (1984). Organizational ecology. *Annual Review of Sociology, 10,* 71-93.

Chandler, A. D., & Dames, H. (Eds.). (1980). *Managerial hierarchies.* Cambridge, MA: Harvard University Press.

Cohen, A. M. (1962). Changing small-group communication networks. *Administrative Science Quarterly, 6,* 443-462.

Cohen, A. M., Robinson, E. L., & Edwards, J. L. (1969). Experiments in organizational embeddedness. *Administrative Science Quarterly, 14,* 208-221.

Cohen, M. D., March, J. G., & Olsen, J. P. (1972). A garbage can model of organizational choice. *Administrative Science Quarterly, 17*(1), 1-25.

Cyert, R. M., & March, J. G. (1963). *A behavioral theory of the firm.* Englewood Cliffs, NJ: Prentice Hall.

Daft, R. L., & Weick, K. E. (1984). Toward a model of organizations as interpretation systems. *Academy of Management Review, 4,* 284-295.

Dalton, D. R., & Tudor, W. D. (1979). Turnover turned over: An expanded and positive perspective. *Academy of Management Review, 4,* 225-235.

Davis, S., & Lawrence, P. (1977). *Matrix.* Reading, MA: Addison-Wesley.

DeGroot, M. H. (1970). *Optimal statistical decisions.* New York: McGraw-Hill.

DeGroot, M. H. (1974). Reaching a consensus. *Journal of American Statistical Association, 69,* 118-121.

Downs, A. (1967). *Inside bureaucracy.* Boston, MA: Little, Brown.

Duncan, R. B. (1973). Multiple decision-making structures in adapting to environmental uncertainty: The impact on organizational effectiveness. *Human Relations, 26,* 273-291.

Dutton, J. M., & Thomas, A. (1984). Treating progress functions as a managerial opportunity. *Academy of Management Review, 9,* 235-247.

Galbraith, J. (1973). *Designing complex organizations.* Reading, MA: Addison-Wesley.

Grofman, B., & Owen, G. (Eds.). (1986). Information pooling and group decision making. *Proceedings of second University of California, Irvine, Conference on Political Economy.* Greenwich, CT: JAI.

Grusky, O. (1963). Managerial succession. *American Journal of Sociology, 49,* 21-31.

Grusky, O. (1964). Reply to scapegoating in baseball. *American Journal of Sociology, 70,* 72-76.

Guetzkow, H., & Dill, W. R. (1957). Factors in the organizational development of task-oriented groups. *Sociometry, 20,* 175-204.

Hastie, R. (1986). Experimental evidence on group accuracy. In F. M. Jablin, L. L. Putnam, K. H. Roberts, & L. W. Porter (Eds.), *Handbook of organizational communication.* Newbury Park, CA: Sage.

Hastie, R., Park, B., & Weber, R. (1984). Social memory. In R. S. Wyer & T. K. Srull (Eds.), *Handbook of social cognition* (pp. 53-71). Hillsdale, NJ: Lawrence Erlbaum.

Hedberg, B. L. (1981). How organizations learn and unlearn. In P. C. Nystrom & W. H. Starbuck (Eds.), *Handbook of organizational design* (Vol. 1). Oxford, UK: Oxford University Press.

Jablin, F. M., Putnam, L. L., Roberts, K. H., & Porter, L. W. (Eds.). (1986). *Handbook of organizational communication.* Newbury Park, CA: Sage.

Johnson, H. T., & Kaplan, R. S. (1987). *Relevance lost: The rise and fall of management accounting.* Boston, MA: Harvard Business School Press.

Johnson, M. K., & Hasher, L. (1987). Human learning and memory. *Annual Review of Psychology, 38,* 631-668.

LaPorte, T. R., & Consolini, P. M. (1988). *Theoretical and operational challenges of "high reliability organizations": Air traffic control and aircraft carriers.* Presented at Annual Meeting of the American Political Science Association, Washington, DC.

Leavitt, H. (1951). Some effects of certain communication patterns on group performance. *Journal of Abnormal and Social Psychology, 46,* 38-50.

Levitt, B., & March, J. G. (1988). Organizational learning. *Annual Review of Sociology, 14,* 319-340.

Lichtenstein, S., & Fischhoff, B. (1977). Do those who know more also know more about how much they know? The calibration of probability judgments. *Organizational Behavior and Human Performance, 20,* 159-183.

Lindblom, C. E. (1959). The "science" of muddling through. *Public Administration Review, 19,* 79-88.

Malone, T. W. (1986). *A formal model of organizational structure and its use in predicting effects of information technology* (Technical report). Cambridge: MIT Sloan School of Management.

Malone, T. W. (1987). Modeling coordination in organizations and markets. *Management Science, 33,* 1317-1332.

March, J. G. (1981). Footnotes to organizational change. *Administrative Science Quarterly, 26,* 563-577.

March, J. G., & Olsen, J. P. (1975). The uncertainty of the past: Organizational learning under ambiguity. *European Journal of Political Research, 3,* 147-171.

March, J. G., & Romelaer, P. (1976). Personal and presence in the drift of decisions. In J. G. March & J. P. Olsen (Eds.), *Ambiguity and choice in organizations.* Bergen, Norway: Universitetsforlaget.

March, J. G., & Shapira, Z. (1982). Behavioral decision theory and organizational decision theory. In G. Ungson & D. Braunstein (Eds.), *New directions in decision making: An interdisciplinary approach to the study of organizations.* Boston: Kent.

March, J. G., & Simon, H. A. (1958). *Organizations.* New York: John Wiley.

Marschak, J. (1955). Elements for a theory of teams. *Management Science, 1,* 127-137.

Masuch, M., & LaPotin, P. (1989). Beyond garbage cans: An AI model of organizational choice. *Administrative Science Quarterly, 34,* 38-67.

McClelland, J., Rumelhart, D., et al. (1986). *Parallel distributed processing: Explorations in the microstructure of cognition.* Cambridge: MIT Press.

McGuire, C. B., & Radner, R. (1986). *Decision and organization.* Minneapolis: University of Minnesota Press.

Mintzberg, H. (1979). *The structure of organizations.* Englewood Cliffs, NJ: Prentice Hall.

Mintzberg, H. (1983). *Structure in fives: Designing effective organizations.* Englewood Cliffs, NJ: Prentice Hall.

Nelson, R. R., & Winter, S. G. (1982). *An evolutionary theory of economic change.* Cambridge, MA: Harvard University Press.

Neustadt, R. E., & May, E. R. (1986). *Thinking in time: The uses of history for decision makers.* New York: Free Press.

Nisbett, R., & Ross, L. (1980). *Human inference: Strategies and shortcomings of social judgment.* Englewood Cliffs, NJ: Prentice Hall.

O'Neill, B. (1984). Structures for nonhierarchical organizations. *Behavioral Science, 29,* 61-76.

Padgett, J. F. (1980). Managing garbage can hierarchies. *Administrative Science Quarterly, 25*(4), 583-604.

Padgett, J. F. (1980b). Bounded rationality in budgetary research. *American Political Science Review, 74*, 354-372.

Panning, W. H. (1986). Information pooling and group decisions in nonexperimental settings. In F. M. Jablin, L. L. Putnam, K. H. Roberts, & L. W. Porter (Eds.), *Handbook of organizational communication*. Newbury Park, CA: Sage.

Perrow, C. (1984). *Normal accidents: Living with high risk technologies*. New York: Basic Books.

Pettigrew, A. (1985). *The awakening giant: Continuity and change at ICI*. London: Blackwell.

Pfeffer, J., & Salancik, G. R. (1978). *The external control of organizations: A research dependency perspective*. New York: Harper & Row.

Preston, J., & Keachie, E. C. (1964). Cost functions and progress functions: An integration. *American Economic Review, 54*, 100-107.

Price, J. L. (1977). *The study of turnover*. Iowa: Iowa State University Press.

Price, J. L., & Mueller, C. W. (1981). *Professional turnover: The case of nurses*. Jamaica, NY: Spectrum Publications.

Radner, R. (1987). Decentralization and incentives. In T. Groves, R. Radner, & S. Reiter (Eds.), *Information, incentives, and economic mechanisms: Essays in honor of Leonid Hurwicz*. Minneapolis: University of Minnesota Press.

Rosenberg, N. (1982). *Inside the black box: Technology and economics*. Cambridge, UK: Cambridge University Press.

Rumelhart, D., McClelland, J., et al. (1986). *Parallel distributed processing: Explorations in the microstructure of cognition*. Cambridge: MIT Press.

Shaw, M. E. (1954). Some effects of unequal distribution of information upon group performance in various communication nets. *Journal of Abnormal and Social Psychology, 49*, 547-553.

Shaw, M. E. (1981). *Group dynamics: The psychology of small group behavior*. New York: McGraw-Hill.

Shaw, M. E., & Rothschild, G. H. (1956). Some effects of prolonged experience in communication nets. *Journal of Applied Psychology, 40*, 281-286.

Simon, H. A. (1947). *Administrative behavior*. New York: Macmillan.

Simon, H. (1973). Applying information technology to organizational design. *Public Administrative Review, 33*, 268-278.

Smith, R. (1980). The contract net protocol: High-level communication and control in a distributed problem solver. *IEEE Transactions on Computers, 12*, 1104-1113.

Steeb, R., et al. (1980). Distributed intelligence for air fleet control. (Technical Report). Santa Monica, CA: RAND.

Steinbruner, J. D. (1974). *The cybernetic theory of decision processes*. Princeton, NJ: Princeton University Press.

Strand, R. G. (1971). An efficient suboptimal decision procedure for associating sensor data with stored tracks in real-time surveillance systems. *Proceedings of IEEE Conference on Decision and Control*. Miami Beach, FL.

Thompson, J. (1967). *Organizations in action*. New York: McGraw-Hill.

Thorndyke, P., McArthur, D., & Cammarata, S. (1981). Autopilot: A distributed planner for air fleet control. *Proceedings of the seventh IJCAI*. Vancouver, BC, Canada.

Tsitsiklis, J. N., & Athans, M. (1984). On the complexity of decentralized decision making and detection problems. *IEEE Transaction on Automatic Control*, AC-30, 440-446.

Tsitsiklis, J. N., & Athans, M. (1989, May). *Effects of CEO and executive team succession on subsequent organization performance* (Technical report). Presented at the NSF-sponsored Conference on Organizational Learning—Carnegie Mellon University.

Tushman, M. L., Virany, B., & Romanelli, E. (1985). Executive succession, strategic reorientation and organizational evolution. *Technology in Society, 7,* 297-314.

Tversky, A., & Kahneman, D. (1971). The belief in the law of small numbers. *Psychological Bulletin, 76,* 105-110.

Tversky, A., & Kahneman, D. (1973). Availability: A heuristic for judging frequency and probability. *Cognitive Psychology, 5,* 207-232.

Tversky, A., & Kahneman, D. (1974). Judgment under uncertainty: Heuristics and biases. *Science, 185,* 1124-1131.

Tversky, A., & Kahneman, D. (1981). The framing of decisions and the rationality of choice. *Science, 211,* 453-458.

Weber, M. (1922). Bureaucracy. In H. Gerth & C. W. Mills (Eds.), *Max Weber: Essays in sociology.* Oxford, UK: Oxford University Press.

Wilensky, H. (1967). *Organizational intelligence: Knowledge and policy in government and industry.* New York: Basic Books.

Williamson, O. E. (1975). *Markets and hierarchies: Analysis and antitrust implications.* New York: Free Press.

Williamson, O. E. (1981). The economics of organization: The transaction cost approach. *American Journal of Sociology, 87,* 548-575.

13

An Organizational Learning Model
of Convergence and Reorientation

THERESA K. LANT
STEPHEN J. MEZIAS

A critical challenge facing organizations is the dilemma of maintaining the capabilities of both efficiency and flexibility. Recent evolutionary perspectives have suggested that patterns of organizational stability and change can be characterized as punctuated equilibria (Tushman & Romanelli, 1985). This paper argues that a learning model of organizational change can account for a pattern of punctuated equilibria and uses a learning framework to model the tension between organizational stability and change. A simulation methodology is used to create a population of organizations whose activities are governed by a process of experiential learning. A set of propositions is examined that predict how patterns of organizational change are affected by environmental conditions, levels of ambiguity, organizational size, search rules, and organizational performance. Implications of this learning model of convergence and reorientation for theory and research are discussed.

(ORGANIZATIONAL LEARNING;
CONVERGENCE; REORIENTATION)

INTRODUCTION

A critical challenge facing organizations is the dilemma of maintaining the capabilities of both efficiency and flexibility; the observation that there

This chapter appeared originally in *Organization Science,* Vol. 3, No. 1, February 1992. Copyright © 1992, The Institute of Management Sciences.

exists a mix of capabilities that enables the organization both to function efficiently and to remain flexible over time is a hallmark of the organization theory literature (Cyert & March, 1963; March & Simon, 1958). Thompson (1967, pp. 148-150) called this the paradox of administration. Various theoretical perspectives have described the nature of this paradox, including ecological theories (Hannan & Freeman, 1977, 1984), contingency theories (Galbraith, 1973; Lawrence & Lorsch, 1967), and bureaucratic theories (Perrow, 1986). Recently, Tushman and Romanelli (1985) observed that organizations experience long periods of convergence punctuated by fundamental reorientations. Convergence is defined as periods of equilibrium characterized by "relatively long time spans of incremental change and adaptation which elaborate structures, systems, controls, and resources toward increased coalignment" (Tushman & Romanelli, 1985, p. 173). The punctuations in these equilibria are called reorientations; they are characterized by: "simultaneous and discontinuous shifts in strategy, the distribution of power, the firm's core structure, and the nature and permissiveness of control systems" (p. 179). This punctuated equilibrium perspective seeks to understand the management of both stability and change by emphasizing the role of top management in producing convergence and reorientation. Tushman and Romanelli (1985, pp. 209-215) and Tushman, Newman, and Romanelli (1986) emphasize managerial vision as the key to the successful management of this process.

The application of a learning model to the punctuated equilibrium perspective can contribute to our understanding of organizational change by offering an alternative explanation for patterns of stability, change, and organizational performance. This alternative explanation is focused on understanding organizational routines; in particular, the role of adaptive performance targets in mediating the probability of organizational change is stressed. This paper argues that a learning model of organizational change can account for a pattern of punctuated equilibria and uses a learning framework to model the tension between organizational stability and change. A simulation methodology is used to create a set of organizations whose activities are governed by a process of experiential learning. A set of propositions is examined that predict a pattern of organizational change characterized by punctuated equilibria. We find general support for the punctuated equilibria propositions of Tushman and Romanelli (1985) despite the fact that we have limited firm level differences, including executive leadership, to a probability distribution.

A LEARNING MODEL

Experiential Learning and Patterns of Change

According to the organizational learning perspective, organizational change can be modeled as the result of a basic learning process (Argyris & Schön, 1978; Cyert & March, 1963; March & Olsen, 1976; March & Simon, 1958); this process entails updating routines based on interpretations of experience (Levitt & March, 1988). This paper proposes that a learning model can account for patterns of organizational change that have been observed in the literature (Tushman & Romanelli, 1985; Tushman et al., 1986). Organizational learning models typically have three basic components (Cyert & March, 1963; Levitt & March, 1988). First, organizations have a target level of performance or aspiration level to which they compare their actual performance; in each period, they determine whether they have performed above or below this aspiration level. The perspective that organizations set goals, or aspiration levels, and compare their actual performance to their goals, is a common theme in learning models (Cyert & March, 1963; Herriot, Levinthal, & March, 1985; Lant, forthcoming), the psychology of decision making (Kahneman & Tversky, 1979; Mezias, 1988; Payne, Laughhunn, & Crum, 1980; Siegel, 1957), and open-system models of organization (Buckley, 1967; Cameron & Whetten, 1981). Second, performance relative to aspiration levels defines the organization's perceptions of success and failure (Cyert & March, 1963; Lant & Mezias, 1990; Milliken & Lant, 1991), affecting the likelihood of observable organizational change. Change in behavior is more likely when performance is below aspiration level, or perceived as failure. This is a typical outcome of trial and error learning; behavior that is associated with success tends to be repeated, while behavior that is associated with failure tends not to be repeated (Herriot, Levinthal, & March, 1985; Levinthal & March, 1981; Levitt & March, 1988). Third, unlike the typical firms of neoclassical economics which optimize in the acquisition and use of information (Varian, 1978), a learning model suggests that the acquisition and processing of information about alternatives takes place in a relatively costly process of search (Cyert & March, 1963; March, 1978; Nelson & Winter, 1982), frequently conducted under conditions of ambiguity (March & Olsen, 1976). In sum, an organizational learning model suggests that the impetus for organizational change and adaptation is triggered by performance below aspiration level, and the content of change depends on the outcomes of the organizational search process.

We propose that the capabilities for both stability and change, and thus patterns of convergence and reorientation, can be described as outcomes of different types of learning. The first type of learning is called *first-order*[1] *learning,* a routine, incremental, conservative process that serves to maintain stable relations and sustain existing rules (March, 1981). Bateson (1972) suggests that this type of learning reflects the organization's ability to remain stable in a changing context. It is basically the process of gaining competence in a certain activity, routine, or technology; Tushman and Romanelli (1985) refer to this as convergence. An example of first-order learning leading to convergence is illustrated in Tushman et al.'s (1986, p. 30) description of General Radio and Company from 1915 through 1972. General Radio designed an organizational system consistent with their mission and strategy to produce innovative, high priced, high quality electronic test equipment. As the environment became more competitive, they made only incremental changes designed to improve their chosen strategy; structures and systems remained intact. Thus, even given environmental changes, their response consisted of learning how to better implement their chosen strategy while maintaining consistency in other organizational systems.

The second form of learning is called *second-order learning* and is characterized by the search for and exploration of alternative routines, rules, technologies, goals, and purposes, rather than merely learning how to perform current routines more efficiently. Second-order learning results from the realization that certain experiences cannot be interpreted within the current belief system, theory-in-use (Argyris & Schön, 1978) or organizational paradigm (Brown, 1978; Pfeffer, 1981). This process of experimentation (March, 1988) can lead to the recognition of new goals or means to achieve goals, new ways of assembling responses or connecting stimuli to responses (Kelley, 1955), and the integration of new constructs into existing cognitive structures (Hedberg, 1981); this is what Tushman and Romanelli (1985) call reorientation. Tushman et al.'s (1986, p. 30) description of General Radio in 1973 illustrates how a firm can shift from first-order learning to second-order learning. Sustained poor performance apparently led to such a degree of dissatisfaction that the current strategy and organizational systems were called into question. Beginning with a change in CEO, General Radio changed its strategy, structure, and control systems simultaneously. They even changed their name to GenRad, thereby symbolically underscoring that they had become a "different organization" (Glynn & Slepian, 1990). Thus, GenRad has discovered and implemented a new set of goals, purposes, routines, and rules. Rather than continuing to improve the "old way of doing things," they had learned how to create a "new way of doing things."

It is the central argument of this paper that routine processes of organizational learning can account for a pattern of convergence and reorientation. The key insight of a learning model of convergence and reorientation is that aspiration levels provide a basis for determining when performance is interpreted as satisfactory or unsatisfactory (Cyert & March, 1963; Glynn, Lant, & Mezias, 1991; Lant, forthcoming; March & Simon, 1958; Mezias, 1988). The basic mechanisms are simple and familiar: satisfactory performance will tend to result in reinforcement of the lessons drawn from the organization's past experiences; the status quo will be maintained and justified, resulting in first-order learning and convergence. By contrast, this tendency toward convergence will be mitigated when unsatisfactory performance calls existing routines and practices into question. As a result, the organization is more likely to undertake major changes in an effort to raise performance above aspiration level. Thus, the equivocal experience associated with failure may produce a level of organizational change consistent with reorientation. It is important to keep in mind, however, that aspiration levels adapt to performance, providing a moving target which complicates the dynamics of stability and change.

PROPOSITIONS

This paper explores the dynamics of stability and change produced by the interaction of learning processes with different organizational and environmental conditions; our focus is on the implications of these interactions for understanding organizational convergence and reorientation. We propose that many of the patterns of change reported in the literature can be explained by the process of organizational learning in an ecology characterized by negative selection and periods of stability and change. In this section, propositions which predict how organizational and environmental conditions affect organizational change are derived from the literature.

Environmental and Organizational Change

The literature on organizational change has generally posited a close relationship between environmental and organizational change (Lawrence & Lorsch, 1967). Tushman and Romanelli (1985, pp. 197-208) suggest several mechanisms by which environmental forces affect the probability of change to core organizational dimensions. We have argued that most organizational activity is driven by routines; organizations enact the environment in the course of routine functioning and apply routine responses to this enacted environment (March, 1981). The application of routines developed in a given environmental configuration will result in decreased performance in the wake of environmental change. This leads directly to performance below aspiration level; current practices and organizational procedures are called into question (Levitt & March, 1988), increasing the probability of organizational change (March & Simon, 1958, p. 183). As March (1981) has pointed out, "most change in organizations results neither from extraordinary organizational processes nor forces, nor from uncommon imagination, persistence or skill, but from relatively stable, routine processes that relate organizations to their environments" (p. 564). Thus, a fundamental restructuring of environments should increase the likelihood of significant organizational change. This is the core prediction of learning models; it also corresponds to the central argument of the punctuated equilibria model (cf. Tushman & Romanelli, 1985, Propositions 9, 10, and 13).

PROPOSITION 1. *Organizational change will increase following environmental change, and will decrease during environmental stability.*

It is our intention to demonstrate that this relation results from a view of organizations as experiential learning systems, without reference to the characteristics of particular firms. In particular, the punctuated equilibria result can be derived without reference to internal consistency (Tushman & Romanelli, 1985, pp. 187-189), increased structural and social complexity (pp. 189-191), length or stability of previous convergent period (pp. 192-195), the characteristics of the executive team (pp. 187-189, 210-213), or the quality of executive leadership (pp. 209-210; Tushman et al., 1986). We posit a process of routine organizational learning in which aspiration levels mediate the interpretation of failure and success while simultaneously adapting to performance. The perspective developed here suggests that organizational change results from a process that is "routine based, history dependent, and target oriented" (Levitt & March, 1988, p. 319). In the sections below, these three characteristics of the learning process serve as the basis for a series of propositions concerning organizational change. These propositions reflect much of the literature, especially as it has been summarized in the punctuated equilibria and learning perspectives.

The Effect of Routines

Tushman and Romanelli (1985, Proposition 14) suggest that organizations can have systematically different patterns of convergence and reorientation. Further, they argue that particular patterns of convergence and reorientation will be more universally effective (Proposition 14A). The apparent genesis of these universally more effective patterns of convergence and reorientation is the quality of executive leadership (pp. 209-213), what Tushman et al. (1986) call visionary executive leadership. By contrast, a learning perspective stresses the difficulty of executive leadership: "Sometimes organizations ignore clear instructions; sometimes they pursue them more forcefully than was intended; sometimes they protect policymakers from their folly; sometimes they do not" (March, 1981, pp. 563-564). A learning perspective offers an alternative explanation for why organizations will have systematically different patterns of organizational change: differences in organizational routines affect responsiveness to environmental change. We suggest that organizations may differ systematically in the process by which they search for information about the relationship between organizational characteristics and outcomes, information about possible changes in organizational characteristics, and information about the viability of such changes. These different routines focus attention on different types of information and will have important consequences for the pattern of convergence and reorientation that characterizes the organizational life cycle.

PROPOSITION 2.   *Organizations with adaptive search routines will be more responsive to environmental change than those with either initiative or garbage can routines.*

We also suggest that organizations may differ systematically in the routines that determine how they respond to performance signals. Conceptually, we argue that organizations are characterized by routines which result in differential propensity to change in response to a given discrepancy between performance and aspiration level; the result is that organizations are heterogeneous with respect to the probability of change. To explore the importance of such heterogeneity of routinized change, we posit a dichotomy between firms which are more likely to change, called high change potential firms, and firms which are less likely to change, called low change potential firms.

PROPOSITION 3.   *Firms with high change potential are more likely to change in response to environmental change than firms with low change potential.*

History Dependence: Past Performance and Size

Tushman and Romanelli (1985, pp. 206-208) suggest that successful organizations have developed the correct balance of stability and change; these organizations will reorient when environmental conditions warrant such a change. They argue that unsuccessful organizations have not learned how to balance stability and change, and will reorient either too frequently or not at all. We argue that the posited relationships among change, success, and environmental restructuring can be generated from the assumptions of a learning model with the differences among firms reduced to a probability distribution. In this model, differential responsiveness results from the process by which aspiration levels mediate interpretations of performance as either success or failure.

PROPOSITION 4. *High-performing firms will exhibit fewer changes than low-performing firms.*

The organizations literature also has argued that large organizations are less likely to change in response to environmental changes than small organizations. Tushman and Romanelli (1985, Proposition 3) propose that increased size leads to increased complexity, increased convergence, and thus, increased inertia. A learning model, however, suggests that inertia develops as a result of a firm's performance history. Large firms tend to be successful; good performance tends to accumulate in the organization as slack (Cyert & March, 1963), and the organization will grow larger with repeated success. Since success reduces the probability of change in a target-oriented organization (Cyert & March, 1963), large organizations will be less likely to change.

PROPOSITION 5. *Large firms will be more inert than small firms.*

Performance Targets and Ambiguity

Tushman and Romanelli (1985, Propositions 2 and 2A) argue that internal requirements for coordinated action and external requirements for account-ability and predictability lead to increased social and structural complexity. These, in turn, lead to increased convergence upon an established strategic orientation and resistance to change in core organizational dimensions. A learning model recognizes the increased complexity of performance programs developed in response to the needs for coordinated action (March & Simon, 1958; Thompson, 1967). However, a learning model also suggests that given such complexity, organizations increasingly seek out clear signals about their performance by focusing on simple, objective outcomes (Cyert & March, 1963; Lant, forthcoming). We argue that the development of inertia may result from an organization's attempts to learn in an ambiguous world. Ambiguity complicates the relationship between firm characteristics and performance (March & Olsen, 1976) and organizational attempts to seek out clear signals based on "objective" outcomes. Under conditions of ambiguity, performance feedback can be thought of as consisting of a systematic component, relating performance to firm characteristics, and a random component. This randomness hinders the ability of the organization to determine the viability of its characteristics based on its performance. Thus, even while increased social and structural complexity focus organizations on simple, objective indicators like performance (Cyert & March, 1963; Lant, forthcoming), ambiguity in the signal may render its usefulness problematic. Although ambiguity makes effective change more difficult, it does not necessarily make change "essentially random with respect to future value" (Hannan & Freeman, 1984, p. 151). However, in a population characterized by negative selection, costly change, and ambiguity, we expect that selection would favor organizations that are less sensitive to the ambiguous information contained in performance.

PROPOSITION 6. *As the level of ambiguity in the relationship between firm characteristics and performance increases, the average sensitivity to changes in performance will decrease.*

Finally, organizations in ambiguous worlds are more likely to remain inert in the face of performance below aspiration level. Relative to selection under unambiguous conditions, selection under ambiguous conditions favors firms that are less responsive to environmental changes. As selection pressures favor those firms that are less sensitive to changes in performance, the average firm in the population is more likely to remain inert.

PROPOSITION 7. *The greater the ambiguity in the relationship between organizational characteristics and performance, the less responsive organizations are to an environmental restructuring.*

METHODOLOGY

We have argued that organizations learn via a longitudinal process of considerable complexity. The longitudinal and evolutionary nature of the suggested theoretical framework makes deriving its implications quite complicated. It is difficult to explicate how the processes develop over time in different contexts to yield various organizational outcomes. The unfolding of these processes can be observed, however, in a computer simulation. A computer simulation can take a complex set of assumptions, simulate a set of organizational processes, and represent the implications of these processes for organizational outcomes. Computer simulations have played an important role in the development of theory on organizational learning (Cyert &

March, 1963; Herriot et al., 1985; Lant & Mezias, 1990; Levinthal, 1990; Levinthal & March, 1981; March, 1988). This paper extends the application of computer simulations of organizational learning in order to derive the implications of a learning model of organizational convergence and reorientation and to test the implications of the set of propositions suggested by such a model. The basic rules which govern the behavior of these organizations are described in the following sections.[2]

Organizational Characteristics and Performance

The key assumption made in order to operationalize organizational characteristics and change is that organizations are completely characterized by four core dimensions (Hannan & Freeman, 1984; Tushman & Romanelli, 1985). For the sake of simplicity, it is assumed that firms have only two choices, e.g., 0 or 1, on each of these dimensions; thus, there are 16 distinct firm types. Contingency theory argues that organizational performance is contingent on the fit between organizational characteristics and the environment (Burns & Stalker, 1961; Child, 1972; Lawrence & Lorsch, 1967). Thus, each of the four dimensions is assigned a performance level for each of the alternative characteristics that firms can adopt on each dimension. An example of the assignment of performance to the four dimensions of firm type and how this assignment changes during environmental restructuring is shown in Table 13.1. The base performance of each of the 16 types is the mean of performance assigned to each of the four dimensions of firm type rounded to nearest integer. For example, the base performance of a firm which was a type 0000, where the assignment of performance to the four dimensions was identical to that displayed in the upper panel of Table 13.1, is computed as follows:

$$\frac{-11 + (-3) + 2 + (-1)}{4} = -4.25$$

which rounds to −4. After the discontinuous change in period 20, a firm of the same type would have a base performance computed using the numbers depicted in the lower panel of Table 13.1 as follows:

$$\frac{10 + (-2) + (-7) + 7}{4} = 2$$

which rounds to 2. An assignment of performance to dimensions is made at the beginning of each run of the simulation. Base performances for all 16 types are derived from this assignment and the firm types may be ranked on this base performance; types having better base performance are regarded as being better fit to the environmental configuration. The assignment of base

TABLE 13.1 Examples of Assignments of Performance Levels to Dimensions in a Typical Run of the Simulation

	Upper Panel: Initial Assignments in Period	
Dimension	Contribution to Base Value of Zero	Performance Value of One
First	−11	9
Second	−3	6
Third	2	−7
Fourth	−1	8

	Lower Panel: Assignments in Period 20: The Discontinuous Change	
Dimension	Contribution to Base Value of Zero	Performance Value of One
First	10	−1
Second	−2	1
Third	−7	15
Fourth	7	−8

performance to the types remains stable for 19 periods before changing at the time of the environmental restructuring in period 20; it then remains stable until period 50 when the simulation ends.

Performance in organizational learning models has been modeled as consisting of both a systematic and a random component (Herriot et al., 1985; Lant & Mezias, 1990; Levinthal & March, 1981; March, 1988). Ambiguity is operationalized as a random component in performance. These random components come from a distribution with a mean of zero; the level of ambiguity increases with the variance of the distribution of these random components. Defined in this way, ambiguity directly and differentially affects each firm in the population in determining actual performance in each period. For propositions that do not address the effects of ambiguity directly, our baseline condition is one where the random components are all set to zero: the no ambiguity condition. However, each of these propositions is examined under conditions of no ambiguity, moderate ambiguity, and high ambiguity; results that are substantially altered as a result of different levels of ambiguity are discussed.

Patterns of Learning: Search Behavior

The initial search conducted by firms is founding search. During founding search, firms search among the firm types to find the highest performing type, and enter the population as this type of firm. The reasoning behind this founding search follows from Hannan and Freeman (1987): "Some foundings initiate an entirely new form and thus contribute qualitatively to the diversity of organizational forms in society. Most foundings replicate an existing form and contribute quantitatively to diversity" (p. 911). Their description suggests two characteristics of the founding process: First, the founding process must be effective at replicating types that achieve high performance in the population when the environment is stable. Second, it must include a mechanism for introducing types that will achieve high performance in the new environmental configuration following an environmental shift. The process of organizational founding in this simulation has both of these characteristics; they emerge from a routinized founding search process that determines the type of the organization. Firms in this simulation face a liability of newness; consistent with Levinthal's (1990) arguments about refined risk sets and the liability of small size, we stress the smaller size of young firms as the cause. Following founding search, the amount of search conducted by organizations in this simulation depends on the relative wealth of the organization and a firm's specific propensity to search.

In addition, firms differ according to the rules governing their search behavior following founding search. It was predicted that different search rules would affect the pattern of organizational change. We examine three search rules that correspond to theoretical perspectives in the organization theory literature.

1. An adaptive perspective argues that change is designed to improve performance (Thompson, 1967; Tushman & Romanelli, 1985). Organizations with an adaptive strategy search for information that reveals the relationship between organizational characteristics and performance. That is, they determine which mix of organizational characteristics is associated with the highest performance and adopt these characteristics.

2. An institutional perspective argues that organizations change in order to become isomorphic with the characteristics of key firms (DiMaggio & Powell, 1983). Key firms, or industry leaders, establish legitimized characteristics. Organizations with this imitative strategy monitor the behavior of industry leaders and change in order to become more like these firms, and thus, more legitimized (Mezias, 1990). In this simulation, size functions as the proxy for the designation of which firm is the industry leader. Firms search for and identify the largest organization in the population and adopt the characteristics of this industry leader.

3. A garbage can perspective (Cohen, March, & Olsen, 1972) explicitly recognizes the difficulty of planned change; it emphasizes the challenges faced by

those who would lead organizations. Following Delacroix, Swaminathan, and Solt (1989), we argue that organizational level change can be viewed as the result of ". . . probabilistic groping along the lines of the garbage can model of decision-making" (p. 249). The information that these firms gather during their search will suggest the adoption of characteristics that have only a random relationship with performance.

Aspiration Levels, Performance, and Likelihood of Change

Organizations have a target level of performance or aspiration level that adjusts over time in response to performance (Cyert & March, 1963; March & Simon, 1958); the aspiration levels of firms in this simulation are updated according to the formula estimated by Lant and Montgomery (1987). In each period, a firm determines whether it has performed above or below its aspiration level. The probability that a firm will change one or more characteristics is higher when performance is below aspiration level than when performance exceeds aspiration level (Cyert & March, 1963). The exact decision rules governing change are probabilistic. For performance below aspiration level, the probability of change is an increasing function of the size of the discrepancy between actual performance and aspiration level. Thus, the worse a firm performs, the more likely it is to change. Although the probability of change is highest when performance is below aspiration level, there is a small probability that firms change even when performance is above aspiration level. In these situations, the probability of change depends on serendipity in the form of a conjunction between the discovery of a good opportunity and the will to act on it even in the absence of performance below aspiration level. The likelihood of change is also affected by a randomly assigned firm specific propensity to change. Change is assumed to be costly (Hannan & Freeman, 1984), and this cost is assumed to be identical for all firms in the population in all periods.

Simulating a System of Organizations

The assumptions described above are used to simulate a number of organizations over time. In each run of the program, a population of 150 organizations is created and simulated over 50 periods. At birth, organizations in the population are assigned randomly to one of the three search rules and high or low change potential. The firms engage in founding search through the 16 firm types and adopt the characteristics of the type which this search suggests will yield the highest performance. Search rule, search potential, and change potential are fixed at the firm level for the duration of the simulation. The organizations commence experiencing their performance, setting aspiration levels, searching, and changing. A firm goes bankrupt when its resources fall to zero; it is replaced by a random draw from the surviving firm types with positive performance. The new firms are assigned the search rule and propensity to change of the randomly chosen surviving firm. As a result, those values of these characteristics associated with positive performance in the current period are favored by selection pressures. Thus, the ecology created by the simulation is characterized by negative selection; this selection process results in the differential reproduction of superior firm types over time. In all other respects, the replacement firms are assigned characteristics in the same way as at the time of initialization of the population. For example, they engage in the same founding search process and are given the same initial resource allocation. The period in which a firm goes bankrupt is the last period in which it is included in the results. In all subsequent periods, the characteristics of the replacement firms are used in the compilation of population statistics; this is consistent with both theoretical and empirical studies in the ecological paradigm. There is an environmental restructuring in period 20, and the simulation ends in period 50. All results are based on 50 runs of the program, and the results reported represent the characteristics of an average firm in the population.

RESULTS

Discussion

The results of the simulation are presented in figures with numbers that correspond to each proposition. The figures present mean levels across 50 simulated populations over time. The first five propositions do not address directly the effects of ambiguity. The figures presenting support for these propositions are for no ambiguity, our baseline condition. Where differing levels of ambiguity substantially changed the results, figures depicting the results under ambiguity are presented. The relationship between organizational change and environmental conditions is depicted in Figure 13.1. The figure plots the average number of changes to core dimensions over time; a discontinuous change in the environment occurs in period 20. The number of changes immediately following the initialization of the population increases briefly then declines until period 20. At period 20 the mean number of changes rises abruptly and then begins to decrease again immediately. By period 30 the number of changes has fallen almost to pre-restructuring levels. The trend in the mean number of changes over time suggests that firms change in response to key population life cycle events: initialization of the population and environmental restructuring.

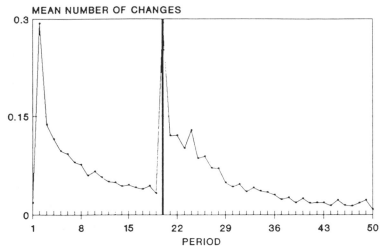

Figure 13.1. Mean Changes by Time

Figures 13.2 and 13.3 show the effects of two types of routines on the relationship between organizational and environmental change. Figure 13.2 shows the mean number of changes by three search rules: adaptive, imitative, and garbage can. Following a founding search process which allows firms to find high-performance types, only garbage can firms change prior to the environmental restructuring. The average level of change in this group decreases over time until period 20, when the restructuring occurs. Adaptive firms exhibit the highest level of change in response to the environmental restructuring; thereafter their level of change drops to about zero for the remainder of the simulation. Imitative firms do not have an immediate response to the restructuring; their number of changes does not increase until two to five periods after the restructuring before dropping off to about zero by the tenth period following the restructuring. Like the adaptive firms, garbage can firms have their highest level of response during the period of the restructuring, but this level is less than half that of the adaptive firms in the same period. Their level of change decreases slightly, but levels off at 0.1, a higher level than that of adaptive or imitative firms.

The relationship between change potential and mean number of changes is illustrated in Figure 13.3. As expected, firms with high and low change potential exhibit different patterns of change. Low change potential firms exhibit fewer changes than firms with high change potential following the

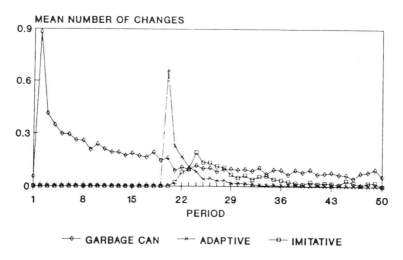

Figure 13.2. Mean Changes by Search Rule

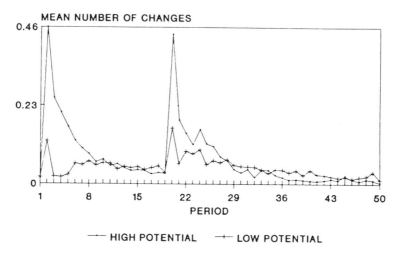

Figure 13.3. Mean Changes by Change Potential

periods of initialization and restructuring. By nine periods after initialization and eight periods after the restructuring, the difference in average levels of change between high and low change potential firms all but disappears. This trend in the relationship over time is particularly interesting; it suggests that differences between the two groups of firms decrease with time following

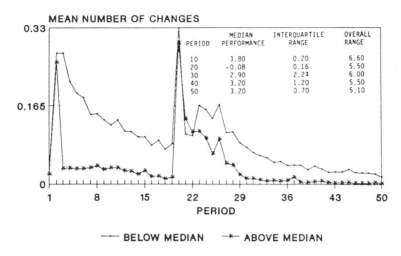

Figure 13.4. Mean Changes by Performance

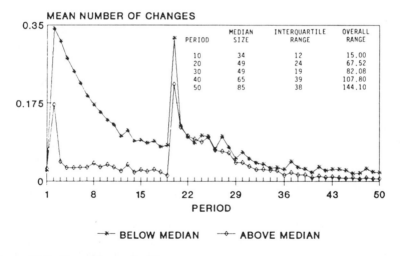

Figure 13.5. Mean Changes by Size

key population life cycle events: initialization of the population and environmental restructuring.

Figures 13.4 and 13.5 illustrate the effect of past performance on the responsiveness of organizations. The direct effect of performance on patterns of change is demonstrated in Figure 13.4 by comparing the number of changes made by firms performing above and below the median performance in the population. Figure 13.4 also reports median level of performance, the interquartile range of performance, and the overall range of performance at ten-period intervals to aid with interpretation of the figure. Although both high and low performing organizations make the same number of changes during the periods immediately following initialization of the population and environmental restructuring, the pattern of changes is different thereafter. High performing firms exhibit a smooth decrease in number of changes following both initialization and restructuring; this number stabilizes near zero by period 3 following initialization and period 29 following the restructuring. The low performing firms exhibit less of a decline following initialization and a less smooth response following the restructuring. In the first periods after the restructuring poor performers change less than high performers. However, poor performers increase their number of changes in periods 23 through 26. After period 26, poor performers exhibit a decrease in number of changes for the remainder of the simulation, but the level of change remains higher than that of high performers.

Figure 13.5 compares the number of changes for firms smaller than the median size and those larger than the median; median size, the interquartile range of size, and the overall range of size at ten-period intervals are also listed to aid with interpretation of the figure. Small firms exhibit a greater number of changes than large firms after the initialization of the population. Both groups exhibit a decrease in the number of changes from periods 3 through 19; for large firms changes drop immediately to just above zero, while for small firms changes drop more gradually to about 0.1 just before the environmental restructuring. Small firms then make more changes than large firms in response to the restructuring. Immediately after restructuring, however, the number of changes for both groups is about equal and decreases to near zero by period 36. Small firms maintain a slightly higher rate of change through period 50.

The effect of ambiguity on the responsiveness of target-oriented organizations is illustrated in Figures 13.6 and 13.7. The relationship between ambiguity and sensitivity to performance signals is demonstrated in Figure 13.6. Sensitivity to performance is measured by the randomly assigned firm specific characteristic called change potential, distributed symmetrically around zero. Firms born with positive values of change potential are more likely to change than firms with values less than zero. Average change potential starts at about zero, as would be expected given random assignment of the variable. Under high ambiguity, change potential begins to decrease rapidly through period 15; it then decreases gradually, stabilizing at about −0.11 from period 33 through 44, and increases slightly thereafter. Change

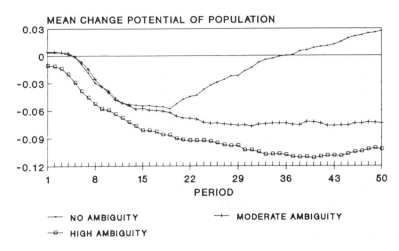

Figure 13.6. Mean Change Potential by Ambiguity

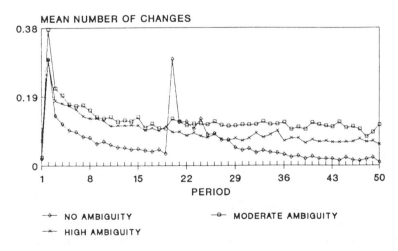

Figure 13.7. Mean Changes by Ambiguity

potential for firms under no ambiguity and moderate ambiguity begins to decrease in period 5, with the decrease being equal for both groups of firms. Under no ambiguity, change potential begins to increase in period 20 when the environment restructures, and shows a fairly rapid increase for the remainder of the simulation. By period 38, the mean change potential for no ambiguity firms is greater than zero. For moderate ambiguity, change potential continues to decline until about period 25, when it stabilizes at about −0.075.

The effect of ambiguity on firms' responsiveness to the environmental restructuring is also illustrated in Figure 13.7, which shows the effects of three levels of ambiguity on the number of changes. Firms under no ambiguity exhibit a pattern similar to that seen in Figure 13.1. The number of changes is high during the period of restructuring, drops quickly thereafter, shows a small second increase in period 24, and then declines throughout the simulation to a level near zero. Changes for firms under moderate and high ambiguity exhibit a pattern that is less of a function of environmental change. The level of change for these firms decreases only slightly after the restructuring, and then remains fairly stable throughout the simulation at a level higher than that of no ambiguity firms.

Unanticipated Results

The results of the simulation are generally consistent with the predictions of an evolutionary model of convergence and reorientation (Tushman & Romanelli, 1985). There are, however, aspects of the results not necessarily anticipated by an evolutionary model that are worth noting. Figure 13.1 exhibits an unanticipated increase in mean number of changes in period 2. This increase is the result of two characteristics of the simulation. First, although firms conduct a founding search in order to enter the population as a good performing type, they are randomly assigned other fixed characteristics such as search rule and change potential. These characteristics may result in a less than perfect fit with the environment, leading to these early changes. In short, birth of the population may be as traumatic as an environmental restructuring. As more appropriate levels of these characteristics are selected for, the number of changes tends to decrease during the periods of environmental stability that follow initialization. Second, all firms in period 1 have the same initial allocation of resources and the same aspiration level. Since the impetus for change depends on aspiration level and relative wealth, firms in period 1 do not perform below their aspiration, and thus do not change. By period 2 there is variance in relative performance and aspiration level; those firms that perform below their aspiration level start changing.

It was predicted that the pattern of changes for low and high change potential firms would differ. Figure 13.3 indicates that these differences occur only following initialization of the population and environmental restructuring. A similar pattern in the number of changes over time is found in Figure 13.4, which compares the number of changes of large and small firms. Although small firms exhibit a higher level of change than large firms, the difference occurs during initialization and environmental restructuring and thereafter decreases over time. The gap narrows between initialization and restructuring and following restructuring. The pattern of change exhibited in Figures 13.3 and 13.4 can be explained by two processes that occur in this ecology. First, high change potential firms and small firms exhibit greater responsiveness to the initialization of the population and the environmental restructuring than low change potential and large firms. These firms make most of their changes soon after these events, and thus exhibit few changes for the remainder of the simulation. Second, the differential selection of firms with different search rules contributes to the decrease in the number of changes over time. Imitative and adaptive firms tend to be selected for, while garbage can firms tend to be selected against. Garbage can firms maintain a higher level of change than imitative and adaptive firms during environmental stability. Thus, the negative selection of garbage can firms results in an overall decrease in average change in the population. Such a result suggests the importance of understanding the dynamics of the selection process with respect to a wide range of organizational characteristics in order to understand the patterns of change exhibited by a population of organizations.

In addition, the unanticipated disappearance of the difference in number of changes made by large and small firms following the environmental restructuring seems to be mediated by the level of ambiguity. Figure 13.5 presents the results for the baseline condition, no ambiguity; the results indicate that there is little difference in mean number of changes for firms above and below the median size in the population. Figure 13.8 compares the number of changes made by firms above and below the median size under conditions of moderate ambiguity; median size, the interquartile range of size, and the overall range of size at ten-period intervals are also listed to aid with interpretation of this figure. The main difference between Figures 13.5 and 13.8 is that the difference in mean number of changes made by firms above and below the median size seems to be maintained in the ambiguous condition.[3] This suggests that part of the underlying causality for the relatively greater inertia of large firms is selection of less responsive firms under ambiguity (cf. Figure 13.6).

Figure 13.6 illustrates an unanticipated pattern with respect to the change potential of firms under no ambiguity. Mean change potential for these firms decreases until period 20, when the environmental restructuring occurs. Subsequently, change potential for these firms increases for the remainder of the simulation. This pattern indicates that sensitivity to changes in performance is selected against during periods of environmental stability, but is selected for following a period of environmental change. This suggests that the timing of environmental changes may have important effects on the ability of organizations to respond to them. If change potential is selected

MEAN NUMBER OF CHANGES

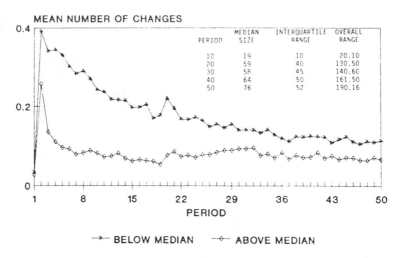

—✳— BELOW MEDIAN   —◇— ABOVE MEDIAN

Figure 13.8. Mean Changes by Size: Moderate Ambiguity

against during periods of environmental stability, as suggested by the first 20 periods of Figure 13.6, then populations of organizations that have experienced long periods of stability may find themselves ill-equipped to deal with environmental change. The rise in average change potential after the restructuring for firms under no ambiguity suggests that a higher level of responsiveness enhances survival following the environmental restructuring. This raises the intriguing possibility that selection pressures at one point in time may result in the selection of firms not well suited to future environmental configurations. Figure 13.6 also illustrates how ambiguity mediates the differential selection of change potential. Under conditions of ambiguity, the effect of the restructuring on the selection of change potential is moderated relative to the unambiguous condition. Instead of sloping upward, the curves for the moderate and high ambiguity conditions merely flatten out. When performance signals are noisy, the negative selection against high change potential moderates following the restructuring, but does not reverse itself.

Figure 13.7, which illustrates the effects of ambiguity on number of changes, had two patterns of change that were not anticipated. First, firms under moderate ambiguity stabilize at a slightly higher level of change than firms under high ambiguity. We believe that the explanation of this result lies in the increasing selection of low change potential firms as the level of ambiguity increases. Second, firms under no ambiguity exhibit a secondary rise in number of changes in period 4 after the restructuring. This effect can be explained by the mix of search rules in this group. As is seen in Figure 13.2, imitative firms exhibit a delayed reaction to the environmental restructuring. This is due to the characteristics of the imitative search rule, which leads to change only when an imitative firm is not the same type as the largest firm in the population. The firm that is the largest prior to the restructuring is likely to maintain its relative size for some time after the environmental restructuring. However, the size of the original industry leader eventually declines, and a firm that is a high performing type under the new environmental configuration eventually becomes the largest firm in the population. Once a new industry leader emerges, imitative firms discover this in their search process and begin to change. Thus, the pattern of change for firms under no ambiguity illustrated in Figure 13.7 is a combination of the pattern exhibited by adaptive firms, which respond immediately to the restructuring, and that of imitative firms, which show a delayed response.

These unanticipated results highlight the importance of considering three factors that affect the pattern of organizational change: differential selection of organizational characteristics, environmental variability, and ambiguity. The importance of these factors as well as their interactions are illustrated clearly in Figure 13.6. Differential selection of firms with different propensities to change is demonstrated by varying levels of change potential in the population. The importance of longitudinal response to environmental restructuring is seen by the shift in the lines indicating mean change potential during the period of the restructuring; this shift is particularly pronounced in the no ambiguity condition, which actually begins to rise, while the others only level off. The importance of ambiguity can be seen in the differences in mean change potential for three levels of ambiguity. Average change potential under high ambiguity is lower than under moderate and no ambiguity. The interaction between selection, environmental restructuring, and ambiguity is demonstrated by the following: the slope of the line indicating average change potential in the no ambiguity condition changes direction following the restructuring. This suggests that the effect of selection pressures on high change potential firms is altered following the restructuring under no ambiguity. Conversely, the slopes of the lines under moderate and high ambiguity flatten out, indicating a somewhat different alteration of the effect of selection pressures on high change potential firms.

CONCLUSIONS

The learning model of convergence and reorientation presented in this paper has paralleled much of the literature on organizational stability and change (Cyert & March, 1963; Hannan & Freeman, 1984; Lawrence & Lorsch, 1967; Tushman & Romanelli, 1985). However, the insights of a learning model are different from much of this work in at least three areas. First, the model developed here highlighted the importance of considering longitudinal dynamics in making predictions about organizational convergence and reorientation. Unconditional statements about the universal value of particular strategies are called into question: A learning model produces many of the results predicted by the punctuated equilibria framework while avoiding claims about the universal functionality of consistency (Duncan & Weiss, 1979; Tushman & Romanelli, 1985), longer and less turbulent periods of convergence (Tushman & Romanelli, 1985), and particular patterns of top management team demography, promotion, and succession (Allen & Panian, 1982; Tushman & Romanelli, 1985). Claims about effectiveness need to be couched in explicitly longitudinal terms with clear conditions for their applicability. The difficulty of making such claims is suggested by Figure 13.6, especially in the no ambiguity condition. The results demonstrate that selection pressures at one point in time can hinder learning in a new environmental configuration (Hedberg, 1981; Lant & Mezias, 1990). Such considerations speak to the applicability of a learning model of organizational convergence and reorientation, with a particular emphasis on the ways that seemingly functional responses become competency traps (Levitt & March, 1988) and the complicated dynamics that can be produced in a population of organizations characterized by a few simple routines (Lant & Mezias, 1990).

Second, the learning model suggests a similarity in the internal processes which generate convergence and reorientation. This is in contrast to the evolutionary perspective: "Organizational processes are fundamentally different between convergent periods and reorientations" (Tushman & Romanelli, 1985, p. 215). Specifically, models of organizational learning processes suggest a variety of ways in which mundane organizational activities sometimes lead to surprises such as reorientation (Harrison & March, 1984; Levitt & March, 1988; March, 1981). The same processes that lead to first-order learning and convergence can provide the raw material for second-order learning and reorientation. The main impediments to second-order learning and change in this learning model are the redundancy and paucity of experience; this is similar to Tushman and Romanelli (1985), but with a focus on "interpretations" of experience, especially in terms of search rules, aspiration levels, and propensity to change. However, the learning model adds the explicit recognition that normal organizational routines sometimes provide the equivocal experiences which lead to second-order learning and change. Thus, the simulation demonstrated that organizations whose behavior was guided by simple experiential learning routines that did not change over time exhibited patterns of change consistent with a punctuated equilibria perspective.

Third, the learning model of organizational convergence and reorientation deemphasizes the role of executive leadership in comparison to much of the literature on strategic management and change (Child, 1972; Miles, 1982). Tushman and Romanelli (1985) maintain this emphasis on executive leadership throughout their discussion of convergence and reorientation; Tushman et al. (1986) push the importance of executive leadership even further, assigning causality for successful performance and adaptation to visionary leadership. By contrast, learning models call attention to the possibility that success has a stochastic element (March, 1988); thus, it becomes important to distinguish between two possible processes that might produce the repeated success that distinguishes consistently high performing organizations. The first is having a strategy which is more effective in some "objective sense." The second is stochastic success, e.g., a lucky draw from the distribution of performance outcomes. There is an ex-post attribution problem when success resulting from the second process is interpreted to signal the efficacy implied by the first process. This ex-post attribution problem is exacerbated in a system where early success tends to become a self-fulfilling prophecy (March & March, 1977) or where organizational growth is a random walk process (Levinthal, 1990). In the former case, stochastic early success has a halo effect which translates into a greater probability of subsequent success. In the latter case, stochastic early failure is fatal, and these organizations that accumulate enough stochastic early successes are buffered from the effects of subsequent failure.

In the simulation presented here, choices about search rules and propensities to change were made through a random assignment. After this assignment, these characteristics were assumed to be inert. The change in core dimensions that did occur was governed by fairly simple rules about search and change. Still, with all these simplifying assumptions, the organizations in this simulation demonstrated many of the patterns suggested by Tushman and Romanelli (1985). In this way, the role of management was reduced to a probability distribution; this view follows from a logic which emphasizes that "there are some reasons for anticipating that careers in top management in many social systems would tend to be nearly random events involving nearly indistinguishable managers" (March & March, 1977, p. 377). It is important to make clear that our view of the role of leadership is quite distinct from the nihilistic conclusion that managers do not matter. Managers occupy well-defined social positions that require a complex bundle of skills to perform competently; as with, for example, championship skiers, the fact that luck may play a large role in determining who wins which prize on which day does not mean that an unskilled novice could descend the slope and win. However, the larger the role of luck, the more difficult it becomes to determine that success is associated with the characteristics of the particular organizations that experience it. Further, the more complex and ambiguous the context, the more problematic such assertions become.

In conclusion, a learning model directs research attention to the fact that most organizational change is produced by conventional, routine activities performed by reasonably competent organizations in ordinary ways. Thus, we would emphasize that "[t]ypically, it is not possible to lead an organization in any arbitrary direction that might be desired, but it is possible to influence the course of events by managing the process of change, and particularly by stimulating or inhibiting predictable complications and anomalous dynamics. Such a view of managing organizations assumes that the effectiveness of leadership often depends on being able to time small interventions so that the force of natural organizational processes amplifies the interventions" (March, 1981, p. 575). This first attempt at using a learning model to understand convergence and reorientation has concentrated on exploring system dynamics to discover some possible complications and anomalous dynamics. Choices about search rules and propensities to change were made through a random assignment and reproduced through differential selection. At the level of the individual organization, these characteristics were assumed to be inert. A fuller exploration of the role of management in such systems, following from the view expressed above, is a logical next step. A first pass at such an exploration of the role of management might involve relaxing the assumption of inertia with respect to these characteristics. The exploration of alternative possibilities for specifying the switching rules that organizations might employ in changing any of these parameters is a useful way to explore the possibility of successful managerial intervention. The application of simulation methodology to questions of strategic management and the use of the population as the unit of analysis serve as useful reminders that system dynamics limit the frontiers of individual efficacy and the possibilities for managerial leadership. We believe that the most useful avenues for understanding the role of leadership in organizations must stay within these bounds. More importantly, these bounds delineate a focus for the study of the role of management which can serve as a useful guide for both theory and practice.

Appendix
Rules Governing Search, Learning, and Change

The following appendix specifies the rules governing the simulation and the choices of parameter values. To the extent possible, we have used empirical estimates to set parameter values. Where no empirical estimates were available, values were set to be consistent with prior theory. The sensitivity of the results to these values is explored at the end of the appendix. In addition to specific parameter values, we have made a number of other simplifying assumptions. For instance, firms in the simulation do not increase their competency with activities over time. The capability of firms to move from one type to another does not depend on size. There are no barriers to entry from capital requirements or returns to scale. Although Tushman and Romanelli (1985, Proposition 12) suggest some factors that affect the probability of success with a reorientation, in this simulation the probability of successful execution of a change, once the organization has decided to undertake it, is unity. The stochastic element of change is embedded in the decision to undertake it, as discussed below in Rules Governing Change.

We have also made crucial decisions by adopting several assumptions from Hannan and Freeman (1977, 1984) and creating organizations that are relatively inert with respect to certain characteristics. Thus, we do not consider the possibility that management can choose to alter their search rules, change potential, or aspiration level adjustment parameters. These characteristics are assigned to a firm randomly at the initialization of each run of the simulation and are fixed for the life of the firm; the effect of managerial choice with respect to these characteristics is reduced to a probability distribution. Since we assume that management discretion is limited after founding, this study does not address the argument that turbulent convergent periods will lead to greater internal dissensus and less resistance to change (Tushman & Romanelli, 1985, Proposition 5, p. 194), or the argument about the relationship between organizational effectiveness and characteristics of organizational demography or promotion patterns (Tushman & Romanelli, 1985, Proposition 7, p. 196).

Firm Types and Base Performance

Firms are characterized completely by four dimensions; on each of these dimensions, the firm has a value of one or zero. The result is 16 distinct combinations of zeros and ones, each of which represents a distinct firm *type*. Each type can be depicted as a unique four-digit combination of zeros and ones. Each of the four dimensions is assigned a performance level for both of the alternative characteristics which firms can adopt on that characteristic. In order to avoid the possibility that performance could be negative for all alternatives on all dimensions, the rule that at least one of the alternatives on all dimensions had to offer the possibility of nonnegative performance was imposed. The randomly assigned performance level assigned to characteristics on each dimension is an integer between −20 and 20 which reflects the degree of fit between the environment and organizations which have the given alternative for the given dimension. The base performance of each of the 16 types is the mean of the performance assigned to each of the characteristics on the four dimensions. This assignment is fixed until period 20, when the discontinuous change in the environment takes place. At this time, all 16 firm types are assigned a new base performance by the process described above. This relationship then remains fixed for the remaining periods of the simulation. The calculation of base performance, BP_{kt}, $k = 1, \ldots, 16$, $t = 1, \ldots, 50$, from a combination of 4 dimensions can be seen in Table 13.1. For instance, Type 1 carries a score of 1 on each of the 4 dimensions, and thus is a 1111. Base performance is calculated by taking the mean of performance assignments for a firm which is a 1 on each dimension and rounding that mean to the nearest integer. Assuming that $t = 1$, then the expression to compute the performance of a Type 1 is given by: $BP_{1,1} = (9 + 6 + (-7) + 8)/4 = 4$. The reassignment of base performance after an environmental restructuring can be seen by comparing the Upper and Lower Panels of Table 13.1. For example, using the numbers in Table 13.1, Upper Panel, $BP_{1,1}$ is 4, $BP_{2,1}$ is 2, and $BP_{16,1}$ is −3. While the environment is stable, the relationship between each firm type and its performance does not change. However, when the environmental restructuring occurs, the relationship between performance and firm type is likely to change due to the new random reassignment of firm types to performance. This is shown in Table 13.1, Lower Panel. Beginning in the period following the restructuring, $BP_{1,20}$ is 2, $BP_{2,20}$ is 6, and $BP_{16,20}$ is 2.

Performance and Resources

P_{it}, the performance of firm i at time t, consists of a systematic component, related to its firm type, and a random component which is different for each firm in each period. This is summarized by the following expression: $P_{it} = BP_{kt} + \mu_{it}$. As defined above, BP_{kt} is the base performance of type k at time t, the value of k depends on the type of firm i. In the unambiguous condition, μ_{it} is zero; in the moderate ambiguity condition, μ_{it} is a draw from the uniform distribution of integers between −10 and 10 for firm i at time t; in the high ambiguity condition μ_{it} is a draw from the uniform distribution of integers between −20 and 20. Performance, whether negative or positive, is added to total resources in each period. The following expression describes this process: $R_{it} = R_{it-1} + P_{it}$, where R_{it}, denotes the resources of firm i at time t, and P_{it}, is defined as above. Firms receive an initial resource allocation of 35 units. This value is chosen so that a firm which experienced the median worst possible performance could survive for 5 periods. This initial resource allocation produces a liability of newness due to small size, but allows firms some time to adjust to the environment before they are selected out of the population. When a firm's resources go to zero or below, it is eliminated from the population and is no longer included in the computation of population statistics to compile the results. That firm is then replaced by a random draw from the surviving firms with positive performance at time t; the new firm inherits the firm type, search rule, search potential, and change potential of the random firm which is selected. The results reported here are most likely quite sensitive to this treatment of births and deaths; it is justified by its consistency with both theoretical and empirical work in the ecological perspective.

Aspiration Level Updating

Aspiration level formation is based on performance, P_{it}. In the initial period, aspiration level AL_{i1} is set to 0.5. In each subsequent period, aspiration levels adjust to the current performance by a weighted average formula as estimated from the data of Lant and Montgomery (1987):[4]

$$AL_{it} = 0.15736 + 1.0987\,(AL_{it-1}) + 1.2571\,(AD_{it-1})$$

where AL_{it} is the current aspired level of performance for firm i at time t. $AD_{it-1} = P_{it-1} - AL_{it-1}$ is defined to be the attainment discrepancy in the last period, that is, last period aspiration level minus the last period performance.

Rules Governing Search

The initial search conducted by firms is founding search, which takes place at the beginning of the organizational lifecycle to determine the characteristics of the organization to be founded. In keeping with the population ecology literature, founding search is modeled as an attempt to discover the relationship between firm type and performance. In this way, new firm types can be introduced to the population and existing types can be replicated. We have assumed that this occurs without ambiguity. All firms in the population search at founding through some subset of the K firm types choosing the type that satisfies the following relation: $\text{Max}_k FP_{ikt}$. The decision rule is that firm i founded at time t becomes the type that founding search has revealed to have the highest base performance.

Subsequent to founding search, firms may search the environment for information about the relationship between the characteristics of firms and survival, size, or performance. In any period, a firm may choose to expend resources on search. The amount of resources dedicated to search by a firm depends on the amount of resources available[5] and a firm specific propensity to search, SP_i, called search potential. SP_i is a random draw from the integers -1 and 1. The maximum number of searches a firm will conduct in a given period is binomial with $n - 4$ and the probability of a search given by π_{it}^*. π_{it}^* is defined to be equal to $(RR_{it} + SP_i/2)/2$, with SP_i, the search potential of firm i defined as above. RR_{it}, defined to be the relative resources of firm i at time t, is a measure of relative wealth; the resources of firm i are stated as a proportion of the resources of the largest firm in the population at time t. This quantity is denoted RR_{it}, $= R_{it}/\text{max}_i(R_{it})$, where R_{it}, as above, measures the resources of firm i at time t and $\text{max}_i R_{it}$, denotes the resources of the largest firm at time t. Each search uses 1.75 units of resources; this is the cost of search associated with each search a firm makes in each period, regardless of the type of search. The cost of each search is equal to 5% of the initial resource allocation. This means that a firm that does all possible searches in every period would die after 5 periods given the initial resource allocation.

We impose the rule that search starts from the neighborhood of current firm type (Cyert & March, 1963). Four types of searches may take place. The first type of search involves examination of the types of firms that the searching firm would become by changing only one dimension of its structure. For example, a firm characterized by 1111 would look at types 1110, 1101, 1011, and 0111. The second type of search involves examination of all the changes of two dimensions. The third type of search involves examination of all the changes of three dimensions. Finally, the fourth type of search involves examination of the type that the firm would become if it changed all dimensions simultaneously. Firms follow different rules for making these 4 types of searches depending on the search rules elaborated below. The purpose of search is to collect information to guide organizational change; in the absence of guidance from search, changes do not occur.

Adaptive Search Rule. The adaptive search rule tries to discover the true underlying relationship between firm type and performance, as given, for example, in Table 13.1. These firms try to determine which changes to the firm's type will improve performance. For a given number of changes, adaptive firms determine which of these changes will yield the highest base performance. For example, if a firm is a 1111, the base performance of 1111 is compared with that of 1110, 1101, 1011, and 0111, to determine which change to a single dimension will enhance performance the most. Analogous processes take place for changes of two, three, and four dimensions. Firms store this information; when the decision is made to make a certain number of changes to the characteristics of the firm, the results of search are used to choose from among change possibilities. Thus, adaptive firms tend to adopt the characteristics of firm types with high base performance. The process of comparing two firm types proceeds as follows. The firm measures the effect of changing from type k, its current type, to type l, some different firm type, by examining the following expression: $D_l = BP_{lt} - BP_{kt} + \mu_{ilt}$, $l \neq k$. In the unambiguous condition, μ_{ilt} is zero; in the moderate ambiguity condition, μ_{ilt} is a draw from the uniform distribution of integers between -10 and 10 for firm i at time t and each type l with which it compares itself; in the high ambiguity condition, μ_{ilt} is a draw from the uniform distribution of integers between -20 and 20. If D_l is positive, then the number of changes, NC, required to change from type k to type l is counted. If $BP_{lt} - BP_{kt}$ is the largest positive value among all changes which require the same number of changes as the transition from k to l, then the result of search, S_{NC}, $NC = 1, \ldots, 4$, is the retention of the largest change in performance that will result from a change to NC dimensions. For example, a Type 1, denoted 1111, operating in an ecology without ambiguity and with the relationship between performance and type depicted in the Upper Panel of Table 13.1 would have a value of 3 for S_1. This is true because the change of one dimension that would result in the biggest increase in performance would be to change to Type 3 with a base performance of 6.

Imitative Search Rule. Firms using an imitative search rule determine the largest firm in the population, and focus their search process on this firm. They determine whether this firm is of a type that would require 1, 2, 3, or 4 changes to core dimensions. The result of search for a given number of changes, S_{NC}, is zero unless that is the number of changes required to move to the firm type of the largest firm in the population. In this case, S_{NC*}, is the number of the firm type containing the largest firm in the population. For example, assume that a firm of Type *1* from Table 13.1, Upper Panel, is doing an imitative search. If the largest firm were a Type 16, four changes would be required. Thus, S_1, S_2, and S_3 would be set equal to zero, and S_4 would equal 16.

Garbage Can Firms. For garbage can firms search results in random noise. Their search provides no real information about firm types or corresponding performance. For example, consider two firm types: k is the current type of the firm, and l is a different firm type. When garbage can firms compare the type which they are currently with another type, the procedure is as follows. The firm measures the effect of changing from type k to type l by examining the following expression: $D_l = \rho_{lit}$, $l \neq k$. ρ_{lit} is a draw from the uniform distribution of real numbers between -1 and 1. If D_l is positive, then the number of changes, NC, required to change from type k to type l is counted. D_l is compared for all changes requiring the same number of changes as the transition from k to l. The largest nonnegative value of D_l for this number of changes is determined, and S_{NC}, $NC = 1, \ldots, 4$, is set equal to the corresponding firm type. If there are no positive draws for that number of changes, S_{NC} is set equal to zero. Despite the fact that this information is not related to performance, the firms use it as the basis for making changes to firm structure.

Rules Governing Change

Failure-Induced Change. The likelihood that a firm will change one or more core dimensions depends on its performance relative to aspiration level and a firm specific propensity to change, CP_i, called change potential. CP_i is a random draw from the integers -1 and 1. In response to performance below aspiration level, firms increase their likelihood of changing some aspect of their type. Each change to one of the core dimensions uses 10% of the firm's resources. The maximum number of changes that a firm will make in a given period, denoted C_{it}, is distributed binomial $(4, \pi)$. The determination of π depends on whether performance is above or below the aspiration level. Failure induced change occurs when performance falls below aspiration level; thus, these rules apply only if $AD_{it} < 0$. The number of changes they will consider is related to the size of the attainment discrepancy. C_i is binomial with $n = 4$ and

$$\pi = \frac{\dfrac{-AD_{it}}{\max_i(-AD_{it})} + \dfrac{CP_i}{2}}{2}$$

AD_{it}, the attainment discrepancy of firm i at time t, and CP_i, the change potential of firm i, are as defined above. $\max_i(-AD_{it})$ denotes the largest negative attainment discrepancy in the population at time t. Thus, the probability of a change in the firm's structure is equal to the negative of the attainment discrepancy as a percentage of the magnitude of the largest negative attainment discrepancy in the population at time t plus one-half times its change potential. Provided the C_{it} observation from this distribution is greater than zero, firms make changes in accordance with the results of search. Adaptive and garbage can firms will make $NC \leq C_{it}$ changes according to a comparison of the best change in performance which search suggests will result from making no more than C_{it} changes. The imitative firms change if and only if $C_{it} \geq NC^*$, where NC^* is defined to be the number of changes required for the firm to become the type that its search has revealed to be that of the largest firm in the population.

Slack Change. A firm with performance above aspiration level will change under limited circumstances. Specifically, a random real number between 0 and 1 is generated. If that number exceeds 0.95 and the results of at least one search are greater than zero, then the firm will change. Results of search are held indefinitely, but are eliminated each time the firm changes its type. In the absence of guidance from search, changes do not occur.

Levels of Ambiguity

Ambiguity is defined as variance in the relationship between firm types and performance; this is true both for the computation of firm performance and adaptive search. In the unambiguous condition, the variance of the random components μ_{it} and μ_{ilt} is zero for all comparisons. Thus, the variance in the relationship between performance and firm type is zero, and firm type predicts performance perfectly. In the moderate and high ambiguity conditions, the variance in the relationship between performance and firm type, σ_P, is equal to the variance of the uniform distributions of μ_{it} and μ_{ilt} described above. The variance of a uniform distribution is equal to the range of the distribution squared divided by twelve.

Sensitivity Analysis

The sensitivity of our results to different parameter values has been explored. A range of performance draws from −10 to 10 is tested along with the range of −20 to 20 used in the reported results. Three levels of ambiguity are tested: under no ambiguity $\mu_{it} = 0$; under moderate ambiguity μ_{it} ranges from −10 to 10; under high ambiguity μ_{it} ranges from −20 to 20. Three slack change parameters are tested, 0.90, 0.95, and 0.975. The impact of the various levels of these three parameters is examined with an ANOVA analysis with mean number of changes in the population as the dependent variable. The results of the ANOVA suggest that the range of performance draws, either 10 or 20, is significant. We have examined all of the plots in the paper using the range of 10 rather than 20; there is no qualitative change to the results. The ANOVA also suggests that the three levels of ambiguity make a difference; where this changed our results we have incorporated the differences into our discussion. The impact of levels of ambiguity can be seen directly in Figures 13.6, 13.7, and 13.8. The levels of the slack change parameter, chosen to approximate what we believe to be a sensible range, make no difference. The interactions of range of performance and level of ambiguity are also significant; again, this made no qualitative difference to the results we report. The two-way interactions with level of slack change and the three-way interaction were not significant. Finally, an earlier version of this paper tested the same propositions and argument using random assignment of performance to the 16 types rather than random assignment of performance to dimensions which then determines the performance of types. Again, the qualitative thrust of the conclusions we draw here is unchanged by this difference.

Acknowledgments

The listing of authors is alphabetical; this work is fully collaborative. The authors would like to thank Joel Baum, Jane Dutton, Frances Milliken, Jim

March, Bill Starbuck, Mike Tushman, and three anonymous reviewers for their comments, and Michael Cohen and Lee Sproull for their superb editorial guidance. In the grand tradition of acknowledgments, we take responsibility for all remaining faults of the paper.

NOTES

1. The terminology first-order and second-order is borrowed from Watzlawick, Weakland, and Fisch (1974) where the terms are applied to types of change at different logical levels. This terminology has also been used in the context of organizational learning and change by Hedberg, Nystrom, and Starbuck (1976). It bears an obvious resemblance to the single-loop and double-loop learning discussed by Argyris and Schön (1978).

2. The technical details of how these rules were operationalized are described in the Appendix. Copies of programs corresponding to each proposition, which were written in Turbo Pascal, can be obtained by writing to the authors.

3. The result is the same for the high ambiguity condition.

4. The constant term used here restates the annual estimate of the constant as a percentage of the average initial allocation of dollars to firms in the Lant and Montgomery (1987) sample.

5. Thus, search depends indirectly on whether performance is above or below aspiration level. However, no distinction is made here between problemistic search, normally thought of as occurring when performance is below aspiration level, and slack search, normally thought of as occurring when performance is above aspiration level (Cyert & March, 1963; Levinthal & March, 1981).

REFERENCES

Allen, M. P., & Panian, S. K. (1982). Power, performance, and succession in the large corporation. *Administrative Science Quarterly, 27,* 538-547.

Argyris, C., & Schön, D. (1978). *Organizational learning.* Reading, MA: Addison-Wesley.

Bateson, G. (1972). *Steps to an ecology of mind.* New York: Ballantine.

Brown, R. H. (1978). Bureaucracy as praxis: Toward a political phenomenology of formal organizations. *Administrative Science Quarterly, 23,* 365-382.

Buckley, W. (1967). *Sociology and modern systems theory.* Englewood Cliffs, NJ: Prentice Hall.

Burns, T., & Stalker, G. M. (1961). *The management of innovation.* London: Tavistock.

Cameron, K., & Whetton, D. (1981). Perceptions of organizational effectiveness over organizational life cycles. *Administrative Science Quarterly, 26,* 525-544.

Child, J. (1972). Organizational structure, environment, and performance: The role of strategic choice. *Sociology, 6,* 2-22.

Cohen, M. D., March, J. G., & Olsen, J. P. (1972). A garbage can model of organizational choice. *Administrative Science Quarterly, 17,* 1-25.

Cyert, R. M., & March, J. G. (1963). *A behavioral theory of the firm.* Englewood Cliffs, NJ: Prentice Hall.

Delacroix, J., Swaminathan, A., & Solt, M. E. (1989) Density dependence versus population dynamics: An ecological study of failings in the California wine industry. *American Sociological Review, 54,* 245-262.

DiMaggio, P. W., & Powell, W. W. (1983). The iron cage revisited: Institutional isomorphism and collective rationality in organizational fields. *American Sociological Review, 48,* 147-160.

Duncan, R., & Weiss, A. (1979). Organizational learning: Implications for organization design. In B. Staw (Ed.), *Research in organizational behavior* (Vol. 1, pp. 75-123). Greenwich, CT: JAI.

Galbraith, J. R. (1973). *Designing complex organizations.* Reading, MA: Addison Wesley.

Glynn, M. A., Lant, T. K., & Mezias, S. J. (1991). Incrementalism, learning, and ambiguity: An experimental study of aspiration level updating. In J. J. Wall & L. R. Jauch (Eds.), *Best paper proceedings of the Academy of Management meetings* (pp. 384-388). Madison, WI: Omnipress.

Glynn, M. A., & Slepian, J. (1990). *An organization by any other name: An examination of institutionalization and adaptation over time.* Paper presented at the annual meeting of the Academy of Management, San Francisco, CA.

Hannan, M. T., & Freeman, J. (1977). The population ecology of organizations. *American Journal of Sociology, 82,* 929-964.

Hannan, M. T., & Freeman, J. (1984). Structural inertia and organizational change. *American Sociological Review, 49,* 149-164.

Hannan, M. T., & Freeman, J. (1987). The ecology of organizational foundings: American labor unions, 1836-1985. *American Journal of Sociology, 92,* 910-943.

Harrison, J. R., & March, J. G. (1984). Decision making and postdecision surprises. *Administrative Science Quarterly, 29,* 26-42.

Hedberg, B. (1981). How organizations learn and unlearn. In P. C. Nystrom & W. H. Starbuck (Eds.), *Handbook of organizational design* (Vol. 1, pp. 3-27). Oxford, UK: Oxford University Press.

Hedberg, B., Nystrom, P. C., & Starbuck, W. H. (1976). Camping on seesaws: Prescriptions for a self-designing organization. *Administrative Science Quarterly, 21,* 41-65.

Herriott, S. R., Levinthal, D. A., & March, J. G. (1985). Learning from experience in organizations. *Proceedings of the American Economic Association, 75,* 298-302.

Kahneman, D., & Tversky, A. (1979). Prospect theory: An analysis of decision under risk. *Econometrica, 47,* 263-292.

Kelley, G. A. (1955). *The psychology of personal constructs.* New York: Norton.

Lant, T. K. (forthcoming). Aspiration level adaptation: An empirical exploration. *Management Science.*

Lant, T. K., & Mezias, S. J. (1990). Managing discontinuous change: A simulation study of organizational learning and entrepreneurial strategies. *Strategic Management Journal, 11,* 147-179.

Lant, T. K., & Montgomery, D. B. (1987). Learning from strategic success and failure. *Journal of Business Research, 15,* 503-518.

Lawrence, P. R., & Lorsch, J. W. (1967). *Organization and environment: Managing differentiation and integration.* Boston: Harvard University, Graduate School of Business Administration.

Levinthal, D. A. (1990). Organizational adaptation, environmental selection, and random walks. In J. Singh (Ed.), *Organizational evolution: New directions* (pp. 201-223). Newbury Park, CA: Sage.

Levinthal, D. A., & March, J. G. (1981). A model of adaptive organizational search. *Journal of Economic Behavior and Organization, 2,* 307-333.

Levitt, B., & March, J. G. (1988). Organizational learning. *Annual Review of Sociology, 14,* 319-340.

March, J. G. (1978). Bounded rationality, ambiguity, and the engineering of choice. *Bell Journal of Economics, 9,* 587-608.

March, J. G. (1981). Footnotes to organizational change. *Administrative Science Quarterly, 26,* 563-577.

March, J. G. (1988). Variable risk preferences and adaptive aspirations. *Journal of Economic Behavior and Organization, 9,* 5-24.

March, J. G., & March, J. C. (1977). Almost random careers: The Wisconsin school superintendency. *Administrative Science Quarterly, 22,* 377-409.

March, J. G., & Olsen, J. P. (1976). *Ambiguity and choice in organizations.* Bergen, Norway: Universitetsforlaget.

March, J. G., & Simon, H. A. (1958). *Organizations.* New York: John Wiley.

Mezias, S. J. (1988). Aspiration level effects: An empirical investigation. *Journal of Economic Behavior and Organization, 10,* 389-400.

Mezias, S. J. (1990). An institutional model of organizational practice: Financial reporting at the Fortune 200. *Administrative Science Quarterly, 35,* 431-457.

Miles, R. E. (1982). *Coffin nails and corporate strategies.* Englewood Cliffs, NJ: Prentice Hall.

Milliken, F. J., & Lant, T. K. (1991). The effect of an organization's recent performance history on strategic persistence and change: The role of managerial interpretations. In P. Shrivastava, A. Huff, & J. Dutton (Eds.), *Advances in strategic management* (Vol. 7, pp. 129-156). Greenwich, CT: JAI.

Nelson, R. R., & Winter, S. G. (1982). *An evolutionary theory of economic change.* Boston: Belknap Press.

Payne, J. W., Laughhunn, D. J., & Crum, R. (1980). Translation of gambles and aspiration level effects on risky choice behavior. *Management Science, 26,* 1039-1060.

Perrow, C. (1986). *Complex organizations: A critical essay* (3rd ed.). Glenview, IL: Scott, Foresman.

Pfeffer, J. (1981). Management as symbolic action: The creation and maintenance of organizational paradigms. In L. L. Cummings & B. M. Staw (Eds.), *Research in organizational behavior* (Vol. 3, pp. 1-52). Greenwich, CT: JAI.

Siegel, S. (1957). Level of aspiration and decision making. *Psychology Review, 64,* 253-262.

Thompson, J. D. (1967). *Organizations in action.* New York: McGraw-Hill.

Tushman, M. L., & Romanelli, E. (1985). Organizational evolution: A metamorphosis model of convergence and reorientation. In L. L. Cummings & B. M. Staw (Eds.), *Research in organizational behavior* (Vol. 7, pp. 171-222). Greenwich, CT: JAI.

Tushman, M. L., Newman, W. H., & Romanelli, E. (1986). Convergence and upheaval: Managing the unsteady pace of organizational evolution. *California Management Review, 29,* 1-16.

Varian, H. R. (1978). *Microeconomic analysis.* New York: Norton.

Watzlawick, P., Weakland, J., & Fisch, R. (1974). *Change: Principles of problem formation and problem resolution.* New York: Norton.

14

Executive Succession and Organization Outcomes in Turbulent Environments

An Organization Learning Approach

BEVERLY VIRANY†
MICHAEL L. TUSHMAN
ELAINE ROMANELLI

This paper explores executive succession as an important mechanism for organization learning and, thus, for organization adaptation. We argue that executive succession can fundamentally alter the knowledge, skills and interaction processes of the senior management team. These revised skills and communication processes improve the team's ability to recognize and act on changing environmental conditions. Especially in turbulent environments, succession may be critical for improving or sustaining the performance of the firm. We explore continuity and change of CEOs and their executive teams as associated with first- and second-order organization learning, which are differentially important under stable versus turbulent environmental conditions. We also link these organization learning ideas to the nature of organization evolution. A series of hypotheses link executive-team succession and strategic reorientation to subsequent organization performance.

Results in a study of 59 minicomputer firms, all founded between 1968 and 1971, indicate that succession exerts a positive influence on organization performance. We also show that it is important to distinguish between CEO succession and executive-team change, which independently improve subsequent organization

---

†Beverly Virany died of cancer in 1987. This paper is a testimony to her dedication and creativity and to her enthusiasm for her emerging career.

performance. The positive impact of succession is accentuated when it coincides with strategic reorientation. Finally we examined how longer term patterns in succession and reorientation affect organization performance. We discovered two modes of organization adaptation in this turbulent industry. The most typical mode combines CEO succession, sweeping executive-team changes, and strategic reorientations. A more rare, and over the long-term more effective, adaptational mode involves strategic reorientation and executive-team change, but no succession of the CEO. Consistently high performing organizations are managed to sustain a relatively high level of learning (through turnover of senior executives and strategic reorientation), and at the same time to maintain links with established organizational competencies (through retention of the CEO).

(EXECUTIVE SUCCESSION; ORGANIZATION
LEARNING; ORGANIZATION PERFORMANCE)

INTRODUCTION

Sustained scholarly interest in executive succession is premised on a basic inconsistency of beliefs about the efficacy of senior organizational leadership. On the one hand, no rationale can be posited for the study of succession other than belief in the power of senior executives to affect organizational activities and thus organizational performance. On the other hand, emphasis on succession implies a basic lack of belief in the ability of incumbent executives to influence organization performance, especially when change is required. This inconsistency is apparently resolved by an implicit assumption that senior executives can be influential and effective, but only for a time, i.e., only during the early years of their tenure (Boeker, 1989; Miller & Toulouse, 1986). Later, due to institutionalization, senior executives become impediments to change. Thus, they must be replaced.

Several studies document difficulties that incumbent executives face in altering established organizational activity patterns. For example, investigations of executive attributions for performance declines (Bettman & Weitz, 1983; Salancik & Meindl, 1984; Staw, McKechnie, & Puffer, 1983) describe the tendency of senior executives to make self-serving attributions regarding corporate performance. Self-serving attributions tend to overemphasize vagaries of environmental conditions and underemphasize executive responsibility for managing the organization toward fit with those conditions. Other studies discuss the inability of senior executives even to recognize environmental changes that threaten the viability of ongoing activities (Kiesler & Sproull, 1982; Staw, Sandelands, & Dutton, 1981). These findings suggest

that executive succession is typically necessary to introduce new perspectives and new ties to the external environment. They suggest as well that
executive succession may be most appropriate when environments are
changing and/or when the organization is experiencing performance declines
(Pfeffer & Davis-Blake, 1986; Pfeffer & Salancik, 1978; Selznick, 1957).

The paper explores executive succession as an important mechanism for
organization learning and, in turn, organization adaptation. Building on the
organization-learning literature (Lant & Mezias, 1992; Levitt & March,
1988), we argue that succession-performance relations can be clarified by
considering succession as a team phenomenon and by associating CEO and
executive-team succession with substantial changes in organizational activities. We distinguish between first- and second-order learning, which are
differentially important under stable versus turbulent environments. Second-
order learning, necessary when environments are turbulent, requires both
new informational inputs from the environment and experimentation for
discovering new relationships of the firm to its environment. CEO succession coupled with turnover in the executive team should contribute more to
increases in information diversity, and to more exchange of information
among senior managers, than CEO succession alone. Substantive changes in
organizational activity, which we consider here in terms of strategic reorientations (Tushman & Romanelli, 1985), further increase the diversity of
information available to senior executives by revealing relationships of
organization actions to outcomes. Where substantial executive-team and/or
organizational change may be associated with disruption, crisis, and performance decline in stable contexts (Friedman & Singh, 1989; Hannan &
Freeman, 1984), in turbulent environments executive succession coupled
with strategic reorientation should improve the organization's ability to
adapt, and thus also the organization's performance.

To explore these ideas, we develop a series of hypotheses that link the
degree of CEO succession, executive-team change, and strategic reorientation to subsequent organization performance. Our study focuses on a cohort
of minicomputer firms founded between 1968 and 1971. We tracked these
firms from their births to 1980. This period was characterized by substantial
technological and competitive turbulence. Results indicate that succession
is a complex phenomenon that, when successful, balances organizational
requirements for stability and continuity with environmentally demanded
needs for change.

EXECUTIVE SUCCESSION,
ORGANIZATION LEARNING,
AND ORGANIZATION EVOLUTION

Organizations evolve through alternating periods of convergence and reorientation (Miller & Friesen, 1984; Tushman & Romanelli, 1985). Convergence refers to incremental and interdependent changes that increasingly stabilize established patterns of activities. During convergent periods, an organization learns to accomplish its strategy in an ever more coherent and efficient manner. Reorientations punctuate convergent periods. Reorientations are system-wide organizational changes involving concurrent shifts in strategies, structures, power distributions, and control mechanisms. During reorientations, organizations do not incrementally improve existing modes of organizing; rather, they shift to fundamentally different operating modes. Senior executives are principally responsible, during convergent periods, for managing symbolic outcomes that sustain established activity patterns (Pfeffer, 1981). During reorientations, however, it is the task of senior executives both to define and legitimize substantively new patterns of activity (Tushman & Romanelli, 1985).

Organization learning is a form of informational updating through which decision makers develop an understanding of relationships between organization actions and outcomes (Fiol & Lyles, 1985; Levitt & March, 1988). There are two contrasting learning modes which are related to convergent periods and reorientation. First-order learning involves incremental updating of established premises regarding the best way to respond to environmental conditions. During convergent periods, first-order learning processes operate to improve existing competencies and standard operating procedures (SOPs) (Lant & Mezias, 1992), as well as to correct errors and adjust inconsistencies about a given set of understandings and objectives (Louis & Sutton, 1989). Second-order learning, by contrast, is characterized by a shift in core assumptions and decision-making premises. Second-order learning involves unlearning prior premises and SOPs and developing new frames, new SOPs and new interpretive schemes (Bartunek, 1984). Where first-order learning reduces behavioral variability, second-order learning increases variability in service of creating a diverse experience base from which new understandings and objectives can emerge (Fiol & Lyles, 1985; Hedberg, Nystrom, & Starbuck, 1976). Organization learning, then, is related to a firm's ability to evolve as environmental conditions change.

Executive Succession and First-Order Learning

First-order learning builds increased competence with a fixed set of decision premises. As organization actors increase their experience with their tasks and with each other, they adjust their activities and understandings toward even greater coherence (Miller & Friesen, 1984). In time, as coherence and efficiency of activity patterns improve, actors come to accept these patterns as appropriate (Gersick & Hackman, in press; Zucker, 1977). First-order learning contributes to institutionalization of activity patterns, to increasingly interlinked behaviors and, in turn, to social and structural inertia.

Several authors (Bartunek, 1984; Kiesler & Sproull, 1982; Levitt & March, 1988) have explored relationships between characteristics of executive teams and first-order learning in organizations. The longer that executive teams are in place, the less turnover in the team and the more homogeneous the team members become with respect to experiences and understandings (Tushman & Keck, 1990). Over time, first-order learning processes overwhelm whatever diversity of experience and knowledge may have characterized the team early on. Habit, SOPs, history, and institutionalization drive out vigilant problem solving (Louis & Sutton, 1989). Katz (1982) and Wagner, Pfeffer, and O'Reilly (1984) have linked these developments to decreased communication with actors outside the group. New information, which might alter established interpretative schemes, does not enter into play. Ancona (1989) has shown that the longer a decision-making group is together, the less the group experiments with new ways of doing things. The longer the period of first-order learning, the longer these inertial processes operate, and the more executive-team history and precedent guide current behavior.

As long as the environment remains stable, first-order learning contributes positively to organization performance. Efficiency improves as the organization practices basic skills (Argyris & Schön, 1978). As the firm establishes reliable and accountable relationships with external actors, uncertainties about flows of resources and revenues are reduced (Hannan & Freeman, 1984). When environments are changing, however, first-order learning also reduces the likelihood that organization actors will perceive the need for new understandings and actions. Inertia associated with first-order learning anchors the organization to its past even in the face of environmental change (e.g., Morison, 1966). The benefits of first-order learning are achieved at the price of decreased ability to adapt as an ever more redundant experience base drives out an executive team's ability to learn outside a given frame (Kiesler & Sproull, 1982; Levitt & March, 1988).

Executive Succession and Second-Order Learning

Lant and Mezias (this volume) argue that second-order learning is triggered by experiences that cannot be ignored and cannot be handled or interpreted by existing competencies and understandings. Increasing pressures from external actors and (eventually) from performance declines lead even the most entrenched executive team to understand that ongoing activity patterns can no longer be maintained. Long-established teams, however, may be trapped by their prior competencies and internal processes, and be unable either to formulate and/or execute alternative actions. Executive succession, then, should be an important mechanism for instigating second-order learning (Greiner & Bhambri, 1989).

Execution succession facilitates second-order learning by affecting the demography of the senior team and its communication and decision-making processes. Executive succession may change the team's competence base and increase its heterogeneity of experiences which form the bases for experimentation (Ancona, 1989; O'Reilly & Flatt, 1989). Reduced executive-team tenure also decreases the team's social integration (O'Reilly, Caldwell, & Barnett, 1989). These demographically younger executive teams revise SOPs and decision-making processes and, thus, potentially alter the premises and core objectives of the firm (Bartunek, 1984; Dutton & Jackson, 1988). Externally recruited executives will retain, at least for a time, communication links with outside sources which further increases the availability of heterogeneous information. New executive teams may also possess less vested interest in established power distributions; indeed, their individual interests may lie in changing existing power balances (e.g., Helmich & Brown, 1972). Finally, as new executives signal to both internal and external actors that change is likely, they obtain a license to alter established decision-making premises (Neustadt, 1980).

Executive-team succession facilitates second-order learning at a cost however. Where younger, more heterogeneous executive teams may be able to deal with uncertainty more effectively than older, more homogeneous teams, these new teams incur liabilities of newness. Newer executives accrue none of the benefits of experience with the particular organization. Heterogeneity, which increases experimentation with alternatives, may also spur dysfunctional dissensus and disruption of effective activity patterns (Grusky, 1963). External actors may not have confidence in the effectiveness of new activities (Hannan & Freeman, 1984). Executive succession and associated second-order learning is a break from history and precedent and, as such, reduces competence accumulated through prior convergent periods.

Nevertheless, when environments are changing in uncertain ways or when established organizational activity patterns are proved ineffective, second-order learning may have more survival potential than sustained attention to the status quo (Watzlawick, Bavelas, & Jackson, 1967; Weick, 1979). Technological discontinuities, environmental jolts, and/or turbulent environmental conditions radically alter organization competence requirements and bases of competition in an industry (Meyer, 1982; Miles, 1982; Tushman & Anderson, 1986). While it may be obvious, under such conditions, that prior competencies have been rendered obsolete, in real time it may not be clear what the new requisite competencies might be. For example, between 1850 and 1970 mechanical escapements were the dominant mode for oscillation in watches (see Landes, 1983). In 1970, this technology was challenged by both tuning-fork and quartz oscillation. All that was known by watch producers in 1970 was that there was technical variation in the product class. It was not until several years later that producers would "know" that quartz oscillation would dominate.

In turbulent environments, then, organization action has uncertain outcomes. Organization learning occurs only after experience has been gained (March & March, 1977). Action, even mistakes, provide new information— fragments of experience—that form the basis for learning (March, Sproull, & Tamuz, 1991). When environments are turbulent, action with uncertain, possibly negative, outcomes may have more survival value than persistent improvements on established activity patterns. In such environments, even random choices between plausible rival actions may enhance organization survival (Weick, 1979).

An organization-learning approach to executive succession suggests that executive succession is a potentially powerful tool for changing organization-environment alignments. Moreover, it suggests that succession is a variable that can moderate the degree of organization learning. Executive succession coupled with change in organizational activities shapes the nature of organization learning and, thus, in turn, affects organization performance. The dual positive and negative succession effects in stable and changing environments indicate further that a balance must be struck between the advantages of learning gained by succession and the liabilities of new executive teams. The following section explores linkages between executive succession, reorientation and organization performance.

EXECUTIVE SUCCESSION AND
ORGANIZATION PERFORMANCE

Much of the executive-succession literature has focused on the change of a single individual, the CEO. This research stream has produced confusing and contradictory results (Carroll, 1984; Friedman & Singh, 1989; Romanelli &

Tushman, 1988). Hambrick and Mason (1984) have suggested that the CEO and his or her executive team may be a more effective unit of analysis for succession research. Simple CEO succession may not introduce sufficient new and diverse experience or knowledge to alter established understandings and entrenched activity patterns. Moreover, even a radically different CEO may be unable to implement changes. Without extensive team changes, incumbent team members with vested interests in the status quo and with stronger ties to the existing organization may undermine a new CEO's attempts at change (Smith, 1988).

Executive-team change initiated by incumbent CEOs, however, also might not introduce sufficient new and diverse experiences into the senior team to alter entrenched patterns of activities. In choosing new team members, an incumbent CEO is as much a product of institutionalized understandings as any member of the old executive team. Due to restricted communication and institutionalization processes (Katz, 1982; Wagner et al., 1984), the incumbent CEO may be as much committed to established understandings developed by this team, and thus as resistant to change, as any other member. It is also likely that the CEO will have been instrumental in placing these individuals in their executive positions. Self-serving attributions reduce the likelihood that the CEO will come to view these executives as ineffective (Bettman & Weitz, 1983). Finally, even if the CEO recognizes need for change in the executive team, he or she may still select new executives in terms of established understandings (Hambrick & Mason, 1984).

It seems, then, that substantial impediments to change confront new CEOs or new executive teams when the other remains in place and unaltered. The combination of CEO succession and substantial turnover in the executive team, however, may provide a sufficient critical mass of new skills and experiences to promote organizational change. Such thoroughly altered executive teams should also possess enough power throughout the organization to overcome more structural resistances to change. Case studies of organizational turnarounds at ICI and Chrysler, for example, indicate that both a new CEO and a completely revised executive team were necessary to implement system-wide changes (Pettigrew, 1985; Tichy & Devanna, 1986).

System-wide change and strategic experimentation associated with second-order learning may or may not be successful, of course. Given uncertainty associated with turbulent environments, effective action can only be known ex-post. Nevertheless, in turbulent environments and/or under performance-crisis conditions, the combination of CEO and executive-team change should be associated with greater organization responsiveness and, thus, with enhanced organization performance rather than incremental change in the executive team.

Hypothesis 1.   In turbulent environments, there will be no direct relationship between CEO change alone or executive-team change alone and subsequent organizational performance.

Hypothesis 2.   In turbulent environments, the combination of CEO succession and executive-team change will be positively related to subsequent organizational performance.

While CEO succession coupled with substantial change in the executive team improves the likelihood that the new executives will perceive alternative, potentially more effective organizational activities, second-order learning typically also requires that substantive action be taken to learn about effective responses to changing conditions. Significant change also signals to internal and external actors that a new order of activity is in place. A number of case histories (Chandler, 1982; Landes, 1983; Pettigrew, 1985) have shown that substantial executive change coupled with strategic reorientation is associated with fundamentally different modes of organization activity. These reoriented organizations were frequently, though not always, more capable of dealing with altered environmental contingencies. In contrast, other studies have shown that, in turbulent environments, change of senior executives without associated change in organizational activities leads either to no performance improvement or, in several cases, to decline and failure (Grinyer & Spender, 1979; Hall, 1976; Lodahl & Mitchell, 1980; Messinger, 1955). In turbulent environments, sweeping executive-team change coupled with strategic reorientation may break the grip of organizational inertia. While the content of successful reorientations cannot be known in advance, even random choice among plausible rival alternatives may have greater survival value than sustained organizational inertia.

Hypothesis 3.   In turbulent environments, the positive effect of combined CEO succession and executive-team change on subsequent organizational performance will be accentuated where CEO and executive-team succession are coupled with strategic reorientation.

There are costs associated with using CEO succession, executive-team change and reorientations as tools for organizational learning. New executive teams must negotiate altered balances of power and incur substantial implementation costs (Greiner & Bhambri, 1989). In turbulent environments, time and cost pressures are great (Eisenhardt, 1989). Given the costs of second-order learning, some maintenance of links to the prior convergent period may still be important.

A number of studies have examined the performance impact of succession where the new CEO was internally promoted versus externally recruited. Promotion of CEOs from inside the organization is often associated with a perpetuation of existing policies and practices (Dalton & Kesner, 1985; Downs, 1967; Helmich & Brown, 1972). In contrast, outsider succession is associated with more change of organizational activities (Carlson, 1961; Helmich & Brown, 1972), less commitment to the status quo, and a broadened knowledge of environmental conditions (Pfeffer & Leblebici, 1973).

All of these studies have examined CEO succession in isolation from associated executive-team changes. While externally-promoted CEOs may be most likely to initiate substantial organizational changes, they do so at a cost of decreasing ties to the old system. A wholly new executive team, especially if led by an externally recruited CEO, will lack well-developed political networks inside the organization and knowledge of the organization's systems. These reconfigured executive teams may have difficulty implementing change. The most effective executive-succession events, then, may be those where an internally promoted CEO initiates substantial changes in the executive team. In this fashion, the new CEO takes advantage of existing systems and relationships even as he or she equips the firm with more heterogeneous expertise and understanding (Dalton & Kesner, 1985; Pettigrew, 1985).

Hypothesis 4.   In turbulent environments, the positive relationship between combined CEO succession and executive-team change on subsequent organizational performance will be accentuated where new CEOs are internally promoted.

It is possible that some firms introduce and execute fundamentally new patterns of interaction without CEO succession. If a CEO has demonstrated that he or she can manage the firm through turbulent times, change of this individual may spawn a lack of confidence in new management from both internal and external actors. While environmental turbulence may still require change in executive-team skills and interaction processes as well as strategic reorientations, performance of high performing organizations may be better sustained by retention of the CEO and change only in his or her executive team. For example, Mintzberg and Waters (1982) described metamorphic change in a retail chain guided by a single chief executive officer. This executive served as an anchor to the company's distinguished past even as he fundamentally altered his team and organization. Theodore Vail at AT&T and Joe Wilson at Xerox were also able to initiate extensive team

changes and organization-wide action as their firms faced evolving environmental conditions (Dessauer, 1975; Smith, 1982).

For consistently high performing organizations, the costs of CEO succession may outweigh potential benefits of change. Effective CEOs, if retained,
can inspire confidence in actors within and outside the organization that
relationships and activities will be sustained even as change in the CEO's
top team signals renewed heterogeneity of perspective and understanding.
Consistently high performing organizations, even in turbulent environments,
may sustain their performance by instituting executive-team change and
reorientations without CEO succession.

> *Hypothesis 5.   In turbulent environments, consistently high performing organi-*
> *zations will experience fewer CEO successions, but the same degree of the*
> *executive-team change and the same number of strategic reorientations as*
> *other firms.*

RESEARCH METHOD

This research employs a cohort-based, longitudinal design. All minicomputer firms (n = 59) that were founded between 1968 and 1971 were
identified (excluding original equipment manufacturers, which simply added
peripherals and/or software to another firm's minicomputer).[1] Data on CEO
succession, executive-team change, and strategic reorientations were gathered over the life spans of 38 of these firms from birth through 1980, or until
a firm was acquired or failed. We were unable to gather extensive data on 21
firms. While our sample has substantial variability in organization fate and
performance, it may be biased by firms that survived more than one year.
The period 1968 to 1980 covered a particularly turbulent time in the minicomputer industry. Concentration ratios and industry-sales conditions were
highly volatile (Romanelli, 1989). Technology was changing rapidly, in
terms both of minicomputer design as well as emergent microcomputers, and
posed significant threat to the minicomputer industry as a whole (Tushman
& Anderson, 1986). Organization-level data were gathered from 10Ks, annual reports, industry journals, business-press articles, and industry contacts.

CEO Succession

The chief executive officer was considered as either the Chair of the Board
of Directors (unless the Chair was listed as an outsider with other full-time
responsibilities), the CEO, or the President of the firm in cases where no

other individual was listed as Chair or CEO. In firms with both a chairperson and CEO, the chair was considered the more senior executive. CEO succession was coded as 1 for any year in which a new individual was installed in office, and 0 otherwise. Successors were also coded as internal promotions or external recruitment. A successor was coded as externally recruited if he or she held a position outside the organization less than one year prior to being appointed CEO; otherwise the new CEO was coded as an insider.

Executive-Team Change

For each year of a firm's existence other than the first year, the membership of the executive team (not including the CEO) was compared with membership of the preceding year. All executives down through the vice-president level were included as members of the executive team. Executive-team change was calculated as the percentage of the team to change in the particular year. In Table 14.4, executive-team change is categorized as either high or low based on a median split.

Strategic Reorientations

Reorientations are defined as discontinuous and simultaneous changes in organization strategy, structure, power distributions, and control practices (Tushman & Romanelli, 1985). Several sources were gathered to obtain a wide range of organizational data. Annual reports, 10Ks and prospectuses were gathered for all public firms ($N = 20$) for all available years. Data were also gathered from industry reports, market-research firms, industry publications, and the general business press. Substantial data on 41 firms were available from these public sources. Our challenge was to develop reliable and valid methods for identifying reorientations from our longitudinal data base. Building on Miller and Friesen's (1984) and Mintzberg and Waters's (1982) methods for capturing organizational activity patterns longitudinally, a multistep, multi-coder process was developed to move from the raw historical record, to company histories, to the determination of reorientations. A three-step process was employed to make maximum use of diverse data and to ensure both independence and consistency of coding procedures.

Step 1. Two independent research teams developed company histories from these data sources. One team (four individuals) used 10Ks, annual reports, and prospectuses, while the second team (two other individuals) used all other industry sources. Histories developed from these two sources allowed us to assess the quality of data obtained from noncompany documents (e.g., business-press articles and information obtained from industry-research firms) in comparison with company 10Ks and annual reports. Data from non-company sources were sufficiently rich and consistent with company sources for us to conclude that information on nonpublic companies was detailed and accurate. The histories also provided a qualitative overview of the lives and events of the companies that aided in the interpretations of more quantitative data.

Step 2. Using these histories and returning to the raw records as necessary, research teams supplemented qualitative histories with concrete data on changes in organizational strategy, structure, and formal control practices. These dimensions of organizational activities were defined and changes were coded as follows:

A. *Strategy* was defined in terms of products and markets. Changes in strategy were coded whenever a company added or deleted a major product line (e.g., minicomputers, microcomputers, telephone switching systems) and/or a company entered or exited a market category. Market categories, which were identified in consultation with industry experts and on the basis of market distinctions used commonly by the organizations themselves, included: end-user sales versus sales to original equipment manufacturers; U.S. versus international; and several categories of end-user applications (e.g., scientific and engineering laboratories, distributed data processing, industrial automation, and process control). For every year, product lines and served markets were identified for every firm. Strategy changed if either product lines, or served markets, or both, changed in a year. Strategy change was coded as either 0 (no change in product lines or markets) or 1 (change in product lines, markets, or both) on a year-by-year basis.

B. *Structure* was examined in terms of changes in distributions of executive-team members' titles, which were coded as functional (e.g., treasurer, vice-president sales), product divisional (e.g., vice-president software, or a particular minicomputer line), market divisional (e.g., vice-president military applications), or geographical divisional (e.g., vice-president, Great Britain). Hybrid titles (e.g., vice-president marketing, Great Britain) occasionally appeared. In all cases these involved the combination of a functional category with a divisional category. Such titles were coded on the basis of their divisional classification.

For all companies, titles were arrayed over all years of the firm's existence for the period of our study. All firms started out with a functional classification. The functional classification was used as the benchmark against which to examine structural change. Structure changed for any year during which titles of any one of the divisional categories reached 25% of the total number of titles or when a category that had been 25% dropped below this threshold.

Firms were coded as retaining a functional structure so long as functional titles were greater than 75% of the total. Given these rules, structure was coded as either 0 (retained functional structure) or 1 (moved to divisional structure) on a year-by-year basis. (It should be noted that title changes do not necessarily correspond to executive changes. It was surprisingly routine in these companies for the same individuals to "change hats" sometimes two or three times.)

C. *Formal Control Practices* reflect management's focus on efficiency and formal processes. Formal control, a generic problem in rapid growth environments, is exercised via inventory controls, management information systems, manufacturing controls, and formal incentives. Data on formal control practices were obtained from 10Ks, annual reports, and industry sources. Any year in which two or more of the above formal control practices were initiated or changed, control practices were coded as having changed (coded as 1), otherwise control practices were coded 0 (no change).

Step 3. The final step in identifying reorientations involved two coders who combined and integrated data gathered in Steps 1 and 2. Reorientations were defined as having occurred only when strategy, structure, and formal control all changed (i.e., all were coded 1) within a two-year period. The most detailed data on control practices were available from 10Ks and annual reports. Information on formal control practices was incomplete for nonpublic firms. For these organizations, reorientations were coded 1 where strategy and structure both changed. Working independently, investigators reviewed both the qualitative histories and arrayed quantitative variables for each company. Over 85% of the reorientations were consistently identified. Discrepancies were resolved by going back to original sources and/or through interviews with industry contacts. Reorientations are sufficiently encompassing to stand out yearly in both the public and private records from more routine organization changes.

This multi-step, multi-method coding process was designed to maximize consistency between independent coders and maximize the use of expensively collected data. These methods also built in a consistent process of combining quantitative with qualitative data in operationalizing reorientations. Given the complexity of the phenomenon and the nature of available data, neither quantitative or qualitative approaches alone would take full advantage of these data. Because of the difficulties in gathering rich organizational data longitudinally, and because of industry differences, specific measures used here may not be appropriate in other industries. The method we have employed, however, should be generalizable to analyses of organization change in any industry.

TABLE 14.1 Descriptive Statistics

	N	Mean (s.d.)	Pearson Correlations (Ns)		
			(2)	(3)	(4)
(1) CEO Succession	278	0.09 (0.28)	0.22*** (148)	0.22** (241)	0.12 (173)
(2) Executive-Team Change	149	0.34 (0.24)		0.14* (147)	0.02 (128)
(3) Reorientation	225	0.36 (0.48)			−0.03 (160)
(4) ROA Change	324	0.03 (0.39)			

***$p < 0.01$.
**$p < 0.05$.
*$p < 0.10$.

Organization Performance

Organization performance was measured by return on assets (ROA). These data were measured yearly for each firm. The percentage change in ROA between the year of succession and two years subsequent to succession was utilized to explore effects of succession and reorientation on organization performance. A two-year interval was employed to provide a time period long enough to permit changes to take place, but short enough not to be confounded by other factors. We also explored one-year ROA differences and the average of one- and two-year differences. These alternative organization performance measures yielded results essentially the same as those reported here.

To test Hypothesis 5, organizations were classified into three historical performance categories by comparing firm ROA to industry-average ROA for each year of a company's life. A firm was categorized as consistently high performing if its ROA was greater than industry-average ROA for all years—excluding the firm's startup and allowing for at most one outlier year of low performance later in the company's life. Fifteen firms were so categorized. Six organizations failed over the period studied. These failing firms performed below industry average ROA for the majority of their years of operation. Those organizations that were neither high performers nor failures were categorized as moderately effective firms; there were 17 of these.

Table 14.1 reports means, standard deviations, and correlations. The n for these measures—i.e., the number of years over all companies' lives for which each measure was taken—vary due to data availability. These observations come from 21 firms with complete data and from 17 firms with incomplete data.

ANALYSES

For the multivariate analyses, our pooled time-series/cross-sectional design creates special requirements to correct for autocorrelation since not all firms were alive for the entire time period. Following Kmenta (1986), we used a two-stage least-squares method to correct for autocorrelation and then heteroscedasticity. Unit specific values used to transform the data were calculated and applied individually to each firm's data. These new autocorrelation-corrected data were then pooled to form the sample for a single generalized least-squared (GLS) regression that meets classical OLS assumptions. Plots of residuals verify that the assumption of first-order autocorrelation was appropriate. Heteroscedasticity was also evaluated since multiple cross-sectional units are included. Plots of residual variances indicated that heteroscedasticity existed. Unit specific variances for each firm were used to correct for this bias. Subsequent plots revealed that heteroscedasticity has been removed.

Hypotheses were tested using generalized least-squares regressions with controls for prior performance change and secular trends.[2] Several models were analyzed to explore both main and interactive effects of CEO succession, executive-team change, and strategic reorientation. R-squared values are not reported in Table 14.2 as they are misleading and cannot be compared across models when generated by these corrected generalized least-squared methods.

RESULTS

Hypotheses 1 through 3 argued that, in turbulent environments, organizational performance would be improved when the CEO and his/her executive team changed simultaneously, and that such improvements would be accentuated when new senior executives implemented organization-wide action. Table 14.2 reports three GLS models for testing these relationships. Model 1 shows main effect relationships of CEO succession, executive-team change, and reorientation on subsequent organizational performance, controlling pre-event ROA change and secular trends in environmental conditions. Model 2 adds the CEO-succession, executive-team-change interaction. Finally, Model 3 adds the three-way interaction of CEO succession, executive-

TABLE 14.2 Generalized Least Squares Regressions: ROA Change as a Function of CEO Succession, Executive-Team Change, Reorientation, and Their Interactions[a]

	Model	Model 2	Model 3
Main Effects			
CEO Succession	0.31***	0.36*	0.19
Executive-Team Change	0.16*	0.17***	0.41***
Reorientation	−0.03	−0.03	0.38***
Interactions			
CEO Succession × Executive-Team Change		−0.06	−0.22
Executive-Team Change × Reorientation			−0.63***
CEO Succession × Executive-Team Change ×			
Reorientation			0.43***
Lagged Performance Change and Secular Trends			
Lagged ROA Change	0.14	0.14	0.19**
1969-73	0.25*	0.25*	0.14
1974-76	0.30**	0.30**	0.15
1977-80	−0.02	−0.02	−0.10
F	4.65***	3.94***	4.56***
d.f.	93	92	90

[a]Standardized betas reported.
***$p < 0.01$.
**$p < 0.05$.
*$p < 0.10$.

team change, and reorientation along with associated lower-order interactions.[3]

All three models indicate positive effects of both CEO succession and executive-team change on subsequent organizational performance. Two of the three CEO-succession coefficients are significant, while all three of the executive-team-change coefficients are significant. The interaction of CEO succession and executive-team-change on subsequent performance (Models 2 and 3), however, is not significant. Contrary to Hypotheses 1 and 2, both CEO succession and executive-team change influence subsequent organizational performance positively, but not their interaction. Evidently, CEO succession and executive-team change, by themselves, are able to bring sufficient expertise and/or change in senior team processes to enhance organization performance in turbulent environments. (*Note*: The consistently positive and, in Model 3, significant lagged ROA change coefficients indicate not regression to the mean, but an acceleration effect. Those firms that had positive ROA change prior to the succession/reorientation event tended to have increased positive ROA change after the event. The rich seem to get richer, and vice versa.)

Hypothesis 3 argued that the positive impact of change in senior management would be accentuated when combined with strategic reorientation. In Model 3, strategic reorientations, by themselves, have a significantly positive association with subsequent organization performance. Evidently in this turbulent minicomputer environment, discontinuous organization change enhances organization performance. Further, in support of Hypothesis 3, the coefficient on the three-way interaction of CEO succession, executive-team change, and reorientation is positive and significant. Where CEO succession and executive-team change together have no significant effect on subsequent performance, when sweeping executive changes are coupled with organization-wide action, organization performance is significantly improved. Reorientations may break the grip of organization inertia and, in turn, help new executive teams shape revised organization action in turbulent environments.

The significantly negative interaction of executive-team change and strategic reorientation and the negative (though not significant) CEO-succession/executive-team change interaction suggest that tentative organization transitions are resisted by either stable CEOs or organization inertia, respectively. On the other hand, the positive and significant interaction of CEO succession, executive-team change, and strategic reorientation indicates that these sweeping organization transformations have positive effects over and above individual main effects.

Hypothesis 4 argued that internal CEO promotions, where the composition of the executive team was simultaneously revamped, would exert a more positive influence on subsequent organizational performance than external CEO recruitment. We reasoned that internally promoted CEOs would be able to utilize links to existing networks and knowledge of the status quo in implementing change in their teams and throughout the organization. While there are too few cases to permit statistical analysis ($n = 10$), the average increase in performance is more than twice as large when the new CEO is internally promoted than when the new CEO is hired from outside the company. In support of Hypothesis 4, the mean increase in return on assets for internally promoted CEOs is 0.51 as compared with 0.21 when the new CEO was recruited from outside.

Another way to investigate the effects of executive succession is to compare succession patterns of different categories of organizations. Hypothesis 5 argued that, for consistently high performing organizations, performance improvements would be accomplished via executive-team change and reorientation without CEO change. Results reported in Table 14.3 support this hypothesis. Historically high performing organizations engage in

TABLE 14.3 Mean CEO Succession, Executive-Team Change, and
Reorientation: Consistently High Performing Firms, With and
Without CEO Succession, Compared With All Other Firms

	High Performing Firms	All Others	High Performing Firms	
			Succession	No Succession
CEO Succession	0.05	0.14**	0.10	0**
	(132)	(99)	(68)	(64)
Executive-Team Change	0.32	0.38 (N.S.)	0.35	0.27**
	(93)	(54)	(51)	(42)
Reorientation	0.41	0.39 (N.S.)	0.46	0.35 (N.S.)
	(128)	(87)	(71)	(57)

**p < 0.05.
N.S. = Not significant.
Ns in parentheses.

significantly fewer CEO successions than all other firms. These companies,
however, exhibit the same degree of executive-team change and frequency
of reorientation as all other firms in the cohort. In the few cases where these
consistently high performers did replace a CEO, the new CEO was internally
promoted in 3 out of 5 cases.

A more in-depth analysis of the 15 consistent high performing organizations found that seven of these companies had no CEO successions at all.
Further, these organizations had significantly less executive-team change
than the other high performers (see Table 14.3). There was, however, no
difference between these two groups in terms of reorientation frequency. The
other eight high performing organizations showed succession patterns similar to those of the rest of the cohort. These firms tended to combine CEO
succession (typically internal succession) with extensive executive team
change and strategic reorientations.

Finally, to explore more completely the relations between CEO succession, executive-team change, and reorientation and long-term organization
performance, we examined the frequency and performance consequences of
these events (and their interactions) for three organizational performance
categories: consistently high performing organizations, moderately effective
organizations, and failures (see methods section). There are important differences in succession patterns between these three categories of organizations.

As shown in Table 14.4, failing organizations either initiated no executive
changes, or initiated excessive executive changes. In 66% of the cases,
failing organizations were inactive, initiating no CEO change or reorientations and infrequent executive-team change. Failing firms were inactive

TABLE 14.4 Event Frequencies and ROA Consequences by Long-Term Performance Classification

	Long-Term Performance			Differences Between Frequencies[3]
	High	Moderate	Failed	
No Action				
Frequency[1]	0.31^b	0.39^b	0.66^a	**
Consequence[2]	0.03	0.08	−0.26	
High Executive-Team Change				
Frequency	0.42^b	0.54^b	0.16^a	**
Consequence	0.06	0.02	0.23	
Reorientation, No CEO Change Little Executive-Team Change				
Frequency	0.26^a	0^b	0.16^b	**
Consequence	0.08	N.A.	0.22	
CEO Succession and High Executive-Team Change				
Frequency	0.04	0.09	0.18	N.S.
Consequence	0.33	0.27	1.20	
CEO Succession, High Executive-Team Change, Reorientation				
Frequency	0.01	0.03	0.17	N.S.
Consequence	0.10	0.27	1.20	

[1]Frequency refers to the number of times an event (or no action or combination of actions) occurred for firms in each long-term performance category over the total number of years for which an event could have occurred.

[2]Consequence refers to mean returns on assets two years following the occurrence of any event for firms in each category.

[3]Compares differences in mean frequencies for *a* firms with pooled sample of *b* firms (**$p < 0.05$).

significantly more frequently than all other firms ($t = 2.3$; $p = 0.02$). The consequence of inaction in the face of crisis was further performance decline (mean ROA decline of −0.26). Similarly, failing organizations used executive-team change significantly less frequently than other organizations ($t = 1.9$; $p = 0.05$). While executive-team change and executive-team change coupled with CEO change and/or reorientations were associated with increases in performance, these levers were rarely used in failing organizations.

Executive succession can also be excessive. In three organizations, extensive change in executive teams over successive years resulted in failure. These firms experienced external CEO changes combined with substantial executive team changes (between 40-100% turnover) repeatedly over successive years. Two of the three firms also initiated reorganizations during the same period. Thus, failing organizations either did not use executive succession as a lever for change or were excessive in their use of these levers. Inaction or too much action in the face of crisis was associated with further decline and, in turn, failure.[4]

Consistently high performing organizations, by contrast, were more moderate in their use of executive team change and/or reorientations. These organizations were not only able to initiate reorientations with significantly fewer CEO successions than other firms (see Table 14.3), they were also significantly more likely to initiate reorientations with low executive-team turnover as well ($t = 3.7; p < 0.01$). High performing organizations apparently take advantage of a relatively stable group of executives even as they initiate as many reorientations as other firms. Consistently high performing firms did not, however, avoid executive succession. These firms initiated major changes in their executive teams in 42% of the observed years. These changes in executive team were most often initiated by the existing CEO.

We also explored the timing of different succession events for each firm. While most firms utilize succession and/or reorientations as a reactive response, high performing firms are unusually proactive. High performers initiated approximately 75% of major executive changes and/or reorientations under increasing performance conditions. These exceptional organizations initiated reorientations and/or shifts in the executive team not to stem organizational crisis, but to enhance their ability to cope with organizational growth and turbulent environmental conditions.

Moderate performing organizations, however, initiated major changes in the executive team as well as CEO change in response to declining performance. Unlike the high performing organizations, in no case did these moderate performers initiate reorientations without either CEO or substantial executive-team change. Unlike failing firms, however, these moderately successful firms did respond to performance decline utilizing executive succession both with and without reorientations.

DISCUSSION

This research has explored CEO succession and executive-team changes as important mechanisms for organization learning and, in turn, for organization adaptation in turbulent environments. First-order learning involves incremental updating of established decision premises and organizing patterns (Fiol & Lyles, 1985; Levitt & March, 1988). This learning mode enhances organization performance when environments are stable by increasing organizational competence with established activity patterns. We argued that long tenured and stable executive teams (including the CEO) enhance organization performance when environments are stable due to increased routinization of decision premises and increased homogeneity of executive perspectives (O'Reilly & Flatt, 1989).

When environments are turbulent, however, second-order learning is required to alter established decision-making patterns (Lant & Mezias, 1992). Second-order learning involves an explicit change of core organization assumptions, as well as experimentation with alternative decision-making premises. CEO succession and executive-team change are fundamental levers for triggering second-order learning. Executive succession is associated with new competence and a shift in executive-team demography as well as revised executive-team processes. While second-order learning produces less consistent and reliable outcomes than first-order learning, this increased variability has enhanced ability to deal with uncertainty and/or crisis conditions (Levitt & March, 1988).

This research has explored these organization-learning ideas by directly investigating the relations between CEO succession and executive-team change on subsequent performance in turbulent environmental conditions. Given social and structural inertia associated with convergent periods, we hypothesized that, while CEO succession or executive-team change by themselves would be resisted by recalcitrant teams and conservative organizations, the combination of CEO succession and executive-team change would alter team demographics and dynamics to enable the senior team to take substantive action in turbulent environments. Further, we argued that the effects of executive-team change on organization outcomes would be accentuated when these revised teams simultaneously initiated system-wide organization change. Finally, we hypothesized that CEOs promoted from within might be better able to take advantage of local networks and politics in implementing executive-team change and/or reorientation than externally recruited CEOs.

Contrary to predictions, in five of six coefficients, both CEO succession and executive-team change were, by themselves, significantly positively associated with subsequent organization performance. There was no interaction effect of executive-team change and CEO succession on organization performance. Evidently, new CEOs are not actively resisted by their executive teams, and revised teams are not blocked by incumbent CEOs. Rather, new CEOs and/or new executive teams seem to provide, on their own, sufficient diversity of expertise and a change in team-interaction processes to facilitate learning in turbulent environments. It appears that even in turbulent environments, first-order learning, associated with incremental executive-team change, keeps senior teams coupled with environmental conditions without the trauma of wholesale executive-team change (Gersick & Hackman, in press).

These findings add an important new dimension to succession research in that they verify the importance of distinguishing between CEO and executive-team succession. Previous research has emphasized change of the CEO almost exclusively. Results presented here suggest that firms employ alternative succession tactics for improving the skill and knowledge diversity of senior management. Some of the contradictory findings from previous studies may be explainable by their collective inattention to succession in the overall management team.

Independent of changes in executive teams, reorientations in this turbulent environment were positively associated with subsequent performance. We should emphasize that this positive relationship was found without any reference to the strategic content of the reorientation. Apparently, in turbulent environments, change alone improves performance. This is consistent with the second-order learning arguments, which emphasize the importance of experimentation. Reorientation coupled with sweeping executive-team change was also positively associated with enhanced performance over and above the main effects. It may be that system-wide change initiated by new senior teams opens the way for pent-up forces for change. Executive succession coupled with reorientation may signal the end of the old order and legitimize sweeping organization change and system-wide learning (e.g., Pettigrew, 1985). While our data are limited, these patterns were accentuated when new CEOs were internally promoted. An internally promoted CEO may be able to take advantage of personal credibility and existing social networks even as he or she initiates widespread changes in the team and throughout the organization.

Added perspective on these succession/performance relationships was gained by exploring succession patterns of three categories of firms with different historical performance records. Failing firms either made no executive changes or initiated excessive changes. In essence, they achieved the worst of both worlds. The firms' executives either limited their capacities for learning about changing environmental conditions by failing to introduce new managers; or the executives lost all benefit of established competences and relationships by overhauling the executive team too extensively and too frequently. In turbulent environments, either sustained stability or radical and frequent change was associated with failure.

Consistently high performing organizations, on the other hand, had fundamentally different succession patterns than all other firms in the cohort. Where low and moderately performing organizations relied on new CEOs and revised executive teams to initiate system-wide organization change, consistently high performing organizations tended to initiate reorientations and executive-team change without CEO succession. In the few cases where high performing organizations did replace the CEO, they were most frequently internally recruited. High performing firms were thus able to take advantage of a stable CEO or an internally recruited CEO even as they initiated sweeping executive-team and organization changes.

High performing organizations were also distinct in that they initiated second-order learning not in response to performance decline, but either in anticipation of environmental change or as a response to elevated performance standards. It may be that the aspiration levels of executives in high performing organizations are set so high that those firms act as if they are perpetually in crisis. These proactive reorientations and executive-team changes stand in contrast to moderately performing firms that reactively rebuilt their teams and initiated reorientations in response to real performance crises, and low-performing firms that were inactive despite poor performance. While proactive change is risky, high performing organizations were able to initiate multiple succession/reorientation events to keep ahead of the turbulent product class. For example, Ken Oshman at Rolm initiated several waves of executive succession and reorientations as Rolm led product and technological change in the minicomputer and PBX product classes.

It seems, then, that there are two fundamentally different learning modes in turbulent environmental conditions. One mode is rare. A subset of high performing organizations had no CEO succession and significantly less executive-team change than other firms in the cohort. These extraordinary organizations had relatively stable executive teams that initiated reorientations to stay ahead of turbulent environmental conditions. Not one of these high performing organizations made it to 1980 without at least one strategic reorientation. Executive teams in these organizations were able to balance relative stability in the senior team along with fundamental organization change. These executive teams initiated second-order learning not through sweeping executive-team and/or CEO change, but through reorientations in the context of executive-team stability. These unique executive teams seem to possess an ability to learn not through executive-team change, but through changes in how they work together (Eisenhardt, 1989; March et al., 1991).

The other learning mode is more turbulent, yet more frequent. The majority of firms in this research initiated second-order learning not with stable teams but through new CEOs and substantially revised executive teams. These reconfigured executive teams, in turn, often initiated reorientations. Some high performing organizations initiated these sweeping changes in advance of performance decline and with internal CEO promotion, while moderately performing firms initiated these changes in response to performance crises.

In sum, results of our study indicate that executive succession can be a powerful lever for improving organization performance, and for sustaining performance where it is already high. Executive succession is also, however, a complex phenomenon. In turbulent environments, succession exerts a direct and positive influence on organization performance. Based on evidence of the consistently high performing organizations, however, succession is best employed in a tempered fashion. The highest performing firms in our sample either retained the incumbent CEO or promoted a new CEO from within, while changing the composition of the executive team rather substantially. These organizations also timed their successions in anticipation of environmental change, as opposed to in response to such changes. Finally, they linked the succession events with strategic reorientations. These patterns of measured executive succession and strategic reorientation reflect a balance between change for learning and stability for competence that is not shown by moderate- and low-performing organizations. If environmental conditions change, building and rebuilding executive teams and strategic reorientations may enhance organization flexibility. If so, executive-team succession must be continually reaccomplished if an organization is to retain its ability to adapt.

Acknowledgments

The authors thank Don Hambrick, Dan Levinthal, Charles O'Reilly, Barry Staw, Lance Sandelands, and the anonymous reviewers for their comments. Michael Cohen has been particularly insightful and supportive during the review process. Sara Keck, Lori Rosenkopf, and Donald Nagle provided methodological assistance. This research was supported by the Innovation and Entrepreneurship Research Center at Columbia University and the Center for Innovation Management Studies at Lehigh University.

NOTES

1. This cohort-based longitudinal design maximizes internal validity. This design controls for many plausible rival hypotheses including age, size effects (at birth), economic conditions, and industry factors. Further, in-depth industry studies permit greater industry specific insight for researchers in interpreting and understanding results. The price paid for this internal validity is greatly reduced external validity. Our results may be limited to this minicomputer cohort. What is more likely is that these results apply to organizations competing in turbulent environments (see Romanelli & Tushman, 1986, for greater discussion of design considerations in comparative-longitudinal research). Future research must explore these organization learning ideas in more stable environments (e.g., Bartner & Tushman, 1990).

2. Dummy variables were used to assess secular trends, with 1968 as the base year. In regressions with all years included, the years 1969-1973, 1974-1976, and 1977-1980 had similar coefficients. These three sets of years were used as secular dummies in Table 14.2.

3. We added lower-order two-way interactions along with our hypothesized three-way interaction in Model 3. Because CEO succession and reorientation are categorical variables, their interaction is a linear combination of the main effects and their hypothesized 3-way interaction. We therefore dropped the CEO succession × reorientation interaction in Model 3. This interaction was not significant in other models (not reported here).

4. These three examples of failure due to excessive executive changes were not included in Table 14.4. This table includes observations only where ROA data two years subsequent to the executive change were available. For these three failing firms, the excessive actions described were immediately followed by organization failure.

REFERENCES

Ancona, D. G. (1989). Top management teams: Preparing for the revolution. In J. Carroll (Ed.), *Social psychology in business organizations*. Hillsdale, NJ: Lawrence Earlbaum.

Argyris, C., & Schön, D. (1978). *Organizational learning*. Reading, MA: Addison-Wesley.

Bartner, L., & Tushman, M. L. (1990). *Executive succession, organization reorientation and performance in stable environments*. San Francisco: Academy of Management.

Bartunek, J. (1984). Changing interpretive schemes and organizational restructuring. *Administrative Science Quarterly, 29*, 355-372.

Bettman, J. R., & Weitz, B. A. (1983). Attributions in the board room: Causal reasoning in corporate annual reports. *Administrative Science Quarterly, 28*, 165-183.

Boeker, W. (1989). The development and institutionalization of subunit power in organizations. *Administrative Science Quarterly, 34*, 388-410.

Carlson, R. O. (1961). Succession and performance among school superintendents. *Administrative Science Quarterly, 6*, 210-227.

Carroll, G. R. (1984). Dynamics of publisher succession in newspaper organizations. *Administrative Science Quarterly, 29*, 93-113.

Chandler, A. D. (1962). *Strategy and structure: Chapters in the history of American industrial enterprise*. Cambridge: MIT Press.

Dalton, D. R., & Kesner, I. R. (1985). Organization of performance as an antecedent of inside/outside chief executive succession. *Academy of Management Journal, 28*, 749-762.

Dessauer, J. (1975). *My years with Xerox*. New York: Manor.

Downs, A. (1967). *Inside bureaucracy*. Boston: Little, Brown.

Dutton, J., & Jackson, S. (1988). Discerning threats and opportunities. *Administrative Science Quarterly, 33*, 370-387.

Eisenhardt, K. (1989). Making fast strategic decisions in high velocity environments. *Academy of Management Journal, 32*, 543-576.

Fiol, M., & Lyles, M. (1985). Organizational learning. *Academy of Management Review, 10*, 803-813.

Friedman, S., & Singh, H. (1989). CEO succession and stakeholder reaction. *Academy of Management Journal, 32*, 718-744.

Gersick, C., & Hackman, R. (in press). Habitual routines in task performing groups. *Organization Behavior and Human Decision Processes*.

Greiner, L., & Bhambri, A. (1989). New CEO intervention and dynamics of deliberate strategic change. *Strategic Management Journal, 10*, 67-86.

Grinyer, P., & Spender, J. (1979). *Turnaround*. London: Associated Business Press.

Grusky, O. (1963). Managerial succession. *American Journal of Sociology, 49*, 21-31.

Hall, R. H. (1976). A system pathology of an organization: The rise and fall of the old *Saturday Evening Post. Administrative Science Quarterly, 21,* 185-211.

Hambrick, D., & Mason, P. (1984). Upper echelons: The organization as a reflection of its top managers. *Academy of Management Review, 9,* 193-206.

Hannan, M. T., & Freeman, J. (1984). Structural inertia and organizational change. *American Journal of Sociology, 49,* 149-164.

Hedberg, B., Nystrom, P., & Starbuck, W. (1976). Camping on see saws: Prescriptions for a self-designing organization. *Administrative Science Quarterly, 21,* 41-65.

Helmich, D. L., & Brown, W. B. (1972). Successor type and organizational change in the corporate enterprise. *Administrative Science Quarterly, 17,* 371-381.

Katz, R. (1982). The effects of group longevity of project communication and performance. *Administrative Science Quarterly, 27,* 81-104.

Kiesler, S., & Sproull, L. (1982). Managerial response to changing environments: Perspectives on problem sensing from social cognition. *Administrative Science Quarterly, 27,* 548-570.

Kmenta, J. (1986). *Elements of economics.* New York: Macmillan.

Landes, D. (1983). *Revolution in time.* Cambridge, MA: Harvard University Press.

Lant, T. K., & Mezias, S. (1992). An organizational learning model of convergence and reorientation. *Organization Science, 3,* 47-71.

Levitt, B., & March, J. G. (1988). Organizational learning. *Annual Review of Sociology, 14,* 319-340.

Lodahl, T., & Mitchell, S. (1980). Drift in the development of innovative organizations. In J. Kimberly & R. Miles (Eds.), *Organization life cycle.* San Francisco: Jossey-Bass.

Louis, M. R., & Sutton, R. I. (1989). Switching cognitive gears: From habits of mind to active thinking. In S. Bacharach (Ed.), *Advances in organizational sociology.* Greenwich, CT: JAI.

March, J. C., & March, J. G. (1977). Almost random careers: The Wisconsin school superintendency. *Administrative Science Quarterly, 22,* 377-409.

March, J. G., Sproull, L., & Tamuz, M. (1991). Learning from samples of one or fewer. *Organization Science, 2,* 1, 1-14.

Messinger, S. L. (1955). Organizational transformation: A case study of a declining social movement. *American Sociological Review, 20,* 3-10.

Meyer, A. (1982). Adapting to environmental jolts. *Administrative Science Quarterly, 27,* 515-537.

Miles, R. (1982). *Coffin nails and corporate strategies.* Englewood Cliffs, NJ: Prentice Hall.

Miller, D., & Friesen, P. H. (1984). *Organizations: A quantum view.* Englewood Cliffs, NJ: Prentice Hall.

Miller, D., & Toulouse, J. (1986). Chief executive personality and corporate strategy and structure in small firms. *Management Science, 32,* 1389-1409.

Mintzberg, H., & Waters, J. A. (1982). Tracking strategy in an entrepreneurial firm. *Academy of Management Journal, 25,* 465-499.

Morison, E. (1966). *Men, machines and modern times.* Cambridge, MA: MIT Press.

Neustadt, R. E. (1980). *Presidential power: The politics of leadership from FDR to Carter.* New York: John Wiley.

O'Reilly, C., & Flatt, S. (1989). *Executive team demography, organizational innovation, and firm performance* (Working paper). Berkeley: University of California at Berkeley.

O'Reilly, C., Caldwell, D., & Barnett, W. (1989). Work group demography, social integration and turnover. *Administrative Science Quarterly, 34,* 21-37.

Pettigrew, A. (1985). *The awakening giant: Continuity and change at ICI.* London: Blackwell.

Pfeffer, J. (1981). Management as symbolic action: The creation and maintenance of organizational paradigms. In L. L. Cummings & B. Staw (Eds.), *Research in organizational behavior* (Vol. 3, pp. 1-52). Greenwich, CT: JAI.

Pfeffer, J., & Davis-Blake, A. (1986). Administrative succession and organizational performance: How administrator experience mediates succession effects. *Academy of Management Journal, 29,* 72-83.

Pfeffer, J., & Leblebici, H. (1973). Executive recruitment and the development of interfirm organizations. *Administrative Science Quarterly, 18,* 449-461.

Pfeffer, J., & Salancik, G. R. (1978). *The external control of organizations: A resource dependence perspective* New York: Harper & Row.

Quinn, J. (1981). *Strategies for change: Logical incrementalism.* Homewood, IL: Dow Jones.

Romanelli, E. (1989). Environments and strategies of organizational start-up: Effects on early survival. *Administrative Science Quarterly, 34,* 369-387.

Romanelli, E., & Tushman, M. L. (1986). Inertia, environments and strategic choice: Quasi-experimental design for comparative research. *Management Science, 32,* 608-621.

Romanelli, E., & Tushman, M. L. (1988). Executive leadership and organizational outcomes: An evolutionary perspective. In D. Hambrick (Ed.), *The executive effect: Concepts and methods for studying top managers* (pp. 129-146). Greenwich, CT: JAI.

Salancik, G. R., & Meindl, J. R. (1984). Corporate attributions as strategic illusions of management control. *Administrative Science Quarterly, 29,* 238-254.

Selznick, P. (1957). *Leadership in administration.* New York: Harper & Row.

Smith, G. (1982). *The anatomy of a business strategy.* Baltimore: Johns Hopkins University Press.

Smith, G. (1988). *From monopoly to competition.* Cambridge, MA: Harvard University Press.

Staw, B., McKechnie, P. I., & Puffer, M. (1983). The justification of organizational performance. *Administrative Science Quarterly, 28,* 582-600.

Staw, B., Sandelands, L. E., & Dutton, J. E. (1981). Threat-rigidity effects in organizational behavior: A multilevel analysis. *Administrative Science Quarterly, 26,* 501-524.

Tichy, N., & Devanna, M. (1986). *Transformational leaders.* New York: John Wiley.

Tushman, M. L., & Anderson, P. (1986). Technological discontinuities and organizational environments. *Administrative Science Quarterly, 31,* 439-465.

Tushman, M. L., & Romanelli, E. (1985). Organizational evolution: A metamorphosis model of convergence and reorientation. In L. Cummings & B. Staw (Eds.), *Research in organizational behavior* (Vol. 7, pp. 177-222). Greenwich, CT: JAI.

Tushman, M. L., & Keck, S. (1990). *Environmental and organization context and executive team characteristics* (Working paper). New York: Columbia University.

Wagner, W. G., Pfeffer, J., & O'Reilly, C. A., III. (1984). Organizational demography and turnover in top management groups. *Administrative Science Quarterly, 29,* 74-92.

Watzlawick, P., Bavelas, J. B., & Jackson, D. D. (1967). *Pragmatics of human communication.* New York: Norton

Weick, K. E. (1979). *The social psychology of organizing.* Reading, MA: Addison-Wesley.

Zucker, L. G. (1977). The role of institutionalization in cultural persistence. *American Sociological Review, 42,* 726-743.

15

Collective Mind in Organizations

Heedful Interrelating on Flight Decks

KARL E. WEICK

KARLENE H. ROBERTS

The concept of collective mind is developed to explain organizational performance in situations requiring nearly continuous operational reliability. Collective mind is conceptualized as a pattern of heedful interrelations of actions in a social system. Actors in the system construct their actions (contributions), understanding that the system consists of connected actions by themselves and others (representation), and interrelate their actions within the system (subordination). Ongoing variation in the heed with which individual contributions, representations, and subordinations are interrelated influences comprehension of unfolding events and the incidence of errors. As heedful interrelating and mindful comprehension increase, organizational errors decrease. Flight operations on aircraft carriers exemplify the constructs presented. Implications for organization theory and practice are drawn.

Some organizations require nearly error-free operations all the time because otherwise they are capable of experiencing catastrophes. One such organization is an aircraft carrier, which an informant in Rochlin, LaPorte, and Roberts's (1987) study described as follows:

This chapter appeared originally in *Administrative Science Quarterly,* Vol. 38, 1993. Copyright © 1993 by Cornell University.

. . . imagine that it's a busy day, and you shrink San Francisco Airport to only one short runway and one ramp and one gate. Make planes take off and land at the same time, at half the present time interval, rock the runway from side to side, and require that everyone who leaves in the morning returns that same day. Make sure the equipment is so close to the edge of the envelope that it's fragile. Then turn off the radar to avoid detection, impose strict controls on radios, fuel the aircraft in place with their engines running, put an enemy in the air, and scatter live bombs and rockets around. Now wet the whole thing down with sea water and oil, and man it with 20-year-olds, half of whom have never seen an airplane close-up. Oh and by the way, try not to kill anyone. (p. 78)

Even though carriers represent "a million accidents waiting to happen" (Wilson, 1986, p. 21), almost none of them do. Here, we examine why not. The explanation we wish to explore is that organizations concerned with reliability enact aggregate mental processes that are more fully developed than those found in organizations concerned with efficiency. By fully developed mental processes, we mean that organizations preoccupied with reliability may spend more time and effort organizing for controlled information processing (Schneider & Shiffrin, 1977), mindful attention (Langer, 1989), and heedful action (Ryle, 1949). These intensified efforts enable people to understand more of the complexity they face, which then enables them to respond with fewer errors. Reliable systems are smart systems.

Before we can test this line of reasoning we need to develop a language of organizational mind that enables us to describe collective mental processes in organizations. In developing it, we move back and forth between concepts of mind and details of reliable performance in flight operations on a modern super carrier.[1] We use flight operations to illustrate organizational mind for a number of reasons: The technology is relatively simple, the coordination among activities is explicit and visible, the socialization is continuous, agents working alone have less grasp of the entire system than they do when working together, the system is constructed of interdependent know-how, teams of people think on their feet and do the "right thing" in novel situations, and the consequences of any lapse in attention are swift and disabling. Because our efforts to understand deck operations got us thinking about the possibility that performance is mediated by collective mental processes, we use these operations to illustrate that thinking, but the processes of mind we discuss are presumed to be inherent in all organizations. What may vary across organizations is the felt need to develop these processes to more advanced levels.

THE IDEA OF GROUP MIND

Discussions of collective mental processes have been rare despite the fact that people claim to be studying "social" cognition (e.g., Schneider, 1991). The preoccupation with individual cognition has left organizational theorists ill-equipped to do much more with the so-called cognitive revolution than apply it to organizational concerns, one brain at a time. There are a few exceptions, however, and we introduce our own discussion of collective mind with a brief review of three recent attempts to engage the topic of group mind.

Wegner and his associates (Wegner, 1987; Wegner, Erber, & Raymond, 1991; Wegner, Giuliano, & Hertel, 1985) suggested that group mind may take the form of cognitive interdependence focused around memory processes. They argued that people in close relationships enact a single transactive memory system, complete with differentiated responsibility for remembering different portions of common experience. People know the locations rather than the details of common events and rely on one another to contribute missing details that cue their own retrieval. Transactive memory systems are integrated and differentiated structures in the sense that connected individuals often hold related information in different locations. When people trade lower-order, detailed, disparate information, they often discover higher-order themes, generalizations, and ideas that subsume these details. It is these integrations of disparate inputs that seem to embody the "magical transformation" that group mind theorists sought to understand (Wegner et al., 1985, p. 268). The important point Wegner contributes to our understanding of collective mental processes is that group mind is *not* indexed by within-group similarity of attitudes, understanding, or language, nor can it be understood without close attention to communications processes among group members (Wegner et al., 1985, pp. 254-255). Both of these lessons will be evident in our reformulation.

Work in artificial intelligence provides the backdrop for two additional attempts to conceptualize group mind: Sandelands and Stablein's (1987) description of organizations as mental entitles capable of thought and Hutchins's (1990, 1991) description of organizations as distributed information processing systems. The relevant ideas are associated with theories of "connectionism," embodied in so-called "neural networks." Despite claims that their work is grounded in the brain's microanatomy, connectionists repeatedly refer to "neurological plausibility" (Quinlan, 1991, p. 41), "neuron-like units" (Churchland, 1992, p. 32), "brain-style processing" (Rumelhart, 1992, p. 69) or "neural inspiration" (Boden, 1990, p. 18). This qualification is warranted because the "neural" networks examined by connectionists are simply computational models that involve synchronous parallel processing among many interrelated unreliable and/or simple processing units (Quinlan, 1991, p. 40). The basic idea is that knowledge in very large networks of very simple processing units resides in patterns of connections, not in individuated local symbols. As Boden (1990) explained, any "unit's activity is regulated by the activity of neighboring units, connected to it by inhibitory or excitatory links whose strength can vary according to design and/or learning" (p. 14). Thus, any one unit can represent several different concepts, and the same concept in a different context may activate a slightly different network of units.

Connectionism by itself, however, is a shaky basis on which to erect a theory of organizational mind. The framework remains grounded in a device that models a single, relatively tightly coupled actor as opposed to a loosely coupled system of multiple actors, such as an organization. Connectionists have difficulty simulating emotion and motivation (Dreyfus & Dreyfus, 1990), as well as everyday thought and reasoning (Rumelhart, 1992). In computational models there is no turnover of units akin to that found in organizations, where units are replaced or moved to other locations. And the inputs connectionists investigate are relatively simple items such as numerals, words, or phrases, with the outputs being more or less accurate renderings of these inputs (e.g., Elman, 1992). This contrasts with organizational researchers who pay more attention to complex inputs, such as traditional competitors who make overtures to cooperate, and to outputs that consist of action as well as thought.

What connectionism contributes to organizational theory is the insight that complex patterns can be encoded by patterns of activation and inhibition among simple units, if those units are richly connected. This means that relatively simple actors may be able to apprehend complex inputs if they are organized in ways that resemble neural networks. Connectionists also raise the possibility that mind is "located" in connections and the weights put on them rather than in entities. Thus, to understand mind is to be attentive to process, relating, and method, as well as to structures and content.

Sandelands and Stablein (1987, pp. 139-141) found parallels between the organization of neurons in the brain and the organization of activities in organizations. They used this parallel to argue that connected activities encode concepts and ideas in organizations much like connected neurons encode concepts and ideas in brains. Ideas encoded in behaviors appear to interact in ways that suggest operations of intelligent processing. These parallels are consistent with the idea that organizations are minds. The important lessons from Sandelands and Stablein's analysis are that connections between behaviors, rather than people, may be the crucial "locus" for mind and that intelligence is to be found in patterns of behavior rather than in individual knowledge.

Hutchins (1990, 1991, p. 289) has used connectionist networks, such as the "constraint satisfaction network," to model how interpretations based on distributed cognitions are formed. These simulations are part of a larger inquiry into how teams coordinate action (1990) and the extent to which distributed processing amplifies or counteracts errors that form in individual units. Hutchins's analysis suggests that systems maintain the flexible, robust action associated with mindful performance if individuals have overlapping rather than mutually exclusive task knowledge. Overlapping knowledge allows for redundant representation that enables people to take responsibility for all parts of the process to which they can make a contribution (1990, p. 210).

The potential fit between connectionist imagery and organizational concepts can be inferred from Hutchins's (1990) description of coordination by mutual constraint in naval navigation teams:

> [The] sequence of action to be taken [in group performance] need not be explicitly represented anywhere in the system. If participants know how to coordinate their activities with the technologies and people with which they interact, the global structure of the task performance will emerge from the local interactions of the members. The structure of the activities of the group is determined by a set of local computations rather than by the implementation of the sort of global plan that appears in the solo performer's procedure. In the team situation, a set of behavioral dependencies are set up. These dependencies shape the behavior pattern of the group. (p. 209)

The lessons we use from Hutchins's work include the importance of redundant representation, the emergence of global structure from local interactions, and behavioral dependencies as the substrate of distributed processing.

Our own attempt to describe group mind has been informed by these three sources but is based on a different set of assumptions. We pay more attention to the form of connections than to the strength of connections and more attention to mind as activity than to mind as entity. To make this shift in emphasis clear, we avoid the phrases "group mind" and "organizational mind" in favor of the phrase "collective mind." The word "collective," unlike the words "group" or "organization," refers to individuals who act as if they are a group. People who act as if they are a group interrelate their actions with more or less care, and focusing on the way this interrelating is done reveals collective mental processes that differ in their degree of development. Our focus is at once on individuals and the collective, since only individuals can contribute to a collective mind, but a collective mind is distinct from an individual mind because it inheres in the pattern of interrelated activities among many people.

We begin the discussion of collective mind by following the lead of Ryle (1949) and developing the concept of mind as a disposition to act with heed. We then follow the lead of Asch (1952) and develop the concept of collective interrelating as contributing, representing, and subordinating, and illustrate these activities with examples from carrier operations. We next combine the notions of heed and interrelating into the concept of collective mind as heedful interrelating and suggest social processes that may account for variations in heedful interrelating. Finally, we describe three examples of heedful interrelating, two from carrier operations and one from the laboratory, and present an extended example of heedless interrelating that resulted in a $38-million accident.

MIND AS DISPOSITION TO HEED

"Mind" is a noun similar to nouns like faith, hope, charity, role, and culture. "Mind" is not the name of a person, place, or thing but, rather, is a dispositional term that denotes a propensity to act in a certain manner or style. As Ryle (1949) said,

> The statement "the mind is its own place," as theorists might construe it, is not true, for the mind is not even a metaphorical "place." On the contrary, the chessboard, the platform, the scholar's desk, the judge's bench, the lorry-driver's seat, the studio and the football field are among its places. These are where people work and play stupidly or intelligently. (p. 51)

That mind is actualized in patterns of behavior that can range from stupid to intelligent can be seen in the example Ryle (1949) used of a clown who trips and stumbles just as clumsy people do. What's different is that "he trips and stumbles on purpose and after much rehearsal and at the golden moment and where the children can see him and so as not to hurt himself" (p. 33). When a clown trips artfully, people applaud the style of the action, the fact that tripping is done with care, judgment, wit, and appreciation of the mood of the spectators. In short, the tripping is done with heed. Heed is not itself a behavior but it refers to the way behaviors such as tripping, falling, and recovering are assembled. Artful tripping is called heedful, not so much because the tripping involves action preceded by thought but because the behaviors patterned into the action of tripping suggest to the observer qualities such as "noticing, taking care, attending, applying one's mind, concentrating, putting one's heart into something, thinking what one is doing, alertness, interest, intentness, studying, and trying" (p. 136). These inferences, based on the style of the action, are called "heed concepts" and support the conclusion that the behaviors were combined intelligently rather than stupidly.

The word "heed" captures an important set of qualities of mind that elude the more stark vocabulary of cognition. These nuances of heed are especially appropriate to our interest in systems preoccupied with failure-free performance. People act heedfully when they act more or less carefully, critically, consistently, purposefully, attentively, studiously, vigilantly, conscientiously, pertinaciously (Ryle, 1949, p. 151). Heed adverbs attach qualities of mind directly to performances, as in the description, "the airboss monitored the pilot's growing load of tasks attentively." Notice that the statement does not say that the airboss was doing two things, monitoring and also checking to be sure that the monitoring was done carefully. Instead, the statement asserts that, having been coached to monitor carefully, his present monitoring reflects this style. Mind is in the monitoring itself, not in some separate episode of theorizing about monitoring.

Heedful performance is not the same thing as habitual performance. In habitual action, each performance is a replica of its predecessor, whereas in heedful performance each action is modified by its predecessor (Ryle, 1949, p. 42). In heedful performance, the agent is still learning. Furthermore, heedful performance is the outcome of training and experience that weave together thinking, feeling, and willing. Habitual performance is the outcome of drill and repetition.

When heed declines, performance is said to be heedless, careless, unmindful, thoughtless, unconcerned, indifferent. Heedless performance suggests a failure of intelligence rather than a failure of knowledge. It is a failure to see, to take note of, to be attentive to. Heedless performance is not about ignorance, cognition (Lyons, 1980, p. 57), and facts. It is about stupidity, competence, and know-how. Thus, mind refers to stretches of human behavior that exhibit qualities of intellect and character (Ryle, 1949, p. 126).

Group as Interrelated Activity

Ryle's (1949) ideas focus on individual mind. To extend his ideas to groups, we first have to specify the crucial performances in groups that could reflect a disposition to heed. To pinpoint these crucial performances, we derive four defining properties of group performance from Asch's (1952, pp. 251-255) discussion of "mutually shared fields" and illustrate these properties with carrier examples.[2]

The first defining property of group performance is that individuals create the social forces of group life when they act as if there were such forces. As Asch (1952) explained it,

We must see group phenomena as both *the product and condition* of actions of individuals. . . . There are no forces between individuals as organisms; yet to all intents and purposes they act as if there were, and they actually create social forces. Group action achieves the kind of result that would be understandable if all participants were acting under the direction of a single organizing center. No such center exists: between individuals is a hiatus, which nevertheless, they succeed in overcoming with surprising effectiveness. (p. 251)

An example from carriers occurs during flight operations. The men in the tower (Air Department) monitor and give instructions to incoming and departing aircraft. Simultaneously, the men on the landing signal officers' platform do the same thing. They are backed up by the men in Air Operations who monitor and instruct aircraft at some distance from the ship. From the aviator's viewpoint, he receives integrated information about his current status and future behavior from an integrated source when, in reality, the several sources are relatively independent of one another and located in different parts of the ship.

The second defining property of group performance is that when people act as if there are social forces, they construct their actions (contribute) while envisaging a social system of joint actions (represent), and interrelate that constructed action with the system that is envisaged (subordinate). Asch (1952) explained this as follows:

There are group actions that are possible only when each participant has a representation that includes the actions of others and their relations. The respective actions converge relevantly, assist and supplement each other only when the joint situation is represented in each and when the representations are structurally similar. Only when these conditions are given can individuals subordinate themselves to the requirements of joint action. These representations and the actions that they initiate/bring group facts into existence and produce the phenomenal solidity of group process. (pp. 251-252)

The simultaneous envisaging and interrelating that create a system occur when a pilot taxies onto the catapult for launching, is attached to it, and advances his engines to full power. Even though pilots have to rely on the catapult crew, they remain vigilant to see if representations are similar. Pilots keep asking themselves questions like, "Does it feel right?" or "Is the rhythm wrong?" The referent for the question, "Does *it* feel right?" however, is not the aircraft but the joint situation to which he has subordinated himself. If a person on the deck signals the pilot to reduce his engines from full power, he won't do so until someone stands in front of the plane, directly over the catapult, and signals for a reduction in power. Only then is the pilot reasonably certain that the joint situation has changed. He now trusts that the catapult won't be triggered suddenly and fling his underpowered aircraft into a person and then into the ocean.

The third defining property of group performance is that contributing, representing, and subordinating create a joint situation of interrelations among activities, which Asch (1952) referred to as a system:

> When these conditions are given we have a social system or a process of a definite form that embraces the actions of a number of individuals. Such a system does not reside in the individuals taken separately, though each individual contributes to it; nor does it reside outside them; it is present in the interrelations between the activities of individuals. (p. 252)

An example from carriers is a pilot landing an aircraft on a deck. This is not a solitary act. A pilot doesn't really land; he is "recovered." And recovery is a set of interrelated activities among air traffic controllers, landing signal officers, the control tower, navigators, deck hands, the helmsman driving the ship, etc. As the recovery of a single aircraft nears completion in the form of a successful trap, nine to ten people on the landing signal officer's platform, up to 15 more people in the tower, and two to three more people on the bridge observe the recovery and can wave the aircraft off if there is a problem. While this can be understood as an example of redundancy, it can also be interpreted as activities that can be interrelated more or less adequately, depending on the care with which contributing, representing, and subordinating are done.

The fourth and final defining property of group performance suggested by Asch (1952) is that the effects produced by a pattern of interrelated activities vary as a function of the style (e.g., heedful-heedless) as well as the strength (e.g., loose-tight) with which the activities are tied together. This is suggested by the statement that, in a system of interrelated activities, individuals can work with, for, or against each other:

> The form the interrelated actions take—on a team or in an office—is a datum of precisely the same kind as any other fact. One could say that all the facts of the system can be expressed as the sum of the actions of individuals. The statement is misleading however, if one fails to add that the individuals would not be capable of these particular actions unless they were responding to (or envisaging the possibility of) the system. Once the process described is in motion it is no longer the individual "as such" who determines its direction nor the group acting upon the individual as an external force, but individuals working with, for, or against each other. (p. 252)

It is these varying forms of interrelation that embody collective mind. An example of interrelating on carriers can be seen when ordnance is loaded onto an aircraft and its safety mechanisms are removed. If there is a sudden change of mission, the live ordnance must be disarmed, removed, and replaced by other ordnance that is now activated, all of this under enormous time pressure. These interrelated activities, even though tightly coupled, can become more or less dangerous depending on how the interrelating is done.

In one incident observed, senior officers kept changing the schedule of the next day's flight events through the night which necessitated a repeated change in ordnance up to the moment the day launches began. A petty officer changing bombs underneath an aircraft, where the pilot couldn't see him, lost a leg when the pilot moved the 36,000-pound aircraft over him. The petty officer should have tied the plane down before going underneath to change the load but failed to do so because there was insufficient time, a situation created by continual indecision at the top. Thus, the senior officers share the blame for this accident because they should have resolved their indecision in ways that were more mindful of the demands it placed on the system.

Although Asch (1952) argued that interrelated activities are the essence of groups, he said little about how these interrelations occur or how they vary over time. Instead, he treated interrelations as a variable and interrelating as a constant. If we treat interrelations as a variable and interrelating as a process, this suggests a way to conceptualize collective mind.

HEEDFUL INTERRELATING
AS COLLECTIVE MIND

The insights of Ryle (1949) and Asch (1952) can be combined into a concept of collective mind if we argue that dispositions toward heed are expressed in actions that construct interrelating. Contributing, representing, and subordinating actions that form a distinct pattern external to any given individual, become the medium through which collective mind is manifest. Variations in heedful interrelating correspond to variations in collective mind and comprehension.

We assume, as Follett (1924, pp. 146-153) did, that mind begins with actions, which we refer to here as contributions. The contributions of any one individual begin to actualize collective mind to the degree that heedful representation and heedful subordination define those contributions. A heedful contribution enacts collective mind as it begins to converge with, supplement, assist, and become defined in relation to the imagined requirements of joint action presumed to flow from some social activity system.

Similar conduct flows from other contributing individuals in the activity system toward others imagined to be in that system. These separate efforts vary in the heedfulness with which they interrelate, and these variations form a pattern. Since the object of these activities ("the envisaged system," to use Asch's, 1952, phrase) is itself being constituted as these activities become more or less interrelated, the emergent properties of this object are not contained fully in the representation of any one person nor are they finalized at any moment in time. A single emergent property may appear in more than one representation, but seldom in all. And different properties are shared in common by different subsets of people. Asch seems to have had this distributed representation of the envisaged system in mind when he referred to "structurally similar representations." This pattern of distributed representation explains the transindividual quality of collective mind. Portions of the envisaged system are known to all, but all of it is known to none.

The collective mind is "located" in the process of interrelating just as the individual mind for Ryle (1949) was "located" in the activities of lorry driving, chess playing, or article writing. Collective mind exists potentially as a kind of capacity in an ongoing activity stream and emerges in the style with which activities are interrelated. These patterns of interrelating are as close to a physical substrate for collective mind as we are likely to find. There is nothing mystical about all this. Collective mind is manifest when individuals construct mutually shared fields. The collective mind that emerges during the interrelating of an activity system is more developed and more capable of intelligent action the more heedfully that interrelating is done.

A crude way to represent the development of a collective mind is by means of a matrix in which the rows are people and the columns are either the larger activities of contributing, representing, and subordinating, or their component behaviors (e.g., converging with, assisting, or supplementing). Initially, the cell entries can be a simple "yes" or "no." "Yes" means a person performs that action heedfully, "no" means the action is done heedlessly. The more "yeses" in the matrix, the more developed the collective mind.

We portray collective mind in terms of method rather than content, structuring rather than structure, connecting rather than connections. Interrelations are not given but are constructed and reconstructed continually by individuals (Blumer, 1969, p. 110) through the ongoing activities of contributing, representing, and subordinating. Although these activities are done by individuals, their referent is a socially structured field. Individual activities are shaped by this envisioned field and are meaningless apart from it. When people make efforts to interrelate, these efforts can range from heedful to heedless. The more heed reflected in a pattern of interrelations, the more developed the collective mind and the greater the capability to comprehend unexpected events that evolve rapidly in unexpected ways. When we say that a collective mind "comprehends" unexpected events, we mean that heedful interrelating connects sufficient individual know-how to meet situational demands. For organizations concerned with reliability, those demands often consist of unexpected, nonsequential interactions among small failures that are hard to see and hard to believe. These incomprehensible failures often build quickly into catastrophes (Perrow, 1984, pp. 7-12, 22, 78, 88).

An increase in heedful interrelating can prevent or correct these failures of comprehension in at least three ways. First, longer stretches of time can be connected, as when more know-how is brought forward from the past and is elaborated into new contributions and representations that extrapolate farther into the future. Second, comprehension can be improved if more activities are connected, such as when interrelations span earlier and later stages of task sequences. And third, comprehension can be increased if more levels of experience are connected, as when newcomers who take nothing for granted interrelate more often with old-timers who think they have seen it all. Each of these three changes makes the pattern of interrelations more complex and better able to sense and regulate the complexity created by unexpected events. A system that is tied together more densely across time, activities, and experience comprehends more of what is occurring because the scope of heedful action reaches into more places: When heed is spread across more activities and more connections there should be more understanding and fewer errors. A collective mind that becomes more comprehensive, comprehends more.

Variations in Heed

If collective mind is embodied in the interrelating of social activities, and if collective mind is developed more or less fully depending on the amount of heedfulness with which that interrelating is done, we must address the issue of what accounts for variations in heed. We suspect the answer lies in Mead's (1934) insight that mind is "the individual importation of social process" (p. 186). We understand the phrase "social process" to mean a set of ongoing interactions in a social activity system from which participants continually extract a changing sense of self-interrelation and then re-enact that sense back into the system. This ongoing interaction process is recapitulated in individual lives and continues despite the replacement of people.

Mead (1934) stressed the reality of recapitulation, as did others. Ryle (1949), for example, observed that "this trick of talking to oneself in silence is acquired neither quickly nor without effort, and it is a necessary condition to our acquiring it that we should have previously learned to talk intelligently aloud and have heard and understood other people doing so. Keeping our thoughts to ourselves is a sophisticated accomplishment" (p. 27). Asch (1952) described the relationship between the individual and the group as the only part-whole relation in nature "that depends on recapitulation of the structure of the whole in the part" (p. 257). The same point is made by

Morgan (1986) and Hutchins (1990, p. 211), using the more recent imagery of holograms: System capacities that are relevant for the functioning of the whole are built into its parts. In each of these renderings, social processes are the prior resources from which individual mind, self, and action are fashioned (Mead, 1934, pp. 191-192). This means that collective mind precedes the individual mind and that heedful interrelating foreshadows heedful contributing.

Patterns of heedful interrelating in ongoing social processes may be internalized and recapitulated by individuals more or less adequately as they move in and out of the system. If heedful interrelating is visible, rewarded, modeled, discussed, and preserved in vivid stories, there is a good chance that newcomers will learn this style of responding, will incorporate it into their definition of who they are in the system, and will reaffirm and perhaps even augment this style as they act. To illustrate, Walsh and Ungson (1991) defined organization as a "network of intersubjectively shared meanings that are sustained through the development and use of a common language and everyday social interactions" (p. 60). Among the shared meanings and language on carriers we heard these four assertions: (1) If it's not written down you can do it; (2) Look for clouds in every silver lining; (3) Most positions on this deck were bought in blood; and (4) Never get into something you can't get out of. Each of these guidelines, if practiced openly, represents an image of heedful interrelating that can be internalized and acted back into the system. If such guidelines are neglected, ignored, or mocked, however, interrelating still goes on, but it is done with indifference and carelessness.

Whether heedful images survive or die depends importantly on interactions among those who differ in their experience with the system. While these interactions have been the focus of preliminary discussions of communities of practice (Lave & Wenger, 1991, pp. 98-100) involving apprentices and experts, we highlight a neglected portion of the process, namely, the effects of socialization on the insiders doing the socializing (Sutton & Louis, 1987).

When experienced insiders answer the questions of inexperienced newcomers, the insiders themselves are often resocialized. This is significant because it may remind insiders how to act heedfully and how to talk about heedful action. Newcomers are often a pretext for insiders to reconstruct what they knew but forgot. Heedful know-how becomes more salient and more differentiated when insiders see what they say to newcomers and discover that they thought more thoughts than they thought they did.

Whether collective mind gets renewed during resocialization may be determined largely by the candor and narrative skills of insiders and the attentiveness of newcomers. Candid insiders who use memorable stories to describe failures as well as successes, their doubts as well as their certainties, and what works as well as what fails, help newcomers infer dispositions of heed and carelessness. Insiders who narrate richly also often remind themselves of forgotten details when they reconstruct a previous event. And these reminders increase the substance of mind because they increase the number of examples of heed in work.

Narrative skills (Bruner, 1986; Orr, 1990; Weick & Browning, 1986) are important for collective mind because stories organize know-how, tacit knowledge, nuance, sequence, multiple causation, means-end relations, and consequences into a memorable plot. The ease with which a single story integrates diverse themes of heed in action foreshadows the capability of individuals to do the same. A coherent story of heed is mind writ small. And a repertoire of war stories, which grows larger through the memorable exercise of heed in novel settings, is mind writ large.

The quality of collective mind is heavily dependent on the way insiders interact with newcomers (Van Maanen, 1976). If insiders are taciturn, indifferent, preoccupied, available only in stylized performances, less than candid, or simply not available at all, newcomers are in danger of acting without heed because they have only banal conversations to internalize. They have learned little about heedful interdependence. When these newcomers act and try to anticipate the contributions of others, their actions will be stupid, and mistakes will happen. These mistakes may represent small failures that produce learning (Sitkin, 1992). More ominous is the possibility that these mistakes may also represent a weakening of system capacity for heedful responding. When there is a loss of particulars about how heed can be expressed in representation and subordination, reliable performance suffers. As seasoned people become more peripheral to socialization, there should be a higher incidence of serious accidents.

We have dwelt on insider participation simply because this participation is a conspicuous phenomenon that allows us to describe collective mind, but anything that changes the ongoing interaction (e.g., preoccupation with personalities rather than with the task) can also change the capability of that interaction to preserve and convey dispositions of heed. Those changes in turn should affect the quality of mind, the likelihood of comprehension, and the incidence of error.

ILLUSTRATIONS OF
HEED IN INTERRELATING

The concepts of heed, interrelating, contributing, representing, subordinating, intelligent action, comprehension, recapitulation, and resocialization come together in the concept of collective mind as heedful interrelating. Applying the language of collective mind to four examples of complex systems, we illustrate the adequate comprehension produced by heedful interrelating and the problematic comprehension produced by heedless interrelating.

Heedful Interrelating

The first example of interrelating that is heedful involves a laboratory analogue of collective mind (Weick & Gilfillan, 1971). Three people who can neither see nor talk with one another are given target numbers between 1 and 30. Whenever a target number is announced, each person is to contribute some number between 0 and 10 such that, when all three contributions are added together, they sum to the target number.

There are many ways to solve this problem (e.g., a target number of 13 can be achieved with a 3s strategy, 4-4-5, or a 10s strategy, 10-3-0). Once a group evolves a strategy, people are removed one at a time, and strangers, who know nothing of the strategy in use, enter. The questions are, how do old-timers interrelate with newcomers, what strategy emerges, how soon does it emerge, and how stable is it?

Austere as these operations are, they have the rudiments of a collective mind. A newcomer knows a number of things: (1) There are others in the activity system but they must be envisioned, since it is impossible to communicate with them (representation); (2) the two other people have had some experience with the system and with the game (there are imagined requirements to which one must subordinate); (3) each contribution is important and must interrelate with the others (contributions must converge, supplement, assist, and be defined in relation to one another); (4) to learn the existing system or to create a new one requires attention, careful calculations, and clear signals of intent (heedful contribution, representation, and subordination); and, (5) casual, indifferent interrelating will not be punished severely, because people are anonymous, and the rewards for participation are trivial (heedless responding is an option).

Just as the newcomers know these things, so do the old-timers. When these three people try to work out and maintain a system that hits each target on the first try, they are attempting to interrelate. They contribute, represent, and subordinate with varying amounts of heed. Their interrelating is better able to distinguish a mistake from an intentional effort to change strategy the more heedfully it was assembled. Likewise, heedful interrelating can "read" a newcomer's intentions quickly, whereas heedless interrelating cannot. These discriminations are not accomplished by single individuals but are accomplished by interrelated activities and the heedfulness with which those activities are defined in relation to one another. Heedful action at any one of these three positions can be undermined if it is not reciprocated at the other two. What is undermined, however, is a pattern of interrelations, not a person. A pattern of nonreciprocated heedfulness represents a loss of intelligence that is reflected in missed targets and slow change.

Heedful interrelating on carriers looks a lot like the pattern of interrelating seen in the common-target game. A vivid example of this similarity is Gillcrist's (1990) account of what it feels like to land and taxi on a carrier deck at night. Having successfully trapped onto the deck, Gillcrist watched the flight director's two amber wands:

> I raised the hook handle with my right hand and simultaneously added a lot of power to get the Crusader moving forward. There was an urgency in the taxi signal movement of the wands, telling me that there must be another plane close behind me in the groove. They wanted to get my airplane completely across the foul line as quickly as possible. Taxiing at night was more carefully done than in the light of day, however. We'd had enough airplanes taxi over the side at night to learn that lesson. . . . The wands pointed to another set of wands further up the flight deck and I began to follow their direction as my F-8 was taxied all the way to the first spot or the bow. "God, how I hate this," I muttered to myself. "Do they really have to do this or are they just trying to scare me?" In spotting me in the first taxi spot on the bow, the taxi director was turning the F-8 so close to the edge of the flight deck that the cockpit actually swung in an arc over the deck's edge. All I could see was black rushing water eighty feet below. "Jesus" I said to myself, "I hope that guy knows what he is doing." (pp. 287-288)

The taxi director does know what he is doing, as does the pilot, but that alone does not keep the plane from dropping off the deck. The interrelating of their know-how keeps the plane on the deck. A command from the director that is not executed by the pilot or a pilot deviation that is not corrected by the director are equally dangerous and not controllable by either party alone. The activities of taxiing and directing remain failure-free to the extent that they are interrelated heedfully.

A third example of heedful interrelating is of special interest because so much of it appears to involve the mind of one individual, in this case, the person responsible for deck operations (the bos'n). One of the people in this position who was interviewed had 23 years of experience on 16 carriers. At the time he joined this carrier's crew, it took six hours to spot 45 aircraft on the deck. He reduced that time to two hours and 45 minutes, which gave his crew more time to relax and maintain their alertness.

This person tries constantly to prevent the four worst things that can happen on a deck: It catches fire, becomes fouled, locked (nothing can move), or a plane is immobilized in the landing area. The more times a plane is moved to prevent any of these conditions, the higher the probability that it will brush against another plane ("crunch"), be damaged, and be out of service until repaired.

This bos'n, who is responsible for the smooth functioning of deck operations, gets up an hour early each day just to think about the kind of environment he will create on the deck that day, given the schedule of operations. This thinking is individual mind at work, but it also illustrates how collective mind is represented in the head of one person. The bos'n is dealing with collective mind when he represents the capabilities and weaknesses of imagined crewmembers' responses in his thinking, when he tailors sequences of activities so that improvisation and flexible response are activated as an expected part of the day's adaptive response, and when he counts on the interrelations among crewmembers themselves to "mind" the day's activities.

The bos'n does not plan specific step-by-step operations but, rather, plans which crews will do the planning and deciding, when, and with what resources at hand. The system will decide the operations, and the bos'n sets up the system that will do this. The bos'n does this by attempting to recognize the strengths and weaknesses of the various crews working for him. The pieces of the system he sets up may interrelate stupidly or intelligently, in large part because they will either duplicate or undermine the heedful contributing, representing, and subordinating he anticipates.

Heedless Interrelating

When interrelating breaks down, individuals represent others in the system in less detail, contributions are shaped less by anticipated responses, and the boundaries of the envisaged system are drawn more narrowly, with the result that subordination becomes meaningless. Attention is focused on the local situation rather than the joint situation. People still may act heedfully, but not with respect to others. Interrelating becomes careless. Key people and activities are overlooked. As interrelating deteriorates and becomes more primitive, there is less comprehension of the implications of unfolding events, slower correction of errors, and more opportunities for small errors to combine and amplify. When these events are set in motion and sustained through heedless interrelating, there is a greater chance that small lapses can enlarge into disasters.

An incident that happened during a nighttime launch and recovery, which was described to us in interviews and correspondence, illustrates the steady loss of collective mind as interrelating became less heedful. This incident began to unfold during a night launch in which one-third of the planes in the mission were still on deck waiting to be launched, even though other planes were already beginning to be recovered.

Aircraft A, which was in the air and the fourth plane in line to land, had an apparent hydraulic failure, although the pilot was able to get his gear and tail hook down. This failure meant that if the plane were landed, its wings could not be folded, and it would take up twice the space normally allotted to it. This complicates the landing of all planes behind it.

While the pilot of plane A was trying to get help for his problem on a radio channel, plane B, an F-14, which was number three in order of landing, had a compound hydraulic failure, and none of his back-up hydraulic systems appeared to work, something that was unheard of. Plane C, which was fifth in line to land, then developed a control problem. Thus, the airboss was faced, first, with several A-7 aircraft that still had to be launched. This is not a trivial complication, because the only catapult available for these aircraft was the one whose blast-deflector panel extends part way into the area where planes land. Second, the airboss had a string of planes about to land that included (1) a normally operating A-7, (2) a normally operating A-7, (3) plane B with a compound hydraulic failure, (4) plane A with a hydraulic failure but gear and tail hook down, and (5) plane C with an apparent control problem.

The first plane was taken out of the landing pattern and the second was landed. Plane B, the one with the most severe problems, was told to land and then had to be waved off because the person operating the deflector panel for launches lowered the panel one second too late to allow B to land. The deflector operator had not been informed that an emergency existed. Plane B and its increasingly frightened pilot were reinserted into the landing pattern behind plane C for a second pass at the deck. Plane B then experienced an additional hydraulic failure. Plane A landed without incident, as did plane C. Plane C had corrected its control problem, but no one was informed. Thus, plane B's second pass was delayed longer than necessary because he had to wait for C to land in the mistaken belief that C still had a problem. The pilot of plane B became increasingly agitated and less and less able to help diagnose what might be wrong with his aircraft. The decision was made to send plane B to a land base, but it ran out of fuel on the way and the pilot and his RIO (radar intercept officer) had to eject. Both were rescued, but a $38-million aircraft was lost. If aircraft B had not been waved off the first time it tried to land, it would have been safely recovered. If we analyze this incident as a loss of collective mind produced by heedless interrelating, we look for two things: events that became incomprehensible, signifying a loss of mind, and increasingly heedless interrelating.

There were several events that became harder to comprehend. The failure of the hydraulic system in aircraft B was puzzling. The triggering of additional hydraulic failures was even more so. To have three of five aircraft on final approach declare emergencies was itself something that was hard to comprehend, as was the problem of how to recover three disabled planes while launching three more immediately.

Incomprehensible events made interrelating more difficult, which then made the events even harder to comprehend. The loss of heed in interrelating was spread among contributions, representations, and subordinations. The squadron representative who tried to deal with the stressed pilot in plane B was not himself a pilot (he was an RIO), and he did not scan systematically for possible sources of the problem. Instead, he simply told the pilot assorted things to try, not realizing that, in the pilot's doing so, additional systems on the plane began to fail. He didn't realize these growing complications because the pilot was both imprecise in his reports of trouble and slow to describe what happened when he tested some hypothesis proposed by the representative. And the representative did nothing to change the pilot's style of contributing.

But heedless interrelating was not confined to exchanges between pilot and representative. The RIO in plane B made no effort to calm the pilot or help him diagnose. The deflector operator was not treated as a person in the *recovery* system. Three different problems were discussed on two radio frequencies, which made it difficult to sort out which plane had which problem. No one seemed to register that the squadron representative was himself getting farther behind and making increasingly heedless contributions. The airboss in command of the tower was an F-14 pilot, but he was preoccupied with the five incoming and the three outgoing aircraft and could not be pulled completely into the activity system that was dealing with the F-14 problem. As heed began to be withdrawn from the system, activities and people became isolated, the system began to pull apart, the problems became more incomprehensible, and it became harder for individuals to interrelate with a system of activities that was rapidly losing its form. The pattern of interrelated activities lost intelligence and mind as contributions became more thoughtless and less interdependent.

Had the pattern of interrelations been more heedful, it might have detected what was subsequently said to be the most likely cause of the failures in plane B. Although the aircraft was never recovered, the navy's investigation of the incident concluded that too many demands were placed on the emergency back-up systems, and the plane became less and less flyable. Sustained heedful interrelating might well have registered that the growing number of attempted solutions had in fact created a new problem that was worse than any problem that was present to begin with.[3]

It is important to realize that our analysis, using the concepts of collective mind and heedful interrelating, implies something more than the simple advice, "be careful." People can't be careful unless they take account of others and unless others do the same. Being careful is a social rather than a solitary act. To act with care, people have to envision their contributions in the context of requirements for joint action. Furthermore, to act with care does not mean that one plans how to do this and then applies the plan to the action. Care is not cultivated apart from action. It is expressed in action and through action. Thus people can't *be* careful, they *are* careful (or careless). The care is in the action.

The preceding analysis also suggests that it is crucial to pay attention to mind, because accidents are not just issues of ignorance and cognition, they are issues of inattention and conduct as well. The examples of incomprehension mentioned above are not simply issues of fact and thinking. Facts by themselves are of no help if they cannot be communicated or heard or applied or interpreted or incorporated into activities or placed in contexts, in short, if they are not addressed mindfully. One "fact" of this incident is that plane B could have landed had it not been waved off because of the extended deflector. Furthermore, individuals within the system were not ignorant of crucial details (e.g., the pilot of plane C knew he no longer had a problem).

One interpretation of this incident is that individuals were smarter than the system, but the problem was more complex than any one individual could understand. Heedful interrelating of activities constructs a substrate that is more complex and, therefore, better able to comprehend complex events than is true for smart but isolated individuals. The F-14 may have been lost because heedful interrelating was lost. Heightened attentiveness to social process might have prevented both losses.

DISCUSSION

We conclude from our analysis that carrier operations are a struggle for alertness and that the concept of heedful interrelating helps capture this struggle. We began with the question, How can we analyze a complex social activity system in which fluctuations in comprehension seem to be consequential? We focused on heed (understood as dispositions to act with attentiveness, alertness, and care), conduct (understood as behavior that takes into account the expectations of others), and mind (understood as integration of feeling, thinking, and willing).

We were able to talk about group mind without reification, because we grounded our ideas in individual actions and then treated those actions as the means by which a distinct higher-order pattern of interrelated activities emerged. This pattern shaped the actions that produced it, persisted despite changes in personnel, and changed despite unchanging personnel. Thus, we did not reify social entities because we argued that they emerge from individual actions that construct interrelations. But neither did we reify individual entities, because we argued that they emerge through selective importation, interpretation, and re-enactment of the social order that they constitute.

In broadening our focus, we conceptualized mind as action that constructs mental processes rather than as mental processes that construct action. We proposed that variations in contributing, representing, and subordinating produce collective mind. Common hallmarks of mind such as alertness, attentiveness, understanding, and relating to the world were treated as coincident with and immanent in the connecting activities. To connect *is* to mind.

For the collective mind, the connections that matter are those that link distributed activities, and the ways those connections are accomplished embody much of what we have come to mean by the word "mind." The ways people connect their activities make conduct mindful. Mindless actions ignore interrelating or accomplish it haphazardly and with indifference (Bellah, Madsen, Sullivan, Swidler, & Tipton, 1991).

As a result of our analysis, we now see the importance of disentangling the development of mind from the development of a group. In Asch's (1952) description of the essence of group life, as well as in other discussions of group cognition, the development of mind is confounded with the development of the group. As a group matures and moves from inclusion through control to affection (Schutz, 1958), or as it moves from forming through storming, norming, and performing (Tuckman, 1965), both interrelating and intimacy develop jointly. If a mature group has few accidents or an immature group has many, it is difficult to see what role, if any, mind may play in this. An immature group of relative strangers with few shared norms, minimal disclosure, and formal relationships might well find it hard to cope with nonroutine events. But this has nothing to do with mind.

In our analysis we have assumed that there is something like a two-by-two matrix in which a group can be developed or undeveloped and a collective mind can be developed or undeveloped. And we assume that the combinations of developed-group-undeveloped mind and undeveloped-group-developed mind are possible. These two combinations are crucial to any proposal that collective mind is a distinct process in social life.

The combination of developed-group-undeveloped mind is found in the phenomenon of groupthink (Janis, 1982), as well as in cults (Galanter, 1989), interactions at NASA prior to the *Challenger* disaster (Starbuck & Milliken, 1988), and ethnocentric research groups (Weick, 1983). Common among these examples is subordination to a system that is envisaged carelessly, or, as Janis (1982, p. 174) put it, there is an overestimation of the group's power, morality, and invulnerability. Furthermore, contributions are made thoughtlessly; as Janis (p. 175) put it, there is self-censorship of deviations, doubts, and counterarguments. And, finally, representations are careless; members maintain the false assumption that silence means consent (Janis, 1982, p. 175). In the presence of heedless interrelating, comprehension declines, regardless of how long the group has been together, and disasters result.

The combination of undeveloped-group-developed mind is found in ad hoc project teams, such as those that produce television specials (e.g., Peters, 1992, pp. 189-200) or motion pictures (Faulkner & Anderson, 1987), and in temporary systems such as those that form in aircraft cockpits (Ginnett, 1990), around jazz improvisation (Eisenberg, 1990), in response to crises (Rochlin, 1989), or in high-velocity environments (Eisenhardt, 1993). The common feature shared among these diverse settings is best captured by Eisenberg (1990), who characterized them as built from nondisclosive intimacy that "stresses coordination of action over alignment of cognitions, mutual respect over agreement, trust over empathy, diversity over homogeneity, loose over tight coupling, and strategic communication over unrestricted candor" (p. 160).

Translated into the language of heedful interrelating, what Eisenberg (1990) depicted were relationships in which shared values, openness, and disclosure, all hallmarks of a developed group, were *not* fully developed, but in which collective mind was developed. Nondisclosive intimacy is characterized by heedful contributing (e.g., loose coupling, diversity, strategic communication), heedful representing (e.g., mutual respect, coordination of action), and heedful subordinating (e.g., trust).

If heedful interrelating can occur in an undeveloped group, this changes the way we think about the well-known stages of group development. If people are observed to contribute, represent, and subordinate with heed, these actions can be interpreted as operations that construct a well-developed collective mind; however, those same actions can also be seen as the orienting, clarifying, and testing associated with the early stages of a new group just beginning to form (McGrath, 1984, pp. 152-162). By one set of criteria, that associated with group formation, people engaged in forming are immature. By another set of criteria, that associated with collective mind, these acts of forming represent well-developed mental processes.

These opposed criteria suggest that groups may be smartest in their early stages. As they grow older, they lose mind when interrelating becomes more routine, more casual, more automatic. This line of reasoning is consistent with Gersick's (1988) demonstration that groups tend to re-form halfway through their history. In our language, this midcourse reshuffling can be understood as redoing the pattern of interrelations that constitute mind, thereby renewing mind itself. If groups steadily lose mind and comprehension as they age, their capability for comprehension may show a dramatic increase halfway through their history. If that is plausible, the sudden surge in comprehension should be accompanied by a sudden decrease in the number of accidents they produce.

The Conceptualization of
Topics in Organizational Theory

Our analysis of collective mind and heedful interrelating throws new light on several topics in organizational theory, including organizational types, the measurement of performance, and normal accidents.

The concept of mind may be an important tool in comparative analysis. LaPorte and Consolini (1991) argued that high-reliability organizations such as aircraft carriers differ in many ways from organizations usually portrayed in organizational theory as (for convenience) high-efficiency organizations. Typical efficiency organizations practice incremental decision making, their errors do not have a lethal edge, they use simple low-hazard technologies, they are governed by single rather than multilayered authority systems, they are more often in the private than the public sector, they are not preoccupied with perfection, their operations are carried on at one level of intensity, they experience few nasty surprises, and they can rely on computation or judgment as decision strategies (Thompson & Tuden, 1959) but seldom need to employ both at the same time. LaPorte and Consolini (1991) concluded that existing organizational theory is inadequate to understand systems in which the "consequences and costs associated with major failures in some technical operations are greater than the value of the lessons learned from them" (p. 19).

Our analysis suggests that most of these differences can be subsumed under the generalization that high-efficiency organizations have simpler minds than do high-reliability organizations. If dispositions toward individual and collective heed were increased in most organizations in conjunction with increases in task-related interdependence and flexibility in the sequencing of tasks, then we would expect these organizations to act more like high-reliability systems. Changes of precisely this kind seem to be inherent in recent interventions to improve total quality management (U.S. General Accounting Office, 1991).

Our point is simply that confounded in many comparisons among organizations that differ on conspicuous grounds such as structure and technology, are less conspicuous but potentially more powerful differences in the capability for collective mind. A smart system does the right thing regardless of its structure and regardless of whether the environment is stable or turbulent. We suspect that organic systems, because of their capacity to reconfigure themselves temporarily into more mechanistic structures, have more fully developed r.nds than do mechanistic systems.

We also suspect that newer organizational forms, such as networks (Powell, 1990), self-designing systems (Hedberg, Nystrom, & Starbuck, 1976), cognitive oligopolies (Porac, Thomas, & Baden-Fuller, 1989, p. 413), and interpretation systems (Daft & Weick, 1984) have more capacity for mind than do M forms, U forms, and matrix forms. But all of these conjectures, which flow from the idea of collective mind, require that we pay as much attention to social processes and microdynamics as we now pay to the statics of structure, strategy, and demographics.

The concept of mind also suggests a view of performance that complements concepts such as activities (Homans, 1950), the active task (Dornbusch & Scott, 1975), task structure (Hackman, 1990, p. 10), group task design (Hackman, 1987), and production functions (McGrath, 1990). It adds to all of these a concern with the style or manner of performance. Not only can performance be high or low, productive or unproductive, or adequate or inadequate, it can also be heedful or heedless. Heedful performance might or might not be judged productive, depending on how productivity is defined.

Most important, the concept of mind allows us to talk about careful versus careless performance, not just performance that is productive or unproductive. This shift makes it easier to talk about performance in systems in which the next careless error may be the last trial. The language of care is more suited to systems concerned with reliability than is the language of efficiency.

Much of the interest in organizations that are vulnerable to catastrophic accidents can be traced to Perrow's (1981) initial analysis of Three Mile Island, followed by his expansion of this analysis into other industries (Perrow, 1984). In the expanded analysis, Perrow suggested that technologies that are both tightly coupled and interactively complex are the most dangerous, because small events can escalate rapidly into a catastrophe. Nuclear aircraft carriers such as those we have studied are especially prone to normal accidents (see p. 97) because they comprise not one but several tightly coupled, interactively complex technologies. These include jet aircraft, nuclear weapons carried on aircraft, nuclear weapons stored on board the ship, and nuclear reactors used to power the ship. Furthermore, the marine navigation system and the air traffic control system on a ship are tightly coupled technologies, although they are slightly less complex than the nuclear technologies.

Despite their high potential for normal accidents, carriers are relatively safe. Our analysis suggests that one of the reasons carriers are safe is because of, not in spite of, tight coupling. Our analysis raises the possibility that technological tight coupling is dangerous in the presence of interactive complexity, unless it is mediated by a mutually shared field that is well developed. This mutually shared field, built from heedful interrelating, is itself tightly coupled, but this tight coupling is social rather than technical. We suspect that normal accidents represent a breakdown of social processes and comprehension rather than a failure of technology. Inadequate comprehension can be traced to flawed mind rather than flawed equipment.

The Conceptualization of Practice

The mindset for practice implicit in the preceding analysis has little room for heroic, autonomous individuals. A well-developed organization mind, capable of reliable performance is thoroughly social. It is built of ongoing interrelating and dense interrelations. Thus, interpersonal skills are not a luxury in high-reliability systems. They are a necessity. These skills enable people to represent and subordinate themselves to communities of practice. As people move toward individualism and fewer interconnections, organization mind is simplified and soon becomes indistinguishable from individual mind. With this change comes heightened vulnerability to accidents. Cockpit crews that function as individuals rather than teams show this rapid breakdown in ability to understand what is happening (Orlady & Foushee, 1987). Sustained success in coping with emergency conditions seems to occur when the activities of the crew are more fully interrelated and when members' contributions, representations, and subordination create a pattern of joint action. The chronic fear in high-reliability systems that events will prove to be incomprehensible (Perrow, 1984) may be a realistic fear only when social skills are underdeveloped. With more development of social skills goes more development of organization mind and heightened understanding of environments.

A different way to state the point that mind is dependent on social skills is to argue that it is easier for systems to lose mind than to gain it. A culture that encourages individualism, survival of the fittest, macho heroics, and can-do reactions will often neglect heedful practice of representation and subordination. Without representation and subordination, comprehension reverts to one brain at a time. No matter how visionary or smart or forward-looking or aggressive that one brain may be, it is no match for conditions of interactive complexity. Cooperation is imperative for the development of mind.

Reliable performance may require a well-developed collective mind in the form of a complex, attentive system tied together by trust. That prescription sounds simple enough. Nevertheless, conventional understanding seems to favor a different configuration: a simple, automatic system tied together by suspicion and redundancy. The latter scenario makes sense in a world in which individuals can comprehend what is going on. But when individual comprehension proves inadequate, one of the few remaining sources of comprehension is social entities. Variation in the development of these entities may spell the difference between prosperity and disaster.

Acknowledgments

We acknowledge with deep gratitude, generous and extensive help with previous versions of this manuscript from Sue Ashford, Michael Cohen, Dan Denison, Jane Dutton, Les Gasser, Joel Kahn, Rod Kramer, Peter Manning, Dave Meader, Debra Meyerson, Walter Nord, Linda Pike, Joe Porac, Bob Quinn, Lance Sandelands, Paul Schaffner, Howard Schwartz, Kathie Sutcliffe, Bob Sutton, Diane Vaughan, Jim Walsh, Rod White, Mayer Zald, and the anonymous reviewers for *Administrative Science Quarterly*.

NOTES

1. Unless otherwise cited, aircraft carrier examples are drawn from field observation notes of air operations and interviews aboard Nimitz class carriers made by the second author and others over a five-year period. Researchers spent from four days to three weeks aboard the carriers at any one time. They usually made observations from different vantage points during the evolutions of various events. Observations were entered into computer systems and later compared across observers and across organizational members for clarity of meaning. Examples are also drawn from quarterly workshop discussions with senior officers from those carriers over the two years. The primary observational research methodology was to triangulate observations made by three faculty researchers, as suggested by Glaser and Strauss (1967) and Eisenhardt (1989). The methodology is more fully discussed in Roberts, Stout, and Halpern (1993). Paper-and-pencil data were also collected and are discussed elsewhere (Roberts, Rousseau, & LaPorte, 1993). That research was supported by Office of Naval Research contract #N-00014-86-k-0312 and National Science Foundation grant #F7-08046.

2. We could just as easily have used Blumer's (1969, pp. 78-79) discussion of "the mutual alignment of action."

3. There is a limit to heedfulness, given the number and skill of participants, and on this night this ship was at that limit. The system was overloaded, and the situation was one that managers of high-technology weapons systems worry about all the time. They call it OBE (overcome by events). Given perhaps only minor differences in the situation, the outcomes might have been different. In this situation, for example, had the carrier air group commander come to the tower (which he often does), he would have added yet another set of eyes and ears, with their attendant skills. Perhaps he could have monitored one aspect of the situation while the boss and mini boss took charge of others, and the situation would have been a more heedful one. Had the squadron representative in the tower been a pilot, he might have searched through his own repertoire of things that can go wrong and helped the F-14's pilot calm down and solve his problem, increasing the heedfulness of the situation.

REFERENCES

Asch, S. E. (1952). *Social psychology.* Englewood Cliffs, NJ: Prentice Hall.

Bellah, R. N., Madsen, R., Sullivan, W. M., Swidler, A., & Tipton, S. M. (1991). *The good society.* New York: Knopf.

Blumer, H. (1969). *Symbolic interaction.* Berkeley: University of California Press.

Boden, M. A. (1990). Introduction. In M. A. Bode (Ed.), *The philosophy of artificial intelligence* (pp. 1-21). New York: Oxford University Press.

Bruner, J. (1986). *Actual minds. Possible worlds.* Cambridge, MA: Harvard University Press.

Churchland, P. M. (1992). A deeper unity: Some Feyerabendian themes in neurocomputational form. In S. Davis (Ed.), *Connectionism: Theory and practice* (pp. 30-50). New York: Oxford University Press.

Daft, R., & Weick, K. E. (1984). Toward a model of organizations as interpretation systems. *Academy of Management Review, 9,* 284-295.

Dornbusch, S. M., & Scott, W. R. (1975). *Evaluation and the exercise of authority.* San Francisco: Jossey-Bass.

Dreyfus, H. L., & Dreyfus, S. E. (1990). Making a mind versus modeling the brain: Artificial intelligence back at a branch point. In M. A. Boden (Ed.), *The philosophy of artificial intelligence* (pp. 309-333). New York: Oxford University Press.

Eisenberg, E. (1990). Jamming: Transcendence through organizing. *Communication Research 17,* 139-164.

Eisenhardt, K. M. (1989). Building theories from case study research. *Academy of Management Review, 14,* 532-550.

Eisenhardt, K. M. (1993). High reliability organizations meet high velocity environments: Common dilemmas in nuclear power plants, aircraft carriers, and microcomputer firms. In K. Roberts (Ed.), *New challenges to understanding organizations* (pp. 117-135). New York: Macmillan.

Elman, J. L. (1992). Grammatical structure and distributed representations. In S. Davis (Ed.), *Connectionism: Theory and practice* (pp. 138-178). New York: Oxford University Press.

Faulkner, R. R., & Anderson, A. B. (1987). Short-term projects and emergent careers: Evidence from Hollywood. *American Journal of Sociology, 92,* 879-909.

Follett, M. P. (1924). *Creative experience.* New York: Longmans, Green.

Galanter, M. (1989). *Cults.* New York: Oxford University Press.

Gersick, C. G. (1988). Time and transition in work teams: Toward a new model of group development. *Academy of Management Journal, 31,* 9-41.

Gillcrist, P. T. (1990). *Feet wet: Reflections of a carrier.* Novato, CA: Presidio Press.

Ginnett, R. C. (1990). Airline cockpit crew. In J. E. Hackman (Ed.), *Groups that work (and those that don't)* (pp. 427-444). San Francisco: Jossey-Bass.

Glaser, B., & Strauss, A. L. (1967). *The discovery of grounded theory: Strategies for qualitative research.* Chicago: Aldine.

Hackman, J. R. (1987). The design of work teams. In J. Lorsch (Ed.), *Handbook of organizational behavior* (pp. 315-342). Englewood Cliffs, NJ: Prentice Hall.

Hackman, J. R. (Ed.). (1990). *Groups that work (and those that don't).* San Francisco: Jossey-Bass.

Hedberg, B. L. T., Nystrom, P. C., & Starbuck, W. H. (1976). Camping on seesaws: Prescriptions for a self-designing organization. *Administrative Science Quarterly, 21,* 41-65.

Homans, G. C. (1950). *The human group.* New York: Harcourt Brace.

Hutchins, E. (1990). The technology of team navigation. In J. Galegher, R. E. Kraut, & C. Egido (Eds.), *Intellectual teamwork* (pp. 191-220). Hillsdale, NJ: Lawrence Erlbaum.

Hutchins, E. (1991). The social organization of distributed cognition. In L. B. Resnick, J. M. Levine, & S. D. Teasley (Eds.), *Perspectives on socially shared cognition* (pp. 293-307). Washington, DC: American Psychological Association.

Janis, I. (1982). *Groupthink* (2nd ed.). Boston: Houghton Mifflin.

Langer, E. J. (1989). Minding matters: The consequences of mindlessness-mindfulness. In L. Berkowitz (Ed.), *Advances in experimental social psychology* (pp. 137-173). New York: Academic Press.

LaPorte, T. R., & Consolini, P. M. (1991). Working in practice but not in theory: Theoretical challenges of high-reliability organizations. *Journal of Public Administration Research and Theory, 1,* 19-47.

Lave, J., & Wenger, E. (1991). *Situated learning: Legitimate peripheral participation.* New York: Cambridge University Press.

Lyons, W. (1980). *Gilbert Ryle: An introduction to his philosophy.* Atlantic Highlands, NJ: Humanities Press.

McGrath, J. E. (1984). *Groups: Interaction and performance.* Englewood Cliffs, NJ: Prentice Hall.

McGrath, J. E. (1990). Time matters in groups. In J. Galegher, R. E. Kraut, & C. Egido (Eds.), *Intellectual teamwork* (pp. 23-61). Hillsdale, NJ: Lawrence Erlbaum.

Mead, G. H. (1934). *Mind, self, and society.* Chicago: University of Chicago Press.

Morgan, G. (1986). *Images of organization.* Beverly Hills, CA: Sage.

Orlady, H. W., & Foushee, H. C. (1987). *Cockpit resource management training.* Springfield, VA: National Technical Information Service (N87-22634).

Orr, J. E. (1990). Sharing knowledge, celebrating identity: Community memory in a service culture. In D. Middleton & D. Edwards (Eds.), *Collective remembering* (pp. 169-189). Newbury Park, CA: Sage.

Perrow, C. (1981). The President's Commission and the normal accident. In D. Sills, C. Wolf, & V. Shelanski (Eds.), *The accident at Three Mile Island: The human dimensions* (pp. 173-184). Boulder, CO: Westview Press.

Perrow, C. (1984). *Normal accidents.* New York: Basic Books.

Peters, T. (1992). *Liberation management.* New York: Knopf.

Porac, J. F., Thomas, H., & Baden-Fuller, C. (1989). Competitive groups as cognitive communities: The case of Scottish knitwear manufacturers. *Journal of Management Studies, 26,* 397-416.

Powell, W. W. (1990). Neither market nor hierarchy: Network forms of organization. In B. M. Staw & L. L. Cummings (Eds.), *Research in organizational behavior* (pp. 295-336). Greenwich, CT: JAI.

Quinlan, P. (1991). *Connectionism and psychology.* Chicago: University of Chicago Press.

Roberts, K. H., Rousseau, D. M., & LaPorte, T. R. (1993). The culture of high reliability: Quantitative and qualitative assessment aboard nuclear powered aircraft carriers. *Journal of High Technology Management Research.*

Roberts, K. H., Stout, S., & Halpern, J. J. (1993). Decision dynamics in two high reliability military organizations. *Management Science.*

Rochlin, G. I., LaPorte, T. R., & Roberts, K. H. (1987). The self-designing high-reliability organization: Aircraft carrier flight operations at sea. *Naval War College Review, 40*(4), 76-90.

Rumelhart, D. E. (1992). Towards a microstructural account of human reasoning. In S. Davis (Ed.), *Connectionism: Theory and practice* (pp. 69-83). New York: Oxford University Press.

Ryle, G. (1949). *The concept of mind.* Chicago: University of Chicago Press.

Sandelands, L. E., & Stablein, R. E. (1987). The concept of organization mind. In S. Bacharach & N. DiTomaso (Eds.), *Research in the sociology of organizations* (pp. 135-161). Greenwich, CT: JAI.

Schneider, D. J. (1991). Social cognition. In L. W. Porter & M. R. Rosenzweig (Eds.), *Annual Review of Psychology, 42,* 527-561.

Schneider, W., & Shiffrin, R. M. (1977). Controlled and automatic human information processing: I. Detection, search and attention. *Psychological Review, 84,* 1-66.

Schutz, W. C. (1956). *FIRO: A three-dimensional theory of interpersonal behavior.* New York: Holt, Rinehart & Winston.

Sitkin, S. (1992). Learning through failure: The strategy of small losses. In B. Staw & L. Cummings (Eds.), *Research in organizational behavior* (pp. 231-266). Greenwich, CT: JAI.

Starbuck, W. H., & Milliken, F. J. (1988). Challenger: Fine-tuning the odds until something breaks. *Journal of Management Studies, 25,* 319-340.

Sutton, R. I., & Louis, M. R. (1987). How selecting and socializing newcomers influences insiders. *Human Resource Management, 26,* 347-361.

Thompson, J. D., & Tuden, A. (1959). Strategies, structures, and processes of organizational decision. In J. D. Thompson (Ed.), *Comparative studies in organization* (pp. 195-216). Pittsburgh: University of Pittsburgh Press.

Tuckman, B. W. (1965). Developmental sequence in small groups. *Psychological Bulletin, 63,* 384-399.

U.S. General Accounting Office. (1991). *Management practices: U.S. companies improve performance through quality efforts* (Document GAO/NSIAD-91-190). Washington, DC: Government Printing Office.

Van Maanen, J. (1976). Breaking in: Socialization to work. In R. Dubin (Ed.), *Handbook of work, organization and society* (pp. 67-130). Chicago: Rand McNally.

Walsh, J. P., & Ungson, G. R. (1991). Organizational memory. *Academy of Management Review, 16,* 57-91.

Wegner, D. M. (1987). Transactive memory: A contemporary analysis of the group mind. In B. Mullen & G. R. Goethals (Eds.), *Theories of group behavior* (pp. 185-208). New York: Springer-Verlag.

Wegner, D. M., Erber, R., & Raymond, P. (1991). Transactive memory in close relationships. *Journal of Personality and Social Psychology, 61,* 923-929.

Wegner, D. M., Giuliano, T., & Hertel, P. T. (1985). Cognitive interdependence in close relationships. In W. J. Ickes (Ed.), *Compatible and incompatible relationships* (pp. 253-276). New York: Springer-Verlag.

Weick, K. E. (1983). Contradictions in a community of scholars: The cohesion-accuracy tradeoff. *Review of Higher Education, 6*(4), 253-267.

Weick, K. E., & Browning, L. (1986). Arguments and narration in organizational communication. *Journal of Management, 12,* 243-259.

Weick, K. E., & Gilfillan, D. P. (1971). Fate of arbitrary traditions in a laboratory microculture. *Journal of Personality and Social Psychology, 17,* 179-191.

Wilson, G. C. (1986). *Supercarrier.* New York: Macmillan.

16

Technological Change and the Management of Architectural Knowledge

REBECCA M. HENDERSON

One of the most difficult and important challenges facing many modern organizations is the need to respond to seemingly ceaseless rapid technological change. Developments in computing technology, in new materials, in medicine, biotechnology, and a wide variety of other fields present firms in industries as diverse as banking, food, capital equipment, and packaged consumer goods with both major opportunities and significant threats.

Many of these developments present a particularly difficult challenge because they cannot be easily classified as either "radical" or "incremental" innovation. Both practicing managers and academic researchers have long accepted the idea that dramatic, radical technological change often creates very significant competitive problems for established firms, whereas more minor, incremental innovation often reinforces their skills and position. The research presented here focuses upon a class of innovations that are intermediate in character between the two—innovations that build upon much of the existing experience and capability of established organizations but that still have very significant competitive consequences. Consider, for example, the case of Xerox and the introduction of small copiers.

Xerox, the pioneer of plain-paper copiers, was confronted in the mid-1970s with competitors offering copiers that were much smaller and more reliable than the traditional product. The new products required little new

Selected passages of this chapter have been reprinted from *Transforming Education*, edited by Thomas A. Kochan and Michael Useem. Copyright © 1992 by The Sloan School of Management. Reprinted by permission of Oxford University Press, Inc.

scientific or engineering knowledge, but despite the fact that Xerox had invented the core technologies and had enormous experience in the industry, it took the company almost eight years of missteps and false starts to introduce a competitive product into the market. In that time Xerox lost half of its market share and suffered serious financial problems (Clark, 1987).

In a recent paper innovation (Henderson & Clark, 1990), Clark and I suggested that this type of innovation should be defined as "architectural." Architectural innovation changes a product's architecture, or the relationships between its components, but leaves the components, and the core design concepts that they embody, unchanged.

Architectural innovation often creates very significant problems for established firms because architectural knowledge is embedded in the implicit knowledge of the organization, particularly its communication channels, information filters, and problem solving strategies, so that its obsolescence is difficult to observe and to correct. This is the kind of innovation that confronted Xerox. It destroys the usefulness of a firm's architectural knowledge but preserves the usefulness of its knowledge about the product's components.

This chapter explores the usefulness of this idea for the understanding of organizational transformation. I begin by briefly summarizing the arguments and evidence presented earlier (Henderson & Clark, 1990). The concept of architectural innovation grew out of work in the semiconductor photolithographic alignment industry, an industry in which the established firms suffered sharp declines in market share following the introduction of equipment incorporating seemingly minor innovation.

I then explore the implications of the concept of architectural innovation for organizational transformation in general. I suggest that the distinction between component knowledge and architectural knowledge has general application beyond problems of product design, and that one of the recurrent themes addressed by the other chapters in this book is the need to rethink the structure of existing systems and to rebuild tacit organizational knowledge to reflect new environmental realities. I close by suggesting that many of the proposals for organizational transformation discussed in this book can be understood as proposals for the creation of organizations that explicitly manage architectural knowledge.

ARCHITECTURAL INNOVATION

To develop the concept of architectural innovation, I focus on the problem of product development, taking as my unit of analysis a manufactured

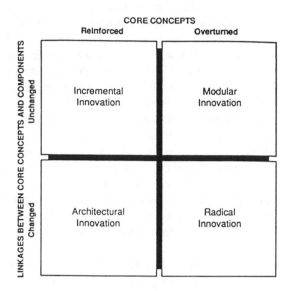

Figure 16.1. A Framework for Defining Innovation

product sold to an end user and designed, engineered, and manufactured by a single product-development organization. Such a product can be usefully understood as both the product as a whole—the system—and the product in its parts—the components. This distinction has a long history in the design literature (Alexander, 1964; Marples, 1961). For example, a room fan's major components include the blade, the motor that drives it, the blade guard, the control system, and the mechanical housing. The overall architecture of the product lays out how the components will work together. Taken together, a fan's architecture and its components create a system for moving air in a room.

Successful product development requires two types of knowledge. First, it requires component knowledge, or knowledge about each of the core design concepts and the way in which they are implemented in a particular component. Second, it requires architecture knowledge, or knowledge about the ways in which the components are integrated and linked together into a coherent whole. Innovations can be understood in terms of their impact on these two types of knowledge. This idea is illustrated in Figure 16.1.

The horizontal dimension captures an innovation's impact on components; the vertical captures its impact on the linkages between components. Framed in this way, radical and incremental innovation are extreme points along both dimensions. Radical innovation establishes a new dominant design and hence a new set of core design concepts embodied in components that are linked together in a new architecture. Incremental innovation refines and extends an established design. Improvement occurs in individual components, but the underlying core design concepts, and the links between them, remain the same. Modular innovation is innovation that changes a core design concept without changing the product's architecture.

The essence of an architectural innovation is the reconfiguration of an established system to link together existing components in a new way. This does not mean that the components themselves remain untouched. Architectural innovation is often triggered by a change in a component—perhaps size or some other subsidiary parameter of its design—that creates new interactions and new linkages with other components in the established product. The important point is that the core design concept behind each component— and the associated scientific and engineering knowledge—remain the same.

The application of this framework can be illustrated with the example of the room air fan. If the established technology is that of large, electrically powered fans, mounted in the ceiling, with the motor hidden from view and insulated to dampen the noise, improvements in blade design or in the power of the motor would be incremental innovations. A move to central air conditioning would be a radical innovation. New components associated with compressors, refrigerants, and their associated controls would add whole new technical disciplines and new interrelationships. For the maker of large, ceiling-mounted room fans, however, the introduction of a portable fan would be an architectural innovation. Although the primary components would be largely the same (e.g., blade, motor, control system), the architecture of the product would be quite different. There would be significant changes in the interactions between components. The smaller size and the co-location of the motor and the blade in the room would focus attention on new types of interactions between the motor size, the blade dimensions, and the amount of air that the fan could circulate, while shrinking the size of the apparatus would probably introduce new interactions between the performance of the blade and the weight of the housing.

These distinctions are important because they give us insight into why established firms often have a surprising degree of difficulty in adapting to architectural innovation. Incremental innovation tends to reinforce the competitive positions of established firms since it builds on their core competencies (Abernathy & Clark, 1985), or is "competence enhancing" (Tushman & Anderson, 1986). In the terms of the framework developed here, it builds on the existing architectural and component knowledge of organization. In contrast, radical innovation creates unmistakable challenges for established firms, since it destroys the usefulness of their existing capabilities. In our opinion, it destroys the usefulness of both architectural and component knowledge (Cooper & Schendel, 1976; Daft, 1982; Tushman & Anderson, 1986).

Architectural innovation presents established firms with a more subtle and potentially equally difficult challenge, because of the way in which architectural knowledge resides within the firm. Since architectural knowledge is usually stable during long periods of incremental innovation, it tends to become embedded in the communication channels, information filters, and problem-solving strategies of the organization. This makes its obsolescence difficult to observe and to correct.

In the first place, established organizations require significant time (and resources) to identify a particular innovation as architectural, since architectural innovation can initially be accommodated within old frameworks. In the second place, even after the need for architectural innovation has been recognized, the building of new architectural knowledge takes time and resources. New entrants to the industry must also build architectural knowledge necessary to exploit an architectural innovation, but since they have no existing assets, they can optimize their organization and information-processing structures to exploit the potential of a new design. Established firms may be used to modify the channels, filters, and strategies that already exist rather than use the significant fixed costs and considerable organizational friction required to start new sets from scratch (Arrow, 1974; Chandler, 1990). But it may be difficult to identify precisely which filters, channels, and problem-solving strategies need to be identified and the attempt to build a new product with old (albeit modified) organizational tools can create significant problems.

These problems are well illustrated in the history of the semiconductor photolithographic alignment industry.

INNOVATION IN PHOTOLITHOGRAPHIC ALIGNMENT EQUIPMENT

Photolithographic aligners are sophisticated pieces of capital equipment used in the manufacture of integrated circuits. The production of semiconductors requires the transfer of small, intricate patterns to the surface of a wafer of semiconductor material known as silicon, and this process of transfer is known as lithography. The surface of the wafer is coated with a light-sensitive chemical, or "resist." The pattern that is to be transferred to the wafer surface is drawn onto a mask and the mask is used to block light

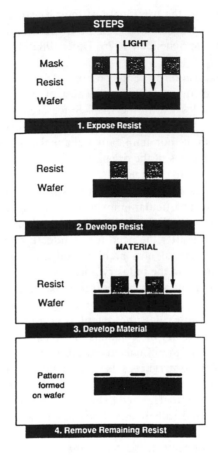

Figure 16.2. Schematic Representation of the Lithographic Process

as it falls onto the resist, so that only those portions of the resist defined by the block are exposed to light. The light chemically transforms the resist so that it can be stripped away. The resulting pattern is then used as the basis for either the deposition of material onto the wafer surface or the etching of the existing material on the surface of the wafer. The process may be repeated as many as twenty times during the manufacture of a semiconductor device, and each layer must be located precisely with respect to the previous layer (Watts & Einspruch, 1987). Figure 16.2 is a very simplified representation of this complex process. A photolithographic aligner is used to position the mask relative to the wafer, to hold the two in place during exposure, and to

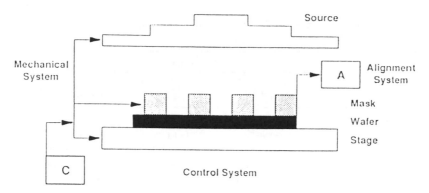

Figure 16.3. Schematic Diagram of a Contact Aligner

expose the resist. Figure 16.3 is a schematic diagram of a contact aligner, the first generation of alignment equipment developed. Improvement in alignment technology has meant improvement in minimum feature size, the size of the smallest pattern that can be produced on the wafer surface; yield, the percentage of wafers successfully processed; and throughput, the number of wafers the aligner can handle in a given time.

A constant stream of incremental innovation has been critical to optical photolithography's continuing success. The technology has also seen four waves of architectural innovation: the move from contact to proximity alignment, from proximity to scanning projection alignment, and from scanners to first- and then second-generation "steppers." (Photolithographic technology is described in much greater detail in Henderson, 1988.) Table 16.1 summarizes the changes in the technology introduced by each generation. In each case the core technologies of optical lithography remained largely untouched, and much of the technical knowledge gained in building a previous generation could be transferred to the next. Yet in each case the industry leader was unable to make the transition.

Table 16.2 shows share of deflated cumulative sales from 1962 to 1986 by generation of equipment for the leading firms. Figure 16.4 shows share of sales over time for three of the leading established firms and new entrants in proximity printers, scanners, and the first generation of steppers. The first commercially successful aligner was introduced by Kulicke and Soffa in 1965. They were extremely successful and held nearly 100 percent of the (very small) market for the next nine years, but by 1974 Cobilt and Kasper had replaced them. In 1974 Perkin-Elmer entered the market with the scanning projection aligner and rapidly became the largest firm in the industry. GCA, in turn, replaced Perkin-Elmer through its introduction of the stepper,

TABLE 16.1 A Summary of Architectural Innovation in Photolithographic Alignment Technology

| | Major Changes | |
Equipment	Technology	Critical Relationships Between Components
Proximity	Mask and wafer separated during exposure.	Accuracy and stability of gap is a function of links between gap-setting mechanism and other components.
Scanning projection	Image of mask projected onto wafer by scanning reflective optics.	Interactions between lens and other components are critical to successful performance.
First-generation stepper	Image of mask projected through refractive lens.	Relationship between lens field size and source energy becomes significant determinant of throughput.
	Image "stepped" across wafer	Depth of focus characteristics—driven by relationship between source wavelength and lens numerical aperture—becomes critical. Interactions between stage and alignment system are critical.
Second-generation stepper	Introduction of "site-by-site" alignment, larger 5× lenses.	Throughput now driven by calibration and stepper stability. Relationships between lens and mechanical system become crucial means of controlling distortion.

SOURCE: Field interviews, internal firm records (Henderson, 1988).

TABLE 16.2 Share of Deflated Cumulative Sales (%), 1962-1986, by Generation, for the Leading Optical Photolithographic Alignment Equipment Manufacturers[a]

| | Alignment Equipment | | | | |
Firm	Contact	Proximity	Scanners	Step and Repeat (1)	Step and Repeat (2)
Cobilt	44		< 1		
Kasper	17	8		7	
Canon		67	21	9	
Perkin-Elmer			78	10	< 1
GCA				55	12
Nikon					70
Total	61	75	99+	81	82+

SOURCE: Internal firm records. Dataquest, VLSI Research Inc.

a. This measure is distorted by the fact that all of these products are still being sold. For second-generation step and repeat aligners this problem is particularly severe, since in 1986 this equipment was still in the early stages of its life cycle.

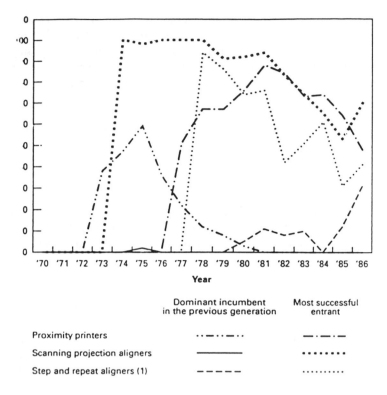

Figure 16.4. Estimated Share of Sales by the Most Successful Entrant and by the Most Successful Established Firm of the Previous Generation

only to be supplanted by Nikon, which introduced the second-generation stepper.

In nearly every case, the established firm invested heavily in the next generation of equipment, only to meet with very little success. A reliance on architectural knowledge derived from experience with the previous generation blinded the incumbent firms to critical aspects of the new technology. They thus underestimated its potential or built equipment that was markedly inferior to the equipment introduced by entrants.

The case of Kasper Instruments and its response to Canon's introduction of the proximity printer illustrates some of the problems encountered by established firms. Kasper Instruments was founded in 1968 and by 1973 was a small but profitable firm supplying approximately half of the market for contact aligners. In 1973 Kasper introduced the first contact aligner to be equipped with proximity capability. Although nearly half of all the aligners that the firm sold from 1974 on had this capability, Kasper aligners were only rarely used in proximity mode, and sales declined steadily until the company left the industry in 1981. The widespread use of proximity aligners occurred only with the introduction and general adoption of Canon's proximity aligner in the late 1970s.

Canon's aligner was superficially very similar to Kasper's. It incorporated the same components and performed the same functions, but it performed them much more effectively because it incorporated a much more sophisticated understanding of the technical interrelationships that are fundamental to successful proximity alignment.

Kasper failed to develop the particular component knowledge that would have enabled them to match Canon's design. More important, the architectural knowledge that Kasper had developed through its experience with the contact aligner had the effect of diverting Kasper's attention from the new problems whose solution was critical to the design of a successful proximity aligner.

Kasper conceived of the proximity aligner as a modified contact aligner. Like the incremental improvements to the contact aligner before it, design of the proximity aligner was managed as a routine extension to the product line. In particular, the gap-setting mechanism that was used in the contact aligner to align the mask with the wafer was slightly modified, and the new aligner was offered on the market. As a result, Kasper's proximity aligner did not perform well. The gap-setting mechanism was not accurate or stable enough to ensure adequate performance, and the aligner was used in its proximity mode. Kasper's failure to understand the obsolescence of architectural knowledge is demonstrated graphically by two incidents.

The first is the firm's interpretation of early complaints about the accuracy of its gap-setting mechanism. In proximity alignment, misalignment of the mask and the wafer can be caused by inaccuracies or instability in the gap-setting mechanism and by distortions introduced during processing. Kasper attributed many of the problems that users of its proximity equipment were experiencing to processing error, since it believed that processing error had been the primary source of problems with its contact aligner. The firm "knew" that its gap-setting mechanism was entirely adequate and, as a result, devoted very little time to improving its performance. In retrospect this may seem like a wanton misuse of information, but it represented no more than a continued reliance on an information filter that had historically served the firm well.

The second illustration is provided by Kasper's response to Canon's initial introduction of a proximity aligner. The Canon aligner was evaluated by a team at Kasper and pronounced to be a copy of a Kasper machine. Kasper evaluated it against the criteria that it used for evaluating its own aligners—criteria that had been developed during its experience with contact aligners. The technical features that made Canon's aligner a significant advance, particularly the redesigned gap mechanism, were not observed because they were not considered important. The Canon aligner was pronounced to be "merely a copy" of the Kasper aligner.

Similar problems that show up in all four episodes of architectural innovation in the industry's history are typified by the case of Perkin-Elmer and stepper technology. By the late 1970s Perkin-Elmer had achieved market leadership with its scanning projection aligners, but the company failed to maintain that leadership when stepper technology came to dominate the industry in the early 1980s. When evaluating the two technologies, Perkin-Elmer engineers accurately forecast the progress of individual components in the two systems but failed to see how new interactions in component development—including better resist systems and improvements in lens design—would give stepper technology a decisive advantage.

GCA, the company that took leadership from Perkin-Elmer, was itself supplanted by Nikon, which introduced a second-generation stepper. Part of the problem for GCA was recognition, but much of its failure to master the new stepper technology lay in problems in implementation. Echoing Kasper, GCA first pronounced the Nikon stepper a "copy" of the GCA design. Even after GCA had fully recognized the threat posed by the second-generation stepper, its historical experience handicapped the company in its attempts to develop a competitive machine. GCA's engineers were organized by component, and cross-department communication channels were all structured around the architecture of the first-generation system. Although GCA engineers were able to push the limits of the component technology, they had great difficulty understanding what Nikon had done to achieve its superior performance.

Nikon had changed aspects of the design—particularly the ways in which the optical system was integrated with the rest of the aligner—of which GCA's engineers had only limited understanding. Moreover, because these changes dealt with component interactions, there were few engineers responsible for developing this understanding. As a result, GCA's second-generation machines did not deliver the kind of performance that the market demanded. Like Kasper and Perkin-Elmer before them, GCA's sales languished and it lost market leadership. In all three cases, other factors also played a role in the firm's dramatic loss of market share, but a failure to respond effectively to architectural innovation was critical.

ARCHITECTURAL INNOVATION
AS A PERVASIVE ISSUE IN
ORGANIZATIONAL TRANSFORMATION

Although the concept of architectural innovation was derived from a study of technological change, the idea is a source of rich insight into some of the most fundamental barriers to organizational transformation.

This is immediately apparent if we think of component and architectural knowledge in more general terms. In general, component knowledge is local, active, focused knowledge about elements of a larger problem, whereas architectural knowledge is knowledge about how these elements fit together. Architectural knowledge is more likely to be diffused within the organization and to be embedded in organizational routines rather than in the minds of individuals because during long periods of incremental innovation it is much more stable than component knowledge.

During periods of incremental innovation, there will be rich, unstructured information flows and problem-solving activities within the boundaries of a component, but the information flow and problem solving that occur across component boundaries will be much more highly structured and more diffuse. "Components" emerge as organizations learn enough about a particular organizational task to be able to fragment it into elements that can be addressed in relative isolation without the need to transport the full range of knowledge about the internal workings of other components across component boundaries. Thus component boundaries are defined simultaneously by an organization's knowledge and problem-solving capabilities and by the internal structure of any particular organizational task.

As an illustration, again consider the room fan company. If information about the design of every element of the fan could be costlessly and instantaneously transferred to all designers, the distinction between component and architectural knowledge would not be a useful one. The designers of a new blade could take full advantage of all available knowledge about motors: all knowledge would be component knowledge in the sense that it would be actively involved in problem solving and locally accessible. Architectural knowledge develops because information transfer is expensive, or, in Von Hippel's (1990) terms, because component knowledge is "sticky." In the case of the room fan, it summarizes the component knowledge of the motor designers into a reduced set that summarizes what the blade designers need to know about motors in order to design adequate blades. Architectural knowledge can thus emerge only after an organization has developed sufficient experience with a problem to be able to fragment it into elements without losing critical information.

In the case of technologies that develop hierarchically in the manner outlined by Henderson and Clark (1990), components will correspond to logically and physically distinct elements of the design, since knowledge about the technology will evolve simultaneously with the design. Thus in our analysis of the nature of architectural innovation in photolithographic design and of the problems that it created for established firms, we were able to interpret each firm's knowledge of the relationship between the physical components of the design as embedded architectural knowledge. In such a case, the component and the architectural knowledge of the organization will be a logical reflection of the internal structure of the technology, and the organization and the products that it builds will mirror each other in very specific ways.

In the case of more general organizational tasks, the development of architectural knowledge is less likely to be guided by a particular technological structure, but we can hypothesize that the information-processing constraints of the organization will nevertheless result in the formulation of architectural knowledge as soon as any particular organizational task is sufficiently stable that it can be fragmented into elements without the overall problem-solving effort suffering too greatly. Architectural innovation will in this sense be more than a technical event—it will be any innovation that requires the firm to rethink the way in which it integrates together any coherent set of organizational tasks.

For example, much of the recent stress on design for manufacturing techniques (see Hauser & Clausing, 1988; Nevins & Whitney, 1988) can be interpreted as a move to manage architectural innovation within the design process. Many manufacturing firms have historically separated their design and manufacturing efforts into "components"—that is, into centers of local problem solving which are integrated together by a reduced set of stable architectural knowledge. In some firms this knowledge took the form of beliefs such as "those guys can build anything smaller than a breadbox" or "anything made out of aluminum held together with rivets." Design-for-manufacturing methodologies represent an explicit realization that this type of architectural knowledge may be outdated or insufficient, and that the organization has to explicitly recognize the existence of a much richer set of potential interactions between design and manufacturing. In this sense richer "rules of manufacturability" (rules such as "all else equal reduce part count") are attempts to build more appropriate architectural knowledge. Extensive simultaneous engineering efforts are attempts to transfer the "component knowledge" of product and process engineers to each other.

This much broader definition of component and hence of architectural knowledge suggests that this research may have immediate relevance to more general problems of organizational transformation and to many of the other chapters in this book. For if component knowledge is local, intense knowledge about particular elements of larger problems, and architectural knowledge is embedded knowledge about the ways in which these elements interact, then many of the major challenges of organizational transformation may involve the reconfiguration of architectural knowledge, and our attempts to create "learning" organizations are attempts not only to create organizations that actively engage in the construction of component knowledge —that is, the building of richer knowledge about particular aspects of a problem—but also to create organizational forms and processes that can actively reevaluate and reconstruct new forms of architectural knowledge. The other chapters suggest that this may be quite as difficult a challenge in other fields of organizational endeavor as it is in the management of technological innovation.

Consider, for example, Bailyn's (1992) discussion of the need to consider family issues in discussions about work and human resources. Bailyn suggests that one of the major challenges facing the modern U.S. corporation is the need to adapt to a significantly different kind of workforce—one with much more diverse needs and expectations. She suggests that this may require a fundamental rethinking of the basic assumptions that most organizations make about personnel policies such as training, job tenure, and promotion. This can be understood as a need to rethink some of the fundamental architectural knowledge of the organization, where local problem solving about the ways in which particular employees should be treated is currently embedded in an overarching and largely implicit structure. The problems of workforce diversity require a reconfiguration of the organization's thinking since the relationships among employees, their families, and the company, and the needs and demands that govern these relationships, are likely to be quite different.

The same concern with organizational change that may completely reconfigure the elements inside the corporation is evident in the discussion of corporate governance issues in chapters by Dore (1992), Useem (1992), and Healy (1992) . Dore suggests that many Japanese corporations are governed by quite different conceptions of the relationships between the multiple stakeholders of the firm. In consequence, the set of implicit assumptions about how the stakeholders of a firm—the employees, owners, customers, and suppliers—work with each other is quite different. He implies that the set of relationships found inside such Japanese corporations may ultimately result in more successful performance, and thus that U.S. corporations may have to rethink the way in which competing interests are mediated inside the firm. The same theme is evident in Useem's work. He suggests that the recent wave of leveraged buyouts and mergers is bringing about a qualitatively different relationship between owners and managers inside some American corporations. Healy's work suggests that these changes also significantly change performance.

All three works strikingly reinforce the idea that architectural innovation can have very significant consequences and be very difficult to implement despite the fact that from some perspectives it appears to be relatively "minor." After all, changes in governance could in principle merely be changes in contractual relationships within the firm. These three works imply that there are major organizational barriers to these types of changes that flow from deeply held assumptions—architectural knowledge—about the ways in which the parts of the firm work together to promote the interests of the whole.

Beyond the identification of the problems that organizations face in responding to these types of architectural innovation, the central concerns of several of the other chapters can be interpreted as the development of a richer understanding of alternative organizational mechanisms that may make organizations much more capable of explicitly managing architectural knowledge.

For example, Kochan and McKersie (1992) suggest that the most success- ful manufacturing organizations are those that are able to take full advantage of the knowledge and capabilities of their workforce. This point is also made forcefully by MacDuffie and Krafcik (1992), who suggest that historically many U.S. manufacturing corporations have maintained assumptions about the need to control and limit the involvement of the blue-collar workforce in the introduction of new technologies—architectural assumptions in that they shaped the ways in which problems were solved inside the organization— that are now actively inhibiting effective performance, but that are difficult to change because they are embedded deeply in the structure of the corpora- tion. For example, Kochan and McKersie (1992) stress that minor innova- tions such as the introduction of quality circles are unlikely to be successful unless they are backed by fundamental changes in the firm's structure and governance.

Senge and Sterman (1992) also address this issue. They suggest that one of the major problems facing organizations today is the fact that managers use inadequate or overly simplistic "mental maps" of the organization and its environment, which are rarely subject to challenge or assessment, and that these may lead them to grossly inappropriate decisions that fail to take account of the interactive, dynamic nature of their environment. They de- scribe the development of computer-based tools that assist managers to develop much more accurate and communally understood mental maps of their environment reflecting the nature of the system with which they are confronted. These tools can be thought of as a way to make the architectural knowledge of senior managers about the interrelationships between elements of the firm and its environment explicit.

RESEARCH ISSUES AND
QUESTIONS OUTSTANDING

A number of critical issues remain for further research. The most immediate is the need to build a richer understanding of the nature of architectural knowledge and the ways in which it is managed and changed within an organization. My research in the photolithographic alignment equipment industry led me to some specific hypotheses about the structure and development of technically derived component and architectural knowledge. Although I believe that these concepts may have relevance to more general problems of organizational change, much more remains to be done to make the concepts concrete and operationally useful in other settings.

For example, it will be important to build a better understanding between the concept of architectural knowledge and the internal mental maps of Senge and Sterman (1992), the concepts of theory in use and unfreezing developed by Schein (1992), and the descriptions of organizational routines of Nelson and Winter (1982). Further field-based studies of these problems should also shed light on this issue.

Another important area for future research is the relationship between the internal structure of the tasks facing organizations and the development of architectural and component knowledge. Clark and I (1990) found the concept of the hierarchy of design extremely useful as a way to understand the development of architectural knowledge in the photolithographic industry. An interesting research question is the degree to which analogous concepts can be of use in the analysis of the development of other types of knowledge.

Answers to these questions will be fundamental to the development of a richer understanding of organizational transformation.

REFERENCES

Abernathy, W. J., & Clark, K. (1985). Innovation: Mapping the winds of creative destruction. *Research Policy, 14,* 3-22.
Alexander, C. (1964). *Notes on the synthesis of form.* Cambridge, MA: Harvard University Press.
Arrow, K. J. (1974). *The limits of organization.* New York: Norton.
Bailyn, L. (1992). Changing the conditions of work: Responding to increasing work force diversity and new family patterns. In T. A. Kochan & M. Useem (Eds.), *Transforming organizations* (pp. 188-202). New York: Oxford University Press.

Clark, K. B. (1987). Managing technology in international competition: The case of product development in response to foreign entry. In M. Spence & H. Hazard (Eds.), *International competitiveness* (pp. 27-74). Cambridge, MA: Ballinger.

Chandler, A. D. (1990). *Scale and scope.* Cambridge, MA: Harvard University Press.

Cooper, A. C., & Schendel, D. (1976). Strategic response to technological threats. *Business Horizons, 19,* 61-69.

Daft, R. L. (1982). Bureaucratic versus nonbureaucratic structure and the process of innovation and change. In S. B. Bacharach (Ed.), *Research in the sociology of organizations* (pp. 129-165). Greenwich, CT: JAI.

Dore, R. (1992). Japan's version of managerial capitalism. In T. A. Kochan & M. Useem (Eds.), *Transforming organizations* (pp. 17-27). New York: Oxford University Press.

Hauser, J., & Clausing, D. (1988, May-June). The house of quality. *Harvard Business Review,* pp. 63-73.

Healy (1992). The effect of change on corporate control on firm performance. In T. A. Kochan & M. Useem (Eds.), *Transforming organizations* (pp. 61-79). New York: Oxford University Press.

Henderson, R. M. (1988). *The failure of established firms in the face of technical change: A study of photolithographic alignment equipment.* Unpublished doctoral dissertation, Harvard University.

Henderson, R. M., & Clark, K. B. (1990). Architectural innovation: The reconfiguration of existing product technologies and the failure of established firms. *Administrative Science Quarterly, 35,* 9-30.

Kochan, T., & McKersie, R. (1992). Human resource, organizational governance and public policy: Lessons from a decade of experimentation. In T. A. Kochan & M. Useem (Eds.), *Transforming organizations* (pp. 169-187). New York: Oxford University Press.

MacDuffie, J., & Krafcik, J. (1992). Integrating technology and human resources for high performance manufacturing: Evidence from the international auto industry. In T. A. Kochan & M. Useem (Eds.), *Transforming organizations* (pp. 209-226). New York: Oxford University Press.

Marples, D. L. (1961). The decisions of engineering design. *IEEE Transactions on Engineering Management, 8,* 55-71.

Nelson, R., & Winter, S. (1982). *An evolutionary theory of economic change.* Cambridge, MA: Harvard University Press.

Nevins, J. L., & Whitney, D. E. (1988). *Concurrent design of products and processes.* New York: McGraw-Hill.

Senge, P., & Sterman, J. (1992). Systems thinking and organizational learning: Acting locally and thinking globally in the organization of the future. In T. A. Kochan & M. Useem (Eds.), *Transforming organizations* (pp. 353-371). New York: Oxford University Press.

Schein, E. (1992). The role of the CEO in the management of change: The case of information technology. In T. A. Kochan & M. Useem (Eds.), *Transforming organizations* (pp. 80-96). New York: Oxford University Press.

Tushman, M. L., & Anderson, P. (1986). Technological discontinuities and organizational environments. *Administrative Science Quarterly, 31,* 439-465.

Useem, M. (1992). Corporate restructuring and organizational behavior. In T. A. Kochan & M. Useem (Eds.), *Transforming organizations* (pp. 44-60). New York: Oxford University Press.

Von Hippel, E. (1990). *The impact of "sticky" information on innovation and problem-solving* (Working paper 3147-90-BPS). Cambridge: MIT Management of Technology Department.

Watts, R. K., & Einspruch, N. G. (Eds.). (1987). *Lithography for VLSI, VLSI electronics— Microstructure science.* New York: Academic Press.

17

Organizational Evolution
and the Social Ecology of Jobs

ANNE S. MINER

The persistence of organizational routines is studied by examining
the survival of formalized jobs. Basic models of evolutionary change
predict that organizational context, job-founding processes, and
whether a job is novel affect job survival. Negotiated order and
social interaction theories predict, however, that the relationship of
the jobholder to the organization and to the job duties should also
affect the persistence of formalized jobs, e.g., the initial incumbent's
familiarity to the hiring department and whether the job was tailored
to a specific person. These predictions are analyzed using partial
likelihood analysis of the hazard rate of "job death" among 347
formalized jobs in a large organization over roughly a six-year
period. Results support most of the predictions. The findings suggest
that organizational evolution should be examined through systematic study of organizational routines.

Two increasingly important models of organizational change—organizational evolution and organizational learning—view organizations as bundles of standard operating procedures or organizational routines (Campbell,

This chapter appeared originally in *American Sociological Review,* Vol. 56, pp. 772-785, December 1991.

1969; Levitt & March, 1988; Nelson & Winter, 1982). While rich qualitative and simulation literatures have supported this view for nearly 30 years, little quantitative field research has examined its plausibility or usefulness. My first goal is to use fundamental concepts from an evolutionary change perspective to examine empirical patterns in the survival of one important type of organizational routine: the formalized job.

A substantial body of research in other traditions implies that the study of routines will be sterile unless it addresses the impact of social and personalistic processes. Social interaction theorists and negotiated order theorists, for example, have long stressed the interaction between formal structure and personalistic processes, while others have stressed the importance of social ties (Berger & Luckman, 1967; Granovetter, 1985; Strauss, 1978). My second goal is to consider whether some of these factors affect the survival of the routines (jobs) themselves.

Using interviews, field observation, archival data, and informant coding of key variables, I explore these issues by examining the relative death rates of approximately 350 jobs in a large organization over roughly a six-year period. I present basic descriptive data on job survival and analyze relative hazard rates for job death.

THEORY AND HYPOTHESES

Many elaborate models of organizational change can be developed from ecologies of routines (Levitt & March, 1988; Nelson & Winter, 1982). I examine evidence regarding one element—selection—in the basic model of organizational evolution. In this model, substantial organizational action occurs through the repetition of standard operating procedures or routines (Cyert & March, 1963; Nelson & Winter, 1982). Variations that occur in these routines may then be incorporated in the ongoing collection of routines that, in turn, guide future action (Campbell, 1969; Weick, 1979). Modern treatments of this process seek to forego facile applications of dubious "biological analogies" (Penrose, 1952, p. 804), to attend to both variation and selection rates, and to avoid functionalist reasoning (Singh & Lumsden, 1990). Organizational evolution, for example, can lead to superstitious learning, "competency traps" and suboptimal performance as well as to adaptation (Granovetter, 1979; Levitt & March, 1988; Miner, 1990).

I use the phrase "evolutionary process" to refer to any change process in which variation, selection and retention occur over time. From this perspective, trial-and-error learning is a particular type of evolutionary process that embodies the purposeful use of variation and selection over time.

Although proposed and embellished for more than two decades, evolutionary models of organizational change have proved difficult to study. One important obstacle has been the definition and measurement of the units on which selection and retention processes operate. Organizational theorists have proposed a variety of definitions and labels for inertial units including standard operating procedures (Cyert & March, 1963), routines (Nelson & Winter, 1982), and competencies (McKelvey, 1982). Examples of the constructs include: skills of individual employees (Aldrich, 1979; Nelson & Winter, 1982); individual human beings (Aldrich, 1979; McPherson, 1990); organizational activity bundles such as jobs, assembly lines, airline reservation systems, accounting principles or rules of war (Allison, 1971; Miner, 1990; Winter, 1990); technologies, rules and procedures (Aldrich, 1979; Levitt & March, 1988); and overall strategies of an organization (Burgelman, 1991).

I define an organizational *routine* as a coordinated, repetitive set of organizational activities. A *job* is "a collection of tasks performed by a single individual" (Heneman, Schwab, Fossum, & Dyer, 1983, p. 547). A job is *formalized* if it has an explicit written "job description" (Pugh, Hickson, Hininger, & Turner, 1968). Formalized jobs are routines, then, and represent a promising vehicle for studying changes in organizational routines. Formalized jobs exist in roughly comparable forms in many organizations and organizations often keep records of at least some aspects of job histories.

I examine organizational routines by asking three simple questions about job death. First, do formalized jobs die at rates consistent with a role as a vehicle of organizational change? Second, do job context and job characteristics affect job death rates, as predicted by evolutionary and learning theories? Finally, if job type affects job death, does the relationship of the job's first incumbent to the organization or to the job duties affect job death?

Turnover in Organizational Routines

The classic Weberian perspective envisions formal organizations as fixed lattices of stable, impersonal jobs (Weber, 1968). Many observers of large bureaucratized organizations see the presence of predominantly formalized jobs as an indication of organizational stability or even rigidity. Systems with large numbers of formalized jobs, for example, have often been contrasted with "organic," informal systems in which job duties are presumed to change more rapidly (Burns & Stalker, 1961; Scott, 1981). Although not always explicit, the assumption that high formalization is linked to job stability pervades many theories of organization structure and has influenced some formal mobility modeling (Spilerman, 1977; White, 1970).

In contrast, I have proposed that formalized jobs are not necessarily stable, and that structural organizational evolution may occur through turnover in jobs (Miner, 1990). A crucial feasibility requirement for any evolutionary model is that substantial stability is coupled with turnover in the relevant routines (Holland, 1975). However, with the exception of a paper by Stewman (1986), there is little systematic evidence regarding the stability of formalized jobs inside ongoing organizations. There is economy-wide evidence of job volatility, but the degree to which this arises from turnover among organizations, growth and decline of individual organizations, or steadystate patterns of job replacement remains unclear (Leonard & Jacobson, 1990). I predict:

> H_1: A nontrivial minority of jobs will disappear over time even in a large organization composed of formalized jobs.

Influences on the Survival of Routines

If jobs do show stability as well as nontrivial levels of job death, what factors affect job survival? While theorists have shown extraordinary ingenuity in speculating about turnover in routines (Levitt & March, 1988; Weick, 1979; Winter, 1990), there is no systematic evidence on the point. However, evolutionary models generally emphasize ways that contextual and founding processes affect the survival of routines.

Organizational Context. Evolutionary theories imply that the context of a routine affects its fate, including the characteristics of its founding context. Stinchcombe's (1965) "imprinting" hypothesis and related research have emphasized founding conditions (Tucker, Singh, & Meinhard, 1990). In the case of jobs, the inertial aspect of context implies that departmental characteristics in the period of job founding affect job death rates.

One fundamental organizational characteristic that should affect survival is size. On the one hand, large departments should be more impersonal and more willing than smaller departments to use efficiency values in evaluating jobs. This suggests job death rates should be higher among jobs founded in large departments. On the other hand, large size may be associated with large resources and a low capacity for monitoring internal efficiency (Pfeffer, 1981). Thus, jobs founded in large departments should have low death rates. In either case, however, I predict:

> H_2: Department size at time of founding will affect the hazard rate for job death.

Types of Routines. Evolutionary theories also predict that the characteristics of the routines themselves should affect their survival. In particular, these theories imply that history matters. Relatively small events can have an impact long after the period in which they occurred (Carroll, 1988; Gould, 1977; Levitt & March, 1988). This emphasis clearly distinguishes evolutionary from rational and political models in which organizational action is related to current or anticipated circumstances. If history matters, the way routines were initially adopted should affect the survival of those routines. In the case of jobs, this means that the founding processes for jobs should affect job persistence rates.

Previous research has shown that jobs arise in different ways (Doeringer & Piore, 1971; Miner, 1987). I have shown that in some cases job duties are formed around the skills or interests of particular individuals within an organization (evolved jobs) or around individuals previously outside the organization (opportunistic hires). Other jobs, of course, are planned in advance by management (planned new jobs). Finally, in many systems, jobs expand enough to receive new titles, but do not alter their basic duties (reclassifications). If basic job characteristics and founding processes affect job survival, then:

H_3: Job-founding type will affect the hazard rate for job death.

If the data support hypothesis 3, however, the question arises, what aspects of the four job types drive their effect on hazard rates? Closer exploration of the effect of job type permits the examination of this question. By creating simple design variables from the four job types, I explore three aspects of these job types without explaining additional variation.

In evolutionary models, current organizational routines represent the organization's memory of what appeared to be successful in the past (Cyert & March, 1963; Nelson & Winter, 1982). Valuable routines are retained and less valuable routines expire. *Novel routines* are those whose content the organization has not previously experienced. Some novel routines prove to be valuable with experience, while others prove to be valueless or even harmful. If the organization has systematically retained valuable routines, however, there should be a lower proportion of valuable routines in any novel group than in an established group of routines. Thus, a higher hazard rate for novel sets of routines should obtain if the organization continues to select on the same criteria (Holland, 1975; March, 1981).

Applying these ideas to jobs implies that while an organization plans for all jobs to contribute, it does not know their value until it has experience with them. After evaluating them, it can terminate jobs that do not contribute as expected. In contrast, any group of pre-existing jobs contains mostly surviving jobs that have proven valuable. Thus, if an organization maintains fairly stable criteria for selecting jobs, I expect that:

H_{3a}: Novel jobs will have a higher hazard rate than pre-existing jobs.

These arguments treat organizational routines as disembodied entities. The word "routine" connotes something impersonal that persists apart from individuals. However, theorists from a variety of perspectives have long argued that social structure both constrains and is formed by individual traits and actions (Berger & Luckman, 1967; Giddens, 1984). Role theorists have argued that formal organizational roles respond to individual action overtime (Graen, 1976; Van Maanen & Schein, 1979). Negotiated order theory (Strauss, 1978) and political models of organizations emphasize that participants actively bargain over formal organizational roles (Barley, 1986; MacKenzie, 1986; Pfeffer, 1981). Finally, Granovetter (1985, 1986) has developed a convincing case for the embeddedness of economic action—including employment patterns—in social relations. These perspectives imply that job survival is linked to the relationship of particular individuals to the organization.

Some organizational routines encompass many people's activities. Routines that are essentially performed by one person, however, have an initial incumbent who first executes the routine. The social interaction perspective implies that the links between that person and others in the organization affect the destiny of the routine (Strauss, 1978). Inertial perspectives imply that the links of early incumbents are especially important (Berger & Luckman, 1967).

In the case of jobs, a first incumbent already familiar to department members has better information on managerial preferences and subtle aspects of departmental priorities. This information can be used to justify the continuation of the job during early job evaluations (Strauss, 1978). In addition, if the department must choose among jobs to cut while the first incumbent is still present and a job's value is ambiguous, simple friendship links could favor jobs held by *familiar incumbents*. Thus, social interaction theories imply that:

H_{3b}: Jobs whose initial incumbents were familiar to the department will have lower hazard rates than other jobs.

Another potentially important relationship is that between the routine's content and its implementer. In general, students of organizational change have focused on change created through selection of individuals over time, or through selection of impersonal routines, rather than the interaction between the characteristics of routines and their implementers. In the case of jobs, many literatures rest on what I define as the "vacancy assumption" which holds that jobs exist prior to and independent of their incumbents. In contrast, I label evolved jobs and opportunistic hires as "idiosyncratic jobs" because their content is designed around the interests and abilities of particular individuals (Miner, 1987, p. 327). If the relationship of a routine's initial implementer to its content affects survival, then *job idiosyncrasy* should affect job survival.

Some observers have argued that idiosyncratic jobs represent temporary concessions extracted by powerful employees, special favors granted to relatives, or simply temporary lapses in effective planning (March & Simon, 1958; Williamson, 1975). If so, they may have a higher failure rate than other jobs. Alternatively, these jobs may persist due to the congruence between the abilities of the incumbent and the tasks. Creators of these jobs may also have identified unusually important needs, so that the jobs tend to survive the first incumbent. Finally, powerful incumbents who have successfully negotiated idiosyncratic jobs may shape the criteria for judging the jobs (Miner, 1990; Strauss, 1978; Thompson, 1967). Because theory suggests idiosyncrasy could increase or decrease hazard rates, the final hypothesis simply predicts:

H_{3c}: Job idiosyncrasy will affect job hazard rates.

METHODS AND MEASURES

The data for this study are from a long-term study of organizational change. Archival data, interviews, and observations were collected over roughly a ten-year period. All jobs studied were created or reclassified between April 1, 1980, and December 31, 1982. The fate of each job up to August 1, 1986, was then traced through a combination of file and computer research. Figure 17.1 shows the time structure of the study.

The organizational setting was a major private university employing between 5,000 and 6,000 nonacademic staff each year during the study period. The organizational context for each job was its individual department. Departments included both academic departments (e.g., Classics) and nonacademic departments (e.g., Buildings and Grounds). The jobs included posts such as groundskeeper, student counselor, secretary, library assistant, accountant, writer, computer programmer, fund raiser, planner, data analyst, research assistant, and steamplant engineer. Because the purpose of the study was to examine ordinary jobs rather than patterns unique to universities,

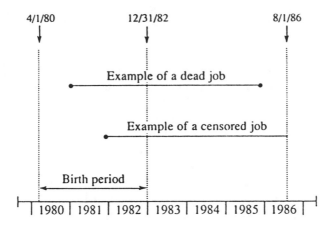

Figure 17.1. Structure of Data Set for Job Outcomes

faculty, research associate, and student positions were excluded. There were no state or public jobs in the sample.

All jobs in the system had written job descriptions, i.e., they were formalized (Pugh et al., 1968). All jobs were assigned to one of approximately 250 detailed job classifications. Each job classification, in turn, was assigned to a formal pay category.

The total job system tended to link official job duties to behavior in several ways. Written job descriptions determine recruiting requirements for job openings and set standards for performance reviews. The descriptions would often affect the expectations of new employees, managers, and other employees and could also become decisive documents in grievance procedures. The attachment of wage levels to specific job descriptions focused attention on formal job traits. Thus, although job descriptions rarely correspond perfectly to the activities of job holders, job descriptions in this organization captured meaningful consistency in behavior.

Independent Variables

In this study, a job "birth" occurs when a department appoints a person to perform duties that have not previously been performed as a single job in that department.

Job-Founding Types. My previous research in this organizational setting showed that job content is sometimes shaped around particular individuals.

"Idiosyncratic jobs" occur when (1) the existence of the job holder prompted the creation of the position in its current form and (2) the combination of job activities was designed to match the perceived abilities, interests, or priorities of the person around whom the job was created (Miner, 1987, p. 327). There are two types of idiosyncratic jobs. *Opportunistic hires* are created around people from outside the department, while *evolved jobs* are created around existing employees (Miner, 1987). For example, a talented head technician in a laboratory proposed new training programs for other technicians, based on her interests and abilities and perceived laboratory needs. The laboratory management then created a full-time administrative position so she could run such programs. This novel job was coded as an evolved job.

Although idiosyncratic jobs occur even in this completely formalized setting, most jobs are defined in advance by management. Such jobs are *planned novel jobs* and include any job first defined by management and filled. A planned novel job may represent a completely new set of duties—a job coordinating accountants in a new project—or, it may represent the addition of a secretarial position whose duties were novel to that department. Thus, all novel jobs can be classified as planned novel jobs, opportunistic hires, or evolved jobs.

Reclassifications, one type of pre-existing job, were studied for contrast. Some jobs, while retaining their basic duties, expand or contract over time. They may be assigned a new job classification or pay group without changing their fundamental duties.

For example, an employee previously classified as a Secretary II might be reclassified as a Secretary III after assuming more independence in scheduling visitors, ordering supplies, and completing budget drafts for approval. Normal reclassifications are not novel jobs because the combination of duties already exists in the department, but they involve administrative action and a change in job title and compensation.

Measurement of Job-Founding Type. For this study, individual jobs were classified using informant ratings of the approximately 1,500 jobs identified from organization records and from a random selection of jobs from appropriate computer files.

In this organization, job openings can be posted only after approval of a formal job requisition. Each job is then posted with the central personnel office for a required length of time. Candidates are considered and a final selection is made. Under exceptional circumstances, the posting process can be waived. In practice, common grounds for a waiver include (1) a proposed candidate represents a selection from an existing candidate pool, (2) a major crisis makes it necessary to hire immediately, or (3) the duties are uniquely matched to the new person's abilities, interests, and priorities. The job requisitions for all waivers granted during the birth period formed the candidate pool for potential opportunistic hires.

For a current employee to be reclassified, a reclassification request must be made by his/her department to the central compensation staff. Each request is supported by written documentation and after review, results in approval, adjustment, or denial. While normal reclassifications represent expansions or contractions of pre-existing jobs, in some cases the new duties represent the creation of a novel job. Reclassification requests during the birth period are candidates for potential evolved jobs.

After measurement development and training sessions, individual members of a panel of 11 compensation analysts and two senior employment representatives from the central personnel staff rated the waiver and reclassification requests for the cases they were familiar with. (Each case was rated by a professional familiar with the details of the original request.) The raters answered the question "To what degree has the content of the job developed around the skills or interests of the person?" Responses ranged from "1" indicating "not to an unusual extent" to a score of "5" indicating "nearly completely." Jobs rated as "4" or "5" were defined as idiosyncratic, i.e., as opportunistic hires or evolved jobs. The Spearman Brown reliability estimate for the evolved job panel members working in training sessions was $r = .97$, while the simple correlation coefficient for the two opportunistic hire raters was .78.

The average confidence level reported by the raters at the end of the study was 4 on a 5-point scale in which 5 represents extremely high confidence. Of a total of 1,273 reclassification requests, raters had enough information to rate 1,158 jobs. Of these, 139 were classified as evolved jobs. Raters were able to rate 354 of a total of 400 waiver requests reviewed by the central personnel office during the period. Sixty of the 354 were classified as opportunistic hires. For further description of these data and procedures, including rater rules of thumb and examples of cases rated idiosyncratic, see Miner (1987).

A matched group of novel job requisitions not created around specific individuals was obtained from a computer listing of all jobs posted during the birth period that were classified as "new jobs" by the hiring department. These posted novel jobs could have been filled by people from inside or outside the department. A random sample of jobs was drawn from this list, stratified by occupation. The distribution of these control jobs was forced to approximate the distribution of idiosyncratic jobs by occupation. Stratification by occupation was done to control for possible occupational effects. To facilitate follow-up studies using department informants, the list from which control cases were selected was restricted to the departments in which idiosyncratic jobs had occurred.

A comparison group of pre-existing jobs was added to the study. All reclassifications that had a rating of "3" or less on job idiosyncrasy were candidates for this group. A random sample of these reclassified pre-existing jobs was selected, again stratified by occupation to match the initial idiosyncratic jobs, and restricted to departments that created idiosyncratic jobs during the birth period.

Because of the sample design, the jobs in this study are not representative of all jobs in the organization. Although idiosyncratic jobs occurred in all occupational groups, they were more likely to occur in professional and administrative categories than in other categories. Thus, the total sample of jobs in this study is skewed toward professional and administrative jobs. In addition, not all departments are represented. The mean size of the departments in this study did not differ significantly from the mean department size in the original study of idiosyncratic jobs and there was no reduction of variance in observed departmental traits. However, examination of the traits of the achieved sample suggests that jobs from larger departments are somewhat over-represented in this study.

Job Characteristics. The four job-founding types differ in the process leading to job creation or continuation. Using information on the practices of this organization, it was possible to generate indicators for specific characteristics of the jobs. Novel jobs were defined as jobs whose combination of duties was novel to their department at the time of first observation in this study. Planned novel jobs, opportunistic hires, and evolved jobs were thus all coded as novel and assigned a value of 1. Reclassifications of preexisting jobs were assigned a value of 0. A dummy variable for job idiosyncrasy was created by coding opportunistic hires and evolved jobs as 1, and planned novel jobs and reclassifications as 0.

A direct measure of the familiarity of the initial incumbent to the department was not available. A rough approximation of this variable was generated as follows. By definition, all initial incumbents for opportunistic hires were from outside the department. All such cases were coded 1. In contrast, all initial incumbents of evolved jobs and reclassifications were current employees. All these cases were coded 3. Planned novel jobs were filled either by current department members or by people from outside the department. The probability that these jobs were filled by persons familiar to the departments is thus intermediate between the other two categories. All these cases were coded 2. While this probabilistic measure of familiarity of original incumbents for planned novel jobs is far from ideal, it does make use of the available information.

Table 17.1 summarizes the four job-founding types and shows the relationship of job-founding type to job characteristics. Table 17.2 shows the

TABLE 17.1 Characteristics of Job-Founding Types

Job-Founding Type	Source of Designation	Job Characteristics		
		Job Duties	Relationship of Initial Incumbent to Department	Source of Job Duties
Opportunistic hire	Job requisition and waiver request	Novel	From outside department	Idiosyncratic
Evolved job	Reclassification request	Novel	From inside department	Idiosyncratic
Planned novel job	Job requisition	Novel	From outside or inside department	Impersonal
Reclassification	Reclassification request	Existing	From inside department	Impersonal

number of cases in each job-founding type. Means and correlations between independent variables used in the same survival models are shown in Appendix A.

Other Variables. The number of department employees at the beginning of the job formation period was obtained from central computer records. Thirteen cases could not be assigned to a department.

Each job was also classified according to whether the original incumbent was replaced during the study period. Dates of any transitions between incumbents were not used in the analysis because the study concerns the fates of jobs, not people. A dummy variable distinguished jobs that had more than one incumbent. Most multiple incumbent jobs had only two incumbents over this period.

Dependent Variable

The dependent variable is the relative unobserved hazard rate for job "death" for different job groups. Jobs are continuously at risk of ending. They "die" when departmental activities are reorganized, changed, or reduced. Routine decision making, budget cuts, and changed priorities or projects could all produce job deaths. The duties of a specific job may disappear, partially disappear, or be divided up and redistributed among other jobs. If the job disappears, the current jobholder may be encouraged to compete for another departmental position, reassigned, laid off, or helped to find a position outside the department.

Estimating the relative hazard rates requires the dates of job births and deaths. Figure 17.1 shows the basic data structure for the study. For each job, the date of birth or reclassification and date of job death, if appropriate, were recorded. The date of appointment of the first incumbent was recorded as the date of birth for planned novel jobs, opportunistic hires, and evolved jobs. The effective date of reclassification was recorded for reclassified jobs because it represented the date of change in job title and duties. In terms of duties, reclassifications are "left-censored" because the initial duties occurred before the start of this study. Their true duration is unknown, but is underestimated in these data. Models were run that omitted the left-censored cases to assess their impact on results. The survival models remained statistically significant and the relative ordering of coefficients remained the same.

Job death was assessed as follows. Consider a planned novel job initially filled by Smith. Paper records tracing Smith's employment were inspected. If Smith left the job, a computerized file of all job requisitions during the entire study period was then searched. If Smith's name appeared as "prior incumbent" for a job on the file, the name of Smith's replacement—say Johnson—was recorded. Johnson's written record was then inspected. If Johnson left the job, the requisition file was searched again. This process continued until the job's death was determined or the cutoff date of August 1, 1986, occurred. A job death occurred if the last known incumbent was never replaced.

In some cases, the original incumbent was reclassified. Reclassifications within a fixed job series (Secretary I, Secretary II and Secretary III, for example) were not treated as job deaths. If Smith was reclassified to a title in another job series (Secretary II to Accountant I, for example), however, the case was reviewed. An informant in the organization assessed whether this change represented the end of the first job. For example, a reclassification from "Miscellaneous professional" to "Coach I" could represent the death of one job and the creation of another or it could represent the continuation of the job of a junior water polo coach given a new title to reflect more responsibility.

Out of 400 cases tracked in this way, 40 could not be fully classified. This outcome resulted from missing data in the organization's records and from cases in which a transition occurred that could not be confidently assessed by informants. As a result, complex cases may have been less likely to remain in the data set. There is no a priori reason to assume these cases have systematically higher or lower chances of job death.

A large number of jobs persisted up to the cutoff point and are thus right censored. Because the source of right censoring is the cutoff date, which is independent of the causal processes of interest, the right censoring should not produce a systematic bias in results (Allison, 1984).

Hazard Rate. The hazard rate can be roughly conceptualized as an instantaneous probability of job death. A Cox proportional hazards model was used to examine the relative effects of job founding type and job characteristics on the hazard rate. In the proportional hazards model:

$$h(t;z) = h_0(t)\exp(\beta'z)$$

where β is a vector of unknown regression coefficients and $h_0(t)$ is an unknown hazard function for an individual with covariate vector $z = 0$ (Hopkins, 1988). The model makes no parametric assumption about the specific nature of duration dependence in the hazard rate. It does, however, assume proportional hazard rates for all jobs, and a loglinear effect for covariates upon the hazard function.

Partial likelihood analysis was used because it is well-suited to exploratory research. In contrast to logistic regression or logit analyses, this approach makes use of available information on the relative survival time of jobs and also uses the information on the jobs still alive at the end of the study. In contrast to maximum likelihood models of the hazard rate, partial likelihood analysis does not require assumptions about the form of duration dependency. Field observation suggests that duration dependency for jobs is unlikely to be monotonic and is worthy of separate study. The focus of this study, however, is the relative effect of theoretical variables on job death. Finally, partial likelihood estimates have reasonable properties as long as sample size is not too small (Tuma & Hannan, 1984). Survival analysis using P2L in BMDP based on Cox models of partial likelihood was used for all hazard rate analyses (Hopkins, 1988).

This analytic approach assumes that the shape of the indeterminate underlying duration dependency is proportional for all jobs (Allison, 1984). Inspection of survival plots and tests of this assumption indicated that it was generally appropriate but might be violated in comparisons between reclassifications and other jobs. The product of reclassification status and the log of measured job duration was statistically significant at the .05 level when included with other variables in several models. Following Allison (1984), this term was therefore included as a control variable—labeled "proportionality control"—in all subsequent analyses to reduce the possibility of spurious results due to nonproportionality.

RESULTS

Table 17.2 presents simple descriptive data on the four job-founding types. Because observation stopped at the end of the six-year study period, a true mean survival time for jobs cannot be estimated. However, for pre-existing jobs (reclassifications) the observed mean survival time is nearly five years. Nearly 74% of these jobs were right censored, i.e., they still existed at the end of the observation period. The true stability among these jobs will be higher than observed here because these censored jobs will live longer. Indeed, interviews revealed that a few jobs in this organization have existed since its founding at the turn of the century—more than 80 years. These findings suggest substantial job stability.

On the other hand, there is evidence of nontrivial turnover in jobs, as predicted. Among reclassifications, about 26% of the jobs died during the study period. A higher proportion of planned novel jobs, 49%, died during that time. These two job types best represent most jobs in the organization. About 30% of the evolved jobs and nearly 60% of the opportunistic hires died during the study period. Thus, both stability and nontrivial levels of job

TABLE 17.2 Descriptive Statistics by Job-Founding Type: Private University, 1980-1982

Job-Founding Type	Number of Cases	Mean Minimal Survival Time (in years)	Standard Deviation	Dead Jobs[a]		Censored Jobs[b]	
				Number	Percent	Number	Percent
Opportunistic hire	57	3.15	1.89	34	59.6	23	40.4
Evolved job	118	4.14	1.64	35	29.7	83	70.3
Planned novel job	98	3.61	1.66	48	49.0	50	51.0
Reclassification	87	4.83	1.30	23	26.4	64	73.6

a. Maximum survival time for dead jobs is 6 years 4 months.
b. Minimum survival time of a censored job is 3 years 7 months.

TABLE 17.3 Partial Likelihood Coefficients for Hazard Rates for Job Deaths on Selected Independent Variables: Private University, 1980-1986

Independent Variable	Coefficient	Coefficient/S.E.
Model 1		
Department size	−.003*	−2.092
	$(.015^{-1})$	
Job-founding type[a]		
Opportunistic hire	.091	.389
	(.234)	
Evolved job	−.808**	−3.514
	(.230)	
Reclassification	−4.447**	−2.897
	(1.535)	
Multiple incumbents	−1.212**	3.948
	(.307)	
Proportionality control	1.017*	2.359
	(.431)	
Model 2		
Department size	−.003*	−2.092
	$(.015^{-1})$	
Novel job	3.997**	2.592
	(1.542)	
Idiosyncratic job	−.359	−1.814
	(.198)	
Familiar first incumbent	−.450**	−3.693
	(.122)	
Multiple incumbents	−1.212**	−3.948
	(.307)	
Proportionality control	1.017*	−2.359
	(.431)	

NOTE: Numbers in parentheses are standard errors. For both models: $N = 347$; log likelihood = −707.6184; global χ^2 = 5801 with 6 degrees of freedom, $p < .001$.

a. The omitted category is planned novel jobs.

*$p < .05$; **$p < .01$

deaths occurred during the six-year period of the study, supporting hypothesis 1.

Hypothesis 2 predicts that department size affects the hazard rate for job death. Model I of Table 17.3 shows the effects of department size on the hazard rate for job death. Because the dependent variable is the hazard rate, a positive coefficient indicates that a variable makes jobs more likely to die and a negative coefficient indicates that the variable impedes job death. Table 17.3 shows that department size significantly decreases the hazard rate for jobs, i.e., jobs in large departments are less likely to die than jobs in small departments.

Hypothesis 3 suggests that job-founding type should affect job persistence. Model I of Table 17.3 shows the effect of job-founding type on the hazard rate for job death, comparing the job-founding types to the omitted group of planned novel jobs. Opportunistic hires have a higher death rate than planned novel jobs, but the effect is not statistically significant. The coefficient for evolved jobs shows that they are significantly less likely to die compared to planned jobs, although the magnitude of the effect is not large. Reclassifications are substantially less likely to die than are planned novel jobs, with a coefficient of nearly 4.5.

Model 2 of Table 17.3 presents the effects of several variables constructed by combining different job-founding types. Although no additional variation is explained in Model 2, it permits exploration of the effects of specific aspects of the job founding types examined in Model 1. Hypothesis 3a, which predicts that novel jobs have a higher hazard rate than pre-existing jobs, is supported.

Hypothesis 3b predicts that a familiar first incumbent decreases a job's hazard rate. Results in Model 2 show that familiarity significantly reduces the chance of job death.

Finally, hypothesis 3c predicts that job idiosyncrasy affects the hazard rate for jobs. However, the effect of job idiosyncrasy on the hazard rate for job deaths is not statistically significant.

In partial likelihood analysis, the underlying duration effects are canceled out across cases rather than estimated, so no parameters are shown for a main effect of duration in Table 17.3 (Allison, 1984; Tuma & Hannan, 1984). Effects for control variables are as expected: multiple incumbency is associated with lower hazard rates and the proportionality control variable is statistically significant, supporting its inclusion in the models.

DISCUSSION

Results suggest that nontrivial numbers of formalized jobs die and that a job's context, origin, and relational aspects of first incumbent may affect its survival rate. The findings and their limitations raise interesting questions.

The results demonstrate the existence of job continuity coupled with nontrivial levels of job deaths. Thus, formalized jobs may provide one engine for systematic change if their survival is nonrandom. This, in turn, supports the plausibility of incremental evolutionary processes through the ongoing selection of jobs.

A cross-sectional study of this organization would have revealed complete formalization of jobs and a rather stable level of total employment, suggesting a typical Weberian bureaucracy. Yet the observed level of job deaths seems surprisingly high. This may arise from norms of flexibility or from the fact that some positions in a research university are funded through "soft money"—external funds. However, the proportion of job deaths among research professionals—who are more likely to be on "soft money"—was only slightly higher than that for nonresearch professionals, and it was approximately the same as that for lower management jobs.

Leonard and Jacobson (1990) concluded from examining economy-wide data on the state of Pennsylvania that substantial job creation and destruction routinely occurs in existing firms through short-term growth and decline. My results suggest the additional possibility that routine job destruction may occur even in the absence of short-term growth and decline. Clearly, the degree to which steady-state job turnover—in addition to employee turnover —characterizes many organizations deserves further attention.

Department size at the time of job founding affects the hazard rate for jobs. This finding is consistent with the broad proposition that founding context affects job survival rates, and is also consistent with the claim of evolutionary theories that founding conditions have effects that may persist. Department size should remain correlated over successive years in many cases. If so, the result could reflect an ongoing effect of department size, supporting the more general claim that organizational context affects survival of routines.

The fact that large size tends to reduce the hazard rate does not support the expectation that more informal norms in smaller departments will lead to longer job survival. It appears more likely that the large resources, reduced capacity to monitor the value of routines, or other traits associated with large departments permit jobs to survive longer. Additional work is needed to determine more precisely the nature of the size effect, as well as the effects of other contextual factors. Certainly fluctuations in resource levels should affect the survival of routines in an evolutionary model.

Whether a job originated as a planned new job, opportunistic hire, evolved job, or reclassification affects its survival prospects. This outcome is not consistent with organizational models in which managers assess organizational activities and make adjustments based solely on current and future factors. In such a world, the nature of job duties, rather than the process by which jobs were created should affect job survival. The data are more consistent with the notion that founding processes have long-lasting effects on the fates of organizational routines (Dornblaser, Lin, & Van de Ven, 1989).

I argued that job novelty should be an important aspect of the observed effects of job-founding type. In particular, I proposed that any set of novel jobs would contain a higher proportion of "bad ideas" when compared to jobs that had survived prior selection processes. The data support the prediction of a higher hazard rate for novel jobs. This outcome is consistent with models of organizational trial-and-error learning that stress selective retention of routines that are judged valuable by the organization. The evolutionary perspective does not preclude conscious choice by managers (Coleman, 1986) as one engine of selection processes, although political and accidental factors may also reduce life chances of novel jobs (Miner, 1990).

The novelty effect could also arise if there is a significant tendency for older jobs to be less likely to die simply because they are old. In this case, the results still imply that job novelty, as measured here, enhances the chance of job death. But the cause would be a changing propensity of all jobs to fail over time rather than a high variance in the value of jobs when they are created. If distinct measures of job novelty and job value were available while modeling duration dependence, the relative impact of these different processes could be explored.

The data also support the hypothesis that jobs first held by familiar incumbents would survive longer. This result contradicts the implicit assumption in many literatures that the destinies of jobs are determined solely by the functional relationship of their current duties to current needs or plans. It is more consistent with negotiated order theory in which activities may need to be constantly justified, and with theories emphasizing social embeddedness in which friendship ties may affect decisions about which jobs to retain in the organization. Selective initial placement of familiar candidates in the most valuable core jobs could also produce the outcome observed here, of course. Also, if departure of a first incumbent triggers a review of a job's value and familiar first incumbents are less likely to leave voluntarily, these results would occur.

While results do not support an effect for job idiosyncrasy at the .05 level, the ratio of coefficient to standard error (1.81) is statistically significant at the .10 level. The negative sign of the coefficient is consistent with theories suggesting idiosyncrasy reduces job deaths because of the effectiveness or political standing of idiosyncratic jobs. In considering idiosyncrasy, it should be noted that the equations include a control variable for multiple incumbency. Logistic regressions using multiple incumbency as the dependent variable indicate that opportunistic hires are significantly less likely to have multiple incumbents. In contrast, job novelty and department size had no statistically significant effect on multiple incumbency. Idiosyncrasy may affect job survival through its impact on the tendency for first incumbents to be replaced after their voluntary departure. Unfortunately, the data do not distinguish between layoffs and voluntary departures of first incumbents, making a definitive interpretation of this additional analysis premature.

To tease out the microprocesses of job death, future studies should estimate duration dependence explicitly and should include measures of both jobs and people (Barley & Tolbert, 1988; Jacobs, 1981). In principle, models exploring the interdependence of jobs and people should include measures of the centrality of jobs, duration of jobs, occupational groups, and degree of job idiosyncrasy. Data on all incumbents of a particular job should include the existence and intensity of social ties (Wegener, 1991), duration in job, and duration in institution, along with traditional human capital and ascriptive variables. The data collection burden of such studies is obviously substantial. Work on estimating the magnitude of effects of specific variables could point to variables whose omission could lead to serious modeling errors.

More broadly, research is needed on other organizational routines if researchers are to develop meaningful models of organizational evolution. The best developed empirical evidence for internal variation-selection-retention sequences comes from qualitative studies of organizational strategies (Burgelman, forthcoming; Mintzberg & McHugh, 1985). Routines that leave archival traces, such as changes in work protocols, accounting practices and categories, formal policies, and programs and departments are especially promising candidates. Indeed, structural contingency theory predicts that departments that mediate crucial broader dependencies will be selected for survival over time (Pfeffer, 1981). While this study has focused on incremental change, periods of massive shifts in the composition of organizational routines may also occur (Miner, Amburgey, & Stearns, 1990; Tushman & Romanelli, 1985).

Overall, the present study is in many ways exploratory. The data include simple measures in a complex world. Nonetheless, the pattern of results is consistent with the argument that structural evolution may occur through the selection and retention of formalized jobs. Because some of the jobs that survive are jobs tailored to particular people, change does not arise solely from impersonal planning. Finally, the results provide preliminary evidence that selection processes in organizational evolution are affected by the relationships of implementers of routines with their organizations.

The findings here are important for two unfolding areas of research. First, the results broadly support the movement toward conceptualizing career mobility and stratification as dynamic and interactive processes (DiPrete & Soule, 1988; Halaby, 1988; Lawrence, 1990). Evidence of substantial job turnover is not incompatible with mobility models that are agnostic on sources of impersonal opportunities. Preliminary evidence that incumbents' traits may affect the survival of jobs raises more serious issues, however. At first blush, such results seem to encourage a return to the idea that individual traits determine achievement unconstrained by organizational structures. This inference is unwarranted. Field observation shows that some jobs in this system, for example, have existed for decades.

In combination with other work on the whole economy (Leonard & Jacobson, 1990), however, this study points to a world in which we cannot automatically equate job formalization with job stability. It may be more appropriate to conceptualize formal organizations as skeletons of some stable, impersonal jobs—such as Controller, Director of Finance, and President —surrounded by other jobs of varying stability that are routinely contested and replaced. If this is so, individual traits—whether education, skills, gender, race, or social ties—will affect mobility not only through recruitment and selection for stable jobs, but also through their relationship with job birth and death itself (Estler, 1981; Miner & Estler, 1985). More generally, career mobility studies may need to examine the social ecologies of the jobs in which mobility patterns arise (Barnett & Miner, 1990).

Second, some theorists have suggested that we must choose between two approaches to organizational change: a world of structural inertia in which organizations rarely change in significant ways (Hannan & Freeman, 1984) or a world in which rational or political managers match organizational action to their goals and environments (Carroll, 1984). Further empirical study of organizational routines will permit more precise examination of less-explored emergent models of organizational change and learning (Aldrich & Marsden, 1988; Huber, 1991). It may permit study of the transmission of routines between organizations (Zucker, 1987) and consideration of nested evolutionary systems of individuals, organizations, populations, and communities of organizations (Gould, 1980; Kaufman, 1985; McKelvey, 1982).

Even if such grand goals are premature, much can be done now to examine organizational evolution prompted by turnover in routines. Evolutionary models can promote dangerous functionalism and sterile mathematical elaboration of inappropriate analogies. However, the study of organizational routines can also permit a study of change that is systematic without being adaptive, change that encompasses unintended outcomes of individual action (Coleman, 1986; Schelling, 1978). Such study can incorporate both social processes and theories of choice. For sociologists and organization theorists, the study of the evolution of institutions through turnover in routines is not only a natural domain of inquiry, it has been underway implicitly for 50 years. It is time to turn attention once more to the evolution of individual organizations where individual and collective behavior so often meet.

Appendix A. Descriptive Statistics and Correlation Matrix for Independent Variables ($N = 347$)

Independent Variable	Mean	Standard Deviation	Correlation Matrix							
			(1)	(2)	(3)	(4)	(5)	(6)	(7)	(8)
(1) Department size	73.121	63.473	1.000	—	—	—	—	—	—	—
(2) Opportunistic hire	.161	.368	-.063	1.000	—	—	—	—	—	—
(3) Evolved job	.337	.473	-.083	-.313	1.000	—	—	—	—	—
(4) Reclassification	.251	.434	.107	-.254	-.413	1.000	—	—	—	—
(5) Multiple incumbents	.199	.400	.060	-.120	-.080	.062	1.000	—	—	—
(6) Novel job[a]	.749	.434	-.107	—	—	—	.062	1.000	—	—
(7) Idiosyncratic job[a]	.499	.501	-.124	—	—	—	-.165	.577	1.000	—
(8) Familiar first incumbent[a]	2.427	.754	.041	—	—	—	.044	-.440	-.098	1.000

a. This variable is not used in the same model as job–founding type because it is a linear combination of job–founding types.

Acknowledgments

Contributions from Ramon Aldag, Joel Baum, Steve Barley, William Barnett, Barbara Lawrence, Arie Lewin, James March, Robert Mare, Kathy McCord, Craig Olson, Pamela Tolbert, and anonymous reviewers have improved the quality of this research. This study was partially funded by the University of Wisconsin Business School Research Fund, the Patricia Ostermann Research Fund, and the University of Wisconsin Graduate Fund. Charles Lehner made important early contributions to the project, and James Ploog provided valuable assistance. Philip Curry provided imaginative support in data collection.

REFERENCES

Aldrich, H. E. (1979). *Organizations and environments*. Englewood Cliffs: Prentice Hall.
Aldrich, H. E., & Marsden, P. V. (1988). Environments and organizations. In *Handbook of sociology* (pp. 361-392). Newbury Park, CA: Sage.
Allison, G. T. (1971). *Essence of decision: Explaining the Cuban missile crisis*. Boston: Little, Brown.
Allison, P. D. (1984). *Event history analysis*. Beverly Hills, CA: Sage.
Barley, S., & Tolbert, P. S. (1988). *Institutionalization and structuration: Methods and strategies for studying links between action and structure*. Paper presented at the Conference on Longitudinal Field Research Methods for Studying Organizational Processes, University of Texas, Austin.
Barley, S. R. (1986). Technology as an occasion for structuring: Evidence from observations of CT scanners and the social order of radiology departments. *Administrative Science Quarterly, 31*, 78-108.
Barnett, W., & Miner, A. S. (1990). *Standing on the shoulders of others: Institutional interdependence in job mobility* (Working paper). Madison: University of Wisconsin School of Business.
Berger, P. L., & Luckman, T. (1967). *The social construction of reality*. New York: Doubleday.
Burgelman, R. A. (forthcoming). Intraorganizational ecology of strategy-making and organizational adaptation: Theory and field research. *Organizational Science*.
Burns, T., & Stalker, G. M. (1961). *The management of innovation*. London: Tavistock.
Campbell, D. (1969). Variation and selective retention in sociocultural evolution. *General Systems, 16*, 69-85.
Carroll, G. (1984). Organizational ecology. *Annual Review of Sociology*, 71-93.
Carroll, G. (1988). *Ecological models of organizations*. Cambridge, MA: Ballinger.
Coleman, J. S. (1986). Social theory, social research, and a theory of action. *American Journal of Sociology, 91*, 1309-1335.
Cyert, R. M., & March, J. G. (1963). *A behavioral theory of the firm*. Englewood Cliffs: Prentice Hall.
DiPrete, T. A., & Soule, W. T. (1988). Gender and promotion in segmented job ladder systems. *American Sociological Review, 53*, 26-40.
Doeringer, P. B., & Piore, M. J. (1971). *Internal labor markets and manpower analysis*. Lexington, MA: Lexington Books.

Dornblaser, B. M., Lin, T., & Van de Ven, A. H. (1989). Innovation outcomes, learning and action loops. In A. H. Van de Ven, H. L. Angle, & M. S. Poole (Eds.), *Research on the management of innovation* (pp. 193-217). New York: Harper & Row.

Estler, S. E. (1981). Evolving jobs as a form of career mobility. *Personnel Management Journal, 10,* 335-365.

Giddens, A. (1984). *The constitution of society.* Cambridge, UK: Polity Press.

Gould, S. J. (1977). *Ever since Darwin.* New York: Norton.

Gould, S. J. (1980). Is a new general theory of evolution emerging? *Paleobiology, 6,* 119-130.

Graen, G. (1976). Role-making processes within complex organizations. In M. D. Dunnette (Ed.), *Handbook of industrial and organizational psychology* (pp. 1201-1245). Chicago: Rand McNally.

Granovetter, M. (1979). The idea of advancement in theories of social evolution and development. *American Journal of Sociology, 88,* 489-515.

Granovetter, M. (1985). Economic action and social structure: The problem of embeddedness. *American Journal of Sociology, 91,* 481-510.

Granovetter, M. (1986). Labor mobility, internal markets and job matching: A comparison of the sociological and economic approaches. In R. V. Robinson (Ed.), *Research in social stratification and mobility* (pp. 3-39). Greenwich, CT: JAI.

Halaby, C. N. (1988). Action and information in the job mobility process: The search decision. *American Sociological Review, 53,* 9-25.

Hannan, M. T., & Freeman, J. (1984). Structural inertia and organizational change. *American Sociological Review, 49,* 149-164.

Heneman, H. G., III, Schwab, D. P., Fossum, J. A., & Dyer, L. D. (1983). *Personnel/human resource management.* Homewood, IL: Irwin.

Holland, J. H. (1975). *Adaptation in natural and artificial systems: An introductory analysis with applications to biology, control and artificial intelligence.* Ann Arbor: University of Michigan Press.

Hopkins, A. (1988). Survival analysis with covariates—Cox Models. In W. G. Dixon (Ed.), *BMDP manual* (pp. 719-744). Berkeley: University of California Press.

Huber, G. (1991). Organizational learning: The contributing processes and a review of the literatures. *Organization Science, 2,* 88-115.

Jacobs, D. (1981). Toward a theory of mobility and behavior in organizations: An inquiry into the consequences of some relationships between individual performance and organizational success. *American Journal of Sociology, 87,* 684-707.

Kaufman, H. (1985). *Time, chance, and organizations.* Chatham, NJ: Chatham House.

Lawrence, B. S. (1990). At the crossroads: A multiple-level explanation of individual attainment. *Organization Science, 1,* 65-85.

Leonard, J. S., & Jacobson, L. (1990). Earnings inequality and job turnover. *American Economic Review, 80,* 298-302.

Levitt, B., & March, J. G. (1988). Organizational learning. *Annual Review of Sociology, 14,* 319-340.

MacKenzie, K. (1986). Virtual positions and power. *Management Science, 32,* 622-642.

March, J. G. (1981). Footnotes to organizational change. *Administrative Science Quarterly, 26,* 563-577.

March, J. G., & Simon, H. W. (1958). *Organizations.* New York: John Wiley.

McKelvey, W. (1982). *Organizational systematics: Taxonomy, evolution, classification.* Berkeley: University of California Press.

McPherson, J. M. (1990). Evolution in communities of voluntary organizations. In J. V. Singh (Ed.), *Organizational evolution: New directions* (pp. 224-245). Newbury Park, CA: Sage.

Miner, A. S. (1987). Idiosyncratic jobs in formalized organizations. *Administrative Science Quarterly, 32,* 327-351.

Miner, A. S. (1990). Structural evolution through idiosyncratic jobs: The potential for unplanned learning. *Organization Science, 1,* 195-210.

Miner, A. S., Amburgey, T., & Stearns, T. (1990). Interorganizational linkages and population dynamics: Buffering and transformational shields. *Administrative Science Quarterly, 35,* 689-713.

Miner, A. S., & Estler, S. E. (1985). Accrual mobility: Job mobility in higher education through responsibility accrual. *Journal of Higher Education, 56,* 121-143.

Mintzberg, H., & McHugh, A. (1985). Strategy formation in an adhocracy. *Administrative Science Quarterly, 30,* 160-197.

Nelson, R. R., & Winter, S. G. (1982). *An evolutionary theory of economic change.* Cambridge, MA: Harvard University Press.

Penrose, E. T. (1952). Biological analogies in the theory of the firm. *The American Economic Review, 41,* 804-819.

Pfeffer, J. (1981). *Power in organizations.* Marshfield: Pitman.

Pugh, D. S., Hickson, D. F., Hininger, R., & Turner, C. (1968). Dimensions of organizational structure. *Administrative Science Quarterly, 13,* 65-104.

Schelling, T. C. (1978). *Micromotives and macrobehavior.* New York: Norton.

Scott, W. R. (1981). *Organizations: Rational, natural and open systems.* Englewood Cliffs, NJ: Prentice Hall.

Singh, J. V., & Lumsden, C. I. (1990). Organizations and evolution. *Annual Review of Sociology, 16,* 161-195.

Spilerman, S. (1977). Careers, labor market structure and socioeconomic achievement. *American Journal of Sociology, 83,* 551-593.

Stewman, S. (1986). Demographic models of internal labor markets. *Administrative Science Quarterly, 31,* 212-247.

Stinchcombe, A. L. (1965). Social structure and organizations. In J. G. Marsh (Ed.), *Handbook of organizations* (pp. 142-193). Chicago: Rand McNally.

Strauss, A. (1978). *Negotiations.* San Francisco: Jossey-Bass.

Thompson, J. D. (1967). *Organizations in action.* New York: McGraw-Hill.

Tucker, D. J., Singh, J. V., & Meinhard, A. G. (1990). Founding characteristics, imprinting and organizational change. In J. V. Singh (Ed.), *Organizational evolution: New directions* (pp. 182-200). Newbury Park, CA: Sage.

Tuma, N. B., & Hannan, M. T. (1984). *Social dynamics: Models and methods.* San Francisco: Academic Press.

Tushman, M. L., & Romanelli, E. (1985). Organizational evolution: A metamorphosis model of convergence and reorientation. In L. L. Cummings & B. M. Staw (Eds.), *Research in organizational behavior* (pp. 171-222). Greenwich, CT: JAI.

Van Maanen, J., & Schein, E. H. (1979). Toward a theory of organizational socialization. In L. L. Cummings & B. M. Staw (Eds.), *Research in organizational behavior* (pp. 209-264). Greenwich, CT: JAI.

Weber, M. (1968). *Economy and society—An outline of interpretive sociology* (G. Roth & C. Wittich, Eds.). New York: Bedminster.

Wegener, B. (1991). Job mobility and social ties: Social resources, prior job and status attainment. *American Sociological Review, 56,* 60-71.

Weick, K. E. (1979). *The social psychology of organizing.* Reading. MA: Addison-Wesley.

White, H. C. (1970). *Chains of opportunity: System models of mobility in organizations.* Cambridge, MA: Harvard University Press.

Williamson, O. E. (1975). *Markets and hierarchies: Analysis and anti-trust implications.* New York: Free Press.

Winter, S. G. (1990). Survival, selection and inheritance in evolutionary theories of organization. In J. V. Singh (Ed.), *Organizational evolution: New directions* (pp. 269-297). Newbury Park, CA: Sage.

Zucker, L. G. (1987). Normal change or risky business: Institutional effects on the "hazard" of change in hospital organizations, 1959-1979. *Journal of Management Studies, 24,* 671-700.

18

Organizational Routines Are
Stored as Procedural Memory

Evidence From a Laboratory Study

MICHAEL D. COHEN
PAUL BACDAYAN

This original, well crafted paper makes a significant contribution to the understanding of organizational routines and extends, in a rather novel way, the treatment and properties of procedural memory. The paper also exemplifies how individual/group laboratory work can be creatively extended to organizational phenomena.

Arie Y. Lewin

Organizational routines—multi-actor, interlocking, reciprocally-triggered sequences of actions—are a major source of the reliability and speed of organizational performance. Without routines, organizations would lose efficiency as structures for collective action. But these frequently repeated action sequences can also occasionally give rise to serious suboptimality, hampering performance when they are automatically transferred onto inappropriate situations.

While the knowledgeable design and redesign of routines presents a likely lever for those wishing to enhance organizational performance, the lever remains difficult to grasp because routines are hard to observe, analyze, and describe. This paper argues that new work in psychology on "procedural" memory may help explain how routines arise, stabilize, and change. Procedural memory has close

This chapter appeared originally in *Organization Science,* Vol. 5, No. 4, November 1994. Copyright © 1994, The Institute of Management Sciences.

links to notions of individual skill and habit. It is memory for how things are done that is relatively automatic and inarticulate, and it encompasses both cognitive and motor activities.

We report an experiment in which paired subjects developed interlocked task performance patterns that display the chief characteristics of organizational routines. We show evidence from their behavior supporting the claim that individuals store their components of organizational routines in procedural memory. If routines are stored as distributed procedural memories, this may be the source of distinctive properties reported by observers of organizational routines. The paper concludes with implications for both research and practice.

(ROUTINES; ORGANIZATIONAL LEARNING;
STANDARD OPERATING PROCEDURES;
PROCEDURAL MEMORY;
ORGANIZATIONAL MEMORY; SKILLS)

Recent work in psychology on "procedural" human memory may help organization theorists explain key properties of organizational routines, including the dynamics of how they arise, stabilize, and change. We view organizational routines as interlocking, reciprocally-triggered sequences of skilled actions. Striking characteristics of collective routines, such as the tendency to occasionally "misfire" in inappropriate circumstances, may be grounded in the properties psychology has demonstrated for the procedural memories of individual participants.

Procedural memory has close links to notions of individual skill and habit. It is memory for how things are done that is relatively automatic and inarticulate, and it encompasses cognitive as well as motor activities. While others (notably, Nelson & Winter, 1982) have pointed eloquently to the similarity of individual skill and organizational routine, we extend the idea by asserting that the similarity is founded on specific characteristics of the memories of organizational members, and we present evidence for the claim from experimentally-induced group routines.

Our argument proceeds as follows. First, we identify the need for improved understanding of organizational routines and the barriers to understanding that must be overcome. Second, we argue for the theoretical fruitfulness of incorporating the concept of procedural memory into our thinking about routines; we also argue that laboratory experimentation provides an especially useful kind of evidence for investigations of organizational routine. Third, we describe our experimental method of establishing routines in laboratory dyads. Fourth, we report two major results: that the behaviors of our subject pairs have the distinctive features of *organizational* routines, and that individual memories of parts in those routines have the characteristics of the procedural mode. Fifth, we close by exploring the implications of our results both for managers and for organization theorists, paying particular attention to organizational learning and bounded rationality.

We aim to begin unlocking the *dynamics* of organizational routines, the ways they arise and change, by demonstrating that they can be induced in the laboratory and by showing that organizational routines emerge from the interaction of procedurally remembering individuals.

THE IMPORTANCE OF ROUTINES AND THE DIFFICULTIES OF UNDERSTANDING THEM

Routines appear prominently and persistently in descriptions of organizational action (Allison, 1971; Cyert & March, 1963; Gersick & Hackman, 1990; Levitt & March, 1988; March & Simon, 1958; Nelson & Winter, 1982). Their properties clearly merit deeper explanation since, for both good and ill, routines structure so much organizational behavior. On the good side, routines are a major source of organizational competence. Routines arise in repetitive situations where the recurring cost of careful deliberation can become a heavy burden; they store organizational experience in a form that allows the organization to rapidly transfer that experience to new situations.

When the experience is transferred to appropriate situations, routines benefit the organization. They not only provide a major determinant of the nature of short-run organizational responses to familiar and unfamiliar environmental stimuli, but they do so efficiently by decreasing the effort spent on decision making and implementation. Without routines, organizations would not be efficient structures for collective action (March & Simon, 1958; Stinchcombe, 1990). When, however, the organization's experience is automatically transferred to inappropriate situations, routines can be bad. Consider, for example, control room operators or pilots whose vigilance erodes when they become so accustomed to answering each safety check "okay" that they don't see trouble when it actually is present (Gersick & Hackman, 1990). Or again, consider the case of civilian-clothed Soviet troops arriving secretly in Cuba who nonetheless formed into ranks on the dock and marched conspicuously away (Allison, 1971, p. 109). Thus routines are like a two-edged sword. They allow efficient coordinated action, but also introduce the risk of highly inappropriate responses.

By "organizational routines," we mean patterned sequences of learned behavior involving multiple actors who are linked by relations of communication and/or authority. Though they are organized by such relations, the actors may have heterogeneous objectives, information, capabilities, or world models. We use "routine" to designate established patterns of organizational action and we distinguish routines from "standard operating procedures" which are more explicitly formulated and have normative standing. Thus the working routines of an organization may or may not be equivalent to its official standard operating procedures. The value of the distinction becomes clear when one observes that "working-to-rule" can be a profoundly disruptive tactic of labor protest. We also reserve "routine" exclusively for organizational actions and use "skill" or "habit" at the individual level.

Given the important role of routines in patterning the behavior of organizations, it follows that in our efforts to create change we often want to design or redesign routines, and for this we need to better understand the forces that create and maintain them. Information technology, for example, is often introduced with the aim of augmenting or replacing existing routines. But research on information technology (Zuboff, 1988), and on other innovations in manufacturing (Womack, Jones, & Roos, 1990), shows us that even the most advanced new systems can end up gathering dust, and that major reorganizations and technical investments can dramatically fail to increase productivity if the technology is founded on a misunderstanding of the underlying system of routines. Such observations make painfully clear both the pressing need for intelligent (re)design of routines and the poverty of our understanding.

The understanding of organizational routines is hampered, however, by three basic characteristics. First, routines are multi-actor, and thus harder to observe and grasp than single-actor phenomena. (Indeed, the multi-actor character of routines is a major way in which organization is constituted out of member individuals.) The distributed character of the action complicates the work of both managers and field researchers. Landing a commercial airline flight is highly routinized, but we cannot understand it only by examining the pilot's part.

A second characteristic of organizational routines that hinders both understanding and design is their emergent quality. Organizations provide fertile conditions for the evolution of behavior patterns by experiential learning rather than explicit decision making. Documentation is typically sparse and turnover eliminates individuals who recall the intended functions of particular acts. Moreover, there is frequently no one with the intellectual grasp or authority to self-consciously analyze or design a major routine in its entirety. Thus organizational routines often emerge through gradual multi-actor learning, and exhibit tangled histories that may frustrate both understanding and reform.

Experiential learning is often accretionary—hence over time routines can become "contaminated" with extraneous, historically-specific and arbitrary components. Most real-world routines will contain, in addition to valuable elements (e.g., those which might maintain dignity of participants, enhance communication of unstructured information, or overcome individual cognitive limitations), less valuable components. Routines may preserve artifacts of old technology (e.g., continuing to do something in an inconvenient way that originally avoided a technological obstacle that no longer exists). Thus a time-and-motion expert studying motorized British artillery crews around the time of World War II was puzzled by a recurring three second pause just before firing. Finally, an old timer watching slow-motion films said, "Ah, I have it. They are holding the horses" (Morison, 1966). Or, as another example, routines may simply sustain accidents of history. So an experimental group's pace and style in working on a second, comparable task resembles that of their first session even though the experimenter has doubled or halved the time available (Kelly & McGrath, 1985). These emergent, historical qualities imply that sorting out the real functions of the different components of a routine can become a very challenging task.

A third, and pivotal, characteristic of routines which hinders redesign is that the underlying knowledge of the parts of routines held by individual actors is often partially inarticulate. Although it may seem that a manager or researcher ought to be able to understand a routine by interviewing the participants, it frequently turns out that they simply cannot put into words what they do and why. For example, the artillery crews mentioned above could not tell the researcher why they paused. This is most striking for nonverbal tasks such as operating machinery (Nelson & Winter, 1982; Zuboff, 1988), but the problem is encountered even when tasks have significant verbal components, such as forms processing or filing (Sheil, 1981; Suchman, 1983).

Organizational actors who cannot give meaningful responses to typical interview questions are like subjects in some experiments who prove unable to give accurate reports of the causes of their own actions (Nisbett & Wilson, 1977), or experts who have difficulty providing clear accounts of the skills to be coded into expert systems programs (Gaines & Boose, 1988). The problem is to surface hard-to-verbalize knowledge and skill. Thus routines reside partially in an "organizational unconscious," which greatly compounds the observational and analytical problems associated with their multi-actor and learned character.

To summarize, routines offer a powerful concept that accounts for much of what happens—both good and bad—in organizations, and the knowledgeable design of routines presents a potential lever to those interested in enhancing organizational performance. This lever remains hard to grasp, however, because the characteristics described earlier block observation, analysis, and description of specific routines. As we will suggest in the following sections, these properties may be due to the storage of the individual actors' parts in organizational routines as procedural memories.

REQUIREMENTS FOR
THEORETICAL PROGRESS

If organizational routines are learned behaviors involving multiple actors, it follows that if we want to control, design, or modify them with increased precision, we need to understand how organizational members learn their parts in routines. And to do this we need advances both in theory and in observation. It may seem strange to call for theory development when routine and standard operating procedure have been cornerstone concepts of behavioral organization theory since Cyert and March (1963). But, in fact, there has been very little advance of basic theory since their path breaking work. There have been many applications of the theory to interpretation of field observations of routine. Thus the *Social Science Citation Index* shows 71 citations of Cyert and March in a recent five-year period, but none of the citing articles attempts to further develop their theory of routines and standard operating procedures. For the most part, the concept of routine has been applied to mop up the "residuals" of rationality, i.e., as *post hoc* explanation of apparently nonrational behavior. The many studies do not seem to have yielded a better theoretical understanding of routines themselves—where they come from or how they change.

Both theory and observation need new impetus. Our approach on the theoretical side is to point out the potential of developments in recent psychological research that, we feel, give hope of improving our grasp of the dynamics of routines (Cohen, 1991). On the observational side, we show here the value of supplementing field work with laboratory studies, where increased control makes it easier to assess the promise of new theory and to arrange observations that have the best chance of generalizing to multiple settings.

Procedural Memory

Psychological work over the last decade has accumulated substantial evidence for several, partially independent modes of memory (Squire, 1987; Tulving & Schacter, 1990). "Procedural" memory appears to be the form that stores the components of individual skilled actions—for both motor *and* *cognitive* skills. It is distinguished from "declarative" memory, which provides the storage of facts, propositions, and events.[1] One of the most striking illustrations comes from work with patients suffering certain forms of amnesia. They may be unable to remember daily exposures to therapists, apparatus, and training, but nonetheless show improvement on tasks as complex as the game of checkers or the difficult puzzle known as "The Tower of Hanoi" (Cohen, 1984). With only procedural memory available, they learn and exhibit improved performance, but are unaware of what (or even that) they have learned. A crucial observation is that they also perform well in priming experiments, producing appropriate responses when cued in context at the same rates as normal subjects, although their ability to recall items from learned lists is severely impaired (Graf, Squire, & Mandler, 1984).

Though normal individuals have both procedural and declarative memory, studies have shown that each mode has distinctive properties. Among the differences of interest to students of organizational routine, we focus on three. Procedural knowledge is less subject to decay, less explicitly accessible, and less easy to transfer to novel circumstances.

The low decay rate of procedural memory corresponds to long-standing casual observations about the durability of skills (e.g., the commonplace claim that "you never forget how to ride a bicycle"). People may forget the grammatical rules of a language studied long before, but still be able to distinguish grammatical sentences in that language after years of nonuse (Bahrick, 1984). Studies of people solving puzzles in sessions separated by intervals of up to three months show that memory for specific puzzles solved earlier decays rapidly, but memory for how to solve puzzles of that type does not (Bunch, 1936). Such disjunctions indicate that procedural knowledge has decayed far less than its declarative counterpart.

The lowered accessibility of procedural memory has been revealed in studies (Graf, Shimamura, & Squire, 1985) in which a response acquired in written mode is not available when cued verbally but is available when cued visually. Declarative memories, in contrast, are more equally available across communication modes. This property appears to lie behind the common experience of a telephone number or lock combination which cannot be stated, but becomes available once a phone or lock is under the hand.

The restricted range of transfer of procedurally encoded skills has been a particular focus of work by Singley and Anderson (1989) who have demonstrated such phenomena in activities such as LISP programming and problem solving in calculus and geometry. Their findings concur with those of others who have shown that physics students fail to apply well-learned methods to the interpretation of nonclassroom physical events (McCloskey, 1983) and that Brazilian school children, who could correctly determine on the street

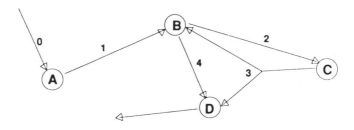

Figure 18.1. A Routine Among Four Actors Shown as Mutual Printing of Procedurally
Stored Actions

the total cost of a purchase such as five lemons at 35 cruzeiros apiece, could
not compute the answer to the matching arithmetic problem 5 × 35 = ?
(Carraher, Carraher, & Schliemann, 1985).

We take it as a significant similarity that the characteristic costs and
benefits of routines discussed above resemble observations by psychologists
on transfer of learning. The development of routines in organizations is good
for reasons parallel to the psychologists' positive transfer effects. Groups of
people get better at doing "the same" thing. That generates rising learning
curves, in which the world business community is today intensely interested;
Senge (1990) is illustrative. On the other hand, the development of routines
in organizations can be bad because of an effect at the individual level similar
to negative transfer. Groups do things in "the same" way when the situation
(as others see it) is not really "the same."

We argue that this similarity of transfer of learning at the individual and
organizational levels is far from coincidental. The properties of organizational routines arise from the way individuals store and enact their parts in
those routines. As individuals become skilled in their portions of a routine
the actions become stored as procedural memories and can later be triggered
as substantial chunks of behavior. The routine of a group can be viewed as
the concatenation of such procedurally stored actions, each primed by and
priming the actions of others (Tulving & Schacter, 1990).

Figure 18.1 gives a schematic example. An action or situation (labeled 0)
triggers action 1 by actor A. This alters the situation so that action 2 is
triggered for actor B. C is then primed to take action 3, which alters the
situation for both B and D. B now takes action 4. D then responds to 3 and
4 with a further step, and the chain may continue.

This model is certainly not entirely new. It is closely connected to Weick's (1979) account of the "double-interact," which itself has a long history (Allport, 1924). And, as we mentioned at the outset, the simile of organizational routine and individual habit has been noted by many others (e.g., Dewey, 1922; Nelson & Winter, 1982; Stene, 1940). But we take an additional step in suggesting a specific psychological mechanism that may generate the phenomenon, and we provide evidence from experimentally-induced routines that supports our claim. Establishing tighter links to relevant individual psychology and adding to our observational repertoire both should help us to unlock the *dynamics* of organizational routines. This will shed new light on their interactions with organizational learning and structure (Drazin & Sandelands, 1992; Levitt & March, 1988).

Experimental Observation

The vast majority of what organization theorists know of routine comes from field observation. But laboratory studies provide a very useful auxiliary approach, especially when the question is a possible linkage to individual psychological phenomena that have also been uncovered with laboratory methods. The enhanced control of the laboratory offers the possibility of carefully testing ideas that claim to explain the rich observations of the field.

Laboratory study of organizational routines is not new, of course. Cyert and March (1963) included such studies in *A Behavioral Theory of the Firm*. And many classic experiments in which small groups repeatedly solve variants of a given type of problem can be regarded as inducing a set of differentiated and interlocked behavior patterns that we would classify as routines (e.g., Laughlin & Shippy, 1983; Shaw, 1954; Weick & Gilfillan, 1971). The early literature is reviewed with great conceptual clarity in Weick (1965).[2]

In the present study we want to be more explicit than has commonly been the case in showing that the behavior patterns of our subject groups have the characteristics commonly reported in field studies of organizational routine. Then we can go on to show that the same experiments provide evidence that elements of the routines are stored by individuals as procedural memory. The experimental instrument we will describe below has been carefully designed not only for the present purpose of demonstrating the linkage of organizational and individual levels, but also to support later studies exploring the impacts on routines of organizational variables such as authority relations, incentive structures, size, and communications channels.

As the first step, then, we want to establish that our procedures generate patterns of behavior in the laboratory with four features characteristic of field-observed routines:

1. *Reliability.* Students of organizational routine have always stressed that a key advantage of routinization is the increased ability of the organization to produce an acceptable result (Allison, 1971; Cyert & March, 1963; Inbar, 1979). Thus we want to show that the patterns of behavior that form in our experiments deliver this same advantage.

2. *Speed.* Along with reliability, routinized behavior is expected to be faster than behavior being generated as deliberate decision making in unfamiliar circumstances.

3. *Repeated Action Sequences.* A characteristic feature of routines is that the actions that compose them are substantially the same over time, so that multiple occurrences can be identified as instances of the same routine. This is a key feature in the definition of group routine offered by Gersick and Hackman (1990).

4. *Occasional Suboptimality.* One of the reasons attention has been drawn to routines is the observed tendency for them to "fire off" in circumstances where, to an observer, some other action would have been more appropriate. This is the "blind-spot" property that makes so striking a story like Allison's (1971) report of soldiers in Cuba failing to achieve disguise. More generally, it is the property usually regarded as a chief cost of routine that must be traded off against benefits such as those mentioned above, and it is evidence that action is occurring without full deliberation, another marker cited by Gersick and Hackman (1990).

EXPERIMENT

After we describe the experimental task, we will show that our subjects' behavior has these four features and thus that our dyads can be seen as miniature organizations with behavior patterns that are organizational routines. Then we will turn to evidence that our individual subjects are encoding their elements of those routines as procedural memories.

Experimental Task

The task we employ in this study is a card game. This is an ideal environment for our purposes, as each hand requires precise rational problem solving, but in the play of many hands there is opportunity for routines to form. The game is played by two players using six cards: the 2, 3, and 4 of a red suit and the 2, 3, and 4 of a black suit. It is played on a board resembling Figure 18.2. Because there are six hundred legal ways to deal the cards in the game, it creates a task setting with a key realistic property: routines can

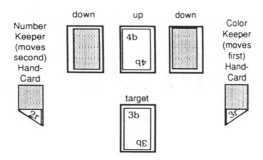

Figure 18.2. Playing Board as It Appeared to Subjects After Deal of Training Hand

form because jobs (deals of the cards) are similar, but each particular job is usually novel in some aspect. When the cards are dealt by the experimenter, each player has a card in hand that cannot be seen by the other player. (The figures indicate this one-sided visibility with a turned-up corner.) On the board, in the marked rectangles, are two face-down cards that neither player can see, and two face-up that both can observe.

In each hand that is played the ultimate object is to maneuver the red 2 (2r in the figure) into the area marked "target." A move in the game is an exchange of the card in a player's hand with one of the cards on the board (or a "pass," making it the other player's turn). Each player is subject to a restriction on moves. The player on the right, called "Color Keeper," may make exchanges with the target area card only if the *color* in the target is preserved. The player on the left, "Number Keeper," may exchange with the target only if the action preserves the *number* in the target area. Exchanges with board areas other than the target are not restricted.

The successive situations in Figures 18.3 through 18.5 illustrate the play of the example hand in Figure 18.2. This is the sequence that was demonstrated to the subjects during training. In Figure 18.3, the Color Keeper has exchanged her card for the down card at the upper left of the figure. (We will use the convention of referring to Color Keeper as "she" and Number Keeper as "he.") The rectangle background is highlighted to show where the most recent action occurred. Her hand now contains the black 2 (2b). The red 3 (3r) has been placed face down on the upper left rectangle of the board without being seen by her partner.

It is now the Number Keeper's turn and he would like to put the 2r in his hand into the target, but the restriction prohibits that. Four other possibilities are available: exchange with the up card; exchange with one of the two down cards; or pass. In the training hand we instructed the subjects to pass. Since the board is unchanged, no separate panel appears in the figures.

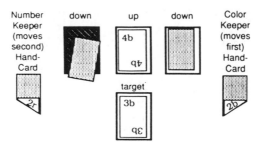

Figure 18.3. Board After Color Keeper Exchanges With Left Down Card

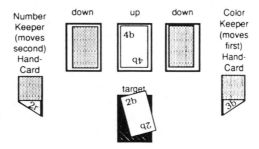

Figure 18.4. Board After Number Keeper Passes and Color Keeper Exchanges With Target Card

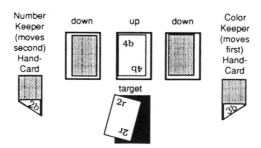

Figure 18.5. Board After Number Keeper Exchanges With Target Card, Finishing Hand

It is the Color Keeper's turn again. This time it is legal for her to exchange her hand with the target, since the action will leave a black card in the target. We instructed the subjects to make this move, and the result is shown as Figure 18.4.

The Number Keeper can now legally exchange his card with the target, which produces the situation shown in Figure 18.5. The hand is finished. Four moves were used to complete it.

The incentive system in the experiment reported here was that subjects had 40 minutes to play up to 40 hands of the game. Each hand they successfully completed earned their partnership one dollar. Each move they made (including passes) cost their partnership a dime. In the example hand they would have netted 60 cents. At the conclusion of a 40-minute session, they split their winnings equally. This arrangement placed the subjects in a fully cooperative relationship with each other, but created a tension between the two performance measures. The team needed to play *quickly* in order to increase the number of hands completed, but they needed to play *carefully* in order to avoid unnecessary moves in completing each hand. The incentives were deliberately quite substantial. Including base pay and variable winnings, a typical subject in the study took home about 35 dollars from two sessions of play.

By design, the experiment incorporates a number of fundamental features characteristic of organizational life. The color and number restrictions create asymmetry of capabilities and thus the potential for division of labor and distinctive roles. On average there are substantial returns to coordination of the multiple actors but when coordination fails performance can actually be worse than what a single actor could achieve. There is uncertainty and asymmetry of information as a result of the face-down cards and hand cards. As each pair develops its method for effectively playing successive hands, it implicitly constructs an interlocked system of roles for the individual members that addresses these classical organizational issues. Their learning creates an organization, albeit one small and short-lived.

Our subjects were graduate and upper-level under graduate students in business, public policy, and the social sciences grouped into 32 pairs at random. They were both male and female. All-male, all-female, and mixed-gender pairs were allocated as evenly as possible into the four experimental conditions. Assignment to partners, game roles, and conditions was otherwise random.

After training, which consisted of reading printed rules and being led through the example hand shown above, each pair played two sessions of 40 minutes separated by a delay. In one experimental condition this delay was a break over dinner time that took two to four hours. In the other condition, the delay was one to two weeks. A second manipulation involved novelty of the second session task. Half the subjects played in a same-task condition. They had identical rules and occupied the same roles at the table as in their first session. The other half were in a novel condition. On their return for the second session, these subjects were asked, without prior warning, to reverse roles. They sat on opposite sides of the playing board from their prior experience and were therefore subject to the reversed form of the restriction on target exchanges. They were also told that their object was now to work the *black* 2 into the target.

The hands played by the pairs were pre-dealt. All pairs got the same sequence of 80 hands, involving 60 distinct deals of the cards. Some deals were repeated to permit comparisons of play early and late in the first session and between sessions one and two. In the experimental context where they were repeatedly rearranging the same six cards, subjects appeared to have little sense that they might have seen any particular deal previously. For the subjects in the novel condition, the second session deals were transformed so that black cards were in the positions occupied by red cards in the deals going to subjects without novel rules. From a logical point of view this means that hands in the novel and same rules conditions were of identical difficulty.

Subjects were strongly urged not to discuss the experiment between sessions and no talking was allowed during play. A factorial design crossing these two manipulations, short versus long delay between sessions and same or novel rules in the second session, yielded four experimental groups. Each contained eight pairs. This design allowed us to test for procedural memory by examining how delay and novelty affected play. The logic of this test is described below.

The experimental sessions were videotaped. The resulting recordings were converted to machine readable records of every move made, and the time period preceding every move. The method was to watch each hand, recording the moves made, then watch each hand again, making a computer keystroke at the moment each card was released onto the playing board. These data are the basis of the analyses below.

RESULTS

We turn now to reporting analyses of the experimental data. These show that routines actually do form as pairs play many hands of the card game and that memory for the actions involved is procedural.

TABLE 18.1 Repeated Measures Analysis of Variance of Average Move Time per Hand for Five Recurring Deals

Source	SS	DF	MS	F	p
Hypothesis	217.894	1	217.894	88.998	< 0.0005
Error	389.281	159	2.448		

Evidence That the Actions Are Routines

We want to assess whether the behavior of our subject pairs displays the four indicators of organizational routinization described above: increasing reliability, increasing speed, the development of repeated action sequences, and occasional suboptimality.

Reliability. We can assess reliability by examining the variation across pairs in the number of moves required to complete play of a hand. The three quartile range reflects this variation well. As fewer pairs encounter serious difficulties in playing a hand, this range should decrease. Over the course of the 40 hands in the first session the moves-per-hand required by the best pair and by the twenty-fifth best pair do grow increasingly similar. The regression of hand number on the three quartile range of moves per hand shows a decrease of about 0.06 per hand ($t = -2.70$; $p < 0.01$, two tail; $r^2 = 0.161$). Because the individual hands vary in difficulty it is at least conceivable that this reflects a trend in the arrangement of the deals. But we can control for difficulty variation by comparing the three quartile range of moves used to complete a hand early in the first session with that of an identical deal later in the session. There are five replicated deals available for this purpose. Each one occurs early and is repeated 25 hands later. The mean of the range is 3.7 moves for the early set, but only 1.8 moves when the set reoccurs. Thus we can say that the performance of the pairs is becoming more reliable.

Speed. The second indicator of routinization was speed. Here we can examine the time used in making a move in any hand of the experiment. This is quite distinct from the number of moves made in that hand. Players could go fast and not necessarily be selecting moves that led to solutions in few steps. In fact, the correlation of moves per hand and average move time in that hand over both sessions is 0.302 (N = 2560; p[r = 0] < 0.0005). As in the previous discussion, it is consistent with the formation of routines that speed increases over time. The regression of hand number on the average move time per hand indicates that each added hand of experience improves performance by about

−0.016 seconds per hand (t = −6.46; p < 0.0005; r^2 = 0.116). And we can control for difficulty of hands by the same repeated measures strategy used earlier. Table 18.1 shows that move time was significantly faster on the second occurrence of each of the repeated five hands. The pairs are taking the steps in their work at increasing speeds.

Repeated Action Sequences. Our third indicator of the formation of routines is the development of repeated action sequences. Steps in playing the card game that occur in the early going while the subjects are proceeding "one move at a time" develop into "chunks" that are run off as units. Our observation is that a number of these chunks form within experimental pairs over the course of a session. Different pairs actually form different stable action patterns. We demonstrate the phenomenon here by reporting on one such sequence, which we refer to as "up-up-anything-target" and abbreviate UU*T. As the name suggests, this is a sequence that begins with either player making an exchange with the nontarget face-up area on the board. The other player then makes an exchange with that same area. The third element of the sequence can be any move. The fourth step is an exchange with the target area.

Figure 18.6 gives an example. Here, as is generally true, the sequence solves the problem faced by a player (Number Keeper here) who has a card in hand (the 2r in this case, but it could be the 2b or something else) that should go into the target. The basic restriction on number (or color) prevents this. Instead the player puts it in the up area, making it known and available. The other player picks it up. The initiating player does something else (frequently a pass). And the partner puts it into the target. A functional interpretation of this sequence is "moving a card you cannot play into the hand of your partner, who can." It nicely exemplifies the teamwork required of a pair to solve the problems they confront and the way the UU*T routine is a property of the group rather than of either of its members.

This sequence occurs 817 times across the 2,560 hands of the two sessions, where the chance expectation would be less than 25 occurrences. The median pair uses the sequence 26.5 times, but some pairs rely on it much more heavily than others (SD = 5.143). The time the sequence takes to run off is instructive. In early play subjects take about the same amount of time to make a move that is part of the sequence as they do to make any other move. In the first two hands the time per move of each type is not significantly different (t = 1.476; df = 25). But as practice accumulates, and the sequence becomes more of a "chunk," a move in the sequence is much faster than a normal move at the same experience level by the same players (t = 3.442; df = 48; p < 0.001). The fastest instances we see by the second session make four moves in less than four seconds. They have virtually overlapping move-

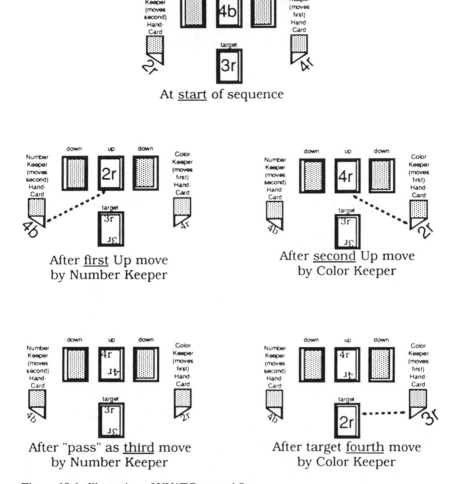

Figure 18.6. Illustration of UU*T Repeated Sequence

ments by the actors. Each knows what the other is about to do. Watching these cases in the lab one is reminded of the way a skilled touch typist rapidly generates a familiar word with overlapping keystrokes—except that here the two hands are on different bodies.

Occasional Suboptimality. A final remark about these sequences such as UU*T is that they contribute to suboptimality, our fourth indicator of routi-

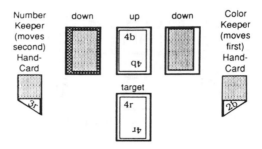

Figure 18.7. Cards Dealt in Thirty-Eighth Hand, Which Has Possible Solution in
Three (or Five) Moves

nization. Across the 32 subject pairs, the number of uses of UU*T is
positively correlated with the average number of moves used in resolving
the 80 hands (r = 0.146; p[r = 0] < 0.0005).

However, there is more striking evidence than this of suboptimality. The
thirty-eighth hand in our first session was dealt as shown in Figure 18.7. This
is a hand in which it is easy to show that the best play would be for Number
Keeper to "stay out of it." The 4r is already in the target. The remaining
problem is for Color Keeper to get the 2r into her hand. If Number Keeper
doesn't interfere, Color Keeper will find the 2r either on her first search of
a down card (finishing in three moves), or on her second search (finishing
in five). Any moves by Number Keeper that bring the 2r into his hand will
only require passing it over to Color Keeper at a cost of four extra moves.

In only 7 of our 32 pairs did both players make two initial moves consistent with Number Keeper staying out of it while Color Keeper searches
and finishes. Most of the remaining 25 pairs used one of two suboptimal
approaches. In 10 of the remaining cases, Color Keeper's opening move was
to exchange with the up pile. This repeats a frequent strategy of making the
2b, or other cards which may be useful, visible to her partner. In 12 additional
cases Color Keeper opened by searching and then Number Keeper searched
as well. Here Number Keeper seems to be adhering to the common approach
in which both players look for the red 2 during the early stages of play.
Unfortunately, Number Keeper actually drew the 2r in nine of these cases.
The unlucky pairs then spent many extra moves undoing the ill effects of
Number Keeper's "success." Thus we have a case where an approach to the
problem that left all the action to one individual would actually be better than
the more organizationally balanced one, but the groups use the approach they
have learned.

We have isolated other deals with similar features. In effect, our pairs are like individuals who have been practicing left turns so long that they will pass by a right turn to make three lefts instead. Action is occurring without full deliberation.

Summarizing, there are four kinds of evidence for the formation of organizational routines in the performance of this task: increasing reliability (decrease in moves required), increasing speed (decrease in time per move), repeated action sequences (recurring dyad-specific sequences of joint behavior), and suboptimality (pairs failing to see solutions superior to their routine methods).

Evidence That Memory for Routines Is Procedural

Having shown that routines emerge in our laboratory task, we turn now to findings on our second question: may these characteristic features of organizational routine that have often been likened to habits and skills derive from the fact that actors store elements of a routine in procedural memory, the same form of memory that psychologists are now arguing is the storage form of individual habits and skills? We proceed by examining the effects of two kinds of experimental manipulations.

First, recall that we earlier characterized declarative memory (for facts, propositions, and events) as being slower than procedural memory. It has been shown by Singley and Anderson (1989) that individuals engaged in skilled activities such as solving calculus or computer programming problems can apply well-learned methods very rapidly to new problems of the familiar type, but are dramatically slowed when novelties are introduced (e.g., differentiating a new form of expression or programming a new type of control structure). They argue that confronting novelties requires switching from skills that are stored in procedural memory to propositional knowledge about possible actions that are stored in declarative memory. The latter is dramatically slower. The novelty of our experimental manipulation after the first session was modest, asking half the subjects to sit on the opposite sides of the table and work with the black two instead of the red two. But if that requires them to revert to declarative processing, then we should expect that *our subjects would be noticeably slowed by the introduction of novelty into the rules of their routinized game.*

Second, Singley and Anderson (1989) also report, and many others have found, that memory for skills (which they view as procedural) decays far less than memory for propositions (which they view as declarative). Thus we should expect that *our subjects, if playing under the same rules for which their routines were built, would not be much affected by the addition of a substantial time interval between sessions of play.*

If we turn to our results, we find these two central expectations are borne out by the repeated measures analysis of variance in Table 18.2. It shows two different comparisons: hand 23 to hand 41; and hand 40 to hand 41. Hand 41 is the first hand of the second session. Hands 23 and 40 are the two hands from the first session with the logical structure most similar, though not identical, to hand 41. Across both comparisons, novelty proves consistently to have significant effects, both within and between subjects. Delay does not.

The nature of the effect can be seen in Figure 18.8, a time series plot of the average time per move for each of the eighty hands for each of the four conditions. The data have been smoothed with the 4253H robust filter of Tukey (Velleman & Hoaglin, 1981). For the two conditions where rules were "Same," the transition from hand 40 to hand 41 makes little difference and, in particular, the long delay group plays quickly despite a break of one to two weeks. For these two groups, the long term steady decrease of time at a decreasing rate suggests typical data for the "power law of practice" that is seen in tasks such as typing (Newell, 1990).

On the other hand, the two "Novel" rule groups have great difficulty for a few hands. One gradually returns to speeds comparable to the "Same" groups. The other, the one with short delay between sessions, seems to have greater trouble in recovering. (We speculate that the short delay may be related to this, perhaps through a mechanism of interference by the still-fresh prior experience. However, from a statistical point of view the apparent effect is not very reliable.)

SUMMARY, INTERPRETATION, AND IMPLICATIONS

Our experiment induces, in the laboratory, behavior patterns that exhibit major characteristics of organizational routines, and the effects of novelty and delay manipulations are consistent with what would be expected if individual memory for elements of routinized performance is procedural. The speed of task performance, itself a principal indicator of routinization, seems to be little affected by delay, but substantially impaired by the introduction of novelty into the task. This is what we should find if elements of those routines were stored as procedural memory, which shows little decay, while subjects' reasoning about response to rule changes required slower declarative memory processing.

The marked suboptimality of our groups on hand 38 can be interpreted as a group *Einstellung* (or set) effect (Luchins, 1942). Seen this way, the subjects in our laboratory are exhibiting *at a group level* what Singley and Anderson (1989) observe to be the characteristic form of negative transfer

TABLE 18.2 Repeated Measures Analyses of Variance of Time per Move in Two Hands From First Session Compared to First Hand of Second Session

Source	Error			Hypothesis				
	SS	DF	MS	SS	DF	MS	F	p
Hand 23 vs. Hand 41								
Between Subjects								
Delay (D)	135.760	28	4.849	6.504	1	6.504	1.341	0.257
Novelty (N)	135.760	28	4.849	30.159	1	30.159	6.220	0.019
D × N	135.760	28	4.849	5.154	1	5.154	1.063	0.311
Within Subjects								
Constant	83.601	28	2.986	29.478	1	29.478	9.873	0.004
Delay	83.601	28	2.986	1.667	1	1.667	0.558	0.461
Novelty	83.601	28	2.986	36.844	1	36.844	12.34	0.002
D × N	83.601	28	2.986	0.360	1	0.360	0.123	0.728
Hand 40 vs. Hand 41								
Between Subjects								
Delay	122.89	28	4.389	1.000	1	1.000	0.228	0.637
Novelty	122.89	28	4.389	22.975	1	22.975	5.235	0.030
D × N	122.89	28	4.389	5.106	1	5.106	1.163	0.290
Within Subjects								
Constant	109.87	28	3.924	48.536	1	48.536	12.370	0.002
Delay	109.87	28	3.924	8.072	1	8.072	2.057	0.163
Novelty	109.87	28	3.924	45.812	1	45.812	11.675	0.002
D × N	109.87	28	3.924	0.382	1	0.382	0.097	0.757

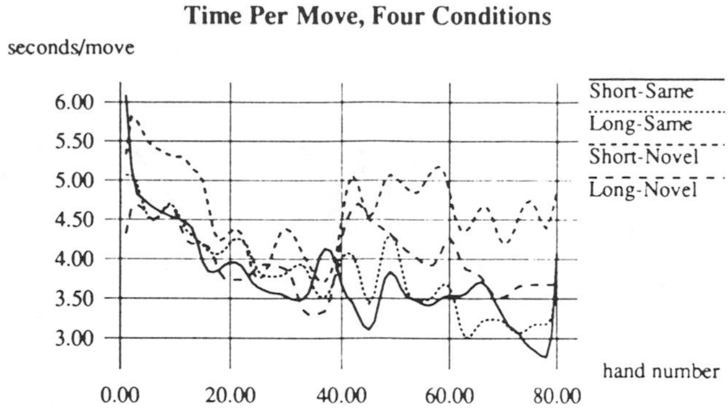

Time Per Move, Four Conditions

Figure 18.8. Time Series of Time per Move for Four Experimental Conditions
NOTE: First session is hands 1-40. Second session is hands 41-80.

of learning for procedurally stored individual skills. Since other group members serve as powerful contextual cues, we might expect them to "prime" responses from each other and thus to trigger inappropriate sequences of action at the organizational level. Thus organizational negative transfer operates by a mechanism akin to that seen in isolated individuals. However, what the behavior of an actor triggers is not further action by the same person, but rather action by another. In short, we believe that, to a significant degree, organizational routines are stored as distributed procedural memories and derive many of their important proper ties from this fact.

If further work establishes a psychologically-informed theory of routines along the lines we propose, it will have significant consequences for research. It can provide a theoretically grounded basis for explaining observed deviations from rationality. This is an important step beyond criticizing rational models and toward an alternative positive theory. In one sense, it offers a return to the original objectives of the bounded rationality research tradition (Simon, 1957). We can transcend the simple cataloging of departures from rationality and begin to explain them in terms of the actual processing capabilities of the individuals and of the system of relations that organizes the actors. But, in another sense, this approach departs somewhat from the typical emphases in the bounded rationality tradition on decision making by individual actors seen as relatively self-conscious, static, emotionally neutral problem solvers. In contrast, our stress is on learning that is dynamic, deeply embedded in a group context, and gives rise to partially unconscious skilled performances. Among the most fascinating opportunities we see are possible connections of our approach to experimental work showing that priming phenomena, which play an important role in procedural memory, are also significant in processes of individual emotional reactions to situations. For example, work by Zajonc and his collaborators have shown that simple prior exposure to a stimulus can increase the chance that it will later be preferred, even when the exposure is so brief that it has no effect on the chance the stimulus will later be recognized (Kunst-Wilson & Zajonc, 1980).

We also see an opportunity to connect our rich experimental data to emerging achievements in the machine-learning field. We hope to compare our subjects' behavior to the way multi-actor versions of learning systems such as Soar (Laird, Rosenbloom, & Newell, 1987) and Holland Classifiers (Holland, Holyoak, Nisbett, & Thagard, 1986; Riolo, 1991) acquire the ability to play the card game. Both systems have good prospects as models of the human acquisition of procedural knowledge. Further, there are many possible experiments that can build upon the demonstration here that routines can be induced in the laboratory. Subjects who have developed routines in one group can be reassigned to other groups to study a laboratory analog of a "clash of cultures." Variations in the card game can accommodate larger numbers of actors and can create conditions that mimic common problems of real organizations, such as conflicting incentives or restrictions on communication due to role asymmetries or physical separation. Then we can observe their effects on the development of routines.

Since routines pattern so much of organizational life—both its possibilities and its limitations—the unfolding of this line of research may hold many significant implications for managers. For example, by drawing on research on the low verbal accessibility of procedurally encoded skills, practitioners may better understand the difficulty that a routine's participants have in articulating their activities to managers or computer systems designers. The findings encourage us to recognize and explore the possibility of an "organizational unconscious," a body of largely inarticulate know-how that underpins so much of an organization's capabilities and which must be accommodated if there is to be effective redesign of organizational processes.

A major contribution to practice could come if improved understanding enables us to reduce the chances of the kind of inappropriate "firing" of routines that we saw from our pairs as they dealt with hand 38. We can probably never eliminate tragic "misfirings" such as the experienced surgical team that worked from a reversed X ray and efficiently removed a patient's one healthy kidney ("Jury gives victim," 1985). But we may find ways to make such cases less likely. There is promise in devices as homely as deliberately varying which team member has responsibility for reading off the items of a safety checklist.

Managers will also benefit from better appreciating the difficulty of transferring procedural knowledge across modes, such as from written to verbal form. This may cast light on some perennial problems. Written rules frequently fail to inform actual practice. Improved practices discovered in one part of an organization often cannot be propagated with written descriptions. These are fundamental limits on the speed and quality of organizational learning (Brown & Duguid, 1991). They may help to explain findings about organizational learning such as the observation that General Motors learned less from circulating careful research reports on its NUMMI joint venture than Toyota did by rotating managers through work in the plant (Krafcik, 1989).

The idea of organizational learning has already contributed significantly to the understanding of "resistance to change" (Argyris & Schön, 1978; Nystrom & Starbuck, 1984). Our conclusion that routines reside in hard-to-access procedural memory offers a different view of the problem, one that provides more precise foundations for the observations in earlier work. In particular, it suggests one detailed mechanism that may give rise to the divergence Argyris and Schön describe between theory-in-use and theory-in-practice. Among other things, it suggests that methods of making actors more conscious of their current practices may facilitate change. Experimental work has explored the use of such methods in the context of improving eyewitness legal testimony (Kassin, 1985). And several of the standard techniques in contemporary systems of "quality management" appear to exploit this principle. Deming (1982), for example, argues that we must abandon slogans in favor of detailed and participative examination of production processes.

With the aid of the distinction between procedural and declarative memory, we may be better able to understand important features of organizational memory (Walsh & Ungson, 1991). We can see how the procedural character of information-handling routines (Cyert & March, 1963) limits the ability of an organization to "remember," as when the seemingly simple task of recovering a misfiled document proves extraordinarily difficult. We may better appreciate how an organization could lose its memory of the reasons for an action (as in our earlier example of artillery teams).

Our argument is not to be taken as "routines are simply procedural memory and only that." It hardly seems likely that normal human action does not intertwine procedural and other forms of memory in intricate relationships. And we fully expect that the psychological literature on procedural memory will continue to develop in complex ways. Nonetheless, the distinctive properties of individual memory for skills that have now been documented are not going to disappear, and our experiments will therefore continue to imply that organization theorists must pay scrupulous attention to the profound ways in which individual memories interact to shape the character of organizational routine.

Acknowledgments

The authors acknowledge with gratitude the support of the National Science Foundation Program on Decision, Risk and Management Science under grant SES 9008853. We thank Jessica Francis for her assistance in coding, Pauline Kelvin and Dr. Richard Kelvin for research assistance, and Mary Tschirhart, Melissa Succi, and LaMont McKim for their help in collecting the experimental data.

NOTES

1. Here we follow Squire (1987) and Singley and Anderson (1989) in using the term "procedural." But see Squire for a listing of contending taxonomies with more than a dozen variant labels including "implicit/explicit," "skill memory/fact memory," and semantic/episodic." Most of these distinctions separate the properties we group under "procedural" from those we group under "declarative." It is conceivable that the procedural/declarative label-pair itself may be superceded. But we are convinced that future results in psychology will continue to support the central ideas used here, that memory is not one homogeneous capacity (Baddeley, 1990), and that memory for skilled actions has properties, especially properties related to "priming" phenomena (Tulving & Schacter, 1990), that distinguish it from other kinds.

2. While the general methods are not new, we observe that the growth of information technology is presenting many fresh laboratory observational possibilities. These include captured keystrokes and messages, and videotape for experimenter analysis and for retrospective reconstruction—a method that collects thinking-aloud protocols while avoiding social contamination from subjects' verbalizing in real time (Kassin, 1985).

REFERENCES

Allison, G. (1971). *Essence of decision: Explaining the Cuban missile crisis.* Boston: Little, Brown.

Allport, F. H. (1924). *Social psychology.* Cambridge, MA: Houghton Mifflin.

Argyris, C., & Schön, D. (1978). *Organizational learning.* Reading, MA: Addison-Wesley.

Baddeley, A. (1990). *Human memory.* Boston: Allyn & Bacon.

Bahrick, H. P. (1984). Semantic memory content in permastore: 50 years of memory for Spanish learned in school. *Journal of Experimental Psychology: General, 113,* 1-29.

Brown, J. S., & Duguid, P. (1991). Innovation in the workplace: A perspective on organizational learning. *Organization Science, 2*(1), 40-57.

Bunch, M. (1936). Amount of transfer in rational learning as a function of time. *Journal of Comparative Psychology, 22,* 325-337.

Carraher, T. N., Carraher, D. W., & Schliemann, A. D. (1985). Mathematics in the streets and in the schools. *British Journal of Development Psychology, 3,* 21-29.

Cohen, M. D. (1991). Individual learning and organizational routine: Emerging connections. *Organization Science, 2*(1), 135-139.

Cohen, N. J. (1984). Preserved learning capacity in amnesia: Evidence for multiple memory systems. In L. Squire & N. Butters (Eds.), *Neuropsychology of memory* (pp. 88-103). New York: Guilford.

Cyert, R. M., & March, J. G. (1963). *A behavioral theory of the firm.* Englewood Cliffs, NJ: Prentice Hall.

Deming, W. E. (1982). *Quality, productivity, and competitive position.* Cambridge: MIT Center for Advanced Engineering Study.

Dewey, J. (1922). *Human nature and conduct; An introduction to social psychology.* New York: Holt.

Drazin, R., & Sandelands, L. (1992). Autogenesis: A perspective on the process of organizing. *Organization Science, 3*(2), 230-249.

Gaines, B., & Boose, J. (1988). *Knowledge acquisition tools* (Vols. 1 and 2). New York: Academic Press.

Gersick, C. J. G., & Hackman, J. R. (1990). Habitual routines in task-performing groups. *Organizational Behavior and Human Decision Processes, 47,* 65-97.

Graf, P., Shimamura, A. P., & Squire, L. R. (1985). Priming across modalities and across category levels: Extending the domain of preserved function in amnesia. *Journal of Experimental Psychology: Learning, Memory, Cognition, 11,* 386-396.

Graf, P., Squire, L. R., & Mandler, G. (1984). The information that amnesiac patients do not forget. *Journal of Experimental Psychology: Learning, Memory, Cognition, 10,* 164-178.

Holland, J., Holyoak, K., Nisbett, R., & Thagard, P. (1986). *Induction: Processes of inference, learning and discovery.* Cambridge: MIT Press.

Inbar, M. (1979). *Routine decision making: The future of bureaucracy.* Beverly Hills, CA: Sage.

Kassin, S. M. (1985). Eyewitness identification: Retrospective self-awareness and the accuracy-confidence correlation. *Journal of Personality and Social Psychology, 49,* 878-893.

Kelly, J. R., & McGrath, J. E. (1985). Effects of time limits and task types on task performance and interaction of four-person groups. *Journal of Personality and Social Psychology, 49,* 395-407.

Krafcik, J. (1989). A new diet for U.S. manufacturing. *Technology Review, 92*(1), 28-34.

Kunst-Wilson, W. R., & Zajonc, R. B. (1980). Affective discrimination of stimuli that cannot be recognized. *Science, 207*(4430), 557-558.

Jury gives victim $5.2 million after bungled surgery. (1985). *Los Angeles Times,* pp. 1, 6, Part II.

Laird, J., Rosenbloom, P., & Newell, A. (1987). Soar: An architecture for general intelligence. *Artificial Intelligence, 33,* 1-64.

Laughlin, P. R., & Shippy, T. A. (1983). Collective induction. *Journal of Personality and Social Psychology, 45,* 94-100.

Levitt, B., & March, J. G. (1988). Organizational learning. *Annual Review of Sociology, 14,* 319-340.

Luchins, A. S. (1942). Mechanization in problem solving. *Psychological Monographs, 54.*

March, J. G., & Simon, H. A. (1958). *Organizations.* New York: John Wiley.

McCloskey, M. (1983). Naive theories of motion. In D. Gentner & A. L. Stevens (Eds.), *Mental models.* Hillsdale, NJ: Lawrence Erlbaum.

Morison, E. E. (1966). *Men, machines, and modern times.* Cambridge: MIT Press.

Nelson, R., & Winter, S. (1982). *An evolutionary theory of economic change.* Cambridge, MA: Belknap.

Newell, A. (1990). *Unified theories of cognition.* Cambridge, MA: Harvard University Press.

Nisbett, R., & Wilson, T. D. (1977). Telling more than we can know: Verbal reports on mental processes. *Psychological Review, 84,* 231-259.

Nystrom, P., & Starbuck, W. (1984). To avoid organizational crisis, unlearn. *Organizational Dynamics, 12,* 53-65.

Riolo, R. L. (1991). Modelling simple human category learning with a classifier system. In R. K. Belew & L. B. Booker (Eds.), *Proceedings of the Fourth International Conference on Genetic Algorithms* (pp. 324-333). San Mateo, CA: Morgan Kaufmann.

Senge, P. M. (1990). *The fifth discipline.* New York: Doubleday/Currency.

Shaw, M. (1954). Some effects of unequal distribution of information upon group performance in different communication nets. *Journal of Abnormal and Social Psychology, 49,* 547-553.

Sheil, B. (1981). *Coping with complexity* (Working paper). Palo Alto, CA: Xerox Palo Alto Research Center, Laboratory for Artificial Intelligence.

Simon, H. A. (1957). *Models of man.* New York: John Wiley.

Singley, M. K., & Anderson, J. R. (1989). *The transfer of cognitive skill.* Cambridge, MA: Harvard University Press.

Squire, L. R. (1987). *Memory and brain.* New York: Oxford University Press.

Stene, E. O. (1940). An approach to the science of administration. *American Political Science Review, 34*(6), 1124-1137.

Stinchcombe, A. (1990). *Information and organizations.* Berkeley: University of California Press.

Suchman, L. (1983). Office procedure as practical action: Models of work and system design. *ACM Transactions on Office Information Systems, 1,* 320-328.

Tulving, E., & Schacter, D. L. (1990). Priming and human memory systems. *Science, 247,* 301-306.

Velleman, P. F., & Hoaglin, D. C. (1981). *Applications, basics and computing of exploratory data analysis.* Belmont, CA: Duxbury.

Walsh, J. P., & Ungson, G. R. (1991). Organizational memory. *The Academy of Management Review, 16,* 57-91.

Weick, K. E. (1965). Laboratory experimentation with organizations. In J. G. March (Ed.), *Handbook of organizations* (pp. 194-206). Chicago: Rand McNally.

Weick, K. E. (1979). *The social psychology of organizing* (2nd ed.). Reading, MA: Addison-Wesley.

Weick, K. E., & Gilfillan, D. P. (1971). Fate of arbitrary traditions in a laboratory microculture. *Journal of Personality and Social Psychology, 17,* 179-191.

Womack, J. P., Jones, D. T., & Roos, D. (1990). *The machine that changed the world: The story of lean production.* New York: Macmillan.

Zuboff, S. (1988). *In the age of the smart machine: The future of work and power.* New York: Basic Books.

19

Culture and Organizational Learning

SCOTT D. N. COOK
DVORA YANOW

Traditionally, theories of organizational learning have taken one of two approaches that share a common characterization of learning but differ in focus. One approach focuses on learning by individuals in organizational contexts; the other, on individual learning as a model for organizational action. Both base their understanding of organizational learning on the cognitive activity of individual learning. However, there is something organizations do that may be called organizational learning, that is neither individuals learning in organizations nor organizations employing processes akin to learning by individuals. This form of organizational learning can be seen in the case of three small workshops that make "the finest flutes in the world." This essay proposes a perspective on organizational learning, drawing on the concept of organizational culture, that can be useful in understanding the case. This perspective provides a fruitful basis for exploring the above distinctions in both theory and practice.

Two questions underlie the phrase "organizational learning": Can organizations learn? What is the nature of learning when it is done by organizations? How these questions have been addressed in the organizational learning literature, directly and indirectly, reveals a particular orientation toward the topic. Our analysis of this orientation and discussion of another view are the subjects of this essay.

This chapter appeared originally in *Journal of Management Inquiry,* Vol. 2, No. 4, December 1993. Copyright © 1993 Sage Publications, Inc.

In writing on organizational learning, most authors (e.g., Argyris & Schön, 1978; Bolman, 1976; Duncan & Weiss, 1979; Etheredge & Short, 1983; Gahmberg, 1980; Hedberg, 1981; Herriott, Levinthal, & March, 1985; Lant & Mezias, 1990; Levitt & March, 1988; March & Olsen, 1976; Miles & Randolph, 1981; Shrivastava, 1983; Sims & Gioia, 1986; Sitkin, 1992; Weick, 1991; Weiss, 1980) have examined how individuals learn in organizational contexts or have explored ways that theories of individual learning can be applied to organizations or both. In the first instance, the typical argument is that organizational learning is a particular sort of learning done in organizations by key individuals whose learning is tied to subsequent organizational change. The second approach holds that organizations can learn because they possess capacities that are identical or equivalent to the capacities that individuals possess that enable them to learn—that is, with respect to learning, this approach treats organizations *as if* they were individuals. Despite their differences, both approaches tend to address the questions just mentioned from a common perspective: They typically base their account of the nature of *organizational* learning, explicitly or implicitly, on an understanding of what it means for an *individual* to learn. This grounding in learning by individuals suggests a link between discussions of organizational learning and theories of cognition. For this reason, we call this orientation the "cognitive perspective" on organizational learning.

Although the cognitive perspective has been and continues to be a wellspring of insight and utility, we have found it less useful in efforts to understand a phenomenon that we believe is central to the subject of organizational learning: specifically, where learning is understood to be done by the organization as a whole, not by individuals in it, and where the organization is not understood as if it were an individual (that is, as if it were in some way ontologically a cognitive entity). We hold that learning can indeed be done by organizations; that this phenomenon is neither conceptually nor empirically the same as either learning by individuals or individuals learning within organizations; and that to understand organizational learning as learning by organizations, theorists and practitioners need to see organizations not primarily as cognitive entities but as cultural ones.

Our intention here is to outline a "cultural perspective" on organizational learning (in keeping with recent attention to organizational culture; e.g., Frost, Moore, Louis, Lundberg, & Martin, 1985, 1991; Schein, 1985). We see this perspective as a complement to, not a substitute for, the cognitive perspective. From the cultural perspective, we argue, the question, "Can organizations learn?" is not an epistemological one about cognitive capacities, but an empirical one about organizational actions—to which the answer is, yes. Further, we hope to show that the second question, "What is the nature of learning as done by organizations?" can be addressed from the cultural perspective in a way that avoids some specific conceptual difficulties found in the cognitive perspective, while also suggesting some new avenues for exploration.

The theoretical argument presented here has grown out of our analysis of three small companies manufacturing flutes. In the sections that follow, we describe what we see as some of the conceptual difficulties inherent in the cognitive view, discuss the meanings of the concept of organizational learning, and outline a cultural perspective on organizational learning, which we illustrate through the case example of the flute companies.

THE COGNITIVE PERSPECTIVE

Most of the literature on organizational learning has addressed the topic from a perspective that entails various concepts traditionally associated with cognition. Many authors, for example, have used the notion of learning from mistakes, a concept central to cognition, to address organizational learning both at the level of the organizational aggregate and at the level of key actors within an organizational setting. In this vein, Etheredge and Short (1983) see governmental learning as a reflection of increased intelligence and behavioral effectiveness: If government behaves more effectively, then we may say that it has learned, often from its own mistakes. Lant and Mezias (1990) hold that "an organizational learning model suggests that the impetus for organizational change is triggered by performance below aspiration level" (p. 149). Some theories of cognition are modeled on principles of systems theory; reflecting this, some authors have understood organizational learning to be tied to the detection and correction of errors linked to a change in course or improved performance. For Bolman (1976) and Argyris and Schön (1978), organizational learning is error detection and correction geared to improving the effectiveness of individual behavior in organizations. Similarly, Sitkin (1991) refers to "the action/failure/feedback/correction cycle" in making the provocative argument that organizations may learn more effectively through "strategic failure" than through a singularly success-oriented strategy of failure avoidance.

However, there are problems inherent in transferring to organizations concepts whose origin is cognition by individuals. These problems, which come both from the nature of cognition and from its application to organizations, are rarely acknowledged or explored. For example, the sorts of activities that we conventionally and unproblematically associate with cognition in individuals (acquiring knowledge of history, mastering skills useful in fixing machines, solving geometric problems, gaining facility at programming or sailing or singing, etc.) are neither conventionally nor unproblematically associated with organizations. Further, it is not readily apparent how the sort of organizational activities commonly described in discussions of organizational learning (e.g., the rearrangement of departmental structure, the adoption of new technologies or strategies, etc.) are in fact activities than can meaningfully be called learning, particularly learning on the part of the organization itself.[1]

A fundamental problem derives from the fact that it is impossible to *see* cognition taking place in the actions of organizations. This has led to the common assertion in the literature that organizational learning has taken place when actions by organizationally key individuals that are understood to entail learning are followed by observable changes in the organization's pattern of activities. In this vein, Miles and Randolph (1981), drawing on Simon's (1991) work, define organizational learning as individuals' insights reflected "in the structural elements and outcomes of the organization itself" (p. 50).

Having accepted generally the inference that organizational learning entails observable organizational change linked to individual cognition, the cognitive perspective splits into two major approaches. One approach has focused on individual learning in an organizational context. The other has used individual learning as a model for understanding certain types of collective organizational activity. Most authors have followed one approach or the other; a few have explored both.

The first approach treats organizational learning explicitly as learning by individuals within an organizational context. For example, March and Olsen (1976) focus on the experiential learning of individuals within organizations. Argyris and Schön (1978) examine the actions of members of organizations, whom they see as agents for the organization. Etheredge and Short (1983) treat governmental learning, in large part, as learning by individual politicians, officials, advisors, analysts, bureaucrats, and other decision makers within government agencies. Weiss (1980) similarly presents societal learning as the accretion over time of government officials' knowledge, which is transferred into the policy-making process. Simon (1991) aligns himself with this approach quite definitively in stating, "All learning takes place inside individual human heads; an organization learns in only two ways: (a) by the learning of its members, or (b) by ingesting new members who have knowledge the organization didn't previously have" (p. 125).

Some authors state that they take organizational learning to be different in some sense from individual learning. Fiol and Lyles (1985), in a review of the literature, found this stance to be one of the points of consensus among theorists. Nonetheless, the accounts and illustrations offered by these authors typically describe episodes of individual learning that occur within organizational contexts. For example, Bolman (1976) treats organizational learning as "learning experiences for key decision makers." For Shrivastava (1983), organizational learning "occurs through the medium of individual members" and involves the development of better interpersonal skills. In a broader sense, for Sims and Gioia (1986), "organizational social cognition" within the "thinking organization" essentially concerns understanding "our own cognitive processes" and "how other people think" (p. x). Organizational learning as approached in such cases, although conceived of as different from individual learning, is nevertheless described as a form of learning by individuals; it is not treated as learning by organizations.[2]

The second approach develops theories of organizational action largely by applying to organizations concepts that are commonly found in models of individual learning. Hedberg (1981) and Gahmberg (1980), for example, extend stimulus-response models of individual learning to explain organizational selection of stimuli and choice of responses. For Weick (1991), the traditional "defining property of learning is the combination of same stimulus and different response," but the fact that this "is rare in organizations" leads him to consider how organizations might employ stimulus-response learning in "nontraditional ways" (p. 117). In a fashion that suggests the themes of adaptation and conditioned response from behaviorist psychology, Cyert and March (1963) see organizational learning as entailed in organizational adaptation that "uses individual members of the organization as instruments" in a way that constitutes "adaptation at the aggregate level of the organization" (p. 123). For them, organizational learning is understood to occur when an organization, in response to "an external source of disturbance or shock," selects "decision rules" that lead the organization "to a preferred state" (p. 99). Lant and Mezias (1991) add the notion of learning to the language of systemic adaptation in describing "an ecology of strategic learning" and arguing that "organizational change is governed by an experiential learning process" within which entrepreneurship is seen as a "search activity" that can bring about "change to the core dimensions of organizational activity" (p. 148). Duncan and Weiss (1979), meanwhile, present a cognitive model of the production of organizational knowledge: Individual decision makers possess specialized knowledge about the organization, which is shared through paradigmatic frameworks that generate a set of beliefs that provide a way of seeing the organizational world.[3] Similarly, in applying the notion of memory to organizations, Levitt and March (1988) argue that "organizational learning depends on features of individual memories . . . but our present concern is with organizational aspects of memory" (p. 326).

It is clear that individuals do indeed learn within the context of organizations, that this context influences the character of that learning, and, in turn, that such learning can have operational consequences for the activities of the organization. Also, there is nothing inherently invalid in applying models of individual learning to organizations. A great deal of important work has come out of these efforts. It is not clear, however, either conceptually or empirically, that such instances of learning constitute learning by organizations. And because it is not obvious, a priori, that organizations are cognitive entities, in drawing on individual cognition as a way of understanding organizational phenomena, we must take care not to lose sense of the "as if" quality of the metaphor, forgetting that organizations and individuals are not the same sorts of entities. The nature of the difference, as we will argue later, bears on how each can be understood to learn.

In both approaches, the application to organizations of a model of learning based on cognition by individuals entails, in our view, at least three substantive problems. First, it raises a set of complex arguments concerning the ontological status of organizations as cognitive entities—specifically, arguments about how organizations exist and how the nature of their existence entails an ability to learn that is identical or akin to the human cognitive abilities associated with learning. In other words, because the cognitive perspective adopts its understanding of learning from theories about individuals, it follows that to discuss cognitive organizational learning, one must first show how, in their capacity to learn, organizations are like individuals.

Further, because theories of cognition already carry with them an understanding of learning, many who have adopted the cognitive perspective on organizational learning have seen *organizations,* although not always *learning,* as the term calling for explanation. In this vein, Argyris and Schön (1978) begin their discussion of organizational learning with the section, "What is an organization that it may learn?" Others (e.g., Duncan & Weiss, 1979; Gahmberg, 1980) similarly begin with definitions and discussions of the concept of organization that, in part, constitute arguments concerning the ontological status of organizations with respect to learning. Morgan (1986) looks at how organizations can be understood to be brains (metaphorically at least) and how this might help us design organizations "so that they can learn and self-organize in the manner of a fully functioning brain" (p. 105). Sandelands and Stablein (1987), meanwhile, consider the existence of the "organizational mind" as a way of understanding an organization's ability to engage in "ideational processes" or a "commerce of ideas" (pp. 138-139). The idea of attributing an ontological status to organizations as cognitive entities, which has been fundamental to the views of the cognitive perspective, has often proven to be conceptually as problematic as it is provocative: What has been taken as self-evident in the case of individuals has proved a lightning rod for debate when applied to organizations. Although this debate has produced many challenging and useful insights, it remains fundamentally unresolved.

Second, the study of individual learning is itself complex, in flux, and bounded by its own theoretical constraints. Adopting the perspective (or the metaphor) of cognition for the study of organizational learning has yielded many insights; yet these insights are limited by what we understand about learning from the field of individual cognition. Although much work is being done that advances our understanding of individual cognition, the absence of an established, commonly accepted model of individual learning leaves its useful application to organizations inherently problematic. Linking our understanding of organizational learning to cognitive theory, at the very least, obligates us to account in organizational terms for developments in that theory or to explain why this is not necessary.

Apart from the problems posed by debates concerning organizational ontology and the nature of theories of individual learning, the cognitive perspective presents a third difficulty: its proposition (often implicit) that learning for organizations is the same as learning for individuals. This is a difficulty for several reasons. In a fundamental sense, it does not follow from anything essential about organizations or about learning that learning must be the same for individuals and organizations. Nor is it clear how two things that are in so many ways so obviously different as individuals and organizations could nonetheless carry out identical or even equivalent activities. Further, even if it were shown that organizations and individuals are ontologically equivalent in the possession of cognitive capacities required for learning, it would not necessarily follow that they would both learn in the same fashion or, as Weick (1991) notes, that the results of their learning would be the same. Indeed, even among individuals, we can observe significantly different "learning styles."[4] This issue has been left largely unaddressed by theorists of organizational learning.

There is a further problematic point that is found in many parts of the literature that derives, we believe, in large measure from its systems origins. Although the idea is not inherent in the concept of cognition itself, organizational learning has typically been linked to organizational change and, particularly, to increased effectiveness. Many authors share the view (or assumption) that "learning will improve future performance" (Fiol & Lyles, 1985). Conversely, the absence of observable change has commonly been taken to mean that learning did not take place or, in fact, that learning was "impeded" (Jenkins-Smith, St. Clair, & James, 1988).

Although change is often associated with individual learning, it seems clear that some forms of learning entail little or no change that is meaningfully discernible, particularly in observable behavior. For example, maintaining the mastery of a technique may involve perceptual or kinesthetic learning that need not involve behavioral change or any observable change in ability—as when a dancer, accommodating an injury, learns new ways to perform the identical movements that were performed before the injury. Likewise, we can learn new knowledge that is not linked at all to behavioral change. One may, for example, learn a phone number and never use it or bring it to mind again. Nor does learning always produce increased effectiveness or improved performance, as the learning of faulty skills or self-destructive habits makes all too clear.

We infer from what has been written in the organizational learning literature a normative concern with learning as change and/or improvement, which typically ignores other notions of learning. The focus on overt behavioral change inherent in the experiments of cognitive psychology may in part account for this tendency to equate learning with change. We will argue, however, that change does not always accompany learning by organizations, and moreover, equating learning with change may leave out much of interest.[5] Here, we turn to an exploration of learning by organizations.

KNOWING AND LEARNING
BY ORGANIZATIONS

Organizations act. The Boston Celtics play basketball. The Concertgebouw Orchestra performs Mahler symphonies. These are activities done by groups; they are not and cannot be done by single individuals. A single basketball player cannot play a game of basketball by herself; only the several players, together as a team, are able to carry out the team's strategies, moves, and style of play. A violinist alone cannot perform Mahler's Third Symphony; the execution of the phrasing, dynamics, and tempi of the piece requires the collective actions of the orchestra as a group.

Further, the ability to play basketball games or perform symphonies, we argue, is only meaningfully attributed to a group, not to individual players. It is not meaningful to say that the ability to play Mahler symphonies is possessed by an individual musician, because no individual person can perform symphonies. An individual musician possesses the ability to carry out merely a portion of what only an orchestra can do. Moreover, musicians can act on that ability only in the context of the orchestra: They may each play their parts alone (to practice, say), but to perform the symphony they must participate in an activity of the orchestra.

Although it has become more common to attribute abilities to groups, there has been an equally common reluctance to attribute to them any form of knowledge or knowing associated with those abilities: Traditionally, it has been accepted, usually unquestioningly, that matters of knowing are exclusively matters about what or how individuals know. This reluctance is consistent with the cognitive perspective's origins in theories of individual cognition. From this perspective, therefore, it would typically be argued that it is the knowledge of all the individuals in an orchestra taken together that constitutes the know-how behind the ability to perform symphonies—and thus it is not know-how possessed by a group. This argument has two shortcomings. First, it implies that the performance of a symphony is meaningfully reducible to the playing of 100 different parts by individuals. This is an implication that belies the experiential reports of musicians and their audiences, and it can never be meaningfully tested because the performance of symphonies is always a group activity. Second, it is conceptually unsound to attribute to individuals know-how that no individual can demonstrate. Just as the ability to perform symphonies is meaningfully attributed only to a group, so is possession of the know-how necessary to do so. Removed from the traditional assumptions of the cognitive perspective, the same reasoning that supports the concept of group abilities would also suggest the concept of group know-how.

In this sense, the statement, "The Celtics know how to play basketball" is meaningful as a statement about organizational knowing. Other "ensembles" that are more commonly thought of as organizations, such as IBM or Saab or the U.S. Environmental Protection Agency, similarly know how to do what they do. The know-how entailed in producing a computer, a Saab 9000, or a set of standards for air quality resides in the organization as a whole, not in individual members of the organization.[6] These are propositions about organizational knowing.

Learning is related to knowing; in one sense, it is the act of acquiring knowledge. Thus the knowledge demonstrated by the Concertgebouw when it plays a symphony or by Saab when it produces a car can be understood as having been learned. The individuals in the organization were not born with the ability to perform their parts of these activities, nor has the organization always possessed these abilities. What can be said of the abilities can be said of the know-how associated with them: It has to be acquired; it has to be learned. The statement, "The Celtics know how to play basketball" suggests something about organizational learning as well as organizational knowing. Organizational learning, then, describes a category of activity that can only be done by a group. It cannot be done by an individual.

In this respect, organizational learning, as we use the term, refers to the capacity of an organization to learn how to do what it does, where what it learns is possessed not by individual members of the organization but by the aggregate itself. That is, when a group acquires the know-how associated with its ability to carry out its collective activities, that constitutes organizational learning.[7]

From the perspective of this understanding, the foregoing examples of organizational activities are descriptions of things that organizations as collectives actually do that can be meaningfully understood as learning. The answer to our initial question is, yes, organizations do indeed learn. We acknowledge that the term *learning* is borrowed from the realm of individual behavior: When individuals demonstrate a new ability, it is meaningful to assert that they have acquired the know-how associated with that ability. However, we believe that the similarity between individual and organizational learning ends there. We do not infer that because there is an apparent likeness in activity, the underlying processes are necessarily alike. In particular, we argue that what organizations do when they learn is necessarily different from what individuals do when they learn. Specifically, we believe that organizational learning is not essentially a cognitive activity, because, at the very least, organizations lack the typical wherewithal for undertaking cognition: They do not possess what people possess and use in knowing and learning—that is, actual bodies, perceptive organs, brains, and so forth. To understand organizational learning, we must look for attributes that organizations can be meaningfully understood to possess and use, that can be seen to give rise to the sorts of activities outlined in the organizational learning examples above. This is a central concern of the arguments that follow.[8]

At this juncture, three additional points can be raised. First, in our view, organizational learning, like individual learning, does not necessarily imply change, particularly observable change. An organization can, for example, learn something in order *not* to change. Second, organizational learning need not, as the systems notion of feedback would suggest, be a response to an environmental stimulus (such as error detection). The impetus for learning can also come from within the organization itself. Third, in a significant measure, organizational knowledge or know-how is unique to each organization. That is, two organizations performing the same task do not necessarily perform it identically. Even two very similar organizations know how to do somewhat different things. The Celtics do not play basketball in the same way as do the 76ers. The Concertgebouw and the New York Philharmonic perform the same Mahler Symphony differently. IBM and Apple have different management styles, although both manufacture computers. Organizational knowing and learning are always in some part intimately bound to a particular organization.

In the case analysis that follows, we examine in greater detail how understanding organizational learning in terms of organizational culture helps address the issues we have identified so far. Organizational culture has been defined and treated in many ways (see, for example, Frost et al., 1985, 1991; Ouchi & Wilkins, 1985; Schein, 1985; Smircich, 1983). For our purposes at hand, we define culture in application to organizations as a set of values, beliefs, and feelings, together with the artifacts of their expression and transmission (such as myths, symbols, metaphors, rituals), that are created, inherited, shared, and transmitted within one group of people and that, in part, distinguish that group from others. This definition is in keeping with an interpretive approach to human action and social reality (see, for example, Berger & Luckmann, 1966; Mead, 1934; Taylor, 1979).[9]

Such an approach to organizational learning builds on the following. Human action includes the ability to act in groups. Over time and in the course of joint action or practice, a group of people creates a set of intersubjective meanings that are expressed in and through their artifacts (objects, language, and acts). Such artifacts include the symbols, metaphors, ceremonies, myths, and so forth with which organizations and groups transmit their values, beliefs, and feelings to new and existing members, as well as in part to strangers. As new members join the group, each acquires a sense of these meanings through the everyday practices in which the organization's artifacts are engaged. Through such "artifactual interactions," shared meanings are continually maintained or modified; these are acts that create, sustain, or modify the organization's culture.[10]

The concept of culture, because it takes human groups as its subject, allows us to begin with the empirical observation that a group of people can and does act collectively—and can do so in ways that suggest learning. The concept of organizational learning, then, is not encountered as a theoretical hypothesis (Can organizations learn?) to be tested and proved. Rather, the concept is addressed through empirical observations that call to be understood. The ontological problem of the existence of an organization as a cognitive entity is, thus, not encountered. The focus of the cultural theorist concerned with organizational learning shifts to the second question, "What is the nature of learning when it is done by organizations?" and the task is to develop concepts with which to describe how a group of individuals acting collectively, as an organization, does those things that might meaningfully and usefully be understood as learning.

THE FINEST FLUTES IN THE WORLD: ORGANIZING CRAFTSMANSHIP

Most of the finest flutes produced in this century have been made in a style reminiscent of old world craftsmanship by three small workshops in and around Boston, Massachusetts: the Wm. S. Haynes Company; Verne Q. Powell Flutes, Inc.; and Brannen Brothers—Flutemakers, Inc. Haynes, the oldest of the three, was founded in 1900. In 1927, Verne Q. Powell, who was shop foreman for Haynes, left the company to make flutes on his own. Two of Powell's mastercraftsmen, Bickford and Robert Brannen, founded Brannen Brothers in 1977.[11]

Instruments made by these three companies have been regarded by flutists internationally as the "best flutes in the world." The idea of excellence has been central to the identities of all three companies. Until the early 1980s, when changing economics and a growing challenge by large-scale, highly tooled Japanese flute manufacturers affected demand, it was common for the Boston companies to have a 5-year backlog of orders.

The companies themselves are rather small, each having begun with 1 or 2 people and expanding slowly to typically about 25. Apart from a secretary or a bookkeeper, all people in the companies work on the instruments. In each workshop, the owners and/or managers (3 to 4 people in each) may have offices and administrative work to do, but each also spends time, in some cases the bulk of it, at a workbench.

The companies are also similar in terms of physical layout. There are areas where work is done with die machines or casting equipment and other areas for cleaning and polishing or storage. But the central area of activity at each shop consists of rows of workbenches stocked mostly with hand tools where flutemakers sit side by side doing the delicate mechanical and aesthetic work that makes the instruments what they are.

The flutemakers themselves are in many ways a varied lot. The range of ages has been wide, yet most of the flutemakers have been in their 20s or 30s. Until recently, they were almost exclusively men; now, at Brannen Brothers, for example, about 40% are women. Some flutemakers are musicians; very few have ever been flutists. A growing number have been to college. Many have hobbies or previous professions that complement the detail and finesse of their work with the flutes (silversmithing, fine woodworking, a "fanatical interest" in high-end stereo equipment, or specialty car engines). Many—for reasons unknown—are astigmatic.

In all three shops, flutes have been made following similar procedures and organization of production. The tube that becomes the body of the flute is made outside the shop to each company's precise specifications. Screws and steel rods for the key mechanism and strips of silver for various parts are also brought in. The parts are collected, carefully inspected, and given an initial polishing. Next, the body is formed. Tone holes are put into the tube, and the structure that holds the key mechanism is soldered on. The key mechanism is assembled and precisely fit to the body. Then, pads are put into the keys and the mechanism adjusted by hand to remarkably fine tolerances. Meanwhile, the head joint and embouchure hole are put together and delicately hand finished. Finally, the flute is polished, packed up, and shipped to its new owner.

At Powell (which we will use here as the primary example), it would take about 2 weeks to make an instrument from start to finish. At all times there would be several flutes at each step of manufacture. Typically, each flute would be worked on by several flutemakers in succession. Each individual craftsman, typically skilled in only a few aspects of the process, would work on his part of a flute (or a small batch) until that work was finished, whereupon the flute (or batch) would be handed on to the next craftsman. The second flutemaker would base her work on the former's. And so on down the line. If at any point a flutemaker felt that earlier work was not right, that person would return the piece to the appropriate prior flutemaker to be reworked to their mutual satisfaction.

In describing why a piece might need to be reworked, a flutemaker would typically make only cryptic remarks, such as, "It doesn't feel right" or "This bit doesn't look quite right." The first flutemaker would then rework the piece until both were in agreement that it had "the right feel" or "the right look." In working on a portion of the key mechanism, say, one flutemaker might tell the previous one that a key "doesn't feel right; it's cranky." This would lead the other to check the key over until he got a sense of how the feel was off. Ultimately he would trace the problem down, for example, to a need for adjusting the way the key fit into the mechanism or, perhaps, to a need to reset the tension on the spring that operates the key. The language in such interchanges is inexact in no small part because many of the actual physical dimensions and tolerances of the flutes have never been made explicit; and many that have been are not commonly referred to in explicit terms by the flutemakers in daily practice. Yet the extremely precise standards of the instruments, on which the flute's ultimate style and quality depend, have been maintained through just these sorts of individual and mutual judgments of hand and eye.

This process has resulted in two very important things. First, it has made sure that at any one step of manufacture not only had work been done properly with respect to the work each flutemaker needed to accomplish, but it was also done properly from the perspective of the next flutemaker who needed to base her work on that of the former. The second result has been that when a flute reached the final inspection at the end of manufacture, almost without exception, it required no further work. The hand-to-hand checking of the flutes has amounted to a very successful, informal quality control system.

Apprentices have typically been trained by sitting at a workbench to do one of the steps of manufacture as would any other flutemaker. As an apprentice finished each piece of work, he would show it to a master-craftsman who would judge it, just as she would judge the work of any other flutemaker: If it did not feel right or look right, it would be handed back to the apprentice to be reworked until it did. Eventually, the apprentice would become a judge of his own work (this would be a mark of the end of his apprenticeship). Similarly, he would become able to judge work by other flutemakers on flutes coming to him for work and be able to recognize when they needed to be taken back because the look or feel was "not right." In this way, at one and the same time, an apprentice would both acquire a set of skills in flutemaking and become a member of the informal quality control system that has unfalteringly maintained the style and quality of these instruments.

No two Powell flutes are exactly alike. Each has its own strengths and quirks, its own personality. Yet a knowledgeable fluteplayer would never fail to recognize a Powell by the way it feels and plays, nor would she confuse a Powell with a Haynes or a Brannen Brothers. Each Powell flute, although unique, shares an unambiguous family resemblance with all other Powells. This family resemblance is the essence of Powell style and quality. And although each Powell has its own personality and aspects of the flute's physical design have been changed from time to time, the Powell style has been maintained. In this sense, a Powell flute made 50 years ago plays and feels the same as one made recently.

This principle is equally true of Haynes and Brannen Brothers flutes. Each company has developed a distinctly recognizable product, transcending individual variations among flutes and design changes over time. Further, this constancy of style and quality has been maintained through the years, even though each instrument has typically been the product of several flutemakers and the workshops have passed through several generations of flutemakers.

ORGANIZATIONAL LEARNING
IN THE FLUTE WORKSHOP

Like playing basketball or a symphony, the knowledge needed to make these flutes of the finest quality resides not in any one individual, but in the organization as a whole. The organization was not "born" with that knowledge; it had to learn it.

We may say that each of the Boston companies, as an organization, knows how to make flutes. Indeed, the know-how required to make one of their instruments from start to finish rarely has been known by a single flutemaker; typically, producing a flute has been a group effort.

Each organization has learned how to produce a flute. The knowledge has been learned collectively, not individually. It is true that each flutemaker knows how to perform his or her individual tasks; but the know-how required to make the flute as a whole resides with the organization, not with the individual flutemaker because only the workshop as a whole can make the flute. This is demonstrated in the fact that when flutemakers have left one of the workshops, the know-how needed to make the flute has not been lost to the organization, as evidenced in the sameness of play and feel of instruments produced by that workshop over the years. The workshop has continued to make flutes of the same quality and style as before because it—the organization, not the individual—possesses the know-how and the ability to make its own particular style of instrument. Typically, neither the flutes nor the way they are made have changed when flutemakers have left one of the workshops.

Moreover, the organizational know-how entailed in flutemaking at each workshop is, in a significant measure, different from that at the others. Although all three know how to make flutes and all follow similar production operations, each makes its own particular flute, one with a unique, unambiguously recognizable style. Thus part of what each workshop knows is unique to it.

Further, such organizational know-how is not meaningfully transferable from one shop to the next; it is deeply embedded in the practices of each workshop. A Haynes flutemaker, for example, could not walk into the Powell workshop, sit down at a bench, and begin making Powell flutes. Over the years, several flutemakers have, in fact, moved from one company to another, and in every instance they have had to be partially retrained, even to do the same jobs they were doing at the other company. They have had to learn a new "feel," a different way of "handling the pieces." Overall, this know-how has been learned not by being given explicit measurements and tolerances, but tacitly, in the hand-to-hand judgments of feel and eye, by working on flutes and having that work judged by the other flutemakers. These judgments are typically expressed in terms of the right look or right feel that are unique to that workshop.

What such a flutemaker knows can be learned only within the context of a specific workshop and only by joining in the collective activity of the workshop as a whole, making its particular instrument. The knowledge of how a finished mechanism, say, should feel can be used only in that workshop. Although each individual possesses the know-how needed to do her portion of the work on the flute, she cannot use that knowledge to produce an entire flute on her own, nor could she produce quality work in the style of a particular workshop except in that particular organizational context.

In this lies an example of organizational learning that does not require overt change on the part of the organization. As a new member, for example, is socialized or acculturated into the organization, learning by the organization takes place: The organization learns how to maintain the style and quality of its flutes through the particular skills, character, and quirks of a new individual. The organization engages in a dynamic process of maintaining the norms and practices that assure the constancy of its product. This is learning in a sense quite different from change-oriented learning: It is the active reaffirmation or maintenance of the know-how that the organization already possesses. We argue that such organizational learning is better explained from a cultural perspective that assumes the group and group attributes as its unit of analysis than from an individually oriented cognitive perspective. We will expand on this reasoning shortly, after considering an example of explicit change at Powell.

POWELL AND THE COOPER SCALE

Along with more routine changes in personnel, one exceptional episode at Powell reflects how an innovation in product design was also a means of maintaining the organization's identity.

In 1974, Powell became aware of a new scale (the particular arrangement and size of a flute's tone holes that determines the way the flute plays "in tune"). Albert Cooper, an independent English flutemaker, had begun making flutes with a scale he had developed himself. Although he produced only a few flutes a year, several flutists had come to favor his scale over any other. Word of the Cooper scale soon came to Powell's attention, and Powell got in touch with Mr. Cooper. Powell's assessment of the Cooper scale led them to consider the possibility of making a Cooper-scale Powell flute.

For Powell, this possibility was not only a matter of the design of the instrument; it also meant that the workshop would have to accommodate something "new and foreign" within what it knew of itself and of flutemaking. What made this possibility challenging for Powell was that the design of the existing flute—already "the best damned flute in the world," as Powell's president at the time put it—was an integral part of the workshop's identity. Its scale had been developed by Mr. Powell himself and was felt to be an intimate part of the Powell flute. The flutemakers were concerned that in changing the scale, they could be changing the style of the Powell flute, and that would be, in their words, "totally unthinkable."

Their concern seems to have been that adopting a different scale would amount to changing the identity of the company. Yet they had been impressed with the Cooper scale, as had a growing number of flutists. The dilemma was summed up when one flutemaker asked, "If the Powell flute is the best there is, and we want to keep it that way, does that mean we need to change when something new and maybe better comes along?"

The debate continued for some weeks. A prototype Powell flute with a Cooper scale was made. Questions were raised and concerns discussed: Is a Powell flute with a Cooper scale still a Powell flute? Can we make a new scale and still be the same company? Can we change and not let go of quality?

The physical changes in design that the adoption of the Cooper scale would entail were actually quite small. In fact, to the eye, the flute with the new scale and those with the old were very hard to tell apart. Nor would the change be any great threat or challenge to the day-to-day aspects of craftsmanship: Virtually every bit of work could be done without noticing which scale a particular flute was built to. Even with respect to tooling, the change would be a minor matter. For example, once dies were made for the new scale, they could be used in place of the old dies, and work could proceed as usual.

Finally, Powell adopted the Cooper scale. By unanimous vote, the company decided to offer its customers the Powell flute with the new scale. But only as a special option: They would continue to make the Powell flute with the original scale, "and we will do so," Powell's president said, "until we die."

Within a few months, Powell, having brought the Cooper scale to the broad attention of the flute world, saw over 90% of its incoming orders opt for the new scale, and most of the orders on the waiting list were changed by customers to the new option. This soon became the normal pattern, with only a few flutists maintaining their preference for the original Powell scale. The workshop viewed Powell flutes with either scale to be consistent with Powell's standards of quality and style and felt that the Powell flute was "still the best there is."

ORGANIZATIONAL LEARNING
AND THE COOPER SCALE

The Cooper scale episode reflects learning by Powell that in some ways entailed observable change and in others did not. Powell became aware of and assessed the new scale and ultimately made new tooling and offered a new product. All of these are observable changes in a meaningful sense. But Powell also learned in other ways that were equally significant but that did not entail overt change, nor was it a matter of change solely through the vehicle of organizationally key individuals. The workshop succeeded in making an innovation that came to constitute an important shift in the history of flutemaking; yet it did so while leaving unchanged the essential style of the Powell flute and the unique culture of the Powell workshop, in particular, its tacit mode of manufacturing know-how.

The flutes that were made with the Cooper scale were accepted by the flutemakers and by fluteplayers as "Powell flutes." No one ever claimed that the style of the Powell flute had been altered by the change. As one flutemaker observed, "We have only made the best, better."

This particular case of technological change did not involve any essential changes in daily work activities. The only explicit changes were some new tooling that produced the nearly imperceptible changes in the physical dimensions of the instrument necessary for the new scale.

In an important sense, the impetus for change was internal, not external: It did not arise out of a need to improve effectiveness or efficiency or to meet any perceived external challenge to market share or to correct an error. At root, Powell adopted a new technology to maintain and reaffirm its own self-image as makers of "the best"—that is, to sustain what the group felt, believed, and valued.

The decision to produce Powell flutes with both scales was not the resolution of a company conflict: There were no warring camps within the organization over which scale was better, nor was there a feeling that the original scale was in error. Offering both scales was Powell's way of accommodating something new while sustaining the organization's image of itself.

The central issue was the question of organizational identity: Could the organization make a flute with a Cooper scale and still be the Powell organization? For Powell flutemakers specifically, this question focused on their product: Could the organization absorb a new scale into its existing image or sense of "the Powell style"? Would the instrument still be "a Powell"? As organizational members put it, "Can we make a Powell flute with the Cooper scale without it ceasing to be the Powell flute?"

In a very real way, this set of questions can be interpreted to mean, Can we change without changing? Can we make a very deliberate design change and manage it organizationally (strategize about it, implement it, incorporate it into company policy, develop new tooling, etc.) without changing the Powell product and organization into different entities?

This suggests a relationship between change and learning that is different from the customary focus of the cognitive approach. In learning how to make the Cooper scale, Powell mostly learned how to build a flute that was subtly but significantly different without changing the style or identity of their product. Powell's primary concern was as much preservative as it was innovative: learning how to do and make something different without becoming a new and different company; learning how to produce a new scale without changing the essence of the Powell flute.

This concern is reflected both in the making of the instrument and in the deliberations about choosing to go with the Cooper scale. Evaluating the possibility of making a Cooper scale at Powell was both an explicit and implicit exercise. A prototype instrument was made, so some things were necessarily explicit: measurements had to be taken, dies had to be cut, and so forth. Yet this was not done to test the Cooper scale: Mr. Cooper had already made flutes with the Cooper scale, which Powell had seen and tested earlier. Making the prototype enabled Powell, almost ceremonially, to go through the motions of making a Cooper-scale Powell flute and in doing so, to assure itself that the flutes and the company's style would be preserved through the Cooper innovation. Powell was not so much learning a new technology as learning—collectively, as an organization—how to maintain its identity in the face of a new undertaking.

Essentially, the exercise of making the prototype and the discussions about being "the Powell style" were actions aimed at preserving the organization's particular identity. The learning accomplished by Powell involved no reorganization, restructuring of tasks, or recasting criteria for effectiveness; it entailed neither explicit reflections on the practice of flutemaking nor the redrawing of organizational maps.

REFLECTIONS ON CULTURAL LEARNING

Several aspects of the cultural perspective on organizational learning can be noted at this point. First, intuitively it is a much shorter conceptual leap to see organizations as cultural entities than it is to see them as cognitive ones. Organizations, being human groups, are more readily understood as being like tribes than they are as being like individuals or brains. Second, because organizational learning here is understood to involve shared meanings associated with and carried out through cultural artifacts, it is understood as an activity *of* the organization, that is, an activity at the level of the group, not at the level of the individual. Accordingly, it is seen as conceptually and empirically distinct from learning by individuals in the organization. Third, it is also, then, unnecessary to argue that organizations learn in a way that is fundamentally the same as or similar to individual learning. The cultural perspective makes it possible to explore the meaning of organizational learning by beginning with empirical observations of group action rather than relying on conceptual arguments about likenesses between theories of individual cognition and theories of organizations. Fourth, it allows us to view organizational learning as both an innovative and a preservative activity, thus incorporating into the discussion of organizational learning the rather considerable amount of effort that organizations, like all human groups, put into maintaining the patterns of activity that are unique to each organization.

The cultural perspective and the cognitive perspective both include the study of the activities of individuals. The difference is one of focus: The cognitive perspective takes individual action as its primary point of reference; the cultural perspective focuses on a group of individuals moving within a "net of expectations" ranging from the organization's "explicit constitution to the most subtle mutual understandings between its members" (Vickers, 1976, p. 6). Within the cultural perspective, organizational knowledge is not held by an individual, nor do we see it as the aggregated knowledge of many individuals. What is known is known and made operational only by several individuals acting "in congregate."

The case analysis presented here exemplifies organizational learning as a collective activity rather than an individual one and, quite importantly, as an activity of preservation as well as one of innovation. From this analysis we derive a definition of organizational learning as *the acquiring, sustaining, or changing of intersubjective meanings through the artifactual vehicles of their expression and transmission and the collective actions of the group.*

These meanings, whether they are acquired by new members or created by existing ones, come about and are maintained through interactions among members of the organization. They need not be face-to-face verbal interactions: meaning-making and meaning-sustaining interactions take place just as importantly through the medium of the artifacts of the organization's culture—its symbolic objects, symbolic language, and symbolic acts. Such "artifactual interaction" happens not only in exceptional circumstances of disruption or change but also routinely as part of "normal" day-to-day work (whether that be production, management, marketing, etc.). Such was the case at Powell.

This means that much of organizational learning, in our view, is tacit, occasioned through experiences of the artifacts of the organization's culture that are part of its daily work. No one says during the course of a typical working day, for example, "Powell values its identity as producer of the flutes with a particular feel to the mechanism." Rather, that part of Powell's culture is incorporated into the artifacts of daily life in the organization. It is reflected, for example, in the company's stories and myths, in the daily judgments of feel and eye, and in the ceremony of making a prototype Powell with a Cooper scale. Through such largely tacit practice and interpretation of artifactual interaction, the members of each workshop sustain their shared "web of meanings" and the group's expectations concerning the quality of workmanship and the style of its product. This sense of artifactual interaction follows Polanyi's formulation (Polanyi & Prosch, 1975) for tacit knowledge: something learned while focusing on something else.[12] Similarly, we argue, organizations learn tacitly, while focusing on "normal" work.

This incorporation of tacit expression and communication is a further point of distinction from the cognitive perspective, which typically requires that those things essential to organizational learning be made explicit, so that they can be communicated. What is to be learned must be "capable *of being stated* [italics added] in terms that are in principle understandable to other members of the organization" (Duncan & Weiss, 1979, p. 86). By contrast, the cultural perspective we propose here argues that what the organization learns may be, and often is, tacitly known, communicated, and understood.

In the flute case, not only do the daily hand-to-hand judgments constitute tacit expressions of organizational know-how, but learning and knowing how to recognize the right feel are also transmitted tacitly—for example, in the mastercraftsman's judgments of an apprentice's work. Indeed, in large measure, it was such tacit knowledge that guided the decision making around the adoption of the Cooper scale.

A central concern of organizational learning from this cultural perspective is how an organization constitutes and reconstitutes itself. We have described organizational learning as the acquiring, sustaining, and changing, through collective actions, of the meanings embedded in the organization's cultural artifacts. Following this, organizational activities, from ordinary daily tasks to major innovations, can be seen to entail the ongoing reconstitution of what is essential to the organization's identity and its ability to do what it does.

One way in which organizations reconstitute themselves is through the acquisition of new members. As new members are successfully integrated into an organization, their actions increasingly exhibit aspects of the group's or organization's culture. Accordingly, the meanings embedded in a new member's actions become compatible with—indeed, become part of—the "web of meaning" embedded in the actions of the group. This is what happens, for example, when an apprentice at one of the workshops begins to use that workshop's metaphors successfully in interactions with other flute-makers or when he becomes able to work within the informal quality control system by judging his own work and that of others as having the right feel, without checking with a mastercraftsman. When a new member's actions "fit in" to group activity, the organization's concerns are thereby confirmed and sustained; that is to say, the organization has reconstituted itself. Organizations also reconstitute themselves through the ordinary day-to-day activities of veteran members. Such activities and their underlying web of meaning mutually confirm and sustain each other.

The flute workshops have engaged in a form of organizational learning that amounts to organizational reconstitution over time as they have passed through successive generations of flutemakers. The personnel have undergone a complete turnover (in some cases more than once), whereas the form of workmanship and the style and quality of the products have remained constant. A provocative parallel can be found in Weick's (1979) example of the Duke Ellington Orchestra continuing long after the Duke had been replaced by his son. Weick reasons that this has been possible because the concept of that orchestra has been continually recreated by the perceptions of its audiences. We suggest that another likely factor is that the orchestra has sustained its identity through long-term organizational learning. Specifically, the ongoing maintenance of the patterns of collective action among the players, intimately bound up with performance itself, has enabled the organization to survive over the years and through a change in personnel (indeed, its leadership!) because the orchestra continued to learn what it needed to do—how it needed to play—to be the Duke Ellington Orchestra.[13]

The focus here is less on what goes on inside the heads of individuals and more on what goes on in the practices of the group (including how those practices are manifested, in part, in individual action). To paraphrase Douglas (1986), rather than seeing the organization as the individual writ large, we would do well to see the individual as the group writ small, each individual carrying those parts of the collective knowledge that make possible individual action with respect to organizational concerns.[14]

Further, organizational reconstitution can be seen as an important feature of organizational change. As the Cooper innovation at Powell suggests, preservation of organizational identity can be a central concern in organizational innovation. Typically, the aim of innovation is for the organization to take on a new situation, not a new identity. Accordingly, a significant part of the effort put into mastering what is new is often concerned with keeping stable what is old. Asking, as the Powell flutemakers did, "Can we undergo this innovation and still remain who we are?" suggests that a major concern of such innovations is the reconstitution of what makes up the identity of the organization, of what it does and how it does it.

In a somewhat similar fashion, Duncan and Weiss (1979), in considering a social basis for organizational learning, focus on shared cognitive frameworks particular to specific organizations. However, echoing the systems view, they maintain that organizational learning involving such frameworks takes place through the detection of a "performance gap" and its closing by the acquisition of organizational knowledge. In contrast, the cultural perspective we have proposed would not limit organizational learning to the closing of performance gaps (although we would certainly wish to include them). The maintenance of patterns of organizational activity (i.e., the reconstitution of the organization) is ongoing, is not dependent on error detection and corrective change, and does not necessarily entail responses to external stimuli. In our view, the dynamic, ongoing preservation of organizational identity is as compelling as an exclusive focus on learning new things and unlearning outlived ones.[15]

CULTURE AND ORGANIZATIONAL
LEARNING: CONCLUSION

We began this article by focusing on two questions: Can organizations learn? What is the nature of learning when it is done by organization? It is our view that in addressing these questions, most authors have adopted a cognitive perspective. They have taken as their common point of reference learning by individuals and have seen organizational learning either as learning by individuals in organizational contexts or as activities of organizations that are akin to learning by individuals. We have argued that the first position tends to blur the useful distinction between learning *in* organizations and learning *by* organizations. The second, we have maintained, raises the conceptually problematic notion that organizations learn the same way people do, which itself entails an unresolved debate about the ontological status of organizations as cognitive entities (an assertion that the cognitive perspective nonetheless seems to require in order to claim that organizations learn). We have noted that, in ways rarely addressed, the cognitive perspective and its insights are dependent on or conceptually linked to theories of individual cognition that are themselves controversial, complex, multiple, and changing. Finally, we have argued that the cognitive perspective's tendency to associate learning with behavioral change derives perhaps as much from its own conceptual predilections as from the realities of organizational life.

By comparison, from a cultural perspective, we have argued (a) that one aspect of the human capacity to act is the ability to act in groups; (b) that a group of people with a history of joint action or practice is meaningfully understood as a culture; (c) that a culture is constituted, at least in part, from the intersubjective meanings that its members express in their common practice through objects, language, and acts; (d) that such meaning-bearing objects, language, and acts are cultural artifacts through which an organization's collective knowledge or know-how is transmitted, expressed, and put to use; and (e) that organizations are constantly involved in activities of modifying or maintaining those meanings and their embodiments—that is, of changing or preserving their cultural identity. Finally, it has been our position that such activities constitute organizational learning. That is, when organizations are seen as cultures, they are seen to learn through activities involving cultural artifacts, and that learning, in turn, is understood to entail organizations acquiring, changing, or preserving their abilities to do what they know how to do.

This is not to suggest that an organization has only one culture—there is always the possibility that an organization will have multiple cultures, no one of which is dominant, or that there will be a dominant culture and one or more subcultures—nor does it indicate that organizational cultures are created only by managers or founders (see Davis, 1985; Louis, 1985; Yanow, 1992, for discussions and examples of multiple cultures, including those not managerially created). Indeed, the flute case illustrates the role of members in sustaining an organization's culture, even when the original ones are long gone. Although we do not wish to minimize the potential for conflict within or across cultural groups, such is not present in this case. What cultural organizational learning might look like in the face of conflict is a subject for future research. What we have described here is the process of learning by a group that does share cultural meanings. In the flute case, the whole organization constituted such a group; in another context, this might not be so.

The cultural perspective we have proposed rests on a particular understanding of culture that is itself part of a debate in the field. Those who understand culture as an organization's artifacts alone may not find in this essay the sorts of stories, rituals, metaphors, and so forth that add up to culture for them.[16]

But because we see culture as the values, beliefs, and feelings of the organization's members along with their artifacts, we do find culture in the case. Powell identified itself, for example, as a maker of "the finest flutes in the world"; this belief, and the value the organization placed on it, ultimately meant for them that they had to learn how to accommodate the Cooper scale within their practice. And they had to learn this in the face of a paradox. They already made what they held to be the finest flute, and it had a Powell scale. This belief was unchallenged. They had to learn how to think of the Powell flute with the Cooper scale as *also* "the finest flute"—in the face of what might appear as a logical and historical impossibility that there could be two different finest Powell flutes at once. This required them to learn to change not just their beliefs—what Gagliardi (1991, p. 13) calls the "logos" or cognitive part of culture—but also their values and feelings—the "ethos" (the moral experience) and the "pathos" (the sensuous experience) of culture. To see culture in the Powell case, one has to have a theory of culture that includes values, beliefs, and feelings along with their artifactual embodiments. Although calling on the study of organizational learning to include organizational culture as well as cognition, we are also joining those who would like to see the field of organizational culture make its work more inclusive of the noncognitive aspects of human action.

In addition to the above, we find a cultural understanding of organizational learning to be a fruitful approach that suggests further areas of exploration. We would like to speculate on some of these.

Organizations commonly acquire new members. As we noted above, such occasions present an opportunity for an organization to learn, where that learning can be understood to constitute the maintenance or preservation of the know-how associated with an organization's activities and abilities. There is a need for a fuller understanding of how the group and the individual come to hold the shared intersubjective meanings that constitute organizational cultures, as well as of processes by which both "agree to disagree." This cultural perspective suggests that organizational socialization is not simply a question of "How do you socialize Smith into IBM?" (because that constitutes learning by Smith, the individual, not IBM, the organization) but rather the fuller question, "How does IBM renourish itself with new members, yet ensure its continuity?" Socialization typically suggests movement in a single direction: IBM socializes Smith, where Smith is relatively passive, a receptive vessel. From the cultural perspective, for Smith to become a member of IBM (or of a unit within IBM), she must form an understanding of the meaning of those elements of IBM's culture that enable her to carry out her role effectively within it (a point where individual cognition may properly and profitably enter the discussion). IBM, meanwhile, must learn how to make Smith's actions compatible with the actions (and underlying meanings) of other members of its culture and to do so in a way that fosters its own continuity, flourishing, and survival. Cultural organizational learning would focus on the *mutual* creation of compatible and shared meanings.

Would one find the same tacit, artifactual interaction in a larger, more highly differentiated organization? We agree with Ed Schein (personal communication, June 1988) that the theoretical premises remain the same, regardless of differences in size and structure. We suggest, however, that cultural learning as we have described it may be more easily seen when size is small and structure is simple. Such would be the case with subunits of large organizations.

Similarly, our presentation of culture as an organization-wide phenomenon may be an artifact of Powell's relatively small size. We do not mean to suggest that organizations have only single cultures. It does seem to us, however, that cultural learning across subcultures within a single organization, even in the presence of differences, disagreements, perhaps hostility, will take place—if at all—through the tacit processes of artifactual interaction we have discussed. The question indeed is whether learning will take place under such circumstances, whether it will be preservative or not, and if so, of what. How and whether it happens is likely to be context specific; that it might be preservative learning is a possibility to entertain in any context. As the field of organizational culture itself develops theories of power, our understanding of cultural learning will benefit.

Finally, from the emphasis on error detection and correction inherited from the systems view, it has been a logical step for the cognitive perspective to develop the normative position that organizations *ought* to have the ability to detect and correct errors. This, in turn, has supported the claim that when organizations detect and correct errors, they have "learned." In this fashion, the cognitive perspective has evolved a substantially problem-oriented and problem-solving understanding of organizational learning: If learning is about correcting errors, then learning is about things that have gone wrong.

But, as Vickers (personal communication, January 1981) has pointed out, an orientation toward what goes wrong does not necessarily yield the sum total of what is interesting or vital about organizational life. What goes right can also be of interest, and is so, we would argue, for the very reason that it accounts for much of what organizations do. We hold that a cultural theory of organizational learning enables one to focus as much on the right as on the wrong and as much on continuity and preservation as on change. We believe this to be a fruitful area for further exploration.

Vickers (1976) intended his focus on the cultural nature of institutional change "to challenge some widely held beliefs about the role and dominance of cognition" (p. 7). We do not assume for ourselves the whole of this challenge, but we would be pleased if our observations were to further the current explorations of the role that culture plays in our lives, particularly that growing portion that is spent in maintaining and changing our institutions.

Acknowledgments

The authors thank Mats Alvesson, Lee Bolman, Gideon Kunda, Craig Lundberg, Ed Schein, Deborah Stone, Sharon Traweek, Barry A. Turner, Karl Weick, and the anonymous reviewers of this essay for their careful readings of the text and for their many helpful suggestions. An earlier version was presented at the Second Annual Symposium of the Public Administration Theory Network, Los Angeles, April 1990.

NOTES

1. This discussion of organizational learning as individual learning has a parallel in organizational behavior that has at times been a source of confusion—specifically, whether "organizational behavior" refers to the behavior of individuals within organizations or to the collective behaviors of organizations themselves. The use of the individual as a model for the group, and vice versa, has a long history. It may be found in philosophy and social science in discussions that trace their lineage, in one sense, to Mead (1934) or, in another sense, to Hobbes (1651/1958). Indeed, it can be found as far back as Plato (Hamilton & Cairns, 1961) when, for example, Socrates suggests that just as large letters can be easier to read than small ones, we should not look first to discover justice in the individual but rather in the state, where the "letters exist . . . larger," and only after finding it there should we look for it in individuals, recognizing then "the likeness of the greater in the form of the less."

2. Duncan and Weiss (1979) develop a similar critique in their finding that individual learning within an organizational setting, as presented by March and Olsen (1976) and Argyris and Schön (1978), has limitations for producing understanding of "systematic organization action."

3. In other respects, however, their work is an exception to the following discussion.

4. For that matter, even within research on individual cognition there is a great deal of attention given to variations in how learning occurs across individuals and within one individual over time (see, for example, Gardner, 1983).

5. It seems to us that the concept of organizational learning began to attract attention in the mid-1970s, in part in response to theories of organizational change from the previous decade that called for radical changes in the social, political, and corporate worlds. The concept of organizational *learning* provided a noncontroversial, conservative, yet dynamic, alternative for addressing the issue of change because, traditionally, learning is not seen as a controversial or radical activity. It also provided a tool for intervention. Its psychological origins made it a manageable tool, in that it targeted problems in single individuals, who could be helped to learn, in contrast with radical change theories rooted in analyses of the sociopolitical structure that demanded change in "the system."

We also note that a learning approach to organizational change addresses implicitly one of the problems that arose in early T-group change efforts. Practitioners using T-groups came to note that although T-groups produced learning and change in individuals, those changes were often challenged when these individuals returned from the training to the organization, and, as a consequence, what those individuals learned was sometimes lost. Seeing organizational change as the result of learning by key individuals within an organization conceptually avoids the problem of translating individual learning into organizational learning.

6. Although inventions and innovations are often the products of single individuals, part of the process of building an organization is a matter of embedding the know-how required for the ongoing production and adaptation of these products into the organization itself. Weick has called to our attention a series of social psychological experiments that modeled cultural transmission within a group, similar to our discussion here, as subjects are replaced over successive generations of the experiment. The research found that the small group's simple strategy survived changes in membership. This research is reported in Weick and Gilfillan (1971).

7. Bateson (1958) was perhaps the first to analyze the problem of learning by a group, in his 1936 study of how the Iatmul culture learned to accommodate change. In his epilogue to the later edition of the book, he elaborated on the concept of "schismogenesis" to describe this process. Much influenced by his interim studies in psychology, Bateson introduced the concept of "deutero-learning"—"learning to learn"—as the way in which groups and individuals manage a changing environment.

8. We are, of course, limited by the English language to describing organizational actions using verbs appropriate to individual action, thereby appearing ourselves to anthropomorphize organizations. This conceptualization of organizational activity is further promoted by the use of a singular verb for group action—for example, the organization *knows*—mandated by accepted rules of English usage. On the other hand, such usage bolsters our conceptualization of the organization as an entity that can take action that is other than the sum of its parts.

9. There is no single definition or theory of culture in either the interdisciplinary field of organizational culture studies or in its disciplinary "homes" of anthropology or sociology. Ouchi and Wilkins (1985) noted this quite thoroughly in their review of the several literatures whose theories and debates underlie and inform work in organizationally oriented culture studies. We place ourselves in the school that considers both meanings and their artifactual expressions to be necessary components of culture. When we refer to a cultural perspective in this essay, we have in mind one informed by such an interpretive theoretical position. We cannot in this article explore the ways in which cultural learning might look different according to one's theoretical position regarding the nature of culture, but we wish to acknowledge that this might be the case and might be a useful area for further research.

10. Properly speaking, symbols, rituals, myths, and so forth are *not* the artifacts of an organization's culture; annual reports, statements of corporate philosophy, award celebrations, daily talk about the specifics of work, and so forth are the artifacts. The former terms are analytic vocabulary that characterize and categorize the actual artifacts. As tools of research, these terms

draw attention to certain features of organizational life; in fact, they incorporate the rules and conventions by which such categories are formed. This point is germane to a central methodological issue in the study of organizational cultures: Because the analytic categories are essentially constructs of the observer, care must be taken not to confuse them with organizational experience itself.

11. This case is based on extensive observation and interviewing over a period of several years, including numerous visits to all three workshops, detailed interviews with all key personnel, and "shop floor" interviews with flutemakers and apprentices at all levels. The case as presented here draws, as well, on Cook (1982). Our theoretical interest in culture as an approach to organizational learning initially grew out of our considerations of the flute case. Since then, we have moved back and forth between theory building and exploration of the case in developing the view presented here. In this sense, both our experience and the form of this essay reflect a recursive interpretive, or hermeneutic, circle.

12. One of Polanyi's examples is of bicycle riding, where balance is learned tacitly while focusing on pedaling or steering or some other target of attention. On a related subject, Brown and Duguid (1991) have explored ways that practitioners communicate and learn skills tacitly in daily practice.

13. We have had this point further confirmed in a personal conversation with a member of the Juilliard String Quartet. Over more than two decades the quartet has replaced all but one of its original members. One of the newest members reports that his experience of learning to play in the style of the Juilliard and his contributions to the evolution of that style were never a subject of explicit conversation but were carried out through the playing of the music itself in rehearsal and performance.

14. For Douglas (1986), such concerns in a societal context include classification systems, institutional memory and forgetfulness, and group identity. She addresses the issue of attributing emotions, behaviors, or thought to institutions, and argues that thinking itself forms the social bond among individuals and binds them in a corporate entity. In a similar sense, Bougon, Weick, and Binkhorst (1977) held that "what ties an organization together is what ties thought together" (p. 626). What we are suggesting is an approach that adds to thinking what Vickers (1973) called "appreciating," that would include values and feelings along with artifacts and practices as the organizational glue.

15. It is possible that we have been disposed to find ongoing conservation, preservation, and reconstitution at work in seeing learning as an aspect of culture. As anthropologists Marcus and Fischer (1986) noted about work in their field, "The drive remains strong . . . to show repeatedly how the tradition and the deep structures of cultures shine through despite change" (p. 181). One of the criticisms levied at phenomenological analyses of human reality is that they are concerned with societal stability and order to the exclusion of change. We hope we have sufficiently illustrated our concern with change as a part of human action. The exception that we take with the cognitive approach to organizational learning is its nearly exclusive concern with change.

16. Related to this, we differ with those who see culture as one of several elements of an organization. Levitt and March (1988), for example, in arguing that organizations learn "by encoding inferences from history into routines that guide behavior," use the term *routines* to include "forms, rules, procedures, conventions, strategies and technologies" along with "beliefs, frameworks, paradigms, codes, cultures and knowledge" (p. 320). Because we understand culture not as something that an organization possesses, but as something constitutive of it, we would not see culture as one of several avenues for carrying out routines, but rather would see routines, as well as many of the other items on their list, as elements or artifacts of an organizational culture.

REFERENCES

Argyris, C., & Schön, D. A. (1978). *Organizational learning.* Reading, MA: Addison-Wesley.

Bateson, G. (1958). *Naven* (2nd ed.). Stanford, CA: Stanford University Press.

Berger, P. L., & Luckmann, T. (1966). *The social construction of reality.* New York: Doubleday.

Bolman, L. (1976). Organizational learning. In C. Argyris (Ed.), *Increasing leadership effectiveness* (pp. 183-210). New York: John Wiley.

Bougon, M., Weick, K., & Binkhorst, D. (1977). Cognition in organizations: An analysis of the Utrecht Jazz Orchestra. *Administrative Science Quarterly, 22,* 606-639.

Brown, J. S., & Duguid, P. (1991). Organizational learning and communities-of-practice: Toward a unified view of working, learning, and innovation. *Organization Science, 2,* 40-57.

Cook, S. D. N. (1982). *Part of what judgment is.* Doctoral dissertation, Massachusetts Institute of Technology.

Cyert, R. M., & March, J. G. (1963). *A behavioral theory of the firm.* Englewood Cliffs, NJ: Prentice Hall.

Davis, T. R. V. (1985). Managing culture at the bottom. In R. H. Kilmann, M. J. Saxton, R. Serpa, & Associates (Eds.), *Gaining control of the corporate culture.* San Francisco: Jossey-Bass.

Douglas, M. (1986). *How institutions think.* Syracuse, NY: Syracuse University Press.

Duncan, R., & Weiss, A. (1979). Organizational learning. *Research in Organizational Behavior, 1,* 75-123.

Etheredge, L. S., & Short, J. (1983). Thinking about government learning. *Journal of Management Studies, 20,* 41-58.

Fiol, C. M., & Lyles, M. A. (1985). Organizational learning. *Academy of Management Review, 10,* 803-813.

Frost, P. J., Moore, L. F., Louis, M. R., Lundberg, C. C., & Martin, J. (1985). *Organizational culture.* Beverly Hills, CA: Sage.

Frost, P. J., Moore, L. F., Louis, M. R., Lundberg, C. C., & Martin, J. (1991). *Reframing organizational cultures.* Newbury Park, CA: Sage.

Gagliardi, P. (1991). Artifacts as pathways and remains of organization life. In P. Gagliardi (Ed.), *Symbols and artifacts* (pp. 3-38). New York: Aldine de Gruyter.

Gahmberg, H. (1980). *Contact patterns and learning in organizations: With a network analysis in two industrial organizations.* Helsinki, Finland: Helsinki School of Economics.

Gardner, H. (1983). *Frames of mind.* New York: Basic Books.

Hamilton, E., & Cairns, H. (Eds.). (1961). *The collected dialogues of Plato.* Princeton, NJ: Princeton University Press.

Hedberg, B. (1981). How organizations learn and unlearn. In P. C. Nystrom & W. H. Starbuck (Eds.), *Handbook of organizational design* (pp. 3-27). London: Oxford University Press.

Herriott, S. R., Levinthal, D. A., & March, J. G. (1985). Learning from experience in organizations. *American Economic Review, 75,* 298-302.

Hobbes, T. (1958). *Leviathan.* New York: Bobbs-Merrill. (Original work published in 1651)

Jenkins-Smith, H. C., & St. Clair, G., with the assistance of James, R. (1988, March). *Analysis of change in elite policy beliefs within subsystems.* Paper presented at the annual meeting of the Western Political Science Association, San Francisco.

Lant, T. K., & Mezias, S. J. (1990). Managing discontinuous change: A simulation study of organizational learning and entrepreneurship. *Strategic Management Journal, 11,* 147-179.

Levitt, B., & March, J. G. (1988). Organizational learning. *Annual Review of Sociology, 14,* 319-340.

Louis, M. R. (1985). Sourcing workplace cultures. In R. H. Kilmann, M. J. Saxton, R. Serpa, & Associates (Eds.), *Gaining control of the corporate culture.* San Francisco: Jossey-Bass.

March, J. G., & Olsen, J. P. (1976). Organizational learning and the ambiguity of the past. In *Ambiguity and choice in organizations* (pp. 54-67). Oslo, Norway: Universitetsforlaget.

Marcus, G., & Fischer, M. M. J. (1986). *Anthropology as cultural critique.* Chicago: University of Chicago Press.

Mead, G. H. (1934). *Mind, self and society.* Chicago: University of Chicago.

Miles, R. H., & Randolph, W. A. (1981). Influence of organizational learning styles on early development. In J. R. Kimberly & R. H. Miles (Eds.), *The organizational life cycle* (pp. 44-82). San Francisco: Jossey-Bass.

Morgan, G. (1986). *Images of organization.* Beverly Hills, CA: Sage.

Ouchi, W. G., & Wilkins, A. L. (1985). Organizational culture. *Annual Review of Sociology, 11,* 457-483.

Polanyi, M., & Prosch, H. (1975). *Meaning.* Chicago: University of Chicago Press.

Sandelands, L. E., & Stablein, R. E. (1987). The concept of organization mind. *Research in the Sociology of Organizations, 5,* 135-161.

Schein, E. H. (1985). *Organizational culture and leadership.* San Francisco: Jossey-Bass.

Shrivastava, P. (1983). A typology of organizational learning systems. *Journal of Management Studies, 20*(1), 7-28.

Simon, H. A. (1991). Bounded rationality and organizational learning. *Organization Science, 2,* 125-134.

Sims, H. P., Jr., Gioia, D. A., & Associates. (1986). *The thinking organization: Dynamics of organizational social cognition.* San Francisco: Jossey-Bass.

Sitkin, S. B. (1992). Learning through failure: The strategy of small losses. *Research in Organizational Behavior, 14,* 231-266.

Smircich, L. (1983). Concepts of culture and organizational analysis. *Administrative Science Quarterly, 28*(3), 339-358.

Taylor, C. (1979). Interpretation and the sciences of man. In P. Rabinow & W. M. Sullivan (Eds.), *Interpretive social science: A reader* (pp. 33-81). Berkeley: University of California Press.

Vickers, G. (1973). *Making institutions work.* London: Associated Business Programmes.

Vickers, G. (1976, November). *Institutional learning as controlled cultural change.* Paper presented at the Division for Study in Research and Education, Massachusetts Institute of Technology.

Weick, K. E. (1979). Cognitive processes in organizations. *Research in Organizational Behavior, 1,* 41-74.

Weick, K. E. (1991). The nontraditional quality of organizational learning. *Organization Science, 2*(1), 41-73.

Weick, K. E., & Gilfillan, D. P. (1971). Fact of arbitrary traditions in a lab microculture. *Journal of Personality and Social Psychology, 17,* 179-191.

Weiss, C. (1980, December). *Policy evaluation as societal learning.* Paper presented at the Pinhas Sapir Conference on Development, Tel Aviv, Israel.

Yanow, D. (1992). Supermarkets and culture clash: The epistemological role of metaphors in administrative practice. *American Review of Public Administration, 22*(2), 89-109.

20

Organizing for Continuous Improvement

Evolutionary Theory Meets the Quality Revolution

SIDNEY G. WINTER

The producers of management advice operate in an economic environment where the tides of fad and fashion run strong. Frameworks, slogans, and buzzwords are brought forth in great profusion with attendant fanfare and claims of novelty. Although large rewards often accrue to successful fashion leaders, it is open to question whether organizations actually perform much better as a result of this activity. To the jaded eye, the latest widely acclaimed insight often looks suspiciously like a fancy repackaging of some familiar platitude or truism. Alternatively, it may be that this year's fashionable ideas are genuinely valuable—but largely because they help to correct a misallocation of attention that was itself produced by an excess of enthusiasm for ideas fashionable in the recent past.

Quality is now a very fashionable word in the management vocabulary. Not too long ago, *Business Week* (1991) devoted a special issue to "The Quality Imperative," declaring in its introduction that a focus on quality is producing a "global revolution, affecting every facet of business" (p. 7). Skeptics are not hard to find, however.

If the quality revolution is as significant as its proponents claim, it may well be the most important management innovation of the 20th (and early 21st) century. If its significance is only a fraction of what is claimed, it could still be quite important. In either of these cases, its importance would relate

This chapter appeared originally in *The Evolutionary Dynamics of Organizations,* edited by Joel A. C. Baum and Jitendra Singh. Copyright © 1994 by Oxford University Press. Reprinted by permission.

not merely to the theory and practice of management, but also to the assessment of the long-term economic outlook. For example, a major part of the "competitiveness" problem of the U.S. economy might be attributable to the follower status of the United States in the diffusion of quality management innovations. On the other hand, if quality management is merely a collection of buzzwords, it is safe to tune out—unless one has a stake in being in touch with current fashion.

That quality management should be taken seriously is the major conclusion of this chapter, but also, in a sense, its major premise: the chapter would not exist if I had reached the opposite conclusion. Quality management ideas provide an interesting perspective on the nature of productive knowledge and the processes by which it is maintained and improved in organizations. It seems clear that their importance as a source of improvement in organizational performance is substantial; how far the revolution may go and what its consequences may be are important and interesting questions. I seek to explain and assess the quality revolution in terms that link its principal ideas to the characterization of firm behavior in evolutionary economic theory (Nelson & Winter, 1982). Many of the perspectives offered here are specifically and obviously *economic* perspectives—but the evolutionary, ecological, and organization-theoretic aspects of evolutionary economic theory also inform this appraisal in significant ways. In particular, the final major section of the chapter sketches some general hypotheses about the ecology of quality management—the characteristics of the organizational and economic niches in which this management innovation is likely to grow and prosper. The chapter may thus serve, indirectly, to link quality management ideas to economics, evolutionary theory, and organization theory generally.

In discussing these ideas, I attempt to minimize the use of quality management jargon and acronyms. Quality management maxims and statements of the recognized "gurus" of the subject are sprinkled in occasionally for clarification and seasoning. One has to concede that "Seek out the low-hanging fruit first!" has a certain appeal relative to its proximate equivalent in economic theory, "Allocate effort to where its marginal product is the highest!"[1]

The ideas and literature of the quality revolution derive from a number of different sources and involve a number of major themes. Most current accounts of the history of thought in the area emphasize the influence of two Americans, W. Edwards Deming and J. M. Juran. There are numerous parallels between the careers of these two men, including their becoming influential in the United States after first being so in Japan, and the fact that both remain vigorous and active in the quality movement at advanced ages. It is clear, however, that the Japanese themselves have not only led the way in making the quality revolution a reality, but have also contributed fundamentally to its intellectual foundations.[2] Further, not only have there been many "follow-on inventions" in the quality field, but there have been numerous precursors, foreshadowers, and independent coinventors of major themes. As a result, attributions of ideas involve more than the usual hazards.

I make only occasional attributions; the principal focus is on the ideas themselves, not on their sources. As a corollary, the account of quality management here is more my own synthesis of what seems particularly interesting than an attempt to reproduce accurately a particular school of thought.[3]

EVIDENCE AND INTERPRETATION

The available evidence that supports the effectiveness of quality management methods is of several kinds. Some of the world's most successful competitors are acknowledged leaders in the practice of quality management and emphatically state their full allegiance to quality management principles —Toyota is perhaps the leading example. Also, there are strong adherents of quality management among executives of struggling or moderately successful companies as well as of highly successful companies. These adherents from less successful companies do not typically blame the quality management tools for their problems; they blame themselves and their fellows for making a late start.

The time required for quality management methods to produce results is, in fact, a key issue. For external observers interested in checking the claims made for quality management, it would be convenient if these tools were touted as the functional equivalent of a magic wand that produces instant, companywide performance improvements. Assuming that the waving of the wand were itself an observable event, it would then be relatively easy to check the validity of the claims. Inconveniently for external observers, the magic wand claim is rarely if ever made. Instead, the usual account is that the introduction of quality management is an incremental, time-consuming (even never-ending) process.

It is not surprising, therefore, that some of the most interesting evidence about quality management methods comes from a very microscopic level, relating to improvements achieved in particular processes. Much of this evidence consists of quantitative anecdotes—accounts of improvements by large factors that were made in particular performance indicators. Among the type of indicators often featured in these stories are defect rates and cycle times. For example, the *Business Week* (1991) special issue contains the following story from Hewlett-Packard: "At one HP factory a decade ago, four of every 1,000 soldered connections were defective, not bad for those days. Engineers were called in, and they cut the defect rate in half by modifying the process. Then, HP turned to its workers. They practically rebuilt the operation—and slashed defects a thousandfold, to under two per million" (p. 16).

As illustrated by the examples of defect rates and cycle times, the performance indicators that typically appear in quality management success stories are not direct measures of profitability.[4] Neither do they relate directly to variables like unit cost or market share, whose links to profitability are familiar themes in economic discussion. In some cases, the indicators may be regarded as proxies for what economists call technical efficiency (at the process level). They are imperfect proxies, however, because the improvements reported in "output" measures typically occur at the expense of increases in some inputs. Further, some investment of resources is always required to bring about the improvement in the first place. Regardless of whether this investment is treated as R&D expenditure for accounting purposes, in economic substance it is process R&D expenditure.

To any individual success story, therefore, a skeptical economist might reasonably respond with "So what?" Not enough information is presented about the bottom-line value of the improvement reported, or about the investment costs and continuing costs of the improvement, to permit an assessment of its economic merit. Further, an economic assessment of the general methods whose power is supposedly illustrated in the success stories would have to address the obvious sampling problem: there are failure stories as well as success stories, and those must be given appropriate weight in an overall assessment. That quality management methods have produced positive results in some organizations is beyond dispute; that these methods are generally economically effective by conventional standards has not been demonstrated.

The phrase "by conventional standards" implicitly invokes an important assumption. Although there is continuing debate about the appropriate goals of the large corporation, economists generally take a narrow view of the matter: they think that private sector managers should concern themselves with profit or present value or perhaps the market value of the firm. Efforts to lower defect rates (for example) may or may not contribute to success in this sense. If they do, fine. If not, the costly pursuit of such technical goals is ill-advised.

Two aspects of this assessment need to be considered, one relating to the actual preeminence of the profit goal and the other to its explicitness. The first involves basic questions about the role of the corporate form in economic organization. If the fundamental social rationale of the corporation is strictly to help investors make money, there may be correspondingly fundamental limits to the efficiency gains achievable by imbuing managers and workers with a culture of mutual trust and cooperation. This issue is discussed further, though of course far from comprehensively, later in this chapter.

The explicitness aspect can again be divided into two parts. First, there is a further perspective on the profit goal. If long-run profit maximization is the goal of the investors who are ultimately in control, it is conceivable that their interests are served by keeping that fact as secret as possible. Perhaps such a deceit is the most effective way to approach the fundamental efficiency limits referred to earlier. There is a school of thought regarding quality management that interprets it as the latest manifestation of a recurring pattern in which owners and/or managers pursue their own interests by attempting to deceive workers—talk of efficiency and cooperation masks an attempt to induce workers to work harder while conceding as little as possible of the resulting product.[5]

There is also the question of whether explicit attention to ultimate goals is otherwise desirable, apart from the fact that it may involve the sacrifice of gains attainable through obfuscation or deceit. In its emphasis on the pursuit of a large number of narrow technical goals, quality management doctrine often appears indifferent to the economic logic of resource allocation. Such indifference may lead to overinvestment in the pursuit of technical achievements that do not actually matter very much. Although this observation has some force, it is simplistic to assume that explicit attention to ultimate goals is always instrumental in achieving those goals. Should the receiver, leaping to catch the pass from the quarterback, be thinking about advancing the ball and winning the game—or should he focus on *catching* the ball? Common wisdom on the subject advises the latter. Similarly, quality management's emphasis on proximate goals and measurable achievements may be sound advice in a world where the effective allocation of scarce attention is a real issue.

QUALITY MANAGEMENT AS
HEURISTIC PROBLEM SOLVING

In the following section, I characterize quality management methods in terms of specific attributes. For present purposes, I require only the following broad characterization of what "quality management" refers to: Quality management is the quest for improvement in organizational routines through the application of a particular collection of problem-solving heuristics and techniques. An important premise underlying most of these heuristics and techniques is that key information required for the improvement of a routine can be obtained only with the active cooperation of those involved in its performance.

A problem-solving heuristic is an approach to problem solving that is useful in spite of limitations deriving in part from vagueness and in part from uncertainty regarding its domain of application. Because of these limitations, shared with all heuristic methods, quality management cannot be expected to *optimize* routines in the sense that optimization is understood in formal economic theory.

At an abstract level, "optimization" means getting the right answer to the problem, and no other approach can logically surpass it. Realistically, however, no approach guarantees getting the right answer, even supposing the formulation of the right question. When real world problems are attacked with optimization methods, it is not the theoretical kind of optimization but optimization-as-heuristic that is at work (Nelson & Winter, 1982, pp. 133, 381).

The optimization heuristic advises that the real problem be described and represented in a way that maps it into the known domain of some well-defined optimization method—an optimization algorithm—and that the algorithm then be applied. The processes of identifying the criterion and the constraints gathering relevant data, and achieving the required representation are part of the optimization heuristic, but they are not part of any algorithm. The cost-benefit analysis of the selection of a particular algorithm, with its associated implementation requirements and costs, is also not within the scope of any algorithm. The optimization heuristic is vague about these matters and offers little guidance regarding the limits of its own applicability.

Assessing the practical merits of any body of heuristic methods is inevitably a chancy business. If there is a leap of faith involved in the adoption of quality management as a problem-solving approach, some such leap is also involved in the practical application of linear programming, capital asset pricing, or computable general equilibrium models.

One difference, important to economists if not otherwise, is that the latter methods carry the cachet of economic theory, whereas quality management in its present form is largely a body of methods that have emerged from practice. A corollary observation is that quality management is more explicit in its guidance regarding practical implementation than are problem-solving techniques whose intellectual roots are in economics or operations research.

KEY FEATURES OF
QUALITY MANAGEMENT

The quality revolution may constitute a major peak in understanding of organization and management, but it is a peak that is often shrouded in a fog of confusion and misunderstanding. A number of conditions contribute to the formation of this fog. The quasi-religious fervor of some advocates is by itself enough to put a reasonable person on guard, and the more so if the advocate is also a seller who stands to profit from a successful pitch. The "empowerment" of employees is a major theme in quality management discussion, and for the casual listener such discussion may be reminiscent of all-too-familiar ideological controversies (just when we thought that chapter of history was safely closed). There is proliferation of jargon, there is aggressive product differentiation effort by purveyors, and there is sectarian controversy—reminiscent, again, of ideological ferment of a political or religious nature (*Business Week,* 1991, p. 53).

Above all, the word *quality* itself invites misunderstanding. Quality in the sense of reliability, durability, product features, and so forth, is clearly important, but does it deserve attention to the utter exclusion of other economically significant measures, such as cost, price, and productivity? The answer is that no such exclusion is involved. Indeed, it is quite possible that the most important contributions of quality management might fall under the familiar heading that economists label "cost reduction" rather than "quality improvement" in the conventional sense.

Process Orientation

This potential for misunderstanding of "quality" derives directly from the most important feature of modern quality management: it directs attention to the improvement of production processes, and not simply to the characteristics of the products. To a degree, it involves a rejection of the original formulation of quality control, which sought assurance that the characteristics of the end-product fell within preassigned tolerance limits. The critical shortcoming of that approach is that it offers a very limited range of responses when instances of inadequate quality are discovered. Defective products can be discarded, but this implies the waste of the labor and capital services that went into their production, and in most cases of materials and components as well. Or additional costs can be incurred to bring the defective units up to standard—repair and rework costs. Deliberately or otherwise, some below-standard products may be delivered to market, where they will ultimately inflict warranty costs, damage to the producer's reputation, or both. Quality management experts and practitioners assert that these various costs associated with poor quality—not just in final products but at any point in the organization's functioning—are, in combination, very large.[6]

By contrast, a quality control approach that treats the entire production process as within its purview can incorporate quality checks and generate diagnostic information at every stage. The intermediate quality checks serve to limit the amount of faulty production generated when individual processes go out of tolerance, prompting corrective action before the units affected encounter the final quality check. More importantly, intermediate checks are directly useful in locating the source of the difficulty and can be supplemented with additional aids to diagnosis. This information can guide not only immediate short-term corrective action, but long-term efforts at improvement. In both the short and long term, the result is not merely the enhancement of the quality of the final product in conventional terms, but also the reduction of production costs by saving resources formerly devoted to producing discards, or to repair and rework.

Customer Focus

Complementing the concern with the production process "upstream" from its nominal end-point is an enhanced sensitivity to what happens "downstream" from that point—to how well the product or service meets customer needs. This involves a rejection of a narrowly technocratic and inward-looking definition of quality in favor of a more comprehensive and outward-looking definition, a switch from "quality is what our engineers say it is" to "quality is what our customers say it is." In this respect the quality management literature follows a long tradition in economic thought, which insists that the truest indicator of quality is provided by the buyer's utility function.

To implement this approach, information on customer needs and reactions must be gathered. A variety of methods are employed to this end, with the mix depending to some extent on the context. In markets where firms supply innovative products produced to order for other firms, design teams may be expanded to include customer technical representatives. In other markets, the channels of communication to customers may be opened by surveys and focus group discussions, or by 800 numbers to facilitate complaints and comments. It is often recommended that management, at all levels, devote some time to receiving customer feedback directly rather than relying entirely on summary information that has been filtered through the system.

There are limitations, ambiguities, and pitfalls in the notion of customer-defined quality. These derive primarily from the limitations of the customer's information and, relatedly, from the distinction between the customer's satisfaction in the short run and in the long. Some attributes that are actually quite important to the customer—such as safety features—may be difficult for the customer to assess. The most obvious candidate for the role of customer—for example, a purchasing agent—may not fully reflect the long-run interests of the more remote customers who are importantly affected by the product. Customers may be overly conservative, perhaps because they have little idea of what options are actually on the menu, or because they are wary of the risks and inconvenience associated with being early users of innovative products.

Finally, from a social point of view, the notion of customer-defined quality is subject to the same critiques applicable to the closely related idea of consumer sovereignty. Warning labels on cigarettes and alcohol, or motorcycle helmet laws, illustrate the expression in the public policy realm of skepticism about the social merits of choices that individual consumers often make.

These concerns are important qualifications to the simple formulation that "the customer is the final arbiter of quality." There is not, however, much sign that the progress of quality management has been seriously impeded by simplistic notions of customer satisfaction. On the contrary, many companies seem quite flexible and creative in their willingness to expand the concept of "the customer" and seek useful information from behind the facade that they directly encounter in the marketplace.

An important link between the process orientation and customer focus of quality management is the concept of the internal customer. This concept emphasizes that relationships within the producing organization—particularly among successive stages in the production process or in new product development—are akin to relationships at the "market interface" between the organization and its customers. The same techniques that are used to enhance the responsiveness of the organization to its customers are applicable to the internal relationships—particularly, the attempt to meet the needs of internal customers better through improved communication between them and their internal suppliers.

The "internal customer" may be viewed as quality management's counterpart to the financial management device of establishing "profit centers." Like the profit center approach, it seeks to infuse the internal relations of a large organization with an element of market discipline, at the same time heightening appreciation of the fact that the success achieved by the organization as a whole is the sum of many smaller successes or failures. In contrast to the profit center approach, it emphasizes measurement and communication to facilitate horizontal relationships among subunits, rather than to establish marketlike incentives for subunits and to facilitate performance evaluation from the top.

Analytical and Factual Basis

Quality management techniques facilitate a *disciplined* quest for process involvement. Random tinkering is not advised; neither is the impulsive implementation of a bright idea, whether from top management or from the shop floor. (Suggestions are strongly encouraged, but for study, not immediate implementation.) These familiar methods of seeking improvement are considered inadequate because of their failure to probe the causes of process shortcomings in sufficient depth or to take adequate account of contextual factors. The consequences of such attempts are expected to be small, temporary, and possibly adverse. "Think of the chaos that would come if everyone did his best, not knowing what to do" (Deming, 1986, p. 19).

The techniques employed to guide and structure the quest for improvements constitute the heart of quality management, and they are too numerous for a detailed survey here.[7] Quality consultants and quality management literature offer a wide selection of quite detailed recipes for implementing quality management—or at least attempting to do so. These recipes describe roles, required actions, and rough timetables for action at all levels of the organization. Whether the effort ultimately succeeds or fails depends, however, on the cumulative effect of a large number of individual quality improvement projects. Such projects address particular problems or "opportunities for improvement"; they are typically conducted by project teams composed at least in part of individuals regularly involved with the subprocess in which the problem arises.

In a variety of formulations, quality management authorities and practitioners urge that the first step toward improvement is to achieve understanding of the process as it currently exists. ("If you want to improve a system or process, you must first understand how it works now.") Flowcharting of the current process is a conceptually simple but powerful tool that often produces surprising insights. ("We cannot improve any process until we can flowchart it.") To encounter difficulty in describing and measuring the current "process" is more ominous than to describe successfully an obviously flawed process. It suggests that there *is* no current process; a portion of the organization is simply adrift. ("Adherence precedes improvement.") Identification of the sources of defects or delays and measurement of their frequency and magnitude serve to focus attention on areas where the payoff to improvement may be greatest. Consultation with internal customers and suppliers of the process under examination may permit the identification of parts of the process that serve no significant purpose and provide a context for review of proposed changes. Measurement and analysis must continue beyond the identification and attempted implementation of a recommended process change, to determine both whether anticipated favorable results have actually occurred and whether *un*anticipated *unfavorable* results have occurred. If the answers are no, yes, or both no and yes, the quest for improvement must be renewed. The refusal to accept "implementation gaps" is built in.

Leadership and Participation Issues

Much of the intensity and fervor associated with quality management derive from its implications for the roles of managers at various levels, as distinguished from the roles of "hands-on" employees. A distinctive feature of quality management doctrine—especially in the Deming formulation—is that it places responsibility for malfunctioning organizations squarely at the door of top management. ("Export anything to a friendly country except American management" [Deming, as quoted in Walton, 1990, p. 13]). Of the many nostrums profitably peddled to American management over the years, few indeed have so clearly identified the clients themselves as the principal culprits in the difficulties their organizations were suffering.

Management is responsible for the problems because management is responsible for the systems, and it is the systems above all that generate the problems. Deming's "85-15 Rule" holds that 85% of what goes wrong is with the system, and only 15% with the individual person or thing (Walton, 1990, p. 20). A related idea is that "the people who know the work best are those who perform it" (Walton, 1990, p. 22). Finally, the general assumption about worker motivation is that pride of workmanship is a powerful motivator. "Give the work force a chance to work with pride, and the 3 per cent that apparently don't care will erode itself by peer pressure" (Deming, 1986, p. 85).[8] On the other hand, people may not know how to do a good job, much less how to do a better job in the face of the numerous constraints the organization imposes on them.

These three propositions—that process problems are predominantly attributable to system flaws, that the experts on the work are the people who do it, and that people are fundamentally motivated to do a good job—together imply a need for major recasting of managerial roles in the interests of organizational effectiveness. Although there may be other significant grounds for favoring such a change, they are redundant once the need for improved organized performance is acknowledged. Management must behave so as to provide a supportive structure within which people at lower levels can act effectively to improve performance. It cannot achieve significant performance improvements by its own unilateral action, for it lacks the detailed knowledge required to do so. It might attempt to force the required knowledge to the surface by fiat, but what is likely to surface instead is an account that is brief, abstract, and simple enough for management to understand, and bowdlerized to conform to perceptions of what management is believed to think should be going on. If the real thing were somehow made to surface, management would immediately collapse from information overload—or perhaps from despair.

From this assessment, the need to involve and empower employees becomes apparent, granting only the premise that the need to improve performance exists. The involvement and empowerment of employees are not, of course, objectives that can be accomplished by announcing them one morning as the new corporate policy. Managers must behave in new ways that neither they nor their subordinates fully understand, and they must overcome a long heritage of distrust and justifiable cynicism about change.[9]

ROUTINES, QUALITY MANAGEMENT, AND EVOLUTIONARY THEORY

Quality management ideas provide an interesting perspective on what organizational capabilities are like in the first place, quite apart from any attempt to improve them. This perspective is similar in many ways to the view of the same issues taken in evolutionary economic theory.

A basic point of contention between the evolutionary theory and orthodox economics is the degree of reality that should be imputed to the orthodox concepts of production sets and production functions—especially long run production functions. As discussed by Nelson and Winter (1982, chap. 3), there are three challenging questions to be raised about the orthodox approach: (1) Where does the knowledge reside? (2) What real considerations could produce a sharp distinction between "technically possible" and "technically impossible" production activities? (3) How does the knowledge possessed by one firm relate to that of others, and to the knowledge environment generally?

On the first point, the orthodox commitment is vague in its details but clearly carries the implication that knowledge is represented in the firm in a form that makes alternative ways of doing things accessible to an effective survey, leading to a choice founded on economic criteria. There is no status quo way of doing things that has special prominence so far as knowledge is concerned; only a costless act of optimizing choice distinguishes the production technique actually used from an alternative that would have been used if prices were different. By contrast, evolutionary theory sees organizational capabilities as fragmented, distributed, and embedded in organizational routines. No individual knows how the organization accomplishes what it actually does, much less what alternatives are available. Although elements of economic choice are built into some routines, the routines themselves are not the consequence of an antecedent choice from a large menu, but of organizational learning.

The quality management perspective is entirely congenial to the evolutionary view but virtually incomprehensible to the orthodox view. Quality management stresses the importance of first *finding out* what process (routine, technique of production) the organization is currently using. Further, this task cannot be approached in a comprehensive way, but only in a fragmented and incremental way that corresponds to the actual distribution of capabilities in the organization. As subprocesses are flowcharted and analyzed, unexpected discoveries are made about how the organization works.

On the second point, the orthodox view sees business firms as operating in a technically efficient manner—right on the cliff edge where the known leaves off and the abyss of the unknown begins. It may be possible to move the cliff edge by investment in research and development, but it is still a cliff edge. Once the engineers have defined the cliff edge, economic choice determines where on that edge the firm operates. On the evolutionary view, there is no cliff edge, and also no sharp distinction between the economics of technical change and the economics of everyday performance. The prevailing organizational routines do not mark the edge of the feasible, but the point where learning stopped—or, more optimistically, the point that learning has now reached.

On the evolutionary view, therefore, it is not particularly surprising that systematic critical scrutiny directed to prevailing routines might turn up major opportunities for improvement in both "technical" methods and "organizational" arrangements. (Evolutionary theory and quality management concur again on the point that the line between the technical and the organizational is not sharply drawn.) There is no general presumption that the prevailing routines ever had such scrutiny in the past. And while "critical scrutiny" may sound simple in principle, quality management teaches that it is anything but simple in practice. Evolutionary theory and quality management doctrine concur again on many specific observations regarding resistance to change—including the important point that such resistance is often functional.

On the third point, evolutionary theory emphasizes that the capabilities of individual firms are not selections from a common technical handbook, but idiosyncratic outcomes of unique firm histories. While imitation across organizational boundaries is a powerful mechanism spreading change through the economy, it is hampered by the general factors tending to stabilize prevailing routines of the imitator and sometimes by attempts at secrecy by the imitatee. The result is something far short of homogenization of method, even within narrowly defined industry categories. The quality management literature takes it for granted that a firm can understand its own methods only by systematic (though fragmented and decentralized) self-study. Methods used by other firms are an important source of ideas for improvement; indeed "competitive benchmarking" is an important branch of quality improvement technique. Effective imitation of the routines of another organization requires, however, at least as much careful analysis and planning as are needed for "home grown" improvement ideas.

In short, there is much common ground between quality management doctrine and evolutionary economic theory with regard to the characterization of organizational capabilities. The improvement program offered by quality management raises somewhat different issues and there is less overlap as a result. (Since evolutionary theory is not a normative approach to management, it is silent on many of the issues that quality management forcefully addresses.) There are, however, some interesting points of contact.

Tacit Knowledge

Evolutionary theory emphasizes that much of the knowledge that underlies organizational capabilities is tacit knowledge; it is not understood or communicable in symbolic form. Two different senses in which this is true have been identified. First, individual skills have large tacit components, and organizational routines involve tacit knowledge to the extent that they involve the exercise of such skills. The second sense relates to the point that organizational knowledge is fragmented. Knowledge that is articulable by some individuals may be inaccessible to others, and to top management in particular. The fact that the organization functions reasonably effectively and is more or less responsive to direction from the top is somewhat mysterious when contemplated from the top—in a sense akin to the CEO's mysterious ability to control his or her car or golf swing, without conscious awareness of how it happens.

The quality management approach to understanding the process as it exists suggests a third, somewhat different perspective on the tacitness of routines. Aspects of a routine that are unknown to any participant may become both known and articulable if the participants get together and talk it over (something they have no occasion to do under routine operation). Together, comparing notes and piecing things together, the team may create an account of how the routine works that simply did not exist before. Such an account provides a framework for predicting the consequences of alterations of the routine and hence an opportunity to plan a successful intervention. Viewed in this light, the injunction "first understand how it works now" calls for an attack on the obstacles to improvement that derive from the tacitness of routines.

This appraisal helps to explain the promise of the method but also suggests some vulnerabilities. There is no chance of articulating all the knowledge that underlies the routine; important areas of tacitness will inevitably remain and can be the source of unintended consequences from improvement efforts. Also, by casting top management in a supporting role in the improvement process, quality management offers relatively little to mitigate the tacitness problem at the top of the organization. It would presumably be helpful for top management to have a better idea of what the organization as a whole can and cannot do; quality management largely defers that problem to some future date—perhaps wisely, perhaps not.

THE ECOLOGY OF QUALITY MANAGEMENT

The preceding discussion suggests that quality management is a promising innovation. More accurately, it is meta-innovation, a loose collection of heuristic methods for producing improvements in organizational routines. In a world of imperfect information and understanding, latent opportunities for performance improvement are always abundant. Quality management methods provide some novel ways of converting a portion of these latent opportunities into recognized opportunities, and recognized opportunities into actual improvements. An attempt to assess the likely future influence of these methods, and to identify their most promising niche in the managerial environment, is in order.

In this connection, the general understanding that has been achieved of the processes of diffusion of innovation is clearly relevant. More specifically relevant—and perhaps discouraging for the prospects for successful prognostication and systematic hypothesis testing—is the literature on the diffusion of relatively "soft" innovations that are characterized by substantial ambiguity of definition. Such innovations mutate as they infiltrate differentiated environments, leaving a puzzling trail of definitional issues for the analyst (Downs & Mohr, 1976; Walker, 1969). Given the diversity and complexity of quality management ideas, this problem looms as a serious one.

Leaving this difficulty to one side, the following discussion explores some of the factors that may shape the application and development of quality management.

The "Buy-In" Problem

It has been argued that the need for a major transformation of managerial roles is an implication of quality management insights regarding the locus of productive knowledge in organizations. While this observation provides sufficient justification for the transformation at the theoretical level, it certainly does not sufficiently motivate it at the practical level. Proponents and practitioners of quality management agree that this transformation is unlikely to occur in the absence of a strong commitment at the top of the organization.[10] The innumerable instances of resistance to change in the organization as a whole can be overcome only if the transformation is fully embraced, supported, and enacted at the top.

In principle, such a commitment might arise from a purely intellectual recognition of the possibility of improved performance and the necessity of organizational change to achieve the improvement. Perhaps the early adopters in Japan were motivated in this way. At the present time and in the American context, however, it seems that the commitment is more likely to arise when it is the necessity of improved performance that is clear and quality management doctrine offers one of the few promising paths available. For example, the willingness of Motorola's management to "buy in" to quality management was stimulated by the discovery that its Japanese competitors had vastly superior quality: "Basically, you had better demonstrate the need or the fear or something that's emotional up front. . . . we put on something we called 'Rise to the Challenge.' The intention of 'Rise to the Challenge' was to make it evident to everybody that there was a need: in fact, this scared the heck out of everybody"—George Fisher, Motorola CEO (Dobyns & Crawford-Mason, 1991, p. 130).

If fear is indeed the most reliable motivator for the adoption of quality management, some significant implications follow. First, an answer is suggested for the economist's perennial question of whether the favored management nostrum of the moment is an offer of free lunch, and if not, who is paying for it. The answer is that quality management is not a free lunch. It requires costly and risky investments in the effort to improve existing routines. Some of these costs may be reflected in a temporary decline in the measured profitability of the organization as resources are diverted to the quality management effort, but much of the finance comes "out of the hides" of organization members, particularly managers.

The desire to assure organizational survival probably looms large among the several motivating factors that lead people to contribute extraordinary effort to quality management.[11] The willingness of individuals to contribute such efforts may depend on assurance that the gains from any improvement in organizational performance will be shared with the contributors. When specialized knowledge that defines a worker's role relates to routines that need dramatic change, or when the quality management task group confronts the possibility of eliminating some of the roles occupied by its own members, the quality management effort may lose its motivational traction and stall.

The Ecology of Inefficiency

Inefficiency in prevailing routines is like high-quality ore for quality management to mine. The more of it there is, the higher the returns to digging it out. Other factors equal (including particularly the commitment to improvement), quality management methods are most likely to deliver good results in organizations where the existing situation is the worst.

Where are the most ample funds of waste likely to be found? To address this question it is helpful to consider the origins of routines in more detail. Under the general interpretation offered here, routines emerge in an organization through a protracted process of organizational learning (Levitt & March, 1988). Although this process may be initiated and partially guided by plans and overt deliberation, a functioning routine involves more details than it is possible to settle at the symbolic level. The initial learning phase ends or fades away when performance that is deemed satisfactory is achieved. Or, to put the point somewhat differently, learning stops when the improvement of the routine is an issue that no longer successfully competes for attention of the kind that is actually needed to produce improvement.[12] The pressure for improvement falls because performance reaches a level that satisfies criteria deriving from general considerations that are remote from the costs and benefits of further improvement in the particular routine—the satisfactory profitability of the organization as a whole, or market acceptance of the final product. It is entirely possible that attractive opportunities for further improvement lie just around the corner when the search for them is abandoned.[13]

The nature of the processes that end an initial learning phase would be of little significant if the timely renewal of improvement efforts could be taken for granted. Attractive opportunities that were missed in the first learning phase would likely be recognized and developed in the second or third. The importance of renewing the search—or maintaining it continuously—is the key admonition of modern quality management. This admonition is far from redundant in the context of typical organizational practice: on the contrary, one of the stronger generalizations about typical patterns in organizations is to just the opposite effect. As Cyert and March (1963) observed, organizational search is "problemistic"—initiated in response to perceived problems, including shortfalls relative to familiar performance standards, and, focused (at least initially) in the vicinity of the problem and its symptoms.[14]

If the environment changes over time in ways that enrich the field of search for improvements, large and widening gaps may develop between actual performance and what could be accomplished if learning were renewed. While the shelf of potential improvements in a given routine becomes increasingly laden with contributions from new technology, new modes of organization, and observable innovations adopted elsewhere, an organization that searches only "problemistically" does not look at the shelf until it suffers a breakdown in that particular routine, or overall performance deteriorates to the point where threats to long-term survival are finally acknowledged and *all* routines are open to question.

The foregoing considerations suggest the following hypothesis about quality management: its potential contribution is the greatest in organizations that have survived longest without being required to reinitiate learning but are now challenged to do so. In such organizations, many routines remain in much the same form they were in when they first stabilized. Few occasions for change have occurred, and a large backlog of opportunities for improvement has accumulated.

More specifically, quality management methods are likely to find their most fruitful application in large organizations marked by long histories of consistent but gradually waning success. An industry founder that went virtually unchallenged for a long period because of its strong position in basic patents, and has encountered serious competition only recently, would be an illustrative candidate. A company that was a vigorous competitor and strong survivor in some now-remote shakeout phase in its principal industry, and has had only gradually mounting challenges since, would be an alternative prototypical example of fertile ground for quality management. Both of these prototypes portray companies that were excellent by the standards of an earlier era, but whose more recent history has been an accumulation of minor disappointments—portending more significant disappointments in the future. Never having received a "wake-up call," these companies have had the maximum opportunity to continue on as living museums for managerial choices that were made long ago—choices that have long hindered rather than guided any quest for improvement.

Although the profile just sketched could fit companies over a wide size range, it is the larger companies that seem most likely to offer the best targets for quality management. Size and complexity make the organization's problems less transparent to top management (there is greater tacitness in the second of the senses identified previously). A larger fraction of the organization's productive knowledge involves routinized relationships, as opposed to personal knowledge held in the heads of a few key individuals. But the stability of relationships and expectations that permit the large organization to function may itself be the most formidable barrier to change. As J. M. Juran remarks,

> Some . . . deficiencies are of an *intra*departmental nature; the symptoms, causes and remedies are all within the scope of one departmental manager. However, the major wastes are *inter*departmental in nature. The symptoms show up in

department X, but there is no agreement on what are the causes, and hence no agreement on what remedial action should be taken. Neither does there exist any organizational mechanism that can help the department managers deal with those interdepartmental problems. (1989, p. 34)

Finally, large size may provide buffers against adversity that postpone the day when a general alarm sounds for the organization as a whole. Selling off a business unit now and then can provide the resources to sustain "business as usual" satisficing behavior in the remainder of the organization.[15]

Organizational Versus Individual Goals

It has been suggested that the most reliable source of fundamental commitment to quality management is a perceived long-term threat to the survival of the organization. At the level of narrow economic motivation, investment in quality management initiatives can be "financed" by extraordinary efforts that are put forward because participants at all levels are prepared to sacrifice a portion of their current well-being to protect their long-term well-being—when the latter is intimately tied to the survival of the organization. This logic does not track unless the "investors" have reasonable assurance that they will in fact be among the beneficiaries of their investments.

This observation connects the ecology of management to a broader set of institutional questions concerning corporate goals and corporate governance. In the 1980s, a surge of activity in the market for corporate control, and of hostile takeovers in particular, was accompanied by a surge of academic commentary endorsing this activity as one of capitalism's most fundamental defenses against managerial sloth and malfeasance. Other commentators, however, took quite a different view. They argued that much of the gain ascribed to the efficiency-demanding discipline of the capital market could equally well be characterized in terms of breach of (implicit) contracts (Shleifer & Summers, 1988). Incumbent—or formerly incumbent—top management was a party to an implicit contract that declared the jobs of middle managers and of key employees at lower levels secure so long as the survival of the corporation itself was not threatened.

Since I have discussed the interpretation of this episode elsewhere (Winter, 1993), I will not address it fully here. Two *Business Week* covers provide a concise metaphor for the issue raised. Five years before the special issue "The Quality Imperative," *Business Week*'s cover story was "The End of Corporate Loyalty?" The story noted the possible threats to morale and productivity resulting from the breakdown of longstanding implicit contracts between middle managers and large corporations. Indeed, nothing that is understood about the requirements for successful response to "The Quality Imperative" suggests that it is compatible with the end of loyalty.

Technical Perfectionism Versus Economizing

The pursuit of improvement relative to measurable, analyzable proximate goals is the heart and soul of quality management. It is this conceptualization of the improvement task that provides the crucial impetus for decentralization and employee empowerment, driving the quest for improvement down the hierarchy to where the relevant resources of knowledge and imagination actually reside. And it is this same conceptualization that makes it possible to prescribe and elaborate a quality management took kit—teachable methods that actually yield results in pursuit of those proximate goals. It is a view that correctly challenges the comfortable but crippling assessment, shared by corporate bureaucrats and most academic economists, that urges the productive forces ever onward in the quest for improvement, and in so doing provides valid and emphatic warning against the dangers of smugness in an environment that is increasingly competitive in increasingly unpredictable ways. These are potent virtues.

Still, there are some inherent problems in quality management ideas that may limit their influence in the long term. As was noted previously, quality management is at least superficially indifferent to the economic logic of resource allocation. For example, many proponents emphatically reject as a fallacy the proposition that improving quality raises unit costs. On the contrary, they say, effectively addressing quality issues generally lowers costs. The preceding discussion gives the reasons why (and the sense in which) they may be right about this. It seems reasonable to assume, however, that sustained attack on the waste in existing routines will ultimately deplete the "ore body"—the fund of chronic waste. At that point, further quests for improvement may resemble, more and more closely, tentative probes in one direction or another along a transformation frontier relating unit cost to quality of the final product or service. Whether a particular probe promises improvement may seem clearer to the project team that proposed it than to the rest of the organization. While the quest for improvement could continue, the effectiveness of the effort might dwindle and its costs rise in subtle as well as obvious ways. In particular, the problem of "interdepartmental" sources of waste, described by Juran, is as much a hazard for quality management as for any other activity. While a project team attempts a coordinated solution to a problem involving the relationship between departments A and B, the quality management effort itself may be generating new costs diffused through departments H, I, J, and K. Indeed, the doctrine that quality can be improved costlessly may actually encourage team members to focus on solutions that generate relatively diffuse and invisible cost increases. For example, the costs may be covered "out of the hides" of numerous participants not represented on the team, who did not volunteer their hides for that purpose. As the quest for improvements demands more trade-off choices and broader participation, effective quality management will itself become more costly and challenging.

While the enthusiasm for quality management is partly a fad and partly the fruit borne by aggressive promotion, the idea of a quality revolution is not merely a media event hyped by the business press. The organizational ailments and dysfunctions that quality management addresses are real phenomena, with sources that lie in the fundamentals of what productive competence is, how it is created, and how it is maintained and improved. Many other observers had noted the existence of these phenomena before the term "quality management" gained currency.

The prescriptions offered by quality management involve more novelty, and also more uncertainty regarding their validity, than the diagnoses. They derive credibility, first, from the fact that they do not directly offer solutions, but a collection of methods for pursuing answers. Also, they are not directed simply to the corporate boardroom or to the offices of top management, but to the entire organization. Finally, they strongly encourage maintaining focus on the quest for problem solutions and attempt to discourage investment in figuring out whom to blame. For these reasons, quality management methods have a much stronger claim to being applicable methods for producing real change in real organizations than the typical management consultant's nostrums of years past.

Substantial investments are being made in the implementation of quality management methods, both in the companies that have adopted programs and in the new service industry that supplies quality management programs and consultation. These investments are being made in full recognition of the fact that quality management does not promise near-term results and that its greatest benefits are achievable only through profound cultural transformation of business organizations.

In this chapter, I have offered some predictions—or theoretically grounded speculations—as to where the principal successes of quality management methods are likely to occur. To assess the likely overall impact of this management innovation is a more hazardous undertaking. It is obvious that there are many identifiable complexities and pitfalls; much winnowing will have to occur to identify the most valuable parts of the contribution, and it is conceivable that the valid core of quality management might be discredited by the bursting of some speculative bubble of extravagant claims. In my view, powerful forces in the global economic situation favor the wide diffusion of quality management methods. With increasing globalization, expanding technical possibilities, and rising sophistication concerning organizational options, few companies will find it possible to compete successfully without committing themselves to continuous improvement. While labels may change and fine points of doctrine remain in dispute, much of what has been identified here as central to quality management will prove indispensable in the struggle for competitive survival.

Acknowledgments

Thanks are due to Jitendra Singh and Don Kash for helpful comments on earlier drafts of this chapter: the usual caveats apply.

Notes

1. The "low-hanging fruit" maxim is the first of several quality management slogans and aphorisms that are quoted in this chapter without attribution. I encountered these phrases in one or more discussions, briefings, or speeches on quality management but cannot at this point provide a citation to a written source.

2. Deming (1986, pp. 486-492) provides a brief account of the origin of the quality movement in Japan after World War II.

3. A GAO report on quality management (U.S. General Accounting Office, 1991) was issued on May 2, 1991. By September 25, 1991, more copies of that report had been distributed than of any other report in the GAO's history, and requests for copies were then coming in at a rate of 1,000 per week. The overview of quality management given here draws on that report as well as other sources.

4. For other examples of success stories, see the "quality stories" sections in several chapters of Walton (1990).

5. See Adler (1993, especially pp. 80-93) for an excellent discussion of this issue set in the context of extensive interview data from the NUMMI plant (the GM-Toyota joint venture in Fremont, California).

6. For example: "In the United States, probably about a third of what is done consists of redoing what was done previously, because of quality deficiencies" (Juran, 1989, p. 78).

7. For discussion of many of these techniques, see Deming (1986), Feigenbaum (1991), Juran (1989).

8. On this point, quality management is aligned with the human relations approach to management, generally, and with "Theory Y" in particular. For a review and critique of the human relations model, see Perrow (1986). The interventions that quality management proposes in order to unleash presumptively constructive worker motivations are quite different from those proposed by the human relations school, although there is significant overlap.

9. See Juran (1989, p. 77) on the "Here-comes-another-one" syndrome as an obstacle to change.

10. The meaning of "top" in this connection is somewhat ambiguous. In a large organization, quality management may succeed at the division, business unit, or plant level without necessarily being embraced at the peak of the full organization. But there is at least a requirement for

tolerance at the peak and commitment at a level that has substantial authority and autonomy in day-to-day operations.

11. Adler (1993) discusses the role of the survival motivation (i.e., fear of unemployment) at NUMMI (pp. 25-26).

12. That is, the end of initial learning may be the result of a satisficing decision (Simon, 1955, 1956, 1987) or something more akin to a lapse of attention. In either case, it reflects the bounded rationality of those whose attention is needed to push learning forward.

13. Of course, even greater benefits might be attainable if commitments made early in the learning process could somehow be reversed and the resources devoted to elaborating those commitments recovered. Chance events early in the process may commit the organization to a learning path that in the long term is markedly inferior to some alternative. Learning itself then reinforces the commitment and makes escape improbable—a "competency trap" (Levinthal, 1992; Levitt & March, 1988).

14. To say that search is "initiated in response to perceived problems" is to say that the satisficing principle applies to the initiation or renewal of search as well as to its termination (Winter, 1971).

15. Some of the points made in the foregoing discussion have been addressed in a large and diverse literature dealing with organizational slack (or "X-inefficiency") and its relationship to risk-taking behavior, performance, and organizational change. See, among others, Bowman (1982), Bromiley (1991), Cyert and March (1963), Leibenstein (1966), Meyer and Zucker (1989), Singh (1986).

REFERENCES

Adler, P. S. (1993). The "learning bureaucracy": New United Motor Manufacturing, Inc. *Research in Organizational Behavior.*

Bowman, E. H. (1982). Risk-taking by troubled firms. *Sloan Management Review, 23,* 33-42.

Bromiley, P. (1991). Testing a causal model of corporate risk-taking and performance. *Academy of Management Review Journal, 34,* 37-59.

Cyert, R. M., & March, J. G. (1963). *A behavioral theory of the firm.* Englewood Cliffs, NJ: Prentice Hall.

Deming, W. E. (1986). *Out of the crisis.* Cambridge: MIT Center for Advanced Engineering Study.

Dobyns, L., & Crawford-Mason, C. (1991). *Quality or else: The revolution in world business.* Boston: Houghton Mifflin.

Downs, G., & Mohr, L. B. (1976). Conceptual issues in the study of innovation. *Administrative Science Quarterly, 21,* 700-714.

Feigenbaum, A. V. (1991). *Total quality control* (3rd ed.). New York: McGraw-Hill.

Juran, J. M. (1989). *Juran on leadership for quality: An executive handbook.* New York: Free Press.

Leibenstein, H. (1966). Allocative efficiency versus X-efficiency. *American Economic Review, 56,* 392-415.

Levinthal, D. (1992). Surviving Schumpeterian environments: An evolutionary perspective. *Industrial and Corporate Change, 1,* 427-443.

Levitt, B., & March, J. G. (1988). Organizational learning. *Annual Review of Sociology, 14,* 319-340.

Meyer, M., & Zucker, L. G. (1989). *Permanently failing organizations.* Newbury Park, CA: Sage.

Nelson, R. R., & Winter, S. G. (1982). *An evolutionary theory of economic change.* Cambridge, MA: Harvard University Press.

Perrow, C. (1986). *Complex organizations: A critical essay* (3rd ed.). New York: Random House.

The quality imperative. (1991, October 25). *Business Week* (Special issue), pp. 7, 16, 53.

Shleifer, A., & Summers, L. H. (1988). Breach of trust in hostile takeovers. In A. J. Auerbach (Ed.), *Corporate takeovers: Causes and consequences.* Chicago: University of Chicago Press.

Simon, H. A. (1955). A behavioral model of rational choice. *Quarterly Journal of Economics, 69,* 99-118.

Simon, H. A. (1956). Rational choice and the structure of the environment. *Psychological Review, 63,* 129-138.

Simon, H. A. (1987). Satisficing. In J. Eatwell, M. Millgate, & P. Newman (Eds.), *The new palgrave: A dictionary of economics, 4,* 243-245.

Singh, J. V. (1986). Performance, slack, and risk taking in organizational decision making. *Academy of Management Journal, 29,* 562-585.

U.S. General Accounting Office. (1991). *Management practices: U.S. companies improve performance through quality efforts* (GAO/NSIAD-91-190). Washington, DC: Author.

Walker, J. L. (1969). The diffusion of innovations among American states. *American Political Science Review, 63,* 880-899.

Walton, M. (1990). *Deming management at work.* New York: Putnam.

Winter, S. G. (1971). Satisficing, selection and the innovating remnant. *Quarterly Journal of Economics, 85,* 237-261.

Winter, S. G. (1993). Routines, cash flows and unconventional assets: Corporate change in the 1980s. In M. Blair (Ed.), *The deal decade: What takeovers and leveraged buyouts mean for corporate governance.* Washington, DC: The Brookings Institution.

21

Learning by Knowledge-Intensive Firms

WILLIAM H. STARBUCK

DISCOVERING EXPERTISE

The General Manager of the Garden Company (a pseudonym) invited John Dutton and me to advise him about what he called their "lot-size problem." He was wondering, he said, whether Garden was making products in economically efficient quantities.

We had no idea what a strange but memorable experience this would be!

The General Manager proposed that we start with a tour of their largest plant, and assigned someone to guide us. Our guide took us first to the model shop, which produced jigs and patterns for use in the main plant. In the model shop, a skilled craftsman would start with a raw piece of metal, work on it with several different machine tools, and end with a finished component. Each successive component differed from those produced before and after, and each craftsman's tasks were shifting continually.

Then our guide took us into the plant itself. To our amazement, we found little difference from the model shop. Many workers were using several different machine tools in succession. Since each worker had several machines, most of the machines were idle at any moment.

Some workers chose to decorate castings' non-functional insides with patterns such as one sees on the doors of bank vaults, each worker inscribing his personal pattern. Quality standards were incredibly high, for the workers saw themselves as artisans who were putting their personal signatures on their products.

This chapter appeared originally in *Journal of Management Studies,* Vol. 29, No. 6, November 1992. Copyright © 1992 by Blackwell. Reprinted by permission.

In the middle of the plant stood a wooden shack. Nails on the wall of this shack represented the distinct areas of the plant. Hanging on each nail were the production orders awaiting work in one area. We saw workers enter the shack, leaf through the orders, and choose orders to work on. Our guide said orders got processed promptly if they called for tasks the workers enjoyed, whereas orders might hang on the nails for weeks if they called for tasks the workers disliked.

Hoppers of partly finished components jammed the aisles. This, our guide explained, reflected raw-materials shortages, misplaced jigs and patterns, and missing components. After work began on an order, a worker would discover that needed raw material was out-of-stock—the order would have to wait while purchasing got the raw material. Or, a worker would be unable to find a needed jig, and a search would reveal that a subcontractor had borrowed the jig and not returned it—the order would have to wait while the jig was retrieved or replaced. Or, a product would be partly assembled and then the assemblers would discover that a component was missing—the incomplete assemblies would have to wait until the missing component emerged from production. Any of these problems might arise more than once during production of a single order. As one result, Garden was taking an average of nine months to deliver standard products that incorporated only a few hours of direct labor.

The plant tour left John and me rolling our eyes in wonder. We could not have imagined less efficient methods or greater disorder. It was hard to believe that Garden could even be making a profit! Yet the main building appeared in good condition, the office areas looked clean, and the General Manager's office had luxurious furnishings.

We told the General Manager that the plant had no lot-size problem, but we wondered whether he would not prefer to have one. A lot-size problem implied that machines would be set up for mass production and that workers would repeat specialized tasks. We suggested, however, that Garden would gain more direct benefit from production and inventory control than from mass production. A computer-based control system could keep raw materials in stock, monitor the progress of production, reduce delays, and make sure that jigs and patterns were available. Inventories could be much lower, machine usage could be much higher, and customers could receive their orders much more quickly.

The General Manager asked for estimates. We told him a control system would have a payback period of roughly two years and the inventory savings alone would cut production costs by at least 10%. To this, he responded, "Why should we want to do that? 10% of our production costs is only 1% of our revenues." He then produced Garden's financial statements for the previous year. After-tax profits had been $40 million on sales of $83.5 million, "And that," he crowed, "was a year in which we had a strike for ten months!"

He went on to explain that Garden made every effort to avoid direct competition. Over a third of Garden's personnel were engineers who were good at designing new products that no other firm was producing. Garden's policy was to continue making a product only as long as its gross margin exceeded 75% of sales. When competition drove a gross margin below 75%, Garden would stop offering that product for sale. The average gross margin across all products exceeded 90%.

Allowing for the corporate tax rate of 52%, we surmised that Garden employed expert tax accountants as well as expert engineers.

John and I had received several lessons in business . . . and the General Manager had not even charged us tuition!

Garden's high profits did not arise from fine steel, unusually skilled craftsmen, or exceptional capital equipment. Its marketing was ordinary. Although Garden delivered high quality, it used no esoteric production technologies, and it often subcontracted production to a broad array of machine shops. It was this subcontracting that had enabled Garden to earn high profits despite a long strike. The profits also did not come from managerial competence of the sort most production firms cultivate. In that domain, Garden appeared utterly incompetent.

The remarkable profits sprang from technical and strategic expertise. The key labor inputs came not from the machinists in the plant, but from the engineers and managers in the office building. These people had created monopolistic opportunities for Garden over and over again. Garden was the only producer of many of its products, and the dominant producer of all of them.

Garden's key input was expertise. It was a knowledge-intensive firm (KIF).

Knowledge intensity has diverse meanings, partly because people use different definitions of knowledge. The next section of this article gives my conclusions about such issues. Two following sections then make empirically based observations about the activities inside KIFs. The first of these sections reviews the kinds of work experts do, and explains why experts find learning hard. The ensuing section then describes organizational learning: KIFs learn by managing training and personnel turnover, and by creating physical capital, routines, organizational culture, and social capital. To see the results of learning, the fifth section looks at KIFs' long-term strategic development, including multinational expansion.

WHAT IS A KIF?

The term *knowledge-intensive* imitates economists' labeling of firms as capital-intensive or labor-intensive. These labels describe the relative importance of capital and labor as production inputs. In a capital-intensive firm, capital has more importance than labor; in a labor-intensive firm, labor has the greater importance. By analogy, labeling a firm as knowledge-intensive implies that knowledge has more importance than other inputs.

Although the terms capital-intensive, labor-intensive, and knowledge-intensive refer to inputs, capital, labor, and knowledge also may be outputs. Why is it useful to classify firms by their inputs? A study of office-equipment or software companies groups firms by their outputs. Such a study emphasizes similarities and differences across customers and distribution channels, and it makes a good basis for analyzing relations with customers or competitors. By contrast, a study of meat packers or machine shops groups firms by their inputs. By emphasizing similarities and differences across raw materials and personnel, such a study makes a good basis for analyzing internal structure and operations. Input classes highlight the effects of resource availabilities, and their determinants, such as governmental policies. As well, Sveiby and Risling (1986) argued that KIFs call for new definitions of ownership and new ways of controlling the uses of capital. Traditional notions of ownership, they said, assume that financial or physical capital dominates labor, whereas human capital dominates the KIFs.

Assessing the importance of knowledge is harder than comparing capital and labor, however. Economists compare capital and labor by expressing them in monetary units, but market prices mainly reflect values that many firms share. At best, prices reflect those aspects of inputs that could transfer readily from one firm to another. Prices ignore inputs' importance for intrafirm activities or for activities that are idiosyncratic to a single firm. Since much knowledge has disparate values in different situations, monetary measures of knowledge are elusive and undependable.

Knowledge itself is almost as ambiguous an idea as value or importance, and it has many guises (Winter, 1987). During a dozen seminars aimed at research about knowledge-intensive firms, almost every speaker devoted time to his or her preferred definition of knowledge. Such discussions have led me to five conclusions.

1. A KIF may not be information-intensive. Knowledge is a stock of expertise, not a flow of information. Thus, knowledge relates to information in the way that assets relate to income (Machlup, 1962, took another view). Some activities draw on extensive knowledge without processing large amounts of current information—management consulting, for example. Conversely, a firm can process much information without using much knowledge. For instance, Automatic Data Processing (ADP) produces payroll checks. ADP processes vast amounts of information, but it is probably more capital-intensive than knowledge-intensive. Producing a payroll check requires little expertise, and many people have this expertise.

The distinction between a KIF and an information-intensive firm can be hard to draw. From one perspective, ADP merely processes data for other firms, using mainly capital in the forms of computers and software. From another perspective, ADP succeeds because it does its specialized task better than its customers can do it themselves. This superior performance may come from both expertise and returns to scale, so expertise and large scale reinforce each other.

2. In deciding whether a firm is knowledge-intensive, one ought to weigh its emphasis on esoteric expertise instead of widely shared knowledge. Everybody has knowledge, most of it widely shared, but some idiosyncratic and personal. If one defines knowledge broadly to encompass what everybody knows, every firm can appear knowledge-intensive. One loses the value of focusing on a special category of firms. Similarly, every firm has some unusual expertise. To make the KIF a useful category, exceptional expertise must make an important contribution. One should not label a firm as knowledge-intensive unless exceptional and valuable expertise dominates commonplace knowledge.

Some forms of expertise may be hard to measure separately from their effects. Why, for example, does one attribute strategic expertise to the Garden Company? One might label Garden a KIF because it employed so many engineers. But many firms employ more engineers with less remarkable results, and Garden's products embodied no technological miracles. These engineers were unusual because they were using their knowledge in ways that gave Garden extraordinary strategic advantages.

Managerial expertise may pose special problems in this regard. It would make no sense to measure managerial expertise by the fraction of employees who are managers or by the wages paid to managers. To judge managers expert, one has to look either at the managers' behaviors or at the results of their behaviors. Do their firms produce unusually high profits? Do the managers show interpersonal skill?

3. Even after excluding widely shared knowledge, one has to decide how broadly to define expertise. One can define expertise broadly, recognize many people as experts, and see the expertise embedded in many machines and routines. This strategy makes KIFs less special, but it removes some blinkers caused by stereotypes about expertise, and it increases the generality of findings about KIFs. Alternatively, one can acknowledge only the legitimated expertise of people who have extensive formal education, and can emphasize high-tech machines and unusual routines. This second strategy makes KIFs appear more special, but produces findings that generalize only to the few firms that use such expertise intensively. It also accepts stereotypes about expertise.

These definitional strategies have political overtones. A broad definition of expertise obscures the influence of social class and social legitimacy, whereas a narrow definition highlights the influence of social class and social legitimacy. Legitimated expertise is normally an upper-middle-class possession. Legitimated experts usually earn salaries high enough to put them into the upper-middle class. They normally gain their expertise through formal higher education, which entails at least the expense of foregone income. Higher education also may give experts entry into recognized professions.

Even jobs widely regarded as unskilled may entail much knowledge (Kusterer, 1978). Skilled trades may be as esoteric and difficult to enter as the professions (Ekstedt, 1989). Yet, people put other labels—such as know-how or skill or understanding—on expertise learned through primary school or on-the-job experience.

Sweden has spawned much of the public discussion and research about KIFs. In 1983, Sveiby started writing about "knowledge companies" in one of Sweden's most prominent periodicals, and Swedish business executives expressed strong interest in this topic. Sveiby and Risling followed in 1986 with a book that became a non-fiction best-seller. Probably this interest reflects Sweden's high incomes and high educational levels.

4. An expert may not be a professional, and a KIF may not be a professional firm. Professionals have specialized expertise that they gain through training or experience, and KIFs may employ people who have specialized expertise. Thus, KIFs may be professional firms.

Many KIFs are not professional firms, however. One reason is that not all experts belong to recognized professions. A profession has at least four properties besides expertise: an ethical code, cohesion, collegial enforcement of standards, and autonomy (Schriesheim, Von Glinow, & Kerrs, 1977). Professionals' ethical codes require them to serve clients unemotionally and impersonally, without self-interest. Professionals identify strongly with their professions, more strongly than with their clients or their employers. They not only observe professional standards, they believe that only members of their professions have the competence and ethics to enforce these standards.

Similarly, professionals insist that outsiders cannot properly supervise their activities.

Management consulting and software engineering, for example, do not qualify as recognized professions. Without doubt, those who do these jobs well have rare expertise. Nevertheless, the ultimate judges of their expertise are their clients or their supervisors, and their employers set and enforce their ethical codes and performance standards. Similarly, despite talk about professional management, managers do not belong to a professional body that enforces an ethical code and insists that its values and standards supersede those of managers' employers. Employers appoint managers without regard for the candidates' memberships in external bodies. Strong loyalty to a professional body would contradict managers' roles as custodians of their employing firms.

Sveiby and Lloyd (1987) divided "knowhow companies" into categories reflecting their managerial or technical expertise. They pointed to law firms as examples of high technical but low managerial expertise. To illustrate firms with high managerial and low technical expertise, they cited McDonald's fast food chain. On the other hand, Ekstedt (1988, 1989, pp. 3-9) contrasted "knowledge companies" with industrial companies, high-technology companies, and service companies "such as hamburger chains." In his schema, both high-technology companies and knowledge companies have high knowledge intensity, but high-technology companies have a higher intensity of real capital than do knowledge companies.

Professional firms can exploit and must allow for all five properties of professions, not merely expertise. Health-maintenance organizations, for instance, must accept doctors' codes of ethics and must allow medical societies to adjudicate some issues. KIFs form a broader company, in which many issues reflect labor markets, interpersonal networks, and experts' individuality, self-interest, and social standing.

Yet, it could be that most KIFs have nearly all the properties that authors have assigned to professional firms. For example, Hinings, Brown, and Greenwood (1991, pp. 376, 390) wrote:

> Bucher and Stelling (1969) suggested that organizations dominated by professionals had a number of special characteristics, including professionals building their own roles rather than fitting into preset roles, spontaneous internal differentiation based on work interests, competition and conflict for resources and high levels of political activity. . . . The *distribution of authority* has long been identified as unique in an autonomous professional organization because of its emphasis on collegiality, peer evaluation, and autonomy, informality, and flexibility of structure (Bucher & Stelling, 1969; Montagna, 1968; Ritzer & Walczak, 1986).

Professionals are not the only experts who build their own roles, divide work to suit their own interests, compete for resources, or emphasize autonomy, collegiality, informality, and flexible structures. Other occupations share these traditions, and some experts have enough demand for their services that they can obtain autonomy without support from a recognized profession.

There is another reason KIFs may not be professional firms.

5. KIFs' knowledge may not be in individual people. Besides the knowledge held by individual people, one can find knowledge in: (a) capital such as plant, equipment, or financial instruments; (b) firms' routines and cultures; and (c) professional cultures.

People convert their knowledge to physical forms when they write books or computer programs, design buildings or machines, produce violins or hybrid corn, or create financial instruments such as mutual-fund shares (Ekstedt, 1988, 1989). Conversely, people may gain knowledge by reading books, studying buildings, buying shares, or running computer programs.

People also translate their knowledge into firms' routines, job descriptions, plans, strategies, and cultures. Nelson and Winter (1982) treated behavioral routines as the very essence of organizations—the means by which firms can produce predictable results while adapting to social and technological changes. Simultaneously, Deal and Kennedy (1982) and Peters and Waterman (1982) were saying it is cultures that perform these functions.

Describing McDonald's as a firm with low technical expertise overlooks the expertise in McDonald's technology and organization. McDonald's success stems from its ability to deliver a consistent quality in diverse environments and despite high turnover of low-skilled people. To get such results, the firm operates extensive training programs and conducts research about production techniques and customers' tastes. Although training at Hamburger University may give McDonald's managers more skill than those at most restaurants, McDonald's managers may have no more skill than those in most production firms. Ceaseless expansion forces McDonald's to concentrate training on new managers. Also, McDonald's substitutes technology and routines for in-person management.

Professional cultures too carry valuable knowledge. For instance, lawyers live amid conflict. Lawyers' culture not only supports conflict, it shows them how to conflict to maximum effect and with minimum damage to their egos and reputations. Lawyers strive to advocate their clients' interests even when this might produce injustice, and they depend on conflict to foster justice by exposing all sides. Lawyers try to keep their roles as advocates for their clients separate from their interpersonal relations as members of the legal profession. They observe behavioral codes strictly and much of their conflict concerns interpretations of and conformity to behavioral codes. When lawyers cannot themselves resolve disagreements, they seek help from above—judges in courts or superiors in law firms. The legal profession also serves as micro environments in which lawyers can cultivate long-term reputations. Some lawyers seek reputations as tough negotiators who yield little and demand much. To nurture such reputations, they may refuse to make concessions that their clients want to make.

A Starting Point

Debates about how KIFs differ from other firms persuaded me to focus on firms that would be knowledge-intensive by almost anyone's definition. As a starting point, I defined an expert as someone with formal education and experience equivalent to a doctoral degree, and a KIF as a firm in which such experts are at least one-third of the personnel. Later, Lawrence Rosenberg pointed out that some expertise takes non-human forms. Some KIFs may even hold most of their expertise in non-human forms, but I have not studied such firms.

I have not been distinguishing firms from other organizations because many KIFs operate at the boundary between government and private enterprise. They are not-for-profit firms that work mainly or exclusively for government agencies.

Although I have interviewed in eight firms satisfying the above criteria, three stand out as excellent examples.

The Rand Corporation and Arthur D. Little are the two firms that came immediately to mind when I first began thinking about the *knowledge-intensive firm*. The Rand Corporation is the prototypic think tank, located near the beach in Santa Monica. Staffed by Ph.D.s, Rand mainly makes policy studies: Rand's personnel evaluate current policies and generate policy alternatives. Rand holds long-term contracts from the U.S. Air Force and the U.S. Army, and it receives short-term grants or contracts from many federal agencies. Its reports are ubiquitous in Washington, D.C.

On the other coast, in a wooded campus near Harvard and MIT, Arthur D. Little is the oldest American consulting firm and an exemplary one. A. D. Little has 21 offices and roughly 1,500 consultants. In a typical year, they complete over 5,000 projects in 60 countries. The project topics range from product technology, to operations management, to economic development and strategic planning.

Partners in Wachtell, Lipton, Rosen and Katz make more money than those in any other American law firm; it is to Wachtell, Lipton that other lawyers turn when they need the very best and they do not care how much it costs. Moreover, not only the partners do well at Wachtell, Lipton: surveys of junior lawyers have repeatedly said Wachtell, Lipton is the best place to work.

Although quite unlike each other, all three firms share similarities, as do the other firms I have studied. Large fractions of their people have advanced degrees. They process information slowly in comparison to information-intensive firms. Their capital equipment is mainly general-purpose office space, office machines, and computers, although A. D. Little also has laboratories.

My observations come mainly from interviews. Indeed, "interview" seems an inadequate label for fascinating conversations with very intelligent, perceptive, articulate people. I had only to point to a few issues that interested me, and they would begin to extrapolate—telling me who else I should interview, what issues *ought* to interest me, where my assumptions seemed wrong, and how their worlds look to them. I often found myself discussing topics or trying frameworks I had not considered before walking into a room.

Are KIFs Peculiar?

One critic complained that all my examples describe peculiar firms that exist solely because their environments have uncorrectable problems. An answer to this charge has three parts.

First, all firms *are* peculiar: we should look for and celebrate their individuality. There are many ways to solve most problems, more opportunities than anyone can pursue, many criteria for judging what is best. It is as important to see how individuals differ—whether individual people, or individual organizations, or individual societies—as to see what they have in common. It is as important to understand complexities as simplicities.

Second, successful firms *cause* their environments to have uncorrectable problems. Firms and their environments change symbiotically. Not only must an environment be hospitable to a KIF, but the existence of a KIF induces its environment to assume that it exists. For example, U.S. military services reassign personnel every two or three years. As a result, military personnel have little experience in their successive jobs, know little of tasks' histories or traditions, and cannot manage long-term projects effectively. Long-term projects would founder if they depended on military personnel. By providing civilian specialists who can have long tenures, the Rand Corporation and the Aerospace Corporation help the military to manage long-term projects, and they reduce the costs of retraining. Yet, having the services of Rand and Aerospace may have kept the military from developing other ways to manage long-term projects and other personnel policies.

Third, I have sought out the most successful firms, and all exceptionally successful firms exploit peculiarities. A modal firm in a competitive industry makes low profits, and it does not survive long. High profits and long survival come from monopolistic competition. Monopolistic competition arises from firms' developing distinctive competencies and mirroring their environments' unusual needs and capabilities.

Wachtell, Lipton shows how exceptional success may feed on peculiarities. The firm's founding partners had disliked their experiences in other law firms: they agreed to follow some unusual policies that would produce a better work environment. These policies have fostered collaboration and given the firm an edge in attracting new lawyers. The founding partners came from a less-well-known law school whose graduates had restricted job opportunities: much better than its reputation, this school supplied highly talented lawyers during the early years. A crisis during the firm's second year led the partners to adopt an unusual policy: Wachtell, Lipton never agrees to represent clients for long periods. This policy has had unforeseen long-term consequences for the types of cases the firm handles.

Success reinforces success, and excellence itself fends off competition. Today, with elegant offices on New York's Park Avenue, Wachtell, Lipton can choose among the top graduates from law schools across America. Potential clients offer the firm four to eight times as many cases than it can handle: it can pick the cases that look most interesting and best suit its abilities. The cases that potential clients bring are non-routine ones that involve large sums, and they often concern immediate threats. Such cases draw attention, as do Wachtell, Lipton's legal innovations.

EXPERTS' WORK

Interactions Between Creating, Applying, and Preserving

The experts in KIFs gather information through interviews or reading; they analyze and interpret this information; and they make written and oral reports to clients and colleagues (Rhenman, 1973, p. 161). An observer cannot overlook the strong, overt similarities across people, sites, and projects.

Nevertheless, experts themselves describe their activities diversely. Some say that they are applying old knowledge to new problems, others that they are creating new knowledge, and still others that they are preserving knowledge that already exists. Experts who see themselves as producing new knowledge emphasize the recency or originality of their data and the differences between their findings and those of predecessors. They may classify such work either as basic scientific research or as applied research on markets, products, or processes. Other experts see their work mainly as applying existing knowledge to current problems. For instance, when most lawyers do research, they analyze and interpret previous cases and they emphasize the continuity over time of knowledge and its meaning. To gain acceptance of their rulings, most judges de-emphasize the innovative quality of their reasoning.

The distinction between creating knowledge and applying it is often hard to make. Lawyers may be more successful if they reinterpret precedent cases imaginatively, or if they conceive original strategies. The Garden Company's engineers were applying known techniques, but they were applying them to products no one else had imagined. Basic research may have direct applicability, and applied research may contribute fundamental knowledge. When it comes to systems as complex as a human body or an economy, people may only be able to create valid knowledge by trying to apply it (Starbuck, 1976, pp. 1100-1103).

To my surprise, several experts described themselves as memory cells. They said their jobs are to preserve information that their clients have difficulty preserving. As mentioned above, because the U.S. military services rotate assignments frequently, military personnel lack job experience and cannot manage long-term projects. Also, military wage scales are too low to attract and retain highly educated experts. To compensate, the military services sign contracts with KIFs that provide long-term continuity of management and expertise. These KIFs employ civilian experts who do not rotate assignments frequently and who either manage long-term projects directly or advise military managers. There may be enough of these KIFs to make up a distinct, long-term memory industry.

Creating, applying, and preserving intertwine and complement each other. At least over long periods, merely storing knowledge does not preserve it. For old knowledge to have meaning, people must relate it to their current problems and activities. They have to translate it into contemporary language and frame it within current issues. Effective preserving looks much like applying. As time passes and social and technological changes add up, the needed translations grow larger, and applying knowledge comes to look more like creating knowledge.

For new knowledge to have meaning, people must fit it into their current beliefs and perspectives; and familiarity with existing knowledge signals expertise. Evaluators assess completed research partly by its applicability and they judge research proposals partly by the researchers' mastery of past research. Thus, Rand Corporation, which depends on research grants for some of its income, makes elaborate literature searches before writing proposals. Rand also employs public-information staff, who highlight the

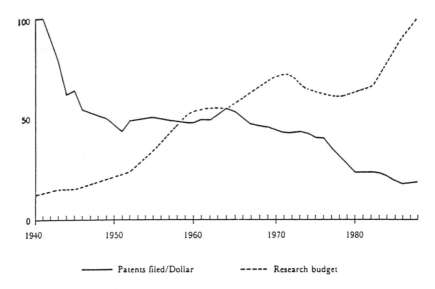

Figure 21.1. R&D by a Large Chemical Firm

relevance of research findings. Similarly, A. D. Little's executives believe
that having credibility with clients requires their firm to specialize in certain industries, technologies, and functions. They want new experts to have
had several years' experience in one of these industries and functions or
technologies.

Ambiguity about the meaning of knowledge creation implies a weak tie,
if any, between knowledge creation and knowledge intensive. Clearly, more
input does not always produce more output. For example, Brooks (1975)
pointed out how rare are the skills needed to create operating systems for
computers. Adding more people to such a programming project does not
accelerate it. On the contrary, more people may slow a project down, by
forcing the experts with rare skills to spend more time coordinating, communicating and observing bureaucratic routines. An example of another kind
concerns R&D by a large chemical firm. As Figure 21.1 shows, this firm has
spent more and more on R&D but incremental dollars have yielded fewer
and fewer patent filings.

Learning

Because experts are learned, one expects them to value learning highly.
Nonetheless, many experts resist new ideas.

Such resistance has several bases. First, clients or even other experts may interpret experts' need to learn as evidence of deficient knowledge. Thus, experts find it risky to discuss their learning needs with clients or colleagues. Second, many experts get paid by the hour, and many others have to account carefully for their uses of time. Explicit learning reduces the time available for billable services. Third, expertise implies specialization, which reduces versatility and limits flexibility. To become experts, people must specialize and move into distinct occupational niches. Required years of education limit entry to these niches; and many experts belong to recognized professions that restrict entrance through licenses and examinations. These niches, however, could become evolutionary dead-ends (Beyer, 1981). Fourth, experts' niches are partial monopolies. Like other monopolies, experts hold favorable positions that confer high incomes and social status. These positions also give experts much to lose from social and technological changes. Fifth, expertise entails perceptual filters that keep experts from noticing some social and technological changes (Armstrong, 1985; Starbuck & Dutton, 1973). Even while they are gaining knowledge within their specialties, experts may overlook exciting and relevant events just outside their domains.

Knowledge creation accelerates the social and technological changes in experts' domains (Wolff & Baumol, 1987). Because employers or clients often seek expertise to help them to understand rapid social and technological changes, experts tend to find employment in rapidly changing domains. Thus, most experts are all too aware that expertise needs updating: they have to seek a dynamic stability in which their apparent knowledge evolves while they retain their favorable positions.

Besides, experts' skepticism about new ideas can enhance their learning. Learning is not adaptation, and it requires more subtlety and complexity than mere change. People can change without learning, and too much readiness to discard current knowledge undermines learning. To learn, one must build up knowledge like layers of sediment on a river bottom. To learn effectively, one must accumulate knowledge that has long-term value while replacing the knowledge that lacks long-term value.

The key issue that experts, like other learners, confront is how to sift out knowledge that will have little value in the future. For this winnowing, expertise itself evidently confers no advantages. Studies of many fields have consistently found that renowned experts predict future events no more accurately than do informed people (Armstrong, 1985; Ascher, 1978; Camerer & Johnson, 1991). Still, few experts know about such studies, and many experts overestimate their abilities as oracles.

ORGANIZATIONAL LEARNING IN KIFs

Personnel Training and Turnover

Learning generally poses different issues for firms than for individual experts. For example, the need to update leads individual experts to spend time reading or attending conferences or courses. By contrast, senior people in a firm see updating as an activity to manage more than to do. Senior people may assign their juniors to take certain courses, or to read certain journals and to summarize what they read. Senior people sometimes deny certain juniors permission to attend conferences and tell others that they must attend and report what they heard.

What individuals find hard, firms may find easy, and vice versa. In particular, individual experts learn little from changing firms, whereas organizational learning readily takes the form of personnel changes. KIFs aggressively pursue new experts with wanted knowledge, and they limit the job security of continuing experts. Since most consulting or research projects have short terms, experts must repeatedly renegotiate their relations with their firms and adapt their knowledge and skills to current tasks. Some small consulting firms give new consultants just three months in which to start bringing in enough business to cover their salaries. A would-be consultant who does not meet this target has to seek other employment. Large consulting firms may not treat each consultant as a separate profit center, but they do ask consultants to account strictly for their time. A. D. Little, for example, expects most consultants to spend 70-75% of their time on activities for which clients are paying, and 20-25% of their time on personal betterment or soliciting new business.

Such development and personnel policies keep expertise closely aligned with environmental opportunities, so rigidity and blind spots may be more troublesome for individual experts than for KIFs. Indeed, such policies make KIFs faddish; and efforts to stay on the cutting edge of rapid technological and social changes accentuate this faddishness.

The policies also make boundaries porous. Just as KIFs may hire experts from their clients or customers, KIFs' clients or customers may add expertise by hiring KIFs' personnel (Stinchcombe & Heimer, 1988). Experts at the forefront of social or technological change usually have many job opportunities. Replacing experts solely to update expertise weakens loyalty to the firm and adds variance to organizational culture. The social networks that make it easy to adopt new ideas also make in-house ideas accessible to other firms, as does the ease of transmitting information. Thus, KIFs find it hard to keep unique expertise exclusive.

Stinchcombe and Heimer (1988) described successful software firms as "precarious monopolies." They are monopolies insofar as they exhibit unusual abilities. Niches evolve naturally as individuals and small groups concentrate on specific streams of innovation. The firms also strive explicitly to develop and maintain unusual abilities. Unusual abilities help the firms to market their services and to avoid head-on competition.

Stinchcombe and Heimer (1988) pointed out that these partial monopolies are constantly at risk, both because technological changes may make unusual abilities obsolete and because key experts may depart. Computer technology has been changing especially rapidly, and the software firms' relations with clients and computer manufacturers repeatedly expose their experts to job offers. To sell their services to clients, software firms have to publicize the talents of their key experts, and this publicity creates job opportunities for the touted experts.

Not all KIFs control distinctive domains of knowledge. Professional firms find it especially hard to sustain monopolistic positions. The recognized professions work at keeping their control of knowledge and at preserving their members' autonomy: firms would run into strong opposition if they would try to convert professional expertise to organizational property. Moreover, many products of professional firms are easy to imitate. For example, Martin Lipton invented the "poison pill" defense against unfriendly corporate takeovers; but, after other law firms saw a few examples, Wachtell, Lipton was no longer the sole source for poison pills (Powell, 1986).

Several modes of organizational learning do convert individual expertise into organizational property. These conversion processes produce at least three types of organizational property: physical capital, routines, and organizational culture. The creation of social capital, such as mutual trust with clients or customers, tends to convert organizational experience into the property of individuals.

Physical Capital

Both KIFs and individuals can gain new expertise by buying capital goods. Computer software affords obvious examples.

Not long ago, expertise was uneven across accountants who handled income taxes. Now, every accountant has low-cost access to software that makes no arithmetical errors, omits nothing, incorporates the latest changes in tax codes, and warns of conditions that might trigger audits by tax authorities.

Lawyers have recently begun to use a computer program, CLARA, to help them do legal research. CLARA helps small law firms to compete more effectively against large firms, and helps novice lawyers to produce results comparable to experienced lawyers (Laudon & Laudon, 1991, chap. 4). Although unfinished, CLARA does research almost as well as law professors. On reading of this achievement, one practicing lawyer sniffed: "Too bad; maybe it will get better someday."

In the short term, KIFs may be able to run expertise into concrete capital. For instance, decades of experience enabled the large public accounting firms to create systematic auditing procedures. The firms then turned these procedures into checklists that novice accountants and clerical staff can complete. Similarly, Rand Corporation's research occasionally produces databases that have value beyond the projects that created them. Rand tries to exploit these databases by proposing new projects that would draw upon them.

Physical capital may be even harder to protect and retain than are people, however. Physical capital also may be less flexible than either the technologies it uses or the markets it serves. The auditing checklists created by firm A work just as well for firm B, so B can easily take advantage of A's experience.

IntelligenceWare wrote superior programs for artificial-intelligence applications. The firm has been seeking to exploit these programs by adapting them to diverse uses. Over the longer term, competing firms can analyze and imitate IntelligenceWare's programs. Also, because IntelligenceWare's programs are too complex for incremental evolution, experience will eventually force the firm to undertake a drastic rewrite.

Databases can be updated piecemeal, but they too gain or lose currency. At Rand Corporation, Brian Jenkins has compiled a database on terrorism. He began this on his own initiative, but the database became a more general asset when terrorist acts escalated and Rand began receiving inquiries about terrorism from the press. Although the press's interest in terrorism fluctuates with the incidence of terrorism, such a database requires continual maintenance.

Orlikowski (1988, pp. 179-267) detailed a consulting firm's efforts to capture its experience as software. Over ten years and many projects, consultants built various software "tools" that help them plan projects and carry them out efficiently. The tools originated separately when consultants saw needs or opportunities, but the firm's general production philosophy implicitly guided these developments and rendered the tools mutually compatible. Also, at first, isolated people used these tools voluntarily, but informal norms gradually made their use widespread and mandatory. Thus, the tools both expressed the firm's culture in tangible form, and reinforced the culture by clarifying its content and generalizing its application. Generalization made the differences among clients' problems less and less important, and it weakened the contributions that clients could make to problem solving.

Generalization also reduced the influence of more technical consultants and increased the influence of less technical consultants. In their interviews, the consultants stressed the tools' strong influence on their perceptions of problems and their methods of solving them. Eventually, the firm started to sell the tools to other firms. At that point, the firm's culture, methods, and experience became products that other firms could buy.

The ease of distributing it makes physical capital an effective way to build organizational culture, and it offers firms opportunities to expand their markets. Easy distribution also can cost firms their competitive advantages. Departing employees can easily take forms, manuals, or floppy disks with them. When firms turn physical capital into products that they sell to competitors, knowledge-intensive capital loses the character of being esoteric and advantageous. In this sense, a portable expert system is self-contradictory. Distributing an expert system renders its knowledge no longer esoteric, and thus no longer expert. It is not only tax accountants who now have low-cost access to programs for filing income taxes; millions of non-accountants are using these programs to file their business or personal taxes.

Routines

Firms also learn by creating routines (Nelson & Winter, 1982; Starbuck, 1983), but formalized routines look bureaucratic. Highly educated experts dislike bureaucracy: conflicts between professions and bureaucracies have attracted much research (Schriesheim et al., 1977), and some of these conflicts apply to expertise in general. Most experts want autonomy, they want recognition of their individuality, and they want their firms to have egalitarian structures.

Some experts derive independent power from their close ties with clients, so service KIFs with multiple clients look more like loose confederations than bureaucracies. Among the service KIFs, only those having long-term contracts with a very few clients seem able to bureaucratize. Even such KIFs must bureaucratize cautiously, for their expert employees have external job opportunities. Of course, a product KIF such as the Garden Company does not run into such problems because its experts have little contact with customers.

The KIFs that can enforce bureaucratic routines can draw benefits from them. Impersonal roles make programs for personnel development possible, and they ease transfers of people to meet shifting tasks. Consistent quality is essential to keeping long-term clients or customers. Bureaucratic clients or customers expect the KIFs they hire to look and behave as they do. For example, the Aerospace Corporation has a seven-layer managerial hierarchy because this structure matches the hierarchy of the U.S. Air Force.

Bhargava (1990) observed that the software firms in which developers interact closely with clients emphasize formalized documentation. These firms devote more effort to planning and systems analysis, to writing user manuals, and to recording the activities carried out and times spent on specific projects. These documents contribute to better client relations and reduce the firms' dependence on developers who might depart.

The Rand Corporation illustrates effective bureaucratization by a KIF. Rand's library staff watch for opportunities to submit proposals, and produce bibliographies to aid technical experts' proposal writing. Some of Rand's experts review others' proposals and reports to assure that they meet Rand's standards for data gathering and statistical analysis. Copy editors suggest ways to make proposals and reports more intelligible. These activities undoubtedly improve final reports' acceptability and the odds of proposals' winning funds. Rand's research proposals have a far-above-average success rate.

Larger KIFs are better able and more inclined to bureaucratize, and larger KIFs can better tolerate and balance the opposing forces in their work. For instance, Brooks (1975) argued that "conceptual integrity" is the key to high quality in systems design. Attaining conceptual integrity, he said, probably requires centralized control by a few key experts, whereas programming and testing a designed system may require many experts. Such work can be troublesome for KIFs with experts who see themselves as equals and substitutes. Large KIFs mitigate these problems by dividing work into projects and allowing experts to specialize in either design or implementation (Bhargava, 1990). Creating routines requires persistence, and both persistence and learning may benefit from specializing with respect to technologies, markets, functions, or locations.

On the other hand, large KIFs may lack knowledge intensity. KIFs are prone to grow by adding support staff instead of experts. Adding support staff promises to increase profitability per expert by using experts more efficiently, whereas growth by adding experts may use experts less efficiently. KIFs also grow by adding activities, products, or services that promise to extract more value from the expertise already in-house. Thus, KIFs tend to lose knowledge intensity as they grow.

Some experts see this loss of knowledge intensity as desirable—a sensible way to get the maximum value from current staff. Other experts see growth as a necessity demanded by large clients or numerous customers. Still other experts see this loss of knowledge intensity as a danger to be combated—by avoiding growth, diversification, and geographic dispersion.

Routinization helps to make knowledge intensity unstable. As with physical capital, converting expertise to routines is risky. Routines may become targets of imitation, spread, and gradually lose the character of being esoteric and advantageous. A routine used by many firms confers small comparative advantages on its users.

Organizational Culture

Cultures have to be built gradually because they are delicate and poorly understood. Building a special organizational culture takes much effort as well as imagination. Imitating another firm's culture is quite difficult, if even possible, because every culture involves distinctive traditions.

Maister (1985) wrote admiringly of "one-firm firms," which stress "institutional loyalty and group effort. . . . In contrast to many of their (often successful) competitors who emphasize individual entrepreneurship, autonomous profit centers, internal competition and/or highly decentralized independent activities, one-firm firms place great emphasis on firmwide coordination of decisionmaking, group identity, cooperative teamwork and institutional commitment" (p. 4). According to Maister, one-firm firms:

take very seriously their missions (usually service to clients),

grow slowly while choosing clients and tasks carefully,

devote much effort to selecting and training personnel,

do R&D beyond the requirements of revenue-producing projects,

encourage free communication among personnel, and

give information freely to their personnel, including financial information.

Maister also warned that one-firm firms may become complacent, lacking in entrepreneurship, entrenched in their ways of doing things, and inbred.

Orlikowski (1988, pp. 152-160) said Maister's idealization accurately describes the consulting firm she studied, except that her firm discourages R&D beyond the needs of current clients. The firm devotes 7% of its revenue to a training program and each consultant spends over 1,500 hours in training during the first six years with the firm. Overtly technical in content, this training involves both self-study and classes at the firm's school. The consultants measure their career progress by their progress through this program. Nevertheless, most consultants seem to agree with the one who said: "The biggest advantage of the school is the networking and socializing it allows. It really is not that important as an educational experience."

Alvesson (1991, 1992) too described a consulting firm that spent much effort on formal socialization. The top managers ran a "project philosophy course." They also sought "to sell the metaphor *the company as a home* to the employees." Designed to foster informal interaction, the building has a kitchen, sauna, pool, piano bar, and large lounge area. The firm supports a chorus, art club, and navigation course. All personnel in each department meet together every second week. Every third month, each department undertakes a major social activity such as a hike or a sailing trip. The firm celebrated its tenth anniversary by flying all 500 employees to Rhodes for three days of group activities.

Interviews with software developers convinced Bhargava (1990) that larger firms work harder to build cultures. They use their cultures to promote free communication, to make them less dependent on key experts, and to ease personnel transfers. He found fewer communication problems and fewer personnel transfers in smaller firms.

Van Maanen and Kunda (1989) vividly described people's ambivalence toward culture-building efforts in a computer firm. Most people readily adopt corporate language and enjoy belonging to a supportive collectivity. Some embrace corporate values and rituals enthusiastically; more do so cynically. Most people also hold themselves aloof from group membership and protect their individual identities.

All the KIFs I have studied select experts carefully, they use teams extensively, they take their missions seriously, they manage growth cautiously, and their people talk openly. Only Wachtell, Lipton, however, comes close to the one-firm model in discouraging internal competition, emphasizing group work, disclosing information, and eliciting loyalty to the firm. The other KIFs depart from the one-firm model in having multiple profit centers, assessing the productivities of individual experts, and revealing only the financial information that laws require. All the KIFs, including Wachtell, Lipton, depart from the one-firm model in decentralizing activities, encouraging entrepreneurship, and not involving everyone in decision making.

KIFs do downplay formal structures, and they achieve coordination through social norms and reward systems instead of hierarchical controls (Nelson, 1988; Van Maanen & Kunda, 1989, pp. 70-93). One reason is experts' sense of their importance as individuals and their desires for autonomy: close control would induce exits. Another reason is common values and norms that result from many years of formal education. KIFs appear to derive some of their properties from universities, and some KIFs employ many who could be university faculty. Third, experts have to work independently because projects involve just a few people (Alvesson, 1992). The instability of projects and services provides a fourth reason: to absorb variations in demands for their services, KIFs need fluidity and ambiguity. Matrix structures are prevalent, and organization charts sketchy. Supervisors counsel non-directively. Experts form liaisons across formal boundaries. Indeed, the Rand Corporation designed its building to foster unplanned encounters.

Still, social norms and reward systems are not equivalent to cultures. KIFs confront serious obstacles to creating and maintaining unusual cultures, especially cultures that embody organizational learning. The attributes that make hierarchical controls troublesome—autonomy, mobility, professionalization, uncertain funding—also make it hard for KIFs to integrate people and to socialize them into unusual organizational cultures. When experts join new firms, they bring with them well-developed values, standards, habits, mental frameworks, and languages. Although they have much in common with their colleagues, the culture they share is supra-organizational.

Social Capital

The Garden Company's customers can easily see whether Garden's products do what the maker claims. The customers do not buy Garden's expertise directly. One result is that Garden's relations with customers are impersonal. Another result is that these relations may be fleeting. The customers readily switch to other suppliers, and Garden itself cuts off relations with customers when it stops making products that are less profitable.

Buyers of expertise itself, by contrast, often have difficulty assessing their purchases. Clients often consult experts because they believe their own knowledge inadequate, so they cannot judge the experts' advice or reports mainly on substance. Clients may be unable to assess experts' advice by acting on it and watching the outcomes: the clients do not know what would have happened if they had acted otherwise and it is frequently obvious that outcomes reflect uncontrollable or unpredictable influences. Clients may not even understand what their expert advisers are saying. Many experts—with awareness—use jargon that obscures their meaning. As a result, clients have to base their judgments on familiar, generic symbols of expertise. Do the experts speak as persons with much education? Have the experts used impressive statistical computations? Are the experts well dressed? Did the experts use data of good quality? Do the experts' analyses seem logical and credible? Do the experts appear confident?

Successful service KIFs, therefore, pay attention to their symbolic outputs. For example, as mentioned above, the Aerospace Corporation uses seven managerial levels that match the Air Force's hierarchy. Aerospace also asks technical experts to practice briefings in-house before presenting them to Air Force officers, and it provides strong support for writing, graphics, and artwork.

Clients also hire experts to obtain legitimacy instead of expertise. In such circumstances, the client-expert relationship is a charade: the clients choose advisers who will give wanted advice. Such selection can be unconscious.

For instance, when the Facit Company was in serious trouble, the board listened to presentations by several would-be advisers (Starbuck, 1989). They then hired McKinsey & Company because that proposal had sounded most sensible: McKinsey's proposal had endorsed the general strategy the board had been pursuing. One result was that the board found it easy to take McKinsey's advice. Another result was that following McKinsey's advice only made the situation worse.

Rhenman (1973) has commented perceptively from his experience:

> [T]here is in the consultant-client relationship an element of conflict. A game is played with all the usual trappings: negotiations, opposing strategies, etc. The client likes to "sound out" the consultant. The client wavers between consultant A and consultant B. He also considers the cost of a particular consultant: will the organization really benefit? Has the consultant perhaps other purposes in mind, beyond his duty to the client? Perhaps he is seeking an opportunity for research or financial reward? The consultant may be particularly anxious to get this assignment. How can he persuade the client to engage him? Or he may be temporarily hard pressed for time. Can he persuade the client to postpone the assignment, or some particularly time-consuming part of it? And during the assignment the consultant is often sure to feel that the client is blind to his own best interests, or that he, as consultant, is becoming involved in internal conflicts. . . .
>
> We have already intimated that political groups may well try to use the engagement of the consultant for their own ends. Other groups may suspect and oppose the engagement on similar grounds; a long and heated struggle can easily develop. The consultant may be aware of what has been going on, or he may realize it only when he discovers that his engagement is tied to certain definite conditions. . . .
>
> But the political system is not simply a part of the background. Soon, whether he realizes it or not, the consultant will become a pawn in the political game: his presence will always have some effect on the balance of power, sometimes perhaps a good deal. If he is not politically aware, various interest groups will almost certainly try to use him for their own purposes. (pp. 160-171)

Over the long term, service KIFs try to convert clients' satisfaction with specific projects into long-term relations. Even in contexts that are initially impersonal, repeated interactions between specific people create bonds. Firm-to-firm ties gradually evolve into person-to-person ties. An expert who repeatedly serves the same client begins to perceive "my" client, and the client comes to think of "my" expert.

Such personalizing can happen with any expert, but the experts having the strongest social skills are not normally those with the greatest technical expertise. Those with superb abilities in both dimensions are rare: one interviewee estimated that only ten people in the U.S. are "great technical lawyers who work well with colleagues, are effective with clients, and show good judgment."

Thus, KIFs use internal specialization, in which socially skillful experts work on building ties with a few specific clients, and technically superior experts provide specialized expertise to many clients. The KIFs offer clients familiar contact persons, who then draw upon *ad hoc* teams with expertise fitting specific projects. To a client, a KIF looks like a single source of diverse expertise that gives high priority to that client's problems.

Formally, American lawyers call the persons whom clients choose to contact "originating attorneys." Informally, they call them "rainmakers." Rainmaking is mysterious and magical, and rainmakers wield power. Their personal and lasting ties with clients give the contact persons divided loyalties as well as power. The divided loyalties serve a quality-control function that nurtures continuing ties between KIFs and clients. The power is a central fact-of-life that KIFs have to appreciate or risk losing long-term clients.

Keith Uncapher once worked at the Rand Corporation, designing information systems for the Defense Advanced Research Projects Agency (DARPA). Rand's top managers declared that the firm should no longer build hardware, but Uncapher believed that DARPA's goals demanded special-purpose hardware. He made a fifteen-minute oral proposal to DARPA, received an initial grant of $10 million, and started a new organization, the Information Science Institute.

As the foregoing implies they should, service KIFs favor client relations over technical expertise. If KIFs allow client relations to dominate too strongly, however, they may lose key technical experts. Instead of thinking that they work for firms, technical experts may think firms exist for their benefit and should be working for them. To remain stable, KIFs have to reconcile their client-relations specialists and technical specialists. Each of these needs the other over the long term, but their mutual dependency may seem obscure at any one moment.

STRATEGIC DEVELOPMENT

This article's second section asserts: "Knowledge is a stock of expertise, not a flow of information." Ironically, firms' stocks of expertise come from the flows in complex input-output systems. Knowledge flows in through hiring, training, and purchases of capital goods. Some knowledge gets manufactured internally, through research, invention, and culture building. Knowledge flows out through personnel departures, imitated routines, and sales of capital goods. Some knowledge becomes obsolete. Fluid knowledge solidifies when converted into capital goods or routines. The sequences of events resembles random walks, and the net outcomes are difficult to foresee. Thus, strategies do not evolve coherently (Greenwood, Hinings, & Brown, 1990).

Diversification

For product KIFs, strategic development calls for regulating numbers of customers and numbers of product lines. Similarly, service KIFs need to regulate numbers of clients and numbers of topical foci. As with other specialization-diversification problems, high risks come from having very few clients or customers and very few topics or product lines. A KIF with very few topical foci must perform superbly in those areas, and a KIF with very few customers cannot afford customer dissatisfaction. The issues, however, do not all lie in the realms of expertise or social skills.

For a year and a half after Wachtell, Lipton began, one client accounted for 75% of its revenue. Then, this client asked Wachtell, Lipton to do something unethical. They replied that they could not take the wanted action. The client countered that Wachtell, Lipton must either do its bidding or lose its business. The partners refused . . . and gave up 75% of their revenue. At that point, unsure their firm could survive, the partners adopted a policy that has had profound consequences: Wachtell, Lipton would work only one-case-at-a-time. It would never again make a long-term commitment to a client.

If Wachtell, Lipton had been more ordinary, this policy might have been deadly. But the firm became one of the rare ones to which corporations turn when their normal legal resources seem inadequate—at least, when corporations don't want to find out whether their normal legal resources would be adequate. In this status, having no long-term clients becomes an asset, for Wachtell, Lipton can be hired by whoever calls first.

Some KIFs serve a few clients contentedly. Keith Uncapher said, "I wouldn't know how to look good to two clients." He designed the Information Science Institute to serve only DARPA, and no other client. The Aerospace Corporation derives 99% of its revenues from a single long-term contract and makes no effort to change this situation.

Most KIFs that begin with narrow foci try to diversify. Like Aerospace, the Rand Corporation initially served a single client, the U.S. Air Force. At the Air Force's urging and with its help, Rand began making strenuous efforts to gain broader support and greater autonomy. These efforts have had partial success. Rand has raised an endowment exceeding $40 million, and it does research for over 80 sponsors annually. Nevertheless, three military sponsors still account for 70% of Rand's revenues, and 80% of its research deals with national security.

A. D. Little has attained broad diversification after developing incrementally for over a century. A. D. Little's precursor, Griffin & Little, began in 1886 as specialists in the chemistry of paper-making. In 1909, when the current firm incorporated, its expertise encompassed paper-making, forest products, textiles, plastics, and sugar. These industries were central to the economy of New England, the firm's home.

Over the years, as the firm expanded its geographic reach, it added a wide range of physical and biological sciences and expertise on a wide spectrum of manufacturing technologies. A. D. Little first studied regional economics in 1916, began financial studies in the 1930s, and moved into management consulting broadly in the 1950s.

These expansions sprang partly from the firm's standards about conflict of interest. After advising a client about a topic, A. D. Little will not advise a different client from the same industry about the same topic. Future projects must change either the industry or the topic.

Just as diversification regarding clients may erode a KIF's ties with its long-standing clients, topical diversification may undermine a KIF's credibility. A few years ago, A. D. Little's senior managers concluded that their firm had become too amorphous. Hiring had become hard because the firm had so few experts in any single specialty. Covering too many specialties for too many dissimilar clients was yielding neither enough profit nor enough client satisfaction. A survey revealed that clients were turning to other consultants to get "focused depth of resources."

Thus, the firm went through a major planning effort, and began to focus on half-a-dozen functions in a handful of industries—mainly chemicals, financial services, health care, and telecommunications. Alfred Wechsler explained, "We try to define our expertise with verb-noun-adverb combinations. For example: we know how *to manufacture a paper cup inexpensively.*"

A. D. Little's strategic development has generally paralleled the developments in its client population—large industrial enterprises. Chandler (1962) described how single-product firms grew into multiple-product, divisionalized firms during the first half of the century. In the same period, A. D. Little was adding many product lines and decentralizing. In the 1970s and 1980s, conglomerates such as ITT decided to retrench into a few core businesses: A. D. Little was making analogous changes at the same time. After 1950, many American firms expanded overseas, and A. D. Little too became multinational.

Its initial foreign venture was an office in Zurich that opened in 1957 to serve American firms that were expanding into Europe. To their surprise, the consultants discovered that European firms also wanted their services. They now have offices in six European cities and in Mexico, Brazil, Venezuela, Saudi Arabia, Japan, Singapore, Hong Kong, and Taiwan. In 1972, they added laboratories in England; these later expanded to Germany.

Multinational KIFs

For KIFs, multinationality poses challenging issues that differ from those facing industrial firms. Many industrial firms use authority and steep hierarchies, and they can often use formal controls or hardware technology to reach performance standards. Consulting firms and other KIFs dare not resort to authority or formal controls and they lack technological wonder pills. They have to depend on autonomous small teams to act ethically and to meet performance standards. This, in turn, means that they need cultural homogeneity.

Nonetheless, A. D. Little has found national differences to be minor problems. One reason may be careful selection of experts. Another reason may be the homogeneity arising from education. Haire, Ghiselli, and Porter (1966) found that managers with similar education espouse similar values no matter what their nationalities. Wuthnow and Shrum (1983) discovered that education erases the ideological differences between managers and professional technical workers. After much education, managers said professionals espouse similar values.

Perhaps because they use authority, formal controls and technology to produce homogeneity, many industrial firms have shown insensitivity toward local values or treated host-country personnel less well than home-country personnel. Yet, insensitivity and inequity have not prevented industrial firms from operating successfully in foreign lands. Consulting firms, on the other hand, would fail if they did allow for local values, and they are apt to treat host-country consultants more than equally.

For instance, A. D. Little is trying to deliver reliable quality across diverse sites, but its clients want services tailored to their individual needs and contexts. Tailoring calls for consultants to act differently, whereas reliable quality and teamwork call for them to act similarly. A. D. Little began its multinational expansion by exporting American experts. Experience promptly convinced the firm that a foreign office must hire primarily experts native to that country. First, devising effective solutions for problems usually requires thorough understanding of the contexts in which those solutions will be tried. Second, clients do not want to waste time explaining basic economic, sociological, or political facts to expensive foreign consultants. Thus, the consultants who staff a foreign office tend to have strong social skills and close ties with their clients. These assets, in turn, tend to give the host-country consultants high status within the firm.

LOOKING BACK AND FORWARD

Summary

Because everyone defines knowledge differently, discussions of KIFs evoke debates about proper definition. Such debates have led me (a) to emphasize esoteric expertise instead of widely shared knowledge; (b) to distinguish an expert from a professional and a knowledge-intensive firm from a professional firm; (c) to differentiate a knowledge-intensive firm from an information-intensive firm; and (d) to see knowledge as a property of physical capital, social capital, routines, and organizational cultures, as well as individual people.

Highly successful KIFs exhibit uniqueness, and they reflect and exploit the peculiarities of their environments. Since they and their environments change symbiotically, their environments reflect and exploit these KIFs.

Whereas experts distinguish between preserving, creating, and applying knowledge, their daily work obscures these distinctions. Not only do pre-servers, creators, and appliers behave similarly, but preserving, creating, and applying are interdependent. Furthermore, experts resist new ideas—even the experts who describe themselves as creators of knowledge. Such resistance arises from self-interest and narrow perspectives. Yet, it may improve learning—by both individual experts and their firms—by making people ask whether knowledge has lasting value.

KIFs learn by hiring, training, and dismissing personnel. They also convert ideas into physical capital, routines, organizational culture, and social capital. Personnel changes and purchases of capital goods generally offer fast ways to pick up new ideas. Training, physical capital, routines, and organizational cultures can turn individuals' knowledge into collective prop-erty. Knowledge in people or in physical capital is easy to lose, and KIFs have difficulty using routines and building special cultures. Social capital transforms a series of successful relations with a client into a long-term relation, but it also converts collective successes into individual property. One consequence is that hierarchies within KIFs reflect social skills as well as technical expertise.

Three themes afford a framework for interpreting KIFs' strategic devel-opment. First, complex input-output systems for knowledge make KIFs' strategic development look erratic. Second, KIFs have to regulate numbers of customers or clients, and numbers of product lines or topical foci. Some KIFs focus on small numbers of clients, customers, product lines, or topics, but most KIFs try to diversify. Third, service KIFs often mirror prominent characteristics of their clients. These similarities are loosely qualitative, however, for KIFs differ from their clients in many ways.

Post-Industrial Currents

One cliché prediction says: future societies will have ever higher proportions of service workers, because machines will replace blue collars much more often than white collars. Perhaps KIFs are also growing more prevalent. But the future is always moot, and more interesting than the general trends are the swirling currents within them.

First, KIFs tend to grow by becoming less specialized and by adding support staff rather than experts. It nearly always *seems* that additional support staff, products, or services will extract more value from the experts already in-house. Individual experts, too, think about broadening their domains as they update their knowledge and see social and technological changes opening new opportunities. But when support staff come to outnumber experts greatly, or when KIFs claim expertise in too many domains, KIFs lose their halos of expertise and their credibility.

Second, all kinds of expertise become less profitable as they grow more prevalent. Esoteric expertise has monopoly power and this power erodes as expertise becomes less esoteric. Neither experts nor KIFs nor KIFs' industry associations should seek proliferation. Yet, experts resist control and they have strong penchants to start new firms. Very small firms can compete successfully if they take advantage of their peculiarities and the peculiarities of their environments. The Garden Company could easily lose out to competitors with better ideas.

Third, some kinds of expertise attract consumers even though their benefits are obscure. Examples include crisis intervention, economic forecasts, investment advice, psychotherapy . . . and management science. Some obscure-benefit expertise seems to have high value partly because the experts are unusual. Such expertise may lose value as the experts come to make up higher proportions of the workforce. On the other hand, such an outcome is not obvious. Placebos make effective treatments although they are very common. Mystery can be routinized. People need help with their problems even when the problems have no solutions—perhaps, especially then.

Obscure-benefit domains may be either more or less stable than the domains in which expertise yields clear benefits. Obscure-benefit domains are stable if they satisfy perennial human needs and no alternatives appear. There were probably economic forecasters before there were humans; even in recent times, the demand for economic forecasts has mounted as organizations have grown larger and more rigid. Obscure-benefit domains can be unstable if beliefs change, if human needs shift, or if more effective substitutes appear. Astrology is a case in point. Clear-benefit domains may themselves wither—as dentists are discovering.

Fourth, physical capital will displace some of experts' activities. Similar changes are occurring across the economy, within firms, and in the work of individual experts. Several new industries are distributing expertise in the form of physical capital. Both firms and individual experts are creating databases and expert systems, and they are buying or building tools to amplify experts' productivity by replacing some of their activities.

These substitutions will enable fewer experts to serve more clients or customers or to invent more products. They also will mean that many clients or customers no longer need experts or that they can make the products they have been buying. Millions of people are already using software to do accounting, to file income taxes, to write wills, to construct leases, or to help them write articles. Computers are revolutionizing product design, manufacturing control, and computer programming. Spiraling medical costs may yet compel the use of software that diagnoses diseases and issues medical prescriptions.

To appreciate such currents' beauty and intricacy, social scientists need to stop averaging across large, diverse categories. The average painting is flat gray, the average day is neither hot nor cold and has 12 hours of daylight, the average firm is mediocre and short-lived, and the average expert knows little about any field. In the social sciences, broad patterns over-simplify and capture only small fractions of what is happening. They leave scientists in worlds that look random. Broad patterns also tend to emphasize what is consistent with the past and to overlook subtle changes.

There is also a world of bright colors, sizzling days, exceptional firms, rare experts, and peculiar KIFs.

Acknowledgments

I owe thanks to many who contributed generously their time, ideas, insights, and contacts. This article reflects help from Mats Alvesson, Tora Bikson, Andrew Brownstein, Mark Chignell, Jess Cook, Joan Dunbar, Roger Dunbar, Tamara Erickson, James Fogelson, Charles Fombrun, Ari Ginsberg, John Jermier, Charles La Mantia, Kenneth Laudon, Martin Lipton, Henry Lucas, Louis Miller, Frances Milliken, Theodore Mirvis, Harold Novikoff, Paul Nystrom, Anthony Pascal, Lawrence Pedowitz, Fioravante Perrotta, Joseph Post, Lewis Rambo, Donald Rice, Harland Riker, James Ringer,

Stephen Robinson, David Ronfeldt, Lawrence Rosenberg, Roberta Shanman, Lee Sproull, Serge Taylor, Jon Turner, Keith Uncapher, Mary Ann Von Glinow, Herbert Wachtell, Alfred Wechsler, Elliott Wilbur, Sidney Winter, and an anonymous referee.

REFERENCES

Alvesson, M. (1991). Corporate culture and corporatism at the company level: A case study. *Economic and Industrial Democracy, 12,* 347-367.

Alvesson, M. (1992). Leadership as social integrative action. A study of a computer consultancy company. *Organization Studies, 13*(2), 185-209.

Armstrong, J. S. (1985). *Long-range forecasting: From crystal ball to computer* (2nd ed.). New York: Wiley-Interscience.

Ascher, W. (1978). *Forecasting: An appraisal for policy-maker and planners.* Baltimore: Johns Hopkins University Press.

Beyer, J. M. (1981). Ideologies, values, and decision making in organizations. In P. C. Nystrom & W. H. Starbuck (Eds.), *Handbook of organizational design* (Vol. 2, pp. 166-202). Oxford, UK: Oxford University Press

Bhargava, N. (1990). *Managing knowledge bases in knowledge-intensive firms: An empirical study of software firms.* Unpublished manuscript.

Brooks, F. P., Jr. (1975). *The mythical man-month: Essays on software engineering.* Reading, MA: Addison-Wesley.

Bucher, R., & Stelling, J. (1969). Characteristics of professional organizations. *Journal of Health and Social Behavior, 10,* 3-15.

Camerer, C. F., & Johnson, E. J. (1991). The process-performance paradox in expert judgment: How can experts know so much and predict so badly? In K. A. Ericsson & J. Smith (Eds.), *Toward a general theory of expertise: Prospects and limits* (pp. 195-217). Cambridge, UK: Cambridge University Press.

Chandler, A. D. (1962). *Strategy and structure.* Cambridge: MIT Press.

Deal, T., & Kennedy, A. (1982). *Corporate cultures.* Reading, MA: Addison-Wesley.

Ekstedt, E. (1988). *Human capital in an age of transition: Knowledge development and corporate renewal.* Stockholm: Allmänna Förlaget.

Ekstedt, E. (1989). Knowledge renewal and knowledge companies. *Uppsala Papers in Economic History,* Report 22.

Greenwood, R., Hinings, C. R., & Brown, J. L. (1990). "P^2-Form" strategic management: Corporate practices in professional partnerships. *Academy of Management Journal, 33,* 725-755.

Haire, M., Ghiselli, E. E., & Porter, L. W. (1966). *Managerial thinking.* New York: John Wiley.

Hinings, C. R., Brown, J. L., & Greenwood, R. (1991). Change in an autonomous professional organization. *Journal of Management Studies, 28,* 375-393.

Kusterer, K. C. (1978). *Know-how on the job: The important working knowledge of "unskilled" workers.* Boulder, CO: Westview.

Laudon, K. C., & Laudon, J. P. (1991). *Business information systems: A problem-solving approach.* Hinsdale, IL: Dryden.

Machlup, F. (1962). *The production and distribution of knowledge in the United States.* Princeton, NJ: Princeton University Press.

Maister, D. H. (1985). The one-firm firm: What makes it successful. *Sloan Management Review, 27*(1), 3-13.

Montagna, P. D. (1968). Professionalization and bureaucratization in large professional organizations. *American Journal of Sociology, 73,* 138-145.

Nelson, R. L. (1988). *Partners with power: The social transformation of the large law firm.* Berkeley: University of California Press.

Nelson, R. R., & Winter, S. G. (1982). *An evolutionary theory of economic change.* Cambridge, MA: Harvard University Press.

Orlikowski, W. J. (1988). *Information technology in post-industrial organizations: An exploration of the computer mediation of production work.* Doctoral dissertation, New York University.

Peters, T. J., & Waterman, R. H. (1982). *In search of excellence.* New York: Harper & Row.

Powell, M. J. (1986). *Professional innovation: Corporate lawyers and private lawmaking.* Unpublished manuscript.

Rhenman, E. (1973). *Organization theory for long-range planning.* London: Wiley.

Ritzer, G., & Walczak, D. (1986). *Working: Conflict & change* (3rd ed.). Englewood Cliffs, NJ: Prentice Hall.

Schriesheim, F. J., Von Glinow, M. A., & Kerrs, S. (1977). Professionals in bureaucracies: A structural alternative. In P. C. Nystrom & W. H. Starbuck (Eds.), *Prescriptive models of organizations* (pp. 53-69). Amsterdam: North-Holland.

Starbuck, W. H. (1976). Organizations and their environments. In M. D. Dunnette (Ed.), *Handbook of industrial and organizational psychology* (pp. 1069-1123). Chicago: Rand McNally.

Starbuck, W. H. (1983). Organizations as action creators. *American Sociological Review, 48,* 91-102.

Starbuck, W. H. (1989). Why organizations run into crises . . . and sometimes survive them. In K. C. Laudon & J. Turner (Eds.), *Information technology and management strategy* (pp. 11-33). Englewood Cliffs, NJ: Prentice Hall.

Starbuck, W. H., & Dutton, J. M. (1973). Designing adaptive organizations. *Journal of Business Policy, 3,* 21-28.

Stinchcombe, A. L., & Heimer, C. A. (1988). Interorganizational relations and careers in computer software firms. In I. H. Simpson & R. L. Simpson (Eds.), *Research in the sociology of work* (Vol. 4, pp. 179-204). Greenwich, CT: JAI.

Sveiby, K. E., & Lloyd, T. (1987). *Managing knowhow.* London: Bloomsbury.

Sveiby, K. E., & Risling, A. (1986). *Kunskapsföretaget—Seklets viktigaste ledarutmaning?* (The knowledge firm—this century's most important managerial challenge?) Malmö, Sweden: Liber AB.

Van Maanen, J., & Kunda, G. (1989). Real feelings: Emotional expression and organizational culture. *Research in Organizational Behavior, 11,* 43-103.

Winter, S. G. (1987). Knowledge and competence as strategic assets. In D. J. Teece (Ed.), *The competitive challenge: Strategies for industrial innovation and renewal* (pp. 159-184). Cambridge, MA: Ballinger.

Wolff, E. N., & Baumol, W. J. (1987). *Sources of postwar growth of information activity in the U.S.* Unpublished manuscript.

Wuthnow, R., & Shrum, W. (1983). Knowledge workers as a "new class": Structural and ideological convergence among professional-technical workers and managers. *Work and Occupations, 10,* 471-487.

22

Organizational Learning

BARBARA LEVITT
JAMES G. MARCH

This paper reviews the literature on organizational learning. Organizational learning is viewed as routine-based, history-dependent, and target-oriented. Organizations are seen as learning by encoding inferences from history into routines that guide behavior. Within this perspective on organizational learning, topics covered include how organizations learn from direct experience, how organizations learn from the experience of others, and how organizations develop conceptual frameworks or paradigms for interpreting that experience. The section on organizational memory discusses how organizations encode, store, and retrieve the lessons of history despite the turnover of personnel and the passage of time. Organizational learning is further complicated by the ecological structure of the simultaneously adapting behavior of other organizations, and by an endogenously changing environment. The final section discusses the limitations as well as the possibilities of organizational learning as a form of intelligence.

INTRODUCTION

Theories of organizational learning can be distinguished from theories of analysis and choice which emphasize anticipatory calculation and intention (Machina, 1987), from theories of conflict and bargaining which emphasize

This chapter appeared originally in *Annual Review of Sociology,* Vol. 14, 1988. Copyright © 1988 Annual Reviews, Inc.

strategic action, power, and exchange (Pfeffer, 1981), and from theories of variation and selection which emphasize differential birth and survival rates of invariant forms (Hannan & Freeman, 1977). Although the actual behavioral processes and mechanisms of learning are sufficiently intertwined with choice, bargaining, and selection to make such theoretical distinctions artificial at times, ideas about organizational learning are distinct from, and framed by, ideas about the other processes (Scott, 1987).

Our interpretation of organizational learning builds on three classical observations drawn from behavioral studies of organizations. The first is that behavior in an organization is based on routines (Cyert & March, 1963; Nelson & Winter, 1982). Action stems from a logic of appropriateness or legitimacy more than from a logic of consequentiality or intention. It involves matching procedures to situations more than it does calculating choices. The second observation is that organizational actions are history-dependent (Lindblom, 1959; Steinbruner, 1974). Routines are based on interpretations of the past more than anticipations of the future. They adapt to experience incrementally in response to feedback about outcomes. The third observation is that organizations are oriented to targets (Siegel, 1957; Simon, 1955). Their behavior depends on the relation between the outcomes they observe and the aspirations they have for those outcomes. Sharper distinctions are made between success and failure than among gradations of either.

Within such a framework, organizations are seen as learning by encoding inferences from history into routines that guide behavior. The generic term "routines" includes the forms, rules, procedures, conventions, strategies, and technologies around which organizations are constructed and through which they operate. It also includes the structure of beliefs, frameworks, paradigms, codes, cultures, and knowledge that buttress, elaborate, and contradict the formal routines. Routines are independent of the individual actors who execute them and are capable of surviving considerable turnover in individual actors.

The experiential lessons of history are captured by routines in a way that makes the lessons, but not the history, accessible to organizations and organizational members who have not themselves experienced the history. Routines are transmitted through socialization, education, imitation, professionalization, personnel movement, mergers, and acquisitions. They are recorded in a collective memory that is often coherent but is sometimes jumbled, that often endures but is sometimes lost. They change as a result of experience within a community of other learning organizations. These changes depend on interpretations of history, particularly on the evaluation of outcomes in terms of targets.

In the remainder of the present paper we examine such processes of organizational learning. The perspective is narrower than that used by some (Fiol & Lyles, 1985; Hedberg, 1981; Starbuck, 1976) and differs conceptually from that used by others. In particular, both the emphasis on routines and the emphasis on ecologies of learning distinguish the present formulation from treatments that deal primarily with individual learning within single organizations (Argyris & Schön, 1978; March & Olsen, 1975) and place this paper closer to the traditions of behavioral theories of organizational decision making (House & Singh, 1987; Winter, 1986), and to population level theories of organizational change (Astley, 1985; Carroll, 1984).

LEARNING FROM DIRECT EXPERIENCE

Routines and beliefs change in response to direct organizational experience through two major mechanisms. The first is trial-and-error experimentation. The likelihood that a routine will be used is increased when it is associated with success in meeting a target, decreased when it is associated with failure (Cyert & March, 1963). The underlying process by which this occurs is left largely unspecified. The second mechanism is organizational search. An organization draws from a pool of alternative routines, adopting better ones when they are discovered. Since the rate of discovery is a function both of the richness of the pool and of the intensity and direction of search, it depends on the history of success and failure of the organization (Radner, 1975).

Learning by Doing

The purest example of learning from direct experience is found in the effects of cumulated production and user experience on productivity in manufacturing (Dutton, Thomas, & Butler, 1984). Research on aircraft production, first in the 1930s (Wright, 1936) and subsequently during World War II (Asher, 1956), indicated that direct labor costs in producing airframes declined with the cumulated number of airframes produced. If C_1 is the direct labor cost of the ith airframe produced, and a is a constant, then the empirical results are approximated by: $C_n = C_1 n^{-a}$. This equation, similar in spirit and form to learning curves in individuals and animals, has been shown to fit production costs (in constant dollars) reasonably well in a relatively large number of products, firms, and nations (Yelle, 1979). Much of the early research involved only simple graphical techniques, but more elaborate analyses have largely confirmed the original results (Rapping, 1965). Estimates of the learning rate, however, vary substantially across industries, products, and time (Dutton & Thomas, 1984).

Empirical plots of experience curves have been buttressed by three kinds of analytical elaborations. First, there have been attempts to decompose experience curves into several intercorrelated causes and to assess their separate contributions to the observed improvements in manufacturing costs. Although it has been argued that important elements of the improvements come through feedback from customers who use the products, particularly where those products are complex (Rosenberg, 1982), most of the research on experience curves has emphasized the direct effects of cumulative experience on production skills. Most studies indicate that the effects due to cumulative production are greater than those due to changes in the current scale of production, transformation of the technology, increases in the experience of individual production workers, or the passage of time (Argote, Beckman, & Epple, 1987; Hollander, 1965; Preston & Keachie, 1964); but there is evidence that the latter effects are also involved (Dutton & Thomas, 1984, 1985). Second, there have been attempts to use experience curves as a basis for pricing strategies. These efforts have led to some well-publicized successes but also to some failures attributable to an inadequate specification of the basic model, particularly as it relates to the sharing of experience across organizations (Day & Montgomery, 1983; Dutton & Freedman, 1985). Third, there have been attempts to define models that not only predict the general log-linear result but also accommodate some of the small but theoretically interesting departures from that curve (Muth, 1986). These efforts are, for the most part, variations on themes of trial-and-error learning or organizational search.

Competency Traps

In simple discussions of experiential learning based on trial-and-error learning or organizational search, organizations are described as gradually adopting those routines, procedures, or strategies that lead to favorable outcomes; but the routines themselves are treated as fixed. In fact, of course, routines are transformed at the same time as the organization learns which of them to pursue, and discrimination among alternative routines is affected by their transformation (Burgelman, 1988; March, 1981).

The dynamics are exemplified by cases in which each routine is itself a collection of routines, and learning takes place at several nested levels. In such multilevel learning, organizations learn simultaneously both to discriminate among routines and to refine the routines by learning within them. A familiar contemporary example is the way in which organizations learn to use some software systems rather than others and simultaneously learn to refine their skills on the systems that they use. As a result of such learning, efficiency with any particular procedure increases with use, and differences in success with different procedures reflect not only differences in the performance potentials of the procedures but also an organization's current competencies with them.

Multilevel learning typically leads to specialization. By improving competencies within frequently used procedures, it increases the frequency with which those procedures result in successful outcomes and thereby increases their use. Provided this process leads the organization both to improve the efficiency and to increase the use of the procedure with the highest potential, specialization is advantageous. However, a competency trap can occur when favorable performance with an inferior procedure leads an organization to accumulate more experience with it, thus keeping experience with a superior procedure inadequate to make it rewarding to use. Such traps are well-known both in their new technology version (Cooper & Schendel, 1976) and in their new procedures version (Zucker, 1977).

Competency traps are particularly likely to lead to maladaptive specialization if newer routines are better than older ones. One case is the sequential exposure to new procedures in a developing technology (Barley, 1988). Later procedures are improvements, but learning organizations have problems in overcoming the competencies they have developed with earlier ones (Whetten, 1987). The likelihood of such persistence in inferior procedures is sensitive to the magnitude of the difference between the potentials of the alternatives. The status quo is unlikely to be stable if the differences in potential between existing routines and new ones are substantial (Stinchcombe, 1986). The likelihood of falling into a competency trap is also sensitive to learning rates. Fast learning among alternative routines tends to increase the risks of maladaptive specialization while fast learning within a new routine tends to decrease the risks (Herriott, Levinthal, & March, 1985).

The broader social and evolutionary implications of competency traps are considerable. In effect learning produces increasing returns to experience (thus typically to scale) and leads an organization, industry, or society to persist in using a set of procedures or technologies that may be far from optimal (Arthur, 1984). Familiar examples are the standard typewriter keyboard and the use of the internal combustion gasoline engine to power motor vehicles. Since they convert almost chance actions based on small differences into stable arrangements, competency traps result in organizational histories for which broad functional or efficiency explanations are often inadequate.

INTERPRETATION OF EXPERIENCE

The lessons of experience are drawn from a relatively small number of observations in a complex, changing ecology of learning organizations. What has happened is not always obvious and the causality of events is difficult to untangle. What an organization should expect to achieve, and thus the difference between success and failure, is not always clear. Nevertheless, people in organizations form interpretations of events and come to classify outcomes as good or bad (Thompson, 1967).

Certain properties of this interpretation of experience stem from features of individual inference and judgment. As has frequently been observed, individual human beings are not perfect statisticians (Kahneman, Slovic, & Tversky, 1982). They make systematic errors in recording the events of history and in making inferences from them. They overestimate the probability of events that actually occur and of events that are available to attention because of their recency or saliency. They are insensitive to sample size. They tend to overattribute events to the intentional actions of individuals. They use simple linear and functional rules, associate causality with spatial and temporal contiguity, and assume that big effects must have big causes. These attributes of individuals as historians are important to the present topic because they lead to systematic biases in interpretation, but they are reviewed in several previous publications (Einhorn & Hogarth, 1986; Slovic, Fischhoff, & Lichtenstein, 1977; Starbuck & Milliken, 1988) and are not discussed here.

Stories, Paradigms, and Frames

Organizations devote considerable energy to developing collective understandings of history. These interpretations of experience depend on the frames within which events are comprehended (Daft & Weick, 1984) They are translated into, and developed through, story lines that come to be broadly, but not universally, shared (Clark, 1972; Martin, Sitkin, & Boehm, 1985) This structure of meaning is normally suppressed as a conscious concern, but learning occurs within it. As a result, some of the more powerful phenomena in organizational change surround the transformation of givens, the redefinition of events, alternatives, and concepts through consciousness raising, culture building, double-loop learning, or paradigm shifts (Argyris & Schön, 1978; Beyer, 1981; Brown, 1978).

It is imaginable that organizations will come to discard ineffective interpretive frames in the very long run, but the difficulties in using history to discriminate intelligently among alternative paradigms are profound. Where there are multiple, hierarchically arranged levels of simultaneous learning, the interactions among them are complex, and it is difficult to evaluate higher order alternatives on the basis of experience. Alternative frames are flexible enough to allow change in operational routines without affecting organizational mythology (Krieger, 1979; Meyer & Rowan, 1977), and organizational participants collude in support of interpretations that sustain the myths (Tirole, 1986). As a result, stories, paradigms, and beliefs are conserved in the face of considerable potential disconfirmation (Sproull, 1981); and what is learned appears to be influenced less by history than by the frames applied to that history (Fischhoff, 1975; Pettigrew, 1985).

Although frameworks for interpreting experience within organizations are generally resistant to experience—indeed, may enact that experience (Weick, 1979)—they are vulnerable to paradigm peddling and paradigm politics. Ambiguity sustains the efforts of theorists and therapists to promote their favorite frameworks, and the process by which interpretations are developed makes it relatively easy for conflicts of interest within an organization to spawn conflicting interpretations. For example, leaders of organizations are inclined to accept paradigms that attribute organizational successes to their own actions and organizational failures to the actions of others or to external forces, but opposition groups in an organization are likely to have the converse principle for attributing causality (Miller & Ross, 1975). Similarly, advocates of a particular policy, but not their opponents, are likely to interpret failures less as a symptom that the policy is incorrect than as an indication that it has not been pursued vigorously enough (Ross & Staw, 1986) As a result, disagreements over the meaning of history are possible, and different groups develop alternative stories that interpret the same experience quite differently.

The Ambiguity of Success

Both trial-and-error learning and incremental search depend on the evaluation of outcomes as successes or failures. There is a structural bias toward post-decision disappointment in ordinary decision making (Harrison & March, 1984) but individual decision makers often seem to be able to reinterpret their objectives or the outcomes in such a way as to make themselves successful even when the shortfall seems quite large (Staw & Ross, 1978).

The process is similar in organizational learning, particularly where the leadership is stable and the organization is tightly integrated (Ross & Staw, 1986). But where such conditions do not hold there are often differences stemming from the political nature of an organization. Goals are ambiguous and commitment to them is confounded by their relation to personal and subgroup objectives (Moore & Gates, 1986). Conflict and decision advocacy within putatively rational decision processes lead to inflated expectations and problems of implementation and thus to disappointments (Olsen, 1976; Sproull, Weiner, & Wolf, 1978). Different groups in an organization often have different targets and evaluate the same outcome differently. Simple euphoria is constrained by the presence of individuals and groups who opposed the direction being pursued or who at least feel no need to accept responsibility for it (Brunsson, 1985). New organizational leaders are inclined to define previous outcomes more negatively than are the leaders who preceded them (Hedberg, 1981). As a result evaluations of outcomes are likely to be more negative or more mixed in organizations than they are in individuals.

Organizational success is ordinarily defined in terms of the relation between performance outcomes and targets. Targets, however, change over time in two ways. First the indicators of success are modified. Accounting definitions change (Burchell, Colin, & Hopwood, 1985); social and policy indicators are redefined (MacRae, 1985). Second, levels of aspiration with respect to any particular indicator change. The most common assumption is that a target is a function of some kind of moving average of past achievement, the gap between past achievement, and past targets or the rate of change of either (Cyert & March, 1963; Lant, 1987).

Superstitious Learning

Superstitious learning occurs when the subjective experience of learning is compelling but the connections between actions and outcomes are misspecified. Numerous opportunities exist for such misunderstandings in learning from experience in organizations. For example, it is easy for technicians to develop superstitious perceptions of a new technology from their experience with it (Barley, 1988). Cases of superstition that are of particular interest to students of organizations are those that stem from special features of life in hierarchical organizations. For example the promotion of managers on the basis of performance produces self-confidence among top executives that is partly superstitious, leading them to overestimate the extent to which they can control the risks their organizations face (March & Shapira, 1987).

Superstitious learning often involves situations in which subjective evaluations of success are insensitive to the actions taken. During very good times, or when post-outcome euphoria reinterprets outcomes positively, or when targets are low, only exceptionally inappropriate routines will lead an organization to experience failure. In like manner, during very bad times, or when post-outcome pessimism reinterprets outcomes negatively, or when targets are high, no routine will lead to success. Evaluations that are insensitive to actions can also result from adaptive aspirations. Targets that adapt very rapidly will be close to the current performance level. This makes being above or below the target an almost chance event. Very slow adaptation, on the other hand, is likely to keep an organization either successful for long periods of time or unsuccessful for long periods of time. A similar result is realized if targets adapt to the performance of other organizations. For example, if each firm in an industry sets its target equal to the average performance of firms in that industry, some firms are likely to be persistently above the target and others persistently below (Herriott et al., 1985; Levinthal & March, 1981).

Each of these situations produces superstitious learning. In an organization that is invariantly successful, routines that are followed are associated with success and are reinforced; other routines are inhibited. The organization becomes committed to a particular set of routines, but the routines to which it becomes committed are determined more by early (relatively arbitrary) actions than by information gained from the learning situation (Nystrom & Starbuck, 1984). Alternatively, if failure is experienced regardless of the particular routine that is used, routines are changed frequently in a fruitless search for some that work. In both cases, the subjective feeling of learning is powerful, but it is misleading.

ORGANIZATIONAL MEMORY

Organizational learning depends on features of individual memories (Hastie, Park, & Weber, 1984; Johnson & Hasher, 1987), but our present concern is with organizational aspects of memory. Routine-based conceptions of learning presume that the lessons of experience are maintained and accumulated within routines despite the turnover of personnel and the passage of time. Rules, procedures, technologies, beliefs, and cultures are conserved through systems of socialization and control. They are retrieved through mechanisms of attention within a memory structure. Such organizational instruments not only record history but shape its future path, and the details of that path depend significantly on the processes by which the memory is maintained and consulted. An accounting system, whether viewed as the product of design or the residue of historical development, affects the recording and creation of history by an organization (Johnson & Kaplan, 1987). The ways in which military routines are changed, maintained, and consulted contribute to the likelihood and orchestration of military engagement (Levy, 1986).

Recording of Experience

Inferences drawn from experience are recorded in documents, accounts, files, standard operating procedures, and rule books; in the social and physical geography of organizational structures and relationships; in standards of good professional practice; in the culture of organizational stories; and in shared perceptions of "the way things are done around here." Relatively little is known about the details by which organizational experience is accumulated into a structure of routines, but it is clearly a process that yields different kinds of routines in different situations and is only partly successful in imposing internal consistency on organizational memories.

Not everything is recorded. The transformation of experience into routines and the recording of those routines involve costs. The costs are sensitive to information technology, and a common observation is that modern computer-based technology encourages the automation of routines by substantially reducing the costs of recording them. Even so, a good deal of experience is unrecorded simply because the costs are too great. Organizations also often make distinction between outcomes that will be considered relevant for future actions and outcomes that will not. The distinction may be implicit, as for example when comparisons between projected and realized returns from capital investment projects are ignored (Häaging, 1979). It may be explicit, as for example when exceptions to the rules are declared not to be precedents for the future. By creating a set of actions that are not precedents, an organization gives routines both short-term flexibility and long-term stability (Powell, 1986).

Organizations vary in the emphasis placed on formal routines. Craft-based organizations rely more heavily on tacit knowledge than do bureaucracies (Becker, 1982). Organizations facing complex uncertainties rely on informally shared understandings more than do organizations dealing with simpler, more stable environments (Ouchi, 1980). There is also variation within organizations. Higher level managers rely more on ambiguous information (relative to formal rules) than do lower level managers (Daft & Lengel, 1984).

Experiential knowledge, whether in tacit form or in formal rules, is recorded in an organizational memory. That memory is orderly, but it exhibits inconsistencies and ambiguities. Some of the contradictions are a consequence of inherent complications in maintaining consistency in inferences drawn sequentially from a changing experience. Some, however, reflect differences in experience, the confusions of history, and conflicting interpretations of that history. These latter inconsistencies are likely to be organized into deviant memories, maintained by subcultures, subgroups, and subunits

(Martin et al., 1985). With a change in the fortunes of the dominant coalition, the deviant memories become more salient to action (Martin & Siehl, 1983).

Conservation of Experience

Unless the implications of experience can be transferred from those who experienced it to those who did not, the lessons of history are likely to be lost through turnover of personnel. Written rules, oral transitions, and systems of formal and informal apprenticeships implicitly instruct new individuals in the lessons of history. Under many circumstances, the transfer of tradition is relatively straightforward and organizational experience is substantially conserved. For example, most police officers are socialized successfully to actions and beliefs recognizable as acceptable police behavior, even in cases where those actions and beliefs are substantially different from those that were originally instrumental in leading an individual to seek the career (Van Maanen, 1973).

Under other circumstances, however, organizational experience is not conserved. Knowledge disappears from an organization's active memory (Neustadt & May, 1986). Routines are not conserved because of limits on the time or legitimacy of the socializing agents, as for example in deviant subgroups or when the number of new members is large (Sproull et al., 1978); because of conflict with other normative orders, as for example with new organization members who are also members of well-organized professions (Hall, 1968); or because of the weaknesses of organizational control, as for example in implementation across geographic or cultural distances (Brytting, 1986).

Retrieval of Experience

Even within a consistent and accepted set of routines, only part of an organization's memory is likely to be evoked at a particular time, or in a particular part of the organization. Some parts of organizational memory are more available for retrieval than others. Availability is associated with the frequency of use of a routine, the recency of its use, and its organizational proximity. Recently used and frequently used routines are more easily evoked than those that have been used infrequently. Thus, organizations have difficulty retrieving relatively old, unused knowledge or skills (Argote et al., 1987). In cases where routines are nested within more general routines, the repetitive use of lower level routines tends to make them more accessible than the more general routine to which they are related (Merton, 1940). The effects of proximity stem from the ways the accumulation of history is linked to regularized responsibility. The routines that record lessons of experience are organized around organizational responsibilities and are retrieved more easily when actions are taken through regular channels than when they occur outside those channels (Olsen, 1983). At the same time, organizational structures create advocates for routines. Policies are converted into responsibilities that encourage rule zealotry (Mazmanian & Nienaber, 1979).

Availability is also partly a matter of the direct costs of finding and using what is stored in memory. Particularly where there are large numbers of routines bearing on relatively specific actions, modern information technology has reduced those costs and made the routinization of relatively complex organizational behavior economically feasible, for example in the preparation of reports or presentations, the scheduling of production or logistical support, the design of structures or engineering systems, or the analysis of financial statements (Smith & Green, 1980). Such automation of the recovery of routines makes retrieval more reliable. Reliability is, however, a mixed blessing. It standardizes retrieval and thus typically underestimates the conflict of interest and ambiguity about preferences in an organization. Expert systems of the standard type have difficulty capturing the unpredictable richness, erratic redundancy, and casual validity checking of traditional retrieval procedures, and they reduce or eliminate the fortuitous experimentation of unreliable retrieval (Simon, 1971; Wildavsky, 1983). As a result, they are likely to make learning more difficult for the organization.

LEARNING FROM THE EXPERIENCE OF OTHERS

Organizations capture the experience of other organizations through the transfer of encoded experience in the form of technologies, codes, procedures, or similar routines (Dutton & Starbuck, 1978). This diffusion of experience and routines from other organizations within a community of organizations complicates theories of routine-based learning. It suggests that understanding the relation between experiential learning and routines, strategies, or technologies in organizations will require attention to organizational networks (Håkansson, 1987) as well as to the experience of the individual organization. At the same time, it makes the derivation of competitive strategies (e.g., pricing strategies) more complex than it would otherwise be (Hilke & Nelson, 1987).

Mechanisms for Diffusion

The standard literature on the epidemiology of disease or information distinguishes three broad processes of diffusion. The first is diffusion involving a single source broadcasting a disease to a population of potential, but not necessarily equally vulnerable, victims. Organizational examples include rules promulgated by governmental agencies, trade associations, professional associations, and unions (Scott, 1985). The second process is diffusion involving the spread of a disease through contact between a member of the population who is infected and one who is not, sometimes mediated by a host carrier. Organizational examples include routines diffused by contacts among organizations, by consultants, and by the movement of personnel (Biggart, 1977). The third process is two-stage diffusion involving the spread of a disease within a small group by contagion and then by broadcast from them to the remainder of a population. Organizational examples include routines communicated through formal and informal educational institutions, through experts, and through trade and popular publications (Heimer, 1985a). In the organizational literature, these three processes have been labeled *coercive, mimetic,* and *normative* (DiMaggio & Powell, 1983). All three are involved in a comprehensive system of information diffusion (Imai, Nonaka, & Takeuchi, 1985).

Dynamics of Diffusion

The possibilities for learning from the experience of others, as well as some of the difficulties, can be illustrated by looking at the diffusion of innovations among organizations. We consider here only some issues that are particularly important for organizational learning. For more general reviews of the literature, see Rogers and Shoemaker (1971) and Kimberly (1981).

Although it is not easy to untangle the effects of imitation from other effects that lead to differences in the time of adoption, studies of the spread of new technologies among organizations seem to indicate that diffusion through imitation is less significant than is variation in the match between the technology and the organization (Mansfield, 1968), especially as that match is discovered and molded through learning (Kay, 1979). Imitation, on the other hand, has been credited with contributing substantially to diffusion of city manager plans among American cities (Knoke, 1982) and multidivisional organizational structures among American firms (Fligstein, 1985). Studies of the adoption of civil service reform by cities in the United States (Tolbert & Zucker, 1983) and of high technology weaponry by air forces (Eyre, Suchman, & Alexander, 1987) both show patterns in which features of the match between the procedures and the adopting organizations are more significant for explaining early adoptions than they are for explaining later ones, which seem better interpreted as due to imitation. The latter result is also supported by a study of the adoption of accounting conventions by firms (Mezias, 1987).

The underlying ideas in the literature on the sociology of institutionalization are less epidemiological than they are functional, but the diffusion of practices and forms is one of the central mechanisms considered (Zucker, 1987). Pressure on organizations to demonstrate that they are acting on collectively valued purposes in collectively valued ways leads them to copy ideas and practices from each other. The particular professions, policies, programs, laws, and public opinion that are created in the process of producing and marketing goods and services become powerful institutionalized myths that are adopted by organizations to legitimate themselves and ensure public support (Meyer & Rowan, 1977; Zucker, 1977). The process diffuses forms and procedures and thereby tends to diffuse organizational power structures as well (Fligstein, 1987).

The dynamics of imitation depend not only on the advantages that come to an organization as it profits from the experience of others but also on the gains or losses that accrue to those organizations from which the routines or beliefs are drawn (DiMaggio & Powell, 1983). In many (but not all) situations involving considerations of technical efficiency, diffusion of experience has negative consequences for organizations that are copied. This situation is typified by the case of technical secrets, where sharing leads to loss of competitive position. In many (but not all) situations involving considerations of legitimacy, diffusion of experience has positive consequences for organizations that are copied. This situation is typified by the case of accounting practices, where sharing leads to greater legitimacy for all concerned.

The critical factor for the dynamics is less whether the functional impetus is a concern for efficiency or legitimacy than whether the feedback effects are positive or negative (Wiewel & Hunter, 1985). Where concerns for technical efficiency are associated with positive effects of sharing, as for example in many symbiotic relations within an industry, the process will unfold in ways similar to the process of institutionalization. Where concerns for legitimacy are associated with negative effects of sharings, as for example in cases of diffusion where mimicking by other organizations of lower status reduces the lead organization's status, the process will unfold in ways similar to the spread of secrets.

ECOLOGIES OF LEARNING

Organizations are collections of subunits learning in an environment that consists largely of other collections of learning subunits (Cangelosi & Dill, 1965). The ecological structure is a complication in two senses. First, it complicates learning. Because of the simultaneously adapting behavior of other organizations, a routine may produce different outcomes at different times, or different routines may produce the same outcome at different times. Second, an ecology of learners complicates the systematic comprehension and modeling of learning processes. Environments change endogenously, and even relatively simple conceptions of learning become complex.

Learning in a World of Learners

Ecologies of learning include various types of interactions among learners, but the classical type is a collection of competitors. Competitors are linked partly through the diffusion of experience, and understanding learning within competitive communities of organizations involves seeing how experience, partly secrets, are shared (Sitkin, 1986), and how organizational actors come to trust one another, or not (Zucker, 1986). Competitors are also linked through the effects of their actions on each other. One organization's action is another organization's outcome. As a result, even if learning by an individual organization were entirely internal and direct, it could be comprehended only by specifying the competitive structure.

Suppose competitors learn how to allocate resources to alternative technologies (strategies, procedures) in a world in which the return received by each competitor from the several technologies is a joint consequence of the potentials of the technologies, the changing competencies of the several competitors within the technologies, and the allocations of effort by the several competitors among the technologies (Khandwalla, 1981). In a situation of this type, it has been shown that there are strong ecological effects (Herriott et al., 1985). The learning outcomes depend on the number of competitors, the rates at which they learn from their own experience, the rates at which they adjust their targets, the extent to which they learn from the experience of others, and the differences in the potentials of the technologies. There is a tendency for organizations to specialize and for faster learners to specialize in inferior technologies.

Learning to Learn

Learning itself can be viewed as one of the technologies within which organizations develop competence through use and among which they choose on the basis of experience. The general (nonecological) expectation is that learning procedures will become common when they lead to favorable outcomes and that organizations will become effective at learning when they use learning routines frequently. The ecological question is whether there are properties of the relations among interacting organizations that lead some of them to learn to learn and others not to do so.

In competitive situations, small differences in competence at learning will tend to accumulate through the competency multiplier, driving slower learners to other procedures. If some organizations are powerful enough to create their own environments, weaker organizations will learn to adapt to the dominant ones, that is they will learn to learn (Heimer, 1985b). By the same token, powerful organizations, by virtue of their ability to ignore competition, will be less inclined to learn from experience and less competent at doing so (Engwall, 1976). The circumstances under which these learning disabilities produce a disadvantage, rather than an advantage, are more complicated to specify than might appear, but there is some chance that a powerful organization will become incapable of coping with an environment that cannot be arbitrarily enacted (Hannan & Freeman, 1984).

LEARNING AS A FORM OF INTELLIGENCE

Organizational learning from experience is not only a useful perspective from which to describe organizational change; it is also an important instrument of organizational intelligence. The speculation that learning can improve the performance, and thus the intelligence, of organizations is confirmed by numerous studies of learning by doing, by case observations, and by theoretical analyses. Since we have defined learning as a process rather than as an outcome, the observation that learning is beneficial to organizations is not empty. It has become commonplace to emphasize learning in the design of organizations, to argue that some important improvements in organizational intelligence can be achieved by giving organizations capabilities to learn quickly and precisely (Duncan & Weiss, 1979; Starbuck & Dutton, 1973). As we have seen, however, the complications in using organizational learning as a form of intelligence are not trivial.

Nor are those problems due exclusively to avoidable individual and organizational inadequacies. There are structural difficulties in learning from experience. The past is not a perfect predictor of the future, and the experimental designs generated by ordinary life are far from ideal for causal inference (Brehmer, 1980). Making organizational learning effective as a tool for comprehending history involves confronting several problems in the structure of organizational experience: (a) The paucity of experience problem: Learning from experience in organizations is compromised by the fact that nature provides inadequate experience relative to the complexities and instabilities of history, particularly when the environment is changing rapidly or involves many dangers or opportunities, each of which is very unlikely. (b) The redundancy of experience problem: Ordinary learning tends to lead to stability in routines, to extinguish the experimentation that is required to make a learning process effective. (c) The complexity of experience problem: Organizational environments involve complicated causal systems as well as interactions among learning organizations. The various parts of the ecology fit together to produce learning outcomes that are hard to interpret.

Improving the Structure of Experience

The problems of paucity, redundancy, and complexity in experience cannot be eliminated, but they can be ameliorated. One response to the paucity of experience is the augmentation of direct experience through the diffusion of routines. Diffusion increases the amount of experience from which an organization draws and reduces vulnerability to local optima. However, the sharing of experience through diffusion can lead to remarkably incomplete or flawed understandings. For example, if the experiences that are combined are not independent, the advantages of sharing are attenuated, and organizations are prone to exaggerate the experience base of the encoded information. Indeed, part of what each organization learns from others is likely to be an echo of its own previous knowledge (Anderson, 1848).

Patience is a virtue. There is considerable evidence that organizations often change through a sequence of small, frequent changes and inferences formed from experience with them (Zald, 1970). Since frequent changes accentuate the sample size problem by modifying a situation before it can be comprehended, such behavior is likely to lead to random drift rather than improvement (Lounamaa & March, 1987). Reducing the frequency or magnitude of change, therefore, is often an aid to comprehension, though the benefits of added information about one situation are purchased at a cost of reduction in information about others (Levinthal & Yao, 1988).

The sample size problem is particularly acute in learning from low probability, high consequence events. Not only is the number of occurrences small, but the organizational, political, and legal significance of the events, if they occur, often muddies the making of inferences about them with conflict over formal responsibility, accountability, and liability. One strategy for moderating the effects of these problems is to supplement history by creating hypothetical histories of events that might have occurred (Tamuz, 1987). Such histories draw on a richer, less politically polarized set of interpretations, but they introduce error inherent in their hypothetical nature.

Difficulties in overcoming the redundancy of experience and assuring adequate variety of experience is a familiar theme for students of organizational change (Tushman & Romanelli, 1985). Organizational slack facilitates unintentional innovation (March, 1981), and success provides self-confidence in managers that leads to risk-taking (March & Shapira, 1987); but in most other ways success is the enemy of experimentation (Maidique

& Zirger, 1985). Thus, concern for increasing experimentation in organizations focuses attention on mechanisms that produce variations in the failure rate, preferably independent of the performance level. One mechanism is noise in the measurement of performance. Random error or confusion in performance measurement produces arbitrary experiences of failure without a change in (real) performance (Hedberg & Jönsson, 1978). A second mechanism is aspiration level adjustment. An aspiration level that tracks past performance (but not too closely) produces a failure rate—thus a level of search and risk taking—that is relatively constant regardless of the absolute level of performance (March, 1988).

A second source of experimentation in learning comes from imperfect routine-maintenance—failures of memory, socialization, or control. Incomplete socialization of new organizational members leads to experimentation, as do errors in execution of routines or failures of implementation (Pressman & Wildavsky, 1973). Although it seems axiomatic that most new ideas are bad ones (Hall, 1976), the ideology of management and managerial experience combine to make managers a source of experimentation. Leaders are exhorted to introduce change; they are supposed to make a difference (MacCrimmon & Wehrung, 1986). At the same time, individuals who have been successful in the past are systematically more likely to reach top level positions in organizations than are individuals who have not. Their experience gives them an exaggerated confidence in the chances of success from experimentation and risk taking (March & Shapira, 1987).

Overcoming the worst effects of complexity in experience involves improving the experimental design of natural experience. In particular, it involves making large changes rather than small ones and avoiding multiple simultaneous changes (Lounamaa & March, 1987; Miller & Friesen, 1982). From this point of view, the standard version of incrementalism with its emphasis on frequent, multiple, small changes cannot be, in general, a good learning strategy, particularly since it also violates the patience imperative discussed above (Starbuck, 1983). Nor, as we have suggested earlier, is it obvious that fast, precise learning is guaranteed to produce superior performance. Learning that is somewhat slow and somewhat imprecise often provides an advantage (Herriott et al., 1985; Levinthal & March, 1981).

The Intelligence of Learning

The concept of intelligence is ambiguous when action and learning occur simultaneously at several nested levels of a system (March, 1987). For example, since experimentation often benefits those who copy successes more than it does the experimenting organization, managerial illusions of control, risk taking, and playful experimentation may be more intelligent from the point of view of a community of organizations than from the point of view of organizations that experiment. Although legal arrangements, such as patent laws, attempt to reserve certain benefits of experimentation to those organizations that incur the costs, these complications seem, in general, not to be resolved by explicit contracts but through sets of evolved practices that implicitly balance the concerns of the several levels (March, 1981). The issues involved are closely related to similar issues that arise in variation and selection models (Gould, 1982; Holland, 1975).

Even within a single organization, there are severe limitations to organizational learning as an instrument of intelligence. Learning does not always lead to intelligent behavior. The same processes that yield experiential wisdom produce superstitious learning, competency traps, and erroneous inferences. Problems in learning from experience stem partly from inadequacies of human cognitive habits, partly from features of organization, partly from characteristics of the structure of experience. There are strategies for ameliorating some of those problems, but ordinary organizational practices do not always generate behavior that conforms to such strategies.

The pessimism of such a description must, however, be qualified by two caveats. First, there is adequate evidence that the lessons of history as encoded in routines are an important basis for the intelligence of organizations. Despite the problems, organizations learn. Second, learning needs to be compared with other serious alternatives, not with an ideal of perfection. Processes of choice, bargaining, and selection also make mistakes. If we calibrate the imperfections of learning by the imperfections of its competitors, it is possible to see a role for routine-based, history-dependent, target-oriented organizational learning. To be effective, however, the design of learning organizations must recognize the difficulties of the process and in particular the extent to which intelligence in learning is often frustrated, and the extent to which the comprehension of history may involve slow rather than fast adaptation, imprecise rather than precise responses to experience, and abrupt rather than incremental changes.

Acknowledgments

This research has been supported by grants from the Spencer Foundation, the Stanford Graduate School of Business, and the Hoover Institution. We are grateful for the comments of Robert A. Burgelman, Johan P. Olsen, W. Richard Scott, and William H. Starbuck.

REFERENCES

Anderson, H. C. (1848). Det er ganske vist. In P. Høybe (Ed.), *H. C. Andersens Eventyr* (pp. 72-75). Copenhagen: Forlaget Notabene.

Argote, L., Beckman, S., & Epple, D. (1987). *The persistence and transfer of learning in industrial settings.* Paper presented at the meeting of the Institute of Management Sciences (TIMS) and the Operations Research Society of America (ORSA), St. Louis, MO.

Argyris, C., & Schön, D. (1978). *Organizational learning.* Reading: MA: Addison-Wesley.

Arthur, W. B. (1984). Competing technologies and economic prediction. *IIASA Options, 2,* 10-13.

Asher, H. (1956). *Cost-quantity relationships in the airframe industry.* Santa Monica, CA: RAND.

Astley, W. G. (1985). The two ecologies: Population and community perspectives on organizational evolution. *Administrative Science Quarterly, 30,* 224-241.

Barley, S. R. (1988). The social construction of a machine: Ritual, superstition, magical thinking and other pragmatic responses to running a CT Scanner. In M. Lock & D. Gordon (Eds.), *Knowledge and practice in medicine: Social cultural and historical approaches* (pp. 33-80). Hingham, MA: Reidel.

Becker, H. S. (1982). *Art worlds.* Berkeley: University of California Press.

Beyer, J. M. (1981). Ideologies, values, and decision making in organizations. In P. C. Nystrom & W. H. Starbuck (Eds.), *Handbook of organizational design* (pp. 166-202). Oxford, UK: Oxford University Press.

Biggart, N. W. (1977). The creative-destructive process of organizational change: The case of the post office. *Administrative Science Quarterly, 22,* 410-426.

Brehmer, B. (1980). In one word: Not from experience. *Acta Psychologica, 45,* 223-241.

Brown, R. H. (1978). Bureaucracy as praxis: Toward a political phenomenology of formal organizations. *Administrative Science Quarterly, 23,* 365-382.

Brunsson, N. (1985). *The irrational organization: Irrationality as a basis for organizational action and change.* Chichester, UK: Wiley.

Brytting, T. (1986). The management of distance in antiquity. *Scandinavian Journal of Management Studies, 3,* 139-155.

Burchell, S., Colin, C., & Hopwood, A. G. (1985). Accounting in its social context: Towards a history of value added in the United Kingdom. *Accounting, Organizations, and Society, 10,* 381-413.

Burgelman, R. A. (1988). Strategy-making as a social learning process: The case of internal corporate venturing. *Interfaces, 18,* 74-85.

Cangelosi, V. E., & Dill, W. R. (1965). Organizational learning: Observations toward a theory. *Administrative Science Quarterly, 10,* 175-203.

Carroll, G. R. (1984). Organizational ecology. *Annual Review of Sociology, 10,* 71-93.

Clark, B. R. (1972). The organizational saga in higher education. *Administrative Science Quarterly, 17,* 178-184.

Cooper, A. C., & Schendel, D. E. (1976). Strategic responses to technological threats. *Business Horizons, 19*(1), 61-63.

Cyert, R. M., & March, J. G. (1963). *A behavioral theory of the firm.* Englewood Cliffs, NJ: Prentice Hall.

Daft, R. L., & Lengel, R. H. (1984). Information richness: A new approach to managerial behavior and organization design. In B. M. Staw & L. L. Cummings (Eds.), *Research in organizational behavior* (Vol. 6, pp. 191-223). Greenwich, CT: JAI.

Daft, R. L., & Weick, K. E. (1984). Toward a model of organizations as interpretation systems. *Academy of Management Review, 9,* 284-295.

Day, G. S., & Montgomery, D. B. (1983). Diagnosing the experience curve. *Journal of Marketing, 47,* 44-58.

DiMaggio, P. J., & Powell, W. W. (1983). The iron cage revisited: Institutional isomorphism and collective rationality in organizational fields. *American Sociological Review, 48,* 147-160.

Duncan, R., & Weiss, A. (1979). Organizational learning: Implications for organizational design. In B. M. Staw (Ed.), *Research in organizational behavior* (Vol. 1, pp. 75-123). Greenwich, CT: JAI.

Dutton, J. M., & Freedman, R. D. (1985). External environment and internal strategies: Calculating, experimenting, and imitating in organizations. In R. B. Lamb (Ed.), *Advances in strategic management* (Vol. 3, pp. 39-67). Greenwich, CT: JAI.

Dutton, J. M., & Starbuck, W. H. (1978). Diffusion of an intellectual technology. In K. Krippendorff (Ed.), *Communication and control in society* (pp. 489-511). New York: Gordon & Breach.

Dutton, J. M., & Thomas, A. (1984). Treating progress functions as a managerial opportunity. *Academy of Management Review, 9,* 235-247.

Dutton, J. M., & Thomas, A. (1985). Relating technological change and learning by doing. In R. S. Rosenbloom (Ed.), *Research on technological innovation, management and policy* (Vol. 2, pp. 187-224). Greenwich, CT: JAI.

Dutton, J. M., Thomas, A., & Butler, J. E. (1984). The history of progress functions as a managerial technology. *Business History Review, 58,* 204-233.

Einhorn, E. J., & Hogarth, R. M. (1986). Judging probable cause. *Psychological Bulletin, 99,* 3-19.

Engwall, L. (1976). Response time of organizations. *Journal of Management Studies, 13,* 1-15.

Eyre, D. P., Suchman, M. C., & Alexander, V. D. (1987). *The social construction of weapons procurement: Proliferation as rational myth.* Paper presented at the annual meeting of the American Sociological Association, Chicago.

Fiol, C. M., & Lyles, M. A. (1985). Organizational learning. *Academy of Management Review, 10,* 803-813.

Fischhoff, B. (1975). Hindsight or foresight: The effect of outcome knowledge on judgment under uncertainty. *Journal of Experimental Psychology, 1,* 288-299.

Fligstein, N. (1985). The spread of the multidivisional form among large firms, 1919-1979. *American Sociological Review, 50,* 377-391.

Fligstein, N. (1987). The intraorganizational power struggle: Rise of finance personnel to top leadership in large corporations, 1919-1979. *American Sociological Review, 52,* 44-58.

Gould, S. J. (1982). Darwinism and the expansion of evolutionary theory. *Science, 216,* 380-387.

Häaging, I. (1979). Reviews of capital investments: Empirical studies. *Finnish Journal of Business and Economics, 28,* 211-225.

Häkansson, H. (1987). *Industrial technological development: A network approach.* London: Croom Helm.

Hall, R. H. (1968). Professionalization and bureaucratization. *American Sociological Review, 33,* 92-104.

Hall, R. I. (1976). A system pathology of an organization: The rise and fall of the old *Saturday Evening Post. Administrative Science Quarterly, 21,* 185-211.

Hannan, M. T., & Freeman, J. (1977). The population ecology of organizations. *American Journal of Sociology, 82,* 929-964.

Hannan, M. T., & Freeman, J. (1984). Structural inertia and organizational change. *American Sociological Review, 49,* 149-164.

Harrison, J. R., & March, J. G. (1984). Decision making and post-decision surprises. *Administrative Science Quarterly, 29,* 26-42.

Hastie, R., Park, B., & Weber, R. (1984). Social memory. In R. S. Wyer & T. K. Srull (Eds.), *Handbook of social cognition* (Vol. 2, pp. 151-212). Hillsdale, NJ: Lawrence Erlbaum.

Hedberg, B. L. T. (1981). How organizations learn and unlearn. In P. C. Nystrom & W. H. Starbuck (Eds.), *Handbook of organizational design* (pp. 3-27). Oxford, UK: Oxford University Press.

Hedberg, B. L. T., & Jönsson, S. (1978). Designing semi-confusing information systems for organizations in changing environments. *Accounting, Organizations, and Society, 3,* 47-64.

Heimer, C. A. (1985a). *Reactive risk and rational action: Managing moral hazard in insurance contracts.* Berkeley: University of California Press.

Heimer, C. A. (1985b). Allocating information costs in a negotiated information order: Interorganizational constraints on decision making in Norwegian oil insurance. *Administrative Science Quarterly, 30,* 395-417.

Herriott, S. R., Levinthal, D., & March, J. G. (1985). Learning from experience in organizations. *American Economic Review, 75,* 298-302.

Hilke, J. C., & Nelson, P. B. (1987). Caveat innovator: Strategic and structural characteristics of new product innovations. *Journal of Economic Behavior and Organization, 8,* 213-229.

Holland, J. H. (1975). *Adaptation in natural and artificial systems: An introductory analysis with applications to biology, control and artificial intelligence.* Ann Arbor: University of Michigan Press.

Hollander, S. (1965). *The sources of increased efficiency: A study of DuPont rayon manufacturing plants.* Cambridge: MIT Press.

House, R. J., & Singh, J. V. (1987). Organizational behavior: Some new directions for i/o psychology. *Annual Review of Psychology, 38,* 669-718.

Imai, K., Nonaka, I., & Takeuchi, H. (1985). Managing the new product development process: How Japanese companies learn and unlearn. In K. Clark, R. Hayes, & C. Lorentz (Eds.), *The uneasy alliance* (pp. 337-375). Cambridge, MA: Harvard Graduate School of Business.

Johnson, H. T., & Kaplan, R. S. (1987). *Relevance lost: The rise and fall of management accounting.* Cambridge, MA: Harvard Graduate School of Business.

Johnson, M. K., & Hasher, L. (1987). Human learning and memory. *Annual Review of Psychology, 38,* 631-668.

Kahneman, D., Slovic, P., & Tversky, A. (Eds.). (1982). *Judgment under uncertainty: Heuristics and biases.* Cambridge, UK: Cambridge University Press.

Kay, N. M. (1979). *The innovating firm: A behavioral theory of corporate R&D.* New York: St. Martin's.

Khandwalla, P. N. (1981). Properties of competing organizations. In P. C. Nystrom & W. H. Starbuck (Eds.), *Handbook of organizational design* (pp. 409-432). Oxford, UK: Oxford University Press.

Kimberly, J. R. (1981). Managerial innovation. In P. C. Nystrom & W. H. Starbuck (Eds.), *Handbook of organizational design* (pp. 84-104). Oxford, UK: Oxford University Press.

Knoke, D. (1982). The spread of municipal reform: Temporal, spatial, and social dynamics. *American Journal of Sociology, 87,* 1314-1334.

Krieger, S. (1979). *Hip capitalism.* Beverly Hills, CA: Sage.

Lant, T. K. (1987). *Goals, search, and risk taking in strategic decision making.* Doctoral thesis, Stanford University.

Levinthal, D. A., & March, J. G. (1981). A model of adaptive organizational search. *Journal of Economic Behavior and Organization, 2,* 307-333.

Levinthal, D. A., & Yao, D. A. (1988). *The search for excellence: Organizational inertia and adaptation.* Unpublished manuscript.

Levy, J. S. (1986). Organizational routines and the causes of war. *International Studies Quarterly, 30,* 193-222.

Lindblom, C. E. (1959). The "science" of muddling through. *Public Administration Review, 19,* 79-88.

Lounamaa, P. H., & March, J. G. (1987). Adaptive coordination of a learning team. *Management Science, 33,* 107-123.

Machina, M. J. (1987). Choice under uncertainty: Problems solved and unsolved. *Journal of Economic Perspectives, 1,* 121-154.

MacCrimmon, K. R., & Wehrung, D. A. (1986). *Taking risks: The management of uncertainty.* New York: Free Press.

MacRae, D. (1985). *Policy indicators.* Chapel Hill: University of North Carolina Press.

Maidique, M. A., & Zirger, B. J. (1985). The new product learning cycle. *Research Policy, 14,* 299-313.

Mansfield, E. (1968). *The economics of technological change.* New York: Norton.

March, J. G. (1981). Footnotes to organizational change. *Administrative Science Quarterly, 26,* 563-577.

March, J. G. (1987). Ambiguity and accounting: The elusive link between information and decision making. *Accounting, Organizations, and Society, 12,* 153-168.

March, J. G. (1988). Variable risk preferences and adaptive aspirations. *Journal of Economic Behavior and Organization, 9,* 5-24.

March, J. G., & Olsen, J. P. (1975). The uncertainty of the past: Organizational learning under ambiguity. *European Journal of Political Research, 3,* 147-171.

March, J. G., & Shapira, Z. (1987). Managerial perspectives on risk and risk taking. *Management Science, 33,* 1404-1418.

Martin, J., & Siehl, C. (1983, Autumn). Organizational culture and counterculture: An uneasy symbiosis. *Organizational Dynamics,* pp. 52-64.

Martin, J., Sitkin, S. B., & Boehm, M. (1985). Founders and the elusiveness of a culture legacy. In P. J. Frost, L. F. Moore, M. R. Louis, C. C. Lundberg, & J. Martin (Eds.), *Organizational culture* (pp. 99-124). Beverly Hills, CA: Sage.

Mazmanian, D. A., & Nienaber, J. (1979). *Can organizations change? Environmental protection, citizen participation, and the corps of engineers.* Washington, DC: Brookings Institution.

Merton, R. K. (1940). Bureaucratic structure and personality. *Social Forces, 18,* 560-568.

Meyer, J. W., & Rowan, B. (1977). Institutionalized organizations: Formal structure as myth and ceremony. *American Journal of Sociology, 83,* 340-363.

Mezias, S. J. (1987). *Technical and institutional sources of organizational practices: The case of a financial reporting method.* Doctoral thesis, Stanford University.

Miller, D., & Friesen, P. (1982). Structural change and performance: Quantum vs. piecemeal-incremental approaches. *Academy of Management Journal, 25,* 867-892.

Miller, D. T., & Ross, M. (1975). Self-serving biases in the attribution of causality. *Psychological Bulletin, 82,* 213-225.

Moore, M. H., & Gates, M. J. (1986). *Inspector-general: Junkyard dogs or man's best friend?* New York: Russell Sage.

Muth, J. F. (1986). Search theory and the manufacturing progress function. *Management Science, 32,* 948-962.

Nelson, R. R., & Winter, S. G. (1982). *An evolutionary theory of economic change.* Cambridge, MA: Harvard University Press.

Neustadt, R. E., & May, E. R. (1986). *Thinking in time: The uses of history for decision makers.* New York: Free Press.

Nystrom, P. C., & Starbuck, W. H. (1984, Spring). To avoid organizational crisis, unlearn. *Organizational Dynamics,* pp. 53-65.

Olsen, J. P. (1976). The process of interpreting organizational history. In J. G. March & J. P. Olsen (Eds.), *Ambiguity and choice in organizations* (pp. 338-350). Bergen, Norway: Universitetsforlaget.

Olsen, J. P. (1983). *Organized democracy.* Bergen, Norway: Universitetsforlaget.

Ouchi, W. G. (1980). Markets, bureaucracies and clans. *Administrative Science Quarterly, 25,* 129-141.

Pettigrew, A. M. (1985). *The awakening giant: Continuity and change in imperial chemical industries.* Oxford: Blackwell.

Pfeffer, J. (1981). *Power in organizations.* Marshfield, MA: Pitman.

Powell, W. W. (1986). *How the past informs the present: The uses and liabilities of organizational memory.* Paper presented at the Conference on Communication and Collective Memory, University of Southern California, Los Angeles.

Pressman, J. L., & Wildavsky, A. B. (1973). *Implementation.* Berkeley: University of California Press.

Preston, L., & Keachie, E. C. (1964). Cost functions and progress functions: An integration. *American Economic Review, 54,* 100-107.

Radner, R. (1975). A behavioral model of cost reduction. *Bell Journal of Economics, 6,* 196-215.

Rapping, L. (1965). Learning and World War II production functions. *Review of Economic Statistics, 47,* 81-86.

Rogers, E. M., & Shoemaker, F. F. (1971). *Communication of innovations.* New York: Free Press.

Rosenberg, N. (1982). *Inside the black box: Technology and economics.* Cambridge, UK: Cambridge University Press.

Ross, J., & Staw, B. M. (1986). Expo 86: An escalation prototype. *Administrative Science Quarterly, 31,* 274-297.

Røvik, K. A. (1988). Organized learning in public administration. *First Scandinavian symposium for organizational research,* Hemsedal, Norway.

Scott, W. R. (1985). Conflicting levels of rationality: Regulators, managers, and professionals in the medical care sector. *Journal of Health Administration Education, 3,* 113-131.

Scott, W. R. (1987). *Organizations: Rational, natural, and open systems* (2nd ed.). Englewood Cliffs: NJ: Prentice Hall.

Siegel, S. (1957). Level of aspiration and decision making. *Psychology Review, 64,* 253-262.

Simon, H. A. (1955). A behavioral model of rational choice. *Quarterly Journal of Economics, 69,* 99-118.

Simon, H. A. (1971). Designing organizations for an information rich world. In M. Greenberger (Ed.), *Computers, communications and the public interest* (pp. 37-52). Baltimore, MD: Johns Hopkins University Press.

Sitkin, S. B. (1986). *Secrecy in organizations: Determinants of secrecy behavior among engineers in three Silicon Valley semiconductor firms.* Doctoral thesis, Stanford University.

Slovic, P., Fischhoff, B., & Lichtenstein, S. (1977). Behavioral decision theory. *Annual Review of Psychology, 28,* 1-39.

Smith, H. T., & Green, T. R. G. (Eds.). (1980). *Human interaction with computers.* New York: Academic Press.

Sproull, L. S. (1981). Beliefs in organizations. In P. C. Nystrom & W. H. Starbuck (Eds.), *Handbook of organizational design* (pp. 203-224). Oxford, UK: Oxford University Press.

Sproull, L. S., Weiner, S., & Wolf, D. (1978). *Organizing an anarchy: Belief, bureaucracy, and politics in the National Institute of Education.* Chicago: University of Chicago Press.

Starbuck, W. H. (1976). Organizations and their environments. In M. D. Dunnette (Ed.), *Handbook of industrial and organizational psychology* (pp. 1067-1123). Chicago: Rand McNally.

Starbuck, W. H. (1983). Organizations as action generators. *American Sociological Review, 48,* 91-102.

Starbuck, W. H., & Dutton, J. M. (1973). Designing adaptive organizations. *Journal of Business Policy, 3,* 21-28.

Starbuck, W. H., & Milliken, F. J. (1988). Executives' perceptual filters: What they notice and how they make sense. In D. Hambrick (Ed.), *Executive effect: Concepts and methods for studying top managers* (pp. 35-66). Greenwich, CT: JAI.

Staw, B. M., & Ross, J. (1978). Commitment to a policy decision: A multi-theoretical perspective. *Administrative Science Quarterly, 23,* 40-64.

Steinbruner, J. D. (1974). *The cybernetic theory of decision.* Princeton, NJ: Princeton University Press.

Stinchcombe, A. L. (1986). *Stratification and organization.* Cambridge, UK: Cambridge University Press.

Tamuz, M. (1987). The impact of computer surveillance on air safety reporting. *Columbia Journal of World Business, 22,* 69-77.

Thompson, J. D. (1967). *Organizations in action.* New York: McGraw-Hill.

Tirole, J. (1986). Hierarchies and bureaucracies: On the role of collusion in organizations. *Journal of Law, Economics, and Organizations, 2,* 181-214.

Tolbert, P. S., & Zucker, L. G. (1983). Institutional sources of change in the formal structure of organizations: The diffusion of civil service reform, 1880-1935. *Administrative Science Quarterly, 28,* 22-39.

Tushman, M. L., & Romanelli, E. (1985). Organizational evolution: A metamorphosis model of convergence and reorientation. In L. L. Cummings & B. M. Staw (Eds.), *Research in organizational behavior* (pp. 171-222). Greenwich, CT: JAI.

Van Maanen, J. (1973). Observations on the making of policemen. *Human Organization, 32,* 407-418.

Weick, K. E. (1979). *The social psychology of organizing* (2nd ed.). Reading, MA: Addison-Wesley.

Whetten, D. A. (1987). Organizational growth and decline processes. *Annual Review of Sociology, 13,* 335-358.

Wiewel, W., & Hunter, A. (1985). The interorganizational network as a resource: A comparative case study on organizational genesis. *Administrative Science Quarterly, 30,* 482-496.

Wildavsky, A. (1983). Information as an organizational problem. *Journal of Management Studies, 20,* 29-40.

Winter, S. G. (1986). The research program of the behavioral theory of the firm: Orthodox critique and evolutionary perspective. In B. Gilad & S. Kaish (Eds.), *Handbook of behavioral economics* (pp. 151-187). Greenwich, CT: JAI.

Wright, T. P. (1936). Factors affecting the cost of airplanes. *Journal of Aeronautical Science, 3,* 122-128.

Yelle, L. E. (1979). The learning curve: Historical review and comprehensive survey. *Decision Science, 10,* 302-328.

Zald, M. N. (1970). *Organizational change: The political economy of the YMCA.* Chicago: University of Chicago Press.

Zucker, L. G. (1977). The role of institutionalization in cultural persistence. *American Sociological Review, 42,* 726-743.

Zucker, L. G. (1986). Production of trust: Institutional sources of economic structure, 1840 to 1920. In L. L. Cummings & B. M. Staw (Eds.), *Research in organizational behavior* (pp. 55-111). Greenwich, CT: JAI.

Zucker, L. G. (1987). Institutional theories of organization. *Annual Review of Sociology, 13,* 443-464.

23

Learning Through Failure

The Strategy of Small Losses

SIM B SITKIN

This chapter concerns the benefits of failing and the liabilities of success and, contrary to the traditional scholarly and managerial emphasis on failure avoidance, argues that failure is an essential prerequisite for effective organizational learning and adaptation. Recent research is drawn on to examine the processes by which failure can enhance learning, adaptation to changing environmental conditions, and systemic resilience when confronting unknown future changes. A conceptual foundation for future empirical research is proposed that distinguishes the critical characteristics of failures that are hypothesized to foster organizational learning. Designs for systemic failure promotion in organizations are conceptualized and illustrated by application to three important organizational concerns —innovation, safety and security, and mergers and acquisitions.

INTRODUCTION

Common sense suggests that failure is something to be avoided. After all, failure can stigmatize: the taint of failure can jeopardize even the most stellar career or the most successful organizational track record (Sutton & Callahan, 1987). Not surprisingly, evidence indicates that organizations, like individu-

This chapter appeared originally in *Research in Organizational Behavior,* Vol. 14. Copyright © JAI Press, Inc.

als, prefer success over failure. There is ample evidence of the influence of failure-avoidance norms (Argyris, 1985; Michael & Mirvis, 1977), including research on risk aversion, the denial of bad news, and the retrospective revision of negative history (Bies, 1990; Browning, 1988; Sitkin & Pablo, forthcoming). Mirvis and Berg (1977) put it well: "In our culture, failure is anathema. We rarely hear about it, we never dwell on it and most of us do our best never to admit to it. Especially in organizations, failure is often simply not tolerated and people avoid being associated with failure of any kind."

But is failure unequivocally bad, or is it possible that failure may actually be a safety and survival-enhancing asset in organizations? In order to provide a framework for responding to this question, this paper systematically examines the benefits of failing and the liabilities of success. In challenging the notion that failure is to be avoided and success pursued, theorists have marshaled varied evidence that suggests that the absence of failure experiences can result in decreased organizational resilience when faced with changing circumstances (Douglas & Wildavsky, 1982; Wildavsky, 1988) and managerial overconfidence in the ability to foresee risks inherent in complex organizational problems (March & Shapira, 1987). Rather than stressing failure avoidance, I will argue that failure is an essential prerequisite for learning, as it stimulates the sort of experimentation that Campbell (1969) and others (March, 1978; Staw, 1983; Weick, 1979; Wildavsky, 1988) have advocated as fundamental for sound policy development and organizational management.

Despite attention to the issue of failure in the organizational literature, previous research has lacked the strong, integrated conceptual underpinning that is essential to cumulative theory development and empirical research. Thus, the goal of this paper is to draw together and extend the disparate efforts of previous authors and to provide a more systematic and explicit framework for further conceptual and empirical research.

This paper is separated into four sections. The first section summarizes arguments concerning the benefits and liabilities of success. The second section explores the value of failure and distinguishes systematic failure from which one can learn, from failure that does not foster learning. The third section highlights the need for organizationally sponsored programs designed to induce constructive failure (referred to as "strategic failure"). In the final section, the implications for organizational theory and managerial practice will be explored, including a brief note on how the strategic failure approach can be applied to several organizational concerns: fostering innovation, safety and security, and mergers and acquisitions.

THE EFFECTS OF SUCCESS

The Benefits of Success

Winning isn't the most important thing: it's the only thing. (Green Bay Packers Coach Vince Lombardi, quoted in O'Brien, 1987, p. 16)

Our theories and our common sense make clear the value of success. Success is helpful in a number of ways—the rewards of success stimulate confidence and persistence, increase the coordinated pursuit of common goals, and enhance efficiency. Organizational success typically results in monetary or symbolic rewards. Furthermore, when we know what works well and feel confident in our competence and achievements, we are more likely to be highly motivated and satisfied. Armed with the rewards of success, individuals are more likely to move ahead confidently, with less hesitation or second-thoughts when faced with minor obstacles or setbacks. Success stimulates persistence not merely because people (and organizations) are rewarded for success, but also because success provides a secure and stable basis for the launching of future activity (Weick, 1984).

By focusing attention and activity on that which is known to work well, an emphasis on success enhances efficiency. Success can eliminate from consideration suboptimal routines, as only the most high performing and/or reliable approaches need to be used. Little time is needed to search for new solutions to problems, since frequently encountered problems can be handled with the use of previously proven, standardized procedural routines. Even if the specific version of the correct course of action turns out to be erroneous, merely having a vision can help in enacting further successful goal achievement because it fosters a more unified, coordinated approach (Weick, 1979).

In summary, if the goal is to promote stability and short-term performance, success provides an excellent foundation for reliable performance. Success tends to encourage the maintenance of the status quo and, so long as current environmental conditions favor such a stance, the operating efficiencies and employee satisfaction associated with "staying the course" can be considerable.

Hypothesis 1. The greater the degree or consistency of prior success, the greater the degree of efficiency can be achieved through the use of focused search and proven, standard procedural routines.

Hypothesis 2. The greater the degree or consistency of prior success, the higher the degree to which goals and values will be shared by employees.

Hypothesis 3.   The greater the degree or consistency of prior success, the more the organizations will exhibit operational stability and coordination among subunits and activities.

Hypothesis 4.   The greater the degree or consistency of prior success, the higher the level of motivation and confidence to persist in the face of minor obstacles or setbacks.

The Liabilities of Success

It is paradoxical but true to say that "failure was born of success." (Nonaka, 1985, p. 13)

The benefits of success are not only well grounded in the literature and in our experiences, they are also intuitive. But what about the drawbacks? While less salient than its benefits, successful outcomes do have four associated liabilities that will be briefly described: complacency, restricted search and attention, risk-aversion, and homogeneity.

Complacency

It is difficult to get people or groups to pursue new ways of doing things when the current ways are relatively successful. Success sends a reinforcing signal that no corrective action is necessary ("if it ain't broke, don't fix it") and thereby reduces the motivation to initiate seemingly unnecessary adaptation. In addition, because successful outcomes are usually credited to the actor's own plans and efforts (Ross & Sicoly, 1979), there is little motivation to pursue new approaches following success. This tendency is likely to be exacerbated to the extent that danger, inconvenience, or embarrassment could be associated with newer and more risky procedures.

A second set of complacency-fostering pressures arise from how blame is allocated in organizations. Simply put, action is more salient than the absence of action. As a result, attributions of causality and blame are drawn to those individuals (or groups) who have acted and failed, more than to those who have failed to act. Thus, there is much more likely to be the risk of blame associated with trying something new, whereas sticking to the old ways of doing things poses very little risk of incurring personal liability for resultant problems (Sitkin & Bies, 1989). That is, there is an inherent risk asymmetry in organizations: problems that result from taking risks often lead to individual punishment, whereas problems that result from the avoidance of risky action are rarely traced to individuals and less often lead to punishment (Browning, 1988; Sitkin & Bies, 1988). Thus, it is not surprising that research has suggested that success tends to perpetuate the status quo by affecting our willingness to take risks. Success has been associated with conservative, risk-averse approaches to decision making (Kahneman & Tversky, 1979; Sitkin & Pablo, forthcoming). Such responses are likely to lead to an avoidance of the risk inherent in new, unproven methods or options.

Weick (1984) has noted that the fear of failure—especially with respect to large-scale social problems—fosters immobilization and the use of dysfunctional performance routines because "the quality of thought and action declines, [and] because processes such as frustration, arousal, and helplessness are activated" (p. 40). In response, Weick has usefully suggested that we formulate large, potentially overwhelming, problems as "mere problems" of a less imposing scale with which individuals can more easily cope. Weick proposed that, by breaking down large scale problems into a series of modest, achievable steps that result in "small wins," we are more likely to be able to motivate constructive action.

Although it is sensible as a way of scaling down problems, Weick's small wins proposal overlooks one important issue: small successes may unintentionally induce low levels of attention and reduced information search. That is, the low level of positive feedback that Weick proposes as a solution (in the form of "wins") is unlikely to draw attention to problems or opportunities or to stimulate learning because it is insufficiently disruptive to attract notice (Weick, 1979, 1986) and, even when attention is drawn, the mantle of success —however modest—still bestows an overconfidence that past routines and assumptions have been proven adequate (Hedberg, 1981; Louis & Sutton, 1991). This sense of system adequacy, in turn, is likely to serve as an obstacle to learning and adjustment, as there is little perceived need to alter that which is operating adequately. Under conditions of low attention and low stimulation, individuals will tend to adhere to old routines, attending only to traditionally relevant information (which reinforces those routines) because there are no signals that indicate the need to try to look for new information or to try new routines.

Homogeneity

When they have been successful, firms tend to stick with their successful "formula," maintaining the same operating procedures and the same (or at least the same type of) personnel. The more uniform and extreme the success of an organization's prior experiences, the greater I would hypothesize would be the tendency to develop homogeneous employee demographic distributions (Kanter, 1977),[1] monolithic corporate cultures (Martin & Meyerson, 1988), and less diverse activity and information sets. I would also expect these changes to have more than a simple additive dampening effect on learning, in that homogeneous hiring and retention practices are likely to further strengthen the pull of inbred coalition and core cultural traditions, making it less likely that suggestions for change or experimentation will even be raised.

Hypothesis 5. The greater the degree or consistency of prior success, the less expansive will be search activities.

Hypothesis 6. The greater the degree or consistency of prior success, the less attention will be paid to whatever discrepant information is made available.

Hypothesis 7. The greater the degree or consistency of prior success, the greater the complacency about experimenting with new or different procedures, personnel, structures, or ideas.

Hypothesis 8. The greater the degree or consistency of prior success, the greater the level of risk aversion.

Hypothesis 9. The greater the degree or consistency of prior success, the greater the proclivity to homogenize personnel, subcultures, and administrative or technical procedures.

AN ALTERNATIVE TO SUCCESS: STRATEGIC FAILURE

With each tottering attempt to walk, our bodies learn from the falls what not to do next time. In time we walk without thinking and think without falling, but it is not so much that we have learned to walk as we have learned not to fall. (Petroski, 1985, p. 13)

Given the abilities and limitations of the success-oriented approaches that have dominated managerial and scholarly thinking, an alternative—one that emphasizes the value of failure—merits closer scrutiny. The analogy between learning to "not fall" and learning from failure suggests that, rather than focusing on the impossible ideal of *learning by avoidance* (without falling), it is more fruitful for both theory and practice to ask how organizations might more effectively pursue *learning by experimentation* (Campbell, 1969; Hedberg, Nystrom, & Starbuck, 1976). Learning through experimentation involves experiencing falls and trying out new adjustments to try "not to fall." Like learning not to fall, the process of learning from failure can be analyzed in terms of the factors that foster more or less effective learning (for recent reviews, see Huber, 1991; Levitt & March, 1988).

The Benefits of Failing

> You have to suffer failures occasionally in order to have successes. You've got to back up risk-takers in order to encourage people to try out new ideas that might succeed . . . I never had much patience with the "play it safe" manager who attempted to minimize failures. Those people rarely have successes. (Former Utah Governor Scott M. Matheson, Matheson & Kee, 1986, p. 226)

It sounds like Orwellian "doublespeak" to say "failing is good." But a closer analysis of the problems associated with success suggests why the seemingly counterintuitive may be advisable. Where success can foster decreased search and attention, increased complacency, risk-aversion, and maladaptive homogeneity, modest levels of failure can promote a willingness to take risks and foster resilience-enhancing experimentation—benefits that complement the liabilities of success.

Attention and the Processing of Potential Problems

Because failure challenges the status quo, it can draw attention to potential problems and stimulate the search for potential solutions (Downs, 1976; Langer, 1989; March & Simon, 1958). Just as success signals that "all is well" and, as a result, does not engender "thoughtful" processing of situational information (Langer, 1978), failure typically represents an exception that does not conform to expectations and thus requires more active, deeper processing. Existing routines are more likely to be maintained when performance remains above aspiration levels, while failure challenges current practices and procedures by drawing attention to previously overlooked problems and inconsistencies. While there is a temptation to dismiss failures as resulting from random processes or isolated events (Bettman & Weitz, 1983; Bies, 1989; Bies, Shapiro, & Cummings, 1988; Salancik & Meindl, 1984), even such public rationalizations can serve to draw attention to a previously overlooked problem.

Ease of Recognition and Interpretation

Performance failure and implementation errors draw attention by providing a clear signal that something is amiss and must be changed. But they do more than just draw attention. As Cameron (1984) has observed, "it is easier for individuals to identify criteria for ineffectiveness—that is faults or weaknesses—than it is to identify criteria for effectiveness—that is, competencies or desirable outcomes" (p. 245). In our terms, failure represents a "clear signal" that facilitates the recognition and interpretation of otherwise ambiguous outcomes. For example, when a "small win" is noticed, it may be unclear whether it represents good news (it was a win), or bad news (it wasn't very big). In contrast, when a small failure is noticed, it is more likely to signal unequivocally that this outcome represents a recognizable problem or (equally valuable) to highlight the need to grapple with a novel type of problem. A heuristic that reflects this perspective on the information value of failure was captured by Lounamaa and March (1987) in their decision rule that "treats performance improvements as confounded but treats performance decrements as containing information" (p. 116).

Stimulating Search Processes

Although large failures are likely to be more effective than small ones in drawing attention, large failures are also less likely than modest ones to be effective in translating that attention into the activation of search processes. In the face of large and potentially threatening losses, organizational responses are more likely to be protective than exploratory. This proposition is consistent with a diverse set of empirical findings on individual and group responses to threat, including hypervigilence (Janis & Mann, 1977), threat-rigidity responses (Staw, Sandelands, & Dutton, 1981), reliance on over-learned behaviors (Weick, 1985), and the escalation of commitment to prior routines (Staw & Ross, 1987). Smaller failures, because they are less threatening, may be able to attain the dual goal of capturing attention while avoiding threat-induced truncation of search.

Motivation to Adapt

Whereas a successful formula fosters little or no impetus to alter existing routines and policies, the experience of failure produces a learning readiness that is difficult to produce without a felt need for corrective action (Cameron, 1984). The reasons that failure stimulates action are straightforward. First, failure provides a clear, identifiable target, and corrective action is more likely to be initiated when there is a specific stimulus or rationale for acting (Cyert & March, 1963; Locke & Latham, 1990). Second, when there is a problem, the sort of action that is undertaken is usually aimed at correcting the identifiable problem—that is, the actions that failure stimulates typically involve adapting to the new circumstances or new difficulties that are suddenly recognized (Hedberg, 1981). Third, the signal that errors have been made and may have negative consequences can also fuel a more general willingness to consider new alternatives and to reconsider institutionalized traditions, even when the identifiable "problem" subsequently shifts (Hedberg,

Nystrom, & Starbuck, 1976). In this sense, errors fuel a Lewinian "unfreezing" process, in which old ways of perceiving, thinking, or acting are shaken and new ways can be accommodated, perhaps for the first time (Louis & Sutton, 1991).

Risk Tolerance

Failure experiences have been associated with increased risk-seeking, just as success has been associated with increased risk-aversion (Kahneman & Tversky, 1979). Although risk-seeking has its obvious drawbacks if taken to an extreme (Singh, 1986), in moderation it is associated with increased innovation and the capacity to adapt to changing circumstances (Sitkin & Pablo, forthcoming). For example, Peters (1987; Peters & Waterman, 1982) has suggested that one of the keys to achieving and sustaining high firm performance is a willingness to take risks and the ability to admit to failure and learn from it. Evidence for this contention can be found in diverse contexts, including merger decision making (Haspeslagh & Jemison, 1991; Jemison & Sitkin, 1986), safety hazard management (Tamuz, 1987), and industrial innovation (Petroski, 1985).

Requisite Variety

Failure can induce experimentation that, in turn, leads to increased variation in organizational response repertoires. March and his colleagues have argued for the value of variation in choice strategies, processes, and outcomes (Herriott, Levinthal, & March, 1985; Levinthal & March, 1981; Levitt & March, 1988; March, 1978, 1988; March & Shapira, 1987) as a means of enhancing performance and promoting learning. Several simulation studies suggested that unequivocally positive feedback fosters faster learning, but may lead to premature specialization in a suboptimal response set and, thus, poorer performance (Herriott et al., 1985; Levinthal & March, 1981). That is, when decision processes are characterized by slower learning, a wider variety of choices may be explored and long-term performance enhanced.

Failure concurrently fuels experimentation and is a natural, unavoidable outcome of experimentation. Because failure stimulates experimentation with new strategies, new methods, and even new personnel, failure can foster additional variety that broader experimentation implies. The more varied the internal capabilities of the organization (in terms of systems, routines, and personnel), the more adaptable the organization will be when confronting unforeseen difficulties (Weick, 1979). Research on technological innovation and biological evolution illustrates this point with reference to mutation:

Simple replication alone will not produce evolutionary change. Random error in the process generates the possibility for successful evolutionary change. . . . Consequently, a life system can suffer from *an amount of error that is insufficient to generate sustainable change.* (DeGregori & Matson, 1987, pp. 4 and 10, emphasis added)

An evolutionary approach to failure-related variation rests on the idea that intelligent choices (equivalent to "selection" in evolutionary theory) rely on the effective production of options from which to choose (through evolutionary "variation"). Unless an organization can produce and retain diverse information, potential choice options will be less varied (Tamuz & Sitkin, 1989) and the opportunity for their intentional or unintentional learning will be reduced (Huber, 1991). As one evolutionary theorist put it, "the more numerous and greater the heterogeneity of variations, the richer the opportunities for an advantageous innovation" (Campbell, 1965, p. 28).

Practice

Failure is not an inherently desirable outcome. Rather, failure is a more effective means of pursuing learning than is success because failure provides "small doses of experience to discover uncertainties unpredictable in advance" (Wildavsky, 1988, p. 26).[2] Because organizations that face changing environmental requirements must learn if they are to survive, an exclusive focus on short-term performance (by solely emphasizing success) jeopardizes concerns essential to long-term organizational effectiveness— and survival.

In arguing for the benefits of risk-taking, Wildavsky (1988) has suggested that when faced with complex problems of major proportions (e.g., managing toxic materials, public health hazards, or transportation safety), the best route to pursue is that of experimentation, rather than the apparently "safer" route of risk avoidance. Wildavsky contends that experimentation is an essential process in nature, by which organisms become more resilient to future environmental changes. It serves this function by providing information about unknown processes, varied experience relevant to unforeseen events, and an orientation that is more flexible and adaptive. That is, experience with small, varied failures reduces the likelihood that unanticipated changes will spark a self-defeating, threat-rigidity response.

Hypothesis 10. The greater the incidence of small prior failure, the more attention will be paid to and the more deeply will be the processing of information about potential problems.

Hypothesis 11.   The greater the incidence of small prior failure, the more potential problems will have been readily recognized and interpreted.

Hypothesis 12.   The greater the incidence of small prior failure, the greater the level of search.

Hypothesis 13.   The greater the incidence of small prior failure, the more flexible and open to change will be the organization, its subunits, and its individual members.

Hypothesis 14.   The greater the incidence of small prior failure, the greater the level of risk tolerance.

Hypothesis 15.   The greater the incidence of small prior failure, the more variety in the personnel and procedures used in the organization.

Hypothesis 16.   The greater the incidence of small prior failure, the more the organization will have obtained experience and practice that is relevant to future, unforeseen problems.

The analysis to this point has distinguished the short-term performance-focused benefits of success from the more long-term learning-focused benefits of failure. This discussion has been necessarily general, drawing a rather crude distinction between success and failure. But, to argue convincingly that failure is beneficial, it is essential to be more precise about what sorts of failure are likely to be beneficial and what sorts of failure are less useful. In the next section, I address this issue.

THE EFFECTS OF SUCCESS AND FAILURE ON ORGANIZATIONAL LEARNING

Learning in organizations can take two forms—it can involve the development of increasingly efficient and reliable routines or it can take the form of increased resilience when confronted with novel situations. These are comparable to the distinction between adaptation and adaptability (Boulding, 1978).

Thus, organizations face a trade-off. To the extent that organizations are successful at adaptation, they are necessarily sacrificing their ability to be adaptive. The essence of the argument is that success fosters reliability, whereas failure fosters resilience. This is depicted in Figure 23.1, which illustrates the hypothesized effects of success and failure on a number of organizational features, and the ultimate effect on short- and long-term performance via enhanced organizational reliability and adaptability.

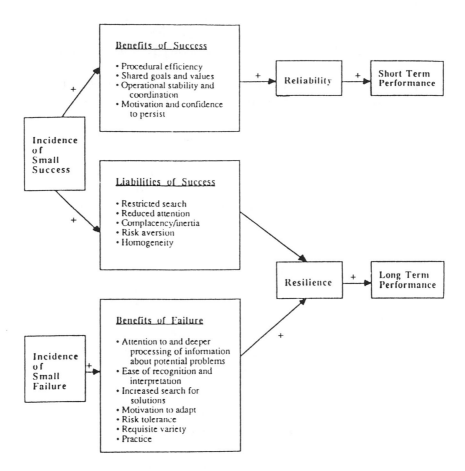

Figure 23.1. The Benefits and Liabilities of Success and Failure

Organizational Reliability

    Reliability is one of the most important goals an organization can achieve.
Sustained, predictable organizational actions and outcomes are most likely
to be achieved by adhering to well established methods and familiar domains.
That is, reliability results from finding a successful formula and then sticking
to it until it can be implemented exceptionally well. The achievement of
reliability implies a number of factors are in place and functioning
smoothly—well trained and motivated personnel, close coordination of
tasks, high degree of agreement about goals and values, as well as a number

of other factors. As noted in the previous sections, many of these factors can be attributed, at least in part, to prior success. Success breeds efficiency in part because employees who associate procedures, leaders, and goals with past successes are more likely to exert the extra effort and care that is required to achieve the predictability and reliability that can assure modest but steady levels of short-term performance.

Organizational Adaptability

By reducing the incentives to experiment, success fosters the repetitive use of highly efficient activity sets. This form of specialization can be a very effective organizational strategy when the firm operates in a stable environmental niche. But, by avoiding the inefficiency of "foolish" behaviors (March, 1976) that could serve as useful preparation for unknown future situations, success enhances short-term performance at the cost of making it harder to learn from experience for the long-term (Wildavsky, 1988). Siu (1968) provides a useful illustration, drawn from the work of Maeterlinck:

> place in a bottle half a dozen bees and the same number of files, and lay the bottle down horizontally, with its base to the window. . . . [T]he bees will persist, till they die of exhaustion or hunger, in their endeavor to discover an issue through the glass; while the flies, in less than two minutes, will have sallied forth through the neck on the opposite side. . . . [The bees' love of light] is their undoing in this experiment. They evidently imagine that the issue from every prison must be where the light shines clearest; and they act in accordance, and persist in too logical action. . . . Whereas the feather-brained flies, careless of logic as of the enigma of crystal, disregarding the call of the light, flutter wildly hither and thither, and meeting here the good fortune that often waits on the simple, who find salvation there where the wiser will perish, necessarily end by discovering the friendly opening that restores their liberty to them. (p. 189)

The root of the problem is that success leads to persistence at the expense of adaptability (Levinthal & March, 1981; March, 1978). Thus, labeling an experience as a "win" is preferable when stability is preferred over change. However, when adaptation is preferred—especially when a general state of adaptability (Nonaka, 1985) or "resilience" (Wildavsky, 1988) is the goal— labeling experience as "minor failure" or "small loss" is more likely to attract attention and stimulate adjustment, without incurring the threat-rigidity response (Staw et al., 1981) or strong negative affective response (Russell & McAuley, 1986; Whitley, 1986) to large-scale failures that Weick (1984) appropriately wished to avoid.

CRITERIA FOR INTELLIGENT FAILURE

Give me a fruitful error any time, full of seed, bursting with its own corrections.
(Vilfredo Pareto, commenting on the scientific contributions of Kepler)

Failure should not be pursued for its own sake. It is a means to an end, not the end itself. If the goal is learning, then unanticipated failure is the unavoidable byproduct associated with the risks inherent in addressing challenging problems. While any *particular* failure cannot be predicted, the probability of *some* failure occurring may be precisely and reliably specifiable.

Not all failures are equally adept at facilitating learning. Those failures that are most effective at fostering learning will be referred to as "intelligent failure" (after Matson, 1989). Five key characteristics that contribute to the intelligence of failures are: (1) they result from thoughtfully planned actions that (2) have uncertain outcomes and (3) are of modest scale, (4) are executed and responded to with alacrity, and (5) take place in domains that are familiar enough to permit effective learning.

Well-Planned Actions

Actions that are well planned and designed can provide a wealth of diagnostic information, regardless of whether they succeed or fail. By instituting a set of actions that have a chance of succeeding, it is possible to glean invaluable information from observed processes and outcomes about alternative ways of acting in the future. For more complex situations, it may be necessary to initiate and coordinate a larger number of independent actions in order to obtain a distribution of outcomes from which underlying probabilities and processes can be estimated. For example, when dealing with low probability events, such as problems in high reliability systems (e.g., Perrow, 1984; Roberts & Rousseau, 1989; Tamuz, 1987), it may be necessary to collect extremely large quantities of data to insure a sufficient number of "observations" to assess the causes of success and failure. One obvious way to increase available data is to increase the level of experimental activity— for example, when executives simultaneously assign the same task to more than one project team (e.g., George, 1981) or when multiple "reforms" are implemented concurrently in independent groups (Campbell, 1969). Another way is to broaden the conception of the problem—for example, when airline accidents are studied by examining "near misses" as well as actual accidents (Tamuz, 1987). In any case, to recognize and learn from feedback, it is essential that actions be thoughtfully designed and executed.

Uncertain Outcomes

Planning is not enough. For failure to be beneficial, the outcome of action must be uncertain. If outcomes are deterministic (i.e., predictable), then the experienced outcome of action provides no new information from which to learn (DeGregori & Matson, 1987; Wildavsky, 1988). Failures that are highly predictable are not "intelligent" because they do not provide any basis for altering future behavior, since no new information has been produced via the experience of failing. It may be important to reemphasize in this context that failure itself is not the goal—the goal is to obtain information that would not be available without the experience.

Modest Outcome Scale

The magnitude of the failure is also important. As Weick (1984) notes, by scaling down problems (i.e., potential outcomes of action) we can make them more amenable to effective human response. To enhance our ability to respond, Weick suggests that our actions should be designed to produce more modest, human scale outcomes (he stresses "small wins," but also refers to "small flops"). A footnote to Weick's observation can be gleaned from Lounamaa and March's caution (1987) that outcome changes must be of sufficient magnitude to rise above the level of background noise. Lounamaa and March's insight recognizes that outcomes do not occur in a pristine, information-free setting, but occur amidst a buzz of organizational action that competes for limited human attention and perceptual capacities. Taken together, the work of Weick and Lounamaa and March suggests that scale is crucial and requires delicate balancing to achieve large enough outcomes to attract attention, but small enough outcomes to avoid negative responses.

Speedy Action Cycles

Learning requires information. Making strategic failure feasible and useful involves insuring that action and feedback happens fast enough that data is quickly generated for evaluation and feedback, so that learning can occur expeditiously. The idea is to continually try out new risky ideas and obtain quick and accurate feedback on whether they seem to work so that equally quick adjustments can be made prior to a new round of experimentation.

The faster the action-failure-action cycle, the more feedback that can be gathered and used for adjustments. Speed is especially important in addressing large, complex interconnected problems for which large quantities of outcome data are needed (e.g., Perrow, 1984). Speedier processes can be manifest in several ways. A number of analysts have noted the importance of engaging in a number of small, rapid-fire experimental actions that provide quick feedback and allow for small, quick adjustments that lead to a new round of small experiments. Argyris and Schön (1978) refer to the importance of "theory in action," Peters and Waterman (1982) refer to "action bias," and George (1981) refers to "trial balloons." The common thread through their varied terms and foci is that learning is facilitated when information is quickly generated, evaluated, and adjusted to. This may be especially important when the organization's competitive or institutional environment is changing rapidly.

Domain Relevance

Although the combination of decreased scale and increased speed are likely to foster faster adaptation and learning, they are not sufficient to define intelligent failure. It is hard to be intelligent about that which is unfamiliar or irrelevant. Failure that occurs in a domain that is not relevant to the organization's future is not likely to be noticed or understood, and is therefore unlikely to stimulate attention, consideration, or responsive action (Payne, 1989). It is essential that the domain of action be familiar enough that novel outcomes are recognizable and interpretable. If the domain is too foreign, it will be very difficult to cull useful lessons from failure experiences, in part because of the difficulty of adequately planning actions or anticipating potential outcomes when in unfamiliar domains (Sitkin, Pablo, & Jemison, 1991).

Double-loop learning (Argyris, 1982; Argyris & Schön, 1978) essentially relies on failures that challenge assumptions. However, when failure challenges *fundamental* organizational assumptions, the implications (or even the facts) of the experience may be ignored or denied if they elicit defensive routines (Argyris, 1985) that serve to protect the integrity of the organization's cultural core. Because "new knowledge is not likely to be accepted if it conflicts greatly with the paradigm held by the organization's members" (Duncan & Weiss, 1979, p. 95), failure is unlikely to be particularly helpful to the extent that it is seen as either unrelated or a fundamental challenge. This is not to suggest that failure in novel areas is useless, but only that actions that extend or modestly challenge existing assumptions, expertise, or strategic goals make learning from failures more likely. Thus, how an outcome is portrayed may have strong implications for whether a failure experience is likely to stimulate learning and which parts of the organization are most likely to learn.[3]

ORGANIZATIONAL CONDITIONS THAT
FACILITATE INTELLIGENT FAILURE

To be successful . . . one must learn to dream of failure. (Henry, 1965)

In the previous sections, the effects and characteristics of intelligent failure were described. In this section, the organizational conditions that are associated with the increased incidence of intelligent failure will be examined to make explicit the implications of the "strategy of small losses" for the design of organizations—a question of substantial importance for applied researchers and practitioners.

By drawing on the work of previous authors (e.g., Cleese, 1988; Matson, 1989; Peters, 1987; Weick, 1984), a number of specific mechanisms can be identified by which organizations can systematically promote intelligent failure. Organizational prerequisites of intelligent failure will be described in terms of four goals: (1) to increase the focus on process (rather than outcomes); (2) to legitimate intelligent failure; (3) to engender and sustain individual commitment to intelligent failure through organizational culture and design; and (4) to emphasize failure management systems rather than individual failure. When put together, these four elements comprise a systematic approach to organizational failure that will be referred to as "strategic failure." These influences are discussed below and shown in Figure 23.2.

Organizational Focus on
Process Over Outcome

Although the discussion has focused on the importance of failure, recall the earlier admonition that failure cannot itself be the goal—instead, the target is to foster the generation of natural outcome distributions that include sufficient amounts of failure. Because problems that are good candidates for intelligent failure are, by definition, problems for which outcomes are uncertain, one cornerstone of a strategic failure approach is to emphasize the processes that foster intelligent failure by trying to remove procedural constraints on natural experimentation. If systems for managing failure are implemented well, then there is no need to directly manage the outcomes, because a varied range of outcomes will be generated naturally. A process focus can be conceptualized in terms of three distinct elements: action independence, challenging aspiration levels, and fast feedback coupled with slow learning.

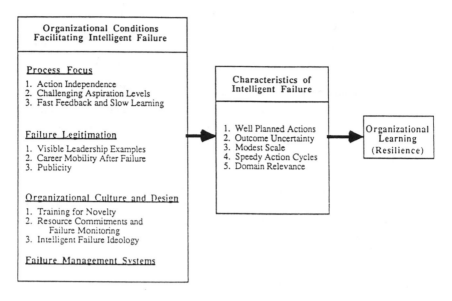

Figure 23.2. Organizational Conditions Fostering Intelligent Failure and Learning

Action Independence

Reducing the scale of action serves several purposes. I have already discussed how scale reductions can enhance the willingness to take risks, in part because the real or perceived consequences of failure are reduced. Scale reductions also increase the degree to which a wide array of independent actions can be generated based on decentralized decision making. In contrast with large scale actions, which can usually be undertaken only by a select group of higher level managers with appropriate levels of authority, actions of modest dimensions can be undertaken by many more lower level employees or independent subgroups, thus generating a larger, more independent database from which to draw implications. With sufficient risk and a sufficiently large number of small "experiments," failure patterns can begin to emerge and be recognized (March, 1976).

Challenging Aspiration Levels

The adjustment of aspiration levels to assure that goals remain challenging is critical to insuring sufficient numbers and modest levels of failure experience. When goals are too easy, aspiration levels will be routinely exceeded, providing no incentive to modify methods used in goal attainment (Cyert & March, 1963). The easy achievement of such "small wins" is also likely to foster a low risk/low effort strategy on the part of individuals, since the expected value of extra effort or creative solutions may be negative when compared with safe, goal directed action (Levitt & March, 1988). The net result of low aspiration levels (i.e., unchallenging goals) on the distribution of outcomes is that many small predictable successes will occur, in part because of how success was defined (i.e., as clearing a low hurdle). In contrast, few failures will be observed, but those that are observed will tend to be large. Both successes and failures may be difficult to learn from, because the underlying distribution from which they are drawn is unknown and the singular goal of such systems is short-term performance and the information necessary to learn from experience may be absent (Lounamaa & March, 1987).

In contrast, there is a strong theoretical and empirical basis for concluding that modestly challenging goals foster higher performance, due to increased effort and attention as well as due to increased learning from experience (Locke & Latham, 1990; Naylor & Ilgen, 1984). Although the substantial literature on individual learning provides a wealth of insight about how to encourage successful learning, only two points from this literature will be raised here. One general finding is that incremental learning (with its ego-building positive reinforcement) is generally effective in building the confidence and skills essential for sustained motivation and performance. This evidence would seem to favor the adoption of a small wins approach because it stresses the value of providing continuous positive reinforcements. However, learning is also built upon increasingly challenging tasks that sustain interest (Locke & Latham, 1990; White, 1959). Furthermore, the strongest form of reinforcement is intermittent, in which feedback is discontinuous— either due to neutral "time outs" from positive or negative feedback or due to the mixing of positive and negative performance feedback. The notion of intermittent reinforcement and its action-sustaining properties is more consistent with a small losses strategy than with a small wins approach since, as I have argued, only by intentionally pursuing intelligent failure can a natural distribution of outcomes (i.e., an intermittent mix of positive, neutral, and negative reinforcements) be attained.

Fast Feedback and Slow Learning

The final element of a process focus is to decouple the speed of action/ feedback from the speed of learning. The case presented previously for the benefits of fast action/feedback/adjustment sequences can be interpreted as implying that quick learning of small lessons is a beneficial thing. However, there is a counter-force that needs to be acknowledged as well. The problem with a fast action/feedback/adjustment process is that it involves quick but potentially misleading learning that can lead organizations to pursue catastrophic policies with undue confidence and little or no reflection. In quick learning, adjustments in plans and beliefs are made on the basis of relatively little outcome information, which may not be representative or accurate and which may be difficult to interpret because of complex contextual changes. This process has been described by Weick (1979) as "deviation amplifying loops" and has also been characterized as a factor in "groupthink" (Janis, 1972) and "escalating commitment" (Staw & Ross, 1987).

Without denying the benefits of quick action and adjustment, we can nonetheless acknowledge that fast learning has its liabilities (Levinthal & March, 1981) in that too frequent adjustments can be "based on observations that are too unreliable. . . . Initiating changes less frequently counteracts the noise by providing a larger sample size and reduces the effect of simultaneous changes" (Lounamaa & March, 1987, p. 121). Lounamaa and March's observation implies that action and feedback be speeded up, but that plan revision (i.e., learning from the feedback) be slowed down until a sufficient number of outcomes have occurred. That is, they essentially propose that we more loosely tie action and learning.[4]

Organizational Legitimation of Intelligent Failure

March (1976) has noted that experimentation-related failure is "intelligent" from the perspective of the organization, but is not necessarily beneficial for the individuals who are generating the failures and must pay its price. Thus, in addition to establishing a supportive set of organization-level processes that can facilitate strategic failure, it is essential to reassure individuals that failure is indeed legitimate in the organization and that intelligent failure will be accepted and supported. Organizational protection of individual risk-taking in effect serves to transform "foolish," high-risk individual experimentation into intelligent, pragmatic individual-level action. This can be done in three ways: (1) having leaders stress the importance of failure; (2) providing evidence of the positive (or at least neutral) effect of intelligent failure on career mobility and rewards; and (3) as part of the first two points, publicizing intelligent failures.

Visible Leadership and Failure

Leadership recognition of the value of failure is important, but more important still is that leaders make a clear public commitment to supporting staff who are willing to undertake intelligent failure. Consider the public statements of two executives (Peters, 1987, p. 315). Soichiro Honda, founder of Honda Motor, has been publicly associated with the following statement: "Many people dream of success. To me success can only be achieved through repeated failure and introspection. In fact, success represents the 1 percent of your work which results from the 99 percent that is called failure." Gordon Forward, President of Chaparral Steel makes a similar point, "You've got to have an atmosphere where people can make mistakes. If we're not making mistakes, we're not going anywhere."

Although it may be difficult for administrators to admit to personal failures, organizational stories that highlight the foibles of executives or other organizational heroes can serve to make the leaders seem more human and understanding of what it takes to get the job done. While Horatio Alger stories can provide a model for how to climb flawlessly to the top, few employees realistically hope to keep their ankles dry while walking on water. Stories which depict a leader mistake that is quickly acknowledged and learned from will tend to send a much more encouraging and realistic message (Cleese, 1988). The point is that visible leadership is a crucial aspect of failure management, both in terms of articulating a firm's strategic failure approach (McCall, Lombardo, & Morrison, 1988) and in exemplifying it through memorable stories (Martin, Feldman, Hatch, & Sitkin, 1983) and other cultural symbols (Trice & Beyer, 1988).

Career Mobility and Failure

If individuals who fail are doomed to wander the back streets of orga-nizational life, then few will take the risks necessary for innovation and fewer still will tackle tough problems when those problems can be passed along to someone else. Consider, for example, when rising stars are identified early in organizational mobility ladders. Under such conditions, the most talented individuals in the firm—those who may be best suited to undertaking the most difficult, failure-prone projects—are placed in a position where they cannot afford to undertake long-term or especially challenging projects because it is so easy to slip from the fast track.

Perhaps the clearest assessment of the link between career development and the legitimacy of failure is offered by Gaertner (1988): "failure should be treated more as an episodic event from which a great deal can be learned and less as an indication of 'unfitness' to manage" (p. 316). Premature judgment can lead to inappropriate and counterproductive judgments of employees. For example, because failure definitions change as aspiration levels, needs, or leader priorities change, today's apparently botched assign-ment may be recognized in retrospect as a critical contribution.[5] If individuals or their contributions are judged too prematurely, valuable careers can be sidetracked unnecessarily.

For assurances of the recognized value of intelligent failure to be meaningful and convincing to employees, there must be visible examples of individuals who have experienced failure and whose careers within the firm were not harmed (Gaertner, 1988). For example, James Burke (Chairman of Johnson & Johnson) tells with pride of how he experienced an early and highly visible failure. Instead of a reprimand or a firing, he reports receiving the personal congratulations of then Chairman General Robert Woods Johnson for his willingness to take a risk in order to try to innovate (Johnson & Johnson, 1988). Burke makes clear the message that risk-taking and task-related failure are not going to hurt an employee's career prospects at Johnson & Johnson, where "a mistake can be badge of honor."

It has been argued that failure should not merely be tolerated, it should be designed intentionally into management development programs (Solomon, 1989). Whether this involves rotating potential leaders into functional areas outside their expertise, putting them into positions that "stretch" their competencies (McCall et al., 1988), or intentionally giving them assignments that they are unlikely to be able to master, the key is that the design of management development reflects an understanding that "executives who have experienced failure on a smaller scale earlier in their careers are probably better able to recognize, learn from, cope with, and avoid larger business failures later" (Gaertner, 1988, p. 316). This basic idea can be built into an organization's human resource management programs from the earliest training programs to the development of well-rounded future executives.

Publicize Intelligent Failures

Exemplars of intelligent failure should be publicized for several reasons. First, by providing salient examples of individuals who failed at tasks and maintained a successful career, a clear message is sent to employees that risk-taking and intelligent failure is legitimate and will be rewarded. When the examples include leaders, the commitment of top management to strategic failure is conveyed. When other employees receive public recognition, then commitment to constructive experimentation can diffuse more rapidly.

A second reason to publicize intelligent failure incidents is that the concept of outcome uncertainty and intelligent failure are not simple for individuals to grasp and operationalize—and they are equally difficult for organizations to institutionalize—in part because they seem to violate so many of the cultural principles we hold dear. When concrete examples of intelligent failure are publicized and explained (Bies & Sitkin, 1991), it not only tends to legitimize failure, but also makes intelligent failure imaginable and provides templates for how to embark on the path of intelligent failure. In addition to the potential benefits of training, practice, and mentoring in experimentation, public examples of intelligent failure may also provide an easy way for employees to see how to operationalize a strategic failure approach in their own work.

Organizational Culture and Design

Organization-level systems for promoting intelligent failure should take into account the natural individual aversion to failure. Three mechanisms for addressing this issue will be discussed here: (1) training and socializing employees; (2) committing necessary resources to implement and monitor a strategic failure approach; and (3) developing an "intelligent failure ideology."

Train for Surprise and Novelty

Training by "inoculation" (i.e., exposure to a small dose of failure in order to develop resilience in the face of full-scale problems) may be one of the most effective ways to prepare employees for uncertain future situations. Through such systematic experiences, employees can also learn how to constructively handle failure experiences—both their own failures and those of their subordinates—since "people can cope with surprise better when they have repeated exposure to it" (Weick, 1985, p. 42). In addition, by incorporating novelty, surprise, and intelligent failure into training, employees can be socialized into understanding that the organization values strategic failure and learning. Put differently, without incorporating surprise and failure into training, what signal is the organization sending to employees about the importance of risk and failure and about the appropriate ways to handle these experiences? If there is no attention paid to such things in socializing employees, it sends the clear signal that failure is a problem—perhaps even a taboo topic—that is to be steadfastly avoided in formal and informal work conversations and decision making (Argyris, 1985; Goffman, 1963; Harvey, 1974; Mirvis & Berg, 1977).

Resource Commitment to and Monitoring of Failure

Firms that are committed to improvement need to operationalize that commitment by allocating staff time to innovation. Arguing that there is room for innovation in every job, Matson (1989) suggests allocating *a minimum of 5 percent* of each employee's time to experimentation, including line workers and secretaries as well as research scientists and managers. This approach is exemplified by John Ferrell, the creative director at advertising agency Young & Rubicam (Peters, 1987, p. 275). Ferrell coupled a speech to his entire employee group on the importance of taking risks with the creation of a new unit, memorably called "The Risk Lab." The Lab's director, who was given the title "Dr. Risk," was authorized to violate cultural norms by providing "quick and dirty" market research tests for unconventional ideas.

Merely allocating resources is not sufficient for "achieving" adequate failure levels. It is also important to monitor and reward failure, just as the firm monitors and rewards other aspects of an employee's or department's performance. In a firm that is serious about strategic failure, employees who are not producing enough of a "scrap pile" (Matson, 1989) might be viewed as devoting inadequate effort to taking risks, dealing with their failures, and to bringing their experiments to resolution. Firm activities could include charting experiments (including failure and success rates, scrap pile sizes, etc.), including experimentation as a formal part of job descriptions and performance reviews, and visibly rewarding experimenters with plaques, dinners, and other symbols tailored to the firm's culture. Building strategic failure into the firm's formal human resource management system and into its formal and informal culture rituals is an integral part of committing resources to intelligent failure and monitoring its implementation.

Developing an "Intelligent Failure Ideology"

Campbell (1969) proposed many of the fundamental concepts underlying strategic failure more than twenty years ago. But the key to sustaining organizational experimentation as a management or policy approach (e.g., Behn, 1976; Staw, 1983; Weick, 1984) is to develop a pervasive organizational understanding of the potential strategic value of failure and to institutionalize the legitimacy of intelligent failure. As Campbell noted, this implies a commitment to solving a problem and an acceptance of the inevitable failures that are a natural part of the problem-solving process. One approach to directly fostering such a way of thinking is to promote the view that regularity and uninterrupted success are a problem and a sign of weakness, rather than an unequivocal sign of strength. Consistent with the arguments posed here, if the absence of failure can be viewed as a signal of inertia, risk-aversion, and an inability to adapt, then the absence of observed problems or mistakes should signal the need to eliminate risk-averse routines and stagnant, unchallenging goals.

Consistent with the arguments posed here, there is a growing body of strikingly parallel evidence outside the domain of organizational research. Much like the organizational need for fits and starts of trial and error in order to learn, grow, and remain healthy, so too it seems biological organisms require performance variation in order to remain strong and viable. For example, there is some evidence that regularity in heartbeats, white blood cell activity, and brain waves are signs of health problems, whereas irregularity signals health: "A healthy heart produces an erratic EKG. A diseased heart produces EKGs with more regular patterns—and EKG patterns during a heart attack are extremely regular" ("If the symptom is order," 1989, p. 69). Thus, regularity may provide a way to predict heart attacks.

This general approach can also be seen in recent work in physics and mathematics (e.g., chaos or fractal theory, fuzzy sets) in which the credibility of smooth, regular, and deterministic definitions of complex phenomena are being challenged (Gleick, 1987). Instead, across these vastly different empirical domains there is an increasing recognition that irregularity and trial and error are characteristics of many natural processes besides the evolution of species.

Failure Management Systems

> Rather than reducing uncertainty, or attempting to control it (which may be impossible anyway), it is posited here that organizations should instead attempt to *learn* from the variance of individual behavior and use that uncertainty as feedback or "signal" . . . (freeing) itself from the classical school of formal organization which treats the variances of individual behavior as "error." (Hall & Fukami, 1979, pp. 138-139)

For all the reasons discussed previously, it is unlikely that individuals can provide a sufficient range of systematic "intentional errors" for learning to occur when complex organizational issues are involved. Individuals are primed to avoid failure, rather than to seek it. Having been rewarded for success rather than failure, the lessons learned from past experiences with success and failure are not so easily overcome. In addition to anticipated instrumental responses (e.g., pay, promotion), the symbolic and social effects of success and failure can be significant deterrents to effective failure on the part of individuals. This is not to suggest that individuals do not fail, for it is quite evident that individuals do indeed fail with unfortunate regularity. We can all think of the individual coworker who so predictably fails at any given assignment that he/she cannot be given responsibility for tasks of even modest importance. But, typically, organizations learn little or nothing from these instances because failure was so predictable that no new information was generated. The point is that isolated individual-level failures were unlikely to produce intelligent failure, as it has been defined here, because individuals are too unreliable to fail systematically.

What is needed is an organization-level perspective on the need for strategic failure. At the individual level, outcome distributions are likely to be skewed toward safe successes or predictable failures. In contrast, the implementation of strategic failure programs at the organizational level should be able to increase the number and diversity of failures, as well increasing the number of innovative successes (through the taking of greater risks and the accumulation of failure-related learning).

Although there has been no systematic research comparing individual and organizational capacities to generate and learn from failure, the analysis presented in this paper implies that organizations need to develop and actively manage failure at the system level, rather than rely on individuals to generate a sufficient supply of intelligent failures from which to learn. Because individuals seek success and avoid failure, even when top management stresses the importance of risk-taking, it is difficult to engender "intelligent failures" through typical organizational processes since organizational culture, traditions, and controls constitute institutionalized biases that insure that truly random distributions of outcomes are rarely observed. As a result, individuals simply do not generate in practice the sort of independent, trial and error experimentation that is essential for organizational learning. Fortunately, "organizations can be playful even when the participants in them are not" (March, 1976, p. 81). By speeding up the action/failure/feedback/correction cycle and by reducing the scale of actions taken, it may be possible to enhance learning by increasing the number of data points in the outcome distribution and by making point estimates in the distribution more fine grained.

Organization-level failure management involves compensatory programs that foster "play" by drawing attention to, legitimating, and rewarding intelligent failure so as to "fill out the distribution" of observed outcomes. But it is difficult to know what a compensatory program should compensate for, without having more information on the outcome distributions produced by individuals acting within an organization's cultural traditions and control systems. To establish a set of baselines that reflect differences in culture and human resource control policies, research is needed that identifies cultural and control characteristics that systematically skew outcome distributions. Based on such results a comparison could be made between the distributions produced by different cultural and control patterns and the outcome distributions produced by strategic failure systems.

IMPLICATIONS FOR FUTURE RESEARCH

There has been a surge of academic interest in the benefits of failure that can be seen across a number of disciplines. Yet, for organizational scholars, the work has lacked a strong, integrative conceptual underpinning that focuses on the central role of failure in organizational learning. The purpose of this analysis has been to draw together the strands of research on the benefits of failure so as to provide the cornerstone for more systematic theoretical and empirical work on the constructive effects of failure in organizations. Although this document provides only a preliminary conceptual outline, the potential relevance of this work to organizational research more generally is substantial.

Implications for Organizational Research

The ideas proposed here are relevant for organizational theorists concerned with commitment processes, learning in and by organizations, procedural justice, decision making and conflict, control and reward systems, culture, innovation, communication, interorganizational collaboration, institutional legitimacy, and organizational effectiveness. Although these links cannot be exhaustively explored here, the research questions listed below are stimulated by these potential connections and suggest the range of fruitful avenues for future work:

- Are there some conditions under which failure is more acceptable than others? For example, what is the effect of rising concerns with litigation on a willingness to admit to failure (Huber, 1985; Sitkin & Bies, 1989)? Does the type of failure matter and how does type of failure interact with specific situational and cultural conditions?
- To what extent do the sequences of confirming and disconfirming outcomes affect the processes described here and how does the mix and sequence of outcomes affect commitment processes (Berlinger, 1990)? In other words, what is the effect of process and outcome history (Sitkin & Pablo, forthcoming) on how current and future risks are perceived and responded to?
- Are there cross-situational similarities and differences in how individuals respond to changes in scale (i.e., modest failures versus small ones), such that learned

helplessness (Seligman, 1975) can be avoided and a sense of self-efficacy enhanced (Gecas, 1989; Wood & Bandura, 1989)?

- What is the effect of human resource management policies on the incidence of experimentation? Under what conditions do the various components (e.g., promotions, pay, symbolic rewards, training, etc.) become more or less important in fostering intelligent failure (Cardinal & Sitkin, 1990)?

- To what extent is the legitimacy of the institution or its top leadership affected by strategic failure? We know that some organizations can survive failures (Meyer & Zucker, 1989), but what are the particular conditions that can serve to buffer intelligent failure without protecting other, less productive forms of failure?

The exploration of these and other questions is the next step in pursuing research on strategic failure.

Application to Organizational Phenomena: Three Illustrations

To illustrate the relevance of the strategic failure framework for organization studies, three organizational issues will be examined briefly. To demonstrate the broad relevance of the framework proposed, these phenomena have been selected to include positive outcomes (e.g., innovation, organizational adaptation), negative outcomes (e.g., hazards, loss of secrets), and significant organizational strategies (e.g., mergers and acquisitions).

Fostering Innovation

There is substantial consensus that successful innovation requires risk-taking, experimentation, and failure. But there is little systematic evidence of what kind of failure promotion systems are being used in these innovative organizations and whether those systems differ from less innovative firms (that is one criticism, for example, of the Peters and Waterman (1982) "excellent company" research). This paper has cited a number of studies and anecdotal evidence that suggests the potential importance of strategic failure as a stimulus for innovation. But the framework needs to be tailored more specifically to innovation concerns. For example, is a small loss approach (e.g., independent trials, faster feedback, novelty training) beneficial in promoting all forms of innovation? Or, alternatively, is an emphasis on small wins better in promoting "incremental innovations," while an emphasis on small losses is most valuable for promoting "radical innovations" (Cardinal & Sitkin, 1990). Recent work on project-level innovation (Van de Ven, 1986), internal corporate venturing (Burgelman & Sayles, 1986), and the use of administrative control mechanisms to foster strategic innovation (Cardinal, 1990) provides a conceptual and empirical base upon which to build this line of research.

Managing Hazards in Organizations

The hazards faced by organizations today are of increasing complexity, defying human capacity to anticipate the unforeseen hazards seemingly innocuous actions can create (Perrow, 1984). Although some hazards may be so catastrophic that "we cannot afford to study failure" (Roberts & Rousseau, 1989, p. 132), the goal of failure-free organizations is illusory since "increasing numbers of serious errors will occur in high-reliability organizations" (Roberts & Rousseau, 1989, p. 138). Yet, as Wildavsky (1988) argues, despite our fears of the consequences of experimenting with serious hazards, the long-term costs of ignoring those hazards may be far more substantial. Thus, even in organizations for which the specter of catastrophe makes failure difficult to routinize, it is essential that large scale problems be reduced to more manageable levels to permit experimentation (e.g., Leary, 1988).

When tragedy accompanies hazard-related failures, it is too easy to overlook the net benefit to society that such failures may have generated (Wildavsky, 1988). For example, Starbuck and Milliken (1988) note that the tragedy associated with the Space Shuttle Challenger accident belies the potential disaster that could have occurred had the Challenger been launched successfully. The next scheduled launch was to have carried nuclear material that Starbuck and Milliken suggest would have contaminated the entire state of Florida had the failure that led to the Challenger's destruction occurred one flight later.

In applying the strategic failure framework to understanding the management of organizational hazards, it is essential that conceptual development clearly focus on the prototypical responses to risk exhibited by both individual and organizational decision makers (Sitkin & Pablo, forthcoming). In addition, it is critical that the distinct information requirements involved in reducing hazards and learning about them to be recognized (Wildavsky, 1988) and modeled (Tamuz & Sitkin, 1989). There is a substantial body of empirical research concerning hazards that can be examined in terms of the failure framework proposed here. This research provides excellent opportunities to apply and extend the failure framework to address issues, such as air traffic safety (Tamuz, 1987; Weick, 1988), nuclear power (Perrow, 1984; Roberts & Rousseau, 1989), industrial use of hazardous materials (Shrivastava, 1988; Shrivastava, Mitroff, Miller, & Miglani, 1988) and other technological (Petroski, 1985) and non-technological liabilities (Sitkin & Bies, 1989).

Approaches to Merger and Acquisition
Decision Making and Integration

Mergers are typically important organizational events of high potential consequence. For most organizations, significant failure in executing an important merger will threaten the organization's performance and may even threaten its viability. Like the pursuit of failure concerning potentially catastrophic hazards, the value of failure with regard to significant strategic decisions is difficult for most organizational leaders to accept.

But there is a consistent finding in the merger and acquisition literature that most such activities result in at least partial failure. In fact, it has been argued that the most insightful and successful executives at managing the merger process are those who not only have a basic strategic plan and a willingness to adjust to changing circumstances, but also have themselves experienced prior merger failures (Sitkin et al., 1991). Consistent with the framework proposed here, acquisitions can be conceptualized as experimenting and learning processes for organizations, rather than as one-time, isolated strategic decisions. Although organizations do make routine acquisitions, most acquisitions involve a significant amount of uncertainty about the validity of the firm's strategic plan, the accuracy of its assessment of its merger partner, and its ability to successfully integrate the two organizations. Thus, the recent emphasis on analyzing mergers and acquisitions as decision processes reflects the inherent indeterminacy of such complex decisions and the need to structure strategic decision making processes so that learning and adaptation can occur effectively (Haspeslagh & Jemison, 1987, 1991; Jemison & Sitkin, 1986; Sitkin et al., 1991; Thomas & Trevino, 1989).

The relevance of the strategic failure approach to mergers and acquisitions is clear in Haspeslagh and Jemison's (1987, 1991) emphasis on "acquisitive strategies." Acquisitive strategies involve an approach to mergers and acquisitions in which each particular merger or acquisition is meaningfully evaluated only in light of the firm's overall strategic goals. Thus, what might appear to be a "failed" acquisition, may in fact be part of a larger, long-term plan in which the firm (or its managers) needed to "acquire" a track record or an experienced management team in a new domain as an early stage in launching a major new strategic thrust. That is, if viewed from a learning perspective, what appears to be a failed acquisition may be more accurately understood as a set of prerequisite experiences necessary to achieve the firm's broader strategic goals. This conception of merger and acquisition activity essentially treats a merger and acquisition program as a series of organizational experiments (i.e., treating each M&A event as an experimental trial) that are guided by and provide feedback on the organization's strategic plans.

Its relevance can also be seen in how merger-related processes are handled at a more micro level. Jemison and Sitkin (1986) noted the severe problems that typically resulted when parent firms were intolerant of subsidiary mistakes. In a useful extension of this idea, Nahavandi and Malekzadeh (1988) suggested that parent firm intolerance of cultural differences can have a systematic negative effect on merger and acquisition success. For example, the failure framework proposed here helps to explain the source of the problems identified by Jemison and Sitkin or Nahavandi and Malekzadeh as being related to how much leeway is given to a newly acquired subsidiary to make mistakes before the parent firm's managers, systems, and culture are imposed.

CONCLUSION

Organizations in the United States are under increasing pressure to assure consistently high short-term performance—often at the expense of less immediate, longer-term objectives. This situation has been blamed, in part, for a competitive disadvantage faced by U.S. firms in international economic competition. Organizational scholars can contribute to this area of inquiry by examining the internal organizational processes that can foster a more long-term perspective, without ignoring the realities of short-term pressures and constraints on decision makers. One form that this interest has taken is in the area of organizational learning, which has drawn increasing attention from scholars in recent years. A focus on learning that includes both reliability and resilience provides a counterbalance to the narrow focus on short-term performance. Such an approach is especially important due to the need for many organizations to be able to adapt to rapidly changing environmental conditions.

This paper analyzes the benefits of failing and the liabilities of success for promoting organizational learning and adaptation. Whereas success, almost by definition, breeds short-term performance improvements, in this paper I have drawn on recent research in organizational behavior, strategic management, engineering, physical and natural sciences, and hazard management to argue that failure enhances adaptation to changing environmental conditions and systemic resilience to unknown future changes, both of which enhance long-term performance. I have distinguished the characteristics of failure that foster organizational learning from failure that does not, suggesting that the key to fostering organizational resilience is the systematic generation of outcome distributions that include failures. Noting that our human predisposition to pursue success implies the need for failure promotion systems at the organizational level, the implications of the idea of "strategic failure" were then applied to several important domains—innovation, safety and security, and mergers and acquisitions.

Although there has been a substantial amount of attention to the benefits of failure, the work has been noncumulative, largely anecdotal or normative, and has not been subjected to systematic empirical testing. Addressing these shortcomings will be of substantial significance to both theorists and practitioners. By drawing together previously isolated streams of research and by proposing a set of empirically testable ideas about the role of failure, this paper is intended to contribute to our understanding and management of innovation, safety and security, strategic change, and other concerns that could benefit from attention to failure management.

Acknowledgments

Portions of this paper were previously presented at the National Meeting of the Academy of Management held in Washington, D.C. in August 1989 and the Texas Conference on Organizations, Lago Vista, Texas in March 1990. Helpful comments on earlier versions of this paper were provided by Larry Cummings, Robyn Dawes, Brian Golden, George Huber, Julie Jacobson, David Jemison, Pam Ryan, Barry Staw, Kathleen Sutcliffe, James Thomas, and Karl Weick.

NOTES

1. This notion is consistent with findings that performance success is strongly correlated with homogeneity. However, the causal direction posited here is the opposite of that proposed by others, who suggest that homogeneity leads to success, whereas I have proposed that success leads to homogeneity.

2. An alternative—that will not be explored here, but merits further study—is the potential value of vicarious failure, in which failure's consequences are observed but not experienced directly (see Huber, 1991, for a general review of the extant research on vicarious organizational learning).

3. This suggests that the question of who decides how to label outcomes (as negative or positive, as well as labeling them as relevant or irrelevant) is a potentially significant form of organizational power that can affect organizational opportunities for learning.

4. However, there is a danger that such an approach, if taken to an extreme, could decay into nonexperiential learning, in which outcomes are decoupled from interpretation/learning (see March & Olsen, 1976). However, the use of faster action routines can minimize this problem, if the quicker pace can generate data quickly enough for learning to be kept at a relatively fast pace (but slower than the pace of feedback) without sacrificing quality. For example, one way to speed up action and feedback is to undertake several parallel experimental actions concurrently by a number of organizational members and subgroups, thus increasing the sample size upon which

learning can be based without prolonging the elapsed time before learning occurs. A problem with this approach is that it assumes sufficient time is available for deferred learning to occur. As was noted previously, time is essential to generate sufficient data upon which to base learning. But time is essential for at least two other reasons as well. First, individual reactions to failure involve a series of relatively predictable stages (negative effect, denial, aggression, and acceptance; Hyatt & Gottlieb, 1987) and it is likely that organizations, like individual members, need to progress to the later response stages before becoming ready to learn from failure experiences. Second, the familiar image of the decisive manager fosters an attribution of poor leadership to those who do not respond to failure quickly. Yet quick reactions are unlikely to be functional for both cognitive (inadequate information and processing time) and affective reasons (only partially processed feelings). Thus, the pressures exerted by organizational cultures makes the deferral of learning particularly difficult to carry out in practice.

5. Furthermore, once a poor performance is labeled as a "failure" versus "a learning opportunity," learning is less likely for both participants and observers (Mitchell, Green, & Wood, 1981).

REFERENCES

Argyris, C. (1982). *Reasoning, learning, and action: Individual and organizational.* San Francisco: Jossey-Bass.

Argyris, C. (1985). *Strategy: Change and defensive routines.* Boston: Pitman.

Argyris, C., & Schön, D. A. (1978). *Organizational learning.* Reading, MA: Addison-Wesley.

Behn, R. D. (1976). Closing the Massachusetts public training schools. *Policy Science, 7,* 51-171.

Berlinger, L. R. (1990). *Managing commitment to increase flexibility: An exploration of processes that strengthen and weaken commitment.* Unpublished doctoral dissertation, University of Texas at Austin.

Bettman, J. R., & Weitz, B. A. (1983). Attributions in the boardroom: Causal reasoning in corporate annual reports. *Administrative Science Quarterly, 28* 165-183.

Bies, R. J. (1989). Managing conflict before it happens: The role of accounts. In M. A. Rahim (Ed.), *Managing conflict: An interdisciplinary approach* (pp. 83-91). New York: Praeger.

Bies, R. J. (1990). *The manager as intuitive politician: Blame management in the delivery of bad news* (Working paper). Washington, DC: Georgetown University.

Bies, R. J., Shapiro, D. L., & Cummings, L. L. (1988). Causal accounts and managing organizational conflict: Is it enough to say it's not my fault? *Communication Research, 15,* 381-399.

Bies, R. J., & Sitkin, S. B. (1991). Explanation as legitimation: Excuse-making in organizations. In M. L. McLaughlin, M. J. Cody, & S. J. Reed (Eds.), *Explaining one's self to others: Reason giving in social context* (pp. 183-198). Hillsdale, NJ: Lawrence Earlbaum.

Boulding, K. E. (1978). *Ecodynamics: A new theory of social evolution.* Beverly Hills, CA: Sage.

Browning, L. D. (1988). *Plausible deniability.* Paper presented at the Academy of Management Meeting, Anaheim, CA.

Burgelman, R. A., & Sayles, L. R. (1986). *Inside corporate innovation: Strategy, structure, and managerial skills.* New York: Free Press.

Campbell, D. T. (1965). Variation and selective retention in socio-cultural evolution. In H. R. Barringer, G. I. Blanksten, & R. Mack (Eds.), *Social change in developing areas* (pp. 19-49). Cambridge, MA: Schenkman.

Campbell, D. T. (1969). Reforms as experiments. *American Psychologist, 24,* 409-429.

Cameron, K. S. (1984). The effectiveness of ineffectiveness. In B. M. Staw & L. L. Cummings (Eds.), *Research in organizational behavior* (Vol. 6, pp. 235-285). Greenwich, CT: JAI.

Cardinal, L. B. (1990). *Implementing strategy through organizational control mechanisms: Transforming strategic intent into innovation in the pharmaceutical industry.* Unpublished doctoral dissertation, University of Texas at Austin.

Cardinal, L. B., & Sitkin, S. B. (1990). *Demystifying the alchemy of strategic innovation: The role of organizational and control mechanisms in implementing strategic intent.* Paper presented at Academy of Management Meeting, San Francisco, CA.

Cleese, J. M. (1988, May 16). No more mistakes and you're through! *Forbes,* pp. 236ff.

Cyert, R. M., & March, J. G. (1963). *A behavioral theory of the firm.* Englewood Cliffs, NJ: Prentice Hall.

DeGregori, T. R., & Matson, J. V. (1987). *Chaos in emerging technology* (Working paper). Houston: University of Houston.

Douglas, M., & Wildavsky, A. (1982). *Risk and culture: An essay on the selection of technical and environmental dangers.* Los Angeles: University of California Press.

Downs, A. (1967). *Inside bureaucracy.* Boston: Little, Brown.

Duncan, R., & Weiss, A. (1979). Organizational learning: Implications for organization design. In B. M. Staw (Ed.), *Research in organizational behavior* (Vol. 1, pp. 75-123). Greenwich, CT: JAI.

Gaertner, K. N. (1988). Managers' careers and organizational change. *Academy of Management Executive, 2,* 311-318.

Gecas, V. (1989). The social psychology of self-efficacy. *Annual Review of Sociology, 15,* 291-316.

George, A. L. (1981). *Presidential decisionmaking in foreign policy: The effective use of information and advice.* Boulder, CO: Westview.

Gleick, J. (1987). *Chaos: Making a new science.* New York: Penguin.

Goffman, E. (1963). *Stigma: Notes on the management of spoiled identity.* Englewood Cliffs, NJ: Prentice Hall.

Hall, D. T., & Fukami, C. V. (1979). Organizational design and adult learning. In B. M. Staw (Ed.), *Research in organizational behavior* (Vol. 1, pp. 125-167). Greenwich, CT: JAI.

Harvey, J. B. (1974, Summer). The Abilene paradox: The management of agreement. *Organizational Dynamics,* pp. 63-80.

Haspeslagh, P., & Jemison, D. B. (1987). Acquisitions—myth and reality. *Sloan Management Review, 28*(2), 53-58.

Haspeslagh, P., & Jemison, D. B. (1991). *Managing acquisitions: From idea to results.* New York: Free Press.

Hedberg, B. (1981). How organizations learn and unlearn. In P. C. Nystrom & W. H. Starbuck (Eds.), *Handbook of organizational design* (Vol. 1, pp. 3-27). New York: Oxford University Press.

Hedberg, B., Nystrom, P. C., & Starbuck, W. H. (1976). Camping on seesaws: Prescriptions for a self-designing organization. *Administrative Science Quarterly, 21,* 41-65.

Henry, J. (1965). *Culture against man.* New York: Vintage.

Herriott, S. R., Levinthal, D., & March, J. G. (1985). Learning from experience in organizations. *American Economic Review, 75,* 298-302.

Huber, G. (1991). Organizational learning: The contributing processes and literatures. *Organization Science, 2*(1), 88-115.

Huber, P. (1985). Safety and the second best: The hazards of public risk management in the courts. *Columbia Law Review, 85,* 277-337.

Hyatt, C., & Gottlieb, L. (1987). *When smart people fail.* New York: Penguin.

If the symptom is order, the patient may be sick. (1989, January 30). *Business Week,* p. 69.

Janis, I. L. (1972). *Victims of groupthink: A psychological study of foreign policy decisions and fiascoes.* Boston: Houghton Mifflin.

Janis, I. L., & Mann, L. (1977). *Decision making: A psychological analysis of conflict, choice, and commitment.* New York: Free Press.

Jemison, D. B., & Sitkin, S. B. (1986). Corporate acquisitions: A process perspective. *Academy of Management Review, 11*(1), 145-163.

Johnson & Johnson, a mistake can be a badge of honor. (1988, September 26). *Business Week,* p. 126.

Kahneman, D., & Tversky, A. (1979). Prospect theory: An analysis of decision under risk. *Econometrica, 47,* 263-291.

Kanter, R. M. (1977). *Men and women of the corporation.* New York: Basic Books.

Langer, E. J. (1978). Rethinking the role of thought in social interaction. In J. H. Harvey, W. Ickes, & R. F. Kidd (Eds.), *New directions in attribution research* (Vol. 2). Hillsdale, NJ: Lawrence Erlbaum.

Langer, E. J. (1989). *Mindfulness.* Reading, MA: Addison-Wesley.

Leary, W. E. (1988, August 19). Purposely flawed shuttle rocket appears to pass crucial test. *New York Times,* p. A7.

Levinthal, D., & March, J. G. (1981). A model of adaptive organizational search. *Journal of Economic Behavior and Organization, 2,* 307-333.

Levitt, B., & March, J. G. (1988). Organizational learning. *Annual Review of Sociology, 14,* 319-340.

Locke, E. A., & Latham, G. P. (1990). *A theory of goals and performance.* Englewood Cliffs, NJ: Prentice Hall.

Louis, M. R., & Sutton, R. I. (1991). Switching cognitive gears: From habits of mind to active thinking. *Human Relations, 44*(1), 55-76.

Lounamaa, P. H., & March, J. G. (1987). Adaptive coordination of a learning team. *Management Science, 33,* 107-123.

March, J. G. (1976). The technology of foolishness. In J. G. March & J. P. Olsen (Eds.), *Ambiguity and choice in organizations* (pp. 69-81). Bergen, Norway: Universitetsforlaget.

March, J. G. (1978). Bounded rationality, ambiguity, and the engineering of choice. *Bell Journal of Economics, 9,* 587-608.

March, J. G. (1988). *Decisions and organizations.* London: Blackwell.

March, J. G., & Olsen, J. (1976). Organizational learning and the ambiguity of the past. In J. G. March & J. P. Olsen (Eds.), *Ambiguity and choice in organizations* (pp. 54-68). Bergen, Norway: Universitetsforlaget.

March, J. G., & Simon, H. A. (1958). *Organizations.* New York: John Wiley.

March, J. G., & Shapira, Z. (1987). Managerial perspectives on risk and risk-taking. *Management Science, 33*(11), 1404-1418.

Martin, J., Feldman, M. S., Hatch, M. J., & Sitkin, S. B. (1983). The uniqueness paradox in organizational stories. *Administrative Science Quarterly, 28*(4), 438-453.

Martin, J., & Meyerson, D. (1988). Organizational culture and the denial, channeling, and acknowledgement of ambiguity. In L. R. Pondy, R. J. Boland, & H. Thomas (Eds.), *Managing ambiguity and change* (pp. 93-125). Chichester, UK: Wiley.

Matheson, S. M., & Kee, J. E. (1986). *Out of balance.* Salt Lake City, UT: Peregrine Smith.

Matson, J. (1989, March 25). Intelligent fast failure. *Management Letter* (Prentice-Hall, Bureau of Business Practice), pp. 7-8.

McCall, M. W., Lombardo, M. M., & Morrison, A. M. (1988). *The lessons of experience: How successful executives develop on the job.* Lexington, MA: Lexington Books.

Meyer, M. W., & Zucker, L. G. (1989). *Permanently failing organizations.* Newbury Park, CA: Sage.

Michael, D. N., & Mirvis, P. H. (1977). Conclusion: Changing, erring, and learning. In P. H. Mirvis & D. N. Berg (Eds.), *Failures in organization development and change* (pp. 311-333). New York: John Wiley.

Mirvis, P. H., & Berg, D. N. (1977). Introduction: Failures in organization development and change. In P. H. Mirvis & D. N. Berg (Eds.), *Failures in organization development and change* (pp. 1-18). New York: John Wiley.

Mitchell, T. R., Green, S. G., & Wood, R. (1981). An attributional model of leadership and the poor performing subordinate. In L. L. Cummings & B. M. Staw (Eds.), *Research in organizational behavior* (Vol. 1, pp. 197-234). Greenwich, CT: JAI.

Nahavandi, A., & Malekzadeh, A. (1988). Acculturation in mergers and acquisition. *Academy of Management Review, 131*(1), 79-90.

Naylor, J. D., & Ilgen, D. R. (1984). Goal setting: A theoretical analysis of motivational technology. In B. M. Staw & L. L. Cummings (Eds.), *Research in organizational behavior* (Vol. 4, pp. 95-140). Greenwich, CT: JAI.

Nonaka, I. (1985). *The essence of failure: Can management learn from the manner of organization of Japanese military forces in the Pacific War?* Unpublished working paper, Institute of Business, Hitotsubashi University.

O'Brien, M. (1987). *Vince: A personal biography of Vince Lombardi.* New York: William Morrow.

Payne, D. (1989). *Coping with failure: The therapeutic uses of rhetoric.* Columbia: University of South Carolina Press.

Perrow, C. (1984). *Normal accidents.* New York: Basic Books.

Peters, T. (1987). *Thriving on chaos.* New York: Harper & Row.

Peters, T., & Waterman, R. H. (1982). *In search of excellence.* New York: Harper & Row.

Petroski, H. (1985). *To engineer is human: The role of failure in successful design.* New York: St. Martin's.

Roberts, K. H., & Rousseau, D. M. (1989). Research in nearly failure-free, high-reliability organizations: Having the bubble. *IEEE Transactions on Engineering Management, 36,* 132-139.

Ross, M., & Sicoly, F. (1979). Egocentric biases in availability and attribution. *Journal of Personality and Social Psychology, 37,* 322-336.

Russell, D., & McAuley, E. (1986). Causal attributions, causal dimensions, and affective reactions to success and failure. *Journal of Personality and Social Psychology, 50,* 1174-1185.

Salancik, G. R., & Meindl, J. R. (1984). Corporate attributions as strategic illusions of management control. *Administrative Science Quarterly, 29,* 238-254.

Schein, E. H. (1985). *Organizational culture and leadership.* San Francisco: Jossey-Bass.

Seligman, M. E. P. (1975). *Helplessness.* San Francisco: W. H. Freeman.

Shrivastava, P. (1988). Editorial: Industrial crisis management: Learning from organizational failures. *Journal of Management Studies, 25*(4), 283-284.

Shrivastava, P., Mitroff, I. I., Miller, D., & Miglani, A. (1988). Understanding industrial crises. *Journal of Management Studies, 25*(4), 285-303.

Singh, J. (1986). Performance, slack, and risk-taking in organizational decisionmaking. *Academy of Management Journal, 29*(3), 562-585.

Sitkin, S. B., & Bies, R. J. (1988). *The architecture of explanation: The process of legitimating actions and outcomes in conflict situations.* Paper presented at meeting of the Academy of Management, Anaheim, CA.

Sitkin, S. B., & Bies, R. J. (1989). *The legalistic organization: A conceptual overview* (Working paper). Austin: University of Texas.

Sitkin, S. B., & Pablo, A. L. (forthcoming). Reconceptualizing the determinants of risk behavior. *Academy of Management Review.*

Sitkin, S. B., Pablo, A. L., & Jemison, D. B. (1991). *A risk-based theory of the acquisition process.* Paper presented at conference on Industrial Organization, Strategic Management, and International Competitiveness. Vancouver, British Columbia.

Siu, R. G. K. (1968). *The man of many qualities: A legacy of the I Ching.* Cambridge: MIT Press.

Solomon, J. (1989, February 17). To nurture managers, expose them to risk. *Wall Street Journal,* p. B1.

Starbuck, W. H., & Milliken, F. J. (1988). Challenger: Fine-tuning the odds until something breaks. *Journal of Management Studies, 25*(4), 319-340.

Staw, B. M. (1983). The experimenting organization: Problems and prospects. In B. M. Staw (Ed.), *Psychological foundations of organizational behavior* (2nd ed., pp. 421-437). Glenview, IL: Scott, Foresman.

Staw, B. M., & Ross, J. (1987). Behavior in escalation situations: Antecedents, prototypes, and solutions. In B. M. Staw & L. L. Cummings (Eds.), *Research in organizational behavior* (Vol. 9, pp. 39-78). Greenwich, CT: JAI.

Staw, B. M., Sandelands, L. E., & Dutton, J. E. (1981). Threat-rigidity effects in organizational behavior: A multilevel analysis. *Administrative Science Quarterly, 26*(4), 501-524.

Sutton, R. I., & Callahan, A. L. (1987). The stigma of bankruptcy: Spoiled organizational image and its management. *Academy of Management Journal, 30,* 405-436.

Tamuz, M. (1987, Spring). The impact of computer surveillance on air safety reporting. *Columbia Journal of World Business,* pp. 69-77.

Tamuz, M., & Sitkin, S. B. (1989). *The effects of information processing on the availability of organizational information about potential dangers.* Paper presented at the American Sociological Association Meeting, San Francisco.

Thomas, J. B., & Trevino, L. K. (1989). *Strategic alliance building: An information processing perspective* (Working paper). Pennsylvania State University.

Trice, H. M., & Beyer, J. M. (1988). Using six organizational rites to change culture. In R. H. Kilmann, M. J. Saxton, & R. Serpa (Eds.), *Gaining control of the corporate culture* (pp. 370-399). San Francisco: Jossey-Bass.

Van de Ven, A. H. (1986). Central problems in the management of innovation. *Management Science, 32,* 590-607.

Weick, K. E. (1979). *The social psychology of organizing.* Reading, MA: Addison-Wesley.

Weick, K. E. (1984). Small wins: Redefining the scale of social problems. *American Psychologist, 39*(1), 40-49.

Weick, K. E. (1985). A stress analysis of future battlefields. In J. G. Hunt & J. D. Blair (Eds.), *Leadership on the future battlefield* (pp. 32-46). Washington, DC: Pergamon.

Weick, K. E. (1986). *The emotions of organizing* (Working paper). Austin: University of Texas.

Weick, K. E. (1988). Enacted sensemaking in crisis situations. *Journal of Management Studies, 25*(4), 305-317.

White, R. W. (1959). Motivation reconsidered: The concept of competence. *Psychological Review, 66*(5), 297-333.

Whitley, B. E. (1986). The relationship of informational attributions to affective response to success and failure. *Journal of Social Psychology, 126*(4), 453-457.

Wildavsky, A. (1988). *Searching for safety.* New Brunswick, NJ: Transaction Books.

Wood, R., & Bandura, A. (1989). Social cognitive theory of organizational management. *Academy of Management Review, 14*(3), 361-384.

Index

Abernathy, W. J., 205, 362
Action, organizational:
  as history-dependent, 517
  ecology of, 167
  learning embedded in, 3
  versus organizational choice, xii
Adaptability, organizational, 553
  through maintaining organizational experi-
    ments, 131
Adaptation, organizational, 125
  by local design, 52-54
  by local interactions, 52
  competing risks in, 198
  environmental selection and, 195-201
  evolution model of organizational change
    and, 377
  organizing work by, 20-55
  through organizational experiments, 131
  through organizational self-appraisals
    and, 131
Adaptive firms, organizational change in,
    281, 287, 296
Adaptive learning models, 198, 200
Adler, P. S., 77, 481, 482
Administration, paradox of, 268
Aguilar, F. J., 137
Aiken, M., 205
Aldrich, H. B., 138
Aldrich, H. E., 378, 397
Alexander, C., 54, 361
Alexander, V. D., 528

Allen, M. P., 290
Allen, S. A., 139
Allison, G. T., xi, 11, 14, 192, 193, 378, 405,
    412
Allison, P. D., 389, 390, 393
Allport, F. H., 411
Alvesson, M., 503, 504
Amado, G., 130
Amburgey, T., 195, 396
Amburgey, T. L., 195, 199, 201
Ancona, D. G., 306, 307
Anderson, A. B., 351
Anderson, H. C., 532
Anderson, J. R., 47, 190, 191, 192, 409, 421,
    422, 427
Anderson, P., 77, 209, 308, 312, 362, 363
Anderson, P. A., 233
Ansoff, H. I., 138
Architectural innovation, 360-363, 373
  architectural knowledge and, 360
  essence of, 362
  established firms and, 360
  in photolithography, 365-366, 371
  organizational transformation and,
    370-374
  product development and, 361
Architectural knowledge, 360, 362, 363, 371,
    372, 373
  definition of, 370
  need for better understanding of, 374
  versus component knowledge, 360, 370

579

Argote, L., 84, 85, 86, 96, 136, 231, 232, 254, 519, 526
Argyris, C., 104, 125, 130, 131, 256, 269, 270, 299, 306, 426, 431, 432, 433, 435, 455, 518, 521, 542, 556, 563
Armstrong, J. S., 497
Aronson, E., 3
Arrow, K., 209, 210
Arrow, K. J., 233, 363
Arthur, W. B., 104, 169, 520
Asch, S. E., 335, 336, 337, 338, 339, 340, 341, 350
Ascher, W., 497
Ashby, W. R., 103
Asher, H., 518
Astley, W. G., 139, 195, 518
Athans, M., 233
Attewell, P., 214

Baddeley, A., 427
Baden-Fuller, C., 353
Bahrick, H. P., 193, 409
Bailyn, 372
Baloff, N., 86
Bandura, A., 568
Bargh, J. A., 10
Barley, S., 396
Barley, S. R., 74, 76, 77, 381, 520, 523
Barnett, C. K., xiv
Barnett, W., 307, 397
Barnett, W. P., 195, 199, 201
Bar-Shalom, Y., 233
Bartner, L., 326
Bartunek, J. M., 78, 144, 305, 306, 307
Bateson, G., 270, 456
Baum, J. A. C., 195
Baumol, W. J., 497
Bavelas, A., 179, 232, 260
Bavelas, J. B., 308
Becker, G. S., 5
Becker, H. S., 525
Beckman, S. L., 85, 86, 96, 136, 231, 232, 254, 519, 526
Beer, M., 130
Beer, S., 126
Behavioral decision theory, 234
Behavioral development, 169
Behn, R. D., 564
Beliefs, organizational:

limits to conservation of, 10
place of events in development of, 4
reliability of learning and construction of, 9-10
reliability of learning and sharing of, 9-10
sustaining existing structures of, 9
validity of learning and construction of causal, 10-14
See also Organizational code
Bell, C. H., 130
Bell, T. E., 13
Bellah, R. N., 350
Bem, D. J., 169
Benjamin, R. I., 225
Berg, D. N., 542, 563
Berger, P., 137
Berger, P. L., 377, 381, 440
Berlinger, L. R., 567
Bettis, R. A., 134, 136, 144
Bettman, J. R., 303, 309, 547
Beyer, J. M., 9, 497, 521, 561
Beyth, R., 4, 12
Bhambri, A., 307, 310
Bhargava, N., 502, 504
Biel, C., 132
Bies, R. J., 542, 544, 547, 562, 567, 569
Biggart, N. W., 528
Bikson, T. K., 210
Binkhorst, D., 457
Björkman, I., 3
Blandin, J. S., 138
Bloch, M., 75
Bloom, B. S., 181
Blumer, H., 340, 355
Boden, M. A., 332, 333
Boehm, M., 521, 526
Boeker, W., 128, 303
Boisjoly, R., 13
Bolman, L., 431, 432, 433
Bond, A., 235
Boose, J., 407
Bougon, M., 457
Bougon, M. G., 145
Boulding, K. E., 131, 551
Bounded rationality, 186
Bourdieu, P., 60, 61, 80
Bourgeois, L. J., III, 135
Bower, G. H., 126, 164
Bowman, E. H., 201, 482
Boyle, K., 210

Braverman, H., 77
Brehmer, B., 8, 531
Bricolage, 68
Brittain, J., 133
Bromiley, P., 482
Brooks, F., 219
Brooks, F. P., Jr., 496, 502
Brown, J. L., 490, 508
Brown, J. S., 69, 426, 457
Brown, L., 204, 207
Brown, R. H., 270, 521
Brown, W. B., 138, 307, 311
Browning, L., 343
Browning, L. D., 542, 544
Bruner, J., 343
Bruner, J. S., 146
Brunsson, N., 4, 9, 523
Brytting, T., 526
Bucher, R., 490
Buckley, W., 269
Bunch, M., 409
Bunn, J. A., 104
Burawoy, M., 80
Burchell, S., 523
Burgelman, R. A., 378, 396, 519, 569
Burgess, C., 222
Burke, James, 562
Burke, W. W., 130
Burns, T., 233, 276, 378
Burt, R., 206, 208, 226
Business computing, institutional features of
        diffusion of, 214-223
    computer bureaus, 215-217
    computer gurus, 223
    computer mavens, 223
    consultants, 218-219
    expertise, 214-215
    interfaces, 221
    manufacturers and knowledge barriers,
        217-218
    recycling software, 219-220
    shells, 221
    standards, 221
    troubleshooting expertise, 221
    user-firm dynamics, 221-222
Butler, J. E., 133, 518

Cairns, H., 455
Caldwell, D., 307

Callahan, A. L., 541
Camerer, C. F., 497
Cameron, K., 269
Cameron, K. S., 547, 548
Cammarata, S., 234
Campbell, D., 2, 376, 377
Campbell, D. T., 542, 546, 550, 554, 564
Cangelosi, V. E., 10, 132, 163, 166, 169, 529
Canonical practice, 59, 60-62, 63
    opus operatum versus *modus operandi*
        and, 60
Cardinal, L. B., 568, 569
Carley, K. M., 231, 232, 233, 234
Carlson, R. O., 311
Carraher, D. W., 410
Carraher, T. N., 410
Carroll, G. R., 196, 197, 231, 308, 380, 397,
        518
Carter, E. E., 139, 140
Carter, R. K., 129
Chambers, C. C., 205
Chambliss, D. F., 171
Chandler, A. D., 50, 189, 232, 310, 363, 509
Chapman, R. L., 132
Child, J., 195, 276, 291
Chow, G. C., 206
Christie, B., 145
Churchland, P. M., 332
Clark, B. R., 13, 521
Clark, K., 362
Clark, K. B., 84, 360, 371, 374
Clark, M., 6
Clark, P., 210
Clausing, D., 371
Cleese, J. M., 557, 561
Cognitive ecology, 50
Cognitive learning theory, 163-164, 431,
        432-437, 438, 448, 452, 454
Cohen, A. M., 231, 232, 259, 260
Cohen, C. E., 9
Cohen, M. D., 9, 104, 132, 165, 233, 234,
        278, 408
Cohen, N. J., 191, 409
Cohen, W. M., 197
Coherence, organizational, xiii
Coleman, J. S., 207, 208, 226, 395, 397
Colin, C., 523
Collaboration:
    as feature of work practice, 66-67
Collective mind, 334, 352, 354

as disposition to heed, 335-339
as pattern of heedful interrelations, 330,
  335, 340, 341
heedful interrelating as, 339-343
in process of interrelating, 340
mutually shared fields and, 340, 353-354
narrative skills and, 343
organization performance and, 330
transindividual quality of, 340
  See also Group mind; Group performance
Collins, A., 69
Communities-of-practice, 71, 77, 79
  emergent, 70-71
  innovating in, 73-76, 77, 79
  learning as LPP in, 59, 72
  learning in, 68-73, 77, 79
  working in, 60-68, 77, 79
Community of interpretation, 68
Competency traps, 197-198, 519-520
  evolution model of organizational change
    and, 377
Competition:
  and importance of relative performance,
    115-117
  for relative position, 119-120
  for strategic action, 119-120
Competitive advantage, 101
  knowledge and, 117-119
  learning and, 117-119
Competitive benchmarking, 473
Competitive processes, 115. *See also* Ecologies of competition
Component knowledge, 362, 363, 372
  definition of, 370
  product development and, 361
  versus architectural knowledge, 360, 370
Congenital learning, 124, 128, 151
Connolly, T., 141
Consolini, P. M., 234, 352
Convergence/reorientation patterns, 267,
  270, 271-272, 290, 305.
    See also Organizational change,
    learning model of
Cook, S. D. N., 457
Cooper, A. C., 363, 520
Corporate intelligence, 135
Crawford-Mason, C., 475
Critical events:
  defining, 9
  focusing intensively on, 3

metaphorical power of, 4
place of in development of belief, 4
place of in history, 4
Crovitz, H. F., 172
Crozier, M., 139
Crum, R., 269
Culnan, M. J., 138, 145
Culture, organizational. *See* Organizational
  culture
Cummings, L. L., 547
Cyert, R. M., 5, 9, 50, 103, 138, 139, 140,
  147, 169, 190, 195, 198, 199, 231,
  232, 256, 268, 269, 271, 274, 275,
  279, 290, 295, 299, 377, 378, 380,
  405, 408, 411, 412, 426, 434, 476,
  482, 517, 518, 523, 548, 559
Czepiel, J. A., 135

Daft, R. L., 60, 73, 74, 75, 137, 140, 142,
  143, 145, 165, 171, 256, 353, 363,
  521, 525
Dalton, D. R., 231, 311
Dames, H., 232
David, H. A., 118
David, P. A., 104
Davies, S., 205
Davis, S., 233, 241
Davis, T. R. V., 452
Davis-Blake, A., 304
Dawes, R. M., 9, 14
Dawkins, R., 54
Day, G. S., 86, 519
Day, R. H., 103
Deal, T., 491
Dearborn, D. C., 4, 134, 144
Decision behavior, self-reinforcing, 3
Decision making, organizational:
  anticipating future benefits and, 3
  anticipating future costs and, 3
  behavioral theories of, 518
  literature on, 130
  logical incrementalism, 130
  successive limited comparisons, 130
    See also Organizational decision-making
    model, proposed
Declarative knowledge, x
  versus procedural knowledge, x, 409
Declarative memory, xi, 190, 191, 193, 409
  definition of, 409

versus procedural memory, 193, 409, 421,
426
Deetz, S. A., 74
DeGregori, T. R., 550, 555
DeGroot, M. H., 232, 233
Delacroix, J., 279
Deming, W. E., 426, 461, 469, 470, 481
Dennett, D. C., 166
Denton, P., 5
DePorras, D. A., 134, 144
Dery, D., 130
Design, local:
    adaptation and, 52-54, 55
    evolution and, 54-55
Dessauer, J. H., 76, 312
Devanna, M., 309
Dewey, J., 411
Diffusion:
    coercive, 528
    dynamics of, 528-529
    mechanisms for, 527-528
    mimetic, 528
    negative consequences of, 529
    normative, 528
    of technical secrets, 529
    through imitation, 528
    See also Innovation diffusion theory;
        Technical diffusion
Dill, W., 9
Dill, W. R., 10, 132, 163, 166, 169, 232, 529
DiMaggio, P. J., 528, 529
DiMaggio, P. W., 278
DiPrete, T. A., 396
Discovering organizations, 73
    versus enacting organizations, 74
Dobyns, L., 475
Doeringer, P. B., 380
Dollinger, M. J., 137
Donnellon, A., 145
Doppelt, N., 132
Dore, R., 372
Dornblaser, B. M., 394
Dornbusch, S. M., 353
Double-loop learning, 521, 556
    versus single-loop, 131
Douglas, M., 126, 451, 457, 542
Downs, A., 138, 232, 233, 241, 311, 547
Downs, G., 474
Downskilling, 58, 61, 77
    approach to training, 62

assumptions behind, 65
practices, 66
Drazin, R., 411
Dreyfus, H. L., 333
Dreyfus, S. E., 333
Driver, M. J., 146
Drucker, P. F., 136
Duguid, P., 69, 426, 457
Duncan, R., 170, 171, 290, 431, 434, 435,
    449, 451, 455, 531, 556
Duncan, R. B., 232
Durkheim, E., 9, 205
Dutton, J., 209, 307
Dutton, J. E., 140, 144, 303, 548, 553
Dutton, J. M., 84, 85, 133, 135, 137, 232,
    497, 518, 519, 527, 531
Dyer, L. D., 378

Ebbesen, E. B., 9
Eckert, P., 79
Ecologies of competition, knowledge and,
    115-120
Ecologies of learning, 518, 529-531
    among competitors, 520
    systems, xiii
    to learn, 530-531
Edwards, J. L., 231, 232
Eells, R., 135
Efficiency, organizational, 267
Einhorn, E. J., 521
Einhorn, H., 9
Einspruch, N. G., 364
Eisenberg, E., 351
Eisenberg, E. M., 145
Eisenhardt, K., 310, 325
Eisenhardt, K. M., 135, 351, 355
Ekstedt, E., 489, 490, 491
Elman, J. L., 333
Emergent phenomena, xiii, 177
Enacting organizations, 60, 73-74, 75
    as adaptive, 77
    as innovative, 77
    versus discovering organizations, 74
English, A. C., 164
English, H. B., 164
Engwall, L., 531
Epple, D., 84, 85, 86, 96, 136, 231, 232, 254,
    519, 526
Erber, R., 332

Esch, K., 13
Estes, W. K., 171
Estler, S. E., 397
Etheredge, L. S., 431, 432, 433
Ettlie, J. E., 213, 226
Evanisko, M., 205
Eveland, J. D., 204, 207, 210, 214, 223
Evolutionary change models, 376
Evolutionary economic theory:
    quality management revolution and, 461,
        471-474
    tacit knowledge and, 473-474
Eyre, D. P., 528
Executive succession:
    as lever for change, 322, 325
    changing environments and, 304
    costs versus benefits of, 312
    first-order learning and, 306, 322-323
    organizational adaptation and, 304
    organizational learning and, 302-327
    organizational performance and, 308-312
    positive impact of, 303
    second-order learning and, 307-308
Experience, organizational:
    experiencing more aspects of, 2-4
    improving structure of, 532-533
    interpretation of, 521-524
    learning from, 1, 2
    simulating, 6-8
    variety of interpretations of, 4-5, 11-12, 15
    See also Histories
Experience curve. See Learning curves
Experiential knowledge, 525
Experiential learning, 124, 151, 407, 518-520
    evaluation of learning from experience
        literature and, 134-135
    experience-based learning curves and,
        133-134
    experimenting organizations and, 131-132
    literature related to, 129-135
    organizational experiments and, 129-130
    organizational self-appraisal and, 130-131
    patterns of change and, 269-271
    unintentional/unsystematic learning and,
        132-133
Expertise:
    discovering, 484-486
    strategic, 486
    technical, 486
Exploitation of old certainties, 101, 121

essence of, 120
rapid improvement of by adaptive
    processes, 104
tendencies to increase, 104
See also Ecologies of competition;
    Exploration/exploitation trade-off;
    Mutual learning
Exploration/exploitation trade-off:
    and social context of organizational learn-
        ing, 105
    and vulnerability of exploration, 104
    in organizational action theories, 102-104
    See also Ecologies of competition; Mutual
        learning
Exploration of new possibilities, 101, 121
    essence of, 120
    sustaining, 121
    tendencies to reduce, 104
    vulnerability of, 104
    See also Ecologies of competition;
        Exploration/exploitation trade-off;
        Mutual learning

Fahey, L., 137, 144
Failing, organizational:
    benefits of, 541, 542, 547-551
Failure:
    career mobility and, 561-562
    effective organizational adaptation and,
        541, 553
    effective organizational learning and, 541,
        542
    implications for organizational research
        on, 567-571
    resilience and, 551
    visible leadership and, 560-561
    See also Failure, intelligent; Failure,
        strategic
Failure, intelligent, 554-556, 566
    action independence and, 558
    challenging aspiration levels and, 558-559
    criteria for, 554-556
    domain relevance and, 554, 556
    fast feedback/slow learning and, 559-560
    modest outcome scale and, 554, 555
    organizational conditions facilitating,
        557-567
    organizational culture/design and, 563-565
    organizational legitimation of, 560-563

process over outcome focus and, 557
publicizing, 562-563
speedy action cycles and, 554, 555-556
uncertain outcomes and, 554, 555
well-planned actions and, 554
Failure, strategic, 542, 557, 564, 571-572
as alternative to success, 546-551
fostering innovation and, 568-569
managing hazards in organizations and,
569
merger and acquisition decision making/
integration and, 570-571
Failure avoidance, 542
managerial emphasis on, 541
Failure ideology, developing intelligent,
564-565
Failure management systems, 565-567
False lessons, learning, 8
Farace, R. V., 142
Faucheux, C., 130
Faulkner, R. R., 351
Faust, D., 14
Feigenbaum, A. V., 481
Feldman, J., 138
Feldman, M. S., 9, 50, 51, 79, 134, 141, 148,
165, 172, 561
Ferrell, John, 564
Finkelstein, S., 139
Fiol, C. M., 125, 169, 433, 436, 518
Fiol, M., 305, 322
First-order learning, 270, 290, 302, 304, 305
benefits of, 306
executive succession and, 306, 322-323
inertia and, 306
Fisch, R., 299
Fischer, G. W., 233
Fischer, M. M. J., 457
Fischhoff, B., 4, 6, 7, 9, 12, 14, 235, 521, 522
Fisher, F., 214, 216, 218, 219
Flannery, L., 222
Flatt, S., 307, 323
Fleischer, M., 205, 209, 212
Flexibility, organizational, 267
Fligstein, N., 528, 529
Focused search, learning by, 138-139
Follett, M. P., 339
Fordism, 189-190
Fossum, J. A., 378
Foushee, H. C., 354
Frame breaking, 78

Framing information, 144, 150
Fredickson, J. W., 140
Freedman, R. D., 135, 137, 519
Freeman, C., 205, 209
Freeman, H. E., 129
Freeman, J., 103, 195, 196, 197, 198, 199,
200, 268, 275, 276, 278, 279, 290,
293, 304, 306, 307, 397, 517, 531
French, W. L., 130
Friedlander, F., 126
Friedman, S., 304, 308
Friesen, P. H., 131, 137, 305, 306, 313, 533
Frost, P. J., 431, 439
Fukami, C. V., 565
Fuld, L. M., 135

Gaertner, K. N., 561, 562
Gagliardi, P., 453
Gahmberg, H., 431, 434, 435
Gaines, B., 407
Galanter, M., 350
Galbraith, J. R., 233, 241, 268
Garbage-can decision organizations, 103
Garbage-can decision processes, 103
Garbage can firms, organizational change in,
281, 287, 297
Gardner, H., 455
Gasser, L., 235
Gates, M. J., 523
Gatignon, H., 207
Gecas, V., 568
Geertz, C., 60
George, A. L., 11, 14, 554, 556
Gershuny, J., 224
Gersick, C. G., 351
Gersick, C. J. G., 306, 323, 405, 412
Gerstenfeld, A., 137
Gerwin, D., 140, 211
Ghiselli, E. E., 510
Giddens, A., 381
Gilad, B., 135
Gilad, T., 135
Gilfillan, D. P., 169, 344, 411, 456
Gillcrist, P. T., 345
Gilovich, T., 167
Ginnett, R. C., 351
Gioia, D. A., 126, 144, 148, 431, 434
Giuliano, T., 332
Glaser, B., 355

Gleick, J., 565
Glueck, W., 138
Glynn, M. A., 270, 271
Goffman, E., 563
Goodman, P., 70, 71
Goore, N., 167
Gottlieb, L., 573
Gould, S. J., 380, 397, 534
Graen, G., 381
Graf, P., 193, 409
Grafting, 124, 128, 136, 141, 151
    through corporate acquisition, 136
    through joint ventures, 136
Grandoori, A., 166
Granovetter, M., 377, 381
Gray, B., 145
Green, S. G., 573
Green, T. R. G., 527
Greenwood, R., 490, 508
Greiner, L., 307, 310
Griffiths, W. E., 99
Grinyer, P., 310
Grofman, B., 232, 233
Group mind, 332-335, 349
    connectionism and, 332-334
    See also Collective mind
Group performance, 336-339
    defining properties of, 336-338
    See also Collective mind
Groups:
    in workplace, 70-71
    versus communities, 70-71
Group theory, 70
Groupthink, 127, 350, 560
Grusky, O., 231, 234, 255, 256, 307
Guetzkow, H., 142, 232

Häaging, I., 525
Hackman, J. R., 70, 172, 353, 405, 412
Hackman, R., 306, 323
Hage, J., 205
Haire, M., 510
Håkansson, H., 527
Halaby, C. N., 396
Hall, D. T., 565
Hall, R. H., 310, 526
Hall, R. I., 533
Halpern, J. J., 355

Hambrick, D. C., 137, 138, 139, 309
Hamilton, E., 455
Hannan, M. T., 103, 195, 196, 197, 198, 199,
    200, 268, 275, 276, 278, 279, 290,
    293, 304, 306, 307, 390, 393, 397,
    517, 531
Harrison, J. R., 3, 132, 134, 290, 522
Harvey, J. B., 563
Hasher, L., 234, 524
Haspeslagh, P., 549, 570
Hastie, R., 231, 232, 234, 259, 524
Hatch, M. J., 561
Hauser, J., 371
Haveman, H. A., 195
Hax, A. C., 7, 130
Hayes, J. R., 181
Hayes, R. H., 84
Healy, 372, 373
Hedberg, B. L. T., 73, 77, 125, 131, 147, 167,
    256, 270, 290, 299, 305, 353, 431,
    434, 518, 523, 533, 545, 546, 548
Heed, variations in, 341-343
Heed concepts, 335, 336
Heedful contributing, 351
Heedful interrelating, 344-346, 351, 352
    as collective mind, 339-343
    examples of, 343-349
Heedful performance:
    productivity of, 353
    versus habitual performance, 336
Heedful representing, 351
Heedful subordinating, 351
Heedless interrelating, 346-349, 351
Heimer, C. A., 498, 499, 528, 531
Helmich, D. L., 307, 311
Henderson, R. M., 360, 365, 366, 371, 374
Heneman, H. G., III, 378
Henry, J., 557
Herbst, P. G., 14
Herriott, S. R., 104, 108, 133, 199, 269, 276,
    277, 431, 520, 524, 530, 533, 549
Hertel, P. T., 332
Hey, J. D., 102
Hickson, D. F., 378, 383
Hierarchies, organizational, 230, 236
    advantages of, 232
    description of, 232
    disadvantages of, 232-233
    learning rate of, 238, 245, 249, 250

learning resilience of, 249
personnel hiring and learning amount, 251
personnel turnover and, 247, 257
ultimate performance of, 241, 242, 243, 244, 249
versus teams, 232
vulnerability of, 248, 258
Higgins, E. T., 10
Hilgard, E. R., 126, 164
Hilke, J. C., 527
Hill, R. C., 99
Hiltz, S. R., 145
Hininger, R., 378, 383
Hinings, C. R., 490, 508
Hirsch, W. Z., 84, 86
Historical events:
experiencing richly, 2-6, 11, 15
organizational pooling of, 2, 15
valid inferences of, 11
See also Critical events; Histories
Histories:
assessing small, 8-14
hypothetical, 7-8, 12-13, 14, 532
improving learning from small, 8-14
near-, 6-7, 12, 13, 14
small, 1-16
See also Historical events
Hitt, M. A., 134, 144
Hoaglin, D. C., 422
Hobbes, T., 455
Hofmeister, K. R., 4
Hogarth, R., 6, 9
Hogarth, R. M., 134, 521
Holland, J. H., 101, 196, 200, 379, 380, 425, 534
Hollander, S., 519
Holyoak, K., 425
Homans, G. C., 353
Hopkins, A., 389, 390
Hopwood, A. G., 523
House, R. J., 135, 196, 518
Huber, G., 397, 546, 550, 567, 572
Huber, G. P., 129, 134, 136, 138, 140, 142, 145, 150, 171
Hunt, H. A., 214
Hunt, L. G., 205
Hunt, T. C., 214
Hunter, A., 529
Hutchins, E., 50, 68, 172, 332, 334, 342

Hyatt, C., 573
Hyatt, J., 169

Iacono, S., 222
Ilgen, D. R., 559
Imai, K., 528
Imitative firms, organizational change in, 281, 287, 289, 297
Immutable mobiles, organizational role of, 76
Inbar, M., 412
Incremental innovation, 361, 362, 363, 370
and success of optical photolithography, 365
as competence enhancing, 362
versus radical innovation, 362-363
Information, soft, 149-150
Information acquisition, 150
Information circulation, 79
Information distribution, 124-125, 141-143, 150
breadth of organizational learning and, 141-142
definition of, 127
information interpretation and, 143
literature, 151
propositions concerning, 142
Information environment, 140
Information interpretation, 124, 125, 143-148, 150, 151
cognitive maps and, 144
definition of, 127
framing and, 144
information overload and, 144, 146
media richness and, 144, 145-146
necessary unlearning and, 144, 147-148
Information overload, 146, 470
Information pooling:
through institutional design, 231-232
Information processing, organizational, 125
Innovating:
in communities-of-practice, 73-76
Innovation, organizational, 58, 59
barriers to adoption of, 203
discontinuous, 77
external sources of, 78
framework for defining, 361
interpretive, 73
organizational learning and, 178-181

organizational memory and, 180-181
organizational research and, 182-183
organizational stability and, 179-180
personnel turnover and, 178-179
preservation of organizational identity
     and, 451
R&D/manufacturing and, 183-184
resisting enacting, 75-76
stories that support, 78
unintentional, 532
See also specific types of innovation
Innovation diffusion theory, 204-206
adopter studies and, 204-205
critiques of current, 207-211
macro-diffusion and, 205-206
See also Technology diffusion
Institutional memory:
analysts and, 248
personnel turnover and, 230, 231
upper management as, 248
Institutional theory, 135
Intentional learning, 125
from feedback, 130
Internal learning, 176
Interpretive organizations. *See* Enacting
     organizations
Ireland, R. D., 134, 144
Isabella, L. A., 144
Isen, A. M., 6

Jablin, F. M., 142, 144, 232, 241
Jackson, D. D., 308
Jackson, S. E., 140, 144, 307
Jacobs, D., 396
Jacobson, L., 379, 394, 397
James, R., 436
Janis, I. L., 11, 127, 350, 351, 548, 560
Jelinek, M., 129
Jemison, D. B., 136, 137, 549, 556, 570, 571
Jenkins-Smith, H. C., 436
Job death, 378, 388, 390, 392, 393
     familiarity and, 393
     hazard rate and, 389-390, 392-393, 395
     job idiosyncrasy and, 393, 395
Job-founding types, 383-384
     characteristics of, 386-388
     evolved jobs, 384, 386, 387, 391, 392,
          394, 398

idiosyncratic jobs, 384, 386, 395, 398
job persistence and, 393
measurement of, 384-386
novel jobs, 386, 393, 395, 398
opportunistic hires, 384, 386, 387, 391,
     392, 394, 398
planned novel jobs, 384, 386, 387, 391,
     394
reclassifications of existing jobs, 384,
     386, 387, 391, 392, 393, 394, 398
Jobs, formalized, 376, 377
as routines, 378
definition of, 378
stability of, 379
Johansen, R., 149
Johnson, B., 210
Johnson, E. J., 497
Johnson, H. T., 232, 524
Johnson, M. K., 234, 524
Johnson, Robert Woods, 562
Johnson & Johnson, 562
Johnson-Laird, P. N., 7
Jones, D. T., 406
Jönsson, S., 533
Jordan, B., 66, 69
Joseph, L., 167
Joskow, P. L., 84, 85, 133
Jowett, P., 205, 214
Judge, G. J., 99
Juran, J. M., 461, 477, 479, 481

Kahneman, D., 7, 14, 103, 144, 148, 234,
     235, 254, 269, 521, 545, 549
Kamien, M., 211
Kanter, H. E., 138
Kanter, R. M., 545
Kaplan, R. S., 232, 524
Karp, L., 6
Kassin, S. M., 426, 427
Katz, E., 207, 208, 226
Katz, M. L., 104
Katz, R., 137, 306, 309
Kaufman, H., 178, 397
Kay, N. M., 528
Keachie, E. C., 232, 519
Keck, S., 306
Kee, J. E., 547
Keegan, W. J., 137

Kelley, G. A., 270
Kelly, D., 195, 199, 201
Kelly, J. R., 407
Kelly, P., 204
Kennedy, A., 491
Kennedy, J. L., 132
Kennedy, M. M., 144
Kerrs, S., 489, 501
Kersten, A., 74
Kesner, I. R., 311
Khandwalla, P. N., 530
Kiesler, S., 8, 12, 145, 303, 306
Kimberly, J. R., 128, 528
Kimberley, J., 205
King, W. R., 137
Klapp, O. E., 167
Klein, J. I., 147
Kling, R., 222
Kmenta, J., 317
Knoke, D., 528
Knowledge, 101
    competitive advantage and, 117-119
    congenital, 128
    depreciation, 91
    inherited, 128
    intensity, 486
    See also specific types of knowledge
Knowledge acquisition, 124, 125, 128-141,
        150-151
    activities toward, 128
    definition of, 127
    informal behaviors toward, 128
    processes of, 124, 128-141, 151
Knowledge-intensive firms (KIFs), 486,
        487-494
    Arthur D. Little, 492, 493, 496, 498, 509,
        510
    as nonprofessional firms, 489-491
    as professional firms, 489
    bureaucratization in, 502
    defining expertise and, 488-489
    definition of, 492
    diversification and, 508-510
    exceptional expertise in, 488, 511
    experts' work in, 494-497
    future of, 512-513
    human capital dominated, 487
    information intensiveness and, 487-488
    learning by, 511

location of knowledge in, 491-492
    multinational, 510-511
    nonprofessionals and, 489-491
    organizational culture in, 503-505
    organizational learning in, 498-507
    peculiar nature of, 493-494
    personnel training in, 498-499
    physical capital in, 499-501
    professionals and, 489
    Rand Corporation, 492, 493, 495, 500,
        502, 504, 507, 508-509
    routines and, 501-503, 511
    social capital in, 505-507
    strategic development and, 507-511
    turnover in, 498
    uniqueness of successful, 511
    use of internal specialization by, 507
    versus information-intensive firms, 488
    Wachtell, Lipton, 492, 493, 494, 504, 508
Knowledge transfer, 83, 86, 209, 210
    extent of, 97
    intra-plant, 96, 97
    model of intra-plant, 92-95
    technical services as alternative to, 213
    See also Technology transfer
Koch, S., 163
Kochan, T., 373
Krafcik, J., 373, 426
Kranzberg, M., 204
Krieger, S., 13, 522
Krone, K. J., 142
Kunda, G., 504
Kunst-Wilson, W. R., 425
Kuran, T., 101
Kurke, L. B., 137
Kurland, M. A., 125, 135
Kusterer, K. C., 489

Laird, J., 425
Landau, M., 129, 139
Landes, D., 308, 310
Langer, E. J., 331, 547
Lant, T. K., 5, 200, 269, 271, 274, 275, 276,
        277, 279, 290, 294, 299, 305, 323,
        431, 432, 434, 523
LaPorte, T. R., 234, 330, 352, 355
LaPotin, P., 233
Latham, G. P., 548, 559

Latour, B., 76
Laudon, J. P., 500
Laudon, K. C., 500
Laughhunn, D. J., 269
Laughlin, P. R., 411
Laurent, A., 130
Lave, C. A., 199
Lave, J., 59, 60, 68, 69, 70, 72, 80, 342
Lawler, E. E., III, 129
Lawrence, B. S., 396
Lawrence, P., 10, 233, 241
Lawrence, P. R., 195, 268, 271, 276, 290
Learning, 58, 68-73, 125-126
    as bridge between working and innovating,
        60
    as form of intelligence, 531-534
    as LLP in communities-of-practice, 59,
        72-73
    as social construction, 69
    by doing, 518-519
    by experimentation, 546
    competitive advantage and, 117-119
    defining property of, 164
    ecologies of, 152
    from direct experience, 518-520
    from others' experience, 527-529
    intelligence of, 533-534
    inter-organizational, 152
    LPP and, 69
    multilevel, 519-520
    transfer of, 85-86, 190, 410
    unintentional, 132-133
    versus training, 68
    versus working, 59
    See also Organizational learning; specific
        types of learning
Learning behavior, organizational, 233-235
    as historically based, 233-234
Learning by doing, 84, 210
    in-house, 225
Learning by searching literature, evaluation
        of, 139-141
Learning by using, 210
Learning curves, organizational, 83, 84, 170
    conventional industrial, 86-88
    experience-based, 133-134
    research on, 84-86
Learning from experience, organizational:
    obstacles to, 134

Learning from experience literature,
        organizational:
    evaluation of, 134-135
Learning-in-working, 59, 62
    conceptual reorganization and, 79
    fostering, 71-73
    stories that support, 78
Learning processes. See Organizational
        learning processes
Learning rate, 92
Leary, W. E., 569
Leavitt, H., 232, 260, 160
Leblebici, H., 311
Lee, T. C., 99
Legitimate peripheral participation (LPP),
    learning and, 59, 69, 72-73
Lehoczky, J., 233
Leibenstein, H., 482
Leifer, R., 129, 138
Leigh, W., 222
Lengel, R. H., 145, 525
Leonard, J. S., 379, 394, 397
Lepper, M. R., 9
Levi-Strauss, C., 68
Levinthal, D. A., xii, 103, 104, 108, 132,
        133, 197, 199, 269, 276, 277, 278,
        291, 299, 431, 482, 520, 524, 530,
        532, 533, 549, 553, 560
Levitt, B., 10, 85, 103, 125, 132, 133, 134,
        135, 152, 165, 166, 197, 200, 210,
        232, 234, 254, 256, 269, 272, 290,
        304, 305, 306, 322, 323, 377, 378,
        379, 380, 405, 411, 431, 434, 457,
        476, 482, 546, 549, 559
Levy, F. K., 85
Levy, J. S., 524
Lewin, K., 130, 147
Lichtenstein, S., 235, 521
Lieberman, M. B., 84
Limited rationality theories, 103
    search in, 103
Lin, T., 394
Lindblom, C. E., 130, 147, 234, 517
Lingaraj, B. P., 150
Lipson, M. Y., 153
Lloyd, T., 490
Locke, E. A., 548, 559
Lodahl, T., 310
Loftus, E., 9

Lombardo, M. M., 561, 562
Lord, C., 9
Lorsch, J. W., 10, 195, 268, 271, 276, 290
Louis, M. R., 305, 306, 342, 431, 439, 452, 545, 549
Lounamaa, P. H., 10, 108, 132, 133, 199, 200, 532, 533, 548, 555, 559, 560
Luchins, A. S., 422
Luckman, T., 377, 381, 440
Lumsden, C. I., 377
Lundberg, C. C., 431, 439
Lyles, M. A., 125, 136, 169, 305, 322, 433, 436, 518
Lyons, W., 336

MacCrimmon, K. R., 533
MacDonald, D., 142
MacDuffie, J., 373
Machina, M. J., 516
Machlup, F., 487
MacKay, Harvey, 169-170
MacKenzie, K., 381
MacNamara, M., 130
MacRae, D., 523
Maddala, G. S., 98, 99
Madsen, R., 350
Mahajan, V., 136, 205, 206
Maidique, M. A., 532
Maier, N. R. F., 11
Maister, D. H., 503
Majluf, N. S., 7, 130
Malekzadeh, A., 571
Malone, T. W., 225, 232
Managerial learning, 257
Mancke, R., 214, 216, 218, 219
Mandler, G., 172, 409
Manis, M., 13
Mann, L., 11, 548
Mansfield, E., 204, 205, 208, 226, 528
Maps:
    canonical, 60-61
    cognitive, 144, 150
March, J., 141
March, J. C., 291, 308
March, J. G., ix, xii, xiv, 3, 5, 8, 9, 10, 11, 50, 79, 85, 103, 104, 108, 125, 126, 132, 133, 134, 135, 138, 139, 140, 141, 147, 151, 152, 165, 166, 169, 175,

177, 190, 195, 197, 198, 199, 200, 210, 231, 232, 233, 234, 241, 254, 256, 259, 268, 269, 270, 271, 272, 273, 274, 275, 276, 277, 278, 279, 290, 291, 292, 295, 299, 304, 305, 306, 308, 322, 323, 325, 377, 378, 379, 380, 382, 405, 408, 411, 412, 426, 431, 433, 434, 455, 457, 476, 482, 517, 518, 519, 520, 522, 523, 524, 530, 532, 533, 534, 542, 546, 547, 548, 549, 553, 555, 558, 559, 560, 566, 572
Marcus, G., 457
Markus, M. L., 145, 206
Marples, D. L., 361
Marschak, J., 232, 233, 260
Marsden, P. V., 397
Martin, J., 10, 13, 72, 431, 439, 521, 526, 545, 561
Maruyama, M., 169
Mason, P., 309
Masuch, M., 233
Matheson, S. M., 547
Matson, J., 554, 557, 563, 564
Matson, J. V., 550, 555
May, E. R., 11, 231, 526
Mazmanian, D. A., 527
McArthur, D., 234
McAuley, E., 553
McCall, M. W., 561, 562
McClelland, J., 239, 240
McCloskey, M., 409
McCulloch, W. S., 191
McGrath, J. E., 351, 353, 407
McGuire, C. B., 232, 233, 260
McGuire, J. W., 145
McHugh, A., 132, 396
McKechnie, P. I., 303
McKelvey, W., 378, 397
McKeown, T., 14
McKersie, R., 373
McKie, J., 214, 216, 218, 219
McNurlin, B., 222
McPherson, J. M., 378
Mead, G. H., 172, 341, 342, 440, 455
    rapidity of feedback and, 145
    variety of cues and, 145
Meehl, P. E., 14
Media richness, 145-146, 153

Meier, R. L., 146
Meindl, J. R., 303, 547
Meinhard, A. G., 379
Mental arithmetic, 20
Menzel, H., 207, 208, 226
Merton, R., 3
Merton, R. K., 526
Messinger, S. L., 310
Meyer, A., 308
Meyer, J. W., 128, 135, 522, 529
Meyer, M. W., 482, 568
Meyerson, D., 545
Mezias, S. J., 200, 269, 271, 276, 277, 278,
    290, 305, 323, 431, 432, 434, 528
Michael, D. N., 542
Miglani, A., 569
Miles, I., 224
Miles, R. E., 291, 308
Miles, R. H., 132, 431, 433
Miller, D., 131, 137, 303, 305, 306, 313, 533,
    569
Miller, D. T., 522
Miller, J. G., 146
Milliken, F. J., 134, 137, 144, 148, 269, 350,
    521, 569
Milliken, F. K., 13
Miner, A. S., 195, 377, 378, 379, 380, 382,
    384, 385, 395, 396, 397
Mintzberg, H., 132, 137, 138, 139, 148, 260,
    311, 313, 396
Mirvis, P. H., 542, 563
Mitchell, S., 310
Mitchell, T. R., 573
Mitroff, I. I., 569
Modular innovation, 361, 362
Mody, A., 133
Mohr, L. B., 14, 474
Montagna, P. D., 490
Montgomery, D. B., 5, 86, 279, 294, 299, 519
Moore, L. F., 431, 439
Moore, M. H., 523
Moore, W. L., 129
Moral density, 205
Morgan, G., 126, 341, 435
Morison, E. E., 306, 407
Morrison, A. M., 561, 562
Mueller, C. W., 231, 254
Muth, J. F., 84, 133, 519
Mutual learning, 105

convergence between organizational and
    individual beliefs and, 121
in knowledge development, 105-115
trade-off between exploration and
    exploitation in, 105
Mutual learning, model of, 106-110
basic properties of in closed system,
    107-115
basic properties of in more open system,
    110-115
environmental turbulence and, 110, 111,
    113-115
features of, 106
learning rate heterogeneity and, 109-110
learning rates and, 107-109
personnel turnover and, 110, 111-113

Nadler, D., 78
Nahavandi, A., 571
Narayanan, V. K., 137, 144
Narration, 75
as feature of work practice, 64-66
See also Storytelling
Nasbeth, L., 209, 226
National Research Council, 6
Naylor, J. D., 559
Negotiated order theory, 376
Negus, R., 216
Nehemiks, P., 135
Nelson, P. B., 527
Nelson, R. L., 504
Nelson, R. R., xi, 50, 148, 189, 190, 197,
    201, 232, 269, 374, 377, 378, 380,
    404, 404, 405, 407, 411, 461, 465,
    471, 491, 501, 517
Neustadt, R. E., 11, 231, 307, 526
Nevins, J. L., 371
Newell, A., 47, 132, 422, 425
Newman, M., 134
Newman, W. H., 268, 269, 270, 272, 273, 291
New York State, 217
Nienaber, J., 527
Nisbett, R., 148, 254, 407, 425
Nonaka, I., 132, 528, 544, 553
Noncanonical practice, 58, 59, 61, 62-64, 65,
    75, 77
of interstitial communities, 75
Nutt, P. C., 134

Nystrom, P. C., 73, 77, 131, 147, 167, 299, 305, 353, 426, 524, 546, 549

O'Brien, M., 543
Oliver, T., 5
Olsen, J. P., 9, 126, 133, 165, 169, 231, 232, 233, 234, 256, 259, 269, 274, 278, 431, 433, 455, 518, 523, 527, 572
O'Neill, B., 233
Open door management, 72
Optimization heuristic, 465
O'Reilly, C., 138, 142, 307, 323
O'Reilly, C. A., III, 306, 309
Organizational across-problem learning, 231
Organizational action theories, exploration and exploitation in, 102-104
Organizational age:
  organizational inertia and, 196, 198
  organizational mortality and, 196-198
  organizational survival and, 197
Organizational change, 125
  adaptation and environmental selection as processes of, 195-201
  adaptive perspective of, 278
  ambiguity and, 289
  architectural innovation and, 370-374
  aspiration level and, 279
  continuous, 200
  core, 199, 200
  differential selection of organizational characteristics and, 289
  effortless, 200
  environmental change and, 271-272
  environmental variability and, 289
  failure-induced, 297-298
  garbage can perspective of, 278-279
  institutional perspective of, 278
  organizational mortality and, 198-200
  peripheral, 199, 200
  population-level theories of, 518
  reorganization as, 199
  slack and, 298
  stability and, 267, 270
  survival rate of organizations and, 195-196
  See also Organizational change, evolutionary model of; Organizational change, learning model of
Organizational change, evolutionary model of, 376, 377, 378-382, 397

adaptation and, 377
competency traps and, 377
selection in, 377
suboptimal performance and, 377
superstitious learning and, 377
survival of routines and, 379-382
trial-and-error learning and, 377, 518
Organizational change, learning model of, 267, 269-271, 289-292, 376
basic components of, 269
effects of routines in, 272-273
environmental and organizational change in, 271-272
history dependence in, 273-274
performance targets and ambiguity in, 274-275, 523
propositions of, 271-275
See also Organizational change
Organizational characteristics:
  and performance, 276-277
Organizational code, 105, 106
  improving knowledge found in, 109
  individual adjustment to, 121
  individuals' beliefs and, 106, 107, 115
  knowledge level reflected by, 113
  knowledge of, 113-114, 115
  of received truth, 106
  personnel turnover and, 112-113
  rapid learning by, 108
  recruitment and, 115
Organizational culture, 58, 453
  definition of, 439-440
  organizational learning and, 430, 431, 439, 444-445, 448-455
Organizational cycle of choice, 169
Organizational decision making model, proposed, 230, 235-240
  as general framework, 256-257
  decision procedure and learning, 239-240
  limitations of, 254-256
  measuring learning and simulation, 243-244
  organizational structure, 236
  simulation of, 230, 235
  simulation results, 244-253
  task, 236-238
  turnover, 240
Organizational design, 20. *See also* Design, local

Organizational development, action research
in, 130
Organizational dynamics, xiii
Organizational experiments, 129-130
Organizational inertia, organizational learning
and, 196
Organizational learning, 84, 125
as form of informational updating, 305
breadth of, 126
cognitive perspective on, 431, 432-437
context of competition for primacy and,
105
cultural perspective on, 430, 431, 439-
440, 444-445, 448-455
definition of, 438
elaborateness of, 126, 127
executive succession and, 302-327
existence of, 126
exploitation in, 101, 102
exploration in, 101-102
innovation and, 178-181
internal learning and, 176
limitations to as instrument of intelligence,
534
mutual learning and, 105
nontraditional quality of, 163-172
organizational inertia and, 196
organizational reconstitution and, 450-451
reliability of as construction and sharing
of belief, 9-10
social context of, 105
thoroughness of, 126, 127
through members' learning, 176
through new members, 176
validity of as construction of causal belief,
10-14
See also Learning; Organizational
learning strategies
Organizational learning literature, 516
Organizational learning processes, 8
Organizational learning research:
computer simulations in, 275-276
dimensions of, xii
Organizational learning strategies:
replace traditional definition, 170-172
retain traditional definition, 168-170, 172
Organizational memory, 124, 125, 148-150,
151, 404, 516, 524-527
computer-based, 149-150
conservation of experience and, 526

definition of, 127
information distribution and, 148
information storage locating/retrieval and,
148-149
information storage norms/methods and,
148
innovation and, 180-181
in organizational learning, 150
membership attrition and, 148
nonanticipation of future needs and, 148
organizational interpretation of information and, 148
organizational routines and, 189
personnel loss and, 148, 180
problems of poor, 148
recording of experience and, 525-526
retrieval of experience and, 526-527
See also Institutional memory
Organizational mind, 435
Organizational mortality, 196
organizational age and, 196-198
organizational change and, 198-200
Organizational performance, 241-244
components for improving, 120
executive succession and, 303, 308-312
ultimate, 241-243
Organizational preferences:
changing dimensions of, 5-6
experiencing more, 5-6
learning and, 5
Organizational reconstitution:
as feature of organizational change, 451
cultural perspective of organizational
learning and, 450-451
Organizational self-appraisal, 130-131, 153
action research as, 130
Organizational simulation of hypothetical
events:
hypothetical histories, 7-8, 12-13, 14
near-histories, 6-7, 12, 13, 14
Organizational structures:
as designs for information acquisition, 189
as designs for organizational improvement, 189
as designs for organizational learning,
188-189
cognitive oligopolies, 353
interpretation systems, 353
networks, 353
self-designing systems, 353

types of, 232-233, 236
variety of, 188
See also Hierarchies, organizational;
Teams
Organizational survival, predicting, 133
Organizational unconscious, routines in, 407
Organizations:
as communities-of-communities, 77-79
as role systems, 178
as systems of interrelated roles, 177
as target-oriented, 517
discovering, 73, 74
enacting, 60, 73-74, 75, 77
experimenting, 131-132
knowing by, 437-438
learning by, 438-440
self-designing, 131
simulating system of, 279-280
Organization theory, 50
cognitive psychology and, 187
conceptualization of topics in, 352-354
normal accidents in, 352
organizational types in, 352
performance measurement in, 352
Orlady, H. W., 354
Orlikowski, W. J., 500, 503
Orr, J. E., 59, 60, 61, 62, 63, 64, 66, 67, 68,
70, 71, 79, 172, 343
Ouchi, W. G., 134, 439, 456, 525
Owen, G., 232, 233

Pablo, A. L., 542, 545, 549, 556, 567, 569,
570
Paconowsky, M., 172
Padgett, J. F., 231, 232, 234
Panian, S. K., 290
Panning, W. H., 232
Paris, S. G., 153
Park, B., 234, 524
Parks, D., 137
Pavitt, K., 209
Payne, D., 556
Payne, J. W., 269
Pea, R. D., 69
Pearson, R. W., 9
Penrose, E. T., 377
Performance, relative:
competition and importance of, 115-117
Performance monitoring, learning by, 139

Perrow, C., 241, 242, 268, 341, 353, 354,
481, 554, 555, 569
Peters, M., 130
Peters, T., 129, 351, 491, 549, 556, 557, 561,
564, 568
Peterson, R., 205, 206
Petroski, H., 546, 549, 569
Pettigrew, A. M., 255, 309, 310, 311, 324, 522
Pfeffer, J., 167, 234, 270, 304, 305, 306, 309,
311, 379, 381, 396, 517
Piore, M. J., 380
Polanyi, M., 121, 449
Pondy, L., 142
Poole, P. P., 148
Porac, J. F., 353
Porter, L. W., 142, 232, 241, 510
Porter, M. E., 125, 135
Powell, M. J., 499
Powell, W. W., 193, 278, 353, 525, 528, 529
Prange, G. W., 7
Pred, A. R., 205
President's Commission, 204
Pressman, J. L., 533
Preston, J., 232
Preston, L., 519
Price, J. L., 231, 254
Problem representation, 185-186, 187
Problem-solving heuristic, 465
Procedural knowledge:
decay rate of, 409
definition of, x
versus declarative knowledge, x, 409
Procedural memory, xi, 190, 191, 193,
403-404
description of, 408-409
individual skill and habit and, 404
low decay rate of, 409
lowered accessibility of, 409
organizational routines stored as, 403-427
versus declarative memory, 193, 409, 421,
426
Product development:
end use and market constraints on, 183-184
innovation and, 183-184
manufacturing constraints and, 184
Productivity, 83
Professional cultures, knowledge and, 491-492
Professionals, 489
versus nonprofessionals, 490
Professions, properties of, 489

Progress curve. *See* Learning curves
Prosch, H., 449
Prospect theory, 103
Puffer, M., 303
Pugh, D. S., 378, 383
Punctuated equilibrium perspective, 267,
     268, 272
Putnam, L. L., 74, 142, 232, 241

Quality:
   in management vocabulary, 460
   misunderstanding of, 466
Quality management, 461, 464, 477
   as heuristic problem solving, 464-465
   customer focus of, 467-468
   definition of, 464
   employee empowerment in, 466
   features of, 465-471
   leadership issues in, 470-471
   participation issues in, 470-471
   process orientation of, 466-467
   See also Quality management ecology;
      Quality management methods
Quality management ecology, 474-481
   "buy-in" problem and, 474-475
   ecology of inefficiency and, 476-478
   organizational versus individual goals
      and, 478-479
   technical perfectionism versus economiz-
      ing and, 479-481
Quality management methods, 462
   implementation of, 480
   quests for improvements and, 468-469
   time required for, 462
   See also Quality management ecology
Quality revolution, 460, 461, 480
   evolutionary economic theory and, 461,
      471-474
Quinlan, P., 332, 333
Quinn, J. B., 130

Radical innovation, 361, 362-363
   versus incremental innovation, 362
Radner, R., 102, 232, 233, 260, 518
Raiffa, H., 4
Raisinghani, D., 137, 138
Rajkumar, R., 233

Randolph, W. A., 132, 431, 433
Rao, H. R., 150
Rapping, L., 518
Rare event learning, 212, 221, 225
Rational search theory, 102-103
Rauch-Hindin, W. B., 150
Ray, G. F., 209, 220, 226
Raymond, P., 332
Reddy, M. J., 68
Reitzel, W. A., 138
Relative position, competition for, 119-120
Reliability, organizational, 551, 552-553
Reliable systems:
   as smart systems, 331
Reorientation, 267
   description of, 268
   See also Convergence/reorientation
      patterns
Research:
   as learning mechanism, 182-183
   innovation and, 182-183
   intelligence function of, 182
   organizational learning, xii, 275-276
Rhenman, E., 494, 506
Rice, R., 210
Riley, P., 165
Riolo, R. L., 425
Risk taking, 101
Risling, A., 487, 489
Ritzer, G., 490
Roberts, K. H., 142, 232, 241, 330, 355, 554,
      569
Robertson, T., 207
Robinson, E. L., 231, 232
Robinson, V., 130
Rochlin, G. I., 330
Rockart, J., 222
Rogers, E., 204, 205, 206, 210
Rogers, E. M., 528
Roles:
   as system of prescribed decision premises,
      177
   structure of, 177-178
Romanelli, E., 137, 198, 231, 234, 255, 256,
      267, 268, 269, 270, 271, 272, 273,
      274, 276, 278, 286, 290, 291, 293,
      304, 305, 308, 312, 313, 326, 396, 532
Romelaer, P., 234
Roos, D., 406

Rorty, R., 9
Rose, N. L., 84, 85, 133
Rosenberg, Lawrence, 492
Rosenberg, N., 210, 211, 232, 519
Rosenbloom, P., 425
Ross, J., 139, 522, 548, 560
Ross, L., 9, 148, 254
Ross, M., 9, 522, 544
Rossi, P. H., 129
Rothschild, G. H., 232
Rothschild, M., 102
Rothwell, R., 205
Rousseau, D. M., 355, 554, 569
Routines, organizational, xi, 268, 272, 476,
    517, 518
  as fundamental building blocks, 50
  as multi-actor, 406
  as source of organizational performance
    reliability, 403
  as source of organizational performance
    speed, 403
  benefits of, 410
  costs of, 410
  definition of, 378
  description of, 50, 165, 405-406
  difficulties in understanding, 406-408
  ecologies of, 377
  emergent quality of, 406-407
  experimental observation of, 411-412
  formalized jobs as, 377
  impersonal, 381, 382
  importance of, 405-406
  inarticulate knowledge of, 407
  individual learning and, 188-193
  inertial perspective of, 381
  influences in survival of, 379-382
  in knowledge-intensive firms (KIFs),
    501-503
  job idiosyncrasy and, 382
  need for improved understanding of, 404
  novel, 380-381
  organizational behavior and, 517
  organizational context and survival of, 379
  persistence of, 376
  procedural memory and, 403-427
  processes that change and, 50
  shifts in composition of, 396
  social interaction perspective of, 381
  tacit knowledge and, 473

  turnover and, 378-379
  types of, 380-382
Rowan, B., 128, 135, 522, 529
Rozin, P., 193
Rule, J., 214
Rumelhart, D., 239, 240
Rumelhart, D. E., 332, 333
Russell, D., 553
Ryle, G., 60, 331, 335, 336, 339, 340, 341

Sabatier, P., 140
Sabel, C. F., 189
Sahal, D., 135
Salancik, G. R., 3, 167, 234, 303, 304, 547
Sammon, W. L., 125, 135
Sandelands, L., 411
Sandelands, L. E., 126, 303, 332, 333, 435,
    548, 553
Satisficing theory, 103, 166
Scanning, learning by, 136, 137-138
Sayles, L. R., 569
Scanlan, T. J., 137
Schachter, D. L., 193
Schacter, D. L., 408, 410, 427
Schalker, T. E., 6
Schein, E., 374
Schein, E. H., 73, 77, 128, 381, 431, 439
Schelling, T. C., 397
Schendel, D. E., 363, 520
Schlesinger, J. R., 146
Schliemann, A. D., 410
Schmitt, B. H., 167
Schneider, D. J., 332
Schneider, S., 131
Schneider, W., 331
Schön, D. A., 104, 125, 131, 256, 269, 270,
    299, 306, 426, 431, 432, 433, 435,
    455, 518, 521, 556
Schriescheim, F. J., 489, 501
Schumpeter, J. A., 101
Schutz, W. C., 350
Schwab, D. P., 378
Schwab, R. C., 138
Schwartz, N., 211
Schwenk, C. R., 134
Scott, W. R., 195, 353, 378, 517, 528
S-curve:
  changing knowledge barriers and, 212

innovation adoption and, 205-206
Searching, learning by, 151, 518, 519, 522
    evaluation of literature on, 130-141
    focused search, 136, 137, 138-139
    founding search, 277-278
    information acquisition through, 124, 128,
        136-141
    noticing, 136, 137
    performance monitoring, 136-137, 139
    scanning, 136, 137-138
    See also Search rules
Search rules, 278-279, 281, 287, 291, 295-297
Second-order learning, 270, 290, 302, 304,
        305
    costs of, 310
    executive succession and, 307-308,
        309-310, 323, 325
Selection, 103
    as element of organizational evolution,
        377
Seligman, M. E. P., 568
Selznick, P., 304
Senge, P., 373, 374
Senge, P. M., xiv, 410
Sevón, G., 9, 141
Sha, L., 233
Shapira, Z., 10, 234, 254, 523, 532, 533,
        542, 549
Shapiro, C., 104
Shapiro, D. L., 547
Shapiro, N. Z., 210
Sharma, S., 136
Shaw, M. E., 231, 232, 241, 411
Shedler, J., 13
Sheil, B., 193, 407
Shiffrin, R. M., 331
Shimamura, A. P., 193, 409
Shippy, T. A., 411
Shleifer, A., 478
Shoemaker, F. F., 528
Short, J., 145, 431, 432, 433
Shrivastava, P., 125, 131, 171, 431, 434, 569
Shrum, W., 510
Sicoly, F., 544
Siegel, J., 145
Siegel, S., 269, 517
Siehl, C., 10, 526
Simon, H., 47, 233
Simon, H. A., 4, 103, 134, 144, 146, 166,
        177, 180, 183, 185, 198, 231, 233,

        241, 268, 269, 271, 272, 274, 279,
        405, 424, 433, 482, 517, 527, 547
Simon, H. W., 382
Sims, H. P., Jr., 126, 144, 431, 434
Singh, H., 304, 308
Singh, J., 549
Singh, J. V., 135, 196, 377, 379, 482, 518
Single-loop learning, double-loop learning
        versus, 131
Singley, M. K., 190, 191, 192, 409, 421, 422,
        427
Sitkin, S. B., 129, 136, 146, 343, 431, 432,
        521, 526, 530, 542, 544, 545, 549,
        550, 556, 561, 562, 567, 568, 569,
        570, 571
Siu, R. G. K., 553
Slepian, J., 270
Slovic, P., 148, 521
Small losses strategy, 557, 559
Small wins strategy, 545, 559
Smircich, L., 439
Smith, G., 309, 312
Smith, H. T., 527
Smith, R., 234
Social construction:
    as work practice feature, 67-68
Social interaction, 20, 33, 37, 52
Social interaction theory, 376
Social learning theory, 164
Solomon, J., 562
Solt, M. E., 279
Sormunen, J., 137
Soule, W. T., 396
Spender, J., 310
Spilerman, S., 378
Spitalnic, R., 125, 135
Sprague, R., 222
Sproull, L., 303, 306, 308, 325
Sproull, L. S., 4, 8, 9, 10, 12, 144, 522, 523,
        526
Squire, L. R., 193, 408, 409, 427
Stability, organizational, xiii
    change and, 267, 270
    innovation and, 179-180
Stablein, R. E., 126, 332, 333, 435
Stalker, G. M., 233, 276, 378
Starbuck, W. H., 9, 13, 73, 77, 131, 134, 137,
        147, 148, 167, 169, 299, 305, 350,
        353, 426, 495, 497, 501, 506, 518,
        521, 524, 527, 531, 533, 546, 549, 569

Stasz, C., 210
Staw, B. M., 129, 139, 303, 522, 542, 548, 553, 560, 564
St. Clair, G., 436
Stearns, T., 196, 396
Steeb, R., 234
Steinbruner, J. D., 231, 234, 517
Stelling, J., 490
Stene, E. O., 411
Sterman, J., 373, 374
Steufert, S., 146
Stewman, S., 379
Stigler, G. J., 5
Stimulus-response learning patterns, organizational:
    different response, same stimulus, 165
    different stimulus, different response, 165, 166
    different stimulus, same response, 164-165, 166
    nonlearning explanations of, 167
    nonlearning sequences of, 165-167
    routines and, 165
    same stimulus, different response, 164, 165, 167
    same stimulus, same response, 165, 166
Stinchcombe, A., 7, 405
Stinchcombe, A. L., 128, 188, 189, 190, 191, 192, 379, 498, 499, 520
Stoneman, P., 206
Storytelling:
    diagnosis aspect of, 66, 70
    enacting and, 74
    giving experience metaphorical force, 4
    preservation aspect of, 66
    process, 63-64
Stout, S., 355
Strand, R. G., 233
Strategic action, competition for, 119-120
Strauss, A., 377, 381, 382
Strauss, A. L., 355
Structural buffering, 257
Success, organizational:
    ambiguity of, 522-523
    benefits of, 543-544
    complacency as liability of, 544-545, 547
    effects of, 543-546
    enhanced efficiency and, 543
    homogeneity as liability of, 544, 545-546, 547

liabilities of, 541, 542, 544-546
    monetary rewards of, 543
    reliability and, 551, 552-553
    restricted search and attention as liability of, 544, 547
    risk aversion as liability of, 544, 547
    strategic failure as alternative to, 546-551
Suchman, L., 61, 80, 407
Suchman, M. C., 528
Sullivan, W. M., 350
Summers, L. H., 478
Superstitious learning, 8, 523-524
    evolution model of organizational change and, 377
Sutton, R. I., 305, 306, 342, 541, 545, 549
Sveiby, K. E., 487, 489, 490
Swaminathan, A., 279
Swidler, A., 350

Tacit knowledge:
    evolutionary economic theory and, 473-474
    routines and, 473
Takeuchi, H., 528
Tamuz, M., 6, 12, 308, 325, 532, 549, 550, 554, 569
Tasks:
    integrated, 234
    quasi-repetitive, 234
Taylor, C., 440
Teams, 71, 230, 236
    advantages of, 233
    description of, 232
    inappropriate employee experience and, 252
    institutional memory in, 258
    learning rate of, 238, 245, 246, 257
    personnel hiring and learning amount, 251
    personnel turnover and, 246-247
    ultimate performance of, 241, 242, 243, 244, 257, 258
    versus hierarchies, 232, 233
    vulnerability of, 248, 250-251, 257
Technical knowledge:
    creation of mediating institutions and, 212
    development of and adoption barrier, 211
    economies of scale and, 212
    immobility of and organizational learning, 211

S-curve and changing barriers to, 212
service as alternative to adopting, 213
technical relationships and, 212
See also Business computing, institutional
features of diffusion of; Technology diffusion
Technological change, management of architectural knowledge and, 359-374
Technology diffusion, 203
communication versus knowledge in,
208-211
individual learning and, 210
knowledge barrier institutional-network
approach to, 211-213, 226
organizational learning and, 210
service to self-service transition in, 213
signaling and, 208-209
technical knowledge (know-how) and,
208-209, 211
See also Business computing, institutional
features of diffusion of; Innovation
diffusion theory; Technical knowledge
Technology transfer, 83. *See also* Knowledge
transfer
Thagard, P., 425
Thayer, L., 142
Theoret, A., 137, 138
Thomas, A., 84, 85, 133, 209, 232, 518, 519
Thomas, H., 353
Thomas, J. B., 570
Thompson, J. D., 232, 241, 268, 274, 278,
352, 382, 521
Thorndike, E. L., 190
Thorndyke, P., 234
Tichy, N., 309
Tipton, S. M., 350
Tirole, J., 522
Trial-and-error learning, 518, 519, 522
organizational evolution model and, 377
Tokuda, H., 233
Tolbert, P. S., 396, 528
Tolman, E. C., 169
Tolstoy, L. N., 12
Tornatzky, L., 204, 205, 207, 209, 210, 212,
214, 223
Toulouse, J., 303
Trevino, L. K., 145, 570
Trice, H. M., 561
Trist, E., 130
Tse, W., 233

Tsitsiklis, J. N., 233
Tuchman, M. L., 306
Tucker, D. J., 196, 379
Tuckman, B. W., 350
Tuden, A., 352
Tudor, W. D., 231
Tulving, E., 193, 408, 410, 427
Tuma, N. B., 390, 393
Tunstall, W. B., 131, 147
Turbulent environments, executive succession
in, 302-327
Turner, C., 378, 383
Turnover, personnel, 240
as beneficial, 231
high task complexity and, 253
information loss and, 256, 257
innovation and, 178-179
in organizational routines, 378-379
loss of history through, 526
low task complexity and, 253
modulating impact of, 249-251
mutual learning model and, 110, 111-113
organizational change and, 186
organizational code and, 112-113
organizational learning ability and,
246-253
organizational learning amount and, 247
organizational learning and, 230-259
organizational learning rate and, 246, 249
organizational performance and, 247, 249
problems from, 231
reduction in institutional memory and, 256
relative effect of executive and analyst,
251-253
Turoff, M., 145
Tushman, M. L., 77, 129, 137, 198, 209,
231, 234, 255, 256, 267, 268, 269,
270, 271, 272, 273, 274, 276, 278,
286, 290, 291, 293, 304, 305, 308,
309, 312, 313, 326, 362, 363, 396, 532
Tversky, A., 7, 14, 103, 144, 148, 234, 235,
254, 269, 521, 545, 549

U.S. General Accounting Office, 352, 481
Ullman, J., 129
Ungson, G. R., 138, 150, 342, 426
United States Department of Commerce,
216, 219
Unlearning:

definition of, 147
discharge of employees and, 147
effects of on learning, 147-148
focused search and, 147
new learning and, 147
organizational inactivity and, 147
socialization of new organizational
    members and, 147-148
Useem, M., 372
Utterback, J. M., 205

Van de Ven, A. H., 139, 195, 394, 568
VanLehn, K., 192
Van Maanen, J., 105, 343, 381, 504, 526
Varian, H. R., 269
Variation, 103
Velleman, P. F., 422
Vicarious learning, 124, 128, 135-136, 141,
    151
Vickers, G., 448, 455, 457
Virany, B., 231, 234, 255, 256
Von Glinow, M. A., 489, 501
von Hippel, E., 76, 78, 205, 206, 209, 370

Wagner, W. G., 306, 309
Walczak, D., 490
Walker, G., 144
Walker, J. L., 474
Walsh, J. P., 150, 342, 426
Walton, A. E., 130
Walton, M., 470
Wang, L., 233
Warner, M., 129
Waterman, D. A., 150
Waterman, R. H., 491, 549, 556, 568
Waters, J. A., 311, 313
Watts, R. K., 364
Watzlawick, P., 299, 308
Weakland, J., 299
Weber, C. E., 140
Weber, M., 232, 378
Weber, R., 234, 524
Web of meanings, 449, 450
Webster's New Collegiate Dictionary, 147
Weeks, W. H., 130
Wegener, B., 396
Wegner, D. M., 332

Wehrung, D. A., 533
Weick, K. E., 5, 8, 9, 54, 60, 73, 74, 75, 113,
    143, 145, 165, 169, 256, 308, 343,
    344, 350, 353, 377, 379, 411, 431,
    434, 436, 450, 456, 457, 521, 522,
    542, 543, 545, 548, 549, 553, 555,
    557, 560, 563, 564, 569
Weiner, S., 9, 10, 523, 526
Weiss, A., 170, 171, 290, 431, 434, 435, 449,
    451, 455, 531, 556
Weiss, C., 431, 433
Weiss, C. H., 129, 134, 140
Weitz, B. A., 303, 309, 547
Wenger, E., 59, 60, 68, 69, 70, 72, 342
Wheelwright, S. C., 84
Whetten, D. A., 520
Whetton, D., 269
White, H. C., 378
White, R. W., 559
Whitley, B. E., 553
Whitney, D. E., 371
Whyte, W. H., Jr., 105
Wiewel, W., 529
Wildavsky, A., 129, 137, 139, 527, 542,
    550, 553, 555, 569
Wildavsky, A. B., 533
Wilensky, H., 233
Wilkins, A. L., 439, 456
Williams, E., 145
Williamson, O. E., 225, 232, 233, 382
Wilson, G. C., 331
Wilson, T. D., 407
Winter, S. G., xi, 50, 103, 148, 189, 190,
    196, 197, 201, 232, 269, 374, 377,
    378, 379, 380, 404, 405, 407, 411,
    461, 465, 471, 478, 482, 487, 491,
    501, 517, 518
Witten, M. G., 145
Wixson, K. K., 153
Wolf, D., 9, 10, 523, 526
Wolfe, D., 144
Wolff, E. N., 497
Womack, J. P., 406
Wood, R., 568, 573
Woodworth, R. S., 190
Work:
    modern idealizations of, 66
    organizing by adaptation, 20-55
Work arounds, 59

Work groups, 71
Work practice, 59
    as conservative, 58
    as resistant to change, 58
    collaboration in, 66-67
    narration in, 64-66
    social construction in, 67-68
Wright, T. P., 84, 518
Wuthnow, R., 510

Yanow, D., 452
Yao, D. A., 132, 532

Yates, J., 150, 225
Yelle, L. E., 84, 133, 518

Zajonc, R., 144
Zajonc, R. B., 425
Zald, M. N., 5, 193, 532
Zegveld, W., 205
Zimmerman, M. B., 85, 133
Zirger, B. J., 533
Zuboff, S., 65, 192, 406, 407
Zucker, L. G., 135, 306, 397, 482, 520, 528,
    529, 530, 568

About the Editors

Michael D. Cohen is Professor of Political Science and Public Policy at the University of Michigan. His research has included laboratory and field studies of organization, as well as theoretical contributions that often use computer modeling techniques. His current work centers on field and laboratory studies of organizational learning and associated computer simulation models.

Lee S. Sproull is Professor of Management at Boston University. She received a Ph.D. from Stanford University and, prior to Boston University, was on the faculty at Carnegie Mellon University. Her research emphasizes information behavior in organizations. Her current work centers on social and organizational dynamics enabled by computer communication technology.

About the Contributors

Linda Argote is Associate Professor of Industrial Administration in the Graduate School of Industrial Administration, Carnegie Mellon University. She received a Ph.D. in Organizational Psychology from the University of Michigan. Her research and teaching interests include organizational learning, productivity, technology, and group decision making and performance. Her research has appeared in *Administrative Science Quarterly, Management Science, Organizational Behavior and Human Decision Processes,* and *Science.*

Paul Attewell is Professor of Sociology at the Graduate Center of the City University of New York. His prior publications on organizational aspects of computing include studies of skill impacts, workplace surveillance, and the use of MIS data for resource allocation. His current research focuses on IT and the "productivity paradox"—the paucity of observable productivity payoffs from IT.

Paul Bacdayan is a doctoral candidate in the Department of Organizational Behavior and Human Resources Management, University of Michigan School of Business. He received an M.B.A. from Dartmouth's Amos Tuck School of Business Administration. He is coauthor (with Robert E. Cole and Joseph White) of "Quality, Participation and Competitiveness," forthcoming in the *California Management Review.*

John Seely Brown is corporate Vice-President and Director of the Xerox Palo Alto Research Center (PARC). He also is cofounder of the Palo Alto-based Institute for Research on Learning (IRL), a nonprofit organization. His multidisciplinary research interests include artificial intelligence, cognitive science, and organizational behavior. He has endeavored to build bridges between these fields and the social sciences. He obtained a doctorate in computer and communication sciences from the University of Michigan.

Kathleen Carley is Associate Professor of Sociology and Information and Decision Systems at Carnegie Mellon University. She received a Ph.D. from Harvard University. She is currently involved in four main research endeavors: examining the impact of training and coordination on organizational performance, examining the impact of individuals on group stability and cultural shifts, developing a combined social and cognitive theory of information diffusion, and encoding mental models from texts. Mailing address: Department of Social and Decision Sciences, Carnegie Mellon University, Pittsburgh, PA 15213.

Scott D. N. Cook is Associate Professor in the Department of Philosophy at San Jose University. His research interests include know-how and technology in the practices of individuals and groups. His works include articles on technology and social change, business ethics, and technological culture and the environment. Most recently, he has been working on a book on know-how, technology, and practice while on sabbatical at Xerox Palo Alto Research Center.

Rukmini Devadas is Assistant Professor in the Department of Management and Organization at the University of Southern California. She received a Ph.D. in Organizational Psychology and Theory from Carnegie Mellon University. Her research interests are in the areas of organizational learning, productivity, and group decision making and performance. She has published in *Organizational Behavior and Human Decision Processes* and is a member of the Academy of Management, the American Psychological Association, and the American Psychological Society.

Paul Duguid is an independent writer and researcher. He was formerly a member of the research staff at the Institute for Research on Learning in Palo Alto.

Dennis Epple is Professor in the Graduate School of Industrial Administration at Carnegie Mellon University. He received a B.S. in Aeronautical Engineering from Purdue University, a Masters of Public Affairs from the Woodrow Wilson School, and a Ph.D. in Economics from Princeton University. His research interests include organizational learning, public economics, and the economics of exhaustible resources. His research has appeared in *American Economic Review, Bell Journal of Economics, Journal of Political Economics, Journal of Urban Economics, Management Science, Public Choice,* and *Science.*

Rebecca M. Henderson is Assistant Professor of Strategic Management at the Sloan School of Management, The Massachusetts Institute of Technology. Her current research focuses on the strategic implications of technical innovation, and she is currently studying the impact of innovation on the pharmaceutical industry. She received her Ph.D. in Business Economics from Harvard University.

George P. Huber is the Fondren Foundation Chaired Professor of Business at the University of Texas at Austin. His research focuses on organization theory, design, and decision making. His 1984 *Management Science* article on the nature and design of post-industrial organizations was awarded First Prize in the International Prize Competition sponsored by The Institute of Management Sciences. Since 1985, he and Dr. William H. Glick have been leading a multi-investigator study of changes in the design and effectiveness of over 100 organizations.

Edwin Hutchins is Associate Professor in the Department of Cognitive Science at the University of California, San Diego. Originally trained as a cognitive anthropologist, he specializes in the study of cognition outside the laboratory. His work includes analyses of real world cognition in village courts in Papua, New Guinea; with traditional navigators in the Western Pacific; on the bridges of large navy ships; and in the cockpits of commercial airliners.

Theresa K. Lant is Assistant Professor of Management at the Stern School of Business, New York University. She received a Ph.D. in Organizational Behavior from Stanford University. Her current research interests include the study of organizational learning and adaptation. Recent publications include a paper in the *Strategic Management Journal.* Mailing address: Stern School of Business, New York University, 90 Trinity Place, New York, NY 10006.

Daniel A. Levinthal is May Department Stores Term Associate Professor of Management at the Wharton School. He received a Ph.D. in 1985 from the Graduate School of Business, Stanford University. His current research interests are interorganizational relationships, organizational learning, and industry evolution. His articles have appeared in *Administrative Science Quarterly, Economic Journal, Marketing Science, Academy of Management Review, American Economic Review,* and *Journal of Economic Behavior and Organization.* He currently serves on the editorial board of *Administrative Science Quarterly.*

Barbara Levitt received her Ph.D. in sociology at Stanford University, where she developed her interest in organizational learning working with her advisor James March. She is currently at Santa Clara University, where she teaches strategic management and gender issues in the work place and continues to do research in organizational learning.

James G. March is Director of the Scandinavian Consortium for Organizational Research and the Jack Steele Parker Professor of International Management (Emeritus) at Stanford University.

Stephen J. Mezias is Assistant Professor of Organizational Behavior at the Yale School of Organization and Management. He received a Ph.D. in Organizational Behavior and an M.S. in Statistics from Stanford University. His current research interests include the study of longitudinal change in institutional environments, the integration of ecological and institutional perspectives, and how authoritative decision-making bodies set their agendas. His work has been published in the *Journal of Economic Behavior and Organization, Strategic Management Journal,* and *Administrative Science Quarterly.*

Anne S. Miner is an Associate Professor at the University of Wisconsin–Madison. Miner's primary theoretical interests concern nontraditional models of organizational change, organizational learning, and the dynamics of change in populations of organizations. Papers include "Accrual Mobility: Job Mobility in Higher Education through Responsibility Accrual" (with S. Estler), her dissertation, "The Strategy of Serendipity" (1985), "Idiosyncratic Jobs in Formalized Organizations" (1987), and "The Social Ecology of Jobs" (with C. Lehner). Recent papers include "Interorganizational Linkages and Population Dynamics" (with T. Amburgey) and "Cooperation and the Shadow of the Future: Effects of Anticipated Future Interaction on Interorganizational Cooperation" (with Jan Heide). Miner's new research concerns organizational learning and the diffusion of organizational routines within populations of child care centers, bargaining units of large industrial employers, and university-corporate research consortia. Miner previously served as Associate director, Annual Fund, Co-Chair of the policy board for the Center for Research on Women, and Assistant to the President and Affirmative Action Officer at Stanford University. She has also served as a consultant to federal agencies and a large manufacturing firm.

Karlene H. Roberts is Professor at the Walter A. Haas School of Business Administration at the University of California, Berkeley, where she received her Ph.D. in Psychology. She is Research Psychologist at the Institute of Industrial Relations and a Fellow of the American Psychological Association and the Academy of Management. Her recent publications include *Handbook of Organizational Communication* and *Managing in Organizations.*

Elaine Romanelli is Associate Professor of Management at the Georgetown University School of Business. Her research focuses on entrepreneurship as a key dynamic in both the strategic development of organizations and the evolution of industry competitive structures. Her current research focuses on the international biotechnology industry and the U.S. motion picture production industry. Both studies are longitudinal, using data going back to the inceptions of the industries. She has published articles in *Administrative Science Quarterly, Academy of Management Journal, Organization Science,* and *Research in Organizational Behavior,* among others. She received a Ph.D. in Management from Columbia University.

Herbert A. Simon is University Professor of Computer Science and Psychology at Carnegie Mellon University. His research has been concerned with decision making and problem solving by individuals and organizations. In 1978, he received the Alfred Nobel Memorial Prize in Economics, and in 1986, he received the National Medal of Science. He is author of many books and papers, including *Administrative Behavior, Organizations* (with James March) and *Human Problem Solving* (with Allen Newell). He received a Ph.D. from the University of Chicago.

Sim B Sitkin is Assistant Professor of Management at the Graduate School of Business, the University of Texas. His primary research interests focus on the effect of legalistic influences and organizational control systems on organizational risk taking, learning, and adaptability. His research appears in edited collections and academic and professional journals, including *Administrative Science Quarterly, Academy of Management Review, Organization Science, Harvard Business Review, Human Communication Research,* and *Research in Organizational Behavior.* He currently serves on the editorial boards of *Organization Science* and the *Academy of Management Review.* He received a B.A. from Clark University, an Ed.M. from Harvard University, and a Ph.D. from Stanford University.

William H. Starbuck is Professor of Business at the NYU Stern School of Business. He earned an A.B. in physics at Harvard University and an M.S. and a Ph.D. in industrial administration at Carnegie-Mellon University. He has served on the faculties of Purdue, Johns Hopkins, Cornell, and London Graduate School of Business Studies, and he was a senior research fellow at the International Institute of Management, Berlin. He has published in the areas of organizational design, decision making, computer simulation, and organizational growth. His memberships include the American Sociological Association, TIMS, and Sigma Xi, and he is a fellow in the American Psychological Association. He is on the editorial board of the *Journal of Applied Social Psychology*, is a former editor of *Administrative Science Quarterly*, and is co-editing the forthcoming three-volume *Handbook of Organizational Design*.

Michal Tamuz received a Ph.D. from Stanford University and is Assistant Professor in the Management Department at Rutgers University. Her research interests include information processing in organizations, organizational learning, and how organizations manage the risks of industrial crises and technological innovation. She is currently studying how organizations adjust for the ambiguities of history as they collect information and learn.

Michael L. Tushman is the Phillip Hettleman Professor of Management at the Graduate School of Business, Columbia University. His research focuses on the nature of technological change and the linkages between technological change, executive team dynamics, and organization evolution. He is currently on the editorial boards of *Administrative Science Quarterly, Human Relations, Journal of Product Innovation Management, Management Science, IEEE Transactions on Engineering Management, and Journal of Business Venturing*. He is coeditor of the Harvard Business School Press book series on the management of innovation and change.

Beverly Virany was a Ph.D. candidate at the Graduate School of Business, Columbia University. She died of cancer in 1987. She received her B.S. at the University of Pennsylvania and her M.B.A. from Columbia University. She was interested in the impact of technological change on executive teams. As a Ph.D. student, she published articles appearing in *Journal of Business Venturing* and *Technology and Society*.

Karl E. Weick is the Rensis Likert Collegiate Professor of Organizational Behavior and Psychology at the University of Michigan and former editor of *Administrative Science Quarterly*. He was trained in psychology at Ohio State University, where he received a Ph.D. He studies and writes about such topics as how people make sense of confusing events, the effects of stress on thinking and imagination, and the consequences of indeterminacy in social systems.

Sidney G. Winter is Professor in the Wharton School of the University of Pennsylvania. He came to Wharton from the post of Chief Economist of the General Accounting Office. He is coauthor, with Richard Nelson, of *An Evolutionary Theory of Economic Change.*

Dvora Yanow is Associate Professor in the Department of Public Administration at California State University, Hayward. She pursues research in interpretive approaches to policy analysis and organizational culture. Recent publications include articles on metaphors, organizational and policy myths, and the role of built space in communicating organizational meanings.